C000128141

BLOODSTAINED SANDS

OSPREY
PUBLISHING

DEDICATED TO
the men at the tip of the spear

BLOODSTAINED SANDS

U.S. AMPHIBIOUS OPERATIONS IN WORLD WAR II

MICHAEL G. WALLING

First published in Great Britain in 2017 by Osprey Publishing,
PO Box 883, Oxford, OX1 9PL, UK
1385 Broadway, 5th Floor, New York, NY 10018, USA

E-mail: info@ospreypublishing.com

Osprey Publishing, part of Bloomsbury Publishing Plc

OSPREY is a trademark of Osprey Publishing, a division of Bloomsbury Publishing Plc.

ISBN: 978 1 4728 1439 5
PDF e-book ISBN: 978 1 4728 1440 1
ePub e-book ISBN: 978 1 4728 1441 8

Index by Angela Hall
Typeset in: Baskerville, Adobe Garamond and Akzidenz Grotesque
Maps by Bounford.com
Originated by PDQ Media, Bungay, UK
Printed in China through World Print Ltd.

17 18 19 20 21   10 9 8 7 6 5 4 3 2 1

Osprey Publishing supports the Woodland Trust, the UK's leading woodland conservation charity. Between 2014 and 2018 our donations are being spent on their Centenary Woods project in the UK.

www.ospreypublishing.com

Front cover and title page: A view from inside an LCVP of the 16th RCT, 1st Infantry Division during its run in to Omaha Beach on D-Day. (NARA)

To find out more about our authors and books visit **www.ospreypublishing.com**. Here you will find extracts, author interviews, details of forthcoming events and the option to sign up for our newsletter.

CONTENTS

ACKNOWLEDGEMENTS

First and foremost to the men who shared their experiences with me either in person, over the phone or in letters. Also, the Army, Navy, Marine, and Coast Guard combat correspondents who captured the men's stories. These courageous correspondents were themselves often in the mist of the fighting.

Once again, thank you to my wife Mary for her unwavering love, faith, moral support, and limitless patience through yet another all-consuming project.

Kate Moore, my editor at Osprey, showed remarkable patience through the often painful process of bringing this project print. My special thanks to the remarkable copyeditor Anita Baker who, with great fortitude, suffered through having to work with me on this project. Also, Gemma Gardner, Chloe May, and the rest of the great staff at Osprey who worked hard with Kate.

Thanks to my agent Kelli Christiansen of bibliobibuli for securing the contract with Osprey and always being supportive.

As special thank you to Mrs. Jean Carrigan for her friendship and for graciously allowing me to use excerpts from her husband Paul E. Carrigan's remarkable book *Flying, Fighting Weathermen of Patrol Wing Four*.

Andrew E. Woods, Research Historian at the Colonel Robert R. McCormick Research Center First Division Museum at Cantigny provided invaluable information and reference sources on the First Infantry Division.

Maneuver Center of Excellence HQ Donovan Research Library Reference, Systems, Virtual Librarian Genoa Stanford assisted with map sources and other important information.

Peter Chen was invaluable in helping me sort out the often confusing information on several operations.

ACKNOWLEDGEMENTS

I am deeply grateful to Cornelius Ryan, James Michener, Bill Mauldin, Samuel Eliot Morison, and William Manchester. It was through their wonderful books that I first gained a glimmer of the horror, terror, selfless sacrifice, and humor of the young men who fought in World War II.

Keep the Faith,
Mike Walling

MAPS

AUTHOR'S NOTE

Before I began writing this book I thought I had a pretty good knowledge of U.S. amphibious operations in World War II. I'd read about them and talked with hundreds of Coast Guardsmen, soldiers, sailors, and Marines over the past 50 years or so. These were the men at the spear's tip, not just once but often multiple times, their odds of surviving growing smaller with each operation. However, I knew there were gaps in my knowledge, even of units I was familiar with, and finding out what lay in those gaps was amazing, funny, and, at times, heart wrenching.

Among my discoveries were Castner's Cutthroats in Alaska, technically the 1st Alaskan Combat Intelligence Platoon, which was dubbed the Alaska Scouts. They were trappers, hunters, fishermen, dogsledders, miners, prospectors, Aleuts, Eskimos, and American Indians. Being tough was the only thing they had in common.

Digging into material about the Aleutian campaign I found the incredible tale of the courageous crewmen of Patrol Wing Four.

The Naval Construction Battalions' Seabees are well known. Less so, the Army Engineering Special Brigades, which I'd also not heard of, even though these tough and resourceful men performed miracles throughout the European and Pacific theaters.

Beach Battalions came to light along with their indomitable courage under fire and finding out about the secretive Beach Jumpers, organized by Lieutenant Douglas Fairbanks Jr., the Hollywood actor turned naval officer, was fun.

Many of us have heard about the Underwater Demolition Teams, and pictured them rolling off rubber boats to reconnoiter a hostile sandy beach. However, finding teams paired with Engineering Special Brigade men in cold waters off the Normandy beaches, blowing gaps in obstacles while taking heavy fire, and later doing the same thing in the Philippines, Iwo Jima, and

Okinawa, among other less than tropical waters, was another knowledge gap filled.

Being an ex-Coast Guardsman I was familiar with the Coast Guard's significant but rarely recognized role in amphibious operations. It was the true extent of what these men did that surprised me. Coast Guard-manned assault transports, LSTs, LCIs, and landing craft crews took part in landings from North Africa through Okinawa, many in both theaters and through the worst assaults.

It is beyond my capability and the scope of any one book to tell the full story of every landing or assault. I've chosen to present some of the well-known ones such as Anzio, Normandy, Tarawa, and Iwo Jima, as well as some not so well known, many of which took place in the Southwest Pacific. For some, days have been covered, while for others, only the first few hours.

I tell the stories, when possible, from the viewpoint and using the words of the landing craft driver, LCI crewman or men in the first assault waves as the ramps dropped, soldiers and Marines under fire as well as pilots flying combat missions or long, often terrifying patrols rather than those of commanders watching from ships offshore. Each man received a pre-assault briefing about the invasion fleet and known enemy strength, something I have tried to do here so that the reader also knows what was facing them. All the quotes are original and some of them contain what is now considered offensive language. To change the wording would make these quotes historically inaccurate which would be a disservice both to the men and the reader.

Above all else my objective with this book is to help keep the often neglected memories of the amphibious forces alive.

BRIEFING

Amphibious Operation

A military operation launched from the sea by an amphibious force to conduct landing force operations within the littorals.

Amphibious Assault

A type of amphibious operation that involves establishing a force on a hostile or potentially hostile shore.[1]

Amphibious warfare and amphibious operations are not new concepts. In the *Iliad*, Homer recorded one of the first amphibious operations in history when the Greeks attacked Troy in the 12th century BC. He describes how, after ten years of war, the Greeks crossed the Aegean Sea, beached their ships near Troy, beat off counterattacks on their ships, and destroyed the city.

In 490 BC the powerful Persian ruler, Darius, launched a waterborne attack against the Greeks that culminated in the Battle of Marathon. The Persians turned their ships into ancient versions of landing ships, pre-dating modern landing ships by almost 2,500 years, when they used gangways to unload their horses from beached ships. Ultimately, Darius failed to conquer the Greeks, however, and he made his landing only to be defeated. A second landing also failed, and the Persians returned to Asia.

One of the most famous and successful amphibious operations was undertaken by William the Conqueror when he crossed the English Channel from Normandy in AD 1066. His boats, which were comparable in length to the smaller landing boats used today, were driven up onto the beach by rowers and a "coxswain" who directed the boat with a large steering oar. Near Hastings, the scene of his landing, William defeated Harold, the English king, and founded a new line of rulers. This was the last successful invasion of England.

Conversely, on July 8, 1775 one of the most disastrous large-scale landing operations occurred when the Spanish sent 50 naval vessels and 240 transports to invade Morocco. The Spaniards only managed to land about a dozen soldiers per trip as a lack of powerboats meant that at least as many men again were needed to row the slow-moving boats through the surf and back to collect the next boatload of hapless soldiers. The initial landing in the Bay of Algiers met little resistance as the roughly 100,000 Moorish soldiers and Berber tribesmen withdrew, drawing the Spaniards into a trap. As soon as the Spanish troops were within musket range the slaughter began. The survivors were driven back to their boats amid carnage and confusion, with many of them being slaughtered as they attempted to retreat. Those who made it to the beach returned to their ships and the Spanish fleet withdrew.[2]

The first U.S. Continental Navy amphibious landing was made during the Revolution when, on March 3, 1776, sailors and Marines landed unopposed six miles from the port of Nassau in the British Bahamas, a landing which went on to the next day. Referred to as either the "Battle of Nassau" or the "Raid on Nassau," the objective was to seize badly needed weapons and gun powder to support the American rebels. The Americans only stayed for two weeks before heading home.

During the Spanish–American War in 1898 the U.S. Navy landed troops in Cuba. With improved landing tactics and rapid ship-to-shore movements, 650 Marines successfully stormed ashore unopposed and captured the key target of Guantanamo Bay.[3]

In April 1915 the first "modern" amphibious assault was launched by a combined British and French task force at Gallipoli in Turkey during World War I. The assault force, composed of British and French naval squadrons, seaplane carriers, and one specially modified landing ship, attempted to put ashore some 78,000 soldiers. Heavy Turkish gunfire swept the assault waves as they came ashore onto beaches laced with barbed wire and sown with improvised mines constructed from torpedo warheads, forerunners of the types of obstacles used in World War II to thwart landings. The landings were not a success and the disastrous campaign resulted in a huge loss of life.

Over the millennia weapons have changed but the basic principles governing amphibious operations have not. However, it wasn't until 1838 that the Swiss-born French general Baron Antoine Henri de Jomini published *Précis de l'Art de Guerre* (*Summary of the Art of War*).[4] In it he listed five key points for any amphibious landing:

1) deceive the enemy as to the point of debarkation;
2) select a beach with hydrographic and terrain conditions favorable to the attacker;
3) employ naval guns to prepare the way for the troops;
4) then use land artillery at the earliest practicable moment;
5) strenuously push the invasion forward by seizing the high ground commanding the landing area, thus securing the beachhead from enemy guns, allowing a quick buildup of supplies ashore, and allowing the conflict to move from amphibious to land warfare.

Jomini's writings were based on his own experiences and observations from the land-centric warfare of the Napoleonic era. Then, as now, there were two primary types of amphibious landings: shore-to-shore and ship-to-shore. In shore-to-shore operations the attacking force is loaded directly onto the landing craft and off-loaded at their target. Ship-to-shore involves embarking the troops onto transports and then off-loading them into smaller landing craft. Many landings are a combination of these two types.

Whether an operation is of the shore-to-shore or ship-to-shore type, each one is broken down into five phases: 1) planning; 2) rehearsal; 3) embarkation; 4) movement; and 5) assault. The planning phase covers the period from when the initiating directive is issued to the end of the operation. The duration of this phase can be anything from a week to several years.

The purpose of the rehearsal phase is to test the adequacy of the plans and communication, the timing of detailed operations, and the combat readiness of the participating forces. Conducting rehearsals is not always feasible because sometimes there is not enough time to gather the task force before the scheduled assault. For example, in 1943 in the Southwest Pacific many of the units were located hundreds of miles apart and the landing ships were engaged in other operations.

Although valuable, in several instances rehearsals have proved costly in terms of men killed and landing craft lost. Before the Anzio landings soldiers drowned as they exited LSTs that had not pulled close enough to shore or fell from nets as they climbed down them into landing craft. Prior to Guadalcanal, irreplaceable landing craft were lost in collisions, had their bottoms ripped open on rock beaches or were smashed against the sides of the transports. In Operation *Tiger*, one rehearsal for the 1944 Allied invasion of Normandy, German E-boats got among the transports and landing craft, causing immense devastation and loss of life.

Phase three, embarkation, involves assigning and assembling the ships and troops that will compose the landing forces, including the necessary equipment and supplies. The fourth phase – the movement of the task force to the amphibious operation area – includes the departure of the ships from the loading points, the sea passage, and their arrival in their assigned positions for the attack. Finally, the assault phase begins when all of the assault elements of the main body arrive at their assigned positions and ends when the unloading is complete.

The men at the tip of the spear leading needed to know the "three Rs" of invasion:

1) the general plan of the operation;
2) the specific plan for their division, regiment, battalion, and company;
3) information about the enemy situation and the target.

Under the first "R," the general plan of the operation, the men were apprised of the overall plan, preferred and alternate, of the attack, which involved two divisions in assault and one in reserve. They were given complete information on the support they would get from naval gunfire and aerial bombardment. They knew that the landing beaches and surrounding areas would be under air attack to "soften up" the target prior to D-Day. They knew, down to the last shell, how much naval gunfire would be dumped on the beaches. They saw aerial photographs taken a few days before D-Day.

The second "R", relating to specific plans for their unit, was dealt with in exacting detail. Information that they were given included details of platoons, companies, and battalions that would land on either flank; the distance from the beach to the first phase line; the direction of attack after the landing; the types of communications available to their unit; code names of all officers; the meaning of pyrotechnic displays; and passwords and countersigns.

The third "R", information about the enemy situation, included making sure the commanders had knowledge of the terrain, gained from a study of aerial photographs and relief maps; climatic conditions; the number and disposition of enemy troops; the type of defense, including the location of all pillboxes, blockhouses, and trenches observed in their zone of action; the probable location of minefields; the direction of expected counterattacks; the number of enemy tanks; and the enemy's air capabilities.

Not only were maps, overlays, and aerial photographs used, but also charts detailing statistical information. Officers used the operations orders and annexes as a "textbook" and passed on every pertinent fact that their men might have to know.[5]

World War II Theaters of War

In the European, Mediterranean, and North African Theaters of Operations U.S. forces were involved in the six major Allied amphibious assaults that were mounted between November 1942 and August 1944: one in North Africa, three in the Mediterranean (Sicily, Salerno, and Anzio), and two in Europe (Normandy and southern France) with each operation coming months after the preceding one. All six were massive undertakings involving hundreds of ships and thousands of men. The North African, Mediterranean, and European Theaters were primarily land battles in which amphibious operations were essential for forcibly reentering German-occupied North Africa and Europe.

The Pacific Theater was divided into two commands. The first, the Southwest Pacific Area (SWPA), based in Australia, covered the Philippines, New Guinea, the Bismarck Archipelago, and the Dutch East Indies. The second, the Pacific Theater of Operations (PTO), based at Pearl Harbor, covered the rest of the Pacific.

The PTO was a maritime theater requiring landings to secure island bases for further operations. PTO forces mounted ten major landings with numerous smaller ones launched to secure islands surrounding the primary targets. The primary objectives included the Gilbert and Marshall Islands, and the Caroline, Mariana, and Volcano Islands. Here, too, landings were often separated by several months and, until Okinawa, were not as large in terms of ships and men as their ETO (European Theater of Operations) counterparts.

Southwest Pacific amphibious operations were different. Often an invasion force consisted of a few landing ships and craft supported by destroyers and land-based aircraft. Sometimes only a few days elapsed between operations as the Allies moved up the New Guinea coast to the northern Solomon Islands and then to the Bismarck Archipelago before major assaults in the Philippines.

Landing Craft

As amphibious warfare evolved from 1921 through 1945, strange-looking ships such as the Landing Ship Dock (LSD) and Landing Ship Tank (LST – referred to as "Large Slow Target" by their crews)* came into being, as did a host of other landing craft — LCTs, LCIs, LCMs, LCPs, LCP(R)s, and LCVPs. To this floating mix were added amphibian vehicles with both propellers and wheels – DUWKs, Seeps, and Water Weasels. The Landing Vehicle Tracked (LVT – tracked vehicles that could carry men across shallow coral reefs) and LVT(A) (armored LVTs fitted with either 37mm cannon-equipped turrets or an 81mm mortar) were used extensively in the Central Pacific and to a lesser extent in Europe.

Existing passenger ships were modified as assault transports (APAs) to handle large numbers of troops and landing craft and new ships were also built specifically for that purpose. In addition to the APAs, specially designed cargo ships (AKAs) were built to handle the massive amounts of equipment, heavy weapons, and other supplies needed to maintain the operations. To man these ships, craft, and vehicles, amphibious tractor and armored battalions were created by the Navy, Marines, and Army, and training schools were established.

Landing Operations

Responsibility for the smooth flow of men and equipment onto and off the beach was the job of Beach Parties, Engineering Special Brigades, and Beach

---

* LSTs evolved from the shallow-draft Lake Maraca Ibo tankers. The British Admiralty began planning the invasion of Europe while their troops were still being evacuated from Dunkirk in 1940. LCTs were an outgrowth of the Continental river barges. The British version was considerably longer than the American.

Battalions. These specialized units were composed of men from the Coast Guard, Navy, Army, and/or Marines. Amphibious operations in the different theaters shared the common goal of getting men and equipment ashore quickly but they differed in the numbers of landings and the logistics involved to accomplish this goal.

Before troops could be put ashore a thorough reconnaissance of the area had to be made. Charts in the Pacific were so poor that sometimes the charted position of an island was off by several miles and its orientation was wrong. Therefore, accurate mapping of the area was needed, which involved discreet aerial photography missions. Teams were also sent in covertly to chart underwater obstacles, ascertain the slope of the beach selected for an assault, record the type of sand, and determine whether the beach could support the weight of heavy traffic. In anticipation of amphibious attacks, the Germans and Japanese expended considerable effort and ingenuity on underwater defenses. A steel rail with one end sharpened to a point and the other embedded in a large block of concrete was a likely device to skewer a landing craft and would be a difficult item to blow up or move away. Mines were interspersed among the various obstacles in such profusion that an invader who timed his arrival for low tide would have a hard time clearing a lane on the beach before the tide had risen enough to complicate operations.

To carry out the critical mission of clearing these obstacles special groups came into being: the Navy Underwater Demolition Teams (initially known as Navy Construction Demolition Units or NCDUs) and, in the Pacific, the Marine Amphibious Reconnaissance Force.

Controlling the flow of men and material onto and off the beach was the responsibility of the Beachmaster and his supporting Beach Party. Here, again, all theaters shared common problems but established slightly different ways of handling them. To some extent during, and then subsequent to, the landings in the Solomon Islands in August 1942 and the North African landings in November 1942, men in the Naval Beach Battalions or Parties were normally assigned to one of four duty classifications: communications, hydrographics, boat repair, or medical. Often under fire from the enemy, these men dug their own slit trenches and foxholes on the beach, fighting alongside the Marines and soldiers to repel enemy attacks while still setting up the beach as a simulated port for the onslaught of supplies, equipment and men that would soon be landed in support of the initial assault troops.

Also part of the first groups into action during a beach assault were the medical personnel administering to assault troops cut down during the first waves and evacuating casualties to naval ships lying off the beaches.

Meanwhile, the Beachmaster and the men trained in hydrographic duties would be surveying the approaches and beach exits, locating and charting underwater obstacles, and determining the best passages for the succeeding waves of landing craft. Enemy gunfire and strafing runs were usually ignored in the early stages of a beach operation as there was no place to go. Navy underwater demolition teams and Army engineering personnel were called in to clear approach lanes and to blow beach and underwater obstacles. Boat repairmen fixed damaged landing craft, or craft that had broached when landing, to get them back into service.

In Europe, Naval Beach Battalions were created as the means of control. When a Beach Battalion went into action, it was organized along the lines of an Army Battalion – three companies, with each company divided into three platoons, the interlocking duties of which embraced every phase of the battalion's task. Company and Battalion Headquarters personnel brought the battalion, at full strength, to 450 officers and men.

Each platoon of a Beach Battalion was under the command of a Beachmaster and his assistant. Each platoon of a Beach Battalion was assigned hydrographic specialists, medical personnel, signalmen, radiomen, and boat repair experts. In a typical beach assault, beach battalion personnel went ashore in one or more of the first three or four assault waves, scattering their equipment over the beach so that not all of the men would be wounded or killed if hit by an enemy bomb or shell.

Beach communications were often instrumental in deciding the course of a battle, and so the communications elements of the Beach Battalion were rapidly established (normally landing with the first assault wave) to link the Beachmaster up with the fleet and the assault troops. Radios, signal lights, and signalmen using semaphore flags were put to immediate and effective use in establishing communications between the beach parties, landing craft, and transports.[6]

In the PTO smaller Shore Parties were established to perform the same functions as the Beach Battalions. The Shore Party was an integral part of a combat division and was organized around a Marine Corps platoon from a Pioneer (shore party company) or Army combat engineer company along with a communications team. In both services the Shore Party formed the nucleus to which the various elements were assigned for an operation. The naval elements included an Underwater Demolition Team, a Naval Pontoon Unit, and a Boat Pool.

The Beach Party of the Shore Party team would land at the objective area and take charge of the beach. The Shore Party was considered to be an instrument of the assault and was relieved by a garrison beach party which unloaded equipment, men, and supplies from ships arriving after the assault.[7] In the Southwest Pacific Area, the Seventh Amphibious Fleet established autonomous Beach Party units that moved from landing to landing.

Naval Gunfire and Tactical Air Support

Two key elements of any successful landing are naval gunfire support and tactical air support. Muzzle velocity and the great weight of projectiles mean that naval gunfire can hit hard; it can be delivered with great rapidity; and, subject to terrain which may shelter targets from its relatively flat trajectories, it makes immediately available the enormous firepower that is necessary for overcoming the initial handicaps of amphibious assault. On the other hand, its effectiveness is limited to the maximum range inland of the ships' batteries; steep terrain may mask targets; radio communications may fail where wire would hold up; and fire from an unstable, moving gun platform can produce large deviations at long ranges, despite the accuracy of modern fire control.

Ships' gunfire helps clear the beaches so that assault waves can land (it was no accident that, even on Iwo Jima, initial resistance to the landing was officially characterized as "light"). After troops are ashore, before artillery can come in, naval gunfire is the only means available for the delivery of continuous close support, if the powerful but necessarily discontinuous assistance of airstrikes is excluded.[8]

During World War II air support became an indispensable feature of any offensive. It had, and still has, two forms: strategic and tactical. These may also be called, respectively, indirect and direct, or distant and close.

Air support of assault landings – both strategic and tactical – may be provided by any combatant air agency within effective range. This support runs the gamut of operations-reconnaissance, both visual and photo, bombing of every kind, strafing, artillery observation and control, combat and antisubmarine patrols, and rescue and transportation services – in short, any or all forms of aircraft activities may be included. Landings in the Western Mandate Islands, as well as the earlier seizures of the Gilberts and the Marshalls, provided classic examples of joint air support of joint overseas assault landings. In the landings in the Marianas Islands, no Allied land airdromes existed near enough to Guam and Saipan, hence carriers furnished the close air support.

When Italy was invaded, tactical air support of the landings was based on fields in Sicily that Allied forces had recently seized. When France was invaded, airdromes in southern England served as bases for Allied support aircraft.

Tactical air support of an assault landing presents one of the most complicated problems in coordination that modern warfare has produced.[9] Men versed in coordinating this element are also among the first waves to hit the beaches as Forward Fire and Air Controllers.

Summary

The five phases of either a landing or assault have to be carefully choreographed or the operation fails at the cost of men lost and equipment destroyed. During World War II the U.S. raised the techniques of amphibious and assault landings almost to an art form. They conducted 168 amphibious landings and 68 amphibious assaults.[10] Remarkably, none of them failed.

Each ship, landing craft, amphibious vehicle Beach Battalion and Beach Party, Engineering Special Brigade, ship's crew providing fire support, and aircraft crew flying reconnaissance or tactical air support played a part in helping the Allies win World War II.

CHAPTER 1

SOWING THE WIND

OCTOBER 1941–JULY 1942

Acting in alliance with the Entente powers during World War I, Japan seized German Central Pacific possessions in the Mariana (except the U.S. territory of Guam), Caroline, and Marshall island groups by October 1914. After the war Japan was granted a mandate to govern these islands in the Treaty of Versailles and at the Paris Peace Conference in 1919, which was further ratified under a Class C mandate by the Covenant of the League of Nations.* Although not a member of the League the U.S. signed a convention with Japan recognizing the League's mandate in February 1922. Part of the terms of the mandate was that the islands were not to be fortified. However, fortified or not, control of these islands shifted the strategic balance of power in the Pacific away from the U.S. to Japan.

Japan's potential threat to U.S. interests in the Pacific was recognized by Marine Corps Major Earl H. Ellis in 1913. Ellis understood the need to defend existing bases in Hawaii, Guam, and the Philippines as well as acquiring bases

---

* There were four distinct Mandates in the Pacific. Japan administered the Carolines, Marshalls and Marianas (except Guam), all north of the equator; Australia, the former German part of New Guinea and the Bismarck Archipelago, with adjoining islands, all south of the equator; New Zealand, the western islands of the Samoan group; and the British Empire, the rich phosphate island of Nauru. With the exception of Samoa, which is in the south central Pacific, the Mandates comprised a large bloc in the west central part of the Pacific, east and southeast of the Philippines. Their land area is greater than that of England, Scotland and Wales. Source: Blakeslee, George H., *The Mandates of the Pacific*, FOREIGN AFFAIRS The Magazine, September 1922 Issue.

on Japanese-held islands. On July 23, 1921 he submitted his ideas in Operations Plan 712 "Advance Base Operations in Micronesia" (FMFRP-12-46) which foretold the course of the war in the Pacific and that Japan would strike the first blow with a great deal of success. Ellis listed Japan's objectives which included the Philippines, Guam, Midway, Wake, and Hawaii. He also detailed the action plan necessary for Japan's defeat which involved seizing the Marshall and Caroline Islands and that the attack on Japan would be made from bases in the Bonin and Mariana Islands. He knew that the job of acquiring new bases would mean attacking the enemy-held territory by amphibious assault, and he went so far as to designate the size and type of units that would be necessary, the kind of landing craft they should use, the best time of day to effect the landing, and other details needed to ensure the success of the plan:

> Japan is a World Power, and her army and navy will doubtless be up to date as to training and materiel. Considering our consistent policy of non-aggression, she will probably initiate the war; which will indicate that, in her own mind, she believes that, considering her natural defensive position, she has sufficient military strength to defeat our fleet.
>
> To effect [an amphibious landing] in the face of enemy resistance requires careful training and preparation, to say the least; and this along Marine lines. It is not enough that the troops be skilled infantry men or artillery men of high morale; they must be skilled water men and jungle men who know it can be done—Marines with Marine training.[*][1]

Between 1922 and 1925 four amphibious operations exercises were held: three exclusively Navy–Marine operations in 1922–24 and the last one in 1925 which was a joint Army and Navy exercise. All of the exercises suffered from the same problems: lack of order among the landing party; superficial naval bombardment; and poor judgment in the stowage of supplies and

---

[*] Ellis died on May 12, 1923 while visiting the Japanese-held island of Palau in the Caroline Islands. The cause of his death remains unclear although several theories have been advanced in the years since his death. One theory is his death was alcohol related compounded by severe depression. Another theory is that the Japanese poisoned his whiskey. Before his body was cremated U.S. Navy Chief Pharmacist Mate Lawrence Zembsch examined the body, but due to a nervous breakdown on his way back to Yokohama, Japan and soon after being killed by falling rubble in the 1923 Great Kantō earthquake, no report was filed. Ellis's maps and papers were confiscated by Japanese authorities and never found after the war.

equipment aboard the transport used. However, the greatest handicap was the lack of adequate landing craft. The next amphibious exercise would not be until 1935.

The development of modern amphibious landing concepts began with the establishment of the Fleet Marine Force (FMF) on December 18, 1933 with Marines from the 1st Battalion, 7th Marine Regiment. The purpose of the FMF was to prepare units for the execution of amphibious missions. The Marine Corps developed a progressive system beginning with basic individual training, followed by the training of units from the squad through to brigade, culminating in joint annual amphibious training in conjunction with the fleet. Since the FMF was organized as a component of the fleet, its training was a matter of direct concern to the Navy.

In July of 1934 the Commander-in-Chief, U.S. Fleet approved a plan of training for the Fleet Marine Force, which was to begin in the Caribbean in 1935. It called for annual fleet landing exercises, known as Fleet Exercises (FLEXs), to develop coordination and teamwork while simulating the conditions of war.[2]

After a hiatus of ten years, major amphibious exercises began again in the winter of 1935. The genesis of these renewed exercises was the publication of the *Tentative Manual for Landing Operations* in January 1934. The title changed to *Manual for Naval Operations* on August 1, 1934, and with a few changes it became the bible for amphibious operations.[*]

Although the *Manual for Naval Operations* laid out the theory for amphibious operations, the theory could only be proven through actual operation, hence the need for exercises. Problems that became apparent included issues with fire support, adequate numbers of suitable transport, close air support, the screening of the transports, antisubmarine tactics, ship-to-shore movement, and beach reconnaissance groups. Ship-to-shore movement alone presented two major problems: the need for the speedy debarkation of the assaulting troops and their equipment into the landing boats and the difficulty in controlling and guiding these craft to their assigned beaches. These problems were exacerbated by the lack of suitable landing craft.

---

[*]   Thornton, Gary J. E., Commander, USCG, *THE U.S. COAST GUARD AND ARMY AMPHIBIOUS DEVELOPMENT*, US Army War College, Carlisle Barracks, PA, March 23, 1987. The Navy accepted it as official doctrine in 1938 under the title of Fleet Training Publication 167, and in 1941 the War Department put the Navy text between Army covers and issued it as Field Manual 314.

While the Navy and Marines refined amphibious operations, Germany was rearming and Japan began expanding its military operations. In 1933 Japan withdrew from the League of Nations and initiated harbor improvements, airfield construction, and the establishment of fuel dumps, bases, and fortifications in its territories including those mandated islands acquired at the end of World War I. According to the Japanese Decisive Battle Plan, the islands would serve as buffers for the homeland and were expendable.*

The first overt provocation against the U.S. came on Sunday, December 12, 1937. In July Japan had launched an invasion of China from bases in Manchuria and by December had reached Nanking on the Yangtze River. The USS *Panay* and three Standard Oil tankers, *Mei Ping, Mei An*, and *Mei Hsia* were anchored near Hoshien, 27 miles north of Nanking. *Panay* displayed a large American flag horizontally across the upper deck awnings, and a 6' x 11' Stars and Stripes displayed from the gaff.

On board *Panay*, the crew, four U.S. Embassy staff members, four U.S. nationals, and four foreign nationals, including one of Universal News's premiere cameramen, Norman Alley, Eric Mayell of Fox Movietone, James Marshall of *Colliers*, photographer Norman Soong of the *New York Times*, United Press's Weldon James, G.M. McDonald of the *London Times*, and two Italian writers, Sandro Sandri and Luigi Barzini, Jr. were at their midday meal when the roar of high-powered aircraft engines, falling bombs, and ripping machine-gun fire shattered the day.

At about 1340, three Japanese B4Y1 Type 96 bi-plane bombers commenced an attack. At least one direct hit was observed, but most bombs missed. Two dive-bombers attacked next, strafing their targets to suppress flak.

---

* The Japanese Navy's Decisive Battle Doctrine (*Kantai Kessen*) was the counterpart to the American Plan Orange. The plan assumed that Japan would quickly seize control of most of the Philippines, both to neutralize the Asiatic Fleet before it could attack Japanese communications and to provoke the Americans into a hasty counterattack. It was assumed that this would take the form of a counteroffensive by the U.S. Navy across the Mandates, with the goal of relieving Manila and blockading Japan. The American Fleet would be met by the Japanese Fleet somewhere in the western Pacific for a decisive battle on the model of the battle of Tsushima in the Russo-Japanese War of 1905. Source: Budge, Ken G., The Pacific War Online Encyclopedia, 2012–2013, http://pwencycl.kgbudge.com/D/e/Decisive_Battle_Doctrine.htm

Panay was hit by two bombs, which disabled her forward 3in gun and wounded Lieutenant Commander Hughes, the commanding officer. The crew fought back with their two .30-caliber Lewis machine guns, but, designed for use against shore and water targets, they could not elevate enough to deliver effective antiaircraft fire. Explosions ripped apart the decks, throwing men into the water. The planes then bombed the three Standard Oil tankers, which were soon engulfed in flames. On board *Mei Ping* members of *Panay*'s crew who were visiting the tanker fought a losing a battle against the fires and had to abandon ship. Finally, nine Nakajima A4N Type 95 bi-plane fighters dropped 18 bombs on *Panay* and also machine-gunned the launches carrying the wounded on their way to shore at nearby Hanshan Island.

Norman Alley and Eric Mayell filmed part of the attack and, after reaching shore, the sinking of the ship in the middle of the river. Navy Coxswain Edgar C. Hulsebus, Storekeeper First Class Charles L. Ensminger, Standard Oil Tanker Captain Carl H. Carlson and Italian reporter Sandro Sandri were killed. Forty-three sailors and five civilians were wounded in the attack.

Two days later in Tokyo, the American Ambassador Joseph C. Grew lodged a formal protest about the USS *Panay* "Incident". Although the Japanese government accepted responsibility for the attack, they stated it had been unintentional. In Shanghai a court of inquiry was presented with incontrovertible evidence that senior Japanese officers had ordered the attack. Ambassador Grew, remembering the public's reaction when the USS *Maine* was blown up in Havana Harbor, expected a declaration of war against Japan. However, although there was outrage and a demand for retribution America was a paper tiger and could do nothing to avenge this outrage.[3]

The Navy did take note of Japan's increasing aggression, which affected both the U.S. and Britain. Later in December Captain Royal E. Ingersoll, the Director of the Navy War Plans Division, was sent to London to informally discuss conditions of U.S.–British naval co-operation in the event both nations were involved in a war against Japan and Germany.

The *Panay* attack made it imperative that the Army and Navy reexamine plans for a U.S. two-ocean war against the Axis powers – Germany, Italy, and Japan. A joint board of Army and Navy planners worked for over a year and in April 1939 they issued a report concluding:

1. Germany and Italy would take overt action in the Western Hemisphere only if Great Britain and France remained neutral or were defeated.

2. Japan would continue to expand into China and Southeast Asia at the expense of Great Britain and the United States, by peaceful means if possible but by force if necessary.

3. The three Axis powers would act together whenever the international situation seemed favorable. If other countries, including the United States, reacted promptly and vigorously to such action then a general war might well follow.[4]

The British Royal Navy was responsible for security in the Atlantic. No mention was made of the need for amphibious operations in Europe and the Mediterranean. North Africa was not a consideration at that time, even though Italy occupied part of Morocco and had conquered the Ethiopian Empire in 1936 which put the Axis power in a position to threaten maritime trade through the Red Sea.

The planners concluded that early in the war Japan would seize all U.S. possessions west of 180 degrees (i.e. the Philippines, Guam, and Wake). They also pointed out that the attacks might begin with an effort "to damage major fleet units without warning," or a surprise attempt "to block the fleet in Pearl Harbor." They stated that American forces would have to fight their way back across the Pacific using a series of amphibious operations using one of four routes:

1. Aleutians;
2. Pearl Harbor–Midway–Luzon (Philippines);
3. Marshalls–Carolines–Marianas–Yap–Peleliu; or
4. Samoa–New Guinea–Mindanao.

The favored routes were Pearl Harbor–Midway–Luzon and the Marshalls–Carolines–Marianas–Yap–Peleliu with the understanding that a combination of the two would most probably have to be used. Forces in Hawaii, Alaska, and Panama were to be reinforced, but not those in the Philippines on the assumption that their loss was a certainty.[5]

Japan's continued conquest of eastern China and Germany's more openly aggressive stance in Europe raised the question of U.S. policy in the event of concerted aggression by all three Axis powers. As options were being examined, events overtook the planners.

On September 1, 1939, the German Army (Heer) and Air Force (Luftwaffe)*
attacked Poland. Two days later France and Britain declared war on Germany,
but other than a brief, inconclusive French incursion into Germany's Saar
region, they were of no help in defending their ally. By September 6 German
forces had occupied Warsaw and the Polish government had surrendered.
Exacerbating the already tense situation was the Soviet Union's invasion of
eastern Poland on September 17.

From October until May 1940, France and Britain built up forces along
Germany's western border in anticipation of invasion. Nothing happened
until April 9, 1940 when Germany attacked Denmark and Norway. Four
weeks later, on May 10, German forces breached its borders with Belgium and
the Netherlands. Within 96 hours German armor broke through French
defenses in the Ardennes Forest and quickly overran the mixed British and
French forces. By June 4, the last British troops had been evacuated from
Dunkirk and France surrendered on June 17. Italy declared war on Britain
and France on June 10, essentially after the major fighting in Europe was over.

By the end of June Germany occupied two thirds of France. The other third
was under the leadership of Marshal Henri Philippe Pétain with its capital in
Vichy in southern France. The Vichy French retained administrational control
of France's overseas colonies, including Vietnam, Syria, Lebanon, Morocco,
Algeria, Tunisia, and Senegal. Vichy French control of Morocco and Algeria,
coupled with the Italian bases in Libya, effectively sealed off the Mediterranean
Sea from Gibraltar to the Egyptian border.

In just ten months all U.S. war plans focusing primarily on operations in
the Pacific with Britain controlling actions in the Atlantic became obsolete.
U.S. Admiral Harold R. Stark, Chief of Naval Operations (CNO), recognized
U.S. security largely depended on Britain's survival. He asserted: "if Britain
wins decisively against Germany we could win everywhere; but that if she
loses the problems confronting us would be very great; and while we might
not *lose everywhere*, we might, possibly, not *win* anywhere."[6]

Admiral Stark also questioned British assurances that Germany and Italy
could be defeated by blockade and bombardment prior to landing troops in
safe harbors, the same tactics used to defeat Napoleon 130 years earlier.

---

*   The *Wehrmacht* (Defense Force) consisted of the *Heer* (Army), the *Kriegsmarine* (Navy)
     and the *Luftwaffe* (Air Force). Therefore, the individual branches will not be referred to as
     the *Wehrmacht* in this work. The *Schutzstaffel* (SS) units were separate from the *Wehrmacht*
     and will be identified as such.

He believed the way to certain victory was "by military success on shore," and for that, bases close to the European continent would be required. "I believe that the United States, in addition to sending naval assistance, would also need to send large air and land forces to Europe or Africa, or both, and to participate strongly in this land offensive."[7]

A secret conference between American, British, and Canadian military staffs (ABC-1) was held in Washington from January 29 to March 27, 1941. Seven key offensive policies were agreed upon at this meeting:

1. To maintain an economic blockade of the Axis by sea, land, and air, and by commodity control through diplomatic and financial means.
2. To conduct a sustained air offensive to destroy Axis military power.
3. To effect "early elimination" of Italy as an Axis partner.
4. To conduct raids and minor offensives.
5. To support neutrals and underground groups in resisting the Axis.
6. To build up the necessary forces for the eventual offensive against Germany.
7. To capture positions from which to launch that offensive.[8]

These policies laid out the "Europe First" strategy in all joint operations stating "the Atlantic and European area is considered to be the decisive theater" and that accordingly it would be where the chief American effort would be exerted, although the "great importance" of the Mediterranean and North African areas was noted.

If Japan launched operations in the Pacific the U.S. would "employ the United States Pacific Fleet offensively in the manner best calculated to weaken Japanese economic power ... by diverting Japanese strength away from Malaysia."[9]

The "Europe First" strategy was further reinforced when Germany invaded Russia on June 22, 1941, and quickly overran a large part of western Russia, laying siege to Leningrad (modern-day St. Petersburg) and Stalingrad (modern-day Volgograd), and coming within sight of Moscow. This further complicated the already major problem of supplying arms and other materials to Britain. Some of these supplies were now diverted to Russia in an effort to prevent her collapse.

The only way to send large land forces into Europe, West Africa, and Italy was by amphibious assault. U.S. forces now faced having to secure bases on

Japanese-occupied islands, as well as positions in North Africa, Italy, and German-occupied France.

––––––––––––

While strategic and geopolitical discussions were being held U.S. forces continued to undertake amphibious exercises. Shortages in landing equipment, and insufficient landing craft, competent boat crews, and transports hampered realistic training. Another sticking point was the lack of joint Army, Navy, and Marine amphibious training. To correct this situation, the 1st Joint Training Force was created in June 1941. It consisted of the 1st Marine Division and the Army 1st Division and subsequently developed into the Amphibious Force, Atlantic Fleet. On the west coast, similarly, the 2d Joint Training Force was created in September, consisting of the Army 3d Division and the 2d Marine Division; this later became the Amphibious Force, Pacific Fleet. Both Forces were under Marine command.

Fleet Exercise 7 (FLEX-7) in August 1941 was the first large-scale Amphibious Force, Atlantic Fleet exercise. It took place off the New River in North Carolina. The Navy made a large contribution, supplying three battleships, nine cruisers, five destroyers, two aircraft carriers and a three-ship destroyer transport group. For the first time the Army and Marines attempted to operate under simulated combat conditions. In addition, new types of landing were being evaluated. However, it wasn't the Navy or Marines who eventually came up with a solution to landing problems, but rather a remarkable businessman named Andrew Jackson Higgins. Higgins's 36ft craft featured a tunnel stern to protect the propeller and a special "spoonbill" bow that enabled it to beach on low banks or beaches and retract easily. It became known as the Landing Craft Personnel (LCP) and later, when it was fitted with a bow ramp, it became the famous drop-ramp Landing Craft Vehicle and Personnel (LCVP).

As well as landing craft, assault troops needed an amphibious tractor to move supplies over the beach. Once again it was a private businessman who came up with the necessary vehicle. Donald Roebling's "Alligator" was a tracked vehicle that derived its propulsion afloat from flanges fixed to the tracks. Designated as Landing Vehicle Tracked (LVT), it was initially armed with only .50 cal. machine guns. However, as the war progressed versions would be fitted with 37mm turrets, mortars, and rockets.

For FLEX-7, the 1st Marine Division embarked on Navy transports and the Army 1st Division embarked on civilian-manned Army transports.

Complications arose when the civilian crews operating the Army transports refused to run without lights to simulate night combat conditions. Then, during the launching and recovery of landing craft, the civilians refused to man the hoisting gear after regular working hours unless guaranteed double wages for overtime. At this time, the ships' civilian cooks refused to prepare meals for soldiers returning late from exercises. Three Navy ships, *Hunter Liggett, Leonard Wood*, and *Joseph T. Dickman* were manned by Coast Guard crews. The Navy, lacking sufficient personnel to man them, with the exception of the medical and supply departments, turned to the Coast Guard for additional manpower.*

In addition, the Navy assigned 600 Coast Guard Surfmen and Motor Machinist Mates from Coast Guard Life Saving stations to duties in landing craft attached to 22 other transports and some supply ships operating with the transports. Maneuvering small boats on and off beaches through heavy surf was not something the Navy practiced and Coast Guard Surfmen were called upon to teach this skill to the growing number of landing craft crews. Men who up to then had put out through storm-whipped breakers to save others now turned to the task of learning how to land soldiers and Marines and soldiers on bullet-swept beaches.

The Coast Guard also played a prominent new role during this exercise by providing Beachmasters who were responsible for the transit of all men and supplies from the line of departure to the water's edge. Lieutenant Commander Walter C. Capron was the Beachmaster for the 1st Marine Division and Lieutenant Commander Dwight H. Dexter served as Beachmaster for the Army 1st Division.[10, 11]

The five-week exercise failed to meet expectations. Troop transports proved to have not only inadequate gear but also inadequate facilities of all kinds. Although the landings were executed in daylight, with a calm sea, men burdened with heavy packs sank as they scrambled out of the boats. Reportedly, a Marine captain was "so mad that he was almost weeping" because the Navy sent his ammunition boats ashore in the first wave without protection. Tanks plunged off ramps into deepening holes in the surf-covered sand. One observer

---

* Earlier in 1941, ten 250ft long *Lake* class cutters were loaned to Britain as part of the Lend–Lease Program. Rear Admiral Wache, Coast Guard Commandant, offered to have the crews man the recently acquired transports. Several hundred officers and men from these cutters were immediately available for this assignment. With the new Coast Guard/Navy agreement establishing full time Coast Guard amphibious responsibilities, the temporary detailing of Coast Guard personnel to landing craft training aboard transports was ended.

remarked: "One tank ... disappeared into a hole and was completely submerged. The driver climbed out and stood disconsolately on the turret looking for all the world like pictures you see of Jesus walking on the water."[12]

Other problems emerged. Shore organization was chaotic; responsibilities for unloading and other beach operations had not been defined, and as a result both Army and Marine combat troops had to serve as stevedores. Boxes of ammunition and rations, handed from the boats to men standing in the surf, were usually saturated. Cardboard cartons of C rations, stacked on the beach, disintegrated, the cans of vegetable hash mingled with the cans of meat stew in a tall silver pyramid that glistened in the sunlight. Once on shore, equipment rusted because essential lubricants had been stowed deep in the ships' holds.[13]

Despite all the problems, some positives did come out of the exercise. FLEX-7 led to better shore party organization and training and the Higgins 36ft landing craft with the bow ramp, along with the 50ft Higgins-designed tank lighters, proved superior to all other designs.

Amphibious operation plans and training progressed against the background of heightening tensions between the U.S., Germany, and Japan. Since 1939 the primary U.S. focus had been assisting Britain. To that end President Franklin D. Roosevelt took a series of unprecedented steps to ensure Britain's survival and to thwart German actions in the western hemisphere. These steps included establishing in 1939 a Neutrality Zone in the North Atlantic to dissuade German naval attacks on shipping in the area; accepting the role of protector of Greenland after Denmark was overrun in 1940; and the March 1941 Lend–Lease Act, which was the principal means of providing U.S. military aid to foreign nations during World War II – it authorized the president to transfer arms or any other defense materials for which Congress appropriated money to "the government of any country whose defense the President deems vital to the defense of the United States."

More provocatively on the part of the U.S., in May the Navy increased its presence in the North Atlantic by agreeing to protect Iceland from the threat of German invasion. The 4,000-man USMC 1st Marine Brigade (Provisional) was sent to Iceland, relieving the British Army occupying force, thus freeing the British troops for combat.

Concurrently, President Roosevelt ordered the Navy to take the steps necessary to maintain communications between the U.S. and Iceland. To accomplish this, the Navy established a base north of Reykjavik in Hvalfjödur

(Whale Bay). This base, along with the one in Argentia, Newfoundland, and the use of the British Naval base in Lisahally, Northern Ireland, would enable the Navy to escort convoys through the mid-Atlantic if necessary.

In great secrecy, and surrounded by warships, British Prime Minister Winston Churchill and President Franklin D. Roosevelt met for the first time in Argentia, Newfoundland, on August 9, 1941. For over three days the two leaders and their staffs discussed plans for the prosecution of the war. Out of this meeting came a joint statement of principles called the Atlantic Charter. It endorsed the rights of all people to choose their own leaders, regain lands lost to them through force, trade freely with one another, have access to raw materials on equal terms, improve the lot of backward countries, disarm aggressors, freedom from want, freedom from fear, and "such a peace should enable all men to traverse the high seas and oceans without hindrance."[14] This last phrase was directed at Hitler's U-boat campaign and served as justification for the U.S. to take part in the battle.

The text of the Charter and photos of the meeting weren't released until the two leaders were safely home in their respective countries. Interestingly, at the time, the Charter didn't exist as a formal document. When a reporter asked President Roosevelt about it, the President is said to have replied: "There isn't any copy ... so far as I know. I haven't got one. The British haven't got one. The nearest thing you will get is the [message of the radio] operator on the [U.S. Navy cruiser] *Augusta* or the [Royal Navy battleship] *Prince of Wales*." * [15]

After returning from Argentia, President Roosevelt issued an Executive Order directing U.S. warships to act as convoy escorts for merchant ships sailing west of Iceland. Also, U.S. warships were not to show lights at night and to be ready for combat at any time. On September 1 the U.S. Navy began escorting convoys across the Atlantic to Britain, coordinating its efforts with British and Canadian forces.

The increasing cooperation between the U.S. and British navies was put to the test on September 4. At 0840 the U.S. Navy destroyer *Greer*, carrying mail and passengers to Argentia, was signaled by a British plane that a U-boat (later identified as U-*625*) had crash-dived some ten miles ahead. Forty minutes later *Greer*'s soundman picked up the contact and *Greer* began to trail the U-boat. The plane, running low on fuel, dropped four depth charges at 1032 and returned to base, while *Greer* continued to dog the U-boat.

---

* A formal document was later drawn up and signed by 14 nations, including the Soviet Union, in September.

At 1248, the U-boat turned and fired a torpedo at her pursuer. Ringing up flank speed, the destroyer turned hard left as her crew watched the torpedo pass 100 yards astern. Then, charging in, *Greer* laid a pattern of eight depth charges, and less than two minutes later a second torpedo passed 300 yards to port. *Greer* lost sound contact during the maneuvers, and began to quarter the area in search of the U-boat. When the encounter ended two hours later, *Greer* had dropped 19 depth charges and U-*625* had fired two torpedoes. Although no damage was done to either ship, the shots blew away the last vestiges of U.S. neutrality in the North Atlantic.

When news of this attack against an American ship on the high seas reached the United States, President Roosevelt declared the German attack to be an act of piracy. He further stated: "in the waters which we deem necessary for our defense, American naval vessels and American planes will no longer wait until Axis submarines lurking under the water, or Axis raiders on the surface of the sea, strike their deadly blow first."[16]

From then on U.S. warships were to shoot on sight at any German warships they encountered. The United States's undeclared war in the Atlantic moved to a new, deadlier phase.

The first U.S. amphibious operation and first face-to-face skirmish between U.S. and Nazi-led ground forces occurred on September 12 in Greenland. Acting on a tip from a dog-team patrol, Commander "Iceberg" Smith sent the Coast Guard cutters *Northland* and *North Star* to investigate a ship that had reportedly landed a party in a fjord.

Commander Carl C. von Paulsen, captain of *Northland*, found the vessel in McKenzie Bay and sent a boarding team over to inspect her. She was the Norwegian sealer *Buskoe*. The boarding team found 27 men who claimed to be on a fishing and hunting expedition. Looking further, the boarding team found not only *Buskoe's* normal radio, but also a portable receiver and transmitter, proof she was servicing radio stations. Questioning turned up the information that a group with radio equipment had been dropped off earlier, several hundred miles up the coast.

Placing a Prize Crew onboard *Buskoe*, the two Coast Guard cutters got underway to search for the base. A day later, *Northland* anchored in Mygybukta, about five miles from where the radio site was believed to be. In darkness, Lieutenant Leroy McCluskey and his armed landing party from *Northland* rowed four miles to a desolate gravel beach. After negotiating the last mile over icy terrain, they reached their goal, a small wooden building.

With weapons loaded, Lieutenant McCluskey kicked down the door. Inside were three very surprised Nazis, their radio gear, confidential codes, and building plans for future radio stations. *Northland*'s men had found the enemy; now the question was what to do with them. Since the U.S. was not at war with Germany or its allies the three men couldn't be considered prisoners of war. However, utilizing a subtle point of international law, the Americans took them into custody as illegal immigrants.

Despite President Roosevelt's statement that U.S. forces would not wait for U-boats to strike, first blood went to the U-boats. In October, five U.S. destroyers, *Kearny*, *Plunkett*, *Decatur*, *Livermore*, and *Greer* were escorting the westbound 49-ship convoy ON-24 when they were diverted to help British escorts defend the fully loaded 52-ship eastbound convoy SC-48. A 13-boat wolf pack had torpedoed two ships on October 14 and was still stalking the convoy. The Americans arrived the next day. During the night of October 16, the U-boats struck again. Shortly after midnight of October 17, U-568 fired a torpedo into *Kearny*'s starboard side, killing 11 men and injuring 22. Surviving crewmembers stopped the flooding, regained power, and *Kearny* limped on to Iceland.

Two weeks later, on October 31, U.S. destroyers *Reuben James*, *Niblack*, *Benson*, and *Hilary P. Jones* were escorting the 43-ship eastbound convoy HX-156. At 0539, *Reuben James* was hunting down a U-boat contact when U-552 fired a torpedo into the destroyer's magazines. The explosion broke *Reuben James* in two. In the flaming hell of those few moments, there wasn't time for her crew to disarm her depth charges. As the *Reuben James* sank, these exploded among the survivors, disemboweling many of them. Only 44 of the 159-man crew lived through that night.[17]

After the *Panay* attack in 1937, Japan did not attack the remaining U.S. Navy and Marine forces in China. Japan did continue its Chinese conquest and occupied French Indochina following the fall of France in 1940. These moves prompted President Roosevelt to freeze all Japanese assets in the United States and ban the export of scrap metal and oil. Scrap metal, and particularly oil, were necessary materials for the Japanese military machine. Negotiations failed to get Japan the materials it wanted and on November 22 Ambassador Kurusu received the last of a series of communiqués from his superiors in Japan setting deadlines for successful negotiations. He was informed that after November 29 things were "automatically going to happen."[18]

The tentative day of attack was set for a Sunday, December 7 (the anniversary of Pearl Harbor). Vice Admiral Chuichi Nagumo, the strike force commander, received orders from Admiral Isoroku Yamamoto on December 2 confirming the chosen date. Taking a northern route to avoid normal shipping lanes his carriers arrived at the launching point right on schedule. At midnight of December 6–7, the Japanese Combined Fleet Operation Order No. 1 informed its readers that a state of war existed with the United States, Britain, and the Netherlands.

At 0630 on December 7, USS *Ward* (DD-139) depth charged and sank an unidentified submarine in restricted waters near the entrance to Pearl Harbor. *Ward*'s radio report to the 14th Naval District was not clear and because of numerous previous false reports nobody took it seriously.

At 0702, two Army operators at the Opana Mobile Radar Station, near Kahuku Point on the northern tip of Oahu, Privates Joseph L. Lockwood and George E. Elliott, detected approximately 50 aircraft about 132 miles away and fast approaching from the northwest. They reported the contacts to First Lieutenant Kermit A. Tyler. Tyler, a fighter pilot assigned to the 78th Pursuit Squadron at Wheeler Field, was working the 0400 to 0800 shift as Duty Officer at the Fort Shafter radar information center. He was new to the job, only having had a walk-through the previous Wednesday, and had never spent a full day there.

Tyler believed it was a flight of U.S. B-17 bombers due in from the mainland. One of the operators then said the U.S. planes would be approaching from the northeast, not the northwest. Tyler then told the operators: "Don't worry about it," and did not pass the information on to his superiors.[19]

It was normal Sunday routine for the Pearl Harbor Naval Base, Hickam Air Field and the Marine Air Base at Ewa. Admiral Husband E. Kimmel and General Walter Short concluded there was no reason to believe an attack was imminent. Aircraft were parked wingtip to wingtip on airfields with empty gas tanks and no ammunition in their guns to prevent sabotage. On board the ships no "Ready Service" ammunition was readily available and the magazines were locked. Watertight doors on the lower decks were open, destroying the ships' watertight integrity. There were also no torpedo nets protecting the fleet anchorage. Many officers and crewmen were on Liberty. Anti-aircraft guns on shore were not manned and the ammunition boxes were locked.

At 0735, the first Japanese assault wave, with 51 "Val" dive-bombers, 40 "Kate" torpedo bombers, 50 high-level bombers, and 43 "Zero" fighters commenced the attack. The first attack wave targeted airfields and battleships.

Sixty-three minutes later the second wave of 171 aircraft consisting of 81 "Vals," 54 "Kates," and 36 "Zeros" hit other ships and shipyard facilities. Lasting until 0945, the attacks sank five battleships and damaged eight others. Three light cruisers, three destroyers and three smaller vessels were lost along with 188 aircraft. The Japanese lost 27 planes out of 355 and five midget submarines which attempted to penetrate the inner harbor and launch torpedoes.

The Japanese also missed the base fuel tanks and did not attack the submarine base. More importantly, the three U.S. Pacific Fleet aircraft carriers, *Lexington*, *Enterprise*, and *Saratoga*, were not in port.

The Navy and Marine Corps counted 2,117 killed or died of wounds, and 779 others wounded in action. There was a total of 696 Army battle casualties, 228 Army men dead or died of wounds, 110 seriously wounded, and 358 slightly wounded. The "bombs" which fell on Honolulu and other civilian parts of the island were Navy 5in antiaircraft shells which had failed to detonate in the air. Explosions in Honolulu started three major fires, and at least 57 civilians were killed and nearly as many seriously injured.[20] Among the dead were 104 men aboard the battleship USS *Arizona*, who died after a bomb exploded in the forward magazine. A day after the attack, the U.S. and Britain declared war on Japan.

Japanese attacks across the Pacific continued unchecked through December and into 1942: December 8, Wake Island; December 10, the Philippines and Guam; December 11, Burma; December 16, British Borneo; December 18, Hong Kong; January 11, 1942, the Dutch East Indies and Dutch Borneo; February 2, Java in the Dutch East Indies; February 8–9, Singapore; March 7, Salamaua and Lae on New Guinea; and March 23, the Andaman Islands in the Bay of Bengal.

The isolated Marine, Army, and civilian defenders on Wake held out until December 23 before surrendering. Of the 449 Marines based there, 49 were killed and 32 wounded. The 68-man Navy contingent lost five killed and three wounded. Of the 1,146 civilians on the island, 70 died and another 12 were wounded. Five defenders were taken and executed on board *Nitta Maru*.[21]

On January 29, Convoy William Sail 12X (Task Force 14.2), which included the Coast Guard-manned transport USS *Wakefield* along with USS *West Point*, and three British transports – the *Duchess of Bedford*, *Empress of Japan*, and *Empire Star* – had delivered supplies and approximately 6,000 British troops and RAF ground personnel to Singapore. The convoy had sailed from Halifax, Nova Scotia on November 10, 1941 before stopping at Bombay.

The next morning at about 0935, while the convoy was tied alongside docks at Kepple Harbor awaiting the arrival of British evacuees, seven Japanese bombers were sighted over the city and were immediately attacked by British "Buffalo" fighters.

While the fighters were trying to stop the seven enemy bombers, a 30-strong bomber force was reported heading for the transports. Bombs straddled *West Point* and *Wakefield*. *Wakefield* took a bomb hit that exploded in the sick bay, killing five men and wounding about 15. A small tanker fueling alongside *Wakefield* also took a direct hit and sank. *West Point* sent fire aid parties to help in the treatment of the injured crewmen on *Wakefield*. Despite the attack, all troops and gear were put ashore. Fortunately the bombers missed the other transports during the attack.

In less than two hours after *Wakefield* was hit 401 British women and children were taken on board. *West Point* embarked 1,276 evacuees made up of naval officers and their families, civilians, a 16-man RAF contingent and 225 naval ratings. Escorted by HMS *Durban* the two American transports cleared Singapore bound for Batavia, where more refugees waited to be rescued.

The attack gave a foretaste of things to come. British General Arthur Ernest Percival surrendered all defending forces of Singapore on Black Friday, February 15 to Lieutenant General Tomoyuki Yamashita. The British general had far more land forces, but he lacked the all-important element of air power.

Eventually, most of the prisoners were marched and transported to Thailand to construct the "Death Railway," which included the bridges over the Kwae Noi River – made famous by the film *Bridge over the River Kwai*.

The decisive Battle of the Java Sea, which commenced on February 27, pitted the combined American-British-Dutch-Australian (ABDA) naval force, under Dutch Rear Admiral Karel W. F. M. Doorman against Rear Admiral Takeo Takagi's Imperial Japanese fleet. The ABDA Eastern Strike Force, as it was known, consisted of two heavy cruisers – HMS *Exeter* and USS *Houston* – three light cruisers, Doorman's flagship HNLMS *De Ruyter*, HNLMS *Java*, HMAS *Perth*, and nine destroyers – HMS *Electra*, HMS *Encounter*, HMS *Jupiter*, HNLMS *Kortenaer*, HNLMS *Witte de With*, USS *Alden*, USS *John D. Edwards*, USS *John D. Ford*, and USS *Paul Jones*. They faced a Japanese fleet of two heavy cruisers, two light cruisers, 14 destroyers, and ten transports.

When it was over two of ABDA's light cruisers and three destroyers had been sunk, the heavy cruiser *Exeter* damaged, and 2,300 sailors killed including Rear Admiral Doorman. Only the cruisers HMAS *Perth* and USS *Houston* remained undamaged. Japanese losses were one destroyer damaged and 36 sailors killed. Both *Perth* and *Houston* were sunk in a night action shortly after midnight of March 1. Of the 1,061 aboard *Houston*, 368 survived, including 24 of the 74-man Marine detachment, only to be captured by the Japanese and interned in prison camps.* *Perth*'s toll was 353 killed: 342 Royal Australian Navy, five Royal Navy, three Royal Australian Air Force, three civilian canteen workers, and the ship's mascot – a black cat called Red Lead. Destroying the ABDA force removed the last Allied naval force threat to the Japanese conquest of the Southwest Pacific.

At first, the Japanese advance through the South and Southwest Pacific had been shielded by their movement into the Central Pacific, where they won initial successes with the occupation of Tarawa and Makin in the Gilbert Islands on December 9, 1941. This had been followed by Japanese penetration of the Bismarck Archipelago, of which Rabaul on New Britain was the hub.

By March, 1942 Japan controlled Malaya, New Guinea, and the Solomon Islands, had invaded Borneo and the Celebes, taken Amboina, and landed in Sumatra. The Japanese established large bases at Rabaul and Kavieng in Papua New Guinea, and Kolombangara in the Solomon

---

* 106 died during their internment: 105 naval and 1 RAAF, including 38 killed by Allied attacks on Japanese "hell ships." The surviving 218 were repatriated after the war.

Islands. On February 19, 1942, they bombed Darwin, Australia, into rubble, and the next day began landing on Timor, the island closest to Australia's northwest coast.

On April 9, 1942, U.S. forces on Bataan surrendered unconditionally to the Japanese and on April 10 the Bataan Death March began. 76,000 Allied POWs, including 12,000 Americans, were forced to walk 60 miles under a blazing sun without food or water toward a new POW camp. As a result, over 5,000 American died.* It was May 6 when General Jonathan M. Wainwright unconditionally surrendered all U.S. and Filipino forces in the Philippines. The last U.S. troops holding out on Mindanao surrendered on May 12.

As one bloody month of defeat flowed into the next, the Allies were losing the war. In Russia not only were the Germans within sight of Moscow, but Murmansk, the only year-round ice-free port, was bombed almost into oblivion by German aircraft staging from bases in Finland only 40 miles away. On June 13, Field Marshall Erwin Rommel's Afrika Korps had pushed British forces back to El Alamein in Egypt. German officers were sending messages making reservations at Cairo hotels, three hours and 160 miles to the east.

Further east in the China-Burma-India Theater, two Chinese armies under the American General Joseph Stillwell were smashed and the overland supply route (the 'Burma Road') from India to China through Burma was closed.

Every night fires from torpedoed ships lit up the east coast of the United States as U-boats prowled almost unmolested offshore. For the seaman and sailors in Atlantic and Arctic convoys it wasn't a question of if you'd be torpedoed, but when. On the west coast of the United States the first Japanese attack on the U.S. mainland came when a submarine shelled an oil refinery near Santa Barbara, California, on May 2.

On the Eastern Front in Russia the Soviet armies were being hard pressed to hold their positions. Soviet Premier Josef Stalin demanded the U.S. and Britain immediately open a second front in Europe, forcing Germany to move forces westward.

---

*   Among the prisoners who died in the POW camp was Coast Guard Lieutenant James E. Crotty, the only Coast Guard POW in World War II. For the full story see: *Lt. Thomas James Eugene Crotty: Mine Specialist, Demolitions Expert, Naval Officer, Artilleryman, Marine and Coast Guardsman in the Battle for Corregidor* by William H. Thiesen, Historian, Coast Guard Atlantic Area, https://www.uscg.mil/history/people/CrottyThomasEbio.pdf

Meeting with Soviet Foreign Minister Molotov in May 1942, President Roosevelt, concerned that the Russians might make a separate peace with Germany, promised Molotov that he "expected" to launch a second front that year.* Churchill and his chiefs of staff were convinced that an invasion of Northern France was not practical at that time. Due to insufficient troops and inadequate landing craft, they believed such a move would fail.

Meanwhile, the Japanese made their next move to isolate Australia – the occupation of Port Moresby on the southwest coast of Papua New Guinea. Their relentless advance had brought them, by May 1942, to a point within 200 air miles of Port Moresby, the main Allied outpost in New Guinea. The possession of this port was vital to both combatants. A heavily escorted invasion force left the Japanese base at Rabaul on May 4 only to run into U.S. Admiral Jack Fletcher's carrier task force.

On May 5 and 6, opposing carrier groups sought each other, and in the morning of May 7 Japanese carrier-based planes sank the U.S. destroyer *Sims* and fleet oiler *Neosho*. Fletcher's planes sank the light carrier *Shōhō* and a cruiser. The next day Japanese aircraft damaged the U.S. carrier *Lexington*, which was eventually scuttled, and damaged the carrier *Yorktown*, while U.S. planes so crippled the large Japanese carrier *Shōkaku* that it had to retire from action. So many Japanese planes were lost that the Port Moresby invasion force, without adequate air cover and harassed by Allied land-based bombers, turned back to Rabaul. For the first time since Pearl Harbor, Japanese plans were blocked.

In the Battle of the Coral Sea the Imperial Japanese Navy (IJN) was beaten in the first aircraft carrier battle in history. U.S. losses included the carrier *Lexington* sunk, the carrier *Yorktown* damaged, one destroyer and one oiler sunk, 69 aircraft destroyed, and 656 men killed. Japan lost a light carrier, one destroyer, three small warships, and 92 aircraft. One fleet carrier, one destroyer,

---

* There are discussions regarding what Roosevelt promised to do. The official transcript reads: "The President then put to General Marshall the query whether the U.S. was preparing a second front. 'Yes,' replied the General. The President then authorized Mr. Molotov to inform Mr. Stalin that we expect the formation of a second front this year." Molotov's summary to Stalin quoted FDR as saying, "This is our hope. This is our wish." Sources: i) Rzheshevsky, Oleg, *War and Diplomacy: The Making of the Grand Alliance*, Taylor & Breach, Abingdon, 1996, pages 179–180, 185–187, 204–206, 219; and ii) *August 1942: Winston Churchill and the Raid on Dieppe. "The People Who Planned It Should Be Shot"*, Churchill Center, Finest Hour 154, Spring 2012, http://www.winstonchurchill.org/publications/finest-hour/73-finest-hour-154/1679-august-1942-winston-churchill-and-the-raid-on-dieppe

two smaller warships, and one transport were damaged, and 966 men were killed. Tactically the Japanese had won, but the strategic victory belonged to the U.S. Although the U.S. lost a carrier, a fleet oiler, and a destroyer, Japan's planned invasion of Port Moresby was stopped.

The turning point in the War in the Pacific occurred on June 3–7 at the Battle of Midway, an island 3,000 miles northwest of Hawaii. After initial heavy aircraft losses, U.S. torpedo planes and dive-bombers from the carriers *Enterprise*, *Hornet*, and *Yorktown* destroyed four Japanese carriers, and a cruiser, and damaged another cruiser and two destroyers. The U.S. lost *Yorktown*, one destroyer, 150 land- and carrier-based aircraft, and 307 men.

Three U.S. airmen, Ensign Wesley Osmus, a pilot from *Yorktown*, Ensign Frank O'Flaherty, a pilot from *Enterprise* and Aviation Machinist's Mate B. F. (or B. P.) Bruno Gaido, the radioman-gunner of O'Flaherty's SBD, were captured by the Japanese during the battle. All three were interrogated, and then killed by being tied to water-filled kerosene cans and thrown overboard to drown.[22]

IJN losses were four fleet carriers, one cruiser, 292 aircraft, and 3,057 men. Five other ships suffered damage. The battle turned back the Japanese invasion force bound for Midway. It also broke the back of Japanese carrier air power and killed the cream of Japanese carrier aircraft pilots.[23]

Through the grim, early days of 1942 Allied planners worked to turn the tide. Command structures in each theater – the Pacific, North Africa/Mediterranean, and China–Burma–India – were established. Competing Navy and Army interests posed a problem in the Pacific. Therefore, on March 30 the U.S. Joint Chiefs established the two Pacific areas – the Pacific Ocean Areas and Southwest Pacific Area – set their geographical limits, named the commanders, and assigned missions.

Admiral Chester Nimitz would command Pacific Ocean Areas and General Douglas MacArthur the Southwest Pacific Area. Nimitz's command encompassed Hawaii, the Gilberts, the Marshalls, the Mandated Islands, and Japan, except for a broad band of ocean off the coast of Central and South America. MacArthur was responsible for Australia, the Philippines, New Guinea, the Solomons, the Bismarck Archipelago, and all of the Netherlands Indies except Sumatra.[24] In the China–Burma–India Theater U.S. Army Lieutenant General Joseph W. Stilwell assumed the position of chief of staff to Chinese leader Chiang Kai-shek.

It wasn't until September 12 that Allied Forces Headquarters, which planned and directed ground, air, and naval operations and military government activities in the North African and Mediterranean theaters, was established. The Commander-in-Chief, Allied (Expeditionary) Force was General Dwight D. Eisenhower. His Deputy Commander-in-Chief, British General Harold Alexander, was responsible for the detailed planning and preparation, and the actual conduct, of combat operations.

The United States and Britain examined the feasibility of a cross-channel attack into France during the summer of 1942, primarily to take pressure off the Soviet Union. Codenamed *Sledgehammer*, the operation was to open with a 15-day air attack, the strategic purpose of which would be to divert the German Air Force from the east. The immediate tactical objectives were to establish control of the air over the English Channel and at least 60 miles inland between Dunkirk and Abbeville, and to inflict the maximum damage on German military installations and lines of communication.

The British chiefs of staff were steadfastly opposed to *Sledgehammer* as they considered it an operation that had no reasonable chance of success. Since it would mainly involve British troops under British command their opposition was decisive.[25] Throughout the discussions, apart from a listing of the barge requirements and a notation that both the Americans and British would have to construct special craft, very little attention was given to the critical problem of landing craft. In July the decision was made to abandon *Sledgehammer* and undertake the invasion of North Africa as the major effort in the Atlantic in 1942.

Despite the decision to invade North Africa, on August 19, Operation *Rutter* (later renamed *Jubilee*) commenced – a raid on Dieppe in France. The two chief purposes of the Dieppe raid were to test German defensive strength and tactics on a strategically important shoreline and to gain experience in combined operations techniques for large forces. Prime Minister Winston Churchill called it "an indispensable preliminary to full-scale operations."[26]

Approximately 5,000 Canadians, 1,000 British troops, 15 Free French commandos, and 50 U.S. Rangers along with 237 ships and landing craft, constituted the assault force. Seventy-four squadrons of aircraft, of which 66 were fighter squadrons, from the Royal Navy, Royal Air Force, Free Polish Air Force, and the U. S. Army Air Force supported the operation. The force landed under British command at six beaches in the vicinity of Dieppe on the German-held Channel coast of France.

The attack was conducted in two phases. Commando units and elements of two Canadian regiments on board LCAs landed at 0450, without gunfire or air support, at four points on the flanks of the main Dieppe assault. They had been ordered to destroy two coastal defense batteries (of 12 6in howitzers each) and to support the main effort. Only the British No. 4 Commando, commanded by Lieutenant Colonel Lord Lovat managed to gain the surprise it sought, destroy the battery assigned to it, and quickly re-embark.

The main landing at Dieppe was preceded by limited destroyer and mortar gunboat bombardment and covered by a smoke screen. A total of 29 British and Canadian tanks in LCTs with accompanying engineers and infantry in LCAs formed the assault waves. Two tanks drowned as they went off the landing craft. The remaining 27, poorly suited for fighting through Dieppe's narrow streets, many of which were lined with reinforced and heavily fortified houses, suffered heavy casualties.

At 1100, under heavy fire, the withdrawal from the beaches began. It was completed by 1400. Tanks that had survived the battle were abandoned by their crews.

Out of the 6,086 men who made it ashore in this "indispensable" raid, 3,367 Canadians, 275 British commandos, and one U.S. Ranger were killed, wounded or taken prisoner. The Royal Navy lost the destroyer HMS *Berkeley* sunk, and 33 landing craft, suffering 550 dead and wounded. The RAF lost over 100 aircraft to the Luftwaffe's 48. The German army casualties were 311 dead and 280 wounded.

The positive results were a few prisoners taken, enemy forces and installations destroyed, and the collection of valuable intelligence about enemy coastal defenses.[27] Allied losses were viewed as a necessary evil. Winston Churchill remarked that, "My impression of 'Jubilee' is that the results fully justified the heavy cost" and that it "was a Canadian contribution of the greatest significance to final victory."[28] However, no other major raid was mounted in the three months leading up to the invasion of North Africa (Operation *Torch*) in November.

In the Pacific, although their invasion of Port Moresby, New Guinea, was blocked by Australian and New Zealand forces in May, the Japanese established a major base at Rabaul on New Britain Island and, further south, the bases on the Solomons and New Guinea. From Lae and Salamaua on the northern coast of New Guinea they threatened the main Australian base at Port Moresby, the key to MacArthur's defense of Australia. In June they began to construct airfields on Tulagi and Guadalcanal at the southeastern tip of the Solomons. These posed an even more grave threat to the Allied positions in New Caledonia and the Fijis.

General George C. Marshall, U.S. Army Chief of Staff, and Admiral Ernest J. King, Chief of Naval Operations, issued a joint directive on July 2, 1942, calling for an offensive to be mounted at once with the ultimate object of seizing the New Britain-New Ireland-New Guinea area. The directive laid down three major phases or tasks:

Task One was the seizure of the Santa Cruz Islands, Tulagi, and adjacent positions;

Task Two, the conquest of the remainder of the Solomons and of the northwest coast of New Guinea;

Task Three, the final assault on Rabaul and the surrounding area.

The Navy chose Guadalcanal and Tulagi as the first U.S. amphibious offensive operation. D-Day was set for August 7.[29]

The die was cast and reconquest was about to begin.

CHAPTER 2
FIRST STRIKE

GUADALCANAL, TULAGI, GAVUTU, AND FLORIDA
SOUTH SOLOMON ISLANDS, AUGUST 1942–FEBRUARY 1943

Although the Japanese forces were turned back in the Battle of the Coral Sea in May 1942, and defeated at Midway in June, they continued to expand their control in the Pacific by occupying the Attu and Kiska islands off Alaska as well as moving down the New Guinea coast toward Port Moresby in the South Pacific. Striking south from Rabaul, they also moved to Bougainville in the British Solomon Islands.

In April U.S. planners decided to halt the Japanese advance by attacking their bases in the southern Solomon Islands. Their objectives were the large island of Guadalcanal and the small islands of Tulagi and Gavutu, just off Florida Island, where the former British governmental headquarters provided modern buildings and equipment. The Japanese reportedly stationed 1,850 men in the Tulagi area and 5,275 on Guadalcanal, just 20 miles south across Sealark Channel to the south.

The need for quick action was reinforced when Australian coast watchers[*] reported that the seaplane base on Tulagi was being augmented with an airfield

---

[*] The Coast Watcher organization was originated by the Australian Navy in 1919 to provide protection along Australia's long coast line. By September 1939, there were about 800 coast watchers The coast watchers' code name "Ferdinand" was chosen after the children's storybook character Ferdinand the Bull as a reminder that their purpose was not to fight and draw attention to themselves, but rather to quietly observe. Source: Feldt, Eric A., *The Coast Watchers*, Ballantine Books, New York, 1946

on Guadalcanal. The Japanese had already established airfields for land-based planes at Rabaul, Kieta on Bougainville, and now on Guadalcanal, along with seaplane bases at Gavutu, Gizo, Rekata Bay, Kieta, Buka Passage, and Tulagi. Aircraft from these bases bombed Darwin on Australia's northeast coast, interdicted Allied convoys bound for Australia, and, if left unchecked, would give the Japanese control over the entire region. As such, preparations for the invasion were accelerated, and D-Day was set for August 7.

Vice Admiral Robert L. Ghormley, USN, was commander of all the United Nations land, sea, and air forces in SWPA with the exception of New Zealand's land defense forces. As there were not sufficient U.S. Army ground forces in the area to mount the invasion, the Marines were given the assignment.

Major General Alexander A. Vandegrift, USMC, was to lead the occupation forces as commander of the 1st Marine Division, the first echelon of which reached New Zealand on June 14, 1942. The operation, codenamed *Watchtower*,* was composed of three major task forces. Task Force Negat, commanded by Vice Admiral Jack Fletcher, USN, would supply aircraft carrier support for the attack. Amphibious Force Task Force Tare, under command of Rear Admiral Richmond K. Turner, was to make the principal attack, transporting and landing the Marines and defending the transport convoys from surface attack. The third and final task force, Mike, with Rear Admiral V. A. C. Crutchley, RN, commanding, would provide aerial scouting and advance bombing of the operations area.

The invasion force, composed of 80 ships, proceeded to Koro Island in the Fijis where rehearsal exercises were held from July 28 through July 31. Only a third of the Marines who were supposed to take part in the rehearsal for an amphibious landing had the opportunity to debark or get any shore-side training. On the positive side, gunfire support ships and the air support aircraft carried out the pre-landing shelling and bombings as planned and learned from the practice drills.

John Colby, one of the landing craft coxswains on board USS *Hunter Liggett* (AP-27) under Commander Louis W. Perkins, USCG, remembers one of the key obstacles they came across when rehearsing the landings: "The coral reefs were tearing up propellers and bottoms of the boats. I went to Commander Dexter [USCG] and recommended we stop before we ran out of boats for the real landings."

---

* Because of the almost ad hoc nature of the operation it acquired the nickname "Operation Shoestring".

The rehearsals would go on, however, Commander C. B. Hunt, USCG, commanding officer of USS *Alhena* (AK-26) recalled:

> Off Onslow Beach in the early days I acted as a spare parts supply ship, doling out engines and propellers to replace those that were burned or beaten up. How well the others had been trained I do not know, but we all certainly heard from the Boss [Rear Admiral Turner] after the first rehearsal in the Fijis. Kelly sounded off in no uncertain terms and no one was spared. We hoisted the boats in and did it again. Times were cut about fifty percent, but still it was not good enough. The third time we all thought that we did a real bang-up job, but not so, according to the Boss. And he was right. After a conference aboard his ship that night we went out to sea, came in and did it again in about one third of the time of our first try and with ten times the precision.

It was planned that 19,546 Marines organized into eight groups would debark over a five-hour period. The first at 0740 would be the 1st Battalion, 2d Marine Division (Combat Team C) landing on the south coast of Florida Island at Haleta and Halavo. The 1st Raider Battalion,* commanded by Colonel Merritt A. "Red Mike" Edson, followed by the 2d Battalion, 5th Marine Division, was to land on Tulagi's south coast at 0800 and was to seize the northwest section of the island.

Marines of the 5th Division (less the 2d Battalion) (Combat Group A) were to land at 0910 on Red Beach, about halfway between Lunga and Koli points on the north coast of Guadalcanal (codenamed "Cactus"), and seize the beachhead. Combat Group B, landing in the same place 50 minutes later, was to pass through the right of Group A and seize a grassy knoll four miles south of Lunga Point. Last, at 1200, the 1st Marine Parachute Battalion (Combat Team B) was to land on the east coast of Gavutu Island at H+4 hours, seize that island, and press on to adjacent Tanambogo (Tulagi and adjacent islands were codenamed "Ringbolt").

The Support Group, with its command post afloat in *Hunter Liggett*, was to go ashore at Red Beach, Guadalcanal, arrange artillery support for the attack, and coordinate antiaircraft and close-in ground defense of the beachhead area.

---

* The first two elite Marine Raider battalions were established in 1942. Their composition was modeled after the British Commandos and the Chinese Communist Eighth Route Army guerrilla organization and tactics.

Division Reserve Group was to be prepared to land Combat Team B on Gavutu Island and attach Combat Team C to the Tulagi Group.

The 3d Marine Defense Battalion was to land detachments on Red Beach, Tulagi, and Gavutu on receipt of orders. Sufficient men were to be left on board the transports to ensure expeditious unloading of all ships, working on a 24-hour basis while shore party commanders were to coordinate traffic in the beach areas. This included calling on troop commanders in their immediate vicinity for assistance in handling supplies from landing beaches to dumps.

Invasion – the 1st Day

Coast Guard Signalman Ray Evans recalls:

> At 0133 on August 7, the dark shore line of Guadalcanal could be plainly seen under the thin crescent of the waning moon. A little later Savo Island was visible. An hour and a half later, the two squadrons separated, Squadron YOKE passing north of Savo Island toward Tulagi and Squadron X-Ray passing east to south of Savo Island along the north shore of Guadalcanal.
>
> There was no challenge and the fleet's arrival was apparently undetected. At 0530 the first planes took off from the carriers. The fifteen transports of Squadron X-Ray steamed along the silent Guadalcanal shore in two columns of seven and eight ships, arranged in the initial debarkation order. At 0613 the bombardment of the coast was begun by the [cruiser] *Quincy* and dive-bombers shortly afterward began attacking enemy shore positions.
>
> In the predawn darkness the flash of gun turrets was like lightning flashes followed by the rushing sound of a train passing and the heart-stopping concussion of their impact on the beaches and inland. We see the explosions on shore, and I remember thinking what sort of hell that must be to be on the receiving end.[1]

At 0547 the transports halted 9,000 yards [four and a half nautical miles] off Red Beach. Boats were hoisted out and the debarkation began. Cruisers and destroyers, which were not giving fire support for the landings, formed a double arc about them to protect against enemy planes and submarines.

Tulagi

The bombardment of the Tulagi area began almost at the same time as that of Red Beach on Guadalcanal. Going into action at 0614, U.S. fighters and dive-bombers started fires, destroyed eighteen enemy planes on the water, strafed the beaches, and pounded every building that might be hiding the enemy.

At 0637 the ships arrived in the Tulagi transport area. They were half an hour behind schedule so the landing force was immediately ordered ashore. H-hour was scheduled at 0800 and remained unchanged so that none of the transports stood idle before their troops were landed. Even the preliminary landing force for Haleta, and the one for Halavo some distance away, both of which were in the USS *President Jackson* (AP-37), made the first landing on time.

Company B, 2d Marines, under the command of Captain E. J. Crane, landed at 0740 near the village of Haleta on a Florida Island promontory overlooking the island fortress of Tulagi. Heavily armed Japanese defenders resisted fiercely. Well entrenched and cut off from escape, they fought to the death.

Louis T. Birch, Boatswain's Mate, Second Class, USCG, on board the fast attack transport USS *McKean* (ADP-5), remembers the landing:

> I was detailed as engineer of one of four landing boats that we carried on our ship. All boat crews were given instructions and maps showing the exact place that our boats were to land. The place chosen for us was directly in front of a graveyard. The landings were supposed to be made on the side of the island where it was shown as unfit for landings in order to help us surprise the enemy.
>
> The boats to be used in this landing from my ship were thirty-six foot Higgins boats, powered by Gray Diesel motors, having three-eighth-inch armor plate in bow and stern and armed with two thirty-caliber machine guns. Most of the landing boats had a four-man crew – coxswain, engineer, and two machine gunners.
>
> About 0715, the four ships in our division proceeded to a position about two and a half miles from the beach at the point we were supposed to land. Boats were loaded at the rail at 0730 and we hit the line of departure at H-hour, around 0830.
>
> Five-inch shells were flying over our heads all the way in, and range of fire was raised a little as we got closer. When we were about five hundred yards from the beach, Jap machine guns opened fire at us. Then the Marine

gunners in the first wave fired back and there was hell to pay. Machine gun bullets hit our boat, but no damage was done.

Suddenly the firing from shore stopped. Birch, standing behind his engine, thought the Japanese were waiting until the boats struck the beach – big targets to be riddled at will. He recalled:

> The time from this point on until we unloaded was really breathtaking, as we were expecting to get drilled with machine gun fire after hitting the beach. The six-inch gun that was only five hundred yards away from the boats did open up just before we hit the beach, but the fire was directed at one of the cruisers shelling the beach. This gun was destroyed by our naval ships lying off from the beach in just a few minutes. Our boat waves hit the beach, unloaded the Marines, and departed safely. After making the landings, we reported back to the ship to await further orders. There were a few amphibian tanks and tanks landed on this island. None of our men were killed during the first day of landings, but a few were injured.

At Tulagi not a single landing craft of the first wave was able to set its Marines directly ashore. All of them were grounded on coral formations at distances varying from 30 to well over 100 yards from the beach line. Assault personnel of Raider Companies B and D, under the command of Colonel Merritt A. "Red Mike" Edson, waded ashore at 0800 through water from waist to armpit deep against no opposition.

"We started to land at southwest corner of Tulagi, but as we approached, machine guns started firing from hospital windows. This was our first experience with Jap trickery, since we had purposely not bombed or shelled the hospital," Bernard Riley, a Navy Electrician's Mate on board one of the landing craft reported:

> We turned away and landed further up the beach out of range. As our boat hit the sandy shore, the first Marine jumped out. He was a husky with a long black beard it must have taken six months to grow. I don't know whether he was an officer or a private. All the Marines in speaking to each other used first names.
>
> Others kept jumping ashore. They took last long drags on their cigarettes, grasped rifles or tommy guns, and plunged into the jungle. After a few

seconds we could hear shooting. They were cool as could be and obviously knew their jobs.[2]

Colonel Edson declared later:

> It was impossible to approach the dugouts except from one direction. One man had to crawl while continuously exposed to deadly fire. And no dugout was wiped out until all the Japs inside were dead.
>
> Many times we held dynamite and hand grenades until the last possible second before tossing them into the dugouts, only to have the Japs toss them back.[3]

The story was told that one doughty sergeant found the Japanese tossing bombs back as fast as he threw them in. When a stick of dynamite was looped gracefully back and splintered his leg, he took off with a roar of rage, ran at the dugout entrance, his tommy gun spouting flame, and killed four Japanese soldiers who were shooting at him with automatic rifles. Eight others lay dead inside the one small limestone cave.

Action similar to this exploded all over the cave-ridden islet. The Marines came up against a strongly defended hill, honeycombed with machine-gun nests and mortar emplacements. Withering fire from pillboxes and dugouts held up the Marine advance for several hours. The battle was finally joined at close range, with Marines crawling up rock slides or sneaking down steep cliffs to trap Japanese concealed in caves and drop hand grenades into cliff holes.[4]

Meanwhile, the Japanese defense forces, concentrated in the southeastern third of the island, realized that an all-out assault was under way. "It was a fine beginning of a successful invasion," Birch said, "but it was tough because of that fire in front of us all the way in. Give me a sneak landing any day. They're cleaner and have more suspense. Then you can really concentrate on the boat work as you go in."

The landing east of Haleta was made to prevent the enemy from using a promontory jutting south from Florida Island to enfilade the boats during the landing on Tulagi Island's Blue Beach. At 0706, landing craft left *Jackson*, covered by a bombardment from *San Juan*, *Buchanan*, and *Monssen*. Once again, the attackers had to wade ashore as Blue Beach was completely surrounded by coral reefs, this meant that the landing boats had to halt before reaching the beach line. However, the beach was only lightly fortified as the Japanese had not expected a landing there because of the reef.

Elsewhere, however, it was a different story. Japanese dug in on Hill 208, which was in the center of Tulagi's southwest coast, had not been dislodged by shelling from *San Juan*. This meant that Company C of the Raiders, coming down the southwestern side of the island, ran into a concentration of machine-gun nests, which held them up for an hour. Gunnery Sergeant Michael J. J. Kennedy's method of dealing with this opposition was typical. When his unit was pinned down by Japanese machine-gun fire, Gunnery Sergeant Kennedy waited for a lull in the fire, charged down the hill road with a grenade in his hand, and threw it at the machine-gun emplacement. The Japanese threw it back at him. Kennedy started back to safety, fell down, and had to crawl back up the hill under heavy fire.

Company D advanced roughly parallel to Company C on the opposite side of the island. In that afternoon's fighting the squad of which Private Methodius C. Cecka was a member lost its squad leader. Cecka took over. He grabbed a Browning Automatic Rifle (BAR) from a Marine who had been killed, and opened fire on the Japanese. They shot the Browning out of his hand. He lost one finger and was shot through the elbow, but he continued firing until he ran out of ammunition. He then used a captured Japanese pistol, firing with his left hand. Although he was wounded at about 1500, he didn't report to the sick bay until 2000. At one point, late in the afternoon, Company C was held up by machine-gun fire from a dugout built up in a ravine. Major Kenneth D. Bailey ran to the top of the dugout and began kicking away the rocks and sandbags on top of it to give Marines an opening for their fire. The Japanese in the dugout shot him through the leg.[5]

Another company entered the jungle and headed directly across the island. By 1012 all the waves had reached the beach. However, the island was nowhere near being secured as Major Justice Chambers reported later.[6]

> Every building that we met had its quota of Japs and we had to drive them out or kill them with hand grenades. We had thought that coconut trees would not have enough branches to conceal snipers. But we found that the Japs were small enough to hide in them easily and so we had to examine every tree before we went by. If they had been good shots, few of us would have survived, but, happily, there was no comparison in marksmanship between the Marines and the Japs.[*][7]

---

[*] Lieutenant Colonel Chambers received the Silver Star Medal for evacuating the wounded and directing the night defense of a battalion aid station on Tulagi, where he himself was a seriously wounded patient.

By nightfall, Company D was on the north side of Hill 281 paralleling A Company on the south side. Company B established itself for the night near the government wharf to the north, while C Company protected A Company's right flank to the southern shore. E Company (Weapons) of the Raiders, commanded by Captain George Herring, was in support along the ridge to the west.

Lines were established before nightfall in front of the Residency, where Colonel Edson had his command post. In a house on top of the hill overlooking the cricket field an Observation Post (OP) of seven men under Lieutenant Adams was set up, with machine guns to right and left and front line forward of the two machine guns. From 1800 to 2100, thirsty men went to this house to get water from the sole available source, and the rattling of their canteens doubtless betrayed the OP's position.

All was quiet, but an enemy counterattack was due. The machine guns and front-line troops withdrew in preparation, leaving the OP high and dry. Meanwhile, the enemy was reorganizing. At 2130 they attacked and broke through two companies of Raiders, isolating one of them, and forcing one amphibious battalion near the shore to evacuate at two minutes' notice. All over Tulagi in the inky, slippery jungle night U.S. Marines fought the Japanese hand-to-hand, without rules or mercy, often without weapons. Knives glimmered, rifles and grenades flashed and thudded, and men died in the dark with a groan. In one incident, a lieutenant with eight men met Japanese attackers head-on, and pushed them over a 100ft precipice.

Successive attempts on the OP were made by the Japanese, and the 2d Battalion, which had two wounded, retired to the front line, the latter being taken over by at least 24 Japanese.[8]

Guadalcanal

Expecting to encounter the greatest resistance on Guadalcanal, most of the landing forces were concentrated there. Zero hour for the Guadalcanal landing had been set for 0910.

Ray Evans recalled:

> The transports arrived off Lunga Point and commenced unloading troops. The USS *Hunter Liggett*, Transport Division command vessel, carried 35 landing craft and four tank lighters. As they were waterborne they formed

four circles off the bow and stern, each boat coming alongside momentarily under a cargo net on which the Marines climbed down to embark. Then the boats, in line abreast, perhaps a mile wide, headed for the beach under the protective umbrella of shore bombardment, which lifted as they reached the beach.

Every person in the fleet expected withering machine gun and cannon fire from the beach, and many casualties, which was deadly true of Tulagi and Gavutu Island 20 miles across Sealark Channel. But at Guadalcanal there was, to my knowledge, not a shot fired from the beach. Intelligence learned that there was a Japanese work force of about 2,000 protected by a very small armed contingent.

At 0913 the 5th Marines (less the 2d Battalion) landed without opposition on Red Beach, between Lunga and Koli Points. The first waves crossed the beaches and headed inland, and by 1030 the landing craft were unloading tractors towing artillery and jeeps pulling trailers loaded with supplies. These tore up the soft sand and the initial orderly unloading descended into chaos as supplies piled up faster than they could be moved to dumps. The only reported casualty was a Marine who cut his hand while opening a coconut.

The Marines intended that half the roughly 600-man 1st Pioneer Battalion would be attached to the Support Group, which was tasked with helping with the unloading and the close-in ground defense of the beachhead area at Red Beach.

Apart from one platoon of 52 men who were sent to Tulagi, the rest of the battalion was split between various regiments as reinforcements. These specially trained men were needed for the unloading of logistic support from landing craft and without them Captain Reifsnider, commander of T, had to resort to ordering each transport and cargo ship to land 15 sailors to assist in handling supplies at the beachhead. However, this move only partially alleviated the problem and left the ships shorthanded. The Boat Group Commander of USS *Barnett* wrote:

There were approximately fifteen or twenty men unloading boats and about fifty others in swimming. I beached my boat and started looking for the Beachmaster, who could not be found. While looking for the Beachmaster, I saw about one hundred men lounging around under the palm trees eating coconuts, lying down shooting coconuts from the trees, also playing around and paddling about in rubber boats. All of these men were Marines that should have been unloading boats.

Eventually the Marines were brought back and put to work unloading the boats.

That afternoon Lieutenant Commander Dwight Dexter, USCG, and 40 Coast Guardsmen arrived on the beach to supervise the boat landings, and their unloading and repair, and to salvage any that were damaged or stranded.

After missing the arrival of the invasion fleet the Japanese were quick to respond. At 1045 Australian coast watchers based in Bougainville alerted the task force that 18 bombers were headed toward Guadalcanal. At 1320, between 20 and 25 twin-engine bombers came in over Savo Island at 10,000ft to 14,000ft. Their attack targeted the transports off Guadalcanal. Two were shot down, two more were damaged, and the rest disappeared behind Guadalcanal's mountains without hitting any of the ships. An hour later, between seven and ten single-engine dive-bombers from the direction of Tulagi suddenly dived on X-Ray Squadron off Guadalcanal. One bomb hit *Mugford* (DD-389), killing eight men and wounding 17. Another 14 men were missing. 4F4 Wildcat fighters from the three carriers engaged Japanese planes throughout the afternoon.

During the day approximately 10,000 Marines were put ashore. By nightfall the 1st Battalion of Combat Group A had reached the mouth of the Tenaru River about two miles west of Red Beach, and established the Marines' right flank. No contact with the enemy had been made throughout the day.

Gavutu – Tanambogo

At around 1000, 394 officers and men of the 1st Parachute Battalion, commanded by Major Robert H. Williams, climbed down the nets and into 12 boats from *Heywood* and one boat from *Neville*. These then formed into three waves with one company per wave. At 1026 the first wave left the assembly area, followed at five-minute intervals by the other two waves. Gavutu is almost surrounded by coral shoals, which meant that the landing had to be made on the northeastern side of the island, not far from the causeway connecting it with Tanambogo.

At Gavutu there were not enough boats for simultaneous landings, making a surprise attack impossible. Also, four hours had passed since the Raiders had staged their attack on Tulagi. Therefore, the 1st Parachute Battalion would be making a frontal assault in the face of machine-gun fire from the hill overlooking the seaplane base; the 148ft-high hill formed most of the island.

Originally the landing was to take place at the concrete seaplane ramps, but heavy naval gunfire and bombing by U.S. forces had left huge blocks of cement in the path of the attacking troops. There was a narrow flat strip facing the harbor and most Japanese construction was located there. Concrete docks and seaplane slips extended into the harbor. Machine shops and repair facilities had been built on the docks and nearby shore.

The boats of the first wave came into the beach at three points about 25 yards apart, all near the destroyed dock. They touched shore at exactly 1200 plus 15 seconds. The Japanese let them land, but opened fire as the Marines started to cross the beach, causing heavy casualties. The enemy, in dugouts near the shore and caves in the face of the hill, allowed the first wave of Marines to land then opened up as the second wave disembarked. Three Marines were hit before they could leave the boat and others were shot down as they splashed ashore. While the boats were backing off one was hit and sunk, apparently by a hand grenade thrown from shore, and two of its crew were killed.

Major Williams was badly wounded while leading his men in the first wave and had to be evacuated. His executive officer, Major C. A. Miller, took command. The heavy gunfire forced the landing craft to withdraw 1,000 yards before making a rendezvous with the boats. There the crews administered first aid to wounded Marines and stood by for any call from the beach.

The senior Marine officer requested that the second wave land only a minute and a half behind the first. Because of the opposition, the third wave landed eight minutes ahead of schedule. Again, several Marines were hit before they could disembark, but the rest stormed ashore in the face of heavy fire, which held up the Marines' advance for almost two hours. The Marines on the left flank, however, managed to advance slowly inland against bitter opposition.

While the Parachutists were coming ashore at the dock, First Lieutenant Walter S. Young, battalion communications officer, found that a dugout near the shore and commanding part of the dock still contained enemy troops firing on the Marines. Although it was beyond his duties as communications officer to do so, Lieutenant Young voluntarily tried to silence the enemy in the dugout and was killed by a shot from within as he tried to force an entrance.

Platoon Sergeant Harry M. Tully had seen some of his best friends killed in the deadly fire that greeted the Parachutists on their landing. An excellent marksman, Tully set about avenging his comrades' deaths. Showing patience that is rare under fire, Tully lay in wait for long periods to make sure of snipers' positions, then got them in his sights and killed them.

The steep, 148ft high hill facing the Marines was honeycombed with machine guns nestled in caves. The Parachutists found the only effective way of sealing these off was by throwing satchel charges of TNT into the holes. Captain Harry L. Torgerson perfected the method and closed up many of the holes by himself. When the Japanese threw out the explosive charges hurled at them in their hideaways, the Parachutists changed tactics and tied the TNT charges to boards and thrust them into the cavern mouths. Covered by the fire of only four of his men, Captain Torgerson rushed from cave to cave with these crude but effective bombs and came out of his daring day's work with only a wrist watch broken and his trousers blasted off.

Second Lieutenant Harold A. Hayes led the way into enemy caves in the final mop-up. Many of the cliff-side holes were still occupied by Japanese who were armed and resisting to the end. Hayes and his men cleaned them out, killing those who still resisted and taking seven prisoners.

By late afternoon the Marines controlled most of Gavutu, but Japanese machine guns still raked the causeway to Tanambogo. At 1500 six boats from *Jackson* were sent to retrieve men from Company B, Combat Team A, 2nd Marines who had landed earlier that day at Haleta. Three of the boats were redirected to northeastern Tanambogo in an attempt to take the Japanese from the rear. The Marines were scheduled to land at 1845, 20 minutes after sunset when the plan literally blew up when one of the last shells from *Monssen* and *Buchanan* ignited a gasoline tank on shore.

Flight Officer Cecil E. Spencer, one of the Australian officer-guides accompanying the expedition, gives this story of the attack, which occurred at about 1900:

> We reached Gavutu about dusk. But by that time Gavutu was under control. The Marines, however, had been unable to cross the narrow causeway leading to Tanambogo. We had about 5 minutes of naval gunfire support prior to landing. As we were coming in, the last shell hit a fuel dump on the beach, lighting up the beach like day, and the Japs opened fire from their dugout on Tanambogo Hill.

Only two boat loads of our men got ashore. The coxswain of the third boat had been hit in the head by a bullet and killed, and there had been some confusion as to who was to take over the wheel. In the confusion the boat got turned around. We on shore were jammed between two piers. The only cover we could get was afforded by the side of the pier. As soon as we opened fire the Japs spotted our tracers, and in addition we were silhouetted against the flaming oil of the fuel dump.[9]

One of the two boats retired, taking the wounded, and Flight Officer Spencer went with it. Shortly after, he returned with the boat to Tanambogo to evacuate the others. According to Spencer:

We found only six men in the boat which had been left at Tanambogo. They said that the Japs had raided our positions along the piers, and that they believed Captain Crane and the other Marines had been wiped out. But Captain Crane arrived with 6 of his men. They had escaped from the Japs by hiding in the bushes. By 9 or 10 o'clock two more Marines returned, swimming naked toward our boats. Our people fired. But the Marines in the water yelled and were saved.[10]

Invasion – the Second Day

Unloading the transports anchored off Guadalcanal and Tulagi continued unabated through the night, but the logistical nightmare of moving supplies off the beach got worse instead of better. Commander Perkins, captain of *Hunter Liggett* reported:

After dark conditions reached a complete impasse. It is estimated that nearly one hundred boats lay gunwale to gunwale on the beach, while another fifty boats waited, some of these up to six hours, for a chance to land. Despite the quiet night, the Marines had failed to clear the beach and very little cargo was worked prior to the air alarm at 1043 [on August 8].

When some fancy cheese broke out of a melted carton, Commander Perkins commented: "Weapons, ammunition prime movers [jeeps and tractors], and canned rations are more worthwhile than fancy groceries during the first days or even weeks of such an operation."

"About 0600, August 8, commenced to notice canned rations floating around about one mile off the beach," wrote USS *Barnett*'s Boat Group Commander. "Upon approaching the beach I found that most of the supplies which had been unloaded during the night had been dumped at the low water mark, and as the tide came in, these supplies, which consisted of many items such as sugar, coffee, beans, cheese and lard, which were all over the sides of the boats lying on the beach, were being ruined."

At Tulagi, according to the transport *Neville*'s War Diary:

> It was not until about midnight that the first word had been received to send the important food rations and ammunition ashore and from then till daylight it went slowly due to insufficient personnel to unload and conflicting orders as to where to land the stores.
>
> Not all the beach trouble was caused by inadequate Pioneer parties. Often the transports and cargo ships overloaded the landing craft. A considerable number of landing boats, chiefly ramp lighters, were stranded on the beach, adding to the confusion. These ramp boats had been loaded too deeply by the head, and could not be driven far enough up on their particular beach to keep from filling and drowning the engine when the ramp was lowered.

The morning of August 8 brought no relief for the hard-worked transport crews. As dawn broke, the battles for Tulagi and Gavutu roared on. The 3d Battalion of the 2d Marines (Combat Team C) from *President Adams* was first ordered to land on Blue Beach but at 0705 the order was changed and the battalion was directed to proceed in boats to Gavutu. *Adams* steamed part of the way toward Gavutu, reducing the distance the boats would have to travel after launching. Meanwhile, the destroyers *Monssen* and *Buchanan* faced Tanambogo to provide close fire support for another attack on that island.

Shortly before 0900, the first wave of boats left *Adams* for Gavutu, landing on the beach there an hour later. The rest of Combat Team C followed in six more waves. Companies I and K joined the Parachute Battalion in exterminating the few remaining Japanese. Persistent sniper fire from Tanambogo slowed operations, and preparations were made to launch a new attack on that island.

Requests from shore fire control parties came in throughout the day and targets on Gavutu and Tanambogo were shelled consistently by *Buchanan* and *Monssen*. They were assisted by air support, with aircraft also bombing nearby islands from which scattered groups of Japanese maintained sniper fire. The shelling and bombing of Tanambogo was so intense that one spectator was recorded as saying that the island changed from "green to red."

At 1049 Coast Watcher Cecil John Mason, Pilot Officer, RAAF, warned from his Bougainville hideout that 44 Japanese planes were headed toward Guadalcanal. Twenty-five Japanese bombers carrying torpedoes approached from the east end of Florida Island accompanied by approximately 20 "Zero" fighters flying high over Sealark Channel at 1159. The task forces, alerted by the warning, maneuvered at top speed. Ships at Tulagi opened up with intense antiaircraft fire as the planes passed them only 50ft above the water, shooting down between nine and 15 planes.

Birch recalled the air raid:

> Three planes came in at our ship to launch torpedoes, but two were shot down and the other was damaged so bad it changed course and proceeded for the beach, later falling between two small islands a few miles away. All 20 Jap planes were shot down by our ships and planes. During the raid, I had only a .30-caliber rifle to fire at the Jap planes, but nonetheless I kept firing at it. I was a little shaky when the first plane came in at our ship, but after firing for a while, I was having a big time – it was just like shooting at ducks, the only difference being that I enjoyed seeing them fall more than ducks.

Motor Machinist's Mate 2nd Class John Gadowski, USCG, on board *Hunter Liggett* when the attack started, remembers:

> One bomber flew along side of us, level with the ship, strafing the *Liggett*. At that time I was on the three-inch gun. We got a lead on him and let loose. Blew his engine right out of the plane. I cannot forget the expression on the Jap pilot's face, he looked so dumbfounded. The plane burst into flames and he tried to crash dive into the ship but couldn't make it. He hit the water a few feet from the ship.

Only three planes passed entirely through and around the transports, and two of these were shot down by screening vessels to the west. One plane crashed onto the deck of the transport *George F. Elliott* (APA-13), setting her afire. The destroyer *Jarvis* was torpedoed, but she was still able to operate under her own power. Coast Guardsman Orviss T. O'Neal remembers the attack:

> I was running between my ship, the transport *Elliott*, and the beach. On one trip, I had just taken a load of gasoline aboard and was moving away from the ship when the air raid alarm sounded. A few minutes later I watched as a flaming Jap plane crashed into the *Elliott*, setting it afire. I hate to think what might have happened to my landing boat if it ever came within reach of those flames.

Coast Guard Boatswain's Mate First Class Fredrick Mann was on board when the plane was shot down and exploded. He carried a fire hose into the troop ammunition magazine to flood the compartment. After almost passing out from the suffocating smoke, Mann reentered the compartment, recovered the hose, and continued his efforts.

Despite all attempts to check the fire on *Elliott* it continued to spread. Finally the order came to sink the stricken ship. However, despite destroyers firing four torpedoes at close range, *Elliott* was still afloat and on fire until finally sinking on the following evening. Eleven of her crew had been killed and 13 wounded in the attack. Lieutenant C. C. Humphreys, USCG, wrote:

> Can you imagine the transports in one of these operations being attacked by high level bombers out of reach of the ship's gunfire, with those damn bombs dropping too close for comfort and now and then finding the mark? Then an attack by squadrons of Jap torpedo planes skimming over the water at 250 or more miles an hour; straight at the transports, twenty or more planes at one time, with flaming planes smacking the water all around and an occasional one going to roost in flames on the deck of a transport. The air full of machine-gun, anti-aircraft and large caliber shells from the transports and their destroyer and cruiser screen, all aimed at the planes but hitting where they may among the closely packed ships. And the falling shrapnel! The terrific din like the inside of forty boiler factories; the whole area within a five-mile radius full of tracers and bursts like an explosion in a fireworks store. And not one plane left to tell Tojo what happened. Just smoke columns rising out of the sea and a blazing transport falling out of line.

The first major objective on Guadalcanal was the airfield and it was captured by 1600 on July 8. Camp sites at the airfield had obviously been left in a hurry with a large quantity of weapons and personal equipment being abandoned. Within a week Seabees (Naval Construction Battalions) using captured Japanese equipment extended the runway to 4,000ft, long enough for Marine and Navy aircraft to use. It was formally named Henderson Field on August 17.[*]

Off Gavutu, two LCTs from *President Adams* (Landing Tank Lighter No. 1, with G. L. D. Sporhase, Boatswain's Mate, Second Class, as coxswain, and Landing Tank Lighter No. 2, B. W. Hensen, Boatswain's Mate, Second Class, coxswain) loaded two M-3 Light tanks of the Third Platoon, C Company, Second Tank Battalion, commanded by Lieutenant R. J. Sweeney, along with Marine infantry to reinforce the hard-pressed Marines on Tanambogo. Sandbags left by the enemy on the Gavutu beach had been loaded on the lighters for extra protection. As the lighters got under way, the crews saw *Buchanan* pouring salvo after salvo into the beach at Tanambogo.

Smoke and fire billowed from oil drums set afire by the destroyer's shells. After *Buchanan* had ceased fire, the tank commander gave orders for the lighters to proceed to the beach. As it passed the destroyer, the captain waved to the men in the lighters and shouted, "Give 'em hell!" The crews began firing their machine guns at the Japanese on shore, and the tank crews opened fire with their 37mm guns. On reaching the beach, Sporhase dropped the ramp and the tank rolled off. Enemy fire was heavy, and a sergeant who was standing forward of the lighter's engine room was killed instantly. Other Marines followed the tank ashore, a few falling as their small line was raked by enemy fire.

Lighter No. 2 ran aground on the coral a few yards from shore. Henson reported:

> When we couldn't get any nearer the beach, I told Lieutenant Sweeney to run right into the ramp and knock it down with the tank when I gave the signal that the stops were off. So the tank knocked the ramp down and started up the beach with fourteen Marines right behind it. Lieutenant Sweeney had his head

---

[*] It was named in honor of Major Lofton Henderson, USMC, the commanding officer of VMSB-241. He became the first Marine aviator to die during the Battle of Midway when his plane was hit while leading his squadron on a bombing run against the Japanese carrier forces.

sticking out the top of the tank, trying to fire the machine gun, and that is the last I saw of him alive. They shot the top of his head off.

After landing the Marines, the boat crews backed the lighters away from the shore, keeping the ramp between them and the enemy's fire. Heading back for Gavutu, the lighters passed a point of land covered with trees that held Japanese snipers. "We spotted the flash from a gun up in one of these trees," Sporhase reported, "and I picked up the Marine's Reising gun and blasted the flash. The Jap fired again. I got a better bead on him, fired, and he come tumbling down like a bird."

On its return to Gavutu, Lighter No. 1 was ordered to ferry 20 Marines to Tanambogo. This time, because of the protection it provided, the ramp was not lowered, and the Marines bailed out over the sides. Although enemy fire from the island was almost continuous the crew again escaped injury.

By 2200, except for a few isolated nests of snipers, Tulagi, Gavutu, and Tanambogo were in Marine hands. Throughout the evening and night boats ferried supplies to the Marines and evacuated the wounded.

On all three islands there had been an estimated 1,500 Japanese of whom 1,000 had been on Gavutu and Tanambogo. Although no accurate body count could be made, since many were left in blasted caves and dugouts, a reasonable estimate was 1,400 Japanese killed, 23 captured, and 70 escaped to Florida Island. Despite the rugged fighting, Marine casualties were eight officers and 100 enlisted men killed, missing, or dead from wounds; and seven officers and 133 men wounded; a total of 248 casualties.

Not all of the casualties were Marines. Louis Birch, from *McKean*, was helping with the final assaults. "During my last trip to the beach, I saw four boats loaded with Marines from a big transport land on a small island in the harbor. Machine-gun fire from the island was hitting around the boats like rain, but they landed the Marines ashore and captured the island with the loss of one coxswain killed."

———

Warnings from the coast watchers that two Japanese destroyers, three cruisers and two gunboats had been sighted at 1127 on August 8 just north of Bougainville added urgency to the task of getting the transports unloaded. That evening the aircraft carriers *Wasp*, *Saratoga*, and *Enterprise* and their escorts began retiring to the south, as their fuel was running low and their fighter strength had been reduced from 99 to 78 planes.

Without adequate air coverage, the transports and cargo ships were ordered to move out at 0600 the next day, August 9. Initially the planners had assumed that the ships would remain in the target area for four days, and even then all available supplies would prove scanty enough, such was the haste with which the assault was mounted. However, a withdrawal early on August 9 would take most of the supplies and equipment away and leave beach supply dumps in a state of chaos.

The weary transport crews were reaching the end of their endurance. Gadowski recalled:

> We kept having alerts one right after the other. We were wishing for rain, for that was the only thing that could save us. Suddenly we got our wish. It began to rain and it really rained. That put a stop to everything. Everyone seemed so relieved, but we were still shaky. Sunday at 2:30 AM, all hell broke loose. Planes came over and dropped flares, lighting up the whole bay for subs to come in. Everyone was so scared, they could hardly speak. It certainly gave us a funny feeling being so helpless. They could see us but we couldn't see them. Then on the horizon we saw flashes and heard the roar of guns. A big sea battle was in progress. Everyone had a prayer on his lips, for we knew that our lives depended on how the sea battle came out.

Enemy flares silhouetted the transports as though a full moon were shining. The transports got underway, and moved into open water off Guadalcanal because of reports that enemy aircraft were approaching.

The Japanese ships, elements of the Eighth Fleet reported earlier that day, had approached Savo Island undetected by the destroyers *Ralph Talbot* and *Blue* on picket duty northwest of the island. They passed the unsuspecting Americans, and headed toward two Allied cruisers, HMAS *Canberra* and USS *Chicago*, and destroyers USS *Bagley* and *Patterson*, which were patrolling the waters between Savo and Cape Esperance. Farther north, cruisers USS *Vincennes*, *Astoria*, and *Quincy* and destroyers *Helm* and *Wilson* were patrolling between Savo and Florida. Down the channel, the transports were covered by two cruisers and their screening destroyers.

With seaplanes from his cruisers scouting for the Allied ships, the Eighth Fleet commander, Rear Admiral Gunichi Mikawa, steamed southeast until he sighted his enemy about the same time Allied ships in Sealark Channel received reports of one or more unidentified planes. However, Admiral Mikawa's surface force was still undetected at 2313 when these reports came in. Admiral Turner had believed that the Japanese ships would anchor in Rekata Bay on Santa Isabel Island and strike at the amphibious force with torpedo-carrying floatplanes.

At 0316 Mikawa ordered independent firing, and two minutes later torpedoes were fired. Two hit *Canberra* in her starboard side, and *Chicago* lost part of her bow, before the Japanese turned in the direction of the Allied ships between Savo and Florida.

In the resulting battle the Japanese inflicted one of the worst defeats they had ever suffered on the U.S. Navy. Cruisers *Vincennes* and *Quincy* were lost; *Canberra* burned all night and was eventually abandoned and sunk; destroyer *Ralph Talbot* was damaged, and another cruiser, *Astoria*, went down at noon the next day. Unaware that the American carriers had departed the previous evening, Mikawa retired without attacking the amphibious shipping farther down the channel.[*]

Godowsky continued his account of events:

> When daylight came we went searching for survivors. Things didn't look so good. There were many horrible sights, and after seeing those casualties, everyone felt downhearted and miserable. That was our first real taste of battle. We also brought a few Jap prisoners aboard. They were so scared they couldn't talk. They didn't know what was going to happen to them. That day we buried seventeen men at sea and next morning a few more.

Shortly before noon on August 9 the transports were ordered to hoist all boats and prepare to get under way. Many survivors and casualties of *Vincennes*, *Astoria*, and *Quincy* were taken on board *Hunter Liggett*. *Liggett*, acting as a guide to X-Ray Squadron, put to sea at 1510 and set course for Noumea, New Caledonia, leaving the Marines on their own with little ammunition – a total of four units of fire per weapon[†] – and only 37 days' supply of food.

---

[*]   The Japanese force did not escape completely unscathed. On the morning of August 10, Admiral Mikawa detached four heavy cruisers, *Aoba*, *Furutaka*, *Kinugasa*, and *Kako*, unescorted to Kavieng, New Ireland. *Kako* was sunk by torpedoes fired by S-44 at 0715. See http://www.combinedfleet.com/kako_t.htm

[†]   Unit of fire – the number of rounds of ammunition that will normally be used by one weapon in one day. In the Central Pacific, the Army unit of fire for each of the main weapons was as follows:

Even when loaded in Wellington, New Zealand, the level of supplies and ammunition had been considered slim. That original loading of 60 days' supplies was below the 90-day levels then considered normal for operations of this kind, and the ships were taking a proportion of these supplies away. As U.S. air support was so sketchy, no one could predict when the transports would come back again. The stacks of captured Japanese rations were a very important supplement for the American forces left behind.

Lieutenant Commander Dexter established Naval Operating Base (NOB) *Cactus* at Lunga Point with a working crew of Navy sailors and Coast Guardsmen from the transports and APDs. The base's personnel consisted of the Naval Local Defense Force, Boat Repair, and the Harbor Signal Stations on Guadalcanal, Gavutu, and Tulagi.

Ray Evans volunteered to go ashore to establish a signal tower and establish ship-to-shore communications for unloading supplies over the weeks and months of the campaign. Later he wrote:

> On the morning of the eighth we landed and made our way to NOB through a plantation of rigidly laid out coconut palm trees in straight rows about ten feet apart. We found Commander Dexter located in the only plantation house on the beach with about thirty-five landing boats and a dozen tank lighters on the beach or anchored just offshore. Eventually we raised a coconut log tower and platform for signaling with Aldus lamps.

It was August 20 when the aircraft mentioned by Evans reached Henderson Field. The force consisting of 18 Marine F4F Wildcat fighters from VMF-223, Major John L. Smith commanding; and VMSB-232's 13 SBD Dauntless dive-bombers led by Lieutenant Colonel Richard Mangrum flew from the escort carrier *Long Island*. Thqese were the lead elements of Marine Air Group (MAG) 23 led by Lieutenant Colonel Charles L. Fike, group executive officer. U.S. Army Air Force 67th Pursuit Squadron, under

† *(continued from previous page)*

WEAPON	ROUNDS
.30-caliber carbine M1	30
.30-caliber rifle M1903 (Springfield)	70
.30-caliber rifle M1 (Garand)	70
.30-caliber automatic rifle M1918A2	750
.30-caliber machine gun	1,800

Major Dale Brannon, with five Army P-400s arriving two days later.[11] This small force was augmented by 11 SBD dive-bombers from the aircraft carrier USS *Enterprise* that were unable to land because of damage sustained during the Battle of the Eastern Solomons on August 24–25.

During the third week in August malaria first appeared among the troops. Marines racked by dysentery and temperatures of 104 degrees manned their defensive positions.

"Our troops' most vicious enemy was malaria and diarrhea. Quinine was an almost unobtainable drug and Atabrine, its substitute, often was in short supply, resulting in many able bodies lying shivering in hospital tents," recalled Ray Evans.

Suppressive Atabrine (an artificial anti-malarial drug) treatment was inaugurated on September 10, but the disease had gained such a foothold that it became the most serious medical problem of the campaign, incapacitating 1,960 men of the division during October.

Due to Japanese air and sea superiority the first reinforcements and a significant amount of supplies didn't reach Guadalcanal until October 13. Though interrupted twice during the day by Japanese bombing raids, the ships landed the men plus jeeps, trucks, 16 British Bren gun carriers, twelve 37mm guns, ammunition, 70 days' rations, 60 days of other supplies, and 1,000 tons of other cargo. Completely unloaded the two ships embarked the 1st Raider Battalion and sailed for Noumea before nightfall. The reinforcements included 164th Infantry Regiment, an artillery battery, and small contingents from service groups of the Americal Division and 210 men of the 1st Marine Air Wing.

Ray Evans watched the Army land.

> The Army stormed ashore with guns at the ready. We laughingly told them there were no Japanese within miles but they did not believe us and set up their .50-caliber machine guns on tripods on the beach.
>
> We always had a security plane flying perimeter guard whenever we had ships at anchor. This day the pilot had been up there for several hours circling the vessels. As he neared the beach an Army gun crew, thinking it was Japanese about to attack opened fire. Before we could get it stopped, they had damaged the plane and it crashed into the water perhaps a hundred feet off the beach. Fortunately, as I remember, the pilot survived.

The reinforcements helped control the situation on land, but the Japanese remained in control of the sea and their bombers still rained destruction on shipping. Coast Guard Chief John Dunlop, while handling landing barges from USS *Alchiba* (AKA-6), at Lunga, featured prominently in the USS *McFarland* (ADV-14) rescue. Dunlop recalls:

We were down to one day's supply of gas on Guadalcanal as no vessel could come in successfully through the Jap task force and its air activities. On October 17, the *McFarland* took a chance and headed in. Together with a coxswain in another Higgins boat, I towed out a pontoon barge loaded with empty drums. We put the barge alongside and hoses were run from the ship filling up these drums with 100 octane gasoline for our planes. We were about half done when suddenly out of a low-lying cloud and over a hill appeared eight Jap dive bombers. I had been laying off a short distance from *McFarland* because they were loading while under way. When I saw these planes attack the ship, I brought my boat alongside the pontoon barge, which was made fast to *McFarland* to pick up the men who were tending the fueling hoses. I got all but two men in my boat. Those had fallen into the water, and we circled around waiting for an opportunity to pick them up. At this moment two more dive bombers came over and their accuracy was far better than that of the first raiders. A bomb hit the stern of the vessel, setting off the ash cans [depth charges], and another hit the edge of the gasoline barge. Now the two men were surrounded by flaming oil.

I had a full boatload of men so I hollered to the coxswain in the other landing boat to pick up one of the victims and I would get the other one. We had to work fast because we might lose not only the men in the water, but would also be endangering the lives of the men in our craft. I headed my boat toward the man in the burning area, broke through the wall of flame, picked up the man and was out again with none of my boatload of men sustaining anything but minor burns. I only had some of my longer whiskers singed.

The other coxswain rescued his man simply by dropping the landing ramp in the bow of his boat, just like a hippopotamus swallowing up a fish with his lower jaw, scooped up his man without even slowing down.[12]

Her crew saved their ship, and for the next two months, *McFarland* received temporary repairs at Tulagi and Espiritu Santo.

On December 9, Army Major General Alexander M. Patch, commanding general of the Americal Division relieved General Vandegrift. A month later, on January 10, 1943, the combined Army–Marine forces mounted a multi-prong offensive against the remaining Japanese forces on the island.

The morning of February 9, advancing American columns met in Tenaru, marking the end of organized fighting on Guadalcanal. General Patch, after the juncture of forces, sent the following message to Admiral Halsey: "Total and complete defeat of Japanese forces on Guadalcanal effected 1625 today ... Am happy to report this kind of compliance with your orders ... because Tokyo Express no longer has terminus on Guadalcanal."[13]

The envelopment was well conceived but executed too slowly to achieve the complete destruction of the enemy: about 13,000 of the enemy managed to evacuate.

The cost of Guadalcanal including Australian sailors lost was 5,041 killed in action. Defeat for the Japanese was more costly: 15,400 killed or missing in action while 9,000 died of wounds and disease. Approximately 1,000 enemy troops were taken prisoner.

"I am proud to possess a Presidential Unit Citation bar on my old uniform awarded to the First Marine Division, Reinforced for its bravery on Guadalcanal," says Ray Evans. "The 'Reinforced' refers to Navy and Coast Guard contingents as well as other marine units assigned to the island. I am proud to say I served at Guadalcanal with the First Marine Division even though I was spared the mud, blood, and rotting jungle they had to surmount to claim victory."[14]

CHAPTER 3

LIGHTING THE TORCH

INVASION OF NORTH AFRICA, NOVEMBER 8–11, 1942

Allied troops from one of the greatest armadas ever put into a single military operation swarmed ashore on the Vichy French-controlled shores of North Africa before dawn on November 8, 1942. Under the supreme command of Lieutenant General Dwight D. Eisenhower, U.S. and British troops landed at Casablanca, Oran, and Algiers. The objectives of the invasion were to secure French North Africa and then strike eastwards and later link up with General Bernard Montgomery's Eighth Army that was fighting its way west from Egypt. The invasion force consisted of 65,000 men and 650 warships.

General George C. Marshall, Chief of Staff of the United States Army, in his official report to the Secretary of War, expressed the Allied objectives in North Africa, as follows:[1]

The final decision was taken in July 1942 to launch an expedition into northwest Africa. In conjunction with the preparations for the advances westward of the British Eighth Army then reorganizing on the El Alamein line. The opening of the Mediterranean would facilitate Allied global operations, and the removal of the constant threat of German activities in western Morocco and at Dakar would add immeasurably to the security of the Allied position while gathering strength to administer the final punishing blows. Furthermore, if our occupation of North Africa could be carried out without fatally embittering the French troops and authorities in that region it would provide a setting for the reconstitution of the French Amy in preparation for its return in force to the homeland. The psychological effect of the conquest of North Africa would be tremendous.

The Allies justified their assault on North Africa by classifying it as a preventative action that was needed to forestall a planned Axis attack against territories controlled by a friendly neutral nation. Plans for the invasion of French North Africa had to take into account political conditions throughout the French empire. The Vichy government, which came into existence after the French surrender to Germany on June 17, 1940, was led by Marshal Philippe Pétain. Prior to the invasion efforts were made to secure Vichy cooperation for the operation. This task fell to American diplomats since the British had no diplomatic relations with Vichy France. The situation was exacerbated by Royal Navy and RAF attacks on Vichy French naval forces in Mers-el-Kébir and Dakar* to which the French retaliated by bombing the British fleet at Gibraltar.

Robert D. Murphy, counselor to the American Embassy in Vichy, sought to enlist the five-star General Henri Giraud. Although professing loyalty to Pétain, Giraud established contact with other French military leaders, especially in Algeria and Morocco, and worked toward an uprising in the spring of 1943, the then estimated date for the North African invasion.

---

*   Under orders from Churchill the attack on Mers-el-Kébir took place on July 3, 1940. The Royal Navy Force H under Vice Admiral Sir James Somerville attempted to negotiate with French Admiral Marcel-Bruno Gensoul. Before the negotiations were formally ended, the British took action. Swordfish and Skua aircraft flew into the harbor to drop magnetic mines, and French H-75 fighters rose to meet them. One Skua aircraft was shot down during the action, killing the crew. At 1754, the warships of the British Force H opened fire. The battleship *Bretagne* was the first French ship to be hit, during the British third salvo, igniting an ammunition magazine which killed 977 by 1809. After about 30 salvos, all French ships were disabled, but coastal guns continued to fire. On July 8, the carrier HMS *Hermes* launched Swordfish torpedo bombers at Dakar, specifically targeting the battleship *Richelieu*. One torpedo hit *Richelieu* below the armored deck. This attack was followed on September 23, when a combined fleet of British and Free French ships reached Dakar to conduct negotiations en force. On 24 and 25 September, the Allied fleet bombarded the coastal fortifications from the sea. Two Vichy French submarines, *Persée* and *Ajax*, left port on attack, but were sunk during the process; submarine *Bévéziers*, however, was able to penetrate the Allied screen and fire her torpedoes at the British battleship HMS *Resolution*. *Richelieu* was badly damaged in the exchange of fire. Source: Chen, C. Peter, British Attacks on the French Fleet, 3 July 1940–25 September 1940, http://ww2db.com/battle_spec.php?battle_id=96. Reprinted with permission.

In late summer of 1942, Murphy began secret talks with General Charles E. Mast, Chief of Staff of the French 19th Army Corps at Algiers, who headed a small underground pro-resistance group in North Africa. Murphy gave assurances that the French would be treated as a fully sovereign ally and furnished with essential arms and other supplies if they were prepared to assist in the landing of American troops.

By mid-October, the negotiations were mainly concerned with the specific details of Allied–French military cooperation. General agreement on these issues was finally reached on October 22, during a secret rendezvous between General Mark Clark, Murphy, and General Mast on the African coast.

French officials asked whether the Americans and British were prepared to send an effective military force to assist them and whether they would also guarantee the integrity of the French colonial empire. According to Murphy's informants, Admiral François Darlan, the minister in charge of Vichy's defense forces, was ready to shift his allegiance, bringing with him the powerful fleet at Toulon, if the conditions discussed were met. However, Darlan's support was not assured.

Also, contrary to Murphy's intelligence reports, most of the French officers and civilians, with the exception of a small pro-Gaullist minority, were either loyal to Pétain or unwilling to run any risk.

The Allies also had the problem of the unanticipated presence in Algiers of Admiral Darlan, who had flown there on November 5. His arrival in Algiers on the eve of the Allied invasion was occasioned by his son contracting polio. It would be Darlan who issued the orders that the Allied landings be resisted despite Murphy's information that the admiral would shift his allegiance.[2]

Vichy French Forces

When the planning for *Torch* began in London, Allied intelligence sources believed French forces in North Africa totaled 120,000 men: 55,000 were said to be in Morocco, 50,000 in Algeria, and 15,000 in Tunisia. The Germans allowed 12 units of motorized field artillery but almost no medium and no heavy artillery. Mechanized cavalry had at its disposal between 120 and 160 obsolete tanks and 80 armored cars in Morocco, approximately another 110 such tanks and 60 armored cars in Algeria, and only 20 armored cars in Tunisia. In each of the three colonies, one regiment of antiaircraft artillery was dispersed, although at the ports supplementary batteries were manned by naval personnel.

The estimated strength of the French Air Force (*Armée de l'air*) varied with most of it concentrated at Moroccan airdromes. From 155 to 170 combat planes could be expected at the first contact, and within two hours after the alarm, from 166 to 207 additional aircraft from airdromes inland.

Vichy French naval forces in Northwest Africa consisted of only submarines and destroyers at Bizerte and Oran, a 6in cruiser, destroyers and the immobile battleship *Jean Bart* moored in Casablanca Harbor, that was nevertheless capable of firing its guns, at Casablanca, and a battleship and three cruisers at Dakar.[3]

Invasion Objectives

The initial objective of Operation *Torch* was the capture of major airfields and ports along the North African coast. This would deny their use to the Germans and allow the Allies to continue operations from the ground, air, and sea. All this was to be accomplished within 24 hours using a three-pronged assault. The final stage of the operation then called for a cessation and settlement of all hostilities in four days in order for the British portion of the convoys to move into Algiers docks and disembark the British First Army, which was destined to attack Rommel's Africa Korps from the West.

The Western Task Force would land at Casablanca in Morocco, 190 miles south of Gibraltar on the Atlantic coast; the Center Task Force would target Algeria and Oran, 280 miles east of Gibraltar; and the Eastern Task Force would land at Algiers, 500 miles east of Gibraltar.

Each task force was to conduct multiple operations within its area, and a total of 21 separate landings were planned, including one by the British 6th Commandos just west of Algiers, and one by American Rangers at Arzew.

The Eastern Task Force, with a complement of 23,000 British and 10,000 U.S. troops and commanded by Lieutenant General K. A. N. Anderson of the British First Army, would attack Algiers. Major General Charles W. Ryder, commander of the 34th Infantry Division, would lead the American element, which consisted of two reinforced regimental combat teams (RCTs), one each from the 9th and 34th Infantry Divisions, and a Ranger battalion. This task force trained in Britain and was escorted to its destination by units of the

OPERATION *TORCH* LANDINGS, NOVEMBER 1942

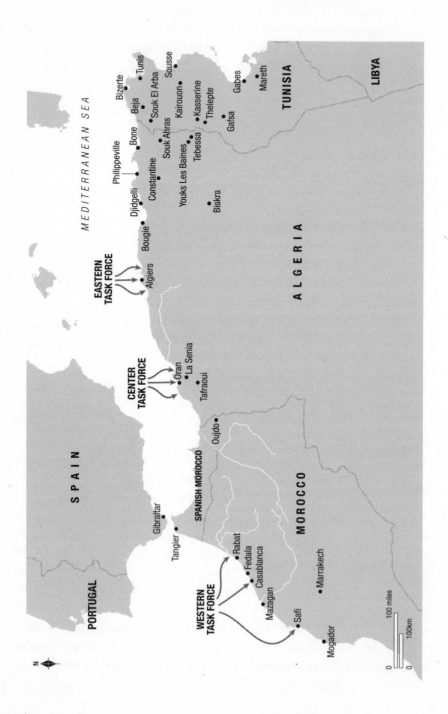

British Royal Navy. General Ryder and his American troops were to spearhead the Eastern Task Force assault in hopes of securing willing cooperation from the French, who were still resentful toward the British because of their bombardment of French Navy ships at Mers-el-Kébir.

A key part of the operation was to prevent the port facilities at Oran and Algiers from being sabotaged. To accomplish this, two destroyers in each task force, loaded with specially trained troops, were detailed to force their way into the respective harbors as the main bodies of troops landed in the surrounding area. Operation *Reservist* targeted Oran while Operation *Terminal* focused on Algiers. Both operations would be launched concurrently with the main assaults.

One phase of the plan for the capture of Oran included dropping 556 paratroops of the 2d Battalion of the 503d Parachute Infantry, commanded by Lieutenant Colonel Edson D. Raff, from 39 C-47s. Two plans were formulated: the "war" plan, which would be used if the French did oppose the landing, entailed most of the paratroops jumping near Tafaraoui and capturing that airdrome; and the "peace" plan, to be implemented if the French did not oppose landings, which would see the planes land at La Senia, where the paratroops would walk in and receive the plaudits of the multitude. The 503d was to take off in Britain on the evening of November 7 and arrive over their target the next morning.[4]

The Center Task Force, under the command of Major General Lloyd R. Fredendall, U.S. Army, was to go ashore on beaches flanking Oran, some 250 miles inside the Mediterranean. The Center Task Force trained in Britain and was convoyed by British warships. Consisting of elements from the U.S. Army II Corps, it was built around the 1st Infantry Division, half of the 1st Armored Division, and a force from the 509th Parachute Infantry Regiment, reinforced by corps troops. In all, the task force comprised more than 40,000 troops.

Commanded by Major General George S. Patton, Jr., the Western Task Force would assault beaches on the Atlantic coast of Morocco in the vicinity of Casablanca. Totaling approximately 34,000 men, it consisted of the 2d Armored Division, the 3d Infantry Division, and two regimental combat teams of the 9th Infantry Division. The Western Task Force trained in the United States and sailed for Africa in ships under the overall command of Rear Admiral H. Kent Hewitt, USN.

Just before the invasion, leaflets explaining that the aims of the invasion were "to protect French North Africa ... and the complete liberation of invaded France" were dropped and at 0100 on November 7, at the moment the landings in Algiers began, President Roosevelt spoke to the French people by short-wave radio, assuring them that the Allies sought no territory and asking for French cooperation against the Nazi regime. He assured the Spanish government also that the invasion was not directed against Spanish Morocco or other Spanish territory in Africa. This was followed by General Eisenhower's proclamation broadcast to the French armies on the land, sea, and in the air in North Africa, which stated, in part:

> Frenchmen of North Africa, the forces which I have the honor of commanding come to you as friends to make war against your enemies.
>
> This is a military operation directed against the Italian–German military forces in North Africa. Our only objective is to defeat the enemy and to free France, I need not tell you that we have no designs either on North Africa or on any part of the French Empire. We count on your friendship and we ask for your aid.
>
> I have given formal orders that no offensive action shall be undertaken against you on condition that for your part you take the same attitude.

Both General Charles de Gaulle, leader of the Free French, and General Henri Giraud, in charge of the French Army in North Africa, broadcast pleas to their countrymen to cooperate with the Allies.

"Arise, every one of you. Help our Allies!" General de Gaulle asked of all French armed forces.

"Join them without reserve! France which fights calls on you!" General Giraud, over Algiers radio, appealed to the French forces in North Africa, exclaiming, "This is our chance of revival!"[5]

Western Task Force Landings

The coast of Morocco is rocky with long, sloping beaches. These meant transports would have to lie a considerable distance from the shore to discharge troops. North Africa's heavy ground swells, high surf and tides were also a problem in planning the landings. Swells towering between 16ft and 20ft were not uncommon along the coast of Morocco. With the approaching winter, bad coastal weather increased. In November weather predictions and

WESTERN TASK FORCE, NOVEMBER 8–11, 1942

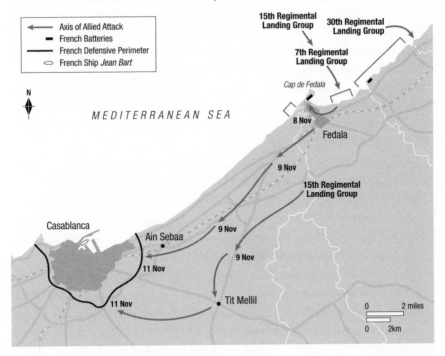

meteorological information had to be accurate to ensure the landings would not be too costly in terms of men and equipment.

In addition to the meteorological and topographical problems, the obstacles facing the invading forces included fixed defenses along the Moroccan coast, supplemented by the mobile strength drawn from the French Army, the French fleet at Casablanca, and both French Army and Navy planes.

After examining intelligence reports, Patton decided that, rather than assaulting Casablanca, where an estimated 50,000 French troops might resist, the task force would come ashore at three detached sites: the Northern Assault Group (*Goalpost*) was to take Mehdia-Port-Lyautey and secure the northern flank of the Western Task Force; the Center Assault Group (*Brushwood*) was tasked with securing Fedala; and the Southern Assault Group (*Blackstone*) was to capture the port of Safi.

Northern Attack Group: *Goalpost*

On the northwestern coast of Morocco, the Navy debarked three landing teams to take Mehdia-Port-Lyautey and secure the Western Task Force's northern flank. *Goalpost* troops, commanded by Major General Lucian K. Truscott, consisted of the 60th Infantry Regiment of the 9th Infantry Division; the 1st Battalion of the 66th Armored Regiment, 2d Armored Division; elements of the 70th Tank Battalion (Separate); and seven coast artillery batteries. With support units, they totaled 9,079 officers and men. The operation's main objectives were airfields at Port-Lyautey and at Sale, 25 miles south near Rabat. To reach them the troops would first have to take the coastal village of Mehdia and the town of Port-Lyautey, five miles inland on the Sebou River.

While the coastline was fairly straight, the Sebou River meandered sharply in an "S" shape to form two peninsulas. The Port-Lyautey airfield lay in the larger peninsula. An advance straight inland from Mehdia was the most direct route to the airfield, but the troops would have to move through a narrow marsh between the river and a lagoon, under the guns of a fortress. From bluffs between the towns, artillery dominated all points. General Truscott decided to land his troops at five beaches along ten miles of shoreline. Two battalion landing teams going ashore south of the river would advance on separate axes to the airfield, while a third would move from the north, down the other peninsula toward Port-Lyautey. If all went as planned the airfield and towns would be under control by sunset of the first day.

Lieutenant Junior Grade Jack Elliott, USNR, with the Naval Beach Party on board USS *Susan B. Anthony* (AP-72), recalls:

> Finally it was here. Suddenly, after dark on the night of November 7, the anchors were dropped, total blackout was enforced for the first time, and the deathly silence after blowers and other machine noises were stopped made us realize that our time to enter the war had come. Around midnight, each of the transports began to prepare for the landing. Cargo nets were slung over the sides of the ships, the landing craft were off-loaded, empty except for the boat crews,* and the signaling flashlights started to signal the beginning of the scariest part of any preparation for landing.
>
> The climbing over a ship's rail in inky darkness, groping with one foot for a piece of the cargo net, carefully finding a hand hold on the net, hopefully two, and then the start down the net, rung by rung, trying to avoid, by feel, stepping on the hands of the man below you, hoping that the man above

---

* The jerry-rigged replacement davits had not been sufficiently tested to warrant entrusting the boats to be loaded with personnel at deck level and then lowered into the sea.

you would also be so kind, realizing, as the net swung out from the ship as it rolled in the tremendous swell, nearer to that part of the African coast, that it was going to swing back in the same pendulum action to smash you and your hands against the rusted, barnacle-encrusted steel side of the ship, hoping as it happened that you wouldn't flinch and cause you to loosen your grip, realizing also that as you swung out from the ship on the outward roll that your weight would probably drop you through the bottom of the landing craft presumed to be down there somewhere in the blackness, with all the guns and ammunition, back packs, and food and water tied to your body one place or another, listening to the cursing and muffled shouts from the boat crew to "get the hell down here, we're in a hurry".

Finally it was over. You had dropped when you could make out the outlines of the landing craft, and, being one of the first over the side, you had fallen into a relatively empty boat, and hadn't squashed any of the beach party under your combat-loaded hulk. You were in a landing craft which, when loaded, would circle with others for an hour or two until enough had been off-loaded to form a line abreast and head for the beach, shepherded by a minesweeper or other shallow-draft ship.

Suddenly, for this particular time of year and segment of the Atlantic Coast of North Africa, you realized that you were embarked in [on], a veritable bucking-bronco making like a latter-day Maid of the Mist. The surf was totally unbelievable.[6]

In fact problems began even before H-Hour, which was set for 0400. While approaching the coast the previous night Navy transports had lost formation and H-Hour was delayed to allow boat crews to improvise assault waves. Heavy seas further slowed debarkation. All landing teams were supposed to go ashore in darkness, but only the first three waves of the 2d Battalion Landing Team managed to make the beach before dawn. Following waves were not only late, but off course. The 1st Battalion Landing Team missed their assigned beach by 2,800 yards while the 3d Battalion Landing Teams missed theirs by five miles.[7]

French opposition caused more confusion and delays. At dawn, French planes strafed the beaches and bombed transports. A strong coast artillery concentration at a fortress near Mehdia rained heavy fire on the transports. To the south, the 1st Battalion Landing Team struggled in the sand for over five hours to regain its beach before rounding the lagoon and starting toward the airfield. However, they were pinned down for the rest of the day by French machine-gun fire and never reached the airfield.

To the rear, French reinforcements from Rabat were firing on landing team outposts. Between the two, the 2d Battalion Landing Team, stopping to await naval gunfire support, was then hit hard by a French counterattack, and was pushed back almost to the beach with heavy losses. While the Navy was firing on the Mehdia fortress, troops ashore did not yet have enough artillery to quiet the French batteries, the fire of which kept tank lighters from landing and forced transports to move out of range before continuing to offload troops and equipment.

Center Attack Group: *Brushwood*

Brushwood's Army contingent, under the command of Major General Jonathan W. Anderson, totaled 1,067 officers, 18,716 enlisted men, and 77 M3 light tanks, and was divided into three parts. The main force – which was to land on four separate beaches near the small town of Fedala – was divided into four columns. Two of those four columns were headed by Coast Guard-manned ships: USS *Leonard Wood* (APA-12), Captain Merlin O'Neill, USCG commanding; and USS *Joseph T. Dickman* (APA-13), Captain Charles William Harwood, USCG commanding.

The measures taken to ensure secrecy and the success of the invasion were attested to by the fact that Casablanca was not blacked out when the task force approached on the night prior to the landings. "They even had a lighthouse lighted," recalled Lieutenant Commander Harry C. Gifford, USCG, Assistant Engineering Officer of *Leonard Wood*.[8]

The necessity for making emergency turns and the use of the emergency turn lights installed on the vessels probably gave the French the first indication that the task force was there. "On the night of our arrival," related Gifford, "immediately upon seeing those lights, the enemy blacked out the entire city within a period of five minutes. The moment that blackout began we knew that we had been discovered. It was about 10 PM."

The transport area about six miles off Fedala was reached a few minutes before midnight on November 7, and the lowering of boats commenced at once. An hour and a half later Scout Boats from USS *Charles Carroll*, and *Joseph T. Dickman* left their rendezvous off the bow of *Leonard Wood* and proceeded to designated points to mark beaches. The debarkation of the landing force was to prove extremely difficult. Considerable confusion was caused by the darkness, which hampered the boats from the combatant ships and those from the transports in their efforts to affect a rendezvous. The waves of boats from *Leonard Wood* were directed toward the beach southwest of Cape Fedala. The waves from USS *Thomas Jefferson* (APA-30), USS *Charles Carroll* (APA-28), and *Joseph T. Dickman* were directed to the beaches between Fedala and the Neffifikh River.

The initial assault objective was to seize a small fort at Pont Blondin on the north side of the wadi, a bridge crossing it, and other points designated as necessary for defense of the beachhead. The landing beach was not considered suitable for landing large quantities of cargo and the adjoining southward beach was designated for that purpose. In view of the expected difficulties retracting boats from the beach, the first five waves hit the beach nearly simultaneously and trusted to skill and good fortune to get back.

The eardrum-bursting pre-invasion bombardment started before daylight. The landing craft, circling offshore, caught the signal and suddenly darted for the beach. "It's all flames, and dive bombers, and red explosions," as one coxswain put it.

A short time later one of the many difficulties that had to be overcome in this operation became manifest. The plans called for 20 boats to be furnished by other vessels to *Dickman*, but the boats became detached from the formation during the maneuvers into the area and only one arrived as scheduled. About half of the total 35 boats needed for the operation were designed to carry vehicles and personnel, and the remainder personnel only. As boats were missing the complicated boat-loading schedule had to be revised under considerable pressure. Fortunately, the Commanding Officer of Troops (Major Bernard) was not a man easily flustered, and a new schedule was quickly arranged with him that permitted 27 of the ship's boats to make up four and a half of the first five waves and to reach the assembly area ahead of time. The destroyer USS *Murphy* (DD-603), acting as control vessel for *Dickman*, escorted these boats to the line of departure then started them into the beach on a signal from the flagship. *Murphy* was hit by a shell from the French battery on Pont Blondin but was not disabled and her return fire was instrumental in silencing the battery.

The 27 boats reached their beach just before the French-manned fort was alerted and unloaded their troops and equipment. Although their return trip was made under fire, not a boat was lost and all 27 returned for another load. A searchlight beam and fire from the fort hit two boats that followed a few minutes later. These two boats were stranded on the rocks, on the northeast side of the Pont Blondin battery, but the troops and crew got ashore without mishap.

The unloading continued and the troops, combat vehicles and equipment landed in good time. At about noon *Dickman* moved closer to the beach, but this advantage was offset by the high surf building up on the beaches, which resulted in the loss of many boats. When the fort at Fedala capitulated the harbor became available but it was too small to accommodate the large amount of supplies being sent in. Lieutenant Elliott later reported about this part of the assault:

> The rapidly rising and falling tide in the small river connecting Fedala and the airport at Port Lyautey, estimated at eleven feet, and the crashing combers along the coastal areas north and south of the Port Lyautey river approach created a combined hazard that wrecked many of our landing craft and caused the drowning deaths of an inordinate number of troops.[9]

No planes attacked the ships, although they were fired upon from a hopelessly long range. Planes did strafe the beaches, shooting up one of *Dickman*'s boats. Two members of the crew, Donald LaRue and R. L. Bucheit, were severely wounded; and the engineman in the boat, Paul Clark, Fireman First Class, took charge, placed the wounded men aboard a destroyer, and completed the boat's mission. He was awarded a Navy Cross for his heroic action. C. C. Curry, a Navy hospital apprentice attached to *Dickman*, was awarded a Silver Star Medal for his courageous treatment of wounded men along the beach while under fire from the planes.

At the beginning of the African invasion, *Leonard Wood* carried six doctors, a dentist, and enlisted medical corpsmen. Lieutenant Richard Campbell, MD, USNR, later told of his experiences: "Nobody knows how many operations we've done – somewhere up in the hundreds. Numbers don't matter, anyhow, it's how many boys you can save." The medical unit, operating almost continuously, survived on black coffee and a quick nap whenever an operating table was vacant.

When landing boats shoved off, the doctors, scrubbed and ready, were at their topside station; the transport had effectively become a floating hospital. The day before, the doctors had taken between 25 and 30 pints of whole blood from crew donors. In response to calls for volunteers, so many eager boys had come forward that as Campbell commented, "It makes you proud to be an American to see those young fellows wanting to do their all even at the moment of going in to face death."

Whole blood was needed in instances of great loss, such as amputation. Plasma, the great lifesaver, was used in the treatment of wound shock. Besides their battle haircuts, the whole crew wore clean clothes, and were shaven against the chance that shrapnel might make them patients also.

Dressing stations were set up all over *Leonard Wood* and could handle 250 casualties. The medical unit rotated at these posts, one doctor and eight corpsmen going in with each beach party. In a foxhole, they set themselves up as a rough-and-ready hospital unit. Doctor Campbell is reported to have said,

> That was where it's really the quick or the dead. On a beachhead, you can only give elementary aid – tourniquets, first treatments of burns, fast dressing to hold a man's insides together. If they're hit bad, you slug them with a half grain of morphine. The LCs bring them back to the ship as fast as we can turn them over. It's not uncommon for a man to go down the landing net into an LC, hit the beach, and be back aboard, wounded in half an hour.
>
> I've never gotten over being surprised at their sheer courage. I've seen a boy propped up against a bulkhead, his leg blown off below the knee; take a cigarette and a glass of grapefruit juice while waiting his turn inside. They never complained. They just sat there, propped up, waiting.[10]

Fifteen minutes after *Leonard Wood* arrived at its assigned debarkation point off Fedala at 0005 on November 8, a beach-marking boat departed to locate and mark the landing Red Beach 2. By 0142 all boats were in the water and the first three waves departed at 0350. The fourth wave departed at 0400 and the fifth wave at 0540.

As the first wave approached the shore, it was illuminated by a searchlight from the direction of Cherugi. Support boats immediately opened fire on the light. A moment later, firing was observed between land batteries at Cherugi and Fedala and U.S. destroyers near the lines of departure. Twenty-one boats from *Leonard Wood* were lost during the initial landing due to striking rocks at the shore line and heavy surf conditions. During the day, a further eight boats were lost trying to run through the surf. Fortunately, there were few personnel casualties either from swamped boats or French gunfire.

"We were scared when the enemy opened fire on us, but it's a cinch we couldn't turn around and go back," is the way Fred Bullock, Seaman Second Class, attached to *Leonard Wood,* expressed himself in relating his feelings about the landing. Before being able to take up his position as a landing barge machine gunner, Bullock had to swim ashore because his boat had been sunk. The majority of the barges lost were capsized due to heavy surf. "We suffered casualties, of course," he observed, "but all that happened to me was that I got wet. Although some transport units were sunk, we managed to land all of the soldiers. I'm glad of just one thing – that I learned how to swim."[11]

When his landing barge was smashed on a reef Douglas M. Pierpont, Jr., Seaman First Class, from *Leonard Wood,* joined the soldiers he had brought ashore and fought alongside them all the way to Casablanca, a distance of 17 miles. "My only close shave," he said, "came when a piece of shrapnel hit my helmet a glancing blow. The opposition was spotty. They'd fire at us until we got near them, and then the French would surrender. It was obvious they didn't want to fight us."

Lieutenant Robert Emerson, a group boat commander from *Leonard Wood,* recalls:

> It was the first landing for all of us, and nothing quite worked out as it does in maneuvers. Landing craft gunboats circled around, protecting us, and we dashed in under destroyers, protecting fire. It was pretty hectic as we laid down our ramps, and soldiers swarmed in under fire. One of the crews couldn't get off in time. They had to get set behind rocks when they heard an enemy platoon approaching. It turned out to be made up of huge black Senegalese with scarred faces and fezzes – Vichy troops. The boys were so surprised at fighting them – just like in an African picture – all they could think of was to yell: "Stick 'em up!" You should have heard them brag about their fancy prisoners.[12]

While his unit was delivering half-ton trucks and soldiers to the shores of Fedala, George Paajanen, Machinist's Mate First Class, from *Leonard Wood,* was badly wounded on the second trip. The men had landed the first truck and boatload of servicemen without incident and gone back to the transport, where they loaded up with another truck and the soldiers to man it. That time, a French plane began a strafing attack against them. "We were about a mile from the beach," related Paajanen, "and by this time the sea had become really heavy. When we landed, the soldier driving the truck said he couldn't get it off the boat because the water was too deep. Waves were breaking over the boat. It seemed the best thing to do was to leave the truck and get ashore." Paajanen then took it upon himself to get the truck ashore. However, it was a hopeless task, so the boat crew gave it up and left the landing barge to get to shore themselves. Just as Paajanen was getting out of the water, a coxswain shouted, "Hit the ground, here comes a plane!" Paajanen turned to look and fell flat on the ground at the same time as the plane let go with a burst of machine-gun fire. He remembers:

> I realized that I'd been hit, but I felt no pain at first. I couldn't walk and my hand was bleeding. The coxswain put a tourniquet on me. Then he went to the First Aid Station and came back with three other Coast Guardsmen and a stretcher. They carried me to the station where a doctor gave me some brandy and morphine shots and put sulfanilamide on my wounds. I was then put on a stretcher again and taken back to the ship's operating room where Dr. Fox went to work on me.[13]

Aboard the transport, Paajanen was given two pints of plasma. It was found that he had a bone broken right above the ankle and one in the thumb. Two bullets had gone through his thighs but missed any bones. Incidentally, the plane that shot him was brought down two minutes later by American antiaircraft fire.

Ensign Robert D. Buckalew, USCGR, in command of the fifth wave to leave *Leonard Wood*, was on a boat carrying an Army jeep and antitank gun, as well as soldiers. As the troop-filled boat drove to shore, the conning tower of a submarine loomed up 300 yards off the port bow. The boat's machine guns were trained on the enemy craft but Buckalew scarcely had time to challenge it before it submerged silently and disappeared. Soon afterwards the boat's steering wheel, which had become loose and which the coxswain was holding in place by pressing his body against it, came off entirely. The boat was stopped and an emergency tiller was rigged. Then the trip was resumed. A landing was made, and the jeep and the antitank gun were driven ashore and the troops followed. Later, the support boat in which Buckalew returned to his ship was sighted by the crew of an enemy gun on the tip of Cape Fedala. By zigzagging rapidly whenever the flash of the gun was seen, Buckalew was able to dodge 18 shells and finally reached his transport, ready for further operations.[14]

Southern Attack Group: *Blackstone*

To seize Safi, Patton selected Major General Ernest N. Harmon, commander of the 2d Armored Division. Harmon's sub-task force *Blackstone* consisted of the 47th Infantry Regiment of the 9th Infantry Division; two reinforced battalions of the 67th Armored Regiment of the 2d Armored Division; elements of the 70th Tank Battalion (Separate); and several artillery batteries. With support units, *Blackstone* troops totaled 6,428 officers and men.

The convoy to Safi halted eight miles offshore, half an hour before midnight on November 7, 1942. The debarkation of troops and equipment was done as quietly as possible since the landing was not preceded by a softening-up bombardment. As the boats turned toward shore, the French let it be known they were not surprised by firing on the transports. U.S. Navy ships immediately returned fire.

As the gun battle went on assault boats from USS *Harris* (APA-2) and USS *Dorothea L. Dix* (AP-67) were loaded with troops and equipment. The ships were rolling badly in the heavy swells. Soldiers carrying 60 pounds of equipment had to go over the rail and down cargo net ladders, clinging on until the fellow ahead was safely in the boat.

Captain James E. Leopold, 47th Regiment, 9th Infantry Division, remembers:

> All was quiet for about two hours and then the rope nets were dropped over the side and the landing boats, which held about forty men each, began to be lowered. When my platoon's turn came, I was the first man down and quickly followed by the rest of my team. There was a heavy ground swell of some twenty feet. As a result the landing boat rose and fell by that much every few moments and the boat's pilot had a tough time holding his small boat against the side of the transport. One of our men, PFC Bridges, was caught on the net at the waterline as the small boat moved away from the ship. The swell came up and covered him. Then the swell moved and Bridges, soaking wet and carrying a load of mortar ammo, was dropped into the water. I got a boat hook to him and held on for a few moments but then he let go and sank out of sight. That was the first war casualty I ever saw and I'll remember the scene clearly for the rest of my life.[15]

It took some boats a full hour to load 36 men and their equipment at the transport's side. Consequently, H-Hour, the date for the rush of landing boats from the departure line, had to be postponed from 0400 to 0430.

The first waves of landing craft plowed through dark swells toward beaches codenamed from north to south "Red," "Blue," "Green," and "Yellow." As naval gunfire pounded French batteries, the first American troops to land in French Morocco – Company K, 47th Infantry – came ashore at 0445 at Green Beach.[16]

During the unloading there occurred the only example in the entire operation of an occurrence common in night warfare – "friendly fire." The tanker attached to each attack group carried on deck, athwart ship, two 63ft gasoline-powered crash boats armed with machine guns, which were intended for use in aircraft rescue. These boats were fragile but unwieldy, very noisy, and of little use except to deliver messages. The two belonging to the Southern Attack Group were nearly lost before daylight.

Around 0430 a motor truck being lowered from *Dorothea L. Dix* into a tank lighter swung with the ship's roll and ruptured a five-gallon gasoline tank that was stowed topside. The gasoline spilled into the tank lighter below and caught fire from the lighter's engine, igniting both the gasoline tank and ammunition. With a flash and roar that could be seen and heard from the other transports, the lighter exploded into a ball of flame.

An unknown radioman began transmitting, "*Dix* torpedoed, *Dix* torpedoed." Just then, the two Southern Attack Group crash boats, which had been laboriously lowered from tanker *Merrimack*, came charging into the transport area from *Dix*'s direction. In the heat of the moment, it was assumed that that they were French motor torpedo boats that had hit *Dix* and were looking for other targets. *Lyon*'s and *Calvert*'s gun crews aimed at the boats and let rip with everything they had. Fortunately, their shooting was so wild that nobody was hurt. The crew of the tank lighter, blown overboard by the explosion, were saved through the quick and courageous actions of the occupants of a landing craft from *Titania*.[17]

The first assault waves from *Dix*, carrying the 2d Battalion of the 47th Regiment, were to have landed at Yellow Beach some nine miles south of Safi, in order to take the town from the rear in case anything went wrong elsewhere. The scout boat located the beach after a considerable search and had marked it with a yellow flare by 0430. However, the explosion on the tank lighter had so disconcerted *Dix*'s crew that by 0523 only one incomplete boat wave was ready to go in with the control destroyer *Knight*. Captain Philips therefore decided to postpone that particular landing until after daylight. His decision was most fortunate because Yellow Beach proved to be a dangerous landing place with heavy surf; and owing to the success in the Safi harbor area, no troops were needed there in any case.

A part of Headquarters Company under U.S. Army Lieutenant J. W. Calton, who had had commando training in Britain, landed on Blue Beach with the first wave and promptly seized Safi's telephone exchange. Other assault troops of Company A moved northward toward the Pointe de la Tour.

Light tanks came ashore in LCMs on Green Beach as early as 0530, and infantry used the same beach. At dawn the 1st Battalion, 47th Regiment, 9th Division deployed and attacked French units that were firing from the hillside; later waves of troops fanned out on either side; and with the capture of Front de Mar at 1000, the initial beachhead was secured.

Offshore unloading of heavy equipment and tanks fell behind schedule. Darkness and heavy seas caused accidents and delays. Many vehicles reaching the beach had drowned engines and faulty batteries. Not until Safi was secured could a deep-draft vehicle transport tie up at the dock and off-load tanks faster and in start-up condition.

The landing of troops did not go much better. Although all battalion landing teams were supposed to be ashore before sunrise only about half the troops met that schedule and the last off the transports did not hit the beach until noon. Despite the problems experienced by the Americans, the French garrison commander understood clearly that he was outnumbered and outgunned. At 1530 he surrendered. Eleven hours after stepping onto French Moroccan territory the Americans controlled Safi.

By daylight on November 9, American troops controlled all of Safi's port facilities, the post office, the telecommunications station, petroleum storage tanks, all roads leading into town, and the civil police force. Reinforced by continuing waves of landing craft, American troops extended their beachhead inland against little more than sniper fire. Sunrise made possible more accurate naval gunfire, and by 1045 all French batteries were out of action. Most resistance to *Blackstone* infantry advancing through town came from a walled barracks, headquarters to the garrison of fewer than 1,000 men. American troops surrounded and isolated the barracks, then moved on to clear the rest of the town. As artillery was off-loaded it was trained on the barracks. However, because Eisenhower and Patton hoped to gain, without a costly battle, the surrender of troops who could later fight Axis armies, they issued no orders to attack.

The next morning French leaders made clear that the surrender at Safi did not apply to other areas. At dawn, several French planes flew through a thick fog over the town and landing area. However, only one managed to drop a bomb, which landed unintentionally on an ammunition storage building. That afternoon U.S. Navy planes raided the airfield at Marrakech destroying over 40 planes on the ground and strafing two convoys of French troops bound for Safi. Moving east of the town, American tanks and artillery overran a machine-gun position and took a bridge, though one tank was lost to mines. On the morning of November 10, after an artillery duel, Harmon decided that the French could be held in position by a small force. He formed most of his tanks and artillery on the road, and at 0900 the armored column raced north to join the ring closing around Casablanca.[18]

Center Task Force

Charged with taking the Algerian city of Oran, Major General Lloyd R. Fredendall's Center Task Force consisted of the 1st Infantry Division with the 1st Ranger Battalion attached and Combat Command B of the 1st Armored Division. Fredendall's troops were to land at three beaches along a 50-mile stretch of coastline: X and Y beaches lay west of Oran, Z Beach to the east. Oran had formidable defenses including 13 French coast artillery batteries, 16,700 troops, about 100 planes, and several destroyers in the harbor.

H-Hour for Center Task Force was 0100, November 8, but a variety of problems delayed most units. At X Beach, 28 miles west of Oran, delays were caused by five French cargo ships unknowingly entering the landing zone. Sailors from British Navy escorts boarded one surprised intruder, then confined the others so close to shore that they ran aground. They also had the same problem as the Western Task Force when lowering boats. Once lowered, the transport crews found that an unexpected current had pushed them farther out to sea than planned. During the lengthened run to the beach one boat engine caught fire, ending any hope of a surprise attack. Despite these problems all assault troops eventually reached shore, although they were late and at varying distances from assigned beaches.

Similar problems continued after assault troops landed on the beaches. Deep-draft tank lighters became stuck on a sandbar 360ft offshore. Engineers worked for three hours to lay a pontoon bridge, which failed to reach shore. Unloaded boats had to be pushed off the beach by bulldozers, a chore that

CENTER TASK FORCE, NOVEMBER 8–11, 1942

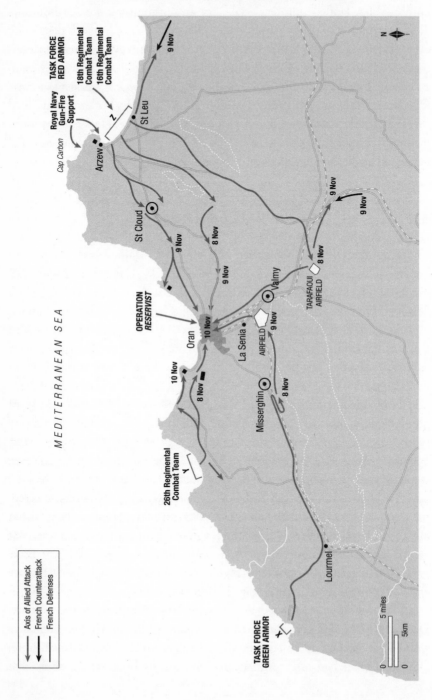

TASK FORCE
RED ARMOR

18th Regimental
Combat Team
16th Regimental
Combat Team

Royal Navy
Gun–Fire
Support

9 Nov

Cap Carbon

St Leu

Arzew

9 Nov

9 Nov

9 Nov

8 Nov

St Cloud

9 Nov

8 Nov

TARAFAOUI
AIRFIELD

9 Nov

Valmy

OPERATION
RESERVIST

10 Nov

La Senia

9 Nov

Oran

AIRFIELD

10 Nov

8 Nov

Misserghin

8 Nov

26th Regimental
Combat Team

MEDITERRANEAN SEA

N

Lourmel

TASK FORCE
GREEN ARMOR

Axis of Allied Attack
French Counterattack
French Defenses

5 miles

5km

0

0

damaged propellers and rudders and put ten of the 13 lighters out of service. Fortunately, no French gunners took advantage of these mishaps.

Once ashore the troops quickly assembled a column of 20 tanks with support vehicles and started toward the village of Lourmel, ten miles inland. One French armored car blocked the road, but a few shots won the cooperation of its crew. By noon Lourmel was in American hands, and X Beach had served its purpose of receiving a sizable armored force.

At Y Beach, 15 miles west of Oran, Brigadier General Theodore Roosevelt's 26th Regimental Combat Team experienced similar problems and found a new one. Ladder rungs on one of the British transports were 2ft apart, slowing the troops' descent into landing boats. Approaching the beach, landing craft crews discovered a sandbar. However, a way around it was found, so the 26th RCT was spared a pontoon bridge-building delay. At about 0645, after most of the troops had come ashore, the French Navy minesweeper *La Surprise* appeared, trying to live up to its name, but was promptly sunk.

At 0800 advancing troops met and destroyed three French armored cars. An hour later a coastal battery hit a transport offshore, threatening the arrival of support weapons ashore. However, British naval gunfire distracted the battery for the rest of the day. Roosevelt's troops pushed inland to clear roads and take two villages by midmorning, when they were stopped by fire from a hill mass five miles behind the beaches.

Z Beach, 20 miles east of Oran, received most of General Fredendall's troops. The 16th and 18th Regimental Combat Teams of Major General Terry Allen's 1st Infantry Division, the attached 1st Ranger Battalion, and most of Combat Command B under Brigadier General Lunsford E. Oliver transferred from transports to landing craft, happily unhindered by the many problems that had delayed landings everywhere else.

In the early morning of November 8, two companies of U.S. Army Rangers under Lieutenant Colonel William O. Darby's executive officer, Major Herman W. Dammer, in rubber rafts, slipped through a boom blocking the entrance to the inner harbor of Arzeu and stealthily approached Fort de la Pointe. After climbing over a seawall and cutting through barbed wire, two groups of Rangers assaulted the position from opposite directions. Within 15 minutes, they had taken the fort and captured 60 startled French soldiers. Meanwhile, Darby and the remaining four companies landed near Cap Carbon and climbed a ravine to reach the Batterie du Nord, overlooking the harbor. With the support of D Company's four 81mm mortars, the force assaulted the position, capturing the battery and taking 60 more prisoners. Trying to signal his success to the waiting fleet, Darby, whose radio had been lost in the landing, shot off a series of green flares before finally establishing contact through the radio of a British forward observer party.[19]

One of the Rangers, Warren "Bing" Evans, tells the story:

On November 8, 1942 in the middle of the night, we dropped anchor in the Arzew harbor. We took smaller boats in to shore from the mother ship, a British vessel. We had trained so hard for this moment. A feeling of excitement and a great deal of anticipation grew within me as we approached the land.

We traveled to a point of land, opposite a buoy, that we had studied carefully. This marked the spot that led us into a gulley – our landing site. We had a little trouble finding it in the dark, though. When we passed our first landmark, I went back and talked with Captain Murray and Captain Schneider. They agreed that we had missed it. Then I talked to Colonel Darby. We were a thousand yards beyond it, and I said, "Colonel, I think we missed our landmark." Darby listened, as was his custom, and ordered our column back about a thousand yards. There was the gulley. That was the only hitch in the whole operation.

After docking, we went up the gulley and climbed the mountain. We made it up to the gun battery about three o'clock in the morning. We took the enemy so much by surprise that they were all asleep, still in their shorts. We got in amongst them before they even knew what was happening. They didn't have any guns in their hands so we didn't have much trouble.[20]

The Rangers weren't the first ashore at Arzew; that honor belonged to the U.S. Marines landing in three groups: 11 men under Colonel Plain, seven under Captain Davis, and six under Sergeant Arnold G. Arrowood. The first assault wave, led by Colonel Plain and his men, met no resistance when they came ashore in British LCA boats at 0100, two hours before the Oran outburst. It was a bit of an anticlimax for the keyed up Marines, armed with M1s, knives and grenades, expecting another action like those at Guadalcanal or Tulagi in the African darkness. As the first landing force tensely prowled up the darkened beach, no one spoke, until the tension was suddenly snapped by a stage whisper from Private Marsh: "Run for your lives, girls. There's a man on the beach."[21]

The 7,092 men of the 18th RCT put ashore unopposed between the villages of Arzew and St. Leu and quickly moved inland, closing in on their objectives. The Rangers infiltrated behind two coastal batteries and took both after brief firefights. The infantry followed and after another brief fight took the town of Arzew, a barracks, and 13 seaplanes. However, they would be the last easy victories. Moving west toward Oran, the 18th RCT met intense opposition at the village of St. Cloud. The two American assaults stalled, and the battle for St. Cloud continued for the rest of the day.

To the east the 5,608 troops of the 16th RCT had an even more successful start to the campaign and took two villages ahead of schedule. By early afternoon it had overcome a French unit and set a defensive line eight miles inland. With the beachhead clear, General Oliver's tanks roared ashore, found a road, and headed directly for Tafaraoui airfield, 25 miles inland. Coordinating with armored infantry, the tanks quickly overran the airfield and 300 prisoners were taken.

At 1630, 26 RAF Spitfires of the 31st Fighter Group, flying via Gibraltar, arrived at Tafaraoui. It had been arranged that four Hurricanes from a carrier would cover their landing. However, four French Dewoitine 520 fighters above the field were mistaken for the Hurricanes and they managed to bring down one Spitfire that was in the circuit just off the end of the airdrome waiting to land; the other Spitfires shot down all four French aircraft. In the dogfight it was very difficult to distinguish the planes of one nationality from those of another. One French pilot bailed out when his plane burst into flames, and another fighter which broke away crashed about ten miles from Tafaraoui.[22]

The 503d Parachute Infantry Regiment troops who were to be part of capturing the airdrome did not make it as planned. Their planes had difficulty in getting into formation in the darkness, in some cases collisions being narrowly averted. Radio and navigator failure made reassembly impossible and the C-47s arrived at widely dispersed points over the North African coast.

Of three that lost their way, one put in at Gibraltar and two reached Casablanca. Three planes landed in Spanish Morocco and their crews and paratroops were interned, and the paratroops of a fourth plane were dropped there and also interned.

Near Lourmel a column of tanks was seen and paratroops jumped from 12 planes. However, the tanks proved to be American. Another landed on an emergency landing field at the west end of the Sebkra d'Oran, a dry salt lake south of Oran. During the morning of November 8 the majority of the aircraft landed there.

Colonel Bentley's plane was among those that reached the Sebkra d'Oran, but after talking with troops who had already landed he instructed his paratroops to jump and turned north to reconnoiter over Tafaraoui and La Senia. However, with his fuel low and one engine misfiring, he was forced to land on a dry sebkra. There he managed to establish radio contact with the ground commander, and reported the situation of the aircraft and paratroops at the west end of the Sebkra d'Oran. Shortly thereafter, with the arrival of French civilian police, Colonel Bentley and the crews of two planes were taken prisoner. On the way to Oran they were joined by the crew and parachutists of a third C-47 that had landed in the vicinity early in the morning, apparently the first to land in Algeria.[*]

As night fell on D-Day, the Americans were well established at three beachheads and held one of two airfields. General Fredendall was in good position to complete the seizure of Oran.

Operation *Reservist*

Operation *Reservist* was the assault on Oran Harbor and the leading role was played by *Walney* and *Hartland*, two former U.S. Coast Guard cutters.[†] Their mission was threefold: to capture Fort Lamoine and the battery near Cape Blanc; to capture and hold the wharves; and to board and hold the merchant ships in the harbor in order to prevent sabotage. To accomplish these missions 400 U.S. Army troops from the 6th Armored Infantry Regiment, 1st Armored Division under the Command of Lieutenant Colonel George C. Marshall were aboard *Hartland*. *Walney* took on board Lieutenant Commander G. D. Dickey, USN, with a 35-man U.S. Naval contingent which included six Marines. British Commando units and a number of specially trained British Navy men were also on board the cutters.

A small but powerful Royal Navy force, led by the cruiser HMS *Aurora*, commanded by Captain W. G. Agnew, RN, was on hand to give support should the cutters be attacked during the approach to Oran and also to deal with any

---

[*]   Colonel Bentley was incarcerated in the prison camp of St. Philippe, where he was courteously treated. He remained there until the 11th, when American armored forces captured the camp.

[†]   These are two of ten 250ft U.S. Coast Guard cutters transferred to Britain in 1941 under Lend-Lease. *Walney* was the former *Sebago* and *Hartland* was *Pontchartrain*.

enemy ships that might try to escape to seaward. The cutters went in flying the American flag in addition to the Royal Navy White Ensign. This unconventional step was part of the plan to attempt to minimize resistance to the operation.

For political reasons, it was considered expedient for the British to be as inconspicuous as possible, particularly in the early stages of the operation, and for their ships to display all the outward appearances of being U.S. warships. However, it could not be assumed that all pro-Allied elements would be sympathetic toward the invasion. Rear Admiral A. C. Bennett, USN, went as far as to express the opinion that the mission was little short of suicidal.

It was vital to the success of *Torch* that the port be taken intact, so the operation was not preceded by any softening-up process. The assignment was all the more hazardous because of the narrow confines of the harbor and the subsequent limitations on maneuverability. Oran Harbor was separated from the sea by a stone breakwater, some 3,000 yards in length. It varied in width from 800 yards at the eastern end, to 500 yards at the western end. Prior to the action taking place, all that was known of the boom was that it comprised an inner and outer obstruction.

Once through, the ships faced one and a half miles of enclosed harbor comprising four main basins, each separated by a broad mole extending from the inshore jetty, which were accessible by a narrow passage between the seaward end of the moles and the sea wall. At the western end of the harbor were two small basins that faced east and were separated by the Mole Centrale.

Such were the confines of the battle area, which was flanked on the southern side by the guns of the Ravin Blanc Battery, and at the western end by forts Lamoine, St. Gregorio and Santa Cruz. In addition, there were several gun emplacements situated on the moles and jetties. These dimensions give a clear indication of just how exposed the cutters were and how little chance they had for evasive action.

The man chosen to head the assault on Oran Harbor was Captain Frederick Thornton Peters, RN, who was typically described by his colleagues as the type of man one would expect to see leading some hazardous operation.

The two cutters made their approach to the North African coast with the main body of ships, designated Group V, and headed for the Eastern Sector landing beaches. They broke off at 2130 on November 7 and headed toward Oran. Just after midnight both ships went to action stations. In the darkness, the crews went quietly and efficiently about the preparations for the coming assault. These were somewhat different, in many respects, from the routine pre-action preparedness to which they had hitherto been accustomed, as the emphasis was on lightweight weaponry. Not only would the main armament be hindered by the confined conditions in the harbor, but an adequate ammunition supply to the guns would have proved difficult due to the presence of over 200 troops on the mess decks on each cutter.

All 5in ammunition was subsequently struck down and the magazines closed off. All close-range ammunition for the .50 caliber machine guns, rifles, automatic weapons, pistols and other small arms, was brought to the upper deck and placed either by the guns, in the forecastle lockers, or in the gun shelter and laundry.

Careful planning had gone into achieving the most efficient and effective deployment of the ship's company. It is in situations like this that the traditional flexibility of the sailor becomes most apparent. The magazine crews and supply parties were to be used as backup for the close-range weapons, as well as for the boarding and landing parties. They were also to be used for turning out the canoes, which were to be used for disembarking the troops. With all this activity, there was little time to contemplate what lay ahead.

Their preparations complete, the two cutters made their approach to the coast at about six knots, making landfall somewhere near Pointe D'Aiguille, about 12 miles east of Oran. They then steered westward and headed towards the port, maintaining a distance of about half a mile from the shore. In company were two motor launches, ML483, with Lieutenant I. H. Hunter, RNVR, in command, and ML480 with Lieutenant J. H. F. Morgan, RNVR, on the bridge. Their task was to provide smoke cover for the cutters' assault on the boom.

The assault came just before 0300, and the ships moved off with *Walney* in the lead. There was a temporary setback when she missed the harbor entrance on the first approach. The group then turned to starboard and performed a full clockwise circle for the next run-in, with *Hartland* approximately 500 yards astern of *Walney*. A last-ditch attempt was made to placate the French, when an announcement was made over the loud hailer. It served little purpose as had all the other previous political ploys and brought an almost instant reaction from the guns ashore.

In unison with the gunfire, the probing beam of a searchlight from Fort Lamoine at the far end of the harbor stabbed the darkness, picking out the cutters while they were less than half a mile from the boom. With the ships now illuminated by searchlight and the gun flashes, the heavy armament of

ORAN HARBOR ASSAULT, NOVEMBER 8, 1942

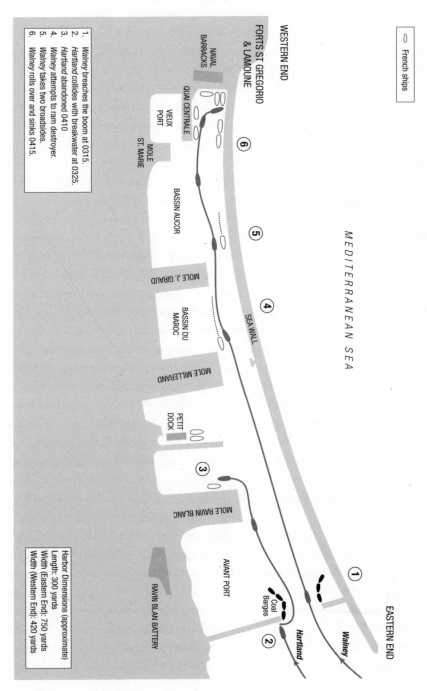

French ships

WESTERN END

FORTS ST GREGORIO
& LAMOUNE

NAVAL
BARRACKS

QUAI CENTRALE

VIEUX
PORT

MOLE
ST. MARIE

BASSIN AUCOR

MOLE J. GIRAUD

BASSIN DU
MAROC

MOLE MILLERAND

PETIT
DOCK

MOLE RAVIN BLANC

RAVIN BLAN BATTERY

AVANT PORT

Coal
Barges

Hartland

Walney

SEA WALL

MEDITERRANEAN SEA

EASTERN END

1. *Walney* breaches the boom at 0315.
2. *Hartland* collides with breakwater at 0325.
3. *Hartland* abandoned 0410
4. *Walney* attempts to ram destroyer.
5. *Walney* takes two broadsides.
6. *Walney* rolls over and sinks 0415.

Harbor Dimensions (approximate)
Length: 300 yards
Width (Eastern End): 750 yards
Width (Western End): 420 yards

Ravin Blanc Battery, together with heavy machine-gun fire from the moles, joined in the devastating barrage at point-blank range.

Hartland bore the brunt of the opening salvoes, while *Walney*, screened by the smoke of the two motor launches, increased her speed to 15 knots and made her run in. In the darkness, nobody could be certain as to the effect of the impact on the ship as she hit first the outer boom and then the inner one, which turned out to be a row of coal barges. Surprisingly, the cutter broke through with hardly a noticeable tremor. The engines were then stopped and the canoes used by the Commandos for landings slipped off the ship with their crews and stores in them. This was achieved in less than a minute. Although all canoes reported themselves clear and under way, one had been damaged by enemy fire before lowering, and sunk shortly afterwards.

As the smoke drifted across the Avant Port, *Walney* was exposed to heavy close-range fire on both quarters from guns mounted on the jetties and moles. It is remarkable that she suffered so little damage from that initial burst of fire.

The situation changed rapidly as *Walney* approached Mole Millerand, as two moored submarines joined in the action. The cutter suffered several direct hits, and all telephonic communications aft were cut. In spite of her decks being swept with enemy fire, the crew managed to complete the launching of the canoes, while the ship moved up harbor at a painstaking four knots. With enemy fire now directed at her from all directions a new hazard presented itself in the form of an enemy destroyer coming towards her in an attempt to flee the harbor. As it approached, *Walney* made a gallant attempt to ram it, but steaming at such slow speed, she was unable to complete the maneuver and the enemy passed down her port side.

Although little more than ten minutes had elapsed since she broke through the boom, the cutter had already fought her way to within 600 yards of her objective at the furthermost end of the harbor. So far her casualties had been light. Illuminated by gun flashes, and raked by machine-gun fire, the order was given to go to boarding stations. The boarding parties, comprising a British naval officer and six ratings, together with seven members of the U.S. Army, clambered into the two port boats, which were then turned out in preparation for when they came alongside the enemy ships. The task of clearing the enemy's decks prior to boarding was in the hands of 16 grenade throwers from the American contingent, mustered on the forecastle. The deck parties were standing by with bow and stern lines ready for use, with power on the winch and capstan.

So far *Walney* had been able to keep all her close-range weapons manned, and had suffered minimal damage. However, the worst was yet to come. As she approached the Quaie Centrale to board *Epervier*, another enemy destroyer attempted to break out. With the attention focused mainly on *Epervier*, which was putting up strong resistance, coupled with salvoes from one of the forts, the cutter was hit by at least two broadsides from the destroyer as it passed down her starboard side. Two shells pierced the ship's side, exploding in the engine-room, devastating the personnel and destroying the lubricating tanks. With the oil supply cut off, the automatic stop valve closed and the main engine shuddered to a halt.

Within seconds of this disaster, another shell detonated in the boiler room, killing most of the men there and totally wiping out the two main boilers. Simultaneously, the wardroom and steering compartment were ravaged by two direct hits on the starboard quarter. With her steering gear out of action *Walney* was now at the mercy of the enemy guns. Another direct hit destroyed the cutter's bridge, killing 16 of the 17 officers and ratings gathered there, among them the ship's Captain, Lieutenant Commander Meyrick. The only survivor, Captain Peters, had a miraculous escape, though he was partially blinded in the explosion.

Of the British military passengers, J. H. Finch later told what happened after *Walney*'s bridge was shot away:

Lofty Pearson and I were both concussed and choking on cordite fumes and smoke as we scrambled from the Asdic compartment over the dead bodies of our colleagues. We managed to make our way to the Gyro room on the starboard side, where kitbags and hammocks were stowed. Other casualties had made their way there. By now, the ship had drifted round so that her starboard side was exposed to the fire. We received a direct hit aft of our position in the storage compartment and the explosion threw me into the pile of hammocks, which collapsed on top of me. I managed to extricate myself and make my way along the row of bunks, between which were the troops. From what I could see, very few had survived.

I crossed the mess-deck to the port passageway and moved aft towards the wardroom. I was suddenly joined by "Nutty" Gardner, the wardroom steward, who informed me that some thirty casualties were gathered there. Together we made our way there, to be greeted by the most appalling sight.

In the dim light, our surgeon and his sick berth attendant were desperately trying to cope with the wounded, many of which were beyond help. I was facing the pantry, with vertical channeling supporting lead-cased cables behind me. Suddenly there was a massive explosion as a shell struck the starboard quarter and exploded in the wardroom. The cables behind me must have given me protection, because I believe I was the only one to survive.

Without power *Walney* drifted closer to *Epervier* and was caught in the French ship's searchlight which was promptly shot out by the cutter's machine-guns. By this time, the cutter had suffered so many casualties that she was unable to keep her guns firing. All the grenade throwers on the forecastle had been killed as had all but two officers and three ratings from the combined boarding parties. In spite of the heavy losses and the severe damage to the ship, the surviving officers and crew members made a gallant attempt to get the cutter alongside *Epervier*. A head rope was finally got to the jetty and Royal Navy Lieutenant Moseley succeeded in getting a stern line out to a depth charge carrier, which lodged between the funnels. However, with no power on the ship, it was impossible to heave-in and *Walney* drifted at right angles to the French ship.

The cutter's guns were finally silenced and she was ablaze forward and amidships. Her crew had been depleted considerably and the carnage among the troops was reported by Lieutenant Moseley as "indescribable." Moseley wrote about what happened next:

I gave the order to un-prime the five-pattern depth-charges still primed, followed by the order to abandon ship. No attempt was made to get away the Carley rafts or other lifesaving equipment since the whole harbour was full of debris by this time and we were still being engaged by the enemy. Our small arms and mortar ammunition was exploding all over the ship, which decided me to get the survivors into the water and away from the ship as quickly as possible. I swam in the direction of *Epervier* and was hauled aboard. Several of the ship's company were killed in the water by riflemen.

Their treatment of me caused me much surprise, as when I came on board they were tending their wounded. They had been hit by a 3in shell or splinters and the forward boiler-room and bridgework, director and searchlights were riddled with bullets. As the blazing remains of *Walney* drifted down at 0700, the ship's company of *Epervier* were too busy to notice me and I was free to have a brief look around.*

Walney's desperate fight, in which she was constantly outgunned, ended only a few yards from the western end of the harbor, where she rolled over and sank.

In contrast, the devastation of *Hartland* began even before she entered the harbor. Although her captain, Lieutenant Commander Godfrey Billot, RNR, could see little of the harbor entrance because of smoke, the sound of the battle from within was clearly audible and the gun flashes and explosions were evidence enough of the reception he could expect.

Hartland, running without lights, began her perilous dash to break the chain that blocked the channel entrance at 0300. Fifteen minutes later she was the center of a raging inferno. As *Hartland* shaped her course into the harbor she was picked up by the Fort Lamoine searchlight and immediately subjected to fire from the Ravin Blanc Battery and the French destroyer *Typhon*.

The opening salvoes were devastating and within minutes most of her guns' crews had become casualties. So quickly did the French react to the cutter being illuminated, she was able to get only three rounds off before there were too few unwounded seamen to man her guns. *Hartland* was a sitting target, illuminated by the searchlight beam and the fires that were raging fore and aft. Her firefighting parties, desperately trying to get the fires under control, were quickly depleted by the continuous enemy fire raking her decks. In addition to the heavy punishment being taken on the upper deck, severe damage was also inflicted below.

Lieutenant Commander Billot was blinded in one eye by shrapnel, and the ship struck the Jettée Du Large, about 6ft from its northern side, before he could recover. Fortunately, the engine room was responding to telegraphs and after some maneuvering, *Hartland* entered the Avant Port, and proceeded, still under heavy fire, towards her appointed billet, halfway down the Quai de Dunkerque, on the western side of the Mole Ravin Blanc. The order to launch the canoes was given, but this was not carried out because both craft had been riddled with bullets and rendered useless.

---

* Lt. Moseley was later imprisoned in the Naval barracks, then moved to a civil prison, and finally lodged in the barracks of the Second Zouave Regiment. "The supply of food for extra mouths was non-existent and the sanitary arrangements -- French," he wrote.

As the ship rounded the mole, she sailed straight into the sights of the heavy armament of the destroyer *Typhon*, the fire of which was joined by the two submarines that had earlier punished *Walney*. At this stage *Hartland* was fully committed and headed for the quay, while the destroyer's guns continued to pound her at a range of less than 100ft. One direct hit put her main motor out of action and all power failed in the ship.

In spite of this setback, she had sufficient way on to reach the jetty, where her First Lieutenant, V.A. Hickson, RN, made a gallant, but unsuccessful attempt to pass a wire ashore. Nothing could be done at the after end of the ship, since the decks were being swept with machine gun fire at point blank range. Anyone who attempted to brave the withering fire was immediately cut down.

With much of her bridge shot away, and out of control, *Hartland* started to drift away from the quay. As the cutter started to drift, Lieutenant Commander Billot gave the order to drop anchor. He then attempted to make a hurried inspection of the ship to ascertain whether further action could be organized. His activities were considerably restricted when he was hit in both legs and a shoulder. With all her guns out of action and flames funnel high, it was obvious *Hartland*'s end was imminent. With the large amount of explosives on board likely to explode at any time, her captain was faced with no alternative but to abandon the ship. In his report of the action, Billet wrote: "Soon after this, the French humanely gave up firing, though we did not heave down our colours."

There followed the task of getting the wounded ashore. This operation was hampered by ammunition going off in all directions. The ship was finally cleared, the wounded forward by Hickson, the First Lieutenant, while a small band of officers were getting the wounded away aft in some haste, as the decks and the ship's side were red hot. These officers were eventually ordered ashore by the captain, who followed at about 0500. By this time, the fires had reached the Crow's Nest and more than half the crew were either killed or wounded. About 25 minutes later *Hartland* was rent apart by a massive explosion, yet stubbornly stayed afloat. It took a further explosion, a few hours later, to finally seal her fate.

Survivors among the troops installed in the two cutters were alarmingly few. Lieutenant Commander Dickey, USN, reported later:

> Upon abandoning ship, officers and men showed the highest kind of leadership and spirit in helping to save the lives of United States soldiers who were unfamiliar with the ship and the use of life jackets. The effort to

rescue men from the water continued long after the ship had been abandoned.

One lone Marine, Corporal Norman Boike, was a witness to the action. From his station by the captain's cabin he saw 4in shells streak through the cutter's sides "like blue flame." Concussion knocked him out, and shrapnel tore away the muscle of his left arm. When he came to, only dead men were below decks. He climbed painfully topside, finding most of the ship ablaze and still under direct fire from the destroyers, although it had swung in close to the French cruiser. British naval units were shelling the harbor.

Boike didn't stand around to admire the fireworks. A Navy lieutenant bound up his arm, gave him a shot of morphine, and together they jumped over the side. The Marine's life jacket was riddled with shrapnel and bullets; he kicked his way through the floating wreckage to a nearby life raft. On it were six British sailors, frantically paddling in circles as they sought to get away from the burning *Harland* and escape the hail of machine gun bullets. Boike crawled aboard and took over, acting as coxswain, until after 150 yards of furious paddling, the raft bumped against a floating dry dock manned by a squad of French soldiers. Weaponless and wounded, there was nothing for Corporal Boike and his "command" to do but surrender. The French were very nice about it. They dressed their wounds, didn't frisk or strip them, and let them rest out in the hot African sun, giving them a ringside seat for the Battle of Oran, until they were taken ashore to the French naval hospital that afternoon.

Meanwhile, back in the gray Algerian dawn, Sergeant Fred Whittaker, and his raiding party of four Marines and a handful of British sailors and Commandos, were trapped below decks on the doomed *Hartland*. They were awaiting orders from topside, but orders never came. The first 6in shell came through about 4ft from Whittaker's head and exploded far back in the hold. The wounded were picked up and laid on a table in the officers' wardroom, which had been converted into a temporary hospital. Just as the British doctor was bending over the first patient to probe for shrapnel, three more shells scored direct hits, and turned the entire below decks into a shambles. Two Marines later reported missing, Private First Class James Earhart. Jr. and Private Robert F. Horr, were believed to have been lost when this salvo struck.

Smoke grew thicker by the minute. The floor was slippery with blood. Men coughed, groaned, and sank to their knees. Sergeant Whittaker decided to hell with orders, he would take over before it was too late. He organized the few men remaining on their feet and climbed the ladder to open the hatch. However, all the hatches were battened down. They beat and yelled for someone on deck to release them, but could not be heard through the din of the bombardment. Besides, no one was on deck.

The situation looked grim for the trapped men. Escape forward was barred by a wall of flame, and the hold was rapidly filling with deadly carbon dioxide gas from the blasted refrigeration plant. Whittaker came down the ladder and held a quick huddle with the remaining Marines and British sailors. One of the British remembered an emergency exit hatch far aft. To get to it they had to climb over bodies, and pull down piled-up sea bags. Working through a fog of choking powder smoke and lethal fumes from the ice plant and engine room, they hammered desperately on the wooden block securing the hatch. It had evidently not been opened for years. Four rifle stocks were broken on it before the hatch cover finally gave way, and a route was cleared out of the deathtrap below decks to the comparative safety of the open deck.

The Marines carried up as many of wounded as they could find and laid them on the scorching deck. Whittaker directed operations, even though he was close to unconsciousness from the searing heat and smoke. He was last to leave the hold, and had just started up the ladder when a Navy corpsman called to him from below. The man had just come to after being knocked out by a shell explosion. Whittaker went back down the ladder, and located the wounded man by his groans. By that time the Marine sergeant was too weak to lift him, and conditions in the aft hold were all but unbearable.

Whittaker directed the wounded corpsman to hang onto his legs, and keep his nose close to the deck, where an inch or two of breathable air remained. Then he crawled toward the emergency exit, dragging the corpsman after him. The Navy man was too weak to climb, and fell at the foot of the ladder. Whittaker kept climbing, made the open deck, and gave directions for another man to go down the ladder for the final rescue. Then he passed out.

When he came to, the deck was ablaze from bow to stern. Piled nearby were cases of ammunition and mortar shells, ready to explode at any minute. An Army sergeant named Mendoza had started to hurl the cases overboard. Whittaker staggered to his feet, got the man next to him into action, and threw overboard all ammunition in direct path of the flames. By now *Hartland* was drifting in toward shore on the other side of the harbor from the abandoned *Walney*. Both ships could blow up at any moment. Whittaker took a hasty look around, located his men, and had them dive overboard with him and head for the shore, some 50 yards away. Marine Private William L. Dickinson had never swum a stroke in his life before, but he made the shore with the rest.

There the Marines were confronted by a concrete seawall that the tired men could not scale. However, as luck would have it, an old tire was hanging over the side. Whittaker hung onto this, but he was too exhausted to get to the top of the wall. The man behind him used Whittaker's body as a ladder and climbed up the wall. Whittaker then was boosted by the man behind him, and so by a kind of human chain, the Marines and their comrades reached the beach at Oran.

The handful of survivors assembled in the shadow of the chalk cliffs, where some earthworks had been thrown up. They dragged in the wounded to within reach, and cleaned and dried what weapons were left to them. They had two .45s and a half dozen grenades. Their position was open to attack from three angles, so Whittaker stationed two men at each side to challenge whoever came along the beach. Overhead, coastal artillery guns on top of the cliffs thundered and spouted death. Machine guns occasionally raked the beach and naval shellfire from British ships at sea had them in range.

As French patrols approached the hideout, they were challenged and captured. Whittaker figured that when his group was picked up by the main body of French troops, they would fare better if they had a few well-treated French prisoners as collateral. For five hours they snapped up unwary French patrols, gathered a few more British survivors, and cared as best they could for the wounded. Later in the morning a British Spitfire plane, manned by an American pilot, flew within 60ft of them and waved encouragement, but could do nothing to aid them. U.S. troops were still battling their way into the outskirts of Oran. The two Marines, Whittaker and Dickinson, with a half dozen British sailors, 14 wounded men, and an equal number of French prisoners, held their beachhead and waited the outcome.

Suddenly *Hartland* blew up. The terrific explosion tore down buildings, rained burning debris and exploded shells over the harbor and beach. They rescued one American whose clothes were blown entirely off his body. A foresighted Marine who wore an extra pair of dungaree pants covered the wounded man's nakedness.

At about 0900 French shore troops spotted the Marine beachhead and moved into action. A hundred men armed with machine guns advanced slowly, surrounding the open position. Whittaker figured resistance was worse than useless, so together with the men who could still move, he walked out onto the open beach and sat down. A French officer came up cautiously, covered by several squads of his riflemen. Whittaker surrendered, the French prisoners were released, and the wounded men were taken off to the hospital.

When dawn broke the full extent of the battle was revealed with debris littering the placid waters and the smell of cordite and smoke still hanging in the air. The harbor was a mess. Ships lay piled end on end as they had been scuttled to avoid being captured. Two enemy submarines had been driven ashore by depth charges. The waves bounced bodies, spars, and wreckage against the seawalls and sunken bulkheads. Many U.S. soldiers and British sailors who had been rescued by French destroyers that first night were later killed by gunfire from their own ships when the destroyers were sunk. Private First Class Earhart's body was recovered a few days later and he was buried in Oran cemetery. Private Horr's never was recovered.

The culmination of this savage conflict by desperate and brave men was a terrible toll of dead and wounded. Eighty-one of *Walney's* crew paid the supreme sacrifice, as did 34 from her sister ship *Hartland*. Also killed on *Hartland* were two U.S. Marines and three U.S. Navy sailors. Only 47 of the 400 1st Armored Division troops survived. A suicide mission had been predicted and that is what it turned out to be.[23]

Eastern Task Force: Algeria[24]

Meanwhile, 220 miles east of Oran the Eastern Task Force had dropped anchor off Algiers in the last hours of November 7. Of the three *Torch* task forces, the Eastern one included the largest British proportion. Not only were naval and air support British, so were 23,000 of the total 33,000 troops. The 10,000 U.S. Army troops landing at Algiers consisted of Colonel Benjamin F. Caffey, Jr.'s 39th RCT from the 9th Infantry Division, and Colonel John W. O'Daniel's 168th RCT and Lieutenant Colonel Edwin T. Swenson's 3d Battalion, 135th Infantry, both from the 34th Infantry Division. These American units and all the British Army units involved in the initial landing were under command of U.S. Major General Charles W. Ryder. Naval support included a Royal Navy flotilla of three aircraft carriers, four cruisers, one antiaircraft vessel, seven destroyers, and 15 transports. Enemy strength was estimated at 15,000 troops with only obsolete tanks, 91 fighters and bombers at two airfields, 12 coastal batteries, and a few destroyers in the harbor.

Both the geography and concept of operations at Algiers closely resembled those of Oran. The city lay in an arc of beaches and bluffs, gradually rising to low hills ten miles inland. Allied troops were to land at three points along a 50-mile stretch of coast: Apples and Beer beaches lay west of the city, and Charlie Beach to the east. After clearing the beaches, the troops would take all roads, villages, and two airfields, then converge behind Algiers and move on the city from three sides.

In this joint campaign, the only parts of the naval force not furnished by the British were four U.S. transports constituting Transport Division Eleven. This division consisted of the flagship USS *Samuel Chase* (AP-56), commanded by Commander Roger C. Heimer, USCG; the USS *Thomas Stone* (AP-59), commanded by Captain Olten B. Bennehoof, USN; the USS *Leedstown* (AP-73), commanded by Lieutenant Commander Duncan Cook, USN; and the USS *Almaack* (AK-27), commanded by Captain Chester L. Nichols, USN. These four ships carried the U.S. contingent of troops in the Eastern Assault Force of which Major General Charles R. Ryder, USA, was in command. Late in the afternoon of November 7, about 160 miles from Algiers, *Thomas Stone* (AP-59) was hit by a torpedo from a Luftwaffe Ju 88. Her troops were put into landing boats, and after a hazardous trip, during which all of the landing craft, but no troops, were lost, succeeded in reaching the Algerian coast. However, by the time they arrived hostilities had ceased.

All vehicles were to be landed on two beaches, extending from Surcouf to the Oued Reghaia. Personnel were to be landed at a third beach, situated halfway between Jean Bart and Ain Taya, which was about 800 yards wide, and at a fourth beach, in front of Ain Taya, which was about half that size. At a transport area chosen about seven miles northeast of the debarkation points, *Samuel Chase, Leedstown, Almaack*, and the civilian merchant cargo ship SS *Exceller* stopped at 2201, on November 7. Boats were lowered at once, and by 2256, *Chase* had all her boats in the water.

Reports indicated there was very little surf. There was a Force 1 breeze, no chop, and a slight ground swell, which did not cause a motion of more than one foot from crest to trough. There was also very little resistance. Debarkation of troops and their equipment continued during the day. However, enemy planes were active over the landing area. At 0225 a low-flying plane was overhead. *Chase* opened fire and the plane was driven off. At 0349, gunfire was observed on the beach and at Cape Matifou. Ensign Heckman, from *Chase*, recalls the landings:

> Hearts began to beat faster and perspiration flowed more freely as Algiers, the North African Paris, lit up like Coney Island in peacetime, came into view. We drew into position, and then came the word, "Take stations for boat lowering. Away all boats." Our boats were lowered, the troops disembarked, and the boats vanished into darkness on their way to the beach. The division then moved into a new position closer to the shore, and the fort surprised us by a searchlight barrage. Caught in the pencils of intense white light, the transports slid along. Suddenly there was a belch of orange flame from shoreward – the fort had opened fire.
>
> A British destroyer, close in, diverted their attention and a battle royal ensued. The fort shelled the tin can and the cocky little can defiantly stood off and answered every salvo. By this time we had successfully rounded the cape and took up a position about three miles from the beach. The boats started to return and we began sending equipment to the army on shore. With each vehicle went a certain amount of ammunition as our combat-loaded cargo began to come out of the holds in priority as needed on shore. By daybreak our boats were making steady rounds to the beach. The same doughty little destroyer, endeared to us by the previous night's action, closed in and again bombarded the fort on the Point. About noon a British cruiser started to pour heavy shells into the fort. This remaining point of beach resistance was finally dive-bombed by carrier planes, and toward evening American troops marched in and found Admiral Jean François Darlan, commander of all Vichy French forces inside.

Landings in the Algiers area met with mixed success. The British 11th Infantry Brigade Group landed on Apples Beach on time and without mishap, making theirs the smoothest of all *Torch* landings. By 0700 the unit had moved 12 miles inland and taken its objective, Blida airfield. However, at Beer Beach a variety of problems – high surf, inexperienced boat crew, absent beach guides, and engine failures – scattered the 168th Team over 15 miles of coastline and delayed the British 6th Commando by over five hours. Fortunately, landings at Apples and Beer beaches were unopposed. At Charlie Beach, however, coastal batteries fired on transports as the landing craft neared the shore. Naval gunfire responded, but then high surf scattered the 39th

EASTERN TASK FORCE, NOVEMBER 8, 1942

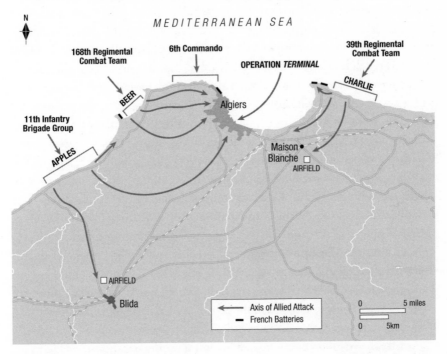

RCT's boats, smashing some against coastal rocks. Leaving the boats, most troops found, instead of gradually rising ground, a vertical bluff with stairs cut for sightseers. Once this difficulty had also been overcome, the troops of the 39th Team moved eight miles inland and took the airfield at Maison Blanche by 0830. However, for the rest of the day a fierce battle raged with a French marine artillery battery. Royal Navy surface and air units eventually prevailed, though Axis bombers managed to damage a transport and destroyer.

In the afternoon of November 8, British ships shelled the fort on Cape Matifou at 1520, and Allied planes dive-bombed it. Less than two hours later, at about 1700, a concerted bombing attack was carried out by Axis bombers and torpedo planes. The bombs from one attack fell 75 yards off the starboard bow of *Chase*, while in another attack a stick of bombs fell 100 yards off the transport's stern. Torpedo planes, which approached over a nearby ledge of rocks, released two torpedoes simultaneously, one of which missed the starboard quarter of *Chase* by about 20 yards, the other passing between the ship's bow and the anchor chain. The enemy plane then banked to the left and flew behind an anchored British attack transport. Using this excellent maneuver he escaped being shot down by the Allied gunners. In this attack, *Leedstown*'s stern was damaged by an aerial torpedo, which resulted in a probable bent shaft and rudder post that immobilized the ship. Hostilities came to an end later that night when word was received that the U.S. Army and the French had agreed an unconditional cease-fire in the Algerian area.

Leedstown was attacked by German aircraft on the evening of November 8, and again on the following afternoon. Surviving these attacks, she was sunk by torpedoes from *U-331* a short time later. Fifty-nine men died in the attacks. As it happened, a similarity in the names of two beaches took a small Coast Guard patrol to an unspecified beach position and led to the rescue of the majority of the crew members, and some of the soldiers, from the torpedoed *Leedstown*. Hunter Wood, Chief Boatswain's Mate, USCG, on *Chase*, later described his dual role on this tour of combat duty, which included lifesaving:

Our transport was bringing men and supplies and we had charge of the landing operations. We arrived at ten o'clock in the evening on November 7, right in the midst of an enemy attack. The soldiers from our transport, the *Samuel Chase*, and others in the convoy were to land on what appeared in the charts as a certain beach. A little farther to the west there was another beach. The Axis bombers were making it hot for the transports. We hid in foxholes on the beach. All the ships got away except the *Leedstown*. Some planes dropped flares and the place lit up like daylight. It gave us a dreadfully helpless feeling, for we wanted to do something about it and couldn't. We just had to wait until the light died down, in the meantime making a perfect target for the enemy. A torpedo plane went directly for our ship. I was on shore at the time and had just come from my foxhole after a bombing and strafing attack. The plane fired two torpedoes directly at the ship, and then swerved off in one of the most beautiful pieces of maneuvering I've ever seen. The torpedoes just missed the bow, one passing on the starboard side, missing by 20 yards, the other missing the port bow by 3ft. The men stood watching the torpedo coming for them and all thought the ship was a goner. But she came through unscathed. The next morning we made firewood out of the tail of a German bomber that had been shot down, and built a fire to cook our coffee. Our ship shot down three of the attacking planes. Meanwhile, the invasion forces were being landed.

A landing of that kind is a big operation, with landing boats shuttling back and forth to the transports. That shore was treacherous, with lots of rocks, and my division under Ensign McLin was keeping the lanes open for the incoming rush of troops and supplies. Some of the boats were disabled and we had to haul them ashore for repairs. The water was cold and the wind was colder. We were wading out up to our necks. After the landing was completed, my men and I left to go to a nearby beach as ordered, to meet my senior officer and the remainder of the division. We arrived at the beach just in time to see *Leedstown* hit by a torpedo. But we didn't see the rest of our division.

The men of the torpedoed vessel abandoned the ship and took to life rafts which floated directly toward the beach. But heavy surf was running and the survivors were thrown from their rafts into the sea a mile and a half from shore. There was bound to be trouble when those rafts hit the rocks offshore. We tried to get the survivors to steer the rafts before they hit the surf so as to avoid being battered. Stripped to the hide, we dived into the icy water and swam out with line to tie to the rafts which we could then pull to shore with the survivors clinging to the sides. The rafts had to be pulled, for the men on them could not steer them clear of the rocks. The surf was throwing the rafts into the air, dumping their human cargoes into the water to be crushed as the rafts were tossed about on top.

We worked for five hours, fighting against a terrific undertow, and finally pulled the survivors to safety. It was a struggle to keep afloat in spite of broken bones, concussions, and shock. Soldiers from a nearby town, and also some French and Arab natives came to assist in the rescue.

The Arabs would cut down large reeds, about 15ft long, then wade into the water, extend them to the men and pull them ashore. All in all, it was a tough job for everybody. The surf was extremely rough, the undertow was strong, and the wind was cold. The French civilians were very cooperative and hospitable. Even the children were down by the waterfront, armed with bottles of wine and brandy which they'd offer the men as they were dragged ashore. Then the survivors were taken to a little movie theatre in the village, straw was spread all around the floor, and they were left there to rest.[25]

It was not until the next day that Hunter Wood discovered that he had gone to the wrong beach and because of the misunderstanding had been on the spot to rescue the survivors of the torpedoed transport.

While the rescue of *Leedstown* survivors was taking place, landing operations continued. "During the afternoon the surf became very high and treacherous and consequently we began losing boats," Ensign Heckman reported.

At one time all of our twenty-six landing boats were stranded on the beach. Mechanics managed to get two in running condition, and a final total of six boats, including two tank lighters, unloaded our ship in the next five days. During this time we were under constant aircraft attack. Every day we would get shot at by high observation bombers, and every morning the Junkers Ju 88s would precede our breakfasts and follow our dinner. Always it was the same: the high precision bombers, the torpedo plane attacks. The ship's complement fought gallantly. Our six salvaged boats ran constantly from the ship to the beach, even under aircraft attack. The unloading continued under fire.

So continued six days at Algiers. When we departed, our official credit was three German bombers. Our crew had unloaded the ship under fire with a few salvaged boats. Living up to the lifesaving traditions of the Coast Guard, the beach party had heroically hauled through the surf the survivors of the American transport *Leedstown*, sunk by aircraft bombing and enemy torpedoes. We had all weathered so many near bomb misses that they became a joke. Proud of the fact that we received commendation from the British Admiralty for gallantry in action, our transport and one other remaining American ship started back to England for more troops. Still in our minds was the message sent in to us from the British battle fleet outside the harbor and just over the horizon. They wanted to know which American battleship had slipped into Algiers, so intense was our antiaircraft fire. Thereafter we were dubbed the 'battleship.'[26]

According to Edward Pearson, Chief Boatswain's Mate, USCG, the convoy was under almost constant attack. He also describes the attack on *Chase*, which appeared almost certain to end in disaster. "It was the closest shave we had," he said:

The torpedoes came head on for our bow. I was assistant battery officer on the forward battery, and while all of us were too occupied firing at the planes to watch the fish I knew they were coming at us. It was plenty tense awaiting the shock that would knock us into kingdom come. Then as one torpedo neared our bow it suddenly veered off and passed astern. The other kept on coming right at us. But it, too, turned at the last minute, just enough to pass between the bow of our ship and the anchor chain.[27]

The first American serviceman to land on the beach at Algiers was said to be Coast Guard Machinist's Mate Second Class Eugene Lowry. He went ashore soon after a British destroyer shattered a huge searchlight that the enemy was using to illuminate the oncoming vessels carrying the U.S. troops. "That destroyer really turned the tables," Lowry declared:

> It helped the landing parties. The beach was bare when we landed. I jumped off and was followed by soldiers and other Coast Guardsmen. When we had completed our unloading, we returned to the ship for more. Quite a few landing barges were damaged in the heavy surf and it took longer to transfer supplies and men ashore then we had anticipated. But everything ran off pretty smoothly. There were only a few casualties.[28]

Operation *Terminal*

As at Oran, the British insisted on an anti-sabotage mission into Algiers Harbor. Operation *Terminal* called for Colonel Swenson's 3d Battalion, 135th Infantry, consisting of 24 American officers and 638 enlisted men, to enter Algiers harbor on two Royal Navy destroyers, debark, and secure port facilities for use in future Allied operations.

Also assigned to the operation were two British destroyers, HMS *Broke* (D83), Lieutenant Commander A. F. C. Layard commanding, and HMS *Malcolm* (D19), Commander A. B. Russell commanding, 74 Royal Navy personnel who were to board and seize ships in Algiers Harbor, and 3 British Army officers. All were in American Army uniforms and under command of Lieutenant Colonel Edwin T. Swenson.

Algiers Harbor extended along the western edge of the bay, more than one and a half miles southward from the Ilot de la Marine. A crescent-shaped sea wall, bowed toward the shore, protected the center of the harbor while two jetties, projecting from the shore beyond the sea wall's extremities, left sheltered gaps for access to the open bay. Both these two entrances were protected by barrier booms. Jutting out from the shore into the harbor were eight concrete moles of varying length and width, which in effect subdivided the entire area into four major basins. At the far north of the harbor was the section controlled by the French Navy, which was protected by powerful fixed batteries mounted on the Jetée du Nord.

The plan of attack called for *Broke* to pierce the barrier, enter the southern basin, and discharge troops and naval boarding parties at the Quai de Dieppe. About 15 minutes later, *Malcolm* was to follow a similar course to the Grand Mole. While a protective cordon was set up barring access by road from the south, platoon-strength teams were to secure an electric power station, a petroleum storage depot, and a seaplane base in the southwestern section of the harbor, and the port offices, graving docks, and adjacent moles farther north.

As the destroyers neared the harbor the city's lights went out. Searchlight beams swept out across the bay and soon fell on the intruders. Shelling followed at once, particularly from the Batterie des Arcades. In the glare and turmoil, both ships twice missed the entrance to the harbor and were forced to circle for a third try.

At that juncture, just after 0400 on November 8, *Malcolm* was badly hit. Her deck caught fire and she was forced to withdraw. *Broke* persisted until a fourth try finally succeeded in taking her at top speed through the barrier, "like a knife through butter." Full daylight was still far away as she entered the port. *Broke* missed the planned point of mooring, either because some anchored vessels barred her path or because she mistook her objective in the darkness, and berthed instead along the Mole Louis Billiard. Half the force, consisting of Company L, one section of Company M, and nine medical troops of the 135th Infantry, with some British naval personnel, had come safely through the heavy bombardment, flattened on the deck of *Broke* and sheltered somewhat by her armored rail. They debarked slowly onto the Quai de Fécamp at about 0520.

By 0800 the troops had secured several objectives and seemed on the verge of success when *Broke*, waiting for their return, came under heavy fire. *Broke*'s siren sounded the recall signal and almost 60 men near the ship hurried aboard. The main part of Colonel Swenson's force could not have reached her for several minutes, and even then, in their commanding officer's judgment, would have been subject to greater danger than if they remained ashore. At 1030 a few men made it aboard as the ship pushed off, but the rest of the unit was surrounded. Shore batteries hit *Broke* as she cleared the harbor.[*]

---

[*] After clearing the harbor HMS *Zetland* (L59) took *Broke* in tow, but the the damage was so severe she sank two days later.

Ammunition was running low when several French light tanks and armored cars arrived about 1130 making the Americans' position hopeless. About 1230, therefore, Colonel Swenson surrendered his group. The port's defenders made no effort to sabotage its installations before the main body of Allied troops took the city two days later.

British losses were 7 killed, 2 died of wounds, and 18 wounded on *Broke*; 10 killed and 25 wounded on *Malcolm*. The 3d Battalion, 135th Infantry, lost 15 killed and 33 wounded. Like Operation *Reservist*, Operation *Terminal* ended in failure but with significantly fewer casualties.[29]

End of the Assault Phase – November 11

As often occurs in wars, politics cost lives. On November 8, a representative of President Roosevelt delivered a message to Marshal Pétain in Vichy France requesting cooperation with all Allied landings. Under close Nazi supervision, Pétain had to refuse but authorized Admiral Darlan to act as he saw fit. Darlan let the invasion continue until further resistance was hopeless before allowing his deputy at Algiers to meet American Major General Charles W. Ryder. Algiers was the first of the three *Torch* objectives to put a cease-fire into effect, at 2000 on November 8.

However, the agreement there did not apply to other areas. French headquarters in Oran did not agree to a separate cease-fire until 1215 on November 10, and at Casablanca the French did not send out a cease-fire order until 1910 on the 10th, but sniper fire continued for days after.[30] Ironically, the cessation of hostilities took place on Armistice Day, the same date that 24 years earlier had marked the end of World War I. Then, the Americans, British, and French had been fighting on the same side.

One hundred and twenty-five thousand soldiers, sailors, and airmen participated in Operation *Torch*; 82,600 of them were U.S. Army personnel. Ninety-six percent of the 1,469 casualties were American, with the Army losing 526 killed, 837 wounded, and 41 missing. Casualties varied considerably among the three task forces. Eastern Task Force lost the fewest Americans killed in action, with 108 killed, while Western Task Force lost 142 killed. Center Task Force lost 276 killed. Without the British-sponsored Operation *Reservist* at Oran, the Center Task Force killed-in-action total would have been in the same range as that of the other task forces.[31]

Lessons Learned

One of the lessons learned from Operation *Torch* was that the landing craft used along Africa's northwest coast were absolutely unsuited for beach landings, except in ideal conditions or in such places as the Solomon Islands where beaches seem to have been selected with a view to proving the effectiveness of the retracting boats. Another lesson learned from the invasion was that specially equipped salvage boats were needed to recover landing craft.

The landing craft crews became experts the hard way. They learned how to hit the beach at the perfect time – neither too early, when they would run into an attack from their own ships and planes, nor too late, when the enemy had had a chance to poke his head aboveground. They learned that the cold precision that the Coast Guard demanded in all assault transports during operations was essential as too little and too late could mean casualties or a lost boat.

The landings also resulted in the organization of Naval Beach Battalions. The 450 or so men of the beach parties that were part of the Western Task Force in this operation, undergoing their initial trial by fire on the beaches of North Africa, were numerically insignificant when compared to the estimated 35,000 men under General Patton's command, but their actions and accomplishments were in no way insignificant.

Lieutenant Junior Grade Jack Elliot recalls:

> In all probability, few in the Hampton Roads naval complex even knew we existed, or had gone, and returned. But the men and officers of the individual beach parties, ordered to the assault transports, ordered to land on the enemy-held beaches, and ordered back home, and finally to the Nansemond Hotel in Oceanview, Virginia, these men and officers – they knew. The nucleus of the First Beach Battalion evolved from this rag-tag "bastard" outfit of army-equipped sailors who had dug their slit trenches and foxholes in the sands of North Africa. There already was a feeling of "belonging," a feeling that we would like to be held together as a group for the future, whatever it held for us. We were the first – we were unique.[32]

For the men at the tip of the spear the price of all lessons in wartime is paid in blood.

CHAPTER 4

UP THE SLOT

SOLOMON ISLANDS, JULY 1942–FEBRUARY 1944

Undaunted by their losses in the Battle of the Coral Sea and the Battle of Midway, on July 21 and 22, 1942, the Japanese landed at Buna, Gona, and Sanananda on the northeast coast of Papua New Guinea. By August 13, 11,000 men had landed and the drive toward Port Moresby began southward across the Papuan Peninsula. For the advance out of Buna the Japanese assembled a force of about 1,800 men, augmented by 1,300 laborers from Rabaul and Formosa, and 52 horses.

To get to Port Moresby they would have to traverse the Owen Stanley Range, a backbone-like barrier rising steeply from the southwest coast then receding more gently to the northeast coast with ranges up to 10,000ft and peaks over 13,000ft. However, the same obstacles facing the Japanese also stood in the way of offensive action on the part of the Allied command. Few areas in the world offer physical barriers to military operations so marked as those of New Guinea. As well as being overshadowed by the lofty Owen Stanley Mountains, their several ranges connected by forbidding foothills and razorback ridges, southeastern New Guinea is also honeycombed with rivers and creeks that drain the upper regions into the swampy lowlands of the coast. A mass of lush and often impenetrable vegetation further complicates the surface of this rugged land. The beach jungle extending inland from the coast is broken frequently by tropical grasslands, where broad-bladed kunai and smaller kangaroo grasses grow. The most extensive vegetation is found along the lower slopes of the central ranges and their connecting ridges. Here a tropical rain forest extends up to about 5,000ft and forms canopies of foliage festooned with thorny vines. Above the 5,000ft line lies a belt of heavy rainfall feeding the mountain forest of bamboo and pine. Here as elsewhere the footing is usually treacherous.[1]

Under the command of Major General Tomitarō Horii the Japanese fought their way across the deep gorges and razor-backed ridges of the Owen Stanley Mountains and descended the southern slopes to within 32 miles of Port Moresby. Here, unexpectedly, they stopped and began withdrawing to Buna. Through message intercepts the Allies learned the Japanese strategic view was that success on New Guinea was directly related to success on Guadalcanal. The Japanese drive against the U.S. Marine beachhead in the Solomons had been repulsed and on September 18 General Horii received orders to withdraw to Buna as his troops might be needed as possible reinforcements for the Imperial Japanese Army forces on Guadalcanal.[*]

While Horii's forces labored toward Port Moresby another Japanese invasion force consisting of the *Kaigun Rikusentai* (Special Naval Landing Forces), accompanied by tanks attacked the Allied airfields at Milne Bay on the eastern tip of New Guinea on August 26. At Milne Bay the Allied force consisted of approximately 7,500 troops, including three companies of U.S. engineers and a battery of U.S. airborne antiaircraft artillery. Named "Milne Force," this two-brigade concentration took positions around two Allied airfields.

Spearheaded by two light tanks, the Japanese mounted night assaults on August 26 and reached Airstrip No. 3. Milne Force stiffened its line and then pushed the enemy into a general retreat.

As U.S. Marines discovered the hard way on Guadalcanal, no mercy could be shown toward a wounded enemy as Sergeant Arthur Trail, 2d Company, 12th Infantry Battalion, Australian Army found out:

> Lying across the [air]strip were dozens of dead Japs ... As our officer crossed in the vanguard a Jap, apparently wounded, cried out for help. The officer walked over to aid him, and as he did the Jap sprang to life and hurled a grenade which wounded him in the face. From then on the only good Jap was a dead one, and although they tried the same trick again and again throughout the campaign, they were dispatched before they had time to use their grenade.

[*]   During the retreat, Horii took a misstep while crossing the Kumusi River and drowned.

Our policy was to watch any apparent dead, shoot at the slightest sign of life and stab with bayonet even the ones who appeared to be rotten. It was all out from then on, neither side showing any quarter and no prisoners were taken.[2]

On September 4 the Japanese called in their navy for evacuation. In this first Allied ground victory – and first significant American action in Papua – Milne Force killed 600 of the enemy, while losing 322 dead and 200 wounded.[3]

Early in September, the 126th and 128th Infantry Combat Teams of the 32d Division (a National Guard unit from Michigan) were ordered to Port Moresby from Australia. Each combat team was composed of a regiment of infantry, a platoon of the 114th Engineers, a Collecting Company and a platoon of the Clearing Company of the 107th Medical Battalion with three 25-bed portable hospitals, and a detachment of the 32d Signal Company.

When the remnants of the Japanese invasion force reached the coast, their positions were roughly at Gona, along the Soputa–Sanananda track, and in a perimeter, based on the sea, with Buna Village its right flank and the coast just below Cape Endaiadere its left flank.

The Buna Combat Zone was located on the low-lying, flat coastal plain stretching inland from Gona and Bunato to the foothills of the Owen Stanley Range. The area is covered with dense jungle, reeking swamps, and scattered patches of kunai grass. Before the campaign it was largely unexplored by foreigners except along a few tracks used by the island's inhabitants, and from the air. Offshore are many uncharted reefs. The sea, however, is usually calm and fog at sea level is unknown.

Throughout the whole of New Guinea, including the Buna Combat Zone, the mosquito was considered as formidable an enemy as the Japanese. Beside the ravages of malaria, dengue fever was also a common malady, while deadly black water fever was less common. Both bacillary and amoebic dysentery were ever-present possibilities, as were jungle ulcers. The smallest scratch or cut had to be treated instantly or infection would set in.

Sand flies were common along the coast. They are small enough to penetrate the average mosquito net, and to scratch their bite is to invite jungle ulcers. Leeches were also fairly common but could be removed with the touch of a cigarette or a burning match. Any break they caused in the skin had to be treated against infection. Scrub typhus, carried primarily by the numerous chiggers (a type of mite) in the area and secondarily by Japanese soldiers infected by fleas carrying the disease, developed during the campaign. There was, and is, no known inoculation against this disease. Ringworm, Dhobi itch, athlete's foot and hookworm were also medical problems in the area.[4]

The troops also suffered from depression and lassitude caused by the climate and inadequate food; salt and vitamin tablets did little more than temporarily alleviate the situation. Within two weeks of being in the area the rate of sickness began to climb, and at all times thereafter a heavy percentage of every combat unit was hospitalized by malaria and other fevers. For every two men who were battle casualties, five were out of action from fever. Daily doses of quinine or Atabrine were compulsory but only suppressed the symptoms.

In a 12-day march from Kapa Kapa to Jaure the men of the 2d Battalion of the 126th Infantry struggled against the worst conditions New Guinea could offer. The heat, the sharp kunai grass, the leeches and fever-bearing insects, and the slippery trail broke down discipline, and the troops discarded large amounts of equipment to lighten their loads. The ration – Australian bully beef (canned corned beef), rice, and tea – made some sick, and diarrhea and dysentery claimed many more.

Five days of steady rain from October 15 made heating food and boiling water impossible and forced the men to wade through neck-deep water when crossing streams. At higher elevations the battalion found razor-backed ridges so steep that the men had to cling to vines to maintain progress. One group stumbled and slid 2,000ft downhill in 40 minutes; it took eight hours to recover the distance.[5]

One man recalled later:

> The men at the front in New Guinea were perhaps among the most wretched-looking soldiers ever to wear the American uniform. They were gaunt and thin, with deep black circles under their sunken eyes. They were covered with tropical sores … They were clothed in tattered, stained jackets and pants … Often the soles had been sucked off their shoes by the tenacious, stinking mud. Many of them fought for days with fevers and didn't know it … Malaria, dengue fever, dysentery, and, in a few cases, typhus hit man after man. There was hardly a soldier, among the thousands who went into the jungle, who didn't come down with some kind of fever at least once.[6]

When the Allies reached the Buna-Sanananda area in mid-November they found a series of beachhead defenses seven miles inland that stretched for

16 miles along the coast. The defenses consisted of bunkers camouflaged with fast-growing jungle vegetation, which were almost impossible to spot in the tangled underbrush. Usually entrances to the bunkers were in the rear, covered by fire from adjacent bunkers, and often angled so that a hand grenade tossed in the door would not kill the occupants.

Approaching troops could not see the enemy bunkers until they were only about 20ft away, by which time the Japanese would have already opened fire. Without armor or heavy artillery and air support infantrymen had to crawl up to each bunker and jam hand grenades into firing slits, a process that was both slow and costly in terms of Allied casualties.

Making a bad situation worse, the Japanese light machine guns and Arisaka rifles gave off no flash, and in the great tent of towering trees sound reverberated so much that the report of a weapon did not aid in finding its location. Each bunker had to be located and then it was either outflanked by soldiers creeping through a swamp or they were forced to charge it again and again until the defenders were killed. One soldier voiced a general complaint: "If we could only see them, it wouldn't take long."[7]

The fighting lasted through December and into January 1943. Reinforced with light tanks the U.S. 41st Division's 163rd Infantry Regiment and Australian troops broke through the last defensive line on January 22, exactly six months after the campaign began.

After months of unimaginative frontal attacks had overcome a well-entrenched foe, General Douglas MacArthur, the Southwest Pacific Area (SWPA) commander, finally had his airstrip and staging base at Buna on the north coast. It was expensive real estate. Besides ruining the Australian 7th and U.S. 32d Infantry Divisions, the campaign had severely taxed the Australian 5th and U.S. 41st Infantry Divisions. To give an example of the losses sustained, one need look no further than the units of the 126th Infantry, which went into the action on the Sanananda front with 1,199 men and officers on November 22; when these units were relieved on January 9, only 165 men and officers came out of the lines. The rest had been killed, wounded or suffered from incapacitating disease. The exhausted Americans needed six months to reconstitute before their next operation. Australian ground forces, despite having heavier losses, became the front line of defense against the Japanese.*

---

* Out of the 13,645-man U.S. force there were 10,879 casualties including 690 either killed in action or died from their wounds, and 17 who died from other causes. However,

THE FIGHT FOR THE OWEN STANLEY RANGE, SEPTEMBER 18–NOVEMBER 15, 1942

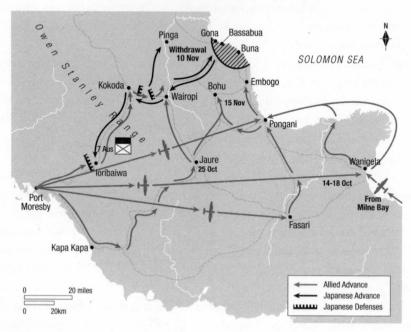

Although the Papua Campaign did not entail significant amphibious operations, other than resupplying Allied forces moving north from Milne Bay, an understanding of the campaign is needed to fully comprehend General Douglas MacArthur's SWPA strategy.

Eliminating the Japanese from Buna cleared the way for the construction of air bases necessary to support amphibious operations to retake the rest of eastern New Guinea, the islands leading to the Philippines and, ultimately, Japan. Once the Japanese thrust south through New Guinea was thwarted planning began for a two-pronged advanced to neutralize the large Japanese base at Rabaul.

---

*   (*continued from previous page*)

the greatest numbers of non-combat casualties were the 7,920 struck by diseases. In addition, the 5th U.S. Air Force lost 525 men. Australian Army casualties were 5,861, with 702 killed in action, and 29,100 sick. The Royal Australian Air Force losses were 310 and the Australian Navy added five to the total number of men killed. Combined Japanese Army and Navy loses were 13,500 killed or died of disease and 5,650 wounded or evacuated due to sickness. Source: The Kokoda Track Casualties, List of casualties for Kokoda, Milne Bay and Buna-Gona, www.kokoda.commemoration.gov.au

The U.S. Joint Chiefs of Staff directive of March 28, 1943 described the Southwest Pacific objectives as a line running across the straits between Finschhafen, New Guinea, and New Britain. Codenamed *Cartwheel*, one prong spearheaded by MacArthur's Southwest Pacific Area forces was to establish air bases on Woodlark and Kiriwina Islands; seize the Huon Peninsula and Madang; and occupy western New Britain. Along the second prong, Allied forces under Admiral Chester W. Nimitz were to move up through the Solomon Islands toward Bougainville, beginning with the New Georgia Islands northwest of Guadalcanal. The Allied forces involved were from Australia, the Netherlands, New Zealand, the U.S., and various Pacific Islands.

For *Cartwheel* MacArthur created "Alamo" Force, an independent operational command that was in reality almost identical to Southwest Pacific's newly created U.S. Sixth Army. By placing Alamo Force directly under General Headquarters, MacArthur removed American troops engaged in tactical operations from the control of Allied Land Forces commanded by the Australian General Sir Thomas Blamey. MacArthur personally selected Lieutenant General Walter Krueger to command Sixth Army. Another American, Vice Admiral Arthur S. Carpender, commanded Allied Naval Forces, which included the U.S. Seventh Fleet. His aggressive assistant was Rear Admiral Daniel E. Barbey, who commanded Seventh Amphibious Force – the ships that would carry the ground forces, their equipment, and their supplies forward into battle against the Japanese during *Cartwheel*. The Allied Air Forces would be under the command of Lieutenant General George H. Brett.[8]

To the poorly armed and inadequately trained Australian militia, traditionally limited in its activity to operations within Australia, were added almost two divisions of desert-toughened Australian fighters recently returned from the Middle East. Two American divisions, the 32d and 41st, rounded out Blamey's much reduced command.[9] This New Guinea Force was assigned responsibility for the eastward thrusts on mainland New Guinea. The U.S. Sixth Army and the Seventh Amphibious Force were to take Kiriwina, Woodlark and Cape Gloucester. Their land forces would be supported by Allied air units under Lieutenant General George Kenney and naval units under Vice Admiral Arthur S. Carpender. The entire strategic concept of the military campaign to drive the Japanese from their positions in the Southwest Pacific Area was predicated on amphibious operations.

Operation *Cartwheel* initially involved 13 separate smaller operations including Rabaul, Kavieng, and Kolombangara. These three were eliminated as being too costly in men and, ultimately, unnecessary. A timetable was established and Army and Marine units were assigned to each operation.

The final operations were divided into two prongs of Operation *Cartwheel* and can be divided as follows:

Prong 1

1. Operation *Toenails* – June 30, 1943.

   The ground troops for all *Toenails* attack forces were designated the New Georgia Occupation Force (NGOF).

   a. Segi Point, New Georgia (4th Marine Raider Battalion) – June 21, 1943.

   b. New Georgia (43d Infantry Division) – June 30, 1943.

   c. Rendova, New Georgia (169th and 172d RCTs) – June 30, 1943.

   d. Zanana, New Georgia (169th and 172d RCTs) – July 5, 1943.

   e. Bairoko, New Georgia (4th Marine Raider Battalion) – July 5, 1943.

   f. Arundel Island (172d RCT, 43rd Infantry Division) – August 27, 1943.

2. Vella Lavella [no codename was assigned to this operation] (35th RCT, 25th Infantry Division, 3d Division New Zealand) – August 15, 1943.

3. Operation *Goodtime* – October 27, 1943.

   a. Treasury Islands (2d Marine Parachute Battalion and 8th Brigade New Zealand).

4. Operation *Blissful* – October 28, 1943.

   Choiseul Island (2d Marine Parachute Battalion).

5. Operations *Dipper*, *Cherryblossom*, and *Hairbrush* – November 1, 1943 (3d Marine Division, 37th Infantry Division).

   a. *Dipper* – Bougainville

   b. *Cherryblossom* – Empress Augusta Bay

   c. *Hairbrush* – Puruata Island

Prong 2

1. Operation *Chronicle* – June 30, 1943.

   a. Woodlark Island (112th Cavalry Regiment).

   b. Kiriwina (158th Regimental Combat Team).

2. Operation *Postern* – September 5, 1943.

   a. Lae, New Guinea (9th and 7th Division Australia, 503d Parachute Infantry Regiment).

3. Operation *Dexterity*
   a. Arawe, New Britain (112th Cavalry) – December 15, 1943.
   b. Cape Gloucester (1st Marine Division) – December 26, 1943.
   c. Saidor (32nd Infantry Division) – January 2, 1944.
4. Admiralty Islands – February 29, 1944 (1st Cavalry Division).
5. Operation Squarepeg– March 29, 1944
   Emirau Island (4th Marine Regiment).[10]

As outlined above, *Cartwheel* would start with amphibious movements in the Southwest Pacific into Woodlark and Kiriwina. Simultaneously, troops in the South Pacific, using diversionary and aggressive infiltration, would move into New Georgia and/or Santa Isabel without committing major forces to action.

All the islands had conditions similar to those experienced during the Buna campaign in New Guinea. All had hot, wet, tropical climates. All were mountainous and heavily jungled. All were pest-ridden and full of tropical diseases, especially malaria. None had motor roads longer than a few miles. There were almost no ports with piers and quays to accommodate unloading of large ships.[11]

Before *Cartwheel* commenced in June, Operation *Cleanslate* was launched to clear the Russell Islands, which are located 25 miles to the west-northwest of Guadalcanal. Although the islands had been briefly occupied by the Japanese in late January 1943, on February 11 a coast watcher reported that they had left the islands. The Japanese had used the islands during the evacuation of Guadalcanal and naval personnel had built a barge-staging post there.

In December 1942, patrol flights taking off from Henderson Field on Guadalcanal, and from the decks of U.S. fleet carriers in the waters around the Solomon Islands, had discovered the Japanese constructing a well-camouflaged airfield at Munda on the Blanche Channel at the northwestern end of New Georgia. This new field posed a definite threat to the Allies still fighting to wrest Guadalcanal from the enemy. It had to be taken or, at the very least, neutralized. U.S. pilots also reported another field being completed on Kolombangara across the Kula Gulf from New Georgia.

Admiral William F. Halsey, Jr., Commander South Pacific, ordered the occupation of the Russell Islands for two reasons. He was worried that the Japanese might attempt to establish a more permanent presence on the Russell Islands, from where they could launch attacks on the recently secured Guadalcanal. He also hoped to develop the islands into a base that could be used in the upcoming invasion of New Georgia.

The invasion force of approximately 10,000 men consisted of the 43d Infantry Division, under Major General John H. Hester, and the 3d Marine Raider Battalion, under Lieutenant Colonel Harry B. Liversedge. As the Japanese had left the islands, the main threat to the Allies was that the Japanese would detect the invasion force and either attack the invasion fleet or land troops on the islands.

Three beaches were chosen for the landings: Yellow Beach, which was Wernham Cove on the southwest coast of Banika; Blue beaches 1 and 2, on opposite sides of the entrance to Renard Sound, an inlet on the northeast coast of Banika; and Red Beach at Paddy Bay, on the eastern shore of Pepesala Point at the northern end of Pavuvu. Late on February 20, the invasion fleet left Koli Point, Guadalcanal, and set course for the beaches.

All units landed at 0600 on February 21. The divisional HQ, most of the 103d Infantry and some of the Marines landed at Yellow Beach, and another battalion from the 103d Infantry landed on Blue beaches 1 and 2. These units had secured Banika by noon.

The 3d Marine Raider Battalion landed on Red Beach, and went on to clear the Pepesala peninsula and Baisen Island. The islands were declared secured at 1200. The next morning the 169th Infantry landed and the garrison was complete. They prepared for a possible Japanese counterattack, but none came. By April 15, Allied aircraft began operating from the first of two new airstrips the Seabees constructed on Banika.[12]

On April 14, as the Allies built up forces for Operation *Cartwheel*, U.S. Naval Intelligence decrypting the Japanese Purple Code tracked the movements of Admiral Isoroku Yamamoto, commander of the Imperial Japanese Navy, on his inspection tour of air units in the Solomon Islands and New Guinea. The decryption revealed that on April 18 Yamamoto would be flying from Rabaul to Balalae Airfield, on an island near Bougainville in the Solomon Islands. He and his staff would be flying in two medium bombers (Mitsubishi G4M "Bettys" of the 205th Kōkūtai Naval Air Unit), escorted by six navy Mitsubishi A6M "Zero" fighters of the 204th Kōkūtai NAU. They were scheduled to depart Rabaul at 0600 and arrive at Balalae at 0800, Tokyo time.

President Franklin D. Roosevelt ordered Secretary of the Navy Frank Knox to "get Yamamoto." Knox passed on Roosevelt's wishes to Admiral Chester W. Nimitz who first consulted Admiral Halsey and then authorized the mission on April 17.

The top secret message sent by Secretary Knox to Admiral Marc Mitscher, Commander Air, Solomon Islands (COMAIRSOLS) read:

SQUADRON 339 P-38 MUST AT ALL COSTS REACH AND DESTROY.
PRESIDENT ATTACHES EXTREME IMPORTANCE TO MISSION.

Codenamed Operation *Vengeance*, the mission was assigned to the 339th Fighter Squadron, 347th Fighter Group, 13th Air Force, whose P-38G Lightning aircraft, equipped with drop tanks, had the range to intercept and engage. Though the mission was to be conducted by the 339th, ten of the pilots were drawn from other squadrons in the 347th Fighter Group.

Eighteen P-38s, based at Kukum Field on Guadalcanal, were tasked for the mission. One flight of four was designated as the "killer" flight while the remainder, which included two spares, would climb to 18,000ft to act as "top cover" for the expected reaction by Japanese fighters based at Kahili.

Led by the squadron's commander, Major John W. Mitchell, the Lightnings departed Guadalcanal at 0725 on April 18. Early on in the mission, two aircraft from the killer group were lost because of mechanical issues, and were replaced with ones from the cover group. Mitchell led the squadron west out over the water before turning north toward Bougainville. To avoid being detected by the Japanese, the Lightnings flew at 50ft or below and maintained radio silence. They arrived at the intercept point one minute early.

Spotting the flight containing Yamamoto, Mitchell's squadron began to climb and the killer group, consisting of Captain Thomas Lanphier, First Lieutenant Rex Barber, Lieutenant Besby Holmes, and Lieutenant Raymond Hine, was ordered to attack. Dropping their tanks, Lanphier and Barber turned so that they were parallel with the Japanese and began to climb. Holmes, whose tanks failed to release, returned back out to sea followed by his wingman. As Lanphier and Barber climbed, a group of "Zeros" dove to attack. Lanphier turned left to engage the enemy fighters, while Barber banked hard right and came in behind the bombers.

Opening fire on one bomber, Barber hit it several times causing it to roll violently to the left and plummet into the jungle below. He then turned toward the water seeking the second bomber. He found it near Moila Point being attacked by Holmes and Hines. Joining in the attack, they forced it to crash land in the water. Coming under attack from the escorts, they were aided by Mitchell and the rest of the flight. With fuel levels reaching a critical level, Mitchell ordered his men to break off the action and return to Guadalcanal. All of the aircraft returned except Hines's which was lost in action and Holmes who was forced to land in the Russell Islands due to a lack of fuel.

The P-38s shot down both Japanese bombers, killing 19, including Yamamoto. In exchange, the 339th lost Hines, who was lost in action along with his plane. Searching the jungle, the Japanese found Yamamoto's body near the crash site. Thrown clear of the wreckage, he had been hit twice in the fighting. Cremated at nearby Buin, his ashes were returned to Japan aboard the battleship *Musashi*. He was replaced by Admiral Mineichi Koga.

General MacArthur referred to the attack as "one of the singularly most significant actions of the Pacific War."[13] The announcement of Yamamoto's death boosted the morale of the hard-pressed Allies but it had no immediate impact on the planned Allied counteroffensives set to begin two months later.

New Georgia Operation Plan

The New Georgia Group is a compact maze of islands, separated by shallow lagoons or narrow reaches of open water that are littered with coral. They lie on a northwest–southeast axis between Bougainvillea, 110 miles to the northwest, and Guadalcanal, 180 miles to the southeast. The group is nearly 150 miles long and 40 miles wide, and comprises 12 major islands surrounded by many smaller islands and formidable reefs. The rugged terrain is covered with dense, forbidding jungle from which rise conical mountains that mark the volcanic origin of the group. The largest island in the group is its namesake, New Georgia.

In November 1942, while still fighting for possession of Henderson Field on Guadalcanal, the Japanese sought another airfield that would bring their fighter planes within shorter striking distance of the southern Solomons. They found the perfect location at Munda Point on New Georgia, about two thirds of the way from Rabaul to Guadalcanal, and started construction on November 21. By December 17, despite multiple bombing raids, the Japanese had an operational 4,700ft-long airstrip that they used mainly for servicing planes after raids on Guadalcanal and the Russell Islands. Despite bombings and occasional shells from ships, the field was never out of service for more than 48 hours, making the airfield at Munda the main objective of the New Georgia offensive.[14]

In the spring of 1943, units that were tasked to take part in the offensive sent reconnaissance parties to patrol the area's designated landing areas. Solomon Islanders acted as guides and scouts led by British resident administrators and Australian Navy intelligence personnel, who, as coast watchers, hid in the hills in the enemy rear areas. From here they radioed information about Japanese troop, air, and naval sightings and movements to Allied listening stations.

The New Georgia landings were set for June 30. The plan was for simultaneous landings at several points on Rendova Island, at Viru Harbor and Segi Point on New Georgia, and at Wickham Anchorage off Vangunu Island, just south of New Georgia. A landing field would then be constructed on Segi Plantation, while Wickham Anchorage and Viru Harbor would be used as staging refuges for small craft. The troops on Rendova were to move across Roviana Lagoon, land to the east of Munda, and capture the airfield. There would be preliminary landings on Sasavela and Baraulu Islands, securing the Onaiavisi entrance to the Lagoon. This attack would be accompanied by the seizure of positions in the Bairoko–Enogai area on northeast New Georgia to prevent reinforcements reaching the Munda garrison. The attack was to be launched from bases on the Russell Islands.[15]

Prior to the landings on June 30 there were reports that the Japanese were moving into the Segi Point area on the southern coast of New Georgia. A force was hastily put together to occupy the point, including two companies of the 4th Marine Raider Battalion (Lieutenant Colonel Michael S. Currin commanding) consisting of five officers and 187 men. The Japanese were moving in on a coast watcher, Donald G. Kennedy, who held the plantation on the point, so Rear Admiral Turner made the decision to bring forward the Segi Point phase of the New Georgia operation in order to keep possession of the beachhead, which for all intents and purposes was already established there, and to protect Kennedy,and his islander guerrillas. During the night of June 20–21, APDs *Waters* (ADP-8) and *Dent* (ADP-9) transited the Slot[*] and early the next morning they threaded their way through the uncharted shoal water between New Georgia and Vangunu to Segi Point. In less than two hours, the two ships had landed their passengers unopposed and had left.

The next day the APDs *Schley* (ADP-14) and *Crosby* (ADP-17) landed two companies of the 103rd Infantry and a survey team. The Army took over on

---

[*] The Marines on Guadalcanal nicknamed New Georgia Sound the Slot. The channel was used by the Japanese to supply its garrison on Guadalcanal.

the 28th and on the 30th the construction of the Segi Point fighter strip began.

Rendova

The second landing took place at Rendova Harbor, on the north side of Rendova Island at 0700 on June 30. Two groups of destroyers patrolled the two entrances of the harbor, while others screened the transports. The assault boats went ashore under a hail of machine-gun fire from the beach. Batteries on Munda Point scored a hit on the destroyer *Gwin* (DD-443), killing three men. However, seven batteries in the Munda Point area were put out of action by *Buchanan* (DD-484) and *Farenholt* (DD-491).

Despite confusion and disorganization, the Allied troops quickly overwhelmed a 120-man Japanese detachment and established a 1,000-yard-deep beachhead. All troops were ashore in half an hour. Once they had landed the main problem was the movement of supplies. They needed to be put ashore and moved inland as quickly as possible. However, the rain turned the ground into red clay mud, and the heavy traffic ruined the island's single mile-long road, making it so muddy that a bulldozer sank. Added to that, inadequately marked supplies, dumped on the beach by troops wading ashore, piled up and became intermixed. So many trucks became mired in the mud that they were ordered to stop traveling to the beachhead, and movement of supplies off the beach became slow and laborious.

As well as resisting on the ground, the Japanese also launched air attacks. Over the course of the morning, a 32-plane combat air patrol from bases on Guadalcanal and the Russell Islands drove off two enemy air attacks. Then, less than hour after unloading had been completed, at 1500 a group of between 24 and 28 enemy torpedo bombers, escorted by an unknown number of "Zero" fighters, was sighted coming in very low over the northwest corner of New Georgia Island. All Allied vessels opened fire and managed to hit a number of the attackers, however, ignoring their losses, the bombers released their torpedoes at 500 yards.

Farenholt was hit by a dud and *McCawley* (APA-4) was struck midship, in the vicinity of the engine room, by three torpedoes. An hour later *McCawley*, dead in the water with a large hole between 18ft and 20ft wide in her side, was attacked by a dozen or more dive-bombers, which were driven off by the salvage crew who manned her guns. When it became apparent that she could no longer be kept afloat all hands were ordered to abandon ship. At 2023 she was struck by three torpedoes and sank. At first an enemy submarine was believed to have fired the torpedoes, but later it was learned that she had been sunk by friendly PT boats who mistook her for an enemy.

The next Japanese air strike against Rendova came two days later killing 30 men, wounding more than 200, and exploding fuel dumps. Another attempt on July 4, however, provided the Americans with a better result. Sixteen Japanese bombers appeared unescorted. A mere 88 rounds of antiaircraft fire brought down 12, and waiting fighters shot down the rest.[16]

Landings on New Georgia moved forward as planned. However, the only maps provided to the attacking force were sketches based on aerial photographs. The drawings outlined jungle areas with conventional symbols that did not reveal the intricate, abrupt mass of hills, ridges, and swamps – jumbled without pattern – that lay under the thick jungle canopy. Contour lines on the maps were based on scouting reports, and, as the soldiers discovered, were usually incorrect. The ridges and hills, bending and twisting in all directions, forced the attacking units to move in one direction, then another.

New Georgia Island

The actual invasion of western New Georgia was not the direct assault on Munda airfield. Late on June 29, lashed by heavy rains, companies A and B of the 169th Infantry Battalion scrambled ashore on the islands that guarded the Onaiavisi entrance to Roviana Lagoon.

Then, on the night of July 2–3, elements of the Army's 172d's 1st Battalion began the move from Rendova to Zanana Beach. The troop transfer was made in landing craft, which towed additional rubber boats carrying soldiers. Torpedo boats escorted the craft across Blanche Channel, and, at the Onaiavisi entrance, local guide canoes took over and directed the landing craft through the lagoon to the beachhead.

The rest of the 169th Infantry Battalion landed on Zanana Beach on July 4 in the midst of a Japanese air attack, which caused unloading activities from the 14 LCIs and four LSTs to be abruptly abandoned. Luckily, no ships were hit. For the men, the bombing attack following a sea-tossed trip from the Russells was a rough introduction to New Georgia. Along with the 172d Infantry Division, the 169th headed for the Barike River and for Munda. Initially there was little Japanese resistance, but this changed and on July 6, short of Barike, the advance halted and the 169th went into camp.

As the Army was fighting its way through heavy jungle and increasing resistance, other objectives on New Georgia were also being targeted. After midnight on July 5, a U.S. Navy task force of seven APDs and one destroyer steamed out of the inky darkness of Rice Anchorage nearby points to open the way for the landing. The Japanese sent up flares, which lit up the convoy, revealing their presence. The Japanese artillery then shelled the invasion fleet but none of the shots reached their mark.

The attacking force was known as the Northern Landing Group assault force and was commanded by Marine Colonel Liversedge. It consisted of the 1st Marine Raider Battalion, the 4th Marine Raider Battalion, the 3d Battalion, 145th Infantry Regiment, 43d Infantry Division, and the 3d Battalion, 148th Infantry, 43 Infantry Division. They landed unopposed from eight APDs and destroyers. However, a narrow beach, difficult landing conditions, and concerns for an enemy naval attack caused the destroyer transport force to depart, taking the Raiders' long-range radio with it. Because speed was so important, Liversedge's force was lightly armed and provisioned, and carried only three days' worth of rations.

During the remainder of the night the men were drenched by a terrific downpour. Sleep was out of the question as ponchos were used chiefly to protect weapons, packs and other gear, rather than for personal comfort. In the morning the invaders were met only by porters and scouts under Australian Flight Officer John A. Corrigan. Lieutenant Colonel Samuel B. Griffith II, 1st Raider Regiment executive officer, described them as small men, "but their brown bodies were wiry and their arm, leg and back muscles were powerful. They wore gaudy cheap cotton lap-lap, or lava-lavas." These 150 New Georgians were the Northern Landing Group's supply transport in a region without roads.

Moving out early on July 5, the men soon learned that, contrary to earlier intelligence reports, the journey to Dragons Peninsula, following the rough trails hacked out of the jungle by coast watchers and New Georgians, would be exceedingly tough. For the first weeks of the campaign, the men were plagued by constant rain, making even more dismal the task of struggling up and down jungle hills, which seemed to be composed in equal parts of sharp coral and thick, clinging vines. The rain also added unforeseen obstacles; one stream soon became a nine-foot-deep river to ford. The men in the 148th's weapons company, laboring under the weight of their heavy machine guns and 81mm mortars, were soon far to the rear.[17]

The story of this early part of the campaign, which was marked by deprivations and bitter fighting, was told in the following eyewitness accounts by two combat correspondents, Technical Sergeants Frank J. McDevitt and Murrey Marder:

The march began at daybreak. Despite the dense vegetation, rain descended in torrents, and soon the jungle floor was a sea of mud. Our march began in the rain and it ended in the rain. All day Monday and Tuesday we sloshed through muck and mire that was knee deep. We were covered from head to foot with mud. Huge fallen trees, slippery with their coats of slimy moss, and the myriad roots of giant banyans, which snaked across our path, helped slow our progress.

The farther we marched the worse the terrain became. Sharp coral-like rocks, thick, overhanging vines and creepers, and prickly plants that pierced our jungle suits, added their hazards. Overhanging branches knocked off our helmets, and sometimes the rifles we carried over our shoulders.

In ravines we lost our footholds as rocks broke from steep slopes. Halts were called frequently. At every stop weapons had to be cleaned and oiled. At dark we laid our ponchos on the ground and made mattresses on the broad leaves cut from the trees. We built lean-tos. Mosquitoes, ants, crabs and lizards crawled all about us. Huge bats flew overhead. Mysterious birds sent weird screeches through the night.

We carried three days' rations, the estimate the march would require. Rain and the jungle conspired to make this a bad guess. By the time our rations were gone, most of our cumbersome gear was gone, too, a trail of sodden blankets, shelter halves, mess gear and field packs littering the jungle.

On July 7, three days after the landings, advance Raider units came across a Japanese patrol at Maranusa; they killed two of the enemy. By mid-afternoon the machine guns and carbines were chattering again. "This time it is a fairly sizeable force – some 150 Jap troopers and naval landing force men," the correspondents wrote later:

They defend a jungle outpost called Triri. The Raiders sweep down on it like hounds after rabbits. By nightfall some 75 Japanese bodies are scattered around the little coral ridge which marks Triri.

Now, some of our buddies are dead, too, although but a handful compared to the Jap toll. We bring them in to the shattered Japanese command post.

Sticks are cut for crosses and the bark shaved off so that they will stand out above the graves against the dark jungle. To the crosses are affixed the identification tags of the dead.

The wounded are brought down into the little valley too, carried in improvised stretchers made of ponchos and branches. Mostly their wounds are superficial – wounds of the arms and legs, and the wounded who are conscious watch quietly as Navy hospital corpsmen attend them. But occasionally there is a feeble cry, "Pain! Morphine! Morphine!"

A series of engagements took place Wednesday night and through Thursday, when we were able to secure two other outpost villages – Maranusa and Baekineru. Early Friday Baevuruno was seized and then the furious struggle for Enogai began. By the morning of July 8th the problem of food became serious. Our command post moved up from Maranusa to Triri. Almost all rations were gone and the men were foraging for Japanese rice and canned fish. Worms got to the rice first.[18]

By afternoon on July 8 the Raiders were on the move again endeavoring to find a passable trail to Enogai. All trails seemed to lead into impassable swamps. The Japanese, who had seemingly wilted at the first attack, were back again. Rifle fire swept the command post at Triri, followed by an attempted Japanese counterattack against Raiders established on a small ridge overlooking Triri. Army units held the left flank, while up on the slope the Marines and Army units withstood the assault. Night falls quickly in the jungle and with it the firing ceased. Down in the valley, Navy hospital corpsmen and Army medics worked feverishly, treating the wounded who were spread out on the floor of a thatched shack.

By this time, rations were exhausted. Although attempts were made to contact the Air Force for parachute drops of rations and ammunition, the heavy jungle growth made communications difficult. The rice that was left was reserved for the wounded.

On July 9, the Enogai defenses were reached and, after an air strike, Liversedge launched an immediate attack. The Japanese were well dug-in and well armed with machine guns and mortars, but their heavy-caliber coast defense artillery could only be used seaward. Richard C. Ackerman, a Marine with Company C, remembered: "We soon came to a lagoon which stopped our forward motion. Our right flank, though, did overrun the enemy's warehouse and food storage area."[19]

The Raiders entrenched quietly and awaited an expected mad *banzai* charge. However, the night passed quietly. At dawn on July 10, the Marines opened up on Enogai with a murderous barrage of 60mm mortars and took Enogai Village. Shells were lobbed into the Japanese camp, creating panic. In the ensuing chaos Japanese soldiers raced about their camp area as if terror stricken. Now and then a grenade sailed up at the attackers on the ridge, but the Japanese offered little organized resistance. Raiders rushed headlong down the slopes and charged the Japanese positions. A sand-bagged machine gun, set up as a road block, was swiftly wiped out. The Japanese fled in mad confusion down a coral road to the beach. Those not hit plunged into the water, attempting to swim to a small mangrove island offshore. Raider machine guns, set on the ridge, mowed them down as they floundered in the water. As a Marine machine gunner put it: "It was like shooting ducks!"

Colonel Liversedge, Lieutenant Colonel Griffith, and Captain Clay Boyd narrowly escaped death in the assault. The trio walked into the line of fire of a hidden Japanese machine gun nest, protected by snipers. With bullets screeching over his head, Colonel Liversedge stood quietly surveying the scene until Lieutenant Colonel Griffith shouted:

"Down, Harry! Get down!"

All three officers escaped injury, but Second Lieutenant Philip A. Oldham, a veteran of Guadalcanal, who had been recently commissioned, was killed as he blasted the nest while leading a grenade-throwing squad.

Finally, in mid-afternoon on Saturday Enogai fell. The position was rushed from all sides. The victorious troops tore through the outer village and across a causeway to the guns in the beach emplacements. The final resistance came from a number of Japanese who remained hidden in the trees and managed to pick off several targets during the night before they were wiped out.

The battalion had fought for 30 hours without rations or water resupply. Army troops carried up water and K-rations and candy bars received in an airdrop. After the battle the Marines erected shaved-stick markers, each with dog tags attached identifying a lost buddy. The area was larger than the small groups of graves at Triri, but the number of Marines killed during the attack was comparatively few.

That night hungry Marines dined on Japanese canned salmon and sardines, as well as meat and vegetables. Rice was prepared and served, as were barley, soy sauce, and dried onions washed down with sake. Stores of Japanese clothing replaced the Marines own mud-caked uniforms.[20]

While the Marines fought their battles, the Army's 169th and 172d troops faced their own kind of hell. The169th's started after it went into camp the evening of July 6.

Accounts of the action during the night of July 6–7 combine fact and fancy. Reports that Japanese riflemen had infiltrated the loose perimeter set up by the 169th's leading battalion caused panic among the soldiers. Although the regiment had been on Guadalcanal and the Russells before landing on New Georgia, the troops evidently were not prepared for jungle combat at night. Soldiers reported the next morning that enemy infiltrators threw grenades, screamed, whistled, shouted invective, and jumped into foxholes to bayonet the occupants. After a wild night of grenade bursts, shooting, and screaming no enemy dead were found in the perimeter. However, U.S. casualties were numerous.

The advance toward Munda continued the next morning with the 172d moving easily along a coastal trail while the 169th slugged through heavy jungle with its open flank screened by a Fiji Scout company. Every step forward was a struggle against a determined enemy and multiple jungle obstacles, dense, vine-choked underbrush, steep ridges, numerous swamps, constant and enervating heat, and almost incessant torrents of rain. Each new enemy attack forced the advancing troops to deploy and strike back to neutralize the threat, slowing down progress. Hidden snipers, pinning down the advance units, held up the regiments for hours.

For the 169th, the advance had been particularly harrowing. They were forced to cross the meandering Barike River a number of times as they slowly pressed forward over steep ridges and through deep swamps in the upper river region. Fatigued from the initial struggle through the jungle from Zanana, and continually harassed at night by enemy soldiers probing at the exposed right flank, the169th was a dispirited outfit. Additionally, with the regiment so strung out, troops were needed to carry food, water, and ammunition to the advanced units as well as to help evacuate the wounded, tasks which further sapped the fighting strength of the outfit. However, despite these incredible hardships, the force pressed on.

The final push on Munda promised the hardest fighting of the campaign. Between the NGOF units and their objective were more than 4,500 yards of low but steep hills, irregular and broken, densely covered with tropical rain forest, and laced with enemy defenses. Reports from patrols combined with observation of bunkers had already indicated that the Japanese soldiers were dug in and covered by low, two-level camouflaged coral and log emplacements with deadly interlocking fields of fire. Trenches bulwarked by coconut logs connected the bunkers. NGOF soldiers were well aware that the enemy would have to be routed from these positions and that resistance until death was standard practice. What's more, the soldiers knew that the Japanese often abandoned one bunker to man another, and then, after the first bunker had been overrun, returned to defend it again. This meant that an area gained in an attack one day had to be cleared again the following one.

The Japanese soldiers, fatigued and muddy, were forced to fight in some instances on only one rice ball a day. Kept irritated and sleepless by the constant bombardment, the Munda defenders were gaunt, weary, and hungry – but still determined. Despite the constant hardships, morale was high and the Japanese soldier was "prepared to die in honor, if necessary."[21]

As the attacks progressed the flamethrower, receiving its most extensive use in the Pacific yet, was coming into its own. Combined with M3A1 Stuart light tanks from the Marine 9th, 10th, and 11th Defense Battalions, the weapon helped Army troops punch through the Japanese defenses barring the way to Munda Point airfield.

The tanks and their crews defied jungle, mud, and suicidal counterattacks to spearhead a slow and deliberate attack. The tank gunners fired 37mm canister rounds to strip away the jungle concealing Japanese bunkers, followed up with high-explosive shells to penetrate the fortifications, and used machine guns to cut down the survivors as they fled. Captain Robert W. Blake, a tank commander who earned the Navy Cross in the central Solomons, noted that "death on the Munda Trail" was noisy, violent, and far from romantic. "I trip the seat lever," he wrote, "and drop down behind the periscopic sight. I level the sight dot at the black slot and press the firing switch. Wham, the gun bucks, a wad of smoke billows through the trees. The concealing branches are left raw and broken." According to one analysis of the fighting, "A handful of Marine tanks, handicapped by difficult jungle, had spearheaded most of the successful attacks on New Georgia."

On August 5, the Marine tanks that survived Japanese fire, formidable terrain, and mechanical breakdown, moved onto Munda Point airfield, which was littered with wrecked aircraft and pockmarked with shell craters. The infantry mopped up on the next day, and the 9th Defense Battalion moved its antiaircraft weapons into position to protect the captured airdrome, while its 155mm guns prepared to shell the Japanese garrison on nearby Kolombangara.[22]

At 1410, the airfield was officially declared secured and Allied troops took over the enemy fortifications ringing the prize which had taken more than a month of bitter combat to obtain.

Along the blasted and cratered runways were hulks of 30 enemy airplanes, some still in revetments. All were stripped of armament and instruments. None would ever fly again. Japanese supplies, including tasty tinned foods, beer, sake, and rice gave triumphant infantrymen a change from the monotony of combat rations.

Patrols, ranging far to the north, reported no opposition. The patrols' only result was the capture of one forlorn Japanese soldier, whom one officer described as typical of the enemy who were thwarted in their attempts to hold their precious airfield: "Injured, tired, sick, no food, dirty torn clothes, little ammunition and a battered rusty rifle."

After a short pause at the airfield, the 161st Infantry joined the 27th Infantry Regiment swung north to complete the destruction of enemy forces in the area between Diamond Narrows and Bairoko Harbor. They encountered little resistance because the Japanese were trying to evacuate the scattered remnants of the New Georgia garrison. After two weeks of locating and eliminating Japanese positions north of Munda, the 27th Infantry declared its zone secured.

The final ground action on New Georgia came on August 25, when the 161st Infantry combined with Liversedge's force to attack the harbor area from three sides only to find the Japanese had just evacuated the area ending one phase of the battle for New Georgia. However, there were still Japanese on New Georgia and the surrounding islands of Arundel, Baanga, Gizo, Kolombangara, and Vella Lavella. These islands had to be captured or neutralized before any action could be taken further up the Solomons chain.

Baanga, Arundel, and Gizo

While the mopping-up operation continued on New Georgia, the 169th Infantry moved onto Baanga on August 11, from where a pair of Japanese 120mm guns had been shelling Munda Point. When the Japanese resisted strongly the 172d was also ordered onto the small island and into the fight.

The two regiments spent ten days driving the Japanese from the southern part of Baanga. The remaining Japanese troops withdrew to Arundel.

The 172d was tasked with clearing Arundel and on August 27 crossed from New Guinea to the southern part of the island. Initially, the island was defended by around 200 men, but the Japanese could easily reinforce it from Kolombangara.

The main fighting took part at the northern end of the island. The north coast has a somewhat unusual layout, with two long narrow gulfs running into the land from the west. The most northwestern point on the main landmass was Bustling Point. The first of these gulfs then separated the main island from the long Bomboe Peninsula, which ran from west to east, joining the north coast about half way along. A second narrow gulf began at this point, bordered in the north by Sagekarasa Island and the Stima Peninsula. The coast then curved around to the south towards Stima Lagoon.

On September 5, the 2d Battalion of the 172d Regiment launched an attack north at Stima Lagoon, but the Americans had finally found the main Japanese defensive positions and the attack was stopped dead.

Three days later both sides committed fresh troops to the fighting on Arundel Island. The Americans moved one battalion from the 169th Infantry onto the island, while the Japanese moved the 3rd Battalion, 13th Infantry Regiment.

The fighting was as bloody and brutal as that during the fight for Munda. One 43d Division battalion commander later described the fighting on Arundel as "the most bitter combat of the New Georgia campaign."[23]

While troops from the 169th held the Bustling Point area, on September 12 the 27th Infantry opened a drive east along the length of the Bomboe Peninsula. The leading battalion, restricted to a narrow strip of island only 400 yards wide and unable to make a flanking attack, could only push straight ahead when it ran into stiff opposition. Small gains with mounting casualties were the inevitable results.

As the front lines inched abreast of Sagekarasa Island, which parallels Bomboe Peninsula, on September 12, a second battalion swam and waded across a lagoon to establish another front on that island.

On the night of September 14–15, Japanese reinforcements on Kolombangara were loaded onto barges for transfer to Arundel to begin a counteroffensive that was supposed to regain the initiative in the Central Solomons. Undaunted by the loss of their colonel and two battalion commanders killed by American artillery fire as their barge beached on the Arundel coast, the Japanese unleashed a near fanatical attempt to break out of the perimeter. The desperate thrust failed. Unable to erase the beachhead in a series of screaming counterattacks the Japanese then hurriedly evacuated their barge base on the extreme western tip of the island.

More U.S. troops arrived on September 16 including M1A1 Stuart tanks of the 9th, 10th, and 11th Marine Defense Battalions.

The Stuarts broached several defensive positions, suffering steady attrition in the process. Some of these tanks were used to support a 27th Infantry attack on the Bomboe Peninsula on September 17 and managed to push the Japanese out of their positions. A second attack on the 18th was less effective and two of the tanks were knocked out.

On September 19, the surviving tanks formed two ranks, the rear rank firing canister shells that stripped the jungle concealment as the tanks opened paths for advancing infantry. This charge proved to be the last major fight during the conquest of Arundel Island.

The Japanese retreat began on the night of September 19–20. On the morning of September 20, the American troops on Sagekarasa discovered that their opponents were gone, and on September 21 the troops on Arundel made the same discovery. The remaining Japanese troops withdrew at night to Kolombangara and the battle for Arundel Island was over.

After the U.S. attack on Barakoma in August General Minoru Sasaki sent 250 Japanese troops from the 2d Battalion, 45th Infantry, and one battery of the 6th Field Artillery Regiment troops to defend Gizo. Around September 20 he evacuated these forces along with those on Arundel.

Kolombangara

Kolombangara was the most heavily garrisoned of the islands with 12,000 troops waiting prepared behind elaborate defenses along the southern beaches with plans already drawn up for counterattacks. Instead of facing another brutal battle to take the island Admiral Halsey and his staff decided to bypass it, instead landing their troops on the lightly defended island of Vella Lavella. At this stage the only Japanese troops on Vella Lavella were some survivors of the naval battle of Kula Gulf on July 5–6 who had managed to reach land.

The Americans badly needed to reconnoiter their new target of Vella Lavella, and on July 21 a scouting party was sent to the island. It landed on the southeastern coast and spent six days exploring. On its return it reported that the island was undefended, had suitable sites for an airfield, and recommended landing in the southeast, at Barakoma. The first American troops, from a scouting party of 45 men, landed on the island on the night of August 12–13.[24]

At dawn on August 15, the advance group of seven APDs arrived off Barakoma with six destroyers as escorts and began unloading troops and equipment. Within an hour they had completed the operation and departed on the return trip to Guadalcanal with a screen of four destroyers. When the second group of 12 LCIs arrived at 0715 it was discovered that only eight of them could be accommodated at one time by the three beaches and the unloading of the last four was delayed until about 0900. Meanwhile, the third group of three LSTs had arrived on schedule at 0800 and was awaiting its turn to land. At 0801 between 15 and 20 enemy fighters and dive-bombers attacked for 20 minutes without managing to cause any damage. At 1227, while the LSTs were still unloading, came the heaviest air attack by between eight and 12 dive-bombers and seven fighters.

The attack was broken up with the loss of ten Japanese planes. At about 1736 yet another attack by eight dive-bombers was broken up by a U.S. fighter plane flying Combat Air Patrol. At 1810 the third group of LSTs got under way for the return trip to Guadalcanal, leaving about 130 tons of supplies still unloaded in order to avoid night attacks while without fighter cover.

The landing on Vella Lavella took place two days after the Japanese Imperial HQ had decided not to send any more troops into the central Solomons. It decided not to try and regain control of Vella Lavella, but instead to establish a barge base at Horainu, on the northeastern shore, for use by ships heading towards Kolombangara. Two army companies and a platoon of naval troops departed from Bougainville on August 17. The U.S. Navy attempted to intercept them, but failed and the Japanese landed safely on August 19. They now had 390 men at Horainu and at least another 200 stragglers on the island.

Within the next 15 days four more echelons, each comprising three or four LSTs with destroyer escort, made the trip from Guadalcanal to Vella Lavella with additional supplies. While all of these were attacked by air only slight damage resulted. One LST was ignited by its own ship's fire and burned to the water, but survivors were taken off by destroyers. However, the Coast Guard-manned LST-167 didn't escape the bombers.

LST-167 was part of a convoy that departed Guadalcanal on September 24 and was ordered to beach at Ruravai, Vella Lavella, a beach not previously used by LSTs. It was consequently without shore defenses and had a minimum of facilities for beaching and unloading. The beaching was made on the 25th at 0745 and all of the 77th Marine Combat Battalion's equipment had been unloaded by 1115. At 1116 the executive officer reported a possible "bogie" about 40 miles out. Thirty seconds later a patrol plane reported "lots of bogies and about 20 angels."

A few seconds later three dive-bombers were picked up coming in directly out of the sun and diving at the ship. At 1117 the order was given to open fire. All 20 guns opened fire but before any of the planes were hit, their bombs had been released. Then one plane burst into flames and another began to smoke heavily. Two bombs struck LST-167, and a third was a near miss. When the bombs struck, the terrific impact knocked nearly everyone off their feet. One bomb struck the main deck port side, exploded, penetrated the deck and came out through the skin of the ship. The second struck the main deck forward and exploded in the provision room. This started a fire on the tank deck in the gasoline and oil that had not been unloaded. Flames immediately leapt up through the cargo hatch and aft ventilators. The electrical circuits were damaged and power could not be kept on. The dead and wounded littered the main deck.

The order was given to secure all engines and abandon ship. Between 1122 and 1135 all living casualties were removed and given first aid at an emergency casualty station in a building on the beach. In fighting the fire on the LST the CO_2 extinguishers were ineffective due to the draft of air through the tank deck. There was no pressure on the fire main. The 40mm ammunition on the main deck began exploding at about 1140, so firefighting was discontinued and the order given to stay clear of the ship.

At 0900 on the 26th the ship was still burning and exploding too heavily to permit inspection. At 1530 when the fire had subsided, a portable fire pump was rigged and water played on the fire. The total casualties were two officers and five enlisted men killed in action, three enlisted men died of wounds, five enlisted men missing in action and one officer and 19 enlisted men wounded in action. All except the wounded embarked on the LST-472 for Guadalcanal and the LST-167 was unbeached and towed to Rendova.[25]

The surviving Japanese troops began to retreat towards the northwestern corner of the island. They were pursued by soldiers from the 14th New Zealand Brigade Group, 3rd Division, under the command of General H. E. Barrowclough. The New Zealanders had replaced the Americans from September 18, and begun an advance along both coasts of the island.

By October 1, the Japanese were pinned back into the northwestern corner of Vella Lavella. A final attempt was made to evacuate the troops on the night of October 6–7 when nine Japanese destroyers and 12 destroyer transports and smaller craft came down to Vella Lavella to rescue the 600 stranded men there. Three U.S. Navy destroyers, USS *Chevalier* (DD-451), USS *O'Bannon* (DD-450), and USS *Selfridge* (DD-357), engaged the Japanese warships northwest of Vella Lavella.

Contact was made in high seas and driving rain, and lasted less than 12 minutes. After firing half of their torpedoes and scoring several hits with gunfire, the U.S. group continued to steam into the line of fire of Japanese torpedoes in order to keep their own guns bearing. At approximately 2205 *Chevalier* was struck on the port bow by an enemy torpedo, which tore her bow off to the bridge, throwing the ship entirely out of control. *O'Bannon*, which was following *Chevalier*, could not avoid the damaged destroyer and rammed her in the aft engine room, flooding that space and stopping *Chevalier*'s port shaft.

While making preparations to abandon ship, *Chevalier*'s skipper, Lieutenant Commander *George Rees* Wilson, ordered the torpedoes in her tubes to be fired at the Japanese destroyer *HIJMS Yugumo*. A hit was scored and the burning Japanese ship blew up soon after. By 2326 it was apparent that *Chevalier* could not be saved and the order to abandon ship was given. The crew was picked up by *O'Bannon*'s boats. *Chevalier* was sunk the following day by a torpedo from USS *La Vallette* (DD-448). Her severed bow was located about a mile to the west and was sunk with depth charges.

Selfridge and *O'Bannon* were both heavily damaged; *Selfridge* by an enemy torpedo, and *O'Bannon* by enemy action compounded by the collision with *Chevalier* just after the latter had gone dead in the water. *Selfridge*'s losses were 13 killed, as well as 11 wounded, and 36 missing and *Chevalier* lost 54 killed, and suffered 36 wounded.[26]

During the battle the transports managed to evacuate the troops stranded almost within the grasp of New Zealand forces.[27]

At this point the Allies had achieved all of their aims on Vella Lavella. Work on an airfield was well under way by the end of August, and the first aircraft landed on September 24. As expected, the capture of Vella Lavella had forced the Japanese to evacuate Kolombangara. Between September 28 and October 2, approximately 12,000 Japanese were reported evacuated from Kolombangara; 3,000 to Choiseul by barge and the remainder to Rabaul by destroyers.

U.S. forces managed to destroy 60 barges and damaged many more during the evacuation operations. By October 3 the Japanese were gone. U.S. troops landed on Kolombangara without opposition on October 6.[28]

Operation *Toenails* was over. For both the victor and the vanquished the campaign was costly. U.S. Army casualties were 1,098 dead, 3,873 wounded, and 23 missing. The figures do not include casualties resulting from disease, combat fatigue, or war neuroses. For example, the 172d Infantry reported 1,550 men wounded or sick, and the 169th Infantry, up to August 5, suffered 958 non-battle casualties. The 103d Infantry had 364 "shelled-shocked" and 83 non-battle casualties. The Marines suffered 600 dead, wounded, and missing. Naval losses were approximately 281 dead, 50 wounded, and 48 missing.

Postwar estimates placed the number of enemy dead at around 2,733, but this does not account for the many more who died in air attacks or at sea when their barges or ships were sunk.[29]

New Georgia Lessons Learned

Although the capture of Munda was essentially an Army operation and the number of Marines participating was proportionately small, the contributions of the Marine Corps tanks, artillery, and antiaircraft units were essential to the success of the operation. The coordinated use of infantry, artillery, tanks, flamethrowers, and air and naval bombardment were an integral part of the story of the campaign.

On a tactical level the armament and equipment of individual units were found to be basically sound. Critiques of the campaign generated a number of valuable equipment improvements particularly in communications where the biggest problem was the lack of a light and easily transported radio set. From the successful operation of Marine Corps light tanks over jungle terrain came a number of recommendations which improved tactics, communication, and fire coordination of the bigger and more deadly machines, which were included in the task organization for future jungle operations.

The battle against Japanese bunker-type defenses on New Georgia also showed the desirability of tank-mounted flamethrowers. Experimental portable models used in the fight for Munda had proved invaluable in taking enemy pillboxes.

Throughout the entire campaign, the improvement in amphibious landing techniques and practices was rapid and discernible. One contributing factor was the increased availability of the ships needed for such island-to-island operations – LCIs, LSTs, LSDs, and the workhorse LCMs.

The efficiency of these ships and craft was, in part, a reflection on the soundness of Marine Corps amphibious doctrines – vindication for the early and continued insistence by the Marine Corps on their development and improvement.

Air support during the Central Solomons campaign was considered of high quality by all commanders. Aviation historian and veteran Pacific War correspondent Robert Sherrod estimated that of the 358 aircraft the Japanese lost during this campaign, 187 were destroyed by Marine Corps aircraft. More significant were the resultant deaths of highly trained and experienced pilots and crews whom the Japanese could not replace.

Bougainville Operations

Bougainville, the largest island of the Solomon Islands chain, is approximately 125 miles long and has an average width of 30 miles. A League of Nations mandate administered by Australia, Bougainville was captured by Japanese forces in April 1942 during their drive towards New Guinea. By 1943, Bougainville had gained strategic importance as it had adequate facilities for basing fleet units and aircraft. Its capture would contain Japanese forces at Rabaul and help neutralize the major enemy base at Truk.

In September 1943, plans were made to establish a base on Bougainville from which aircraft could strike at Rabaul. The choice of location was narrowed down to the Kieta area on the east coast and the Empress Augusta Bay Area on the west coast. The latter was chosen after reports from reconnaissance patrols that had landed from submarines just off Cape Torokina; near the northern end of Empress August Bay were two small islands, Puruata and Torokina.

On October 1, 1943, Admiral Halsey notified General MacArthur that the beaches on Empress Augusta Bay in the middle of Bougainville's west coast would be the main objective. This location was selected as the point to strike because with the main Japanese forces 25 miles away at the opposite north and south ends of the island, it would be the point of least opposition. In addition, it provided a natural defensive region that would give protection to the Marines once they had landed and their airfields had been gouged out of the swamp and jungle. Finally, the target area would provide a site for a long-range radar installation and an advanced naval base for patrol torpedo (PT) boats.

It promised to be another campaign in a miserable location. There were centipedes three fingers wide, butterflies as big as little birds, thick and nearly impenetrable jungles, bottomless mangrove swamps, crocodile-infested rivers, millions of insects, and heavy daily torrents of rain with enervating humidity.

For this operation, Lieutenant General Alexander A. Vandegrift, Commanding General, I Marine Amphibious Corps (IMAC) had under his command the 3d Marine Division, the 1st Marine Parachute Regiment, the 2d Marine Raider Regiment, and the 37th Infantry Division, USA (in reserve).

The Marine riflemen in these units were given a wide range of support: 155mm artillery; motor transport; amphibian tractors; signal; medical; special weapons; Seabee (naval construction); and tank battalions. The 3d Division had its own engineers and pioneers in the 19th Marines and artillery in the 12th Marines. D-Day was set for November 1, 1943.[30]

Two diversionary operations were incorporated into the final plan. One on the Treasury Islands (Operation *Goodtime*) was assigned to the New Zealand 8th Brigade Group, 3d Division, under Brigadier R. A. Row, with 1,900 Marine support troops, U.S. Navy Seabees, and U.S. radar specialists. They were to land on October 27 and capture or destroy Japanese forces located in the area, establish long-range radars and an advanced naval base so that a staging refuge for landing craft and operating facilities for motor torpedo boats could be put into operation.

The Treasury Islands consist of Mono and Stirling Islands, with the deep, sheltered waters of Blanche Harbor dividing them. Blanche Harbor fulfilled all the requirements for a staging base for naval and barge traffic. A radar station was an imperative accessory to the Bougainville landing to give warning of approaching enemy air and surface craft, and a site for it was tentatively selected on the northern coast of Mono Island, a densely wooded cone seven miles by three, rising to a height of 1,100ft. On flat, irregularly shaped Stirling Island, three and a half miles long by anything from 300 to 1,500 yards wide, a site for an airfield was chosen that would be excellent once its dense covering of forest had been removed.[31]

The second diversion would be an attack on the 80-mile long by 20-mile wide Choiseul Island (Operation *Blissful*), located east of the Treasury Islands and 45 miles from Bougainville. Choiseul is overgrown and choked with rank, impenetrable jungle and rain forest. The mountain ranges in the center of the island extend long spurs and ridges toward the coasts, thus effectively dividing the island into a series of large compartments. Where there are beaches, they vary from wide, sandy areas to narrow, rocky shores with heavy foliage growing almost to the water's edge. Some compartments end in high, broken cliffs, pounded by the sea.

The First Marine Parachute Regiment, Lieutenant Colonel Robert H. Williams commanding, with Lieutenant Colonel Victor H. Krulak commanding its 2d Battalion, were assigned to land at Voza, Choiseul, during the night of October 27, not only to conduct a raid but also to be prepared to establish a permanent base if warranted.

Krulak was to select a site for a PT boat base and withdraw after 12 days if the Navy decided it did not want to establish the base. Lieutenant Junior Grade Richard Keresey, a former PT boat skipper, accompanied the Marines to help locate a suitable PT base in case the Americans took the island.

The landing would be made on unguarded beaches in the vicinity of the abandoned village of Voza, on the northern portion of Choiseul's southwest coast between two relatively light concentrations of Japanese soldiers at Sangigai and Choiseul Bay.

There were also some 3,500 transient enemy troops on Choiseul, who were bivouacked and waiting to be shipped the 45 miles north to Bum on Bougainville, where there was already a major Japanese garrison force. General Vandegrift wanted to be sure that the Japanese were focused on Bum. His orders to the diversionary force were to get ashore and stir up the biggest commotion possible: "Make sure they think the invasion has commenced..."[32]

Operation *Goodtime* – Treasury Islands, October 27

In the gray light of breaking day, and wrapped in a drizzle of warm rain, the convoy lay off the western entrance to Blanche Harbor – eight APDs, eight LCIs, two LSTs, and three LCTs, protected by a screen of six American destroyers. Overhead circled a fighter cover of 32 aircraft, including New Zealanders of Nos 15 and 18 Squadrons, Royal New Zealand Air Force (RNZAF), which patrolled from first light. Rain squalls came down as the assault troops descended the rope ladders into the landing craft, which rose and fell below them on the lazy swell, in readiness for the two-mile dash up the harbor.

By 0600, as the light revealed the scene in detail, the first wave of landing craft was on its way to the beaches in an atmosphere of noise, rain, and excitement. Destroyers were unable to maneuver in the harbor, so newly converted LCI gunboats, recently arrived from Noumea, were used experimentally for the first time. They moved on the left flank of the assaulting waves, pouring streams of tracer-like colored water from a hose into the undergrowth along the shore, knocking out at least one deadly Japanese 40mm twin mount gun and a couple of enemy bunkers.

A simultaneous landing was made on the opposite, north, side of Mono Island, at Soanotalu. The Japanese reacted quickly to the Soanotalu landing and hurled themselves against the perimeter. On one occasion, between 80 and 90 Japanese attacked 50 New Zealanders who waited until they saw "the whites of their eyes" before they opened fire. They killed 40 of the Japanese and dispersed the rest. All enemy resistance in the immediate vicinity of the landing was overcome soon after midday and the invaders dug in along their perimeters from 400 to 600 yards in the jungle, which was much thicker than information had led them to believe.

There was unexpected machine-gun fire on Stirling. One Seabee bulldozer operator attacked the machine gun with his big blade. An Army corporal, a medic, said he couldn't believe it, "The Seabee ran his dozer over and over the machine gun nest until everything was quiet… It all began to stink after a couple of days."

Outmanned, the Japanese drew back to higher ground, were hunted down, and were killed. Japanese dead totaled 205, and the 8th Brigade took only eight prisoners. The operation had secured the seaside flank of Bougainville.

Operation *Blissful*, Choiseul Island, October 28

At 0021 October 28, Lieutenant Colonel Victor H. Krulak's three parachute companies reinforced by a communications platoon, a regimental weapons company with mortars and light machine guns, and a detachment from an experimental rocket platoon (bazookas and rockets), Keresey, a few local guides, and an Australian coast watcher with a road map went ashore from four APDs: *McKean*, *Crosby*, *Kilty*, and *Ward*. The force totaled 30 officers and 626 men. Landing unopposed at Voza, the operation was completed in less than 45 minutes.

They had four LCP(R)s with their crews to facilitate mobility up and down the coast. Once they had landed, they dug in for the night, first camouflaging the boats on the Zinoa Islands, two small coral islands just off the shore. A detachment was left to guard them.

Krulak sent out patrols in both directions to study the approaches to the nearby Japanese positions. He led the group heading southeast to Sagigai himself. During the reconnaissance patrol a group of ten Japanese soldiers unloading a barge were found and attacked, marking the start of the raid's active period.

The next day Krulak launched a larger attack on Sagigai, supported by an air strike. He planned to use two companies to envelop the Japanese position. One company would attack along the beach while the other would circle around inland and attack from the east. As so often happened in the Solomon Islands this plan failed to take into account the difficulties of movement in the jungle. The beach force reached its starting positions on time and launched its attack a few minutes after H-Hour at 1400.

At this point Krulak and the inland company were still some way from their starting point. If the Japanese had stood and fought then Company E, on the beach, might have been in trouble. However, the Japanese abandoned the village and retreated into pre-prepared defensive positions. This move brought the Japanese straight into Krulak and Company F, and an hour-long battle began. The Americans came through the fight better than the Japanese, and when it eventually ended they counted 72 Japanese bodies, having only lost four dead themselves.

During day Krulak sent Company G's Second and Third Platoons of 87 Marines, led by Major Warner T. Bigger, on a mission to the northwest to the mouth of the Warrior River. Unfortunately, they were cut off and needed to be rescued. Krulak sent a request for PT boat assistance. The only boats available were PT-236 commanded by Lieutenant Junior Grade Charles F. Ridgewood, Jr. and Lieutenant Junior Grade John F. Kennedy's PT-59.

The two PT boats reached the Choiseul coast and began looking for a landing craft to help guide them to Bigger's force. At around 1800 Kennedy spotted the boat 300 yards off Voza. On board were Krulak and Keresey, who immediately transferred to PT-59.

Kennedy was surprised to see Keresey, who, as skipper of PT-105, had been on patrol with Kennedy the night that PT-109 had been cut in half by a Japanese destroyer. Kennedy asked him what he was doing on Choiseul. Keresey replied, "Never mind that, we have to haul ass up the coast. There's a bunch of marines trapped!"

At the Warrior River, as the marines were trying to get aboard two LCP(R) landing craft, the Japanese began lobbing mortar rounds at them, and a heavy rain began falling. One landing craft, having taken on more than 30 Marines, reversed its engine and began moving away. As it did, the boat scraped the coral reef, which bent the rudder and made steering difficult. Bigger and some 25 Marines boarded the other craft. As that boat began moving out to sea, it too began scraping along the coral reef and taking on water. Soon the motor was flooded out, and the boat began drifting dangerously close to the shore and Japanese fire. It finally came to rest on the coral, less than 100 yards from the beach.

Only gradually did it dawn on those aboard that their feelings of relief and security were a complete illusion. Under the weight of the load and the hammering of the waves the leaking boat was sinking. Fear gripped the men. In the rising water the engine stalled. The frenzied efforts of the crew could not get even a cough out of it. The other LCP(R) had vanished in the night. The exultation of escape was snuffed out by the terrible realization that the waves were pushing the Marines back to the Japanese waiting on the shore.

Luckily, before that happened they saw PT-59 coming toward them through the waves. They could hear the welcome sound of throbbing engines and splashing exhaust. By now they were so low in the water that the motor torpedo boat loomed unnaturally large and formidable. Her two 40mm guns pointed to the dark sky, and the rows of machine guns along her sides where the torpedo tubes used to be were trained on the shore. Helmeted men scurried about the deck making ready to come alongside the sinking boat.

Idling his engines, Kennedy steered between the foundering landing craft and the shore. The Japanese might concentrate heavy fire on him at any moment. He dared not think what a perfect target PT-59 would be a few hundred yards off shore if but a single flare should burst above them now. When he edged the boat against the landing craft, the PT crew began hauling aboard the soaked Marines.

Some 40 to 50 Marines were spilling over into every foot of space on the boat. The deck swarmed with them. They were perched on the day-room canopy, crowded into the fantail, jammed into the crew's quarters. There was scarcely room for the PT sailors to move about in.

"Any left?" Kennedy called back from the cockpit. In addition to the threat of fire from the shore, he was worried that the Japanese might come out in barges to attack them.

"Major Bigger," a Marine called, "this here officer," pointing to Kennedy, "wants to know if everybody is aboard."

"It's okay to go," Bigger said.

At 0230 on November 3, IMAC sent a message to Krulak indicating that the Japanese were closing in on his position and that he needed to evacuate that day. They would be extracted that evening by landing craft. Five PT boats, including PT-59, would cover the extraction of Krulak's battalion that night. The PT boats, already loaded with fuel and ammunition, would rendezvous with the three craft heading toward Choiseul and escort them to their destination.

Before leaving, they left behind numerous booby traps, including a rocket suspended in a tree. Booby traps and mines were placed at various approaches to Voza. Double-edged razor blades were worked into palm trunks to discourage snipers from clambering up.

While waiting at the beach, the Marines set up a semicircular perimeter and learned that locals working for Seton had come across Lieutenant Samuel Johnston's body, one of two Marines captured during the operation. He had been tied to a tree, carved up with knives while alive, and then executed. The other Marine, Corporal Gallaher, was found a few days earlier stripped naked, tied to a tree, and dead, having been used for bayonet practice by his captors.

As darkness fell at Voza, the craft had not arrived. Native scouts reported that Japanese forces were moving closer and soon were less than a mile away. Shortly thereafter, they reported that Japanese barge traffic was moving in large numbers from Moli Point toward Voza.

At 2230 the Japanese craft were out in the channel somewhere beyond Zinoa. Krulak and Seton immediately boarded a landing craft and went out to find them and guide them to the shore. The PT boats patrolled offshore, screening the seaward approaches. A half hour later, a Japanese patrol several hundred yards from the perimeter set off one of the booby traps. Minutes later another booby trap exploded. To the Marines this meant the Japanese were nearby, and they began to worry about mortar shelling.

Three LCIs appeared offshore at a designated spot north of Voza to embark the withdrawing Marines. Much to the parachutists' amusement, the LCI crews nervously tried to hurry embarkation, expecting enemy fire momentarily. Krulak's battalion, however, loaded all supplies and equipment except rations, which were given to the coast watchers and the natives. Embarkation was completed in less than 15 minutes.

The PT boats escorted the slow-moving landing craft back toward Vella Lavella, and when it was clear they would safely reach their destination, the PTs left the flotilla and returned to their base at Lambu Lambu on Valla Lavella. When the craft arrived at Vella Lavella, they were met by the regimental commander, selected members of the IMAC staff, and a section of the Amphibious Corps band. That morning, coast watchers reported the Japanese had occupied the former Marine base.

A single scout was left behind and later taken off by a PBY Catalina flying boat. He gave this terse summary of the Japanese advance:

"The enemy attacked at dawn of November 4th. The morning, thereafter, was replete with cries of disappointment and explosions of mines and booby traps. As they penetrated our positions, they found nothing but empty ration cans."

The mission had accomplished its primary goals. The Japanese sent reinforcements to Choiseul, delaying reaction to the Bougainville landing. The Choiseul operation also killed at least 143 Japanese, destroyed several hundred tons of enemy fuel and supplies, sank two barges, and destroyed the barge station at Sangigai, disrupting Japanese barge traffic along the coast of Choiseul.

In addition, captured documents allowed the Navy not only to navigate the waters around Bougainville more safely but also to mine areas that the Japanese believed were clear, which resulted in the sinking of two Japanese warships.

The Marines lost nine men killed, 15 wounded, and two missing. They left behind 143 Japanese dead on Choiseul.[33]

Operations *Dipper, Cherryblossom*, and *Hairbrush* – November 1, 1943

After a period of training at Efate and Guadalcanal the first echelon of *Cherry Blossom* troops and craft, consisting of eight attack transports, four attack cargo ships, seven destroyers, four destroyer minesweepers, and two fleet tugs, assembled south of Guadalcanal on October 31. Keeping well out to sea on the southwest side of the Solomon Islands, the first echelon, led by the Coast Guard-manned attack transport *Hunter Liggett,* approached Cape Torokina early on the morning of November 1.

The troops were to land on 12 color-coded beaches, running from north to south down the cape. The six beaches to the south (Yellow 2, Blue 3, Blue 2, Green 2, Yellow 1, and Blue 1) were assigned to McHenry's 3d Marines and

Lieutenant Colonel Alan Shapley's 2d Raider Regiment (less one battalion). The five to the north (Red 3, Red 2, Yellow 4, Red 1, and Yellow 3) and Puruata Island (Green 1, opposite Green 2) were the objectives of Colonel Edward A. Craig's 9th Marines and Lieutenant Colonel Fred D. Bean's 3d Raider Battalion. The Koromokina River divided the north and south beaches.

The morning was one to be remembered by those who survived, with torpedo bombers roaring overhead, gray destroyers firing at the beaches, the two lines of transports and cargo ships swinging on their anchors, and the landing craft full of Marines churning toward the enemy. This scene was laid against a natural backdrop of awesome beauty. The early morning tropical sun shone in a bright blue sky. The sea was moderately heavy, and at the shore a white line showed where the surf pounded on the black and gray beaches, which were fringed for most of their length by the forbidding green of the jungle. Behind were the rugged hills, and Mount Bagana, towering skyward, emitting perpetual clouds of smoke and steam.

By 0645, when all transports were anchored in line in the transport area, about 3,000 yards from the shoreline, with the AKs (attack transport cargo ships) in a parallel line some 500 yards to seaward, the traditional signal "Land the landing force" was executed. Marines clambered over the sides to take their places in the LCVPs and LCMs. For many this was their first assault. They were just boys, aged around 19 and 20, who had left pleasant homes back in the eastern part of the United States to train for a year in the jungle for this moment and they weren't going to show what they were feeling inside. When the order "Over the side," came they threw a leg over the rail and silently clambered down the cargo nets into the waiting landing boats, which were pitching in the swell beside the transports.

On the way to shore no one spoke, except for the officers: "Stay down," "Run for cover," "Stay together," "Remember what I told you."

The schedule of the 3d Marines provided for simultaneous landing by four landing teams on beaches from Cape Torokina to the Koromokina River, the 1st Battalion landing on Cape Torokina (Beach Blue 1), the 2d Raider Regiment (less the 3d Battalion) landing west of the 1st Battalion (Beach Green 2), the 2d Battalion to the west of the Raiders (Beach Blue 2), and the 3d Battalion between the Koromokina and the 2d Battalion (Beach Blue 3). The 9th Marines scheduled landings of its 1st, 2d, and 3d Battalions from left to right in that order on beaches Red 3, Red 2, and Red 1, and provided for simultaneous landing of the 3d Raider Battalion (less Company L, which landed on Beach Green 2) on Beach Green 1, Puruata Island, in order to destroy all anti-boat defenses which might be emplaced there.[34]

The signal to start the first assault wave for boats of *President Adams* (APA-19) carrying elements of the 1st Battalion, 3d Marines (reinforced), which had a 5,000-yard run to the most southerly target beach (Blue 1), was executed at 0710. Simultaneously, the fire-support destroyers *Anthony* (DD-515), *Wadsworth* (DD-516), *Terry* (DD-513), and *Sigourney* (DD-643), which had been firing intermittently since about 0547, commenced their prearranged attack.

This attack lifted at 0721, and immediately thereafter 31 Marine SBD Dauntless dive-bombers from VMSB-144 flying from Munda bombed and strafed the beaches for about five minutes. The first boats to hit the beach were those of *President Jackson* (APA-18), carrying elements of the 2d Battalion, 3d Marines (reinforced), which grounded at 0726 on Blue Beach 2, four minutes before H-Hour.

Surf conditions were worse than had been previously observed and some 91 LCVPs and LCMs broached and were abandoned. Of the 12 beaches, the three northernmost were unusable. This necessitated doubling up on the three closest beaches. The beaches were narrow and steep which made unloading cargo a difficult and arduous task. Although the conditions were hazardous, the landings on the northern beaches were almost unopposed.

However, the landings on the six southern beaches and the single beach on Puruata Island were in stark contrast to the northern zone. The Japanese defenders of Cape Torokina on November 1 consisted of the 2d Company, 1st Battalion, 23d Infantry plus 30 men from the Regimental Gun Company. In addition to their usual weapons, this force was equipped with one 75mm gun. Total strength numbered approximately 270 officers and men under the command of Captain Ichikawa. The entire headland was ringed with 15 bunkers, nine of them facing to the southwest and six of them overlooking the beaches on the southeast side of the cape. Behind this protective line and farther inland was another defensive line of eight bunkers that covered the first line of fortifications. Two other bunkers, about 750 yards inland, provided additional cover for the first two lines.

Constructed of ironwood and coconut logs that were 2ft thick, the bunkers were bulwarked by sandbags and set low into the ground. Camouflaged by sand and tangled underbrush, they were hard to detect and difficult to knock out without flamethrowers or demolitions. The Japanese also had a 75mm field gun sited on the beaches.

As the boats came into range, this gun began to fire at them, and succeeded in destroying about four and damaging ten others with 50 high-explosive shells. One boat to come under fire was No. 21, from *President Adams*. Embarked were Lieutenants Byron A. Kirk and Harris W. Shelton, with two squads of Kirk's 2d Platoon, Company C, a detachment of 1st Battalion Headquarters Company, and a demolition squad, Company C, 19th Marines. Less than 20 seconds before this boat was to reach the beach, three shells from the Japanese 75mm gun hit the boat in rapid succession. The first shell killed the coxswain and put the boat out of control, and the second and third shells killed both lieutenants and 12 enlisted men, while wounding 14 others. Some survivors, under Sergeant Dick K. McAllister, went over the side, and by aiding one another were able to get to the beach, where they immediately engaged the Japanese defenders with rifles and hand grenades. Since the only way to get aid for the wounded was to get them back to the ship, Corporal John McNamara decided to attempt to get the boat underway. By this time the boat had drifted up on the beach, so McNamara and a seaman climbed aboard and backed it into the sea. Having been damaged, however, the craft was not seaworthy, and sank. Only four or five of the wounded survived. The fate of boat No. 21 and her occupants was typical of that of other boats hit.

In the meantime, the Boat Group commander's boat had been shot to pieces by the 75mm gun, and the boat waves were completely disorganized. As a result, assault companies of the 1st Battalion, 3d Marines, landed in an order practically the reverse of that planned. To make matters worse, the Japanese opened up with their beach defense machine guns, and those Marines who were able to get ashore unscathed had to cross the beach through a hail of fire.

As the second and third waves approached the shore – all within a matter of seven minutes – the 75mm got the range and scored direct hits on three boats. Only six men got out of one boat, and then without weapons. However, before the landing became a complete disaster, the 75mm was silenced. In an act of true bravery, Sergeant Robert Owens took four men to cover him and he charged the gun emplacement. Although he was killed instantly by a grenade, he first managed to drive the Japanese gun crew out of a rear door where they were shot down. A shell that might have meant death for a boatload of Marines was in the barrel. He was awarded the Medal of Honor for his bravery and sacrifice.

There was confusion on Blue Beach 1 at first. The landing boat coxswains had put one company ashore 150 yards from the designated spot. The men were crouching in the tall underbrush just off the beach, disorganized and leaderless, when Major Leonard Mason, the commander of the 1st Battalion, 3d Marines, came ashore. Noticing a serious gap in the Marine line and a group of men crouched in the bushes apparently unwilling to move, he raged up and down behind them until he had convinced them that the firing directly ahead was their own. Major Mason's gallantry cost him dear. The Japanese in the pillboxes, hearing above the din the sound of his voice giving orders, turned a machine gun on him. He was badly wounded in both legs. Then, while he lay helpless, grenade fragments struck him in the chest. His wife's picture kept a piece of shrapnel from his heart.

Medical corpsmen who reached him wanted to evacuate him to a transport immediately. However, he refused. Afterward he said it was because he thought the landing was in danger of becoming a disaster and he didn't want to be the only one to get away.

By 0800 Marines were scattered throughout the cape in the high grass around the pillboxes, pinned down by Japanese machine-gun fire and the bullets of snipers in the coconut trees overhead. Three-man fire teams were working to destroy the pillboxes. They consisted of one BAR man and two riflemen with M1s, all three using grenades whenever possible.[35]

The battle can well be told in the story of one company, under the command of Captain Clifford Quilici, a soft-spoken young man. This company didn't do all the work, but it did its share under adverse conditions and if it hadn't been there the cape would not have been taken.

The company landed in the wrong place and the ramp of one landing boat stuck and had to be battered down with rifle butts under a hail of Japanese machine-gun fire. However, all 160 men got ashore unharmed and flopped in the bush at the base of the cape, close to the Japanese 75mm gun. It was from there that Sergeant Owens saw the devastation the shells were causing and made the decision that cost him his life, but saved so many others.

First Lieutenant Lavon Crain, commander of the first platoon, got his men together and started up the cape, the men half crawling, half walking. They came up against three pillboxes and had to stop. First Lieutenant Young Broussard brought his second platoon up alongside Crain's. However, they too were stopped by the pillboxes. The third platoon, under First Lieutenant Jules Rouse from Los Angeles, swung farther inland and up. It was stopped by a concentration of ten pillboxes.

For the next two hours a bitter battle was fought under the sizzling equatorial sun. It was a battle of small actions, undertaken by individuals or little groups of soldiers. Deafened by the din of guns and grenades, a Marine would crawl through the grass and hurl a grenade into a pillbox. Maybe he'd crawl back safely or maybe a Japanese grenade would get him and he'd lie out there dying, sometimes being shot again and again. Sometimes a Marine with an automatic rifle would creep behind a coconut tree and let rip against the riflemen in the pillbox trench. Maybe he'd get back. Maybe a sniper would see him and he wouldn't.

Thus, slowly and painfully, the three pillboxes were taken. It was a war of the little man. In the hell of fire each private made his own decisions. He was his own general and he lived or died because of the decisions he made.

Rouse's men in the third platoon had a somewhat better start to the campaign, particularly Platoon Sergeant William Wilson, a bull-necked boy from Drew, Mississippi. Wilson and a private surprised 15 Japanese soldiers scampering from a trench to the safety of a pillbox. They killed every one.

A few minutes later Wilson trapped an enemy soldier outside a pillbox and fired, but his rifle jammed. Ever versatile, he threw it away and leaped on the back of the then fleeing man, slashing at his throat with a knife. The Japanese soldier fell dead after 15ft. Shot through the chest a little later, Wilson killed a sniper on his way back for first aid, had his wound bandaged, and returned to action.

However, when they came upon the ten pillboxes, Rouse's men had more than they could handle, and were just about holding their own, when Captain Frank Vogel's company arrived on the scene. Vogel and his men had driven all the way across the cape, knocking off pillboxes as they went.

Vogel, known to all ranks as "Shorty," sent his men in behind the pillboxes that were pinning down Rouse's platoon. The rear was the blind side for the Japanese. They had hewn firing slits in the front and both sides of the bunkers but neglected the rear. Marines in some cases were able to crawl up the sides of the pillboxes, poke a hole in the sand roof and drop grenades through.

Vogel's appearance seemed to turn the tide. Officers and privates said the same thing. "Shorty saved us." And this was despite the fact that his company that had been hardest hit by the 75mm. All three of the boats that were hit were full of his men.

After 1030 there wasn't much action on the cape itself. Most of the enemy were dead or dying. Six pillboxes still held out in the jungle at the lower end of the cape and it took all afternoon and large quantities of TNT and 75mm shells to blast them to pieces. However, by 1100 Cape Torokina was cleared. Most of its defenders were dead, and those who survived had retreated inland.

The cape was a scene of death and desolation. All around were scarred trees, battered pillboxes, Japanese equipment strewn everywhere, and the bodies of the dead Japanese soldiers, with their neat wrap-around leggings. Of the 270 Japanese who manned the pillboxes, some 50 machine guns and the 75mm beach gun, 202 were killed on the cape. The other 68, including the captain in command, either escaped into the jungle or dragged themselves away to die in solitude.

The Marine C-Company landed with 160 men and ended the day with 126; seven were killed and 27 wounded. One of the dead Marines was Private First Class C. J. Price, a 19-year-old from Munhall, Pennsylvania. Lying horribly wounded and left for dead, he somehow managed to gather enough strength to throw a hand grenade and kill two more Japanese before succumbing to his wounds.[36]

Taking Puruata Island wasn't much easier for Lieutenant Colonel Fred D. Beans' 3d Marine Raider Battalion's I and K Companies. Landing with one reinforced company in the assault and the remainder of the battalion as reserve and shore party, only sporadic fire hit the boats as they neared the island. However, once landed, the Raiders met stiff opposition in the form of Japanese riflemen and machine gunners in well-concealed pillboxes, covered by riflemen in rifle pits and trees. The terrain was overgrown by heavy brush and afforded poor visibility.

Private First Class "Dutch" Doornbos, a rugged BAR man, was in the raider assault force and recalled the death of Marine Gunnery Sergeant Leyden in the early stages of the assault:

Our company came in on the first wave against opposition light by Tarawa standards. However, there were casualties from rifle and mortar fire in almost every Higgins boat before we hit the beach. "K" company came in right after ours.

It took us only a few minutes to get organized and the two companies pushed inland, spread out thin so as to beat out the whole island. We advanced 200 yards against light opposition until "K" company, on the right flank, ran into heavy machine guns and several light Nambus.

While they were cleaning out this machine gun nest, some of us advanced across the native village compound. The Japs laid down a heavy knee mortar barrage into the village. They had the range down pat. We had a lot of casualties.

Our platoon leader responded to that barrage by ordering us to charge right through to the beach and kill every Nipper that got in the way. The mortars stopped firing as we charged and we killed a lot of Japs on our way to the beach. But when we got there, no Nippers were in sight. Apparently, they'd picked up their knee mortars and dived into the dense brush and just let us charge past them.

It wasn't until we'd moved back to the village and dug in that we learned about Leyden. He had been wounded by rifle and mortar fire and was lying out in the brush somewhere.

A corpsman from "K" company went out and found him. While he was dressing the gunny's wounds, a sniper shot the corpsman in the leg. PFC Red Howard and the battalion's chaplain, Father Robert J. Cronin, then moved out into the brush to get the wounded men.

Leyden was dying. But until a few minutes before he died, he kept training his field glasses around in the brush trying to pick up the sniper who'd wounded the corpsman. Leyden did have the satisfaction of seeing Red kill the sniper.

A couple of minutes later, Father Cronin, Red Howard and the corpsman had to hit the deck and lie flat in the brush. Dozens of Japs were passing by them. As soon as the Japs got up ahead a little, though, Howard heaved every grenade he had at them and shot several with his M-1.

We didn't have time to wonder about the chaplain, though, because just about then the Nippers made a banzai charge on our positions in the village. They threw everything they had at us except the kitchen sink. But the two companies in the village just mowed down the charging Nips. After that charge the Japs were finished on Puruata except for a few snipers and the like.

In all this confusion, Father Cronin and Red Howard, dragging the wounded corpsman, got back to our lines, though they had to go under pretty heavy sniper fire. Red was wounded in the hand.

That was about all that happened to us on Puruata – but none of us will ever forget that Gunny Leyden.[37]

Puruata was not declared secured until mid-afternoon of the following day. A two-pronged attack, launched by the Raiders early on the morning of

November 2, swept over the island against only sporadic rifle fire, and by 1530 all Japanese resistance on the island had been erased.

Only 29 Japanese dead were found, although at least 70 were estimated to have been on the island. The remainder had apparently escaped to the mainland. The Raiders lost five men killed and 32 wounded in the attack.

One unique unit made its first combat assault on Bougainville. That was the First Marine Dog Platoon, consisting of 48 enlisted men working in pairs with 21 Doberman Pinschers and German Shepherds as part of Colonel Shapley's 2d Raider Regiment. They came in under fire on November 1 and, still under fire, were dispatched to various companies on Bougainville according to a prearranged plan. The unit immediately proved its worth when a vicious crossfire pinned down the Raiders. The lieutenant signaled to Private First Class Rufus G. Mayo to send his dog Caesar back for reinforcements. Mayo scribbled the message, tucked it into a battered first aid packet attached to the collar around the neck of the big German Shepherd at his side. Then Mayo snapped loose the dog's leash.

"Report!"

The word was spoken gently into Caesar's ear and Mayo gave the dog a last pat. Caesar started for the beach at a steady lope and was swallowed up by the jungle. When Caesar arrived at the battalion command post a few minutes later, the first message ever carried by a Marine war dog in combat was delivered. Throughout the day, Caesar repeated the operation, making his way back and forth through the jungle carrying messages, maps and papers through enemy fire, running the only communications lifeline that existed between the Marine Raider company and its command post.

That same day, Andy, a Doberman Pinscher scout dog, led another company of Marine Raiders safely through the Japanese-infested jungle to a trail-block position 300 yards in from the beach. Twice along the way, Andy stopped short and looked from right to left to "alert" the Raiders to the presence of Jap snipers. That night, the dogs were the night security for both the regimental and the 2d Battalion command posts.

During a later patrol, a dog named Rollo, in the vanguard of the patrol, suddenly alerted. The men hit the deck. Nothing happened so Rollo and his handler, Private First Class Russel T. Frederick, moved ahead to investigate. Enemy fire roared and Private First Class Frederick went down. He had stumbled in front of the muzzles of a Japanese pillbox. Some of the men saw that the dog had not been hurt and tried to call him to safety. However, the dog wouldn't come. He lay down by Frederick. The Japanese guns continued to blaze away and dog and man died together.[38]

By the end of November 1, 14,321 Marines and most of the supplies had been landed, at a cost of 70 killed or missing and 124 wounded. Half the enemy force was killed and the remainder fled inland. Allied fighter cover of 34 planes from New Georgia airfields drove off most of the enemy planes, which made two attacks during the day. Japanese bombs dropped in the transport area missed the transports, which got under way and maneuvered during both attacks, shooting down four planes.

During November eight more transport echelons were sent to Cape Torokina, three of them consisting of attack transports and cargo ships, and five of high-speed transports, LSTs and LCTs. The unloading of the LSTs took longer than expected due to inadequate personnel and bad organization on the beaches. By the end of November, 44,430 officers and 40,338 tons of supplies and equipment had been landed. During this time, air harassment was constant and several U.S. craft were hit, including LCI-70, PT-167, and the transports *Fuller* and *President Jackson*.

The venerable USS *McKean* (ADP-5) with 185 Marines on board was sunk by a "Betty" torpedo plane on November 17. At 0350 the torpedo struck the starboard side, exploding the aft magazine and depth charge spaces and rupturing fuel oil tanks. Flaming oil engulfed *McKean* aft of the No. 1 stack, and she lost all power and communications. Burning oil on the water killed men who were blown or jumped overboard. Her skipper, Lieutenant Commander Ralph L. Ramey, ordered her abandoned at 0355, and at 0400 she began to sink by the stern. Lieutenant Commander Ramey went over the side 12 minutes later. Her forward magazine and oil tank exploded at 0415, and her stacks disappeared at 0418. Sixty-four of her complement and 52 of her embarked troops died from the explosions or flames. The survivors were picked up by rescuing destroyers.

There was no thought of carrying out a large-scale campaign for the conquest of Bougainville. The objective was to establish a firm foothold over an area sufficient for use as an airstrip. By the end of November a beachhead 9,000 yards wide and 7,000 to 8,000 yards deep had been carved out. Work on the airstrip began on December 9 and it was used for an emergency landing on the 24th. It was located near Piva, two and a half miles north of Cape Torokina.

The Green Islands was the last of Admiral Halsey's Operation *Cartwheel* objectives.

Operation *Squarepeg* Green Islands

Nissan, the largest of the Green Islands, was not only close enough to Torokina for Aircraft, Solomons (AirSols) fighter support, but it was also weakly defended. Located 37 miles northwest of Buka and 55 miles east of New Ireland, Nissan had room on its narrow, flat main island for a couple of airstrips. However, with Rabaul only 115 miles away and Kavieng about 100 miles farther off, it would be vulnerable to enemy counterattack once it was taken.

As a preliminary to the attack, 300 officers and men of the New Zealand 30th Battalion, commanded by Lieutenant Colonel F. C. Cornwall, landed on Nissan at midnight on January 30–31, 1944, to carry out reconnaissance. This action was prompted by the need of accurate information concerning enemy strength, the suitability of landing beaches, areas for the construction of airfields, and a site for a motor torpedo boat base. Air photographs disclosed that the only beaches suitable for a landing were inside the lagoon, the entrances to which were too shallow to allow anything but small landing craft. The outer coast of the island consisted for the most part of low cliffs pitted with caves and was in many places protected by an outer reef, which made landing there impossible. Little was known of the Japanese garrison.

Twenty-five specialists from Admiral Wilkinson's headquarters, as well as ten officers from the New Zealand artillery, engineers, and Army Service Corps units, accompanied the raiders. Captain H. M. Denton, from the division staff, and Lieutenant F. P. Archer, a plantation owner then attached to the British Solomon Islands Administration, were also attached. Lieutenant Archer's task was the interrogation of local inhabitants as he was an expert in pidgin English.

The raiders landed without opposition on the beach at Pokonian Plantation, a few hundred yards inside the entrance to the lagoon, and formed a perimeter where Lieutenant Colonel Cornwall established his headquarters for operations. Captain F. R. M. Watson commanded the party at Pokonian, and Major A. B. Bullen commanded the party that crossed the lagoon at first light the following morning to investigate the Tangalan Plantation area where the airfields were to be sited. Working quickly the specialists made their investigations and landing craft chugged around the lagoon from beach to beach, examining those best suited for a landing and consolidation. Everything was going according to plan.

Some erratic enemy sniping from the jungle broke the silence but did not injure anyone. While returning from a reconnaissance of a deserted mission station on the morning of January 31, a barge party led by Lieutenant P. O'Dowd noticed some enemy craft hidden under trees overhanging the water of a small bay and moved in cautiously to investigate. Suddenly, the concealed Japanese opened fire, killing the American coxswain and gunner and another gunner who tried to take his companion's place. Lieutenant O'Dowd was wounded and died later.

A sharp exchange followed and the enemy was silenced, mainly by Private J. W. Jefferis with his Bren gun, and the barge was able to withdraw. Later the Japanese craft were put out of action by mortar fire and 17 of their crew were killed. During this action six enemy dive-bombers attacked the New Zealand landing craft and once they were seen off by machine guns, fearing that other aircraft might return to the attack, all reconnaissance parties were recalled to the perimeter at dusk and the raiders embarked on their landing craft, moving out into the lagoon to wait there until they could board the APDs at midnight.

Getting the raiding force back on board was a difficult operation in the darkness, as a strong wind had risen and outside the lagoon a ten-foot swell tossed the little craft against the sides of the old destroyers. It took hours to get the men aboard. During the raid Brigadier Potter awaited the result from USS *Fullam* (DD-474), which stood off Empress Augusta Bay. [39]

Morning in the tropics was invariably a spectacle and February 15 was no exception. Piles of rose-tinted clouds towered against a pale jade sky, which deepened to blue as the light strengthened. Nissan lay like a dark smudge on an oily sea over which, for miles, landing craft moved slowly awaiting their turn to enter the lagoon. Captive balloons, trailed by the LSTs as protection against dive-bombers, rose in the air. Overhead a screen of aircraft circled at great speed anticipating the enemy, a few of which broke through and dropped their bombs, badly shaking one LST. Six Japanese planes took a final plunge into the ocean as Allied fighters swept them from the skies, where bursts from antiaircraft shells hung for a moment like dusky mushrooms and then dissolved. Far out on the horizon was the cordon of destroyers.

Because of the character of the lagoon entrances, the attack forces included no capital ships. It consisted of eight APDs, 12 LCIs, 7 LSTs, and 6 LCTs, screened by 17 destroyers accompanied by numerous smaller craft. Task Force 39, consisting of three light cruisers and five destroyers, covered the operation to the east and north. Task Force 38, composed of two light cruisers and five destroyers, operated in the area between the Green Islands and St. George's Channel. The attack and garrison forces were units of the 3rd New Zealand Division. The attack group left the northern coast of Bougainville during the night of February 14–15. Task Force 38 was attacked at dusk by six "Val" dive-bombers, one of which made a hit on USS *St. Louis* (CL-49) killing 23 men and wounding 30.

The high-speed transports arrived at their assigned area off the lagoon entrance at 0620 on the 15th. Their landing craft put troops ashore on Nissan Island at 0655. There were no mines or obstructions and no opposition on the beach. At 0645, 15 "Vals" attacked, concentrating on the LCI and LST groups off the entrance channel. Task Force 33 fighter planes and vigorous antiaircraft fire from landing craft and destroyers eliminated six "Vals," and although there was a near miss on LST-486, there was no damage done. The barrage balloons flown by the LSTs may have prevented a more successful attack.

In the opalescent light of early dawn the assault troops entered the lagoon, landing craft moving in single file. There was no opposition. Patrols declared their areas clear and established their defense lines from coast to coast. It was all rather like a perfect battle practice. The Japanese garrison had gone to ground.

The troops landed at Pokonian Plantation just south of the southern entrance channel and at Tangalan Plantation on the eastern side of the lagoon. LCIs followed the waves of assault boats from the high-speed transports and the LSTs arrived and beached at 0835. The LCT group arrived at 1335. There was no opposition from the small Japanese garrison of about 500 on the island or from enemy planes. The last of the LCIs and LSTs retired at 1730 after landing 5,806 men with 4,344 tons of supplies and equipment.

Intelligence reports revealed that an unknown number of Japanese had taken refuge on Sirot, one of the islands at the entrance to the lagoon. The task of clearing them was allotted to B Company, 30th Battalion, and attached troops from the 14th Brigade Defense Platoon. The task of clearing Sirot developed into a sharp and bitter action that lasted for some hours. It was fought out in intensely thick jungle where the Japanese, armed with machine guns and grenades, were well sited and so hidden that for a time it was impossible for the New Zealanders to pinpoint them. However, the New Zealanders eventually triumphed and when the island of Sirot was cleared 20

Japanese had been accounted for. The New Zealanders lost five men killed while several were injured.

Between February 15 and 20, New Zealand infantrymen hunted down and killed the Japanese garrison on Nissan. Ten New Zealanders and three Americans were killed; 21 New Zealanders and three Americans were wounded.

By March 17, 16,448 men and 43,088 tons of supplies had been sent to the Green Islands. The 22d Naval Construction Regiment had begun work as soon as they landed and within two days of the landings a PT boat base opened. This extended the range of the torpedo boat patrols to New Ireland and along the entire northeast coast of Bougainville. By March 4, a 5,000ft fighter field was ready, and in late March a 6,000ft bomber field was opened.

Allied occupation of these low and thickly wooded islands effectively blocked the barge supply route from Rabaul and Kavieng to the beleaguered Japanese garrisons in the northern Solomons, which were estimated to number about 20,000 men. This left the enemy on Choiseul, Bougainville, and Buka Islands virtually isolated from the principal Japanese bases to the north.

For all strategic military purposes this completed the campaign for the Solomon Islands, which had begun at Guadalcanal on August 7, 1942, and continued throughout 1943 with the conquest of the New Georgia group and the establishment of the beachhead on Empress Augusta Bay, Bougainville Island.

Admiral W. F. Halsey, when detached as Commander South Pacific Force and Area, summed up the Bougainville operation as follows:

> The Bougainville campaign was intended to accomplish the destruction of enemy air strength in the Bismarcks; not only was this accomplished, but the by-products of the campaign were so extensive that the subsequent operations at Green Island and Emirau were accomplished virtually without enemy opposition, and the entire enemy offensive potential in the Bismarcks area was destroyed. In the matter of ultimate achievement and importance in the Pacific war, the Bougainville operation was successful beyond our greatest hopes.[40]

CHAPTER 5

ISOLATING RABAUL

SOUTHWEST PACIFIC, JUNE 1943–FEBRUARY 1944

As mentioned in the previous chapter *Cartwheel* was a two-pronged operation aimed at isolating the large Japanese base at Rabaul. While Admiral Chester Nimitz's forces moved up one prong along the Solomon Islands to Bougainville and the Green Islands, General Douglas MacArthur's *Alamo* force in the Southwest Pacific simultaneously tackled the second prong in the following assaults:

6. Operation *Chronicle* – June 30, 1943
    c. Woodlark Island (112th Cavalry Regiment)
    d. Kiriwina, Trobriand Islands (158th Regimental Combat Team)
7. Operation *Postern* – September 4–22, 1943
    a. Lae-Finschhafen-Madang, Huon Peninsula, New Guinea (Australian 3d, 5th, 6th, 7th, 9th, and 11th Divisions, U.S. 162d Regimental Combat Team, 32d Infantry Division,
8. Operation *Alamo* – September 5, 1943
    Nadzab, New Guinea (503d Parachute Infantry Regiment and Australian 2/4th Field Regiment)
9. Operation *Dexterity*
    a. Operation *Director*, Arawe, New Britain – December 15, 1943, (112th Cavalry)
    b. Operation *Backhander*, Cape Gloucester, New Britain – December 26, 1943 (1st Marine Division)

   c. Operation *Michaelmas*, Saidor – January 2, 1944 (32d Infantry
      Division)
10. Operation *Brewer*
    Admiralty Islands – February 29, 1944 (1st Cavalry Division)
    a. Los Negros
    b. Manus
       i. Hauwei
       ii. Lorengau
       iii. Pityilu
       iv. Ndrilo and Koruniat
11. Emirau Island, Bismarck Archipelago, New Guinea
    March 29, 1944 (4th Marine Regiment)

Although the Japanese had been pushed back from Port Moresby and over the
Owen Stanley Range in 1942, they still occupied several key areas along the
eastern New Guinea coast. Over a year later the Australians and American
forces were still locked in a series of battles to drive them out. The strategy
essentially involved first securing places where airfields could be built and
forward operating bases as well as supply bases established. The second part
was the use of these bases to launch operations designed to strike not at the
main concentrations of Japanese forces but rather in areas where they hadn't
established defensive positions. Then, as the final phase, the Allied would
surround and eliminate the Japanese area by area in coordinated pincer
movements.

   As the initial phase of the offensive, the Allies planned to make simultaneous
landings on Woodlark Island, Kiriwina Bay, and Nassau Bay on the morning
of June 30, 1943. In its final form the plan called for the Sixth Army to be
transported by the Seventh Amphibious Force. Air cover was to be supplied
by Fifth Air Force fighters based on Goodenough Island and Dobradura.

   Landings on Woodlark and Kiriwina and the subsequent construction of
airdromes at these locations would bring Rabaul and the northern Solomons
within range of U.S. fighters and medium bombers. Roughly 200 miles off
the eastern tip of New Guinea, these small islands would also serve as way
stations for planes as they shifted from one area to another, flying missions in
support of either MacArthur or Admiral William F. Halsey, Jr., Commander
South Pacific.

Operation *Chronicle*

The *Chronicle* forces assembled, Woodlark's garrison (codenamed *Leatherback*) at Townsville, Australia and Kiriwina's garrison (codenamed *Byproduct*) at Milne Bay on New Guinea.

Woodlark Island

For the 112th Cavalry troopers landing on Woodlark Island this meant giving up their horses. The 112th was originally part of the Texas National Guard before being mobilized for active duty on November 18, 1940. The regiment disembarked at Noumea, New Caledonia, on August 11, 1942, where it was attached to the Americal Division and began acquiring horses to continue its role as mounted cavalry.[1]

A garrison unit on an island with a major headquarters, the 112th was often called on for ceremonial duties and guard details, but it hadn't had any training in assault landings or jungle warfare, nor in field maneuvers or weapons firing, all of which would have better prepared the unit for combat. With the exception of a few defense exercises, combined arms training with armor and field artillery units and practice in the use of air support were simply non-existent. Contact with amphibious craft only came if these special boats were in the bay while the troopers were unloading ships for the Navy.

This all changed abruptly in April 1943 when Halsey transferred the 112th Cavalry out of South Pacific Area (SOPAC) and into Southwest Pacific Area (SWPA), where it fell under the control of Lieutenant General Walter Krueger's Sixth Army and drew the *Woodlark* mission. The 112th turned over its horses to First Island Command and left New Caledonia in May 1943. These developments came as a shock to the troopers, many of whom believed they would never fight the Japanese. They expected the unit to remain mounted and, as such, unsuited for jungle warfare. Lieutenant Colonel Clyde Grant, in charge of 2d Squadron, recalled, "We couldn't see sitting there all during the war with this regiment of horses parading for dignitaries."

Now dismounted, the unit faced the challenge of determining how to carry the mortars, machine guns, and radios that had long ridden on the backs of its horses.

Admiral Daniel E. Barbey, commander of the Seventh Amphibious Force Operations under MacArthur, described *Chronicle* as "a tryout of the organization and of the capabilities of beaching ships and crews under unusually difficult navigational conditions. If no enemy was encountered, it would in effect be an advanced training exercise, and we hoped it would turn out that way."[2]

Reaching the waters off New Guinea's Guasopa Peninsula just after midnight on June 23, 260 men under the 112th's Major D. M. McMains plowed through high-speed winds and choppy waves toward the beach.

To test the Sixth Army's amphibious assault techniques under realistic conditions and to guard against complacency, General Krueger allowed his forces to think that they might come across enemy soldiers on Woodlark – despite intelligence suggesting otherwise. In this regard, the general's plan almost backfired.

Scrambling out of the surf at 0400 and ready for a possible clash with the Japanese, the advanced party just barely avoided a disastrous encounter in the predawn light with an unsuspecting coast watcher and a group of armed locals as the Australian coast watcher had not been informed before the landing.

When told that troops were coming ashore he formed his local guerrillas in skirmish line and got ready to fight. Fortunately, before anything tragic happened, he heard American voices and joined the "invading force." After linking up with this officer from the Royal Australian Navy, McMains and his men prepared landing sites for the main body. A week later, the first echelon of the Woodlark task force arrived and began unloading on the night of June 30. Unloading of the LSTs at their beaching points was rapid. Emptied of their loads, the slow-moving LSTs cleared Woodlark before daylight.[3] The first phase was complete.

Kiriwina, Trobriand Islands

The Kiriwina Task Force, under Colonel J. Prugh Herndon's command, consisted of the 158th Infantry (less the 2d Battalion) Regimental Combat Team, the 148th Field Artillery Battalion (105mm howitzers), plus additional 155mm gun units, the 46th Engineer Combat Company, medical, antiaircraft, and quartermaster troops. The Task Force was to capture and hold Kiriwina and construct an airdrome.

As the 112th were landing without problems, Herndon's landings were not going as smoothly. Twelve Landing Craft Infantry (LCI) and six escorting destroyers had sailed from Milne Bay the previous noon, and began landing their 2,250 troops. Trouble accompanied the landing from the start. The LCIs had great difficulty getting through the narrow, reef-filled channel to Red

Beach, the designated landing point near Losuia. And the water shoaled near shore so much that they grounded 200–300 yards from the shoreline. The landing progressed slowly.

At sunset on June 30, 12 LCTs and seven LCMs arrived. Again there were problems. Heavy rains were falling. The tide was out. Only one LCT was able to cross a sandbar which blocked the approach to the jetty at Losuia. Other LCTs got hung up on the bar and were forced to wait for the tide to float them off. The remainder made for Red Beach but grounded offshore with the result that much of the gear on board had to be carried ashore by hand. Some of the vehicles were driven ashore, but several drowned out in the salt water. LCTs in subsequent echelons avoided some of the difficulties by landing on the north shore of Kiriwina where the coral causeway had been built. But the heavy rains continued and added to the engineers' troubles in building and maintaining roads as well as constructing the airfield.[4]

Regardless of these handicaps, Seventh Amphibious Force carried 12,100 troops to Woodlark and 4,700 to Kiriwina without a casualty, while a total of 42,900 tons of supplies and equipment were unloaded without loss of ship or landing boat.[5]

The Woodlark–Kiriwina operations gave much needed experience to the new Seventh Amphibious Force and provided a protective buffer to the New Georgia operation which was underway at the same time.

Nassau Bay

Although not a part of Operation *Chronicle*, Allied troops also landed at Nassau Bay, New Guinea on the night of June 29–30.

Consisting of the combined elements of Colonel Archibald R. MacKechnie's American 162d Regiment as well as Australian units, MacKechnie's Force embarked from Mort Bay at dusk on 29 June 1943. PT boats PT-142, PT-143, and PT-120 of the Seventh Fleet took aboard 210 men of the 1st Battalion, 162d Infantry Regiment, with PT-68 providing escort. Twenty-nine LCVPs (Landing Craft Vehicle and Personnel), two requisitioned Japanese barges of the 2d Engineer Special Brigade, and one Landing Craft Mechanized (LCM) of the 532d Engineer Boat and Shore Regiment took the other 770 men of the 1st Battalion, 162d Infantry Regiment on board at Mageri Point. The landing force was organized into three waves.

It turned into a hell of a night. A strong head wind whipped up waves and heavy surf, drenching the men, making many of them seasick. Each coxswain strained his eyes for a fleeting glimpse of the white wake of the boat ahead. Some, unable to see, or with motor trouble, unsurprisingly fell out of the column and lost their way.

Colonel MacKechnie wrote about the landing:

> Near the beach the white surf could be seen ahead. What would we find in another minute or two? Were the Japs ready and waiting to pour deadly rifle and machine gun fire into our helpless men? No, there was a signal light on the beach. The Australian patrol which was to work its way through the swamps to meet us was there and had two guide lights up.[6]

At Nassau Bay, a platoon of D Company, 2/6th Australian Infantry Battalion of the 17th Brigade, from Mubo set landing markers to guide the landing craft into the beachhead. As the first wave with PT-142 arrived at Nassau Bay, PT-143 arrived with the second wave landing craft. The landing began, in rainy darkness, shortly after midnight. The Australian platoon on shore had lost its way and arrived at Nassau Bay in time to install only two instead of the planned three lights.

MacKechnie continued:

> Into the surf went our boat. Standing up forward near the ramp I could see boats ahead on the beach, broached, foundered, and wrecked by the heavy seas. A wave half-filled our boat as we hit the open ramp of a boat on the beach. Everyone was knocked flat. My helmet flew off but I still held my Tommy gun, and as the ramp went down, we jumped off into two feet of surging water and struggled up to the beach.

The first two waves of landing craft intermingled and landed together on the same stretch of beach. The landing craft were pushed far up on the beach, with 17 unable to get off the beach which became breached and filled with water.

The LCM, after unloading a bulldozer, was able to proceed back out to sea and retrieved the troops off PT-142 and then returned to the beach, where it became swamped. The landing had been unopposed with 770 men beached at Nassau Bay. The breached landing craft were wrecked and most of the radios were damaged by salt water. PT-143 returned to the advanced PT Base at Morobe, while PT-142 and PT-68 provided seaward protection.

Of the 32 boats which started, only 22 reached the beach that night. The others, lost in the darkness, took refuge on nearby islands and beaches, and came in two or three days later. Of the 22 which landed, 18 breached immediately and filled with water, including the one LCM carrying two Jeep-mounted radios.

The third wave of landing craft with PT-120 arrived hours after the first two waves and decided not to land until the surf had abated. They took shelter in a cove down the coast, until the storm had subsided and then returned to Nassau Bay but failed to find the beachhead. The wave returned to Mageri Point.

At dawn on June 30, the beach was cleared of all ammunition, equipment, and supplies. Machine guns salvaged from the wrecked landing craft were set up in the beach defenses. There was neither enemy opposition nor any casualties. The Japanese in an outpost at the beach had fled into the jungle, believing, prisoners reported later, that the bulldozer was a tank.

MacKechnie said of the landing:

> At that we were lucky. Not a man was lost at sea or in the landing. Not a shot was fired. Although we landed on a strange beach at night during a storm, the second wave before the first, the beach strewn with wrecked boats, life jackets and supplies, there was little or no confusion.

Small bands of enemy soldiers appeared the following day, but after confused nighttime skirmishes in a tropical downpour the outnumbered Japanese fled into the concealment of the thick jungle.

The next morning Company C, under Captain Del Newman, moved out to the south, sweeping the jungle from the beach to the swamps without encountering any Japanese. The Company C platoon on the south, led by Lieutenant Bob Brown, was ordered back to the beachhead at dusk. When it started back it found a force of Japanese had infiltrated across the Tabali River and through the swamps to a position between it and the beachhead. Lieutenant Brown was killed while covering the withdrawal of his platoon, most of which reached the beachhead perimeter just before dark.

On the night of June 30–July 1 the Japanese attacked, calling out in English such things as "Company A fall back" and "Company B come out and unload these boats" in an attempt to create disorder and confusion. All night the yelling and shooting continued. At dawn a few snipers were killed in trees

172

inside the perimeter but the remainder pulled back into the swamps at daylight.[7]

By this point the Americans had lost four officers and 17 men killed and 27 others wounded. The enemy left behind 50 dead.

MacKechnie summarized the 162d's achievements:

> By the night of 1 July we held two and a half miles of beach from the mouth of the Tabali to the mouth of the Bitoi. Our troops, who had never before been under fire had met the wily Jap in his own back yard and had given him a taste of what he was to continue to get until the end of the war.[8]

Seizure of the bay provided a means by which the Australians, who were getting ready to attack Salamaua, could be supplied by water to supplement the air drops, and would also provide a staging point for the shore-to-shore movement of an entire Australian division to a point east of Lae.[9]

Operation *Postern*

Plans for Operation *Postern* involved a landing 15 miles east of Lae on the Huon Peninsula from which drives in two directions, one toward Lae and one toward Finschhafen, were to be initiated. Meanwhile Nadzab, an unused field 15 miles west of Lae, was to be seized by joint use of paratroop and glider units.

The Australian 7th Division and U.S. troops in the vicinity of Salamaua were to complete the destruction of Japanese forces in that area. In addition to transporting the troops to landing points, the Seventh Fleet was assigned the task of blockading any of the Japanese seaborne reinforcements and providing antisubmarine patrols. The Allied Air Force was to support the operation by: 1) intensive aerial bombardment prior to and during the amphibious movement; 2) antisubmarine escort; 3) air blockade of the Lae–Salamaua area; and 4) close support of ground troops.[10]

Lae – September 4

The plan was to by-pass Salamaua, to seize Lae by a shore-to-shore amphibious movement, and to join this maneuver with an airborne landing for the capture of Nadzab, some 15 to 20 miles inland on the Markham River. The assault troops would land on the beaches at Bulu Plantation and at the mouth of the Busu River, less than 20 miles from Lae.

The landings were undertaken by the Australian 20th Brigade, 9th Infantry Division, along with the U.S. Army 2d Engineer Special Brigade and artillerymen. Transportation was provided by the Seventh Amphibious Force.

The 2/13th Battalion would land at and capture "Yellow Beach" on the right flank; the 2/15th Battalion would capture the right-hand half of the main landing beach designated "Red Beach;" the 2/17th Battalion would capture the left-hand half; and the 2/23d Battalion would land on Red Beach immediately after the other two and lead the advance to the west. Soon after landing, the 2/13th and 2/15th would send patrols to link up between Red and Yellow beaches, while the 20th Brigade would proceed to capture their first, second, and third objectives, known as "Bardia," "Tobruk," and "Benghazi."

Lauded as The Rats of Tobruk for the division's exploits there in 1941, the 9th Division had stayed in the Middle East when other troops returned to Australia in 1942, and had fought in the First and Second Battles of El Alamein between June and November 1942. This was to be the 9th Division's first full campaign in New Guinea.[11]

A newspaper correspondent, describing the embarkation, wrote:

> Roads and tracks were swarming with green shirts. They resembled nothing so much as the long lines of chlorophyll-coloured ants that march up and around the trees of the rain-forests of New Guinea and North Australia. Packs that bristled with jungle knives, axes, and spades; MT [motor transport] bashing the mud under loads of ammo and HE [high explosive], guns and gear, everything from a bullet to a bulldozer, it was all there, a perfect picture of the battle eve.[12]

Reveille on September 4 was at 0430, when the assault troops were given hot tea or coffee, and a meal.

At 0618, 18 minutes after the sun rose, five destroyers fired a ten-minute bombardment on the beaches. Then 16 landing craft from the APDs* started for the beaches carrying the assault waves. At 0631 the 20th Australian

---

*   APDs (Auxiliary Personnel Destroyers) were high speed destroyers and destroyer escorts converted to carry up to 200 troops, UDT, Army Rangers or Marine Raiders and, when necessary, provide gunfire support to these units.

Infantry Brigade began going ashore at Red Beach, near Bulu Plantation and some eighteen miles east of Lae. This landing was unopposed. Two minutes later troops of the 26th Australian Infantry Brigade landed at Yellow Beach, 18 miles east of Lae, east of the Bulu River. A small group of Japanese on Yellow Beach ran away at the approach of the Australians. Scouts of the 2d Engineer Special Brigade landed with the Australian infantry.[13]

As the fifth wave, comprising 7 LCIs, approached Red Beach six Japanese fighters followed by three bombers, flying at 1,500ft, strafed and bombed the LCIs which had dropped their stern anchors. The bombers dropped 12 bombs, one of which exploded on the deck of LCI-339 just forward of the bridge, killing the commander of the 2/23rd Battalion, Lieutenant Colonel Wall, a company commander, Captain Reid and five men, and wounding 28 including six officers. LCI-341 received a near miss which blew a large hole in the ship's side and flooded two compartments. The LCIs were so crowded that men were unable to obey their first impulse and throw themselves flat, but could only crouch and hope for the best.

The captain of LCI-341, finding his ship listing to port because of the gaping hole through which the water was pouring, shouted "Every man to starboard." Under their weight the ship gradually righted itself and beached without further trouble. By the skillful handling and determination of Ensign James M. Tidball, LCI-339 landed on time and disembarked the troops. Tidball radioed the flotilla commander, who ordered him to abandon ship. The crippled LCI remained on the beach for a week, a target for Japanese airmen, before it was towed clear, and then it drifted on to a reef.[14]

After the attack the 2d Engineering Special Battalion, about 1,060 men, and its equipment were landed on Red Beach from LCVs, LCMs, and LCTs. From the first of the landing craft, tractors, road graders, wire mesh to make passable roads over sand and swamp, and power-driven saws to fell palm trees for corduroying roads, were unloaded. The unloading parties cleared stores from Red Beach and established dumps inland, while Australian and American engineers pushed the roads ahead. At 0814 the six LSTs began to unload. Describing the scene, the historian of the Second Engineering Special Battalion wrote:

As these ponderous hulks drove to the beach even the longshoremen working frantically in their unloading of the smaller craft stopped to view these monsters as they magically opened their bows and dropped immense ramps slowly to the edge of the surf... Ton after ton of equipment was unloaded and, interspersed with the vehicles and materiel, companies of infantry filed out while artillerymen rode guns drawn by tractors.[15]

Although the air force provided an air umbrella over the convoys going to and coming from Red Beach, it could not prevent all enemy aircraft from breaking through toward Morobe. Four dive-bombers attacked the destroyers guarding the retiring convoy, scoring near misses on two, including the USS *Conyngham* (DD-372). At 1400, when the six LSTs of the second landing group were 25 miles off Cape Ward Hunt, Japanese torpedo and dive-bombers attacked. Six dive-bombers attacked LST-473 and scored two hits and two near misses. Eight Americans were killed and 11 Americans and 26 Australians wounded. LST-471 was attacked by two torpedo bombers. One torpedo hit the port side, wrecking the ship's stern, killing 43 troops and sailors, and wounding 30. Among the casualties were 34 killed or missing and seven wounded from the 2/4th Independent Company.

The four remaining LSTs continued to Red Beach where they arrived at 2300. The commanders of the two crippled LSTs, Lieutenants Rowland W. Dillard (LST-473*)* and George L. Cory (LST-471), were able to keep their craft afloat until LSTs 452 and 458, returning from Red Beach, were diverted to their assistance and took them in tow.[16]

The Japanese did not attack the jammed landing beaches at this time, but returned in the evening to blow up an ammunition dump, damage two beached LCIs, and kill two men.

As the troops moved from the beachhead they faced formidable natural barriers in the form of rivers swollen by recent rain. They came to a halt at the Busu River, which could not be bridged for two reasons: the Australians lacked heavy equipment, and the far bank was occupied by Japanese soldiers.

Patrols attempted to force a crossing on the morning of September 9, but the combination of Japanese bullets and the swift current forced them back. In the late afternoon elements of four rifle companies got across in rubber boats and by wading and swimming. Several men were drowned and many weapons lost in this act of gallantry, but the four companies seized a bridgehead on the west bank and held it against enemy counterattacks.

Meanwhile the troops on the east bank loaded men, weapons, and ammunition onto the 2d Engineer Special Brigade's landing craft and sent them to the west bank. For the next 60 hours, the landing craft plied back and forth until the entire 24th Brigade had been transferred to the west bank. Rain, mist, and darkness helped hide the boats from the Japanese, who nevertheless tried to hit them with artillery, machine-gun, and rifle fire.

Once clear of the river, the troops were ready to resume the advance and effect a junction with the troops of the 7th Australian Division that were advancing east out of Nadzab.[17] The Allied pincer slowly closed around the Japanese.

While the Americans pushed along the coast from Nassau Bay, Australian troops advanced on a western axis from Wau through the Markham Valley and pushed out of the landing zones at Lae. The mainstay of the Japanese defense was a lone infantry regiment. In such rugged jungle terrain, however, a few determined men could slow down a division successfully. Numerous streams cut the coastline into a swampy, muddy bog that impeded the American push. The few jungle trails capable of bearing basic logistic support made the direction of the Australian overland thrust predictable.

Japanese infantrymen dug in along key terrain dominating the obvious approaches. A grueling ordeal followed in the jungle wilds under appalling conditions. Patrol-size probes lurching through overgrown and tangled vegetation became the principal maneuver elements. Ambush and sudden death awaited the careless or unlucky because it was often impossible to see more than a few feet into the undergrowth.[18]

To help close the gap and provided better logistical support, an air assault was planned to take control of the abandoned Japanese airdrome at Nadzab.

Operation *Alamo* – September 5

The occupation of Nadzab, which lies northwest of Lae, would cut off the Japanese in the Lae–Salamaua area from their natural route of escape and give the Allies control of the Markham River valley.

This mission was assigned to Colonel Kenneth H. Kinsler's 503d Parachute Infantry Regiment[19] and elements of the Australian Army's 2/4th Field [Artillery] Regiment with its 25-pounder guns. The 54th Troop Carrier Wing (commanded by Colonel Paul H. Prentiss) C-47s would transport the paratroopers. This was the first combat parachute operation in the Pacific.

Early in the morning of September 5 the C-47s warmed their engines and loaded the U.S. 503d and Australian units for a drop onto the kunai-grass plains of Nadzab. At 0825, the first C-47 rolled down the runway. Within 15 minutes three flights, totaling 79 planes, were airborne.

Over Thirty-Mile Airdrome (located near Rorona [Rarona], roughly 30 miles northwest of Port Moresby), the unarmed transports met the first part of a fighter escort comprised of 48 P-38 Lightning fighters from the 35th and 475th Fighter Groups, 12 P-39 Air Cobras from the 36th Fighter Squadron, 8th Fighter Group and 48 P-47 Thunderbolts from the 348th Fighter Group.

The C-47s crossed the Owen Stanleys at 9,000ft. Above Marilinan, they maneuvered into 6-plane elements in step-up right echelon, all three flights abreast, and dropped from 3,500ft to between 400 and 500ft. At 0948 the paratroopers were alerted and 21 minutes later were given the red light.

At 1022 the first paratrooper made his jump. Eighty-one C-47s carrying the 503d were emptied in four and a half minutes. All men of the 503d but one, who fainted while getting ready, left the planes. Two men were killed instantly when their chutes failed to open, and a third landed in a tall tree, fell 60ft to the ground, and died. Thirty-three men were injured. The Australian artillerymen and their guns parachuted down in the afternoon.

There was no opposition from the enemy, either on the ground or in the air. Once they reached the ground, the 503d battalions laboriously moved through high kunai grass from landing grounds to assembly areas.

The operation was witnessed by Generals MacArthur and Lieutenant General George C. Kenney* from a flight of three B-17s high above. MacArthur was in one, Kenney in another, and the third B-17 was there to provide added fire power in case the Japanese turned up.

By 1204 all transports had returned safely to Port Moresby. The paratroopers met with no resistance, and in late afternoon made contact with the Australians who had reached the area by crossing the Markham River in rubber boats and on a folding boat bridge as soon as the paratroop drop began. At the same time, a Papuan infantry company, which had also come overland, swung westward to cover approaches to Nadzab from that direction. Within 24 hours the area was secured.[20]

The Allied circle around the enemy at Lae began to tighten rapidly. Advance troops of the Australian 7th Division joined the paratroopers and drove along the Markham Road to approach Lae from the west. The 9th Division closed in from the coast while the Allies increased the pressure from the air and on the Salamaua front to the south.

---

* Kenney commanded the Allied Air Forces consisting of the U.S. Fifth Air Force and the Royal Australian Air Force Command.

The Japanese were surrounded except for one narrow route of escape northward through the dense jungles and almost impassable mountain trails of the Huon Peninsula. As the Allied gradually closed them off from all hope of aid, the Japanese yielded their positions and, discarding almost all equipment, began a precipitous flight through jungle and mountains toward Kiari in a desperate effort to escape complete annihilation.[21]

Finschhafen

Finschhafen was the final part of Operation *Postern*. Finschhafen was the strongpoint that guarded the western side of the 60-mile-wide straits separating New Guinea and New Britain. The Japanese regarded Finschhafen as the key defensive position. Possessed of two good harbors – Finschhafen itself and Langemak Bay – and a small airfield, it had long been used as a barge staging point. About 3,000 Japanese construction and engineer troops defended from fortified Satelberg Ridge. This high ground overlooked the entire coastline about Finschhafen and blocked any further ground push northward toward Sio. The Japanese perched on the jungle-covered ridgeline waiting for the inevitable Allied landing.

The beach selected for the landing, designated "Scarlet," lay six miles north of Finschhafen at the mouth of the Song River and 90 miles from Lae. The beach was 900 yards long (north to south), 30ft wide, and was marked by coral headlands to the north and south. Behind the shore a coral track led directly south to Finschhafen, a little more than six miles away, commencing near Heldsbach and passing through Salankaua coconut plantation. South of the plantation the Kakakog area, a narrow spur between the coast and the steep foothills, was thought to be occupied by the enemy in some strength.

Troops of Australian 9th Division's 20th Brigade, half the shore battalion of the 532d Engineer Boat and Shore Regiment (EBSR) with its medical and signal troops, and Papuan Infantry Battalion made up the assault force. Ten LCMs, 15 LCVPs, eight LSTs, 16 LCIs, ten destroyers and four APDs from the Seventh Amphibious Fleet would once again provide the transportation and fire support.

Wednesday, September 22, was another misty dawn. Crouched in their small, square-nosed landing craft, men of the 20th Brigade sped toward Scarlet Beach, still not yet visible in the murky blackness. These men, who had made the assault on Red Beach less than three weeks before, had met no opposition there. Here, they did not know what lay in front of them.

Destroyers bombarded Scarlet Beach, and during darkness, at 0445, the first Australian assault wave touched down. But, this time something out of the ordinary in New Guinea, that land of dank dampness and persistent rains, delayed the landing for a full eight minutes – clouds of dust, kicked up by the exploding shells on the beach, combined with smoke haze from the same shells, so obscured the beach that the commander of the first wave held his boats offshore until the haze cleared. Then he sent the boats ashore, their weapons fire striking the beach and the edge of the jungle 30 to 40ft beyond the shore line with marked effect upon enemy defenders. The first boats grounded on the beach at 0453.[22]

First ashore were the amphibian engineer scouts, followed by four companies and supporting elements of the 20th Brigade. There was little opposition initially from the Japanese. The darkness and lingering dust clouds caused part of the first wave to land along the southern portion of the beach near the mouth of a small waterway known as Siki Creek. The engineer scouts who landed from these craft quickly became aware they were too far south and that offshore boats would cause the larger landing craft in succeeding waves to ground before reaching shore. The scouts accordingly started making their way as speedily as possible to the proper positions at the north end of the beach, in order to erect range lights and beach markers to guide in the later waves.

However, by that time the second wave, made up of eight LCIs, was coming in. As yet the beach lights were not in position. Most of the LCIs, accordingly, had the same difficulty in locating the proper section of the beach as had been encountered by the first wave. As the LCIs approached the shore, the pre-dawn twilight was blasted by streams of tracer bullets searing across the beach front. Red, blue, orange, they chased one another, some spurted out toward the oncoming craft. It was a kaleidoscope of death. And ever surely – too fast it seemed to those watching from the larger craft standing off shore – the small, frail assault craft rode the swell toward that danger line.

Now came the answering fire from the sea. Over the heads of the crouching troops, continuous fire was brought to bear on to a ridge approximately 30ft above sea level and some 40 yards inland.

The LCIs gave that beach everything they had with their 20mm guns. It did not seem possible that anything could remain alive under such a torrent of fire. But there was no slackening of that colored dance from the shore. It seemed, when the boats got closer, that it reached crescendo.

The third wave in seven LCIs, consisting of reserve rifle companies, battalion headquarters, and supporting arms, including the Papuan Infantry Battalion section, and 20th Brigade Headquarters, became the actual assaulting troops on Scarlet Beach. Japanese mortar, machine-gun, and rifle fire from the jungle's edge grew heavy as the troops landed, the gunners on the landing craft replying with all weapons. They had landed, in the main, on Siki Cove, beyond the southern point of Scarlet Beach, and on Arndt Point headland, some 1,000 yards south from Scarlet Beach.

Wave three attacked strongly until the arrival on Scarlet Beach of the assault troops from Siki Cove. Then, together, they routed the enemy. It was bayonet-point fighting in many instances, courage, and grim determination to make that beach no matter what the cost the order of the day.[23]

At least three of the LCIs, being well to the south of the beach area assigned as their landing place, grounded on a sand bar offshore and came under heavy fire. For the troops it was a matter of get to the shore as best they could. An Australian observer reported that the third wave of LCIs dropped their ramps too soon, well before the craft were on the beach, with the result that men were drowned, equipment was lost, and ramps were damaged. The charge of early dropping of ramps at Finschhafen is substantiated by the award of the George Medal to Sergeant Iaking Iwagu, Royal Papuan Constabulary for rescuing his company commander from drowning after the ramp of their assault boat in the third wave had been lowered in 12ft of water. The officer jumped into the water to swim ashore, but was wounded by a Japanese bullet. Iwagu, seeing him sink, went to his aid and, although under heavy fire, succeeded in bringing the wounded officer ashore and stayed with him on the beach until the arrival of stretcher-bearers. Unfortunately, the officer died the same day.[24]

In spite of casualties among the Australians and boat crews, the Japanese were quickly routed from the beach by troops of the third wave aided by Allied forces already ashore from the first and second waves, who hurried to the combat area as soon as they were able to determine, in the darkness, where the fighting was in progress. The troops found that the Japanese had been protected within well-concealed beach defenses, including ten log pillboxes 50 yards apart with shallow connecting trenches.

The Japanese survivors retired to rising ground about a half mile inland and some sharp fighting ensued with hand grenades and bayonets. While the battle was in progress the engineer amphibian scouts, having finally reached Scarlet

Beach proper against increasing resistance, proceeded to set up range lights and flank markers, made a swift survey of the beach, and radioed the results of their reconnaissance to ships offshore. The scouts also searched the beach for Japanese mines and attempted to determine if coral reefs existed in the offshore waters.

Road construction proceeded so rapidly that at one time work was keeping abreast of the moving combat front, where Australian troops were pushing through the jungle driving the Japanese before them. The amphibian engineer medical detachment swiftly set up aid stations and a clearing station, and soon afterward a portable surgical hospital and a collecting station.

The beachhead was firmly established by 1630 and all scattered pockets of enemy resistance had finally been mopped up.

But, the Japanese were not prepared to lose Finschhafen. On October 15, Major General George Wootten, General Officer Commanding, 9th Australian Infantry Division, received a decoded Japanese order which warned him to expect a two-regiment attack from Satelberg, coupled with a seaborne assault. The Australians made ready.

At 0300, October 17, Japanese planes bombed the Allies. Following the bombing, 155 men of the Japanese 10th Company, 79th Infantry, equipped with rifles, machine guns, flame-throwers, and demolition sets, barged silently down the coast under the cliffs north of the Song River to land during a heavy rainstorm in the beating surf on the southern side of the river mouth. Visibility was almost zero. The Japanese let their ramps almost down when 600 yards offshore, cut their motors and quietly paddled their boats in for the landing.

Sergeant John Fuina, in charge of the beach detachment, had remained on the alert to rouse the others if anything happened. Another member of the crew, Technician Fifth Grade Raymond J. Koch, was restless, and, unable to sleep, got up to take a stretch and smoke a cigarette. Gazing out into the sea the two men noticed four smudges on the skyline. Holding their breath, and clutching each other's arms, they waited. The smudges gradually took more distinct shapes as they moved toward the shore. They had the decidedly peaked prows of Japanese landing barges – and they were only 400 yards away. It hardly seemed possible, but there was no mistake.

Fuina yelled an alarm and ran toward his 37mm antitank gun to fire an alert. One shell ripped through the ramp of the leading Japanese craft, smashed its engine, and then penetrated a second craft. But the two boats came on, one broaching in the surf as they beached.

Private Van Noy, awakened by Sergeant Fuina's first yell, was already in his gun position. His loader, Corporal Stephen Popa, was right after him. Their gun was only 15 yards from the water's edge and, when some of the larger guns to their rear opened up, firing blindly, Van Noy held his fire.

Then the Japanese started to hurl grenades by the handful, and one burst in Van Noy's gun emplacement. It was just a lucky toss for the Japanese still couldn't see the gun position and Van Noy had held his fire for that one reason. The shrapnel shattered one of Van Noy's legs and wounded Popa. It looked as if they had waited too long and lost the gamble. A sergeant to the rear of Van Noy, seeing that they couldn't hope to hold out, shouted to them to get back from the beach. Australian Bren gunners, between bursts, yelled, "Come out of there, you bloody fools." But the two gunners refused.

The first to fall to their fire were two Japanese officers trying to scorch the gunners out of their position with flame throwers. Behind them other Japanese flopped on the sand, firing and throwing grenades. Van Noy was seen to install a second belt of ammunition on his gun and reopen fire with enemy soldiers only a dozen feet away. His gun traced patterns among their forms as they tried to crawl forward. One after another was hurled into eternity as his gun flashed. But in the darkness he couldn't hope to see all the Japanese edging toward him. His gun finally went silent, but only a handful of Japanese had escaped his withering fire. Because of their positioning, none of the other guns on the beach could fire on the particular spot where the Japanese landed.

A third barge, under continuous fire from shore, was struck twice by shells and failed to make a landing; it was seen to head north up the coast, and observers on shore reported hearing the sound of wailing aboard the craft, indicating some personnel had been wounded.

Of some 75 Japanese who landed, 39 were killed on the beach by Van Noy, the other amphibian engineers, and the Australians. Thirty-six more Japanese sought shelter behind a sand shelf cut into the beach at the water's edge by wave action and succeeded in making their way northward and across the mouth of the Song River. There, when day dawned, the Australians hunted them out and killed them all.

After it was all over they found Van Noy dead, his finger still on the trigger, the last round fired from his gun. Popa, alive but unconscious, lay with a dead Japanese soldier sprawled across his body. Badly wounded, he had managed to grab a rifle and fire a bullet into the head of the Japanese coming at him with a bayonet. For their actions that night, Popa was awarded the Silver Star, and

Private Van Noy was awarded, posthumously, the Medal of Honor – the first engineer soldier in World War II to win this highest possible award.[25]

The Japanese counterattack on Finschhafen did not slow down the Australian and U.S. troops' relentless advances in eastern New Guinea. As the men advanced slowly but steadily against the retreating enemy, supported all the while by the 2d Engineer Special Brigade craft, they found many sick, wounded, and dead Japanese who had fallen by the wayside as the weakened Japanese 20th Division retreated.

A look at the casualties just from June to mid-September gives some idea of how brutal the campaign was for both the Allies and Japanese. American losses were 81 killed and 396 wounded while the Australian 15th Brigade alone suffered 112 killed, 346 wounded, and 12 missing. Japanese losses surpassed 1,000 men; just one man in five was able to bear arms after the retreat across New Guinea's Huon Peninsula.

The battle casualties tell only part of the struggle, as another deadly battle was waged against nature in the jungle wilds. Men on both sides collapsed, exhausted from the debilitating tropical heat and humidity; soldiers shook violently from malarial chills or from a drenching in tropical downpours. Others simply went mad. The neuropsychiatric rate for American soldiers was the highest in the Southwest Pacific Theater (43.94 per 1,000 men). The same monotonous field ration – bully beef and biscuits for the Australians, C-rations for the Americans – left soldiers undernourished and susceptible to the uncountable tropical diseases that flourished in the warm, moist jungle.[26]

On January 15, 1944 the Australian 9th Division entered Sio, on the north coast of the Huon Peninsula. Fighting on the peninsula was not yet over, but the main strategic objectives – the airfield sites and the coast of Vitiaz Strait – were now in Allied hands. When the Lae-Nadzab road and the airfields were completed, the Allies could control the air over the straits and bring in more bombers and fighters to attack Japanese bases to the north and the west.[27]

New Britain

New Britain forms the southern boundary of the Bismarck Sea and bridged the gap between two Allied drives in the fall of 1943. On the east, South Pacific forces were advancing through the Solomons toward Rabaul. On the west, Southwest Pacific forces were moving along the east coast of New

Guinea. Japanese strength in New Britain was concentrated on the Gazelle Peninsula and at Cape Gloucester.

From Rabaul on the Gazelle Peninsula, the Japanese exercised partial control over straits connecting the Bismarck and Solomon seas. The conquest of western New Britain, the neutralization of Rabaul, and the capture of the Admiralty Islands assured Allied domination of the Bismarck Archipelago.

A crescent-shaped group of islands, lying between northeastern New Guinea and the northern limit of the Solomon Islands, comprises the Bismarck Archipelago. New Britain and New Ireland, the largest islands in the archipelago, form the main part of the crescent. New Hanover, separated from New Ireland by an island-studded channel, and Manus in the Admiralties are the other principal land areas.

New Britain, narrow and mountainous, is strategically the most important as well as the largest island in the archipelago. It is separated from New Guinea by straits 55 to 65 miles wide, in which lies Umboi, a volcanic island suitable for air warning installations and light defenses. Dampier Strait, between Umboi and New Britain, was a Japanese supply route to the eastern coast of Papua New Guinea and islands of the Solomon Sea.

New Britain has a coast line of about 1,000 miles with numerous anchorages for small vessels as well as several harbors. Simpson Harbor in Blanche Bay, at the northeastern end of the island, is unexcelled in the New Guinea–Bismarcks–Solomons area as a base for military operations. Rabaul lies on the north shore of Blanche Bay, in the shadow of volcanic cones which may erupt at any time.

New Ireland, lying like a huge barrier reef northeast of New Britain, possesses an excellent harbor at Kavieng which was an important staging point on the Japanese supply routes to Rabaul and beyond.

The climate, always warm or hot, is extremely humid. In November the northwest monsoon strides the northern islands then spreads over the entire archipelago by December. Heavy rains are common until March when more moderate conditions prevail. Even in the summer months clouds cover from one-third to four-fifths of the sky the majority of the time. These climatic conditions, in addition to being hazards to air operations, were the cause of many incomplete vessel interdiction missions and unsatisfactory bomb runs, especially since the period of most intensive air operations coincided with the monsoon.[28]

General MacArthur decided formally to open the campaign, Operation *Dexterity*, with December assaults on the western tip of New Britain.

Possession of this area would provide the Allies with Cape Gloucester and the small harbor of Arawe, facilitating control of the Vitiaz and Dampier Straits. Local beaches were suitable for amphibious landings, and Japanese defenses were expected to be light.

Operation *Dexterity*

The operation was subdivided into three parts: Operation *Director* to take Arawe; Operation *Backhander* was the assault on Cape Gloucester; and Operation *Michaelmas* aimed at securing Saidor on Papua, New Guinea. General Krueger's Sixth Army was responsible for all operations.

SWPA and Sixth Army originally planned to supplement the primary landing at Cape Gloucester with an attack on Gasmata. Destroying the enemy at this advanced base on New Britain's southern coast offered key advantages to the Allies, but the choice of this location drew criticism from Barbey and Kenney because its proximity to Rabaul would subject the landing force to bomber strikes that Fifth Air Force would be hard-pressed to parry. In addition, it appeared that the enemy was reinforcing the area.

MacArthur and his subordinates met to discuss the issue on November 21 and, the next day, substituted the assault on Gasmata with one 80 miles to the west at Arawe. Because Japanese strength there was presumed to be substantially lower than at Gasmata, Krueger shelved his original plan, which had earmarked a regimental combat team from the 32d Infantry Division, and called upon the smaller 112th Cavalry plus artillery, engineers, and other supporting forces. The 112th would land on December 15.

The north shore of Cape Gloucester was the designated landing area for the 1st Marine Division under the command of General William H. Rupertus. This would be the first action in which the division would participate since Guadalcanal. A two-pronged attack on Borgen Bay at Silimati Point and Tauali was set for December 26. Final plans called for one regimental combat team to land on two beaches on the north coast of New Britain between Silimati Point in Borgen Bay and the airfield at Cape Gloucester, while a second (less a battalion landing team) landed immediately behind, passed through the first, and attacked toward Cape Gloucester to the airfields.

One battalion landing team was to land near Tauali on the west coast of New Britain to block the coastal trail and prevent reinforcement of the airdrome area from the south or retreat of the airdrome garrison to the south.

The Japanese defenders consisted of 9,500 men of the 65th Brigade under the command of Major General Iwao Matsuda, the commander of the forces that had fought at Guadalcanal. A large number of Matsuda's men were already on half-rations and suffering from malaria, dysentery, and numerous fungal infections. Monsoon rains had destroyed their primitive shelters and their health. Matsuda's troops, as physically depleted as they were, would put up a desperate fight to the death to keep the U.S. from taking another Japanese-held island. The main defense on Aogiri Ridge was laced with 37 bunkers that were mutually supported with interconnecting tunnels.

Operation *Director*

The Arawe landing was a feint to deceive the Japanese as to the later more important landing to be made on Cape Gloucester on the northern coast. Indeed, the Arawe force was to be the bait to attract the Japanese while the larger force moved around to Cape Gloucester.[29]

For the Arawe operation MacArthur formed the Director Task Force under Brigadier General Julian W. Cunningham, who as a colonel had led the invasion of Woodlark. Its assault units included Colonel Alexander M. Miller's two-squadron 112th Cavalry; the 148th Field Artillery Battalion; the 59th Engineer Company; Headquarters and Headquarters Battery, 236th Antiaircraft Artillery (Searchlight) Battalion; and C and D Batteries, 470th Antiaircraft Artillery (Automatic Weapons) Battalion. In reserve was the 2d Battalion, 158th Infantry. Supporting garrison units, to be moved to Arawe after December 15 (Z Day), consisted of several engineer, medical, ordnance, and other service detachments. All these units had been attached to the ALAMO Force for the invasion of the Trobriands in June, and were still occupying the islands.[30]

Since their landing on Woodlark Island the 112th Cavalry troops had been on garrison duty there. They were not notified until November 24 of the impending operation. Having conducted no significant live firing for five months, the 112th rushed to reacquaint its men with a skill they were certain to employ during their upcoming mission. Exacerbating the situation was the fact that the 112th had been issued new weapons without getting the necessary training to go with them. Officers, who had recently received the new .30 caliber carbines, fired these weapons for the first time. Soldiers were given rifle grenades that fitted on the end of their M-1s and finally an opportunity to fire them. Squads in the line troops also received one BAR and one Thompson submachine gun. Some troopers were also issued 2.36in rocket launchers (bazookas) and flame throwers.[31]

In three days of training, the cavalrymen also became acquainted with the special boats that would take them to the shores of Arawe. This operation saw SWPA's first use of the Landing Ship, Dock (LSD), a huge vessel designed to transport smaller craft over long distances to a point where they could steam out of its stern from a flowed well deck and cover the last leg of the voyage to the beach.

Attached for the operation was Company A, 1st Marine Division's Amphibian Tractor Battalion, manning the newer, heavier Buffalos as well as their own Alligators LVTs (Landing Vehicles, Tracked). The LVTs included 29 unarmored LVT(1) Buffalos and 10 LVT(A) (2) armorer Alligators which traveled to the scene aboard USS *Carter Hall* (LSD-3). This was also the LVTs debut with Sixth Army and Seventh Amphibious Force.

Krueger also attached part of the 592d Engineer Boat and Shore Regiment, 2d Engineer Special Brigade, with 17 LCVPs, nine LCMs, two DUKWs equipped with 4.5in rocket pods, and one repair and salvage boat. Like the LSDs and LVTs this was the first time in the Pacific area that rockets were used in a combat landing.

Jutting southwest from the mainland the Arawe Peninsula was 5,000 yards in length and less than 1,000 yards wide in most places. There were several beaches that landing craft could use, of which the two best were House Fireman on the west coast of the boot-shaped Arawe peninsula and the village of Umtingalu on the mainland, 1,700 yards east of the peninsula's base. The rest of the coast line consisted of stone cliffs about 200ft high, interspersed with low ground that was covered by mangrove swamp. Reefs fringed all the beaches, and it was clear that LCVPs could not get to the shore until detailed reconnaissance for passages was made.

Totaling 36 vessels in all, the convoy consisted of ten destroyers, a group of patrol boats, the submarine chaser SC 742 as Landing Wave Control craft, and various transports and amphibious craft. In addition to the 112th's C Troop and 1st Squadron headquarters, HMAS *Westralia* carried the beach and shore parties that would prepare House Fireman for the arrival and unloading of heavier follow-on craft.

The actual assault was broken into four operations: a small surprise landing west of Cape Merkus using rubber boats, a full-scale attack on Cape Merkus, and two separate support landings on the islands of Pilelo and Arawe. The 592d's boats participated in the main attack on Cape Merkus and in the support landing on Arawe Island.

Two APDs, *Sands* and *Humphreys*, were assigned to transport A and B Troops who would make the rubber boat landings. A Troop had the mission of cutting the coastal road near Umtingalu village on the Mekus Peninsula. B Troop was to take the Japanese by surprise and silence a radio station that was reported at the village of Paligmete on the islet of Pilelo, across Pilelo passage from the peninsula.

Dawn was still one hour away when 150 men of A Troop, who had been aboard *Sands*, started for the beach. They had been ordered to make a landing in darkness at H minus 1 hour and block the coastal trail that was the Japanese escape and reinforcement route to the east. To get the extremely vulnerable rubber boats safely ashore required surprise: landing under cover of darkness with no forewarning.

However, at about 0525, when the other group's boats were nearing shore, moonlight disclosed the boats of the other group about 100 yards short of the eastern beach, where they were hit by heavy fire from a Japanese 25mm dual purpose gun and machine guns, which promptly sank all but three of the rubber boats. The fire continued while the troops floundered in the water divesting themselves of their light combat packs and outer clothing.

Shaw lay some 3,000 yards offshore in this sector, prepared to deal with targets of opportunity, but in the uncertain light her gunners could not discern the boats against the darkly jungled shore, nor immediately spot the source of enemy fire and held their own fire for many agonizing minutes until sure of not hitting friendly troops. Once she opened, *Shaw* silenced the enemy with two salvos. Later that morning two Alligators picked up the survivors of A Troop who later landed without arms and almost naked at House Fireman Beach. Twelve men were killed, four missing, and 17 wounded in this repulse.

B Troop left *Humphreys* on 15 rubber boats at the same time that A Troop left *Sands*. B Troop had planned to surprise the enemy but when the Japanese started firing on A Troop it was obvious that the element of surprise was lost. B Troop changed its course 90 degrees and made haste for its alternate landing site on the west shore of Pilelo. Once ashore the troopers started on foot for Winguru; the leading platoon reached Winguru at 0615 and met fire from Japanese in two caves on the rising ground south of the village. Leaving one squad to contain these Japanese defenders, B Troop pushed on to Paligmete, found neither Japanese nor radio, and returned to Winguru to mop up.

Bazooka fire pummeled one cave entrance, which collapsed, trapping an estimated eight enemy. Protected by built-up logs, the other cave proved impervious to rocket launcher and machine-gun fire. The flame thrower team came forward and discharged its weapon from a distance of 15 yards. Hand grenades were tossed into the entrance closely behind the stream of fire. B Troop then moved in, tossed grenades, and the action was over. One trooper was killed in the attack and seven dead enemy were found. The action ended at about 1130.[32]

Destroyers bombarded House Fireman Beach with 1,800 5in rounds from 0610 to 0625, whereupon B-25s took over. Three squadrons had been assigned to air alert over Arawe under control of an air liaison party aboard *Conyngham*, and the first of these bombed and strafed the peninsula and the beach, after which the two rocket-equipped DUKWs laid a barrage on the beach to cover the assault waves of LVTs.

Disembarkation began at 0445. The plan called for all the amphibious tractors to be governed by the limit of visibility until daybreak, when they were to form five waves, the first to reach Beach White at 0630, the others to follow at three-minute intervals. Instead of proceeding to Beach White, Buffalos were halted about two miles from Cape Merkus and ordered to lay to until further notice. The Alligators in assault formation had reached a point 2,000 yards off Beach White at about 0614, when they were ordered to return and rendezvous with the Buffalos. At about 0700 all but the LVTs again proceeded, travelling in column until about 600 yards off the old jetty on Beach White, where each wave executed in turn a right flank. One Buffalo drowned upon leaving ship and subsequently sank while being towed. At 0728 the first wave crossed the beach followed by succeeding waves at about three-minute intervals. The troops disembarked under cover and immediately advanced toward the three-mile objective.

Meanwhile, the 592d's craft were being formed and, as they were more powerful and could better cope with the winds and currents, they proceeded to the beach behind the Alligators without difficulty. The beach itself presented another problem as it was far too narrow to accommodate a full wave of boats. Moreover, it was badly congested with the tracked vehicles. The LCVs and LCMs went in as far as possible, dropped their ramps, and the troops had to wade ashore between the Buffalos and Alligators. The operation proceeded much slower than was anticipated but, fortunately, there was no opposition and all troops were landed safely. The naval bombardment and the rocket fire had been too much for the enemy. The Amphibs carried out the third phase of the operation by landing a force on Arawe Island without difficulty. By noon of D-Day the front line was established at the neck of the peninsula.

At 1300, a reinforced platoon from C Troop investigated the rugged terrain running along the east coast of the neck from Cape Merkus. Combing the crevasses of the over-hanging cliffs, the troops killed two enemy riflemen and came across several Japanese dead and many pieces of equipment, including two field guns – presumably abandoned during the intense American bombardment. However, the sweep through this troublesome spot was not thorough enough, and, when Japanese snipers climbed up from one of the defiles to harass the regimental Command Post, the 112th began to gain an appreciation for the enemy's ability to use natural camouflage and terrain to good advantage.

Everyone awaited the Japanese air reaction, for it was certain they would not allow this landing near the fortress of Rabaul without strong air attacks. Soon there was a Red Alert. Allied covering fighters were seen to speed off to the north to meet the approaching Japanese.

It was a ruse that worked for, while the fighters were drawn off to the north, a second group of bombers came in from the east. Nineteen enemy aircraft bombed and strafed the beach and landing craft. Bombs dropped all around the naval craft and the Allied landing boats. All guns fired on the attackers and the 592d was officially credited with destroying one of them. Considering the number of bombs dropped the casualties were light; one LCVP was hit and three men were wounded. Numerous and more intensive raids were to follow.

Of the 3,000 troops of the 112th who went ashore on the first day, there were 13 killed, 29 missing, and 25 wounded. The enemy losses totaled 60 killed.

The morning after the assault, several reconnaissance missions were carried out along the coast and among the adjacent islands. To give added speed and still retain the maximum fire power on these missions, the two rocket-equipped DUKWs were each loaded on LCMs. They encountered no opposition on their first missions and it was believed that whatever enemy forces may have been in the vicinity to resist the first surprise landing had either been wiped out or had fled to inland installations. That was later proved to be an erroneous assumption for many Japanese still remained only a short distance away to continually plague the Allied advance.

Indeed, the Japanese had not yet given up at Arawe. When the 17th Division commander received word of the landing he ordered Major Komori, who was then proceeding by boat and overland march to Arawe from Rabaul, to make haste. The Americans soon became aware of the approaching Japanese.

On the second day Arawe was again heavily bombed and several small naval ships in the harbor were severely damaged. One of the Naval patrol vessels was struck with a direct hit. With bombs and strafing fire raining all around them, the Amphibs went to the rescue in their small boats. They succeeded in saving all personnel of the patrol vessel, which sank in just four minutes.

On December 18 two Japanese armed barges attacked a 112th Cavalry patrol on board two of the 2d Engineer Special Brigade's LCVPs. The Japanese scored direct hits; the patrol abandoned the LCVPs and made its way east to Arawe on foot six days later.

For two weeks, multiple raids took place almost daily – mostly in the early morning hours. During this period, over 350 planes flew against Arawe, strafing House Fireman Beach and dropping approximately 570 bombs on supply dumps and vessels involved in unloading operations. Sorties in December put several landing craft and their escorts out of action. Less severe was the toll taken on forces ashore, as the regiment suffered no casualties – only sleepless nights, fear, frustration, and minor damage to equipment.

With all these Japanese barges in the vicinity the most important job of the boatmen was patrolling, especially at night, to prevent a Japanese surprise landing. Encounters with Japanese planes were frequent. On the day after Christmas one of the LCMs, crewed by Technician Fourth Grade Clyde W. Eidson, Technician Fifth Grade Fred L. Torres, and Private Isadore Pahoski was struck by a falling Japanese plane. The plane swooped down in a strafing attack and the crew, hurriedly manning their guns, returned as much fire as possible. They evidently killed the pilot, for the plane continued in its dive and crashed into the stern of their LCM. The barge did not sink immediately, but none of the crew could be found. After a thorough search in the barge, ashore, and in the water, the surrounding area failed to disclose any evidence of the missing men. They were presumed to have been blown up by the resulting explosion.

On January 6, 1944 Cunningham reported to Krueger the existence of the Japanese positions. Cunningham's forces now totaled almost 4,750 men and his short front line –700 yards – was a strong position with fields of fire cut, barbed wire emplaced, and artillery and mortar data computed. There were only about 100 Japanese with rifles and a half-dozen machine guns, but lack of visibility and the fact that the Japanese moved their guns frequently made them almost impossible for artillery and mortars to hit. Cunningham asked for tanks and more troops.

F Company, 158th Infantry, and B Company, 1st Tank Battalion, 1st Marine Division, reached Arawe between January 10 and 12.

On the morning of January 16, attack and medium bombers struck at the Japanese positions, artillery and mortars shelled them, and the Marine light tanks, two companies of the 158th Infantry, and C Troop of the 112th Cavalry attacked. The tanks led, with infantrymen and cavalrymen following each tank. Direct communication between tanks and foot troops was successfully attained by a device which the tank company improvised; it installed an EE8 field telephone at the rear of each machine. The attack went well and carried forward for 1,500 yards. The next day B Troop demolition teams and a detachment of bulldozers came forward and destroyed the foxholes and coconut-log pillboxes. The losses inflicted on the Japanese included a 75mm field gun, ten machine guns, and 139 enemy dead.

Despite the efforts to secure it, Arawe never became an air base. The only airstrip ever used was one for artillery liaison planes that engineers hastily cleared on January 13.[33]

Operation *Backhander*, Cape Gloucester

The Japanese had occupied Cape Gloucester in December, 1942 and by December, 1943 were estimated to have about 10,000 troops in the area. These were not concentrated in strength along the coastal flat but principally in two rear areas. Once in possession of Allied forces, however, this high ground would give the Allies a clear strategic advantage over the enemy.

The northwestern tip of New Britain is dominated by three volcanic mountains. On the west, from Cape Gloucester south to Cape Bushing, lay an ideal beach area with good anchorage and no reef offshore; but the Japanese, of course, had concentrated their defenses there. The coastal flat, narrowing to 300 yards northeast of these fingers, became a treacherous corridor for advancing troops, threatened on the left flank and left front by high ground, abounding in strategic and covered locations for static defensive positions. High ground also provided the Japanese with advantageous jumping-off points and natural corridors for sharp flanking thrusts at any invaders.[34]

To the east of the mountains was a comparatively low valley running from Borgen Bay south to the mouth of the Itni River. After study, the Marine planners selected two beaches, Yellow 1 and Yellow 2 in Borgen Ray northwest of Silimati Point. With the western third of New Britain in U.S. hands, Rabaul would be effectively neutralized for the duration.

The plan to capture Cape Gloucester called for simultaneous landings east and west of the airfields, each site approximately seven miles from the point of the cape itself. On Green Beach near Tauali, Lieutenant Colonel James M. Masters, Sr., would land his battalion, 2/1, 1st Marine Division, and its attached units, seize a limited beachhead, organize it for defense, and hold it against enemy forces attempting to use the coastal trail to reach the airfields or to withdraw from them. On the opposite side of the cape, on two beaches (Yellow 1 and 2) near Silimati Point, Colonel Frisbie's 1st and 3d Battalions, 7th Marines would land in assault followed by 2/7, with the mission of seizing a beachhead, organizing it for defense, and covering the landing of the rest of the assault force. The 17th Marines' 2d Battalion, the division's pioneers, formed the backbone of the shore party.

Admiral Barbey assigned himself as Commander, Task Force 76, the "Backhander" Attack Force, nine APDs, 23 LSTS, 19 LCIs, 12 LCTs, and 14 LCMs to transport, land, and maintain the assault and garrison troops. The LCTS and LCMs plus five LCIs were assigned to the Western Assault Group (Green Beach) under Commander Carroll I. Reynolds; the rest of the LCIs, the APDs, and the LSTs were part of the Eastern Assault Group scheduled for the Yellow beaches. Barbey commanded the ships at the main landing as well as the naval phases of the whole operation.

For fire support duties, Commander Reynolds had two destroyers and two rocket-equipped DUKWS carried in LCMs. To cover the landings on the eastern side of Cape Gloucester, Barbey had 12 destroyers in addition to his flagship and two rocket-firing LCIs.

Escorting and supporting the attack force was Task Force 74 under Vice Admiral V. A. C. Crutchley, RN, who had two Australian and two American cruisers with eight destroyers.[35]

The 592d U.S. Army Engineering Special Brigade (ESBR) boatmen, working this time with the famed 1st Marine Division, veterans of Guadalcanal, would put the Marines ashore in simultaneous landings on Green and Yellow beaches. One task group under the command of Major Rex K. Shaul of Akron, Ohio, landed Marines on Green Beach, near Tuali, only a few miles south of the main objective: the Cape Gloucester airstrips. The other group under the command of Lieutenant Colonel Ralph T. Simpson landed a force on Yellow Beach farther north and around the tip of New Britain.[36]

The assault troops were loaded from bases on New Guinea and by the evening of December 24, 1943, all of the troops were aboard and the convoy had rendezvoused in Buna Harbor.

The irony of their warlike mission on a day of peace did not escape the men as the convoy moved out at 0300 Christmas morning. "The heat below decks was intense," says the action report, "and men slept topside either in vehicles or on the deck."

When, the next morning, an extrovert who had once been in vaudeville tried to start the men singing Christmas carols, he got nothing but silence as a reward. "He started with 'Silent Night'," recalls a man who was on the same LST. "Response was weak. Tentatively he began, 'Oh, Come All Ye Faithful,' and found his voice echoing back across the water. Somehow those songs seemed irreverent that day."

Not to be suppressed, the ex-vaudevillian tried a secular tune. It was "Pistol-Packin' Mama." This one seemed all right and "brought in half the ship a-singing, more and more of them joining in from the darkness where they were talking, or thinking of home, or wondering if they'd be alive next week. It made everybody feel better."

On another ship that day, a corporal who had left divinity school to fight as a Marine gathered a small group of men around him and read the Christmas story from the Bible. But that did not disturb a larger group of men playing poker on the deck nearby. They did not lower their voices for a while, at least until one of the players rose from the deck and cried out angrily: "This is one of those days when it doesn't pay to get up."

A Marine private, a former master at fashionable Choate School, was complaining that day to one of his friends. His Christmas packages had arrived just before he went aboard ship. "All I could do," he grumbled, "was pass them around, let everybody have a mouthful, and throw away the rest."

Most of the men sat quietly, alternately thinking and snoozing, propped and humped around the sharp and inflexible edges of the gear of war which littered the decks, keeping whatever thoughts they had to themselves as Christmas Day came and went.[37]

At 0300 of the twenty-sixth, which would in fact be Christmas Stateside, the Marines were aroused for the inevitable D-Day breakfast of steak and eggs.

Then there was nothing to do but square away gear for the hundredth time. Silent groups gathered on the blacked-out decks to watch the loom of the land to starboard take form in the gradually graying dark that presages a tropic dawn.

First dawn paled the sky to show the brooding bulk of Mount Talawe looming off to the south, but darkness still lay upon the water at 0600 when the cruisers and destroyers opened fire on their predetermined targets. For the next hour and a half distant thunder beat upon the eardrums, and concussion shook the air. Only one Japanese gun replied – with a single round.

The two rocket-equipped LCIs moved first through the wide opening in the barrier reef, marked by the wreck of a Japanese destroyer that was hung up on the reef 7,000 yards offshore, and took positions off the flanks of the designated beaches, with the dual function of serving as guideposts and firing in support of the assault.

At 0748, the first LCMS grounded on Green Beach and dropped their ramps. The Marines of the assault companies moved quickly across the volcanic sand, mounted the slight bank bordering the beach, and then advanced cautiously into the secondary growth that covered the rising ground beyond.

Conditions were significantly different on the Yellow beaches. From 0700 to 0720, while naval gunfire was concentrated on the beaches and airfields, five squadrons of B-24s dropped 500lb bombs on the Target Hill area. Then, on schedule, at the call of a command plane aloft, naval gunfire on the beaches lifted and a squadron of B-25s streaked in over Target Hill to release eight tons of white phosphorous bombs on its naked crest. Smoke soon obscured the vision of any enemy who might still have been using the hill as an observation post, and three B-25 squadrons began working over the beaches.

Smoke from Target Hill drifted down across the landing beaches pushed on by a gentle southeast breeze. By H-Hour the shoreline had disappeared in a heavy haze, and within another half hour the approach lanes were obscured as far as the line of departure, 3,000 yards out. Coxswains of the leading boat waves handled their craft boldly, however, and the smoke created no severe problems of control or orientation.

When the boats were 500 yards out, rockets from the LCIs began dropping ashore and worked inland as the Marines approached the beach. At 0746 on Yellow 1 and 0748 on Yellow 2, the landing craft grounded and dropped their ramps. Charging ashore to the sound of their own shouts, the Marines splashed through knee-deep water onto narrow strands of black sand. There was no enemy response, no sign of human opposition, just a dense wall of jungle vegetation. In fact, on many stretches of Yellow 1, the overhanging brush and vines touched the water; there was only a hint of actual beach.[38]

The Marines got through somehow to reasonably dry ground beyond. On the left 1/7 drove for Target Hill with such determination that they reached this commanding but exposed eminence before the Japanese defenders had got around to reoccupying the installations they had abandoned under the heavy bombardment, and that flank of the perimeter was firmly anchored. In the center 2/7 reached their objective against weak, scattered sniper fire and set up their defense line partly in a kunai patch, at a maximum depth of about 1,200 yards from the shore. 3/7 set up their right, or western sector with even less difficulty.

Once the perimeter line had been seized, the function of the 7th Marines became purely defensive, so far as this phase of the operation was concerned. The crucial attack on the airdrome had been assigned to the 1st Marines, less one battalion. These units, 3/1 and 1/1, landed respectively at 0830 and 1300 and moved at once to the right. About midmorning 3/1 passed through 3/7 and commenced their inexorable westward drive.

Shortly after 1000 the 3d Battalion, 1st Marines, pushed ahead, advancing in a column of companies because a swamp on the left narrowed the frontage. They ran into trouble almost at once from camouflaged bunkers which fired point-blank into the advancing troops, killing two captains, Joseph A. Terzi, commander of Company K, and his executive officer, Philip A. Wilheit, within a few seconds of each other. More casualties quickly followed. There was little room for maneuver. Flame throwers proved ineffective owing to the density of the jungle and the sturdy bunkers proved impervious to bazooka rockets, which failed to detonate in the soft earth covering the structures.

An ammunition-carrying LVT arrived, and its crew of three volunteered to double for a tank against two bunkers which had been definitely located. It so happened that two of the crew of this particular amphtrack were twin brothers: Privates Leslie E. Hansen, one of the gunners, and Paul L. Hansen, the driver. Machine guns blazing and motor roaring, it crashed through the heavy undergrowth until it became inadvertently wedged between two trees too large for it to bowl over.

Instantly Japanese swarmed out of the jungle. The LVT gunners managed to kill many of the attackers, but the rest were all over the machine before the supporting troops could check them. Leslie E. Hansen was wounded and the other gunner, Sergeant Robert J. Oswald, Jr., was dragged over the side where he was beaten and knifed to death. Paul Hansen, however, managed to extricate himself successfully from the amphtrack. Lunging ahead, he caved in one bunker, silencing its fire and enabling Marine riflemen to isolate three other bunkers and destroy them in succession, killing 25 Japanese.[39]

A feature of the campaign made its appearance that first day: the peril of falling trees. Indeed, one of the first fatalities the division sustained resulted from this. This danger is ever present in rain-forest jungle where excessive wetness and excessive heat accelerate the decay of lush growth. Even the healthiest looking trees could be rotten to the core, ready to collapse at the slightest shock. Here the shattering effect of intensive aerial bombing and naval gunfire had been superimposed upon natural causes, multiplying the peril a hundredfold. Twenty-five Marines were killed during the Battle of Cape Gloucester by huge falling trees in the course of the campaign, many more were injured, and the constant danger came to constitute something of a mental hazard to all.[40]

There were no morning air attacks on the beachhead. The expected attack came, however, between 1430 and 1510 in the afternoon. The presence of "Vals" made Rabaul the likely base of the attack. An estimated 25 "Vals" were escorted by 30 to 60 "Zekes", "Oscars", and "Tojos". The attacking force was first plotted at 1420 and again at 1425. The destroyers' radar lost the plot, however, and the two squadrons sent for interception were out of position when the attack came in. Although there were 49 P-38s, 16 P-47s, and 16 P-40s in the area, the dive-bombers got through to the convoy.

Coast Guard-manned LSTs 22, 26, 66, and 465 were caught in the attack. At 1418 LST-22 beached along with the LST-465 and LST-26 and unloading began at 1428. At 1440 15 "Vals" attacked the first LST echelon, which was at that time standing out through the reefs, and many bombs appeared to be striking the water near these ships. At 1445 one Japanese "Val," which apparently had been driven off from the group attacking the first echelon, came in from astern of the LST-22 strafing the stern and after-deck house. As the plane swung slightly to the southwest and began to parallel the ship, it came within the range of the LSTs' guns. When directly on the starboard beam, the plane burst into flames. It was seen to pass close over the trees fringing the beach and did not reappear. It was reported to have crashed a short distance inland.

On board LST-66 seven Japanese dive-bombers suddenly attacked this ship as it stood in the bay. Signalman 3rd Class Joseph Gerczak and Motor Machinist Mate 3rd Class Frank C. Russo manned one of the antiaircraft guns and were the first to open fire. When the planes came in and struck from starboard, Gerczak poured his drums of ammunition into the attackers with unrelenting fury, blasting two from the sky and into the sea near his vessel. With his ship struck by bomb fragments, each bursting successively closer, he continued delivering a blistering stream of bullets against the enemy until he was fatally struck down by a violent blast which forced shrapnel into his gun shield and finally silenced his weapon. LST-66 shot down three enemy planes after a near miss which killed Gerczak and wounded Russo along with one enlisted Navy man.[41]

As the LSTs fought off the attacks aimed at them, a dive-bomber hit the USS *Brownson* (DD-518) with two bombs at 1442. The bombs struck to starboard of the centerline, near number two stack. A tremendous explosion followed and the entire structure above the main deck, as well as the deck plating, was gone. The ship listed 10 to 15 degrees to starboard and settled rapidly amidships with the bow and stern canted upward.

The wounded were placed in rafts and at 1450 the order to abandon ship was given. The amidships section was entirely underwater by this time. There was a single ripple like a depth charge explosion and the ship sank at 1459. *Brownson* suffered the loss of 108 of her crew. The remainder was rescued by *Daly* (DD-519) and *Lamson* (DD-367).[42]

Unfortunately, the "Vals" made their attack just as the B-25 group was going in to strafe Hill 150 – in fact, the "Vals" flew straight through the B-25 formation. The ships' antiaircraft opened up on both groups and scored more heavily on the B-25s (two shot down and two badly damaged) than it did in getting just one "Val".

In the attacks the Japanese had lost 22 out of the 25 dive-bombers and probably more than 24 of their fighters against an Allied loss of two P-38s, two P-47s, and one destroyer as well as damaging three others and two LSTs.

In a second attack at 1715, 15 torpedo-carrying "Bettys" tried to reach a convoy of LSTs. The 341st and 34d Fighter Squadrons, covering the area with 26 P-47s, intercepted the two attacking waves and destroyed 14 of the "Bettys" and two "Tojos", and claimed the other "Betty" as probably destroyed. Again, the ships' own antiaircraft guns shot down one P-47 of the 342d Squadron.* [43]

The 592d EBSR's rocket-equipped DUKWs again proved their worth on Yellow Beach that day. The rocket-equipped DUKW under the command of 1st Lieutenant Vermeil A. Beck was called into action was when a Marine advance was halted by a Japanese pillbox at a strategic road junction. Access to the pillbox other than by a frontal attack was impossible and that would have cost the lives of several men. When the DUKW was brought into range Lieutenant Beck fired just 20 rounds at the target. The story goes that the Marine commander jumped up and down with joy when he looked at the damage it had caused. On another occasion a DUKW shelled a deep ravine through which Japanese forces were passing. The Japanese thought that they were well masked from artillery fire, but they evidently had not heard of the new American rockets. Over 200 Japanese bodies were mute evidence to the effectiveness of the fire.

The DUKW was also used to rescue a wounded Marine who was lying in an exposed position on a long, narrow sand spit extending from Natamo Point near Yellow Beach. Two Marines had already endeavored to rescue him but, once on the sand spit, had been pinned down by enemy fire and could not get off. Landing craft volunteered to go to their assistance, but sand bars prevented them from getting close enough. The rocket-equipped DUKW was called into action and the crew laid down a 105-round barrage inland from the sand spit. Under its protection the two Marines crossed to safety. Unfortunately, the third Marine was already dead. [44]

---

* Sadly, these were not the only incidents of "friendly fire" casualties. During the month of February the 592d detachment on Cape Gloucester received many casualties due to air attacks – both by Japanese and American planes. One LCVP was sunk when it received a direct hit by an enemy bomb and two nearby LCMs were severely damaged by shell fragments. One officer and four men could not be located and were presumed to have been killed in the attack. On two separate occasions American pilots who must have mistaken the 2d ESB craft for enemy barges zoomed down in strafing attacks. When they came close enough to see the flags and identifying insignia on the boats they immediately ceased firing, but their aim was good and usually by the time they noticed their error, it was too late, and members of the boat crews had already been hit. It was just one of those unfortunate accidents of war. Fortunately, by keeping as close liaison as possible with the Air Force, only two such attacks occurred.

All along the front in perimeters around Green and Yellow beaches the Marines were busy tying in their positions as darkness fell, cutting fire lanes through jungle growth, and laying out trip wires to warn of infiltrators. For the 1st Division Marines it was Guadalcanal all over again, the Americans waiting in the jungles for the inevitable Japanese night attack. The thick overhead cover was dripping as the result of an afternoon rain that drenched the beachhead and all that were in it. The dank swamp forest stank, the night air was humid and thick, and the ever present jungle noises mingled with the actual and the imagined sounds of enemy troops readying for an assault.

Occasionally the adversaries caught a glimpse of the flash of fire at a rifle or machine gun muzzle or the momentary flare when a mortar or artillery shell exploded, but, in the main, the battle was fought by sound. One man, one gun, one group fired and drew a response from the other side who aimed at the sound of the firing; then the tempo would pick up sharply and firing would break out all along the front to die away slowly, only to break out again at another point.[45]

The first night ashore at Gloucester was miserable. Drenching rains of the northwest monsoon poured down in torrents; more trees fell. The rains lasted for hours and recurred at least once nearly every day for the next three months. The division had landed light, without tentage. Men in front-line fox holes were soon up to their necks in water; those in jungle hammocks farther back not much better off.

The fighting at Cape Gloucester was a jungle slugging match, where flame throwers were useless, it was often impossible to throw a grenade more than 10ft ahead, and the bazooka usually failed to detonate upon striking the soft earth of the Japanese field works.

> The terrain was as rugged and treacherous as the Japanese. The direction of the advance necessitated what is known technically as cross compartment fighting, that is moving at right angles to the natural watershed. This meant that instead of following valleys and ridges, an interminable succession of these had to be crossed.
>
> Men would scale one ridge, wiping out the prepared positions, which cluttered both the forward and reverse slopes, then plunge down into another valley where they might or might not find a river which showed on none of their crude maps, with the enemy entrenched on the far bank. One such stream had to be crossed nine times before a bridgehead could be secured.

Or perhaps there would be a swamp, neck-deep or worse. Then another fortified ridge, another unknown valley. And always the rain and the mud, torrid heat and teeming insect life, the stink of rotten jungle and rotting dead; malaria burning the body and fungus infection eating away the feet, and no hot chow for weeks. And fury by day and terror by night and utter weariness all the time. And death.[46]

The experience of the average Marine rifleman in this situation was vividly described by one of the 1st Division's scout officers: "You'd step off from your line in the morning, take say ten paces, and turn around to guide on your buddy. And – nobody there, Jap or Marine. Ah, I can tell you it was a very small war and a very lonely business."[47]

The final action fought by the Leathernecks took place on April 22, when an ambush sprung by the 2d Battalion, 5th Marines, killed 20 Japanese and resulted in the last Marine fatality of the campaign. In seizing western New Britain as part of the isolation of Rabaul, the division suffered 310 killed in action and 1,083 wounded, roughly one-fourth of the estimated Japanese casualties.

On the same night that the 392d boatmen landed the Marines on Cape Gloucester, another 592d provisional group, consisting of Company D and some attached medics and boatmen and an Australian radar detachment, effected a successful landing of their own on Long Island. That small island, 103 miles north of Finschhafen and at the head of the Vitiaz Strait, provided an excellent location for radar installations and a lookout station. The task group of about 200 officers and men under the command of Major Leonard Kaplan of Hempstead, New York, proceeded to Long Island on PT boats, arriving there shortly after midnight on December 26.

As they had been told to expect, the landing was unopposed. Three days before the actual landing Major Kaplan and two amphibian scouts had reconnoitered the island and found no trace of enemy occupation. This landing was the deepest Allied penetration into Japanese-controlled territory up to that time and the absence of opposition was a disappointment to the shore engineers who were well armed and anxious for a crack at the enemy. It turned out that while the Japanese had never garrisoned Long Island it had been used as a staging point for Japanese barges en route from Rabaul to Wewak. The seizure of Long Island stopped this traffic.[48]

Cape Gloucester never became an important air base. The Arawe and Cape Gloucester invasions were of less strategic importance than the other *Cartwheel* operations, and with the benefit of hindsight were probably not essential to the reduction of Rabaul or the approach to the Philippines. Yet they were neither completely fruitless. The 1st Marine Division scored a striking tactical success at the cost of 310 killed and 1,083 wounded. And the Allied forces of the Southwest Pacific Area had, by means of these operations, broken out through the narrow Dampier and Vitiaz Straits.[49]

Saidor: Operation *Michaelmas*

With the landings on New Britain and Long Island so successful, General Krueger's Sixth Army followed up with another landing, this time at Saidor between Sio and Madang on New Guinea's north coast, to cut off the Japanese retreating from the Huon Peninsula.

Saidor, on the north coast of the Huon Peninsula, lay slightly northeast of Mounts Gladstone and Disraeli, which glower at each other from their 11,000ft peaks. It had a prewar airstrip, and had been used as a barge staging point by the Japanese. Lying 110 nautical miles from Finschhafen, 52 from Madang, and 414 from Rabaul, it was well situated to support the advance westward and the move northward.

There was neither time nor opportunity for ground reconnaissance of Saidor; the landing beaches were chosen from aerial photographs. The 32d Infantry Division provided the majority of the units that made up the task force. The main combat power for the task force was the 126th Infantry. The task force commander was Brigadier General Clarence A. Martin, assistant commander of the 32d Division. Colonel Joseph S. Bradley was commander of the 126th Infantry. Three beaches, designated Red, White, and Blue from the left (in the south) to the right on the west shore of Dekays Bay just east of Saidor, were selected. They were rough and stony but were chosen because they were close to the objective, the beach gradient was steep enough to enable the troops to make a dry landing, there was solid ground behind them, and Dekays Bay could be expected to offer protection from the northwest monsoons.

The main elements of the force were embarked from Goodenough Island in nine ADPs, several LCIs, and two LSTs during the last days of December 1943.

On January 2, 1944, three days after the Marines at Cape Gloucester seized their airdrome objective, other SWPA forces sailed through Vitiaz Strait, now secure on both shores, and landed at Saidor. H Hour was set for 0650, 15 minutes before sunrise – the earliest possible minute that would allow adequate light for the earlier naval bombardment. The beaches were obscured due to rain and a very overcast sky; the delay would improve visibility for naval gunfire and landing beach identification. Under the command of Lieutenant Colonel Robert J. Kasper the Shore Battalion of the 542d EBSR and a small boat detachment of six LCMs plus two rocket-equipped DUKWs landed at Saidor with troops of the 32d Infantry Division.

When they reached shore the rifle battalions began to push inland while the artillery established itself and the shore party moved supplies off the beach. Japanese resistance was limited to a few rifle shots. General Martin reported that only 15 enemy soldiers had been near the beaches at the time of the landing, and 11 of these were killed by the bombardments and by soldiers of the 126th.

Japanese land and air resistance to the Allied landing was negligible. For more than eight hours, no enemy aircraft appeared, by which time all landing craft had unloaded their cargoes and were heading back toward Oro Bay. The first raid came shortly after 1600, by nine "Helen" bombers escorted by perhaps twenty "Zeke" and "Tony" fighters. The enemy pilots were not particularly enthusiastic, and when twelve P-40s approached, several of the bombers jettisoned their bombs and with some of the fighters beat a hasty retreat. One American enlisted man was killed and another wounded by the hastily released bomb loads. In the combat that had meanwhile developed overhead, one P-40 was seen to go down in flames, and two "Helens" and three enemy fighters were destroyed.

As soon as the beachhead was established, patrols were pushed inland to prevent movements between the Japanese bases farther west along the coast and the forces now trapped between Saidor and the Australians operating against them from the east. In the first landings the battalions of the 126th Infantry had come ashore on three beaches. The 3d Battalion had taken Red (north) Beach, and the 2d Battalion White (center) and Blue (south) beaches. The 1st Battalion then came in on White Beach, passed through the 2d, and kept on west to seize Saidor Village and the airstrip by it. Casualties on D-Day numbered one soldier killed, five wounded, and two sailors drowned at Blue Beach.

The efficiency of Saidor operations, when compared, for example, with the Kiriwina invasion of the previous year, showed the SWPA's amphibious operations improvements. Yet there are flaws in even well-executed operations as was demonstrated the next morning.

The *Michaelmas* Task Force expected six LSTs to arrive at 0700, January 3, which would be after daylight. However, when three vessels came dimly into view about a hundred yards from the north shore at 0400 and failed to identify themselves, the shore defenses opened fire. Several hits were scored and the vessels put out to sea. After daybreak it was discovered that these were in fact Allied LSTs which had lost their escort. One man was killed and three wounded by this fire.

Once again the Japanese found themselves forced to flee into the rugged mountains in order to escape encirclement. As they sidestepped inland around Saidor, the retreating Japanese left a trail of abandoned equipment. On January 15, an Australian patrol pushing through Sio after the fleeing enemy discovered a half-buried trunk in a stream bed. It held the complete cipher library of the Imperial Japanese Army's 20th Division. The find was immediately returned to Central Bureau, MacArthur's Allied cryptanalytic agency in Brisbane, Australia. Central Bureau used the captured code books to solve the Japanese Army's main cipher system. This intelligence windfall arrived exactly when MacArthur was most prepared to take advantage of it.

The Saidor landing completed the seizure of the Markham-Ramu trough and the Huon Peninsula for the Allies and obtained one more airfield to support operations against the Admiralties and enemy bases to the west.

Operation *Cartwheel* was completed by the seizure of Saidor, and subsequent operations on the Huon Peninsula were anticlimactic strategically, however bitter and tragic they were for those who fought and died in them.

But, General MacArthur and Admiral Halsey were not yet finished with the Japanese in the Southeast Area. By the end of 1943 Rabaul had not yet been completely neutralized, and before the approach to the Philippines could begin there remained a set of subsidiary, transitional operations to be accomplished, including the Treasury Islands.[50]

Admiralty Islands, Operation *Brewer*

The Admiralties lie some 200 miles north and east of New Guinea and 260 miles west of the tip of New Ireland. Manus is the larger of the two main islands and has steep mountains, dense jungle, and a few coconut plantations.

Separated from Manus by a shallow, creek-like strait, Los Negros is generally flat, with hills only in the southwest, and extends in a rough horseshoe curve to form a natural breakwater for Seeadler Harbor, the most extensive of several anchorages. A series of smaller islands, running parallel to the northern coast line of Manus, outpost the harbor. Its principal entrance is a passage between Hauwei and Ndrilo Islands, shown on charts as a free channel, one and a half miles wide and 100ft deep. The surveyed portion of the harbor is six miles wide and more than 20 miles long. Depths ranged up to 120ft. From a military standpoint, Seeadler Harbor, the settlement of Lorengau with its auxiliary landing field, and the central part of Los Negros, site of the large Momote airfield, were the most important areas on the islands.[51] Seizure of the Admiralty Islands would complete the encirclement of the Japanese base and provide the Allies with operational and logistic bases.

On February 24 Alamo Force Headquarters at Finschhafen received orders for the immediate reconnaissance landing on the Admiralties. The 1st Cavalry Division had been designated as the nucleus of the task force assigned to this operation. Major General Innis P. Swift, commanding the division, and his staff were at Finschhafen and had been included in the conferences at Alamo Force Headquarters. The division was at Camp Borio in the vicinity of Oro Bay, staging area for the Brewer Operation, and was training intensively for its first combat duty.[52]

The initial objectives were now on the eastern side of Los Negros, where Hyane Harbor offered the only known landing beach. Earlier intelligence as well as recent aerial studies showed the advantages and drawbacks of Hyane Harbor as the attack area. At the harbor entrance, two flanking points of land only 1,700 yards apart might enable the enemy to lay down effective cross-fire against the landing craft as they maneuvered through the 50ft break in the reef which encircles the island. Within the harbor, boats would have to head for the south and southwest part of the bay, since the north and northwest shores were swampy.

The beach at the south was not more than 1,200 yards long and was composed of firm sand and shingle, passable to motor transportation. Beyond the beach only the jetty area was cleared. Elsewhere the ground was covered with secondary growth and the trunks of fallen coconut trees. The shortest route to the Momote airdrome would be about 150 yards across this jungle terrain.

Information from some 40 islanders who had made contact at various points confirmed that 2,450 Japanese were present in the Momote-Salami

Plantation area; for reserves 750 in the Papitalai-Lombrum region could be counted on, and possibly 1,100 more on Manus Island in the vicinity of Lorengau. The duty of the 2,450 supposed to be located near Momote would be primarily that of guarding the airdrome; therefore field fortifications might be expected. In particular, dual-purpose 25mm pompoms were reported to be organized in depth in a perimeter around the airdrome.

Admiral Thomas C. Kinkaid's, Commander Allied Naval Forces, Southwest Pacific Area, and the Seventh Fleet, (known as "MacArthur's Navy") and Barbey's plans, issued on February 26 provided for transporting and landing the reconnaissance force, then reinforcing it or withdrawing it if necessary. With the cruisers *Nashville* (CL-43) and *Phoenix* (CL-46) and four destroyers Rear Admiral Russell S. Berkey was to provide cover during the approach to the Admiralties and to deliver supporting gunfire against Los Negros, Lorengau, and Seeadler Harbor during the landings. The attack group, which Barbey placed under command of Rear Admiral William M. Fechteler, his deputy, consisted of eight destroyers and three APDs.

The participation of the 592d EBSR in the Support Task Force began only a few days before it actually embarked. Major (later Lieutenant Colonel) Kaplan, the Shore Battalion Commander, received sudden orders late in February to prepare certain units of the regiment for an immediate combat mission. E Company, with Captain Henry M. Seipt Jr. in command, was expanded into a provisional task group by the addition of medical, communication, and weapons sections. Six LCMs and six LCVs represented the Boat Battalion in this initial mission.

The cruisers were added to the force because General MacArthur elected to accompany the expedition, and to invite Admiral Kinkaid to go with him, to judge from firsthand observation whether to evacuate or hold after the reconnaissance.

An indication that the operation might prove more difficult than anticipated came on 27 February when a six-man reconnaissance patrol landed on Los Negros. They reported that the island was "lousy" with Japanese. MacArthur's headquarters disregarded this report after General Kenney, the Fifth Air Force commander, argued that the information was too vague to justify changing the operational plan.

On the morning of February 29, U.S. forces assaulted Hyane Harbor, located on the east side of Los Negros. The site was close to Momote Plantation airfield, one of the early assault objectives. The Japanese had not anticipated a landing there because the harbor had a narrow entrance and a small beach. The bulk of their forces were concentrated on the other side of the island to defend the beaches of Seeadler Harbor. Only a few coast artillery, antiaircraft batteries, and machine guns were positioned to oppose the initial assault on D-Day without being challenged.

At 0817, the first wave of boats landed at Hyane Harbor. Japanese gunners on both sides of the mouth of the harbor continued to fire on the next three waves of landing craft, but naval gunfire and driving rain limited their effectiveness. The landings proceeded on schedule with only four boats sustaining damage. Shortly after noon the entire reconnaissance force was ashore and had secured a small perimeter around Momote Plantation airfield. Reconnaissance patrols did not encounter any Japanese troops but found ample evidence of enemy activity.

The entire landing force of 1,026 men had to land in 12 LCP(R)s. If evacuation had become necessary, it is doubtful if many of these boats would have survived the enemy opposition forcing evacuation, and most of the landing force would have been wiped out. Close support was rendered by destroyers, which moved in to within less than a mile of the shore as the landings progressed.

Support plans called for naval gunfire to stop at 0755 (H minus 20 minutes) so that B-25s could bomb and strafe at low altitudes, but at 0755 no B-25s could be seen nor could any be reached by radio. The ships fired, therefore, until 0810, and then fired star shells as a signal that B-25s could attack in safety. Soon afterward three B-25s bombed the gun positions at the entrance to the harbor.

The first wave of landing craft reached the shore at H-Hour plus 2 minutes. It received only slight enemy fire. As the boats came in, a Japanese machine-gun crew on the beach hastily carried their weapon to cover. The boats grounded roughly on the beaches near the three small jetties while their .30-caliber machine guns, mounted forward, two to a boat, incessantly sprayed the vegetation near the water's edge. The first boat's party, soldiers of G Troop, led by 1st Lieutenant Marvin J. Henshaw, rushed beyond the narrow beach to the edge of a coconut plantation where there were fallen trees and kunai grass for cover. Here they lay prone, forming a rough half-circle with a 50-yard radius. They saw scattered groups of the enemy fleeing inland, some as far away as the other side of the air strip. Lieutenant Henshaw killed one with a long-distance shot, and members of his platoon killed another. Not one of the soldiers who landed in the first wave was a casualty.

The Japanese resumed their positions at north and south arms of the harbor entrance, which were only 750 yards apart, when the naval shelling ceased and fired at the LCP(R)s as they returned to the APDs. *Mahan* (DD-364) steamed to within a mile of shore and fired 20mm and 40mm guns at the southern point. She could not put fire on the point opposite because the LCP(R)s were in the way. As the second wave started through the entrance so much enemy fire came from the skidway and from the northern point that it turned back. The destroyers *Flusser* (DD-368) and *Drayton* (DD-366) then put their fire on the north point while *Mahan* pounded the southern. When the enemy fire ceased, the landing craft re-formed, went through the passage, fired their machine guns at the skidway, and landed 150 men of the second wave at H-Hour plus 8 minutes.

The effectiveness of Japanese fire on one of the LCPRs was described by a *Yank* correspondent:

> As we neared the channel, the Navy men in the bow hollered to us to keep our heads down or we'd get them blown off. We crouched lower, swearing, and waited.
>
> It came with a crack; machinegun fire over our heads. Our light landing craft shuddered as the Navy gunners hammered back and answered with the .30-calibers mounted on both sides of the barge.
>
> As we made the turn for the beach, something solid plugged into us. "They got one of our guns or something," one GI said. There was a splinter the size of a half dollar on the pack of the man in front of me.
>
> Up front a hole gaped in the middle of the landing ramp and there were no men where there had been four. Our barge headed back toward the destroyer that had carried us to the Admiralties.
>
> White splashes of water were plunging through the 6-inch gap in the wooden gate. William Siebieda. S 1 / c, of Wheeling, W. Va., ducked from his position at the starboard gun and slammed his hip against the hole to plug it. He was firing a tommy gun at the shore as fast as wounded soldiers could pass him loaded clips. The water sloshed around him, running down his legs and washing the blood of the wounded into a pink frappe.

Two soldiers and the coxswain died. The other man of the four was uninjured.[53]

Under cover of naval bombardment and heavy rain, the entire reconnaissance force had been landed by H plus 4 hours 35 minutes. By 0950 the Momote airstrip had been occupied, and the patrols began to fan out. The evidence brought in by the patrols indicated a considerable Japanese force in the area.

The rain let up shortly after 1400. When General MacArthur and Admiral Kinkaid came ashore, General MacArthur decorated the first man to land, Lieutenant Henshaw, with a Distinguished Service Cross. He commended General Chase: "You have all performed marvelously. Hold what you have taken, no matter against what odds. You have your teeth in him now – don't let go."[54]

As dusk fell Japanese riflemen and the American outposts began a firefight, whereupon the outposts were recalled. Groups of seven to 15 Japanese kept edging in, flinging grenades at the weapons that fired. The only way the Japanese could be seen was by the light of grenade explosions or when the attackers got close enough so that a cavalryman crouched in a fox hole could see them silhouetted against the sky. Some managed to infiltrate through the line and cut nearly all the telephone wires.

Nevertheless, communications were not greatly missed, since the only way to hold this small jungle area at night against an infiltrating enemy was for each man to stay in his fox hole and fire at anything that moved. Alertness was the best defense; on one occasion an officer sleeping in a hammock above his fox hole was killed by a Japanese soldier using a sword.

The heaviest attack was against the southern part of the perimeter. Some Japanese, using life preservers, swam in behind the American lines and landed. Another group broke through along the shore at the point of contact of the left (east) flank of E Troop and the right (south) flank of the field artillery unit, which was holding the beach. The Americans defended by staying in their foxholes and firing at every visible target and at everything that moved. After the infiltrators had been cleaned up the next morning, 66 Japanese dead were counted within the perimeter for an American loss of seven dead and 15 wounded.

At 0900 on March 2, a second echelon of six LCTs, six LSTs, three destroyers and two minesweepers arrived. The LSTs, besides carrying essential materiel, had embarked troops which included 1,300 combat and 1,000 constructional corps. On arrival off Hyane Harbor the LSTs were met by a barge from shore. The LCMs which they each were towing slipped tow and all proceeded into the harbor without incident. During the day six Japanese "Zero" fighters attacked two B-17 Flying Fortresses that were circling the destroyers, but the attacks were frustrated. An attempt to sweep Seeadler Harbor was abandoned after the minesweepers were opposed by fire from Japanese 3in guns as they were closing the harbor entrance. The LSTs began leaving the harbor late in the afternoon and were all clear and formed up by 1815.

Through the night of March 2–3 the enemy continued attempts at infiltration, but the perimeter was held with a total Japanese loss for the two days counted as 147 men.

By March 3, the Momote airstrip was completely cleared of the enemy. Their casualties of the night before, which must have been considerable, had apparently been taken back with them. But, another large attack was expected that night.

At approximately 0300 the next morning the enemy with a force of about 1,500 men stormed the right flank of the perimeter. Supported by mortar fire, the enemy troops made no attempt at surprise. They talked and sang as they moved automatic weapons up and charged the American positions. Those in front were cut down by the fire of the protective line, but more kept coming.

Three times during the fighting the cavalry, engineers, and Seabees withdrew to prevent being cut off by infiltrating Japanese. In this withdrawal movement they took the bolts from the machine guns and their ammunition, but left the guns in their defensive positions. From their new line of resistance they repulsed the Japanese attack and later, when the situation permitted, returned to their forward gun emplacements.

One gunner, Corporal Joseph E. Walkney, C Company, 592d EBSR, obeyed these instructions but with reluctance. He could not see the sense in leaving his gun in the face of an attack. The idea to go back to his gun obsessed him until he couldn't resist. Grabbing a bolt and some ammunition he cautiously crawled back to his old gun position. The rest of his crew tried to stop him but he paid no attention. Singlehandedly he put his weapon into action and waited for an appropriate target. It was a dark night and he could scarcely distinguish the swiftly advancing forms of Japanese infantry, but he could hear their blood-curdling screams.

There they were – right in front of him! His left forefinger squeezed the trigger and his gun sputtered a trail of hot lead. Corporal Walkney did not live long enough to see the damage he had caused or even to know that he alone had smashed the Japanese charge. At dawn he was found dead behind his gun. In front of it lay many dead Japanese sprawled in grotesque positions.

Undoubtedly he had wounded others who had very probably crawled from his line of fire only to be killed by someone else's bullet. Through his efforts there was no break through the American defense lines that night.[55]

That night heroism was not uncommon. Sergeant Troy McGill's squad of G Troop was defending a revetment about 35 yards in front of the main perimeter when the Japanese launched an attack. Soon, all but McGill and one other soldier had been killed. The sergeant ordered his companion to escape to the perimeter while he continued to defend the position. When his rifle eventually jammed, he used it as a club until he was killed himself.

Near dawn, the Seabees left their foxholes to reinforce the battered cavalrymen along the perimeter. As they advanced, they encountered a Japanese soldier inside the perimeter who had taken over a U.S. machine gun position. A few Seabees quickly dispatched the enemy and recovered the position, while their compatriots manned another gun position near the beach. The night engagements were a harrowing experience for everyone inside the perimeter.[56]

At daylight there were almost 200 dead enemy soldiers piled in front of the perimeter and it is believed that many more casualties had been dragged away.

But the fighting was by no means one sided for a checkup of the 592d personnel revealed one officer and three men killed and several wounded. Most of these casualties were received at one time when the engineers had taken a temporary refuge with some cavalrymen in a dugout. Suddenly two men with submachine guns appeared at each entrance to the dugout and sprayed the inside with .45-caliber slugs. Perhaps the gunners were Japanese. Perhaps American. The mystery remains, but the bullets killed all the same, sad to say.

An hour after daybreak, 50 Japanese shouting hysterically and singing "Deep in the Heart of Texas" again charged the perimeter. Not one survived.[57]

By dawn of March 4 it was clear that the enemy's best effort had been met and matched. During the day, over 750 enemy dead were counted against 61 Americans killed and 244 wounded.

Once Japanese resistance had been eliminated on Los Negros plans were made to send patrols to the Butjo Luo group and Bear Point on Manus, just west of Loniu Passage, to determine enemy strength and look for artillery positions. The island patrols, consisting of detachments from the 302d Cavalry Reconnaissance Troop plus artillery officers, left Salami on March 11. Bear Point, though not occupied by the enemy, had so poor a beach that artillery could not be landed. Butjo Mokau, the most northerly of the Butjo Luo group, offered good artillery positions and bore no signs of enemy occupation. In late afternoon F Troop, 7th Cavalry, occupied both islands of the group.

The Hauwei patrol ran into heavy resistance. One of the 592d Battalion's LCVs, coxswained by Technician Fourth Grade James C. Breslin, covered by a single PT boat, landed a reconnaissance patrol of some twenty-five cavalrymen. Aerial photographs of the island and information from friendly locals indicated the island was unoccupied. As the patrol moved ashore, Major Carter S. Vaden spotted a well-camouflaged bunker and threw two hand grenades into it. When they exploded, concealed Japanese mortars and machine guns commenced firing on the patrol. Other Japanese opened up on the PT boat and the lone LCV. The landing barge was armored and managed to turn the enemy fire but the PT boat's skipper had been wounded and had returned to its tender.

The patrol made a fighting withdrawal to the beach, supported by fire from the PT boat and the LCV. Sergeant Breslin, seeing the patrol in trouble on shore, headed his boat back to the beach and, although under continuous fire the full distance, he succeeded in picking up eight survivors, five of whom were wounded. Retracting from the beach he spotted another group up the beach were frantically signaling for his assistance. Again he pushed his craft to the shore and succeeded in picking up those men. He retracted a second time. Meanwhile, Japanese mortar fire was hitting all around the small boat which veered to the right and then to the left to throw the Japanese off their aim. Their luck ran out for a shell hit very closely and fragments penetrated the boat's armor. It began to sink. The crew during this time had managed to get life jackets on all the passengers, including the wounded. Sergeant Breslin, who was now seriously wounded, set the engines at full speed and went far out to sea and out of range of the enemy.

After three hours in the water, the 18 men, suffering from exposure to the sun and water, were picked up by a PT boat while a destroyer shelled Hauwei. Six men of the reconnaissance troop and two artillerymen had been killed, three were missing, and every survivor was wounded as well as burned. The LCM's crew – Sergeant Breslin, Sergeant Franklin Armstrong, Corporal Walter Wilson, and Private Henry Renfroe were highly praised by the cavalry commander for their heroic action. The next day a cavalry force, supported by three LVTs, one flak LCM, and two rocket LCVs, made a successful landing on the same beach and wiped out the entire Japanese garrison. Observers said that the rocket assault was the heaviest yet launched in a pre-landing barrage.[58]

Manus Island

Estimates of Japanese strength on Manus Island could not be made with any degree of certainty, but for planning purposes it was calculated that at least 2,700 Japanese were concentrated on the island. It was also ascertained that the Japanese would probably make a stand at or near Lorengau, which was known to be fortified. Plans called for a landing near Lugos, a mission and plantation area two and a half miles west of Lorengau. Two landing beaches were selected; one on the west side of the small Liei (Lihei) River was designated Yellow Beach 1; the other, on the east side, was designated Yellow Beach 2. Assault units were to be A and C Troops, 8th Cavalry, with A Troop landing on Yellow Beach 2 and C Troop on Yellow Beach 1. After both beaches were secured, the remainder of the 8th Cavalry was to go ashore, with the 7th Cavalry to follow and to be held in reserve for future ground operations. The 592d EBSR Group was to provide landing craft to take the assault troops ashore and the 2d ESB Support Battery, with the assistance of 592d EBSR craft, was to blast the beaches with rockets and gunfire prior to the landing. H Hour for the Yellow Beach landings was set for 0930.

At 0900, as the LVTs waited offshore for H Hour, 18 B-25s of Fifth Air Force swept in from Nadzab, New Guinea, and began bombing and strafing the Yellow beaches. For 25 minutes the B-25s worked over the beaches, then roared away as the first wave of LVTs headed in to shore. The rocket LCVPs, the combat LVT, and the LCM (flak) began hurling rockets into the landing area as the cargo LVTs neared the beaches. When the assault craft were 500 yards from shore all LVTs, the rocket LCVPs and the LCM (flak) began peppering the shore with machine-gun fire.

The first wave of LVTs hit the shore at 0937, followed one minute later by the second wave. At that moment a Japanese machine gun opened up from east of the landing beaches. Immediately the LVTs swept the area with machine-gun fire, the LCM (flak) turned its guns on the area, and two PT boats moved in. The Japanese position was quickly silenced.

Troops moved east along the coast and by afternoon were within half a mile of the airfield, encountering some enemy mortar and machine-gun fire. The airfield was captured during the night. Stubborn resistance was met, but assisted by shelling from destroyers and artillery the forces crossed to the east bank of the Lorengau River and on March 18 captured the town of Lorengau.

A second force moved inland from the beachhead to flank the airfield and town and cut off Japanese troops who might attempt to flee into the hills south of the

Lorengau area. Overcoming considerable opposition it moved in on the town from the southwest as the other force advanced from the west. The remnants of the enemy force retreated into the hills. By March 29 all major Japanese resistance had been overcome, with probably not more than 900 effective enemy troops remaining on the islands. At least 2,594 Japanese were known to have been killed in the fighting up to that time.[59]

While fighting was in progress on Manus Island, 5th Cavalry units were mopping up those Japanese forces still on Los Negros. Rocket barrages followed by cavalry assaults on the several beaches were very effective. Pityilu Koruniat and Ndrilo Islands north of Manus were seized without much struggle. In rapid succession invasions were made on the islands of Rambutyo and Pak on the southern fringes of the Admiralty group. In all of these operations the boatmen and cavalrymen worked in close cooperation. Detachments from the shore party participated in each assault to unload supplies, construct roads, evacuate casualties, and maintain the dump areas.

Opposition on all of these islands rapidly diminished until it was entirely eliminated. The campaign was not officially closed until May 18. The islands of the Admiralty Group were now in American hands. Although the official count of their dead did not include those removed for burial by the enemy, the total was 3,280 Japanese killed and 75 captured, which almost equaled the original intelligence estimate of the garrison's size. American losses were 326 killed, 1,189 wounded, and four missing.

Emirau – March 20, 1944

With the Admiralties captured, the Allies entered the final phase of the Bismarck Archipelago Campaign. MacArthur wanted Halsey to attack the Japanese base at Kavieng. The Admiral, however, argued that the Japanese withdrawal from the region diminished the importance of Kavieng and that a costly assault was unnecessary. In his view, the Allies could isolate Kavieng and establish a forward support base on a smaller island.

With the support of Admiral Nimitz, Halsey convinced the Joint Chiefs of Staff to change the final campaign objective from Kavieng to Emirau Island, midway between Kavieng and the Admiralties, that was thought to be lightly defended.

No opposition was expected on Emirau, but strong naval and air support was provided. A covering force under Rear Admiral Robert M. Griffin, consisting of the battleships *New Mexico*, *Mississippi*, *Idaho*, and *Tennessee*, accompanied by the escort carriers *Manila Bay* and *Natoma Bay*, and 15 destroyers, carried out part of the original Kavieng plan – the bombardment of Kavieng and the surrounding area. In all, some 1,079 rounds of 14in and 12,281 rounds of 5in ammunition were fired. The bombardment gave Rear Admiral Ryukichi Tamura, commander on Kavieng, the impression that the expected invasion by Allied forces was imminent and he gave the order to kill all the European prisoners currently held in Kavieng. At least 23 of them were executed in the Kavieng Wharf Massacre.[60]

The Attack Group was composed of one APA, the Coast Guard-manned *Callaway*, three LSDs, nine APDs, two ATs, and nine destroyers. On March 14 the newly created 4th Marine Regiment assaulted Emirau and found the island unoccupied. Emirau's islanders told the Marines that only a handful of Japanese had been on the island and they had left about two months before the landing. Intelligence indicated there were enemy fuel and ration dumps on Massau and a radio station on a nearby island.[61]

The landing on Emirau was said to have accomplished as much as a direct assault on Kavieng or Rabaul and it saved many American lives. With the occupation of Emirau the Allied noose around Rabaul was complete.

Summary

Allied tactics of guaranteeing naval, air, and artillery superiority to Allied troops in each operation were making the heavy proportion of Japanese casualties an expected result in the Pacific. In the Admiralties invasion, fire from destroyers kept the enemy under cover during the landing and Allied artillery gave the troopers an enormous advantage.

From the new base in the Admiralties, Allied air and naval forces could now launch surprise attacks on the Dutch New Guinea coast and threaten essential enemy sea lanes within a 1,500-mile radius including the Marianas, the east coast of Mindanao, and the southern limits of the Celebes Sea. Finally, with the neutralization of enemy positions flanking the Admiralties, these islands could become the largest staging area for the eventual Philippines invasion.[62]

CHAPTER 6
HELL ON ICE

ALEUTIAN CAMPAIGN, JUNE 1942–AUGUST 1943

Setting the Stage

Harking back to early 1942, Japanese forces controlled the Central Pacific and Southwest Pacific, occupied much of China's east coast and threatened northern Australia from bases in the South Solomon Islands and New Guinea. The destruction of U.S., British, and Dutch bases completed the first of two phases of Japan's overall strategic plan for control of the Pacific. The second phase was to "enlarge and secure" the strategic positions gained in the first phase and force a speedy end to the conflict by keeping the enemy always on the defensive.[1] This included invading the Aleutians, Midway, Fiji, Samoa, and New Caledonia. The way the islands are situated meant that they could provide mutual and overlapping support for each other using air or naval assets, thereby creating a protective shield for the Empire of the Rising Sun. The aim of the phase was to expand the Japanese perimeter in order to secure new gains, sever U.S.–Australian lines of communication, and provide a buffer against enemy attacks. The buffer would also mean that the Japanese would have early warning of enemy attacks. Japan saw the Aleutians as a strategic location capable of protecting Midway's flank from a northern attack.[2]

In the spring of 1942 the Japanese Imperial High Command, Imperial Army, and Admiral Isoroku Yamamoto developed a two-prong plan to occupy strategic points in the Western Aleutians as well as Midway Island on the western tip of the Hawaiian chain of islands. Yamamoto envisioned these two sites as anchors for a defensive perimeter in the north and central Pacific. By using the Aleutians and then Midway as bait, Yamamoto intended to lure the U.S. fleet, including the carriers he missed during the Pearl Harbor attack, from Pearl Harbor and annihilate it before new construction could replace the losses sustained on December 7, 1941.

Yamamoto's Midway invasion fleet included 176 warships and auxiliaries including four large and two small aircraft carriers. The Northern Area Fleet, commanded by Vice Admiral Boshiro Hosogaya, with a force of two small aircraft carriers (*Junyo* and *Ryujo*), five cruisers, 12 destroyers, six submarines, and four troop transports, along with supporting auxiliary ships, left the Kurile Islands to attack the Aleutians. By assigning two carriers to the Northern Area Fleet, Yamamoto's available carrier aircraft strength was reduced during the fight for Midway on June 4–5. Initially, the Aleutian gambit was only to be a diversion and not a sustained mission lasting through the winter.

The plan was that the Northern Area Fleet would first launch an air attack against Dutch Harbor, Alaska, then follow it with an amphibious attack on the island of Adak, 480 miles to the west. After destroying the reported American base on Adak (there was, in fact, no base on Adak), his troops were to return to their ships and become a reserve for two additional landings: the first on Kiska, 240 miles west of Adak, the other on the Aleutians' westernmost island, Attu, 180 miles from Kiska.

On June 3, 1942, as Japanese and U.S. aircraft fought for survival and dominance in the clear blue skies west of Midway Island, far to the north other Japanese carrier aircraft sought to destroy American forces in fog-bound Dutch Harbor.

However, as at Midway, the Americans knew a Japanese task force was in the area so the attack was no surprise, partly because the U.S. cryptographers had broken the Japanese Purple Code and were reading at least some of the Japanese Navy signals. However, they didn't know exactly when the attack would be launched.

At 0545 on June 3, 17 Japanese bombers and fighters reached Dutch Harbor. Several fighters swept over Fort Mears and the naval installations at Dutch Harbor in a strafing run. Ten minutes later the first of four waves of bombers attacked the area. The attackers ran into a hailstorm of antiaircraft fire, which shot down two planes. Four Japanese seaplanes, launched from two cruisers, flew over Umnak. P-40 Warhawk fighters from the 11th Squadron attacked them. Lieutenant John B. Murphy with Lieutenant Jacob W. Dixon immediately shot one plane down into the Umnak Pass at the end of the runway and another was damaged.

The attack destroyed a Navy barracks, killing 25 men, and damaged a Navy patrol plane. The Japanese lost three planes shot down, another seaplane crashed near its cruiser, and an unknown number crashed into the sea.

Two PBY-5A Catalina amphibians, one from VP-41 piloted by Lieutenant Junior Grade Jean Cusick and the other from VP-42 piloted by Lieutenant Junior Grade Lucius Campbell, were in the skies during the morning of June 3. At 1000 Cusick was on the return leg of his regular patrol, 200 miles from Dutch Harbor, when "Zeros" from *Junyo* attacked. Bullets knocked out Cusick's starboard engine, setting the wing on fire, destroyed the radio and wounded Cusick in his shoulder. The attack happened so quickly there was no time for Cusick's radioman to transmit a contact report. Helped by his copilot, Cusick safely landed the burning aircraft. Although the five-man crew survived the landing, Cusick died of his wounds and one crewman died from hypothermia in the icy water. The Japanese cruiser *Takao* picked up the three remaining crewmen.

Campbell had slightly better luck. He sighted five enemy vessels about 80 miles off Umnak Island and transmitted a warning to Dutch Harbor before diving into cloud cover. However, he was too late and fire from the "Zeros" hit his plane before it reached safety. Machine-gun and 20mm explosive cannon fire quickly reduced the PBY into a flying wreck. Bullets cut the rudder control cables, wounded one of Campbell's waist gunners, Aviation Machinist Mate Third Class B. T. Gillis, in the thigh, and stitched holes in the starboard gas tanks, setting the plane on fire. Despite flying a seriously crippled plane, Campbell successfully made it safely down, only to start sinking as water poured in through the shot-up fuselage. The radioman repaired his equipment, which had been damaged by gunfire, and sent out an SOS and another contact report. The Coast Guard cutter *Nemaha*, patrolling nearby as part of Admiral Theobald's early-warning line, picked up Campbell's SOS/contact report and headed in the direction of the signal. It was three days later, when *Nemaha* put into the Shumagin islands, that Campbell found out his two reports had been too garbled to read.[3]

June 4 brought rain and low visibility, hampering U.S. search efforts and delaying the follow-on Japanese attack. Only one wave was launched, consisting of a total of 15 Mitsubishi A5M Type 96 "Zeke" fighters (the carrier version of the Mitsubishi A6M "Zero") and 11 Aichi D3A "Val" dive-bombers from both carriers and six Nakajima B5N "Kate" torpedo planes, loaded with bombs, from *Ryujo*.

At 1800, ten of the fighters swept over the naval air station at Dutch Harbor in a strafing attack, followed by the 11 dive-bombers, whose bombs inflicted considerable damage upon fuel installations and upon *Northwestern*, a station ship that was being used as barracks. Ten minutes later three more bombers unsuccessfully attacked. Finally, at 1825, five more were overhead, killing four naval personnel as their bombs struck an antiaircraft emplacement.

Junyo's strike group did not know about a secret U.S. airstrip that was located on Umnak Island, and had selected a rally point at the west end of Unalaska Island. There, four dive-bombers and four fighters met eight P-40s of the 11th Squadron's forward echelon. The action occurred directly over Umnak, and because of their lack of advance information about the island's installations the Japanese lost two dive-bombers and two fighters, which were shot down by Lieutenants Chancellor, Dale, White, and J. J. Cape. Unfortunately, Cape in turn was shot down by a "Zeke" fighter, while one other P-40 crashed on the island – its pilot, Lieutenant Winfield E. McIntyre, walked unaided into camp. Antiaircraft fire claimed another bomber, and one more bomber failed to reach home apparently because its radio receiver, which had been knocked out in the action at Umnak, failed. All other planes got back to their carriers.

During the afternoon two B-17 and five B-24 bombers attacked the carrier force, and three more B-26s struck the cruiser *Takao*. No hits were scored and two bombers failed to return.

By the end of June 4, U.S. forces on Unalaska Island had lost 750,000 barrels of diesel oil; 43 had died at Dutch Harbor (33 of them Army personnel, the rest civilians); and about 50 were wounded. The Army Air Force had lost two P-40s in action, one B-17 that had been shot down, and one B-26 that was lost. Additionally, one B-26 was damaged by antiaircraft fire, and one was wrecked in landing. Finally, one LB-30 Consolidated four-engine bomber was wrecked at Kodiak. A total of 78 aircrew were lost in operations over the two days. However, for the defenders the most critical loss was that of radar equipment, for which spare parts were not available except at the cost of radar sets scheduled for delivery to South Pacific bases.

Nine of the Navy's patrolling PBYs were also lost to the "Zekes". After 40 hours of almost continuous operations in wretched weather, pilots and crews were at the limit of their endurance and only 14 of the original 23 planes remained operational. Japanese combat losses for the two days were about ten aircraft.[4]

Following his defeat at Midway, Yamamoto decided to continue the invasion of the western Aleutians. However, the attack on Adak was cancelled as faulty intelligence indicated it was occupied by a large U.S. force.

Japanese Kiska and Attu Occupations

On June 6 at 2227 the Japanese No. 3 Special Landing Party and 500 Marines went ashore at Kiska, capturing a ten-man U.S. Naval Weather Detachment (and a puppy named Explosion, who later escaped).[*][5] Two men, Aerographer's Mate Second Class W. M. Winfrey and Radioman Third Class M. L. Courtenay, were wounded in the attack on their radio shack. One man, Aerographer's Mate First Class William C. House managed to get away from the base. The Japanese believed that he had starved or frozen and soon forgot about him.

Fifty days later he surrendered, making the following statement to his captors:

> Is it 50-odd days? I kept track of the days at first but in the end I forgot. I wandered here and there around the shore of the island, and at times I slept at the foot of the mountain, covering myself with dry weeds, and at times slept in the caves near the shore. During the nights, the wind and the snow blew away the dry grass which I used to cover myself and I thought that I would die of cold … though I existed by eating grass which grew along the shore. I couldn't bear it any longer, so I surrendered. Please look at these skinny legs.

---

* The men were: Petty Officer In Charge, Aerographer's Mate First Class William C. "Doc" House; Pharmacist's Mate First Class Rolland L. Coffield; Radioman Second Class Harold E. Echols; Radioman Second Class Robert Christensen; Radioman Third Class M. L. Courtenay; Aerographer's Mate Second Class James L. Turner; Aerographer's Mate Second Class Walter M. "Whimpy" Winfrey; Seaman First Class Gilbert Palmer; Seaman First Class W. I. Gaffey; Seaman First Class John C. McCandless. Some references include an unnamed lieutenant, but no officers were part of the detachment. All people taken prisoner survived the war.

House weighed 80 pounds and his thigh was no larger than a child's arm.[6]

At 0300 on June 7, the 301st Independent Infantry Battalion landed in Holtz Bay, Attu. The island's population consisted of 45 indigenous Aleuts, and two Americans: Charles Foster Jones, a 60-year-old amateur radio operator and weather observer, and his 62-year-old wife, Etta Jones, a teacher and trained nurse. They both worked for the Bureau of Indian Affairs, and lived in the little village of Chichagof Harbor, which consisted of houses around the harbor where Jones had a radio.

The Joneses were not expecting the Japanese when some men debarked from a huge transport off Chichagof Harbor. Earlier, word had come that an American ship was due to evacuate all the people on Attu. A few soldiers or sailors would maintain the radio station and continue to send weather reports. The Joneses simply mistook the Japanese ship for this vessel.

A short time later Mrs. Jones heard a series of rifle shots echo through the valley. Almost immediately afterwards a woman rushed into her cabin and cried, "The Japs are here!" Mrs. Jones quickly looked out the window to see the Japanese pouring over the hills surrounding the valley, shooting as they came and yelling wildly. Some of the locals were wounded by the haphazard fire, but none seriously.

Even as bullets hit the cabin windows and walls, Mr. Jones was transmitting messages to Dutch Harbor. When the Japanese were almost in the house, he walked out and gave himself up. Right after Mr. Jones gave himself up an officer thrust himself into the cabin and confronted Mrs. Jones with a bayonet. He poked the bayonet against her body and asked in English, "How many are here?"

"Two," Etta replied. "How many have you?"

"Two thousand," was the answer.

Early the next morning Mr. Jones was taken to the Japanese commander for further questioning. That was the last time Mrs. Jones saw her husband alive. She never learnt how he was killed.

Mrs. Jones and the remaining Aleut population were at first held prisoner and later sent to Japan along with the Americans captured on Kiska.[7] After securing both islands without loss the Japanese began setting up defensive positions and building an airstrip on Kiska.

Although Midway was a great victory for the U.S., Admiral Nimitz had lost two of his four carriers. On June 11, he decided not to risk them against the Japanese carriers and land-based planes flying from Attu and Kiska. Therefore, initially the only assets the U.S. had available to fight back with were Army Air Force bombers, Navy Catalinas and Navy warships. These quickly went on the offensive, and on June 11 the 11th Air Force bombers struck for the first time. Five B-24s and five B-17s hit Kiska harbor installations and shipping. Low-altitude runs scored near misses on two cruisers and a destroyer at the cost of one B-24 shot down. Four Japanese fighters chased the other B-24s back to Umnak where U.S. fighters drove them off.

The next day shipping in Kiska Harbor was bombed by six B-17s and one B-24, which damaged a heavy cruiser and a destroyer. Despite the lack of significant results, operations continued unabated. So far most of the losses had been to enemy action. However, on June 19 weather claimed a bomber and two of its crew. The pilot Major Ira F. Wintermute related what happened.[8]

On our first mission we started in a flight of three B-24 Liberators. The weather wasn't bad, but halfway to Kiska we ran into a solid front of fog. We couldn't see anything and felt hemmed in by some evil genie.

I asked Lieutenant H. T. "Peewee" Freeman, navigator, what course to fly and he gave me a heading. My copilot, R. A. Ryden, kept saying, "We'll make it," and told the crew members to quit worrying. I asked the radio operator to contact something – anything – and said to the crew, "We're lost."

There was a dead silence. The crew sat back on the flight deck and prayed silently. I did some praying myself, and kept hoping. We were pretty young; I was 27 and probably the oldest. We didn't have much fuel and flying-time left. Ryden and I talked about how to land in the ocean.

Knowing we couldn't make it back to Kiska, we dropped our bombs to lighten our load and make our fuel last longer. Three hours later, we broke through the fog but could see nothing but ocean. There was no way of knowing whether we were north or south of the island chain. Hour after hour, we flew in wide circles trying to catch a radio signal or sight of land. Nothing!

We had been flying 14 hours and were exhausted. It was time to ditch. "Peewee" gathered maps, Ryden removed the compass in case we needed to do some ocean navigating and others gathered drinking water. The eight of us gathered on the flight deck near the emergency-exit hatch and started to nose down. The plane plowed into the sea and up-ended on its nose. From then on every man was on his own!

Water poured over the top of the plane. It was pitch-dark under the water as I unbuckled my safety belt and started for the hatch. The next thing I knew, I was on top of the water. I swam to a wing and thought I saw all of the crew swimming. Our assistant engineer, Staff Sgt. R. P. Hicks released and inflated our two life rafts. In the last minute before the plane went down, we counted heads. Only six! Two were gone.

We were on those two rafts, tied together, for 18 hours without food or water. Soaking wet, we huddled together to escape the bite of the freezing wind that whipped across the waves. Most of us were sick either because of the motion or from swallowing salt water. No one slept – just sat there like dead men.

The next morning, we brought out paddles and started to push toward what we thought was land. Suddenly, someone yelled, "I hear a plane!" We screamed, "Why don't they see us?" or "Please God, see us!" We got out some flares and started shooting them like mad, cussing when some didn't go off. Finally the plane, a big Navy consolidated patrol boat headed our way. We thanked God for the PBY and cheered the Navy.

When my crew finally did find clear enough weather to get over Kiska to bomb, we found it was definitely a game for keeps. After unloading our eggs and starting back, we were generally attacked by "Zeke" fighters who would rather kill us than save their own necks. They had no regard at all for their own lives.

Air strikes alone weren't going to dislodge the Japanese. The bombers and Catalinas had to fly long distances from their bases and missions were often aborted due to heavy fog and unpredictable bad weather. The same weather plagued U.S. Navy warships trying to shell Japanese bases. The weather, terrain, and long distances made the Aleutians one of the worst places in the world to fight a war.

Aleutian Islands: Geography, Terrain, and Weather

The Aleutians stretch 1,200 miles from mainland Alaska to Attu, the westernmost American island, and encompass approximately 120 islands. In a straight-line measurement, Dutch Harbor on Unalaska Island lies roughly 675 miles east of Kiska, and 850 east of Attu, but it's rare to travel in a straight line due to weather and navigation hazards.

The islands are volcanic in origin, uniformly rocky and barren, with precipitous mountains and little vegetation. The mountains are conical in shape and covered with volcanic ash which resembles cinders. There are no trees on the islands, except a few stunted spruces at Dutch Harbor, and no brush. The lowlands are blanketed with muskeg (a grassy bog), which can be up to 3ft thick. This growth forms a spongy carpet which makes walking difficult and driving mechanical vehicles a nightmare. Below the muskeg is volcanic ash which has been finely ground and water soaked until it has the consistency of slime. In many places water is trapped in ponds under the muskeg. The bogs are deep enough to swallow up a man.

Throughout the Aleutians jagged shorelines and submerged rock formations render sea navigation hazardous. Conditions are least unfavorable in the eastern islands. Unalaska has two comparatively good anchorages, Dutch Harbor and Captain's Bay, while Umnak has three, of which Nikolski Bay on the west coast is the most important. Farther west, protected anchorages are scarce: Atka has two fair harbors; Adak has three small bays on the west coast; and Amchitka offers one small bay on the east coast. Neither Kiska nor Attu possesses a harbor that is entirely suitable for larger vessels. Kiska has a broad, moderately deep indentation on the eastern shore, which is protected by Little Kiska Island, lying across its mouth. Attu has four less adequately guarded bays – Holtz, Chichagof, and Sarana on the northeast side, and Massacre Bay on the southeast.

Weather conditions become progressively worse as the western end of the island chain is approached. On Attu five or six days a week are likely to be rainy, and there are rarely more than ten clear days a year. The rest of the time, for the most part, even if rain is not falling, fog of varying density covers the islands. The weather is highly localized, however, and areas of high visibility will often be found within 20 miles of fog concentration.

Dense cloud cover hovers over the Aleutians 90 percent of the time in summer and 50 percent in winter. Between 60 and 70 percent of the time the ceiling is below 1,000ft, with only two to four clear days per month during June to August. In the winter months rain, sleet, and snow, often in combination, make the islands one of the most uncomfortable regions of the world.

Throughout the islands annual rainfall averages 40 to 50in, spread over most of the year. Precipitation is rarely heavy, but reaches a peak in fall and early winter. On average it rains 260 days a year.

A special hazard to sea and air navigation are the "williwaws" (gusts of wind) that sweep down from the mountainous area with great force, sometimes travelling in excess of 100mph. The columns of spray and mist resulting from the williwaws frequently resemble huge waterfalls. Winds generally are gusty because the steep mountain slopes deflect the air currents. In the Aleutians, curiously enough, winds and fogs may persist together for many days at a time.

The warm currents of the Pacific Ocean meet the icy waters of the Bering Sea at the Aleutian chain, causing many of the unique weather conditions in the region. Average temperatures for the summer can range from 40 to 60 degrees Fahrenheit (4.5 to 15.5 degrees Centigrade), with 20 to 40 degree Fahrenheit (-6.5 to 4.5 degrees Centigrade) temperatures in the winter. The wind chill factor, however, can be a major casualty producer at any time of year.

While the Aleutian weather was a constant impediment to the military operations of the United States and Japan alike, the Japanese enjoyed one advantage – weather in the northern hemisphere moves from west to east with the result that the Japanese always knew in advance what conditions were likely to prevail in the islands.[9] However, this advantage did them little good in their defense of the islands.

The U.S. Counteroffensive

Adak

While Army Air Force bombers and Navy Catalinas engaged in an unrelenting air campaign, plans were made to construct bases on Adak, which was within 250 miles of Amchitka Island, almost 300 miles from Attu and 246 miles east of Kiska.

Adak D-Day was slated for August 30 and the landing site would be Kuluk Bay. The expeditionary force was composed of an odd assortment including transports, a few old freighters, a fishing scow or two, several converted barges, a side-wheel paddle river boat, and a little tug hauling a four-masted schooner loaded with gas. This ramshackle collection would transport the 4,500-strong assault force from the 4th Infantry Division.[10]

However, before the landings could take place a reconnaissance mission was needed to locate suitable sites for an airstrip. On August 28 the U.S. submarines USS *Triton* and USS *Tuna* surfaced four miles due east of Kuluk Bay and a 37-man U.S. Army intelligence-gathering unit, led by Colonel Lawrence Varsi Castner, disembarked. The unit was known as "The Alaska Scouts," or more affectionately as "Castner's Cutthroats," and it was a unit unlike any in the U.S. Army since Teddy Roosevelt's Rough Riders in the Spanish American War. Led by Castner, an Army intelligence officer, the band was created and organized to give the Army a unit that was fully functional with only minimal outfitting. Castner chose men with the skills to flourish in the tough conditions of the Alaskan wilderness, including native Aleuts and Eskimos, sourdough prospectors, hunters, trappers, and fishermen. Their backgrounds in survival and hunting made them ideal scouts. Hard and dangerous men, their names were often in keeping with their unit's nickname – names such as "Bad Whiskey Red," "Aleut Pete," and "Waterbucket Ben."

Thirty-six hours before the scheduled landings on August 30, Navy Aerographer's Mate Paul E. "The Black Irishman" Carrigan and Aviation Third Class Radioman Red Cochrane paddled a rubber raft ashore at Kuluk Bay. A couple hundred pounds of equipment, a BAR, and a Thompson submachine gun were dropped from a PBY and the men were given orders to send weather and surf observations every three hours.

Carrigan recalled what happened when his commanding officer, Lieutenant John F. Tatom, suggested they take weapons:

"You'd best be armed, just in case," Tatom answered.

"But there aren't any Nips on Adak are there?"

"We don't believe there are at this moment but we have evidence they have visited the island several times. Colonels Castner and Verbeek with three dozen of their Alaska Scouts went ashore tonight from two submarines. They are combing the island to make certain."

I'd seen Colonel Lawrence v. Castner, Lieutenant Colonel William J. Verbeck, and a few of their deadly efficient looking native Alaska commandos at the Dutch Harbor weather office several times during the past spring and summer. They had a reputation of slitting throats first, hence their nickname: Castner's Cutthroats. The thought of them sneaking around silently in the night and stumbling upon me sent a chill up my spine. I wanted to ensure there would be no case of mistaken identity in the coming operation.

"Does Colonel Castner know that the radioman and I will to be on the island?"

"Not at present," Tatom admitted, "but I'll have the PBY pilot try and locate Castner and let him know."

My skepticism must have showed because Tatom was quick to add, "You'll be there alone only one night if everything goes as planned. There's nothing to worry about."[11]

During the night of August 29–30, Carrigan and Cochrane huddled in a cold, soggy tent, their only food unheated field rations. Carrigan picks up the story of what happened on D-Day:

> The wind continued to mount in fury and howl forlornly. On one observation I recorded a southeasterly wind speed of 52 knots. It was a miserable night without sleep but fortunately our tent didn't blow down.
>
> Instead of breaking, dawn of August 30, 1942 was more a graying of black. We stepped outside into horizontally slashing rain. Kuluk Bay's waters were whipped into a white froth. At six second intervals, swells that I estimated to be seven feet high were crashing with a roar onto the landing beach. I took an observation and we transmitted. Afterward, we relaxed, certain that the occupation of Adak would be postponed because of surf and weather conditions.

This was not to be the case, though. The official U.S. Army and Army Air Force publications[12] report the landing as unopposed by Japanese forces, which is true. However, that did not mean that the landings were not costly in terms of men and material. Carrigan was there and recalled the experience:

> Because of the high surf and wind conditions this was predictably and rapidly turning into a disaster. Even if the monstrous surf line had been parallel to shore the situation would have been dangerously difficult for landing craft coxswains to maintain control throughout the three steps of beaching, unloading, and backing off. With these breakers crashing onto the beach at a forty-five degree angle it was virtually impossible for coxswains to complete all three phases without mishap.
>
> Landing craft were broaching one after another. Some were swamping in the high surf and drifting ashore only to be rammed by others that did not have time to stop or back off. One barge that had disgorged its load of men and backed off safely was hit by a fully loaded landing craft on the way in. This empty craft sank. Red and I saw several others sink as well. One landing craft grounded fifty yards farther offshore than the others when it ran upon a submerged object. When I looked in that direction later this craft was no longer there. That afternoon a soldier told Red that this

landing craft also sank. Its boatload of soldiers was forced to jump from the doomed craft into water far over their heads. Some of these men were rescued by landing craft but many others went under with their hundred pound combat packs and drowned.*

Wrecked landing craft washed ashore broadside in the crashing surf. Landing barges carrying supplies and equipment started coming in and this added to the confusion as many got into trouble and either wrecked or sank. Red and I helped two soldiers ashore. Both were crawling weakly on hands and knees in the battering surf. Beyond, I could see several soldiers lying face down on the beach. I could not tell if they were in a state of exhaustion or had drowned. Other soldiers were being given artificial respiration. Through the mass of humanity jammed on the narrow shore it appeared that these scenes were repeated at intervals along the entire beach.

I have no idea what the total casualty figure was on the unopposed landing at Kuluk Bay, Adak on August 30, 1942 but it must have been considerable. In materiel alone the cost was high. At the time, I heard that twenty-three of the first twenty-five landing craft broached and either wrecked or sank. Although I didn't count the smashed, swamped hulks littering the shore I had no reason to doubt this figure. This avoidable tragedy was never made public.

That is hardly surprising because even on Adak the official stance seemed to be that it never happened. Whether a candid report exists in some dusty file would be conjecture. Volcanic peaks were not the only things shrouded in Aleutian fogs and mists.

What was the point in having me send accurate weather reports if they were to be totally ignored? Why wasn't the landing delayed until the surf subsided? What was the great hurry? It had all been so senseless and costly. The more I thought about these nagging questions the sadder I felt and the madder I got at Tatom.[13]

No casualty figures were released for losses suffered by those units forced to come ashore on that rocky beach in high surf.

---

*   Amphibious landing troops could not wear a standard life jacket or inflatable rubber vest because of the sheer bulk of their combat packs. Instead, they wore a small life belt. The ones in use during World War II provided some buoyancy in chest-high water, but could not keep a man and 100 pounds of equipment afloat for very long especially if he was injured or weakened rapidly because of his struggles.

The objective of securing Adak was to build an airfield. However, due to the mountainous terrain no acceptable site was available to build a landing strip. Instead, Castner's Cutthroats dammed a lagoon, drained it, and used the sandy bottom floor as a temporary landing strip. Later, Army engineers improved the area and, in a herculean effort, completed the airfield by September 12. Two days later the first B-24s hit Kiska from their new base.[14]

The next step was Amchitka, located less than 300 miles from Attu and roughly 74 miles southeast of Kiska.

Amchitka

Autumn had passed before naval and ground forces could be gathered for the landing. Final approval wasn't granted by the U.S. Joint Chiefs of Staff until December 18. The operation was set for January 5, 1943, but, having learned from previous operations not to depend on the weather cooperating, this time the final date would be determined by weather conditions. On December 18, a Navy PBY landed Lieutenant Colonel Alvin E. Hebert and a small party of Army engineers on Amchitka. After a two-day survey, the engineers reported that a steel-mat fighter strip could be constructed in two to three weeks. Sites also existed for a main airfield with some dispersion on which a runway 200ft by 5,000ft could be built in three to four months.

For this operation the transport group consisted of the Coast Guard-manned USS *Arthur Middleton* (commanded by Captain Paul K. Perry, USCG), the Army transport S.S. *Delarof*, the merchant ship S.S. *Lakona*, and the cargo vessel *Vega* (Commander Arthur C. Smith). Protection was provided by the destroyers *Dewey* (Lieutenant Commander Joseph P. Canty), *Gillespie* (Commander Chester L. Clement), and *Kalk* (Commander Charles T. Singleton, Jr.). Rear Admiral John W. Reeves, Jr., commanded the Alaskan Sector Escort Group of one gunboat, one minesweeper, and three fast minesweepers, while Rear Admiral McMorris commanded the Strike Group with the cruisers *Indianapolis*, *Raleigh*, and *Detroit*, and four destroyers. Aboard *Arthur Middleton* were 102 officers and 2,060 enlisted men from the 813th Engineer Aviation Battalion and a detachment of the 896th Company under Brigadier General Lloyd E. Jones.

January 12 dawned cold and bleak as the task force approached the deep, U-shaped Constantine Harbor on Amchitka's southeast coast. In a now well-established pattern of amphibious operations, 36ft Higgins boats and 50ft tank lighters were lowered from transports, and loaded with troops and equipment before heading toward a shallow, rocky beach in a biting

30F degrees. In the vanguard was the boat group commander Lieutenant Commander R. E. Smith, USCG, who had been formerly stationed in the area, and who was among the first to set foot on the island.

The weather stayed calm all morning. However, even in the relatively good conditions coxswains had trouble backing off the rocky beach without damaging their boats. Then in the early afternoon a williwaw struck. High winds and heavy seas smashed landing craft onto the rocks. To save the boats men put on rubber suits and waded out to their armpits in the harbor, unloaded barges and passed supplies hand over hand to keep them above water and the scum of oil from the ships.

They worked steadily as the wind increased to gale velocity before nightfall. Despite every precaution, most of the landing barges had been wrecked during the storm. At 2307 of that first day, *Arthur Middleton* went aground on her port quarter, although her boats continued unloading operations in the harbor.

USS *Worden*, one of the Strike Force destroyers, wasn't so fortunate. A strong current swept her onto a pinnacle, tearing a hole in her hull beneath the engine room and causing a complete loss of power. Her sister destroyer *Dewey* passed a towline and attempted to tow her free, but the cable parted, and the heavy seas began moving the powerless *Worden* inexorably toward the rocky shore. The destroyer broached and began breaking up in the surf. Commander William G. Pogue, *Worden*'s commanding officer, ordered the ship to be abandoned. However, as he was directing that effort, a heavy wave broke over the ship and he was swept overboard into the wintry seas.

When the distress call came from *Worden*, a Coast Guard landing boat, under Lieutenant Commander Smith, rushed to the scene with instructions to investigate the wreck and render every possible assistance. The Coast Guardsmen from *Arthur Middleton* pulled their boats near to the vessel and passed lines aboard to enable the men to slide down into the rescue craft. All this was accomplished amid mountainous seas that threatened to swamp the landing boats in each successive wave. On their way back to *Arthur Middleton*, a Coast Guard boat picked up two more survivors, who were struggling against death in the freezing water. Pogue was among the fortunate ones, and he was hauled, unconscious, out of the sea. The Coast Guard and Navy crews saved six officers and 169 men. Fourteen others drowned. *Worden* was a total loss.[*]

---

[*]   For their bold rescue work, five Coast Guardsmen were awarded the Navy and Marine Corps Medal. The recipients were Ensign J. R. Wollenberg, Coxswains Russell M. Speck, Robert H. Gross, and George W. Prichard, and Signalman John S. Vandeleur.

The next day a blizzard started that lasted two weeks and racked the island with snow, sleet, and biting winds. When it finally subsided, a Japanese scout plane from Kiska located the American beachhead on Amchitka. Having located the Americans, "Rufes" ("Zero" fighters mounted with floats) bombed and strafed the burgeoning base as engineers desperately continued work on an airfield. Despite the raids, by February 18, the new fighter strip was ready, and with P-40 Warhawks and P-38 Lightnings now in the air overhead there was little danger from enemy bombers. It had been an amazing feat of skill and endurance for both the fleet of landing craft and the 2,100 troops who had planted another base on a flat, muddy, uninhabited island.[15]

Now that the necessary bases were complete it was time to tackle the Japanese on Attu and Kiska. The easy part was over.

Attu and Kiska Operations Prelude

As American forces advanced westward, and particularly taking into account the air base on Adak, the Imperial Headquarters was forced to consider the possibility this was a prelude to an invasion of northern Japan. This changed Japan's initial plans from a short-term engagement to an order to hold the islands at all costs. To implement this new strategy, reinforcements consisting of infantry, engineers, and antiaircraft units, were sent to the Aleutians. Determined to stop Japanese convoys en route to the Aleutians, an American naval task force, led by the heavy cruiser *Salt Lake City*, arrived off the Soviet Union's Komandorski Islands west of Attu. On March 26, the ships' radar picked up a column of eight Japanese warships and two transports carrying supplies for the Aleutians. Both sides opened fire simultaneously, but although each scored hits, the battle ended inconclusively when both forces withdrew. After the battle no further attempt to reinforce or resupply the Aleutians was made using surface vessels. From then until the American invasion in May only submarines succeeded in delivering a trickle of materiel to Attu and Kiska.[16]

Kiska, which had the only operational airfield and a better harbor, was more important militarily than Attu. U.S. intelligence estimated there were 9,000 Japanese on the island. To take it the U.S. would need at least a 25,000-man reinforced infantry division and the necessary shipping to support it. However, because of operations in the Pacific and Europe the necessary forces weren't available, so it was decided that Attu would be invaded instead. Initially, U.S. intelligence estimated Japanese strength on Attu to be between 500 and 1,500 – mostly antiaircraft personnel and labor troops who were probably equipped as infantry. In fact, the actual number was 2,100, the majority of whom were seasoned combat troops.

Attu – Operation *Landgrab*

Attu is a rugged mountainous island, about 20 by 35 miles, with sharp crags and snow-summited peaks, reaching more than 3,000ft into the stormy sky. Its valleys are covered with moss-grown tundra through which the advancing troops sank knee-deep into the muddy marsh beneath. The coast is deeply indented but safe landing is rendered difficult by the severe winds and storms that prevail. Cold, damp, foggy weather, combined with ice, rain, and snow, add to the desolate character of the island. It is unlike any environment the U.S. Army had fought in before.

The 7th Infantry Division, stationed near Fort Ord, California, was the unit detailed to recapture Attu. Trained as a motorized force and scheduled for duty in the deserts of North Africa, the 7th was reported to be in a high state of readiness, and because of its location near the coast, it could readily undergo the amphibious training required for its new mission. Along with 7th Division troops, the 1st Combat Intelligence Platoon (Provisional) Alaskan Scouts were also assigned to the operation.

On April 23 the assault force was embarked on six transports and supported by a naval task force of three battleships, three cruisers, three light cruisers, 19 destroyers, five submarines, and assorted tenders, oilers, and minesweepers. The task force also included the escort carrier USS *Nassau* with Composite Squadron VC-21, with 30 officer pilots, one enlisted pilot, 1 Air Combat Intelligence officer, and 27 enlisted men. VC 21was the main air support for the Army troops. VC-21 had 26 F4F-4 Wildcat fighters in two squadrons – VF-3 and VF-22. The U.S. Marine Corps "Ready Teddy" VMO-155, a three-plane Grumman F4F-3P Wildcat detachment, was also on board to provide photo reconnaissance capability for the Navy's air wing. The total complement of planes was 26 F4F-4s, three F4F-3Ps, and one Curtis SOC-3A scout observation biplane. *Nassau* was the first escort carrier to sail in Alaskan waters, the first to operate aircraft in that area, and the first escort carrier to participate in an amphibious landing.

Several VF-3 pilots, such as 26-year-olds Lieutenant Junior Grade John P. "Johnny" Altemus and Francis R. "Cash" Register, were combat veterans fresh from the bloody air war over Guadalcanal. Both men had six confirmed aerial kills. After fighting in tropical skies Alaska's rough seas, thick fog and strong winds came as a huge shock to the pilots, and made for abysmal flying conditions, especially during ground-support missions.[17]

D-Day was scheduled for May 8 with H-Hour set for 0740. However, it was no surprise that due to the weather conditions the landings were delayed until May 11.*

The tactical plan for *Landgrab* was to force the Japanese Army into the Chichagof area and divide it into two segments. The U.S. troops were, therefore, split into two forces. The larger Southern Force, consisting of the Regimental Landing Group 17 (less Battalion Combat Team 17-1) with Battalion Combat Team 32-2 attached was to land on Yellow Beach and Blue Beach in Massacre Bay and attack and destroy the enemy in the Holtz Bay and Chichagof Harbor area over a ridge to the east. One platoon of the 7th Reconnaissance Troop was to land at Alexai Point (Rainbow Beach) on the southwestern part of Massacre Bay. The Northern Force, consisting of the remainder of Combat Team 17-1, was to land in the west arm of Holtz Bay (Red Beach). Subsidiary landings were to be made by parties of Alaskan Scouts and reconnaissance troops – including the one at Alexai Point (Rainbow Beach), east of Massacre Bay. The Alaskan Scouts, sailing independently of the main convoy, were to be landed by the submarines *Narwhal* and *Nautilus* on the north coast (Scarlet Beach).

It was estimated that the reoccupation of Attu would take just three days. Food and ammunition loads were calculated for that period of time. This would allow enough time for supply dumps to be established on the beachhead.

The Japanese defense was based on daring, deception, and the excellent use of terrain to tempt a landing on the south side of the island. They established their defenses in two sectors: Holtz Bay and Chichagof Harbor. At Holtz Bay, four successive defensive positions were well prepared with a fifth final position at the valley head. Each arm of Holtz Bay was defended by a four-gun antiaircraft battery. Holtz-Massacre Pass (later to be named Jarmin Pass) leading into Massacre Valley was covered by a mountain artillery battery. Within Massacre Valley a weak yielding defensive center

---

* Before sailing much of the individual equipment was issued. Each soldier received Blucher boots with two pairs of insoles, an Alaskan field jacket, an overcoat, wool underwear and socks, a rucksack, a sleeping bag with the cover (not waterproof), snow glasses and a two-piece rain suit very similar to that issued today. The 7th Division staff turned back the Kersey-lined Alaskan trousers. The Blucher boots were not waterproof and wore out quickly in the harsh environment of the Aleutians. Most of the frostbite and trench foot suffered could be attributed to this inadequate footgear.

would allow a U.S. force to build up and lure them into a fire trap at Jarmin Pass.

Chichagof Harbor had substantial beach defenses including a four-gun antiaircraft battery, but the key defensive effort for the harbor was based on well-prepared defensive positions in Massacre Valley on Cold and Black Mountains and the fire trap at Jarmin Pass. Sarana Valley defenses were established on Gilbert Ridge, Point A, Sarana Nose and Buffalo Ridge.

Major final defensive positions were emplaced on Prendergast and Fish Hook Ridges. These were built on some of the most rugged terrain to be found on Attu and the camouflage of all positions was outstanding.

Unlike on the Gavutu and Florida Islands (see Chapter 2: First Strike), the Japanese tactics were to draw the U.S. forces in from the beach, away from their supplies, and engage them from the high ground surrounding the valley with the aim of annihilating them or forcing their withdrawal. The Japanese assumed the U.S. forces would land at Massacre Bay, hence the successive defense of Holtz Bay throughout the valley and in the Sarana Valley, which is constricted by Lake Nicholas. Japanese planners knew vehicles, supplies, and artillery would not get off the beaches in large numbers because of the tundra and mountainous terrain.

Weapons, ammunition, and equipment were available to the Japanese in ample quantities and supply caches were established to prevent reliance on tenuous supply lines across the mountains and tundra. Most importantly, the Japanese troops were properly dressed and equipped mountain troops, trained in north Manchukuo. Having trained in such an environment and being acclimatized to those conditions, the mountain troops could lay motionless for hours in camouflage ready to ambush U.S. soldiers as they passed.[18]

May 11 – D-Day

First ashore on May 11 were the Alaskan Scout teams from the 7th Scout Company. Captain William H. Willoughby led 244 men off submarines *Narwhal* and *Nautilus* toward Scarlet Beach at 0300. First Sergeant Fenton Hamlin, a member of the team, tells the story:

The company got aboard the submarines … at Dutch Harbor on April 28 and started rehearsing our debarkation. The crews of the two submarines had worked with Marine Corps raider battalions and they completely revised our methods, cutting the time required right in two. Their system consisted of inflating the rubber boats and shoving them onto the after-deck. Then, with the men sitting in them, the submarine was partially submerged, leaving the rubber boats floating free.

It was bitter cold at 0100 on May 11. We were about four thousand yards off Attu as the black water gurgled around the submarines, and the rubber boats floated free. The men began to paddle and the little boats moved silently through the foggy night toward Scarlet Beach (Austin Cove).

It was a long way in, and the men were tired when they hit the beach. There was no resistance. The two sections made contact and moved inland, as a signal light blinked out to the submarines that the landing was complete.[19]

It took the men two hours to reach the shore through 5,000 yards of thick fog, and the temperature dropped sharply from 27 degrees Farenheit to 20 degrees as the wind rose. Once ashore the force faced steep, approximately 300ft cliffs that had to be scaled to get off the beach.

The Japanese had expected no one to land in a place such as Scarlet Beach. One of Willoughby's men commented, "It was easy to get completely turned around in the thick, moving mist that made everything vague." The Scouts did eventually make a wrong turn in the fog, which cost them valuable time getting over the mountains to their objective.

At noon, the second wave consisting of 165 men of the 7th Division's Reconnaissance Troop (less one platoon) landed at Scarlet Beach and moved to join the scout company. Upon linkup, the two units, which constituted a provisional battalion, were to occupy the head of the valley where a pass gave access to one of the valleys leading back from Holtz Bay.

As the provisional battalion left Scarlet Beach, fighters from the carrier USS *Nassau* mistakenly strafed and sank all the rubber boats used by the battalion to come ashore. Now they had no choice but to complete the 4,000ft climb to their objective. Beyond it was the worst terrain on the island. Captain Willoughby's men lacked communication with the other U.S. forces and possessed only one and a half days' rations. It was a formidable task.

The job of the 25-man scout team under Captain Thompson on board the Navy transport USS *J. Franklin Bell* was to reconnoiter Red Beach as a landing spot for the Northern Force troops. The beach was only three miles from the main Japanese camp at Holtz Bay. At 0830 the team left aboard LCVPs.

About 1,000 yards from shore, they climbed over the side into whale boats and rowed ashore under the cover of heavy fog.

Al Brattain was at Red Beach.

> We were sent in first to reconnoiter a suitable spot to land the main force. The fog was thick, visibility under 100 yards. Given a heading by the destroyer, we rowed to the beach. I was in the bow of the first boat to touch land. About 100 foot inland was a low bank, maybe two feet high. I reached it as fast as I could just in case there was a Japanese soldier waiting to dispute my right to be there.

At Yellow and Blue beaches, another group of Castner's Cutthroats would go in ahead of the Southern Force and the Scout battalion. The beaches were small and surrounded by steep, jagged cliffs, and the Army wasn't sure if a landing was even possible.

The unopposed landing of the 2d and 3d Battalion Combat Teams of the 17th Regiment on the beaches, which were approximately six miles south of Chichagof Harbor, was delayed until 1620 because of dense fog and high seas.

The minelayer USS *Pruitt* used its radar to guide approximately 100 landing craft toward Yellow and Blue beaches. The fog was as thick as soup, with the cloud ceiling at 1,500ft; visibility was down to 500 to 600 yards. At 100 yards from shore, all 100 landing craft came together in a concentrated mass of confusion. In the resulting chaos, the second wave landed first followed by the simultaneous landing of the first and third waves of the Southern Force. During the confusion, 11 crowded landing craft capsized, losing men and equipment overboard.

Company F, 32d Infantry landed with the first wave at Yellow Beach rather than at Cascoe Cove as planned. The company had to advance southwest on foot to their allocated area of operations. They soon found the tundra-covered ground mushy under foot, causing their pace to be slow and fatiguing. A pause for rest had to be taken every 300 to 400 yards.

The mission was clear. Lieutenant Paulson had the 1st Platoon of F Company, 17th Infantry reinforced with a section of light machine guns and a 60mm mortar. He later recalled his orders.

Land in Massacre Bay; move to the right. Protect the right flank of the battalion, block the pass through the mountains from Sarana Bay; move up Sarana Valley, and join the battalion in the vicinity of Clevesy Pass…

A little after 1600 on the afternoon of the 11th, it was, when we took off to the right and headed up into the mountains. The ground was new to us; the tundra and the holes and the snow gave us a bad time all the way. Some of the slopes were so straight up that we used ropes to haul our guns over them. We traveled all night the first night and got over onto the Sarana side early the next morning. God, we were tired!

Getting the artillery ashore and set up proved to be tough, as Staff Sergeant Stanley E. West, Staff Sergeant Allen W. Robbins, and Corporal Howard B. Campbell of Battery C, 48th Field Artillery Battalion told later:

The advance party with Lieutenant James West were already moving up Massacre Valley into the fog, when the barges with the big 105mm rifles and the heavy cats crunched against the sand of the beach. The motors roared and the cats backed the big guns out of the barges onto Attu.

In a few minutes they had turned around and were struggling over the steep bank up from the beach. Three of the guns had landed, and one was still coming in from the ship. The battery was busy getting up its own fire-direction center, as the big tractors ["cats"] lumbered onto the spongy, yielding tundra dragging the guns slowly behind. About seventy-five yards from the beach the treads of the first cat chewed through the tundra and began to slip. In just seconds it was wallowing helplessly in the black oozy mud.

The other two cats soon shared the same fate. When the tundra broke, the big treads turned round and round and only dug the machine deeper into the mud. What the hell, seventy-five yards was far enough initially!

Stumbling through the muskeg the 2d and 3d Battalions worked their way up both sides of Massacre Bay. At 1900 the Japanese opened fire from well-camouflaged positions, pinning down the troops. Attempts by the 3d Battalion, on the left (southwest), to reach Jarmin Pass, the regimental objective at the head of the valley, failed, resulting in heavy losses.

In another sector, Scout Corporals Al Levorson and Theron Anderson were guiding a 50-man patrol from the 17th Infantry tasked with taking out an enemy machine gun position on the jagged slopes of Sarana Ridge above

Rainbow Beach. Having been informed by his scouts, who had crept forward, that the Japanese also had mortars, the patrol leader tried to radio his commander to report the situation. The radio was dead, so he sent Anderson and Levorson back to the command post to relay the information. The pair crept, crawled, and skidded through snow, over slick mossy rocks and down slippery ravines, until the Command Post was in sight. Then the enemy opened fire. Soldiers at the Command Post returned fire. The Scouts, hugging dirt, were pinned down for several hours until darkness finally allowed them to reach friendly lines.[20]

By 2000 the troops at Red Beach had advanced 1,500 yards, noting some firing, which was presumed to come from their own forces. By 2130, 1,100 troops were ashore at this beach, 2,000 at Yellow and Blue, and 400 at Scarlet. At midnight the first casualty report reached the task force commander. Forty-four officers and men had been killed during the first day.

When dawn of D-Day+1 arrived, it was discovered, however, that Battalion Combat Team 17-2 in Massacre Valley was not 1000 yards from its objective as had been assumed (the pass leading to Sarana Bay), but 1500 yards from it. Meanwhile, Battalion Combat Team 17-3 had mistaken blind Zwinge Valley for Holtz Bay pass and was 2,000 yards south of its objective rather than the 600 yards reported on D-Day evening.

On the north side of the island Battalion Combat Team 17-1 had dug in for the night on what it believed was Hill X. However, they discovered the next day that they were actually on a hill 900 yards short of their objective and during the night the Japanese had in fact occupied Hill X.

Meanwhile, Captain Willoughby and his Scouts had climbed all day in the fog and had reached an altitude of 2,500ft as darkness fell. Their maps were blank beyond this point, so rather than risk venturing farther into the mass of peaks, ridges, and cliffs ahead they bivouacked in deep snow for the night.

It was becoming increasingly clear that the U.S. landing forces would face a long, drawn out, bitter struggle to recapture Attu. No vehicles could move over the muskeg without bogging down, so supplies, food, and ammunition were carried by hand. In the thick fog, without adequate maps, units got lost in the mountains. On short rations to begin with, the men soon ran out of food. Boots fell apart, and wet feet combined with cold temperatures led to trench foot, which was not helped by the fact that it sometimes took over 24 hours to reach medical help.

Indeed, at the end of D-Day the situation was far worse than expected. Heavy terrain, faulty maps, and stiff Japanese resistance all contributed to the

Americans failing to reach their initial objectives. Forty-eight hours later the situation had not greatly improved, and by the third day men were desperate for food and warmth. First Sergeant Fenton Hamlin of the 7th Scout Company tells us what it was like:

> We had repulsed an enemy counterattack the morning of the 14th, and the fight had settled down to bitter, deadly machine-gun duels and grenade and sniper fights. We were bottled up in the canyon and only very slowly making progress to get out. We needed supporting weapons. The ammunition for the 81mm mortars had been exhausted and other ammunition was getting low. Overhead the motor of the supply plane with food, ammunition, and sleeping bags, roared blindly through the fog making futile efforts to locate us. The fog pressed in like wet cotton around the signal flares we had fired as the plane went over us. Finally the motors droned away again over the mountain. The men looked at each other, silently, then rolled back to face the Japs.
>
> It was the third day in the canyon. The cold was intense and some of the men were vomiting green bile from their empty stomachs. We could catch glimpses of the Japs ahead through the fog, as their bullets twanged off the rocks around us. The situation was tense, and nerves were drawn as tight as fiddle strings. No one was talking. A vicious burst of machine-gun bullets crackled over the heads of Sergeant Thomas and his gunner, Morochek. Thomas looked at Morochek and very matter-of-factly broke the silence. "You know," he said, "I think those guys are trying to kill us." He stated, so calmly what was so terrifyingly obvious to everyone, that they laughed. It broke the tension. Some of the cold, hungry men even moved forward to better positions.
>
> The supply plane was droning overhead again. It was exasperating. The men in the canyon were freezing and most of them were vomiting bile now with every drink of water they took. There, overhead, like a promise from heaven, was a load of food and ammunition and sleeping bags. But it was foggy. It was always foggy. The fog was cold and wet and thick and blinding. The frustrated men even thought of firing tracers up at the plane, but realized that the pilot would think they were Japs if they did.
>
> We needed supporting fire badly but the only time that the shore-fire party had been able to contact a ship, a submarine scare had driven the ship out to sea.

U.S. troops aboard a landing craft prior to the landings at Oran during Operation *Torch*. (Photo by Lt. F. A. Hudson/ IWM via Getty Images)

U.S. battleship group in transit across the Atlantic to North Africa as part of Operation *Torch*. (Photo by Time Life Pictures/National Archives/The LIFE Picture Collection/Getty Images)

World War II landing operations at Kiska in the Aleutian Islands. (Photo by Time Life Pictures/U.S. Navy/The LIFE Picture Collection/Getty Images)

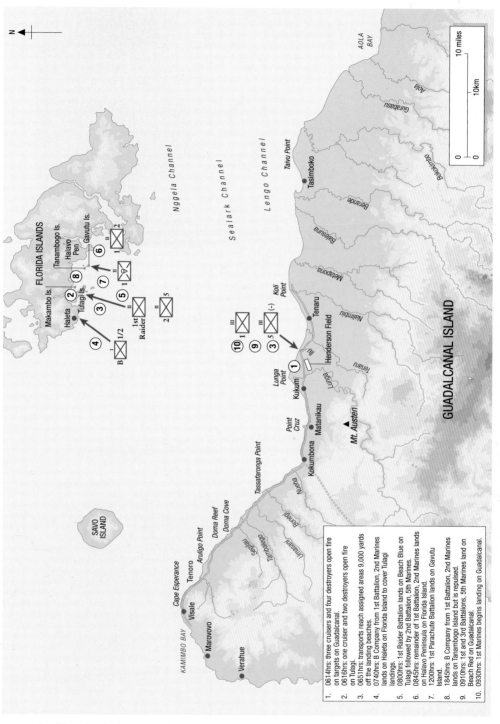

Guadalcanal and adjacent islands and the initial American landings on August 7, 1942. (Copyright Osprey Publishing)

1. 0614hrs: three cruisers and four destroyers open fire on targets on Guadalcanal.
2. 0616hrs: one cruiser and two destroyers open fire on Tulagi.
3. 0651hrs: transports reach assigned areas 9,000 yards off the landing beaches.
4. 0740hrs: B Company from 1st Battalion, 2nd Marines lands on Haleta on Florida Island to cover Tulagi landings.
5. 0800hrs: 1st Raider Battalion lands on Beach Blue on Tulagi followed by 2nd Battalion, 5th Marines.
6. 0845hrs: remainder of 1st Battalion, 2nd Marines lands on Halavo Peninsula on Florida Island.
7. 1200hrs: 1st Parachute Battalion lands on Gavutu Island.
8. 1845hrs: B Company from 1st Battalion, 2nd Marines lands on Tanambogo Island but is repulsed.
9. 0910hrs: 1st and 3rd Battalions, 5th Marines land on Beach Red on Guadalcanal.
10. 0930hrs: 1st Marines begins landing on Guadalcanal.

"I THOUGHT YOU SAID THE COAST GUARD NEVER LEFT CHESAPEAKE BAY."
—Pvt. Jack Ruge

YANK, The Army Weekly, vol. 1, no. 45, April 30, 1943.

Landing boats pouring soldiers and their equipment onto the beach at Massacre Bay, Attu Island, May 11, 1943. The American and Canadian troops took control of Attu within two weeks, after fierce fighting with the Japanese occupying forces. (Photo by Galerie Bilderwelt/Getty Images)

Soldiers unload landing craft on the beach at Massacre Bay, Attu, on May 13, 1943. LCVPs in the foreground are from USS *Zeilin* (APA-3) and USS *Heywood* (APA-6). (NARA)

Two days before the invasion of Sicily, LSTs are lined up and waiting for tanks to be placed onboard, at the French naval base of La Pecherie, Tunisia, July 1943. (Photo by Office of Strategic Services/Interim Archives/Getty Images)

Allied landing craft on the shores of Sicily, during the first stages of the invasion, August 10, 1943. (Photo by U.S. Navy/FPG/Getty Images)

September 14, 1943: LST boats are loaded with troops and equipment as the U.S. prepares to invade the docks of Palermo, Sicily. Barrage balloons were used to form a protective covering against the flight paths of enemy aircraft. (Photo by A. E. French/Hulton Archive/Getty Images)

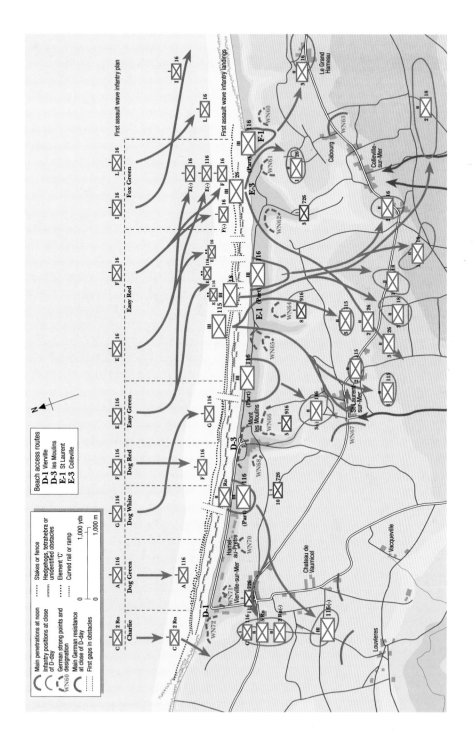

Operation *Overlord*: V Corps D-Day Operations, June 6, 1944. (Copyright Osprey Publishing)

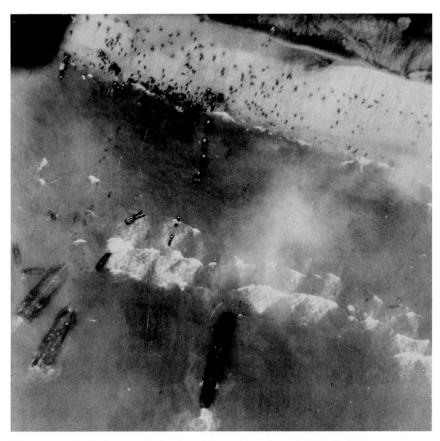

Men and assault vehicles storm the beaches of Normandy on June 6, 1944. (NARA)

Coast Guard landing barges hit the French Coast with the first wave of American troops under heavy fire from German beach nests. This photo, taken from a landing barge by a Coast Guard combat photographer, shows the troops waist deep as they wade ashore. (NARA)

At around 1100hrs LCI-554 and LCT-30 successfully charged through the obstacles immediately in front of the Fox Green sector of Omaha beach. This encouraged other skippers, and LCI-553 came ashore almost immediately in front of a German strongpoint near the Colleville draw. It struck two mines and was later disabled by artillery fire and abandoned on the beach. (NARA)

American assault troops of the 3rd Battalion, 16th Regiment, 1st U.S. Infantry Division, who failed in their attempt to storm across a narrow strip of beach in Colleville-sur-Mer, Normandy, gain the comparative safety of a chalk cliff a few hundred feet from the surf. Omaha Beach, June 6, 1944. (NARA)

The "Water Buffalo" Amphibious Tractor LVT(2) – one of the first types of amphibians produced for the Army, Navy and Marines. It revolutionized amphibious warfare with its ability to negotiate heavy seas and smash over reefs and up onto shore. It carried a crew of three and had a capacity for 24 troops or 8,000lb cargo. (Author's own collection)

A water buffalo loaded with U.S. Marines churns through the water headed for the beaches at Tinian island, near Guam. (Photo by Time Life Pictures/U.S. Coast Guard/The LIFE Picture Collection/Getty Images)

INVASION OF IWO JIMA, VOLCANO IS.

A combat artist's impression of the approach to Iwo Jima with Mount Suribachi in the background. By Chief Specialist John J. Floherty of the U.S. Coast Guard. (Author's own collection)

The price of war. (NARA)

The landings on Okinawa were the largest simultaneous amphibious assault in the entire Pacific War. Here, assault troops of the 1st Marine Division churn ashore aboard a landing vehicle, tracked Mk 3 (LVT[3]) amphibian tractor. (U.S. Marine Corps)

This dramatic shot from the rear of a landing craft shows the chaos into which the Marines were deposited – volcanic ash up to their ankles, enemy pillboxes and bunkers straight ahead, and more troops arriving every five minutes. (U.S. Library of Congress)

It was the fourth day without food. Lieutenant Stott and Sergeant Petruska were in a foxhole together when Lieutenant Stott found two old dirty pieces of candy that had been in his pocket for weeks. Petruska's eyes got as big as saucers and he began to drool over the beaten-up, lint-covered candy sprinkled with tobacco grains. Lieutenant Stott claimed that Petruska would have murdered him if he hadn't offered him a piece of candy. Petruska said, "Gee, that was one of the best things that ever happened to me." Later that day the plane was heard again, feeling its way through the fog above. It dropped some rations just with the chance hope that they might come close, and one small bundle fell where we could get it.

During that night, the 15th, the enemy pulled back, and about 2300 we got a message from the 3d Battalion of the 32d Infantry, informing us of their attacks from the north. We pushed off down the canyon. The Japs had left in a hurry, leaving guns, ammunition, and dead bodies strewn everywhere.

We limped out of the canyon on frozen feet, and our flank patrol killed three snipers, the last vestige of resistance in the canyon. We contacted the 32d Infantry at 1600 near the beach in the west arm.

It had been a long, hard ordeal. The evacuation of the wounded was begun that night, and continued into the next day. We had lost an officer and ten men killed in the bitter six days since we paddled the rubber boats to the beach. The freezing cold and fog had been a harder enemy to fight than the Japs. Ninety per cent of the Scout Company and three-fourths of the 7th Reconnaissance Troop suffered from severe exposure. [21]

As the Army fought hunger, cold, and the Japanese, *Nassau*'s pilots flew ground-support missions. Each time a flight returned to the ship, they were literally "sweated" aboard by all who were watching. Some pilots reported they could not see the ship until they came down to the level of the top of the ship's mast. On only three days were no flight operations conducted, and that was because the fog had completely closed in all targets on the island. However, as in all combat, not everyone came home.

On May 11, two F4Fs and one F4F-3P were lost, but their pilots made it back to *Nassau* safely. On May 14, two F4F pilots, Lieutenant Commander Lloyd K. Greenamyer and Lieutenant Commander Lieutenant Douglas Henderson crashed into mountains around Massacre Valley during a strafing run. On the same mission two other pilots, Ensigns Kelly and E. D. Jackson had to ditch their planes.

Navy Aerographer's Mate Paul Carrigan watched the attack.

Visibility was good under an overcast 500 foot ceiling. Four Wildcats were sent in to drop small bombs and strafe enemy positions along Gilbert Ridge. Someone came into the office after taking a weather observation and reported Wildcats shooting things up on the far side of the valley.

I don't know how many passes had been made by the time I stepped outside. Perhaps one fighter had already crashed. Three were in sight. One was streaking in from seaward. A second was completing a banking turn to follow the first. A third was flying seaward after emerging from the valley.

I watched about two go-rounds. For the eye to flit from plane to plane was distracting like viewing a tennis match. I picked up and focused on a fighter midway through its run. After a sharp left bank and 180 degree turn at the head of the valley this fighter was so low it disappeared behind the hogback bisecting the valley.

I'd shifted my gaze to the bay and picked up another incoming fighter. A split-second later, directly in my line of sight, there was an exploding ball of fire. Black smoke mushroomed like a fat exclamation point. I had not seen the first fighter emerge from behind the hogback but it had evidently crashed about a quarter mile short of the bay.

An additional shock came several days later with an official announcement: all four fighters had been lost on the mission. Three were either struck by williwaws or flew into cloud obscured mountains at the head of the valley. A fourth crash-landed at sea short of Nassau but the pilot was rescued.

It would have taken great flying skill, judgment, and concentration not to crash. In a fast fighter it required split second timing to know when to execute the banking turn. If the planes had been struck by williwaws the pilots wouldn't have had a chance. [22]

Two days later, two more F4Fs were lost. Lieutenant Junior Grade "Cash" Register crashed near Holtz Bay while Sergeant Breen made it back, but had to ditch his plane at sea.

For a full week the Japanese prevented the Northern and Southern forces from joining in Jarmin Pass. Then the Japanese began withdrawing slowly toward Chichagof Harbor and its surrounding ridges. Two more weeks of bitter fighting occurred before the 7th Division and its reinforcements succeeded in driving the enemy from the snow-covered cliffs of Fishhook Ridge and Clevesy Pass, which opened the way to Chichagof on May 28.

Driven from high ground, the noose tightened, and with his back to the sea, the Japanese commander, Colonel Yasuyo Yamazaki, had about 1,200 men left by the night of May 28–29. Approximately 400 of these were hospital cases incapable of further combat. His troops were exhausted and almost out of food and ammunition. He knew that neither help nor evacuation was possible. Yamasaki's brilliantly conceived and executed delaying action had exacted a terrible toll in U.S. casualties, but now it was almost over. Yamasaki chose to mount an all-out attack in one desperate gamble. His daring plan was to break through the weakest point in the American line in Chichagof Valley. As the U.S. troops commanded the heights on both sides, Yamasaki selected nighttime for his suicidal charge.[23]

His objective was the concentration of 105mm howitzers that had been painstakingly dragged up to the head of Massacre Valley over a part creek, part mud trail laid out by the Army Corps of Engineers. If Yamasaki could reach these guns he could turn them on the Americans and then raid and destroy the vast supply dumps in Massacre Valley. With food, guns and ammunition he planned to retreat into the southern mountains to continue the fight with whatever forces he had left. Yamasaki ordered that all Japanese wounded who could not walk or fight to be killed by injections of morphine or by grenades.[24]

In the early hours of May 29, the Japanese made a screaming *banzai* attack out of Chichagof Harbor, up Siddens Valley toward American positions in Clevesy Pass and against Engineer Hill, killing and being killed. Troops of the 50th Combat Engineers who were bivouacked on Engineer Hill succeeded in organizing a thin defensive line and breaking the attack. Joseph Sasser later wrote:

> It was in the AM that we heard shouting that the Japs were coming and some had already gotten behind us. Two of our comrades were bayoneted in their sleeping bags. Finally, after much difficulty, all of our troops were concentrated along the road bed. Having this protection probably saved the lives of many but not all. A medical officer, John Bassett from San Diego, was killed next to me. I didn't realize that he'd been shot for I never

heard a sound. He'd been hit squarely in the forehead.

I don't remember at what time the gun fire stopped. The ravines were full of dead Japs, stacked on top of one another. There was evidence some had taken their own lives with hand grenades.[25]

First Sergeant Jessie H. Clout, Jr. was in Company D, 50th Engineers when the attack came:

We had worked all night and up until noon of the 28th carrying supplies up to the front, then we slept four hours and worked almost all night again. We were so tired when we finally did get into our sacks that I didn't think anything could wake us up, but the 37mm shell that smacked through the tent did it.

The shell was the first indication we had that the Japs had broken through. We had just gotten up before they hit us and things really began to pop. It was foggy and dark, which made it almost impossible to tell American from Jap during the early part of the fight. Lieutenant John H. Green saw a man walking out ahead of him, and he hollered for the guv to get the hell down in a hole; the fellow replied, "Me do, me do," but he didn't get down fast enough because Lieutenant Green shot him. They were right in with us.

We put two BARs in, one on each flank of our line, and they got in some good licks with tracer ammunition which marked our own line for our men, and also pointed out targets. The line we had established held, and very few Japs got through it.

When daylight came we discovered a whole bunch of Japs pinned in a ditch in front of the road along which we had been fighting. While the boys kept firing to keep the Japs down, several others of us crawled up the bank and threw grenades into them. Helmets, rifles, and Japs flew out of the ditch. We were astonished at the mess of them. They had been lying three deep in the ditch trying to hide.[26]

The aid station, which was located about 200 yards behind the 3d Battalion's Command Post, had also been hit by that last, desperate attack by the Japanese.

I recalled that I had been unusually lucky all my life; that the breaks always came at the right time; that – well – it was about time it changed, and here it was. Also, strangely enough, I was grateful for my insurance.

That was Captain Charles Yellin's thought as the Japanese swarmed around outside the aid station on the morning of May 29.

On the evening of May 28 the Japanese dumped several large shells in the area around the Aid station. They were after a nest of 37s that had been set up on the hill to the right, and they were missing. After the excitement of the shelling had subsided, Lieutenant Herbert Friedberg, assisting Captain Yellin in the station, began talking. He had a premonition, a feeling that something was going to happen to him…

Casualties were lying along one side of the tent. They could not be moved over Engineer Hill until morning and were spending the night in the station. Before long other casualties began to arrive. The sounds of fighting up the valley echoed into the tent. By 0300 there were 15 casualties lined up on the floor of the clearing station. Captain Yellin and Lieutenant Friedberg worked among the men with no thought of sleep…

Suddenly the Japs struck. Noise and confusion and death crashed over the tent like an avalanche. The turmoil that followed garbled the sequence of brutal happenings into a maddening jumble of flashes and explosions, screams, and flying steel. "Banzai! We die, you die!" the Japs screamed, as they ripped and slaughtered and smashed everything in their path. The back of the tent was riddled with machine-gun bullets. A bayonet slashed into the canvas, tearing a great rip through which four grenades were thrown onto the men lying inside. Another Japanese attacker thrust the muzzle of an automatic rifle into the hole and sprayed bullets through the tent. Then they discovered the kitchen and stormed it.

The first orgy was over. The men alive inside the tent were helpless. They had few weapons and outside they could hear many Jap voices jabbering deliriously and much running back and forth around the riddled tent… Every man in the tent had been hit by a bullet or a fragment. Lieutenant Friedberg was hit in the head with a grenade fragment. His premonition had been right. He was dead… Chaplain Turner had come into the tent as the Japs struck. He crawled among the men, his presence and good spirits comforting them.[27]

In the early afternoon the Americans had organized resistance around their positions, and grim patrols moved over the hills and across the valleys forcing the scattered Japanese into pockets and destroying them.

The Japs were all around outside. One wounded Jap, lying just beyond the tent, was struggling to reach his rifle, which had dropped into the tent as he fell. One of the wounded men who could move reached another Jap gun with a bayonet on it and stabbed him. On a rise in the ground a few yards behind the station a Jap had set up a machine gun and all through the long, seemingly endless morning he fired short bursts over the tattered clearing station at troops moving in the valley below. He was picked up by American mortar men, and soon the heavy shells began bursting around the gun, within a few yards of the tent, hurling fragments of steel that ripped additional holes in the canvas, no square foot of which did not already have a bullet hole in it.

The next night one of the last groups of Japs still not wiped out passed over the deserted station again and completed the job of destruction, utterly ripping to pieces every piece of equipment in the place before they were cornered and killed. It was a miserable anticlimax to the night before, a fiasco.[28]

On the morning of May 30, Japan announced the loss of Attu. However, the word didn't reach the Japanese on Attu. For many days afterwards American forces continued mopping up operations and continued taking casualties. Sergeant Carmen J. Calabrese, L Company, 17th Infantry took part in the mopping up of Chichagof Village:

It's a very rough soiree that we got ourselves into on the evening of May 30. The Japs are all over since we have never completely straightened things out from the breakthrough on the morning of the 29th. It all starts when our 1st Platoon gets way out ahead on the left flank and leaves the rest of us on a little ridge overlooking the Jap village in Chichagof Harbor.

We spot some good ground over to our right rear and head for it. During the move, of course, we lose some of our control and the men are more or less on their own. They are just straggling up on the high ground as the Japs open up. Lieutenant Beegle, Albert Bianchi, Sergeant Thomas, and myself are up on this high ground already so we start firing back. Then we get an order to move to our left rear toward some higher ground, and the first thing I know Thomas, over on my left, is dead, shot through the mouth. On the right I see Lieutenant Beegle go down from a wound in his shoulder, and then Bianchi topples over a little cliff from a bullet in his shoulder, which is his second wound.[29]

Instead of lasting the projected three days it took until May 31 before Attu was declared secure. Attu cost U.S. forces 549 dead and 1,148 wounded. An unusually high number of men were lost because of the weather and disease. Because of the severe cold weather 1,200 soldiers suffered extreme frostbite and trench foot. These were the first cold-weather casualties of the war. Diseases, primarily those brought on by exposure, such as pneumonia, accounted for 614 casualties. Accidents, mental breakdowns, and self-inflicted injuries took another 318 from the front lines.[30] To the total killed we can add three F4F pilots.

Of the 2,234 Japanese defending the island only 29 survived as prisoners. The rest either died in battle or committed suicide.

Many of the U.S. dead were buried in a cemetery on the shores of Massacre Bay. On July 4, a simple ceremony was held in camp for those unable to cross the pass to the cemetery. Before the 17th Division left the island, the 32d Battalion was assembled. First Lieutenant Robert J. Mitchell recalled:

> Major Charles G. Fredericks read the Roll Call of the men who had fallen. Lieutenant Colonel Glen A. Nelson spoke. A sergeant sang *My Buddy*. And Padre Habetz repeated a prayer.
>
> After the volley, the last note of Taps echoed over the mountains. Then it was over.
>
> Captain Robert C. Foulston said, "Forward ..." but the "march" stuck in his throat. With chins clamped hard and wet eyes blinking, the silent fighting men marched off the field.
>
> It had been paid for. Attu was ours.[31]

Kiska – Operation *Cottage*

It was assumed that taking Kiska would prove to be an even more formidable task than securing Attu. An estimated 10,000 well-entrenched Japanese occupied the island. To counter this force the U.S. fielded 34,426 troops, including 5,500 Canadians, more than double the original strength planned for the operation earlier in the year. Although the U.S. force was bolstered by the additional Canadians, this joint venture was complicated by the fact that many of them spoke only French.

These troops consisted of the 17th Infantry, 53d Infantry, 87th Mountain Infantry, 184th Infantry, First Special Service Force, 13th Canadian Infantry Brigade Group, and headquarters troops. The First Special Service Force, a combined U.S.–Canadian unit,* consisted of about 1,800 men who were especially trained in commando tactics, rubber boat handling, and parachuting.

The ships involved were three battleships, one heavy cruiser, one light cruiser, 19 destroyers, five attack transports, one attack cargo vessel, ten transports, three cargo vessels, one fast transport, 14 LSTs, nine LCI(L)s, 19 LCT(5)s, two light minelayers, three fast minesweepers, two tugs, one harbor tug, and one surveying ship.

Kiska is approximately 25 miles long by eight miles at the widest part and 1.8 miles at the narrowest part. It is practically two islands in one as it is made up of two great land masses separated by a deep narrow gorge known as Middle Pass. Its shoreline is characterized by precipitous rocky cliffs, hidden reefs, rocks, rip tides, and treacherous undertows. The surf to windward is usually up to 7ft high, with as high as 35ft being recorded.

Early in the morning of August 15 the invasion fleet anchored 1,500 yards off the middle of Kiska's north shore. The Special Service Forces had started moving ashore at 0230, followed by the first wave at 0600.

"It was a weird scene that greeted the assault troops as they came out on the decks of the transports and filed to their designated landing craft," Lieutenant Colonel Kenneth Ward wrote later:

---

*   The volunteers for the 1,800-man force consisted primarily of enlisted men who had responded to advertising at Army posts, which stated that preference would be given to men previously employed as lumberjacks, forest rangers, hunters, game wardens, and the like. Much feared for their fighting prowess, the moniker "The Black Devils" was adopted after the discovery of the personal diary of a German officer referring to "die schwarzen Teufeln" ("The Black Devils"). With blackened faces, small units would often overwhelm German defenders without firing a shot, and then disappear into the night.

Force members received rigorous and intensive training in stealth tactics, hand-to-hand combat, the use of explosives for demolition, parachuting, amphibious warfare, rock-climbing, mountain warfare, and as ski troops.

The formation patch was a red spearhead with the words "USA" written horizontally and "CANADA" written vertically. The branch of service insignia was the crossed arrows formerly worn by the U.S. Army Indian Scouts. The unit wore red, white, and blue piping on their garrison cap and on the breast oval behind their parachutist wings. Members of the unit also wore a red, white, and blue fourragère, lanyard, or shoulder cord made out of parachute shroud lines. Source: The First Special Force web site: net/history.html

Overhead the sky was partially overcast, and during the few moments when it did clear, Kiska could be seen in the eerie moonlight. The men moved as phantoms must move; silent and breathless. You could see where their faces should be, yet their faces could not be seen. Daring the night, all assault forces had applied face make-up as recommended by leading make-up men in Hollywood. The object was to break the familiar shape and shadows of the face by skillful use of brown and green grease paint. It was very effective.[32]

The first landing craft approached the beach only to learn what aerial photographs had failed to disclose. Huge rocks just below the surface of the water prevented the craft from approaching the beach with any speed. Instead, the boats crept in. They were forced to limit landings to one boat at a time. Troops moved ashore slowly, most of them by jumping into the icy water and wading to the beach. The rubber boats brought in by the Special Service Forces were used to build temporary docks which aided, to some extent, in speeding up operations. A bulldozer made its way onto shore and unloaded, was used to push rocks aside and clear a landing beach that could handle two small craft.

Major James L. Low recalled the feeling as the first waves landed:

> The quiet that prevailed over the entire area was awesome. Every person was tense with expectation. Each man, as he toiled up the slopes of the ridges, watched those above him and wondered at what moment the first shot would ring out and which man would be the first to fall. The suspense was terrible and was rapidly producing mass jitters.
>
> The first report from the Special Service Forces was relayed to us at approximately 0915. This now famous report was the first indication as to enemy movements. It stated "Enemy outpost over-run, all personnel have left. Hot coffee still on the stove." The message was passed on and everyone felt relieved. Some positive action would soon follow. Surely the main garrison knew of the landing by now and would make a move that would permit our troops to gain contact with them.[33]

When they landed the Americans found Japanese jeeps and trucks, half buried under the earth by explosions, shattered windows, four burned-out ships in the harbor, and practically every object, including the roofs of huts, punctured with bullet holes and shrapnel. However, initially, there were no Japanese forces.[34] They also found the puppy Explosion who had escaped the Japanese weeks before.

The landings forces did find quartermaster warehouses bulging with clothing, food, fruit, vegetables, fish, ammunition, and some big guns. They found a sign from the Japanese that said, in effect, "out to lunch." Ominously, on the wall of the main Japanese command hut was scrawled, "We shall come again and kill out separately Yanki jokers."

As evening closed in Colonel Sutherland, Commanding Officer of the Southern Sector, ordered that extreme precautions be taken by all units to prevent any enemy infiltration and that patrols be kept active. Without knowing the enemy's position the invading force was completely blind. Sutherland later wrote:

> Perhaps they [the Japanese] had withdrawn to the southern part of the island for a last ditch stand. Perhaps they had evacuated but that thought could not be entertained – yet. Sporadic firing of small arms and machine guns could be heard all through the night. Occasionally the sharp blast of a hand grenade gave credence to the thought that we were at last in contact with the enemy. Such reports that men had been bayoneted while asleep and that they, the enemy, could be seen moving in the fog led us to believe that tomorrow would bring great battles.
>
> When morning broke, our casualties for the night were brought down from the hills to the hospital set up near the beach. Some told harrowing tales of close combat while others told of being shot at in the dark without even seeing the enemy. The dead were put to one side, away from the view of the troops.
>
> Something was wrong here, however. Not one Japanese body had been found. In fact, nothing could be found to indicate that the enemy had even been near our lines. Only American blood had been spilled. Were we a match for this cunning or had we killed our own men? That was a tough question to ask ourselves.[35]

Something was wrong, the Japanese had gone. The entire 5,183-man Japanese force had slipped through the air and surface blockade on July 28, almost three weeks earlier. Between then and D-Day, Kiska had been under attack and close surveillance by American naval units and the 11th Air Force, but the erroneous reports of flak and Japanese activity which observers brought back had not been questioned by intelligence offers or anyone else.

The only guns fired were those of friend against friend in error. Twenty-four soldiers died in the shooting, four others were killed by mines and booby-traps, 50 were wounded by these means, and scores were wounded in various accidents. Casualties totaled 313. Included in this figure were over 125 cases of trench foot in spite of the bitter lessons learned on Attu.

The Navy lost the destroyer USS *Abner Read* (DD-526) when she struck a mine on August 18. The blast tore a huge hole in her stern and ruptured her smoke tanks. Men sleeping in aft compartments suffered from smoke inhalation. In the darkness a few men fell through holes in the deck into the fuel oil tanks below. Soon the stern broke away and sank. Once in the water, the men recovered from the effects of the smoke and could breathe. Nonetheless, 70 men were killed or missing and another 47 were wounded.[36]

On August 24, Kiska was declared secure, ending the 14-month Aleutian Campaign. The Japanese threat to the northwestern U.S. flank was eliminated. From Aleutian bases 11th Air Force bombers conducted harassing attacks on Japan's Kurile Islands. To counter this threat Imperial Japanese Headquarters maintained a large defensive force totaling about one-sixth of Japan's air strength.

Lessons Learned

Lessons learned by the Army in preparing and equipping troops to survive the rigors of combat in wretched weather and difficult mountain terrain would prove useful during the upcoming Italian campaign.

Many amphibious warfare techniques developed during the Attu landings were refined for Kiska and were further improved and applied to advantage in later amphibious operations in the Pacific. Other lessons learned included:

a. Beaches must be thoroughly cleared before being established as beaches suitable for landing craft;

b. A landing should not be made on a falling tide when bottom and gradient conditions are unknown;

c. Unless extreme precautions are taken, a blockade cannot completely encircle an island and prevent a determined enemy from reinforcing, supplying, or evacuating; and

　　d. Army and Navy communications and techniques have to be standardized
　　or placed under a joint command.[37]

Estimated U.S. casualties were 1,481 killed, 3,416 wounded, 640 missing, and eight captured, while Japanese were 4,350 killed and 28 captured.

From the standpoint of casualties, Attu was the second most costly in terms of U.S. forces killed and wounded compared to Japanese killed (71 Americans versus 100 Japanese). Only Iwo Jima, two years later, was more costly.

No casualty list includes the hundreds of men lost from Army Air Force aircrews, soldiers who drowned during unopposed landings, or sailors lost in shipboard accidents or battles with Aleutian weather or to the Imperial Japanese Navy.

It was a campaign fought and forgotten in fogs and williwaw-driven storms.

CHAPTER 7

THE SOFT UNDERBELLY

SICILY AND ITALY, JULY 1943–JUNE 1944

During late October and early November 1942 the tide of Axis advances had been turned in three crucial theaters. The Russians triumphed in the epic seize of Stalingrad and the Soviet Army was on the offensive; the British Eighth Army's victory at El Alamein in the eastern desert had driven the German and Italian Armies into their final retreat in northwest Africa; while in the Pacific Japanese aggression was thwarted when Australian and American forces invaded New Guinea, and on Guadalcanal the Marine and Army lines held.

As Allied and Axis forces continued their bitter battles President Franklin D. Roosevelt, Prime Minister Winston Churchill and the Combined Chiefs of Staff met in Casablanca, Morocco, on January 14, 1943, to plan future operations. The main problem to be resolved was where to go once North Africa was secure. The U.S. advocated the invasion of northern France that summer, but the British pushed for more limited operations in the Mediterranean. An examination of the logistics did indeed show that a European invasion was simply not feasible before May 1944.

Churchill stated his opinion of the situation to Roosevelt:

> The paramount task before us is first, to conquer the African shores of the Mediterranean and set up there the naval and air installations which are necessary to open an effective passage through it for military traffic; and,

secondly, using the bases on the African shore to strike at the underbelly of the Axis in effective strength and in the shortest time.[1]

It was agreed that the next Allied offensive would focus on the Mediterranean and the aim would be to force Germany and Italy to widely disperse their forces by making them fight not just along the coasts of Italy and Greece but also on Sardinia, Corsica, and the Greek Dodecanese Islands in the southeastern Aegean Sea. The prime objective of the Mediterranean operations would be to knock Italy out of the war, which would force Germany to assume the defense of the Italian peninsula and replace the Italian troops who were garrisoning the Balkans. Finally there was the possibility that a successful campaign in the Mediterranean might provide a strong inducement to Turkey to enter the war and so open the Black Sea supply route to Russia and provide the Allies with a base for operations against the Romanian oil fields.

The Chiefs of Staff considered whether the Allies had the strength to attack Italy directly and if not, what might be the best intermediary steps. They reached the conclusion that Allied forces needed to capture either Sicily or Sardinia before tackling Italy.

After examining the respective cases for taking Sicily or Sardinia a firm decision was reached. On January 19 the Combined Chiefs of Staff agreed "that after Africa had been finally cleared of the enemy the island of Sicily should be assaulted and captured as a base for operations against Southern Europe and to open the Mediterranean to the shipping of the United Nations."[2]

Four days later they appointed General Dwight D. Eisenhower as Supreme Commander and British General Harold Alexander his deputy. Admiral of the Fleet Andrew Cunningham, RN, was to be the Naval Commander and Air Chief Marshal Arthur Tedder, RAF, the Air Commander. The target date of the operation, codenamed *Husky*, was to be the period of the favorable July moon.

Operation *Husky*

The position and terrain of Sicily made it admirably suited for defense against invasion from anywhere except Italy itself. Separated from the Italian peninsula by the Straits of Messina, which at its narrowest is only two miles wide, the island had long provided a natural springboard for the projection of Axis troops into Tunisia – Cape Bon on the African mainland is but 90 miles from

Sicily's western tip. In the event of an Allied assault on the island, enemy reinforcements could be expected to pour in from the toe of Italy, by sea ferry from the Calabrian ports, or by transport aircraft from the airfields of Naples and Brindisi. It was estimated that the train ferries at Messina could move up to 40,000 men, or 7,500 men and 750 vehicles, in 24 hours.

To stem the flow of this traffic and then reverse it by defeating it would be no easy task, for Sicily's topography would overwhelmingly favor its defenders. Almost the whole surface of the island is covered with hills and mountains, which fall either directly to the sea or to restricted coastal plains or terraces. The only extensive flat ground is the east central plain of Catania, above which towers the massive cone of Mount Etna; more limited low-lying areas are to be found along the southeastern seaboard and at the western extremity of the island. Once attacking forces had penetrated into the mountainous areas of the interior, their lines of advance would be restricted to the few existing roads, and their rate of progress hampered by the enemy's well-known skill in mine warfare and demolition.

Along the 600-mile coastline that forms the perimeter of the Sicilian triangle, more than 90 stretches of beach were reported by Allied intelligence as topographically satisfying the requirements for landing operations. These ranged from less than 100 yards to many miles in length and, although offshore gradients were in several cases unfavorably shallow and the beaches themselves of unpromising soft sand, most of them gave reasonably convenient access to the narrow coastal strip encompassing the island. However, only in two sectors could disembarkation be covered by land-based Allied fighter craft. These were the beaches in the southeastern corner of the island, between the Gulf of Noto and Gela, which were within range of the Malta airfields, and those in the southwest, between Sciacca and Marinella, which could be reached from airfields in Tunisia.[3]

Invasion plans were finalized on May 12 and consisted of five phases:

1) preparatory measures by naval and air forces to neutralize enemy naval efforts and to gain air supremacy this also involved deception operations as to the actual invasion site;

2) predawn seaborne assaults, assisted by airborne landings with the object of seizing airfields and the ports of Syracuse and Licata;

3) the establishment of a firm base upon which to conduct operations for the capture of the ports of Augusta and Catania, and the Gerbini

    group of airfields;

4) the capture of these ports and airfields;

5) the reduction of the island.

An extensive deception plan (Operation *Barclay*) was conducted to lead the Axis to believe that a fictitious British 12th Army would attack the Balkans and an American army under Lieutenant General George S. Patton would invade southern France. The deception plan also called for an assault on Crete on July 24, the Peloponnesus Islands off Greece on July 26, Sardinia and Corsica on July 31, and southern France on August 4.

Various Allied activities were conducted to reinforce the illusion of the deception plan, including aerial bombing attacks. The Allies developed a complete plan that called for a feint to invade Sicily to support the real invasion of Sardinian and a feint to invade the Dodecanese Islands to support the real invasion of the Peloponnesus. The most famous part of *Barclay* was Operation *Mincemeat* in which a deceased man dressed up as a Royal Marine officer with the plan in a briefcase handcuffed to his wrist was dumped off the coast of Spain.*

Based on the false documents, on May 12 Hitler himself ordered that "measures regarding Sardinia and the Peloponnese take precedence over everything else." The Germans reinforced the Italian army on Sardinia in July 1943 with the 90th Panzergrenadier Division consisting of about 40,000 men. The unit could have made a significant difference had it been deployed on Sicily.

In addition to the deception plan, Allied forces conducted preparatory operations against the Pelagie Islands (Lampedusa, Lampione, and Linosa) and Pantelleria located between Tunisia and Malta, south of Sicily. Pantelleria and Lampedusa hosted Radio Direction Finding stations, which were observation posts from where the movement of aircraft and ships, and movement on airfields, could be detected.

Plans for the conquest of Pantelleria (Operation *Corkscrew*) included the first Allied attempt to conquer enemy territory essentially by air action. The real offensive against the island began on May 18 under a plan calling for 50 medium bomber and 50 fighter-bomber sorties per day throughout

---

* The story of this amazing, successful deception was well told in Ewen Montagu's book *The Man Who Never Was: World War II's Boldest Counterintelligence Operation,* J. B. Lippincott, Philadelphia (1954).

June 5 (D-Day-6). Initially the air campaign did not succeed despite two messages to Vice Admiral Gino Pavesi, military governor of Pantelleria, asking him to surrender.

On the night of June 10–11 the British 1st Infantry Division embarked at Sousse and Sfax in three convoys, two fast and one slow. The fast convoys, protected by fighters of the North African Coastal Air Force and by surface craft, were met off Pantelleria at about daybreak of the 11th by a British naval squadron from Malta. Eight miles from the harbor entrance to Porto di Pantelleria the ships lowered their assault craft in readiness to move ashore. While the troops were going ashore a message forwarded from Malta brought the information that Vice Admiral Gino Pavesi had formally asked to surrender.

Lampedusa had excellent defenses. It was well covered by pillboxes, machine-gun nests, trenches, and barbed wire; it had four minefields, each in an area where a landing might be effected; its coastline was almost a continuous cliff some 400ft high, broken by numerous small bays and inlets; it held more than 4,300 troops, a platoons of tanks, and 33 coastal and AA guns.

More than 450 sorties were flown by medium and heavy bombers of the Tactical Air Force between June 10 and 11, but the island's commander refused to surrender. Before midnight on June 11 a British naval task force of four light cruisers and six destroyers, accompanied by an LCI carrying one company of the Coldstream Guards, reached Lampedusa from Pantelleria and began shelling installations, while the air attacks continued. The island, having failed in an effort to surrender to an RAF sergeant pilot who had landed on the airfield because of motor trouble, displayed white surrender flags at around 1900. Thereafter, negotiations were completed quickly, although the local commander initially refused to sign the surrender terms "until he was reminded that we had another 1,000 bombers at our call; then he borrowed a pen and signed."[4]

The Coldstream Guards went ashore to take charge of some 4,000 military and 3,000 civilian personnel and on the morning of June 13 the island officially came under Allied control. With the occupation of Linosa and Lampione by British naval units the entire Pelagie group, and thus all islands in the Sicilian strait, were under Allied control. Neither of these last two had to be bombed or shelled.[5]

Further, the Allies enlarged and expanded Malta's airfields to support over 600 aircraft. After Pantelleria was captured, Allied air forces focused their attacks on Axis airfields in Sicily and Sardinia in order to destroy the enemy air force. In addition to attacking Axis air assets, Allied air forces conducted deep attacks against Axis communications. These attacks focused on Naples, the Sardinian harbors of Olbia and Golfo Aranci, and on Messina's port and ferries. The Allies' intent was to cut the Axis lines of communication to the island of Sicily.[6]

Invasion Forces

There were two primary assault task forces: the Eastern Naval Task Force comprising Royal Navy and British Army units and the Western Naval Task Force made up of U.S. Navy and Army components.

The Eastern Naval Task Force, commanded by Admiral Sir Bertram Ramsay, carrying 115,000 British and Canadian troops of the British Eighth Army under General Bernard Montgomery, would land four divisions, an independent brigade, and a commando force along a 40-mile front stretching from the Pachino Peninsula north along the Gulf of Noto to a point just south of the port of Syracuse. Elements of the British 1st Parachute Brigade would drop behind Axis lines (Operation *Fustian*) while a glider landing by the 1st Airlanding Brigade would assist the amphibious troops in capturing Syracuse (Operation *Ladbroke*).

The Western Naval Task Force, commanded by Vice Admiral Henry K. Hewitt, would transport 66,000 troops of the U.S. Seventh Army under Lieutenant General George S. Patton. Three divisions were to land over an even wider front in the Gulf of Gela. The U.S. assault was to be supported by parachutists from the 82d Airborne Division's 505th Parachute Infantry Regimental Combat Team and the 3d Battalion, 504th Parachute Infantry (PIR) (Operation *Husky-Bigot*).

The combined Eastern and Western task forces totaled 2,590 warships (including 1,614 from the Royal Navy with two Royal Indian Navy escorts, 945 U.S. Navy ones, and 31 from Allied nations), merchant ships, and major and minor landing craft.* Mediterranean Air Command, consisting of 113 British and 146 American squadrons employing more than 4,300 aircraft, would support the invasion.

---

*   The Royal Navy total includes the covering force that was to prevent interference by the Italian fleet. The main group under Vice Admiral Sir A. U. Willis of Force H included the battleships *Nelson*, *Rodney*, *Warspite*, and *Valiant* and the fleet carriers *Formidable* and *Indomitable*.

Once ashore the Eighth Army would thrust northward, capturing in succession Augusta, Catania, and the airfield complex at Gerbini before making the final push on Messina. The Seventh Army's initial objectives were several airfields between Licata and Comiso, after which it would advance to a position approximately 20 miles inland, designated the Yellow Line. From the Yellow Line the Seventh Army would control the high ground that ringed the U.S. beaches and protect the western flank of the Eighth Army's beachhead. Once this had been secured, the Seventh Army was to push slightly forward to a second position, termed the Blue Line, from which it would control the vital road network that emanated from Piazza Armerina.[7]

Assault Plans

The Western Naval Task Force

The Western Naval Task Force, under Vice Admiral Hewitt, was divided into three main attack forces – *Dime*, *Cent*, and *Joss* – and sailed from Oran, Algiers, and Bizerte.

Dime Attack Force, under the Commander Amphibious Force, Northwest African Waters, Rear Admiral John L. Hall, Jr., USN, had as its initial objective the capture of Gela and the airfield at Ponte Olivo. Aboard the *Dime* flagship was Major General Terry Allen, commanding the 1st Division (consisting of the 1st and 4th Ranger Battalions; the 1st and 2d Battalions, 16th Regimental Combat Team (RCT); and the 1st and 2d Battalions, 26th RCT). They would land in the vicinity of Gela over beaches codenamed Red, Green, Yellow, Blue, Red 2, and Green 2. This group would strike at the center of the beach area.

Cent Attack Force, under the Commander Sixth Amphibious Force, Rear Admiral Alan G. Kirk, USN, had as its objective the capture of Scoglitti, and the airfields of Corniso and Biscari. *Cent* Force would land the 45th Division troops (consisting of the 1st and 2d Battalions of the 157th RCT; the 1st and 2d Battalions of the 179th RCT; and the 1st and 2d Battalions of the 180th RCT), under the command of Major General Troy H. Middleton. This group would strike on the right flank. *Cent* Force also included the 505th Parachute Combat Team (Reinforced) which was to land at night prior to the main assault (D-Day-l/D-Day).

Joss Attack Force, under the Commander Landing Craft and Bases, Northwest African Waters, Rear Admiral Richard L. Conolly, USN, had as its first objective the port and airfield at Licata. Aboard its flagship was Major General Lucien Truscott, Commander of the 3d Division (Reinforced) (consisting of the 2d Ranger Battalion, 1st, 2d, and 3d Battalions of the 7th RCT; the 1st, 2d, and 3d Battalions of the 15th RCT; and the 1st, 2d, and 3d Battalions of the 30th RCT). Operating as part of the force was LCI(L) Flotilla Four, under the command of Commander Miles H. Imlay, USCG. Its landing position would be Red, Green East, Green West, Yellow, and Blue beaches on the left flank of the beach area.

The *Kool* reserve force composed of Combat Command B, Second Armored Division, and the 18th RCT of the 1st Infantry Division would remain on ships until needed.

In all three areas, the initial assault troops were landed in LCVPs, whether they had been brought to the area in transports or in the larger types of landing craft. In addition, there were minesweeping and mine-laying groups, destroyer divisions and squadrons, light cruisers and destroyers for shore bombardment prior to troop landings, PT boat squadrons, and smaller auxiliary patrol craft and landing craft, all of whose duties were to be part of the *Husky* Naval Operation Plan.

Fighter Cover and Air Support

Close air support and fighter cover was to be provided by USAAF P-40s from Pantelleria and RAF Spitfires operating from Malta. There were, on average, ten fighters over each of the areas, *Dime*, *Cent*, and *Joss*. There were several "holidays" in the schedule when no cover existed over one or two of the areas and, on two occasions, there were no fighters in any of the areas. Adding to the difficulty of providing adequate coverage were the great distances from operating fields to assault areas, which severely limited the time of cover provided by each sortie.

If close support was requested, and granted, it could not be delivered for at least two hours. In one of the few close air support requests that were requested during the invasion, the time lag was 12 hours. Under these conditions the shore air support liaison parties had little or no value.

Also, with the limited amount of cover, patrols could be maintained at one level only, thus making interception of both high- and low-level attacks difficult. Although there were sufficient fighter aircraft in the theater to provide additional cover, large numbers were tasked to provide fighter escort for the many bombing missions.[8]

Three new types of amphibious vessels would be employed for the first time in the landings: the Landing Ship Tank (LST), the smaller Landing Craft Infantry Large (LCI (L)), and the ungainly amphibious DUKW* (D – designed in 1942; U – utility; K – all-wheel drive; and W – dual rear axles). The U.S.-designed and built LST of World War II was 328ft long and 50ft at the beam, with a large, open deck area that could serve as another transportation deck for supplies, weapons, and vehicles. The bow was blunt and high, with doors that swung open to permit the lowering of a steel ramp. Although the ship was designed for ocean travel as well as beaching, the bow seemed to push a lot of water when the LST was fully loaded and sitting low. It was not "sleek or fast", having a top speed of 10.8 knots, hence the nickname "Large Slow Target."

The LCI(L) ("Elsie Item") was designed to carry 200 troops at up to 15 knots and be as capable at landing as the LCA. About 158ft long with a 23ft beam, it weighed 400 tons, had quarters aboard for 25 crewmen and 210 troops, and had a bridge that looked like the conning tower of an old-fashioned submarine. The design incorporated two fretted ramps that thrust forward and downward from the shell of the craft "like turtle limbs" on either side of the bow for disembarking troops.

The DUKW was a six-wheel-drive, 2 1/2-ton capacity, 6x6 truck modified with a watertight hull and a propeller. It had a steering wheel and peddles like its truck progenitor. The DUKW's main advantage was being able to carry men and equipment from ships over the beaches, and well inland as needed.

These three craft enabled men and equipment to be offloaded directly onto the beaches without having to transfer everything to landing craft first.

Assault – July 10

What should have been an easy crossing from North Africa to Sicily turned into a nightmare when the convoys were hit by a fierce, 40mph gale, dubbed the "Mussolini wind" by seasick GIs, which whipped up the seas, seriously endangering some of the smaller craft. In the words of Lieutenant John Mason Brown, USN, on board the command ship USS *Ancon* (AGC-4):

*   Pronounced "Duck."

As the waves rose under sullen skies, they subjected the little PC boats now with us to a terrible beating. The destroyers were surf-bathing uncomfortably. Even the largest transports were wobbling. One by one, three of their barrage balloons were blown away from them, as easily as a child's balloon slips through his fingers in the park. By 5 o'clock the gale had increased until, as darkness came on, the waves swelled into more and more sizable mountains. The PC boats were by then egg-shelling their way, not so much through as on the heavy seas. Many of us remembered the Spanish Armada's fate. We did not want to remember it, but we did. Nature had undone that formidable Spanish Task Force, dashed its galleons to pieces on the rocks, and scattered them, when in full and proud array it had reached England's shores. We were a far larger armada. Would we be the victim of the same misfortune?

Some transport planes, carrying our paratroops, were reported off to starboard shortly. Although I could not see the planes, I heard the roar of their motors, full of power, full of defiance.[9]

While the weather made it rough for the men at sea, it was significantly worse for the British and American paratroopers. Buffeted by the winds and confused by an overly complex flight plan, the inexperienced pilots ferrying Allied airborne forces became disoriented in the darkness and strayed from their courses.

The British 1st Airlanding Brigade's 1,730 men in gliders scattered anywhere up to 30 miles from their landing zones, some further still. Many had been released far out to sea, much further than the prescribed distance of two miles, so 73 gliders out of an initial 144 ditched in the Mediterranean. Only 56 ultimately reached Sicily, and of these just 12 had come down on or within a respectable distance of their intended zones. Of these 1,730 men, 326 drowned. The majority survived, yet those who were too far out to sea had no choice but to cling to the wings for up to ten hours in the hope that the Royal Navy would find them in the morning.[10]

In the American sector the time set for the drop was 2346 on July 9. Colonel James M. "Slim Jim" Gavin's 3,400-man combat team were even more widely scattered than the British by 35mph winds in the landing area. One plane was shot down and seven others failed to return although the parachutists had cleared them before they were lost. Unable to locate their respective drop zones (DZs), three planes returned with full loads. The objective was to parachute behind enemy lines into an egg-shaped area around Gela, Sicily.

The paratroops would then close off roads leading to the landing beaches and secure the drop zone for further use. Especially important near the drop zone was a series of 16 concrete pillboxes from which German gunners controlled movement on all nearby roads.

Only 15 percent of the combat team had been delivered to the correct drop zone. Gavin himself landed 25 miles southeast of his intended drop zone. Many isolated groups scattered in the British area of operations attached themselves to Canadian forces, and worked and fought with them.

Despite being spread over a wide area, small groups of paratroopers cut every telephone line that they found, devastating the communications of the Axis forces. However, the wide dispersion of paratroopers seriously jeopardized Seventh Army's invasion plan by weakening the buffer these men were supposed to form in front of the 1st Division's beachhead. The parachute drops also alerted the island's commander, Italian General Alfredo Guzzoni, that the invasion had started, although this came as no surprise to him. Axis air reconnaissance had spotted Allied convoys moving toward Sicily earlier that day, and Guzzoni had ordered a full alert at 2200 on the 9th. Based upon the reported airborne drops, Guzzoni correctly surmised that the Allies intended to come ashore in the southeast, and at 0145 on July 10 he issued orders to counteract the invasion, and began moving his mobile forces to the threatened areas. Among these forces was the German Hermann Göring Panzer Division, which was ordered to Gela.

While the paratroopers fought ashore, LSTs, LCIs, and LCTs were still fighting their own battles against winds and heavy seas to reach their assigned positions. Once there they were exposed to the westerly wind that was churning up the surf, the LSTs carrying the U.S. 3d Infantry Division's 7th Infantry Regiment had great difficulty hoisting out and launching the LCVPs. On the transport *Florence Nightingale* a 25-ton LCM broke loose as it was being hoisted outboard, and began to swing like a pendulum with the roll of the ship, banging up against the ship, then by the bridge, then by the fantail. Every time she struck the ship's side something gave, with a booming crash that could be heard through the entire transport area. Little rocket boats were smashed and sank as soon as they hit the water.

Fully exposed to the westerly wind that was churning up the surf, the LSTs carrying the 7th Infantry had great difficulty hoisting out and launching the LCVPs that would take the assault waves to Red Beach. When one davit gave way and dumped a boatload of men into the water, nine men were lost.[11]

H-Hour was set for 0245. The heavy weather and difficulty in launching boats delayed the start. Just after 0300, 15 minutes later than the time scheduled for touchdown on the beach, the attack group commander ordered the LCVPs in to shore. However, there were casualties even before the first landing craft made it to the beaches.

On board LST-375 Ensign John J. Parle, USNR, officer-in-charge of small boats from LST-375, discovered a smoke pot had accidentally ignited in a small boat loaded with high explosives, setting fire to fuses and risking detonating ammunition. If those explosives were to detonate, it would have endangered his ship and revealed the presence of the Allied fleet to the enemy. Undaunted by fire and blinding smoke, Ensign Parle entered the craft and extinguished the fuses. After failing in his desperate efforts to extinguish the fire pot, he finally seized it with both hands and running topside threw it overboard, preventing grave damage to his ship and its crew and ensuring the security of the invasion. The fumes seriously damaged his lungs and he tragically died of pneumonia three days after the incident.* [12]

Almost four hours before H-Hour a team of combat engineers landed on *Dime* Force's Green Beach from a Coast Guard-manned LCI. Chief Photographer's Mate Bill Forsythe was with them:

> Coming into the beach in the dark, we hit a sandbar about fifty yards from the beach. The LCI boat I was in, operated by Coast Guardsmen, got stuck on it; so we bailed out. Luckily, I had enough foresight to waterproof my equipment, with a .45 [pistol] in one hand and a camera in the other I started for the beach. Our Coast Guard gunners opened fire with two .30 caliber machine guns to give us a covering fire in order that we might have a chance to make it. The surf was so heavy that I was knocked under; when I came up the .45 [pistol] was full of sand and unable to fire.
>
> I was completely soaked and cold as hell but I ran up on the beach. I never ran so fast in all my life, but it seemed very slow – water-soaked clothing certainly drags one down. The enemy fire was intense. On my right about 300 yards, an LCI was on the beach and was unable to get off; and on my left, at a distance of about 500 yards, was an Italian fort that kept firing on the LCI and shelling the landing boats and keeping the beach under fire,

---

*   For valor and courage above and beyond the call of duty Ensign Parle was posthumously awarded the Congressional Medal of Honor. He was 23 years old.

with me in the middle. The beach was mined, but this was unknown to us at the time and there we were digging for dear life – and I do mean life.[13]

At San Mollarella, three miles west of Licata, Major Herman W. Dammer's 3d Ranger Battalion, scheduled to land at 0300, went ashore on *Joss* Force Green Beach at 0257. Six companies landed abreast. Companies A, B, and C, led by Dammer, landed to the left of Rocca Mollarella. Companies D, E, and F, under the Executive Officer Major Alvah Miller, beached to the right of the rock. On the extreme left, A Company breeched the wire at the base of Mount Polisca then climbed the steep slopes and cleared the enemy off the high ground. Machine gun fire briefly delayed B Company, with a platoon from C Company, before the Rangers cleared the beach and moved east of Mount Polisca, eliminating Italian positions at the west of the basin between the high ground. Part of C Company established a base of fire using rocks along the shoreline.

At Gela, the 1st and 4th Ranger Battalions, under Darby and Major Roy Murray left the USS *Joseph T. Dickman* (APA-13), HMS *Prince Leopold* (4.251) and HMS *Prince Charles* in LCVPs. The designated Red and Green beaches in front of the town had a combined length of about 1,000 yards and were separated by a 900ft concrete pier. Red Beach to the left of the pier was some 50 yards deep, while Green Beach to the right was roughly 80 yards deep. The 1st Battalion landed on the western half of Red Beach and the 4th Battalion on the eastern half of Green Beach. Facing the Rangers was an extensive defensive ring surrounding Gela comprising concrete pillboxes and barbed wire built by the Italian 429th Coastal Battalion, XVIII Coastal Brigade.

As the Rangers approached the beach Italian searchlights flicked on illuminating the boats. The U.S. Navy response was quick and accurate. Naval gunfire-support ships including the destroyer *Shubrick* (DD-639) and cruiser *Savannah* (CL-42) shot out the lights. The Italians then blew up the Gela pier with a tremendous roar. Five hundred yards offshore, the Rangers came under machine-gun fire, and some of them answered, as best they could, with rockets from their M1A1 recoilless antitank rocket launchers.

"About the time that the boats started hitting the beach," said *Dickman*'s Lieutenant Brown, USCG:

cruisers, battlewagons and destroyers were opening up with everything that they had upon shore installations of guns and lights. The tracer streams are weird but very beautiful. Watching the 4-gun salvos from the Limey 15 inchers was quite a sight. Each shell was tracer and the flight from start to finish – and I do mean "finish" – was rather amusing. The things seemed to float and float and float – quite slowly, too, so it seemed. Our support boat near the beach let go with her barrage which lit upon a pill box emplacement. The explosion of that emplacement was almost beyond imagination – a column of flame shooting upwards about a thousand feet and all of sixty feet in diameter. Later reports said that that blast cleared out many machine-gun nests, enabling our boys to advance into the town.

One landing craft hit a sandbar and began to capsize. Thinking they were in shallow water, the Rangers jumped off. Dragged down in deep water by the weight of their equipment, Lieutenant Joseph Zagata and 16 men of E Company, 1st Ranger Battalion, drowned. Other boats stopped to help, which created a situation where elements of the second wave landed before the first. Seaman First class Thomas A. Sheridan, USCG, shed his clothes and dived into the pitching surf to rescue nine soldiers. He hauled them ashore one at a time, together with their 90-pound packs. Sheridan also picked up 33 men of the same group in his boat and landed them. As the enemy fire continued, the Rangers touched down at 0335, 50 minutes late, followed shortly by the 39th Engineers.

Green Beach was a maze of wire obstacles and antipersonnel and antitank minefields. Many of the 4th Battalion Rangers were seriously wounded. In D Company alone, all the officers were casualties. One Ranger, 29-year-old First Sergeant Randall Harris, was seriously wounded, but still led the men while holding his exposed intestines in place with his cartridge belt. He, and his men, carried on fighting for two hours after he was wounded. Fighting their way through enemy beach defenses, the Rangers swept into Gela, fighting house to house. Harris survived and later received the Distinguished Service Cross and a battlefield commission.

Donald J. Hunt, a crewman on board LST-313, recalls the run for the beach:

On the morning of July 10, 1943, in extremely heavy seas, we were scheduled to launch away and escort five 2 1/2 ton ducks to the beach. Everyone was sick from the violent storm, which had engulfed us. We all felt that the invasion should be cancelled until the ocean waves subsided, but unfortunately, the 82nd airborne paratroopers had already been dropped behind the beach and had to be backed-up with reinforcements or suffer being cut off and wiped out.

The die was cast, and over the side we went. Somehow, with the help of God, plus good luck, we managed to lower away from the davits and get away from the ship. Several huge waves nearly dashed us to bits, as we hung from the davit cables. The waves pounded us against the ship. They tossed us straight out of the water, and dropped us back down, jerking the davits and placing great strain on the cables.

We rendezvoused at the bow of the ship and waited for our five 2 1/2 ton ducks to waddle down the bow and off the ramp. But, unfortunately, it wasn't that simple. The waves would lift and slap the ducks against the side walls of the ramp opening. And if I recall correctly, one of the men lost his leg or sustained severe damage to his leg when the duck was thrown against the ship as it was coming off the ramp. The injured man was brought along side of the ship, and hoisted aboard for emergency medical treatment.

It was 2:00 AM. We were at least fifteen miles or more from shore, when our mission began. With no moon and in total darkness, we headed for what we thought was the beach.

In one stream of light from a passing shell, we could see that one of our ducks had been taken by the sea. As the duck disappeared beneath the waves, the surviving soldiers were left bobbing in the jet black sea. The ocean pulled them up and down, like little wooden puppets. The waves crashed all around them, rolling them close together and then separating them by 30 feet or more. They were in serious jeopardy if we didn't act immediately.

The rescue was not easy, as the men were lost in the darkness, and with only sporadic light from the flying shells, the success rate was low. And when you thought you had a soldier close enough to throw a life ring to, the waves would pick him up and toss him 30 feet or more away. Miraculously, we managed to pull every man out, and again, focused on our objective: the beach. Once underway a second, waterlogged, duck sank. Again, the same difficult rescue mission commenced, and fortunately, we successfully retrieved all the soldiers.

All of the men, soldiers and sailors alike, were sick, tired, wet, and vomiting. Even those who had nothing left to expel, took to dry heaves and suffered from disorientation. After what seemed like an eternity, we finally approached the beach. We were unable to land, however, as the beach was completely jammed with small, overturned vessels and broached craft, that we couldn't find a place to beach.

We finally found a spot large enough to run in and beach. We dropped our ramp and got our soldiers to the beach just as the incoming waves picked us up and threw our stem around, allowing the next wave to broach and roil us over on our side. Our lone DUKW managed to successfully reach the beach; and that, along with our 50 soldiers, who were wet, tired, sick, and totally unprepared, were now expected to complete their prime directive. Unfortunately, they had no weapons, no guns, no ammunition, *no nothing*. They were lucky to be alive, and fortunate to land on a part of the beach which was secured.[14]

From the transport *Jefferson*, Lieutenant Colonel Irving O. Schaefer's 2d Battalion started toward shore at 0303. While, battling wind and sea, and grazed by what appeared to be friendly fire from supporting warships, the control vessel veered off course and at 0355 finally touched down, not on Green Beach 2, but on the southern end of Yellow Beach 2, close to Point Braccetto. The first troops ashore were greeted by a few rifle shots, but there were no casualties. There was little will here to contest the invasion and a machine-gun crew surrendered without firing a shot.

Jefferson's second wave veered off even farther to the right. About 50 yards offshore, the boat crews finally realized that they were heading straight for the rocks at Point Braccetto and into a 10ft to 12ft surf. It was too late to change course, and the first two landing craft broadsided into the rocks and capsized. Weighed down by their equipment and pounded against the submerged rocks, 27 men drowned. The other landing craft managed to get to the point without capsizing, and their passengers laboriously crawled ashore. Three more men would have drowned had it not been for Sergeant Jesse E. East, Jr. of F Company, 157th Infantry, who, after scrambling ashore, tossed off his equipment and dove back into the surf three times to save fellow soldiers. He tried a fourth time, but, apparently tired from his previous efforts, failed, and drowned with the man he was trying to save.

Six of the seven landing craft from the third wave followed close behind. The men already on the rocks tried in vain to wave off the approaching boats. Only two of the six incoming craft grounded on sand. Four hit the rocky area along the north side of Point Braccetto, and though able to unload their troops and cargo, were unable to retract. The seventh boat, far off course from the beginning, landed most of G Company north of Scoglitti on the 179th RCT's beaches.[15]

The landing of the 45th Division's 180th Regiment under Lieutenant Colonel Roy E. Moore was also delayed. The previous night's storm had built up rough seas, seas which drove landing craft out of position. The troops did not land until 0430 on *Cent* Force Red Beach, a shallow cove, which had a seaward approach that was clear of rocks and shoals. By the time the 180th Regiment, 45th Division landed it was scattered over a ten-mile front.* The *Cent* beaches proved to be not as favorable as anticipated. There was soft sand, shifting sandbars, and heavily fortified exits that were dominated by artillery, which also dominated most of the beaches – numerous machine-gun positions were near the center and western end, and there was an extensive defensive position along some 350 yards of the bluff line containing three coast artillery pieces and another ten machine gun emplacements connected by a series of trenches. Six LCIs bearing Major Everett W. Duvall's 2d Battalion, 7th Infantry, started their run into *Joss* Force Red Beach near Licata at 0415 as the sky began to get light. The LCIs were about 450 yards from the beach in a wide, shallow V-formation just opening into a line abreast formation when enemy artillery batteries opened fire directed chiefly at the left half of the line.

The LCIs on the right side of the line escaped the heaviest fire because the Italian gunners could not depress their gun tubes enough for the shells to reach them. Five of the LCIs beached successfully, although heavy surf had hampered them. One lost both ramps soon after they were lowered and was able to land its troops only after salvaging the port ramp. Soldiers in some instances became casualties before they reached the ramps, others were hit while disembarking.

The LCI on the left flank drew the heaviest fire, a flanking fire from both left and right. The Italians shot away her controls and communications as she beached, and though able to lower both ramps, she started to broach almost immediately and had to cut the ramps away. She then swung around completely until her stern rested on the shore, and the troops scrambled over her stern and dropped to the beach.

Shortly after daybreak Admiral Conolly took the Amphibious Force Command ship USS *Biscayne* (AVP-11) close in to shore so that both he and General Truscott could see the beaches. The progress they saw of the assault

---

* The seas were so bad that between 150 to 200 landing craft had been driven ashore by midmorning.

the troops had made securing the beaches and advancing inland was encouraging. First Lieutenants Oliver P. Board and Julian W. Cummings, flying Piper L-4 grasshoppers that had taken off from an LST equipped with an improvised flight deck, flew over the beaches for more than two hours and reported enemy positions and the locations of friendly units, confirming Conolly's and Trescott's impressions.[16]

As dawn broke Luftwaffe and Italian fighters and bombers attacked. Messerschmitt Bf 109s, Junkers Ju 88s, and Italian fighter-bombers dropped flares and attacked the *Cent* Attack Force Area. Eleven enemy dive-bombers attacked the cruiser USS *Philadelphia* (CL-41) and USS *Thomas Jefferson* (APA-30).

The first victim of the air attack was USS *Maddox* (DD-622), which was steaming alone on antisubmarine patrol when she was hit by a bomb dropped by an Italian Ju 87 Stuka at 0421. One of the bombs exploded *Maddox's* aft magazine, causing the ship to roll over and sink within two minutes, taking 210 of her crew with her. The Stuka returned, strafing the 74 survivors before departing.*

The minesweeper USS *Sentinel* (AM-113) was next. At around 0500, a bomb exploded about 200ft off her starboard quarter. Flares inshore of the minesweeper illuminated her for the enemy aircraft. After surviving five more attacks, during which nine of her 60-man crew were killed, and shooting down two Messerschmitt Me 210 bombers *Sentinel* was about finished. After the more seriously wounded had been evacuated on LCI-33 and SC-530, the remainder of her crew boarded PC-550. The gallant little ship capsized at 1030 and went under at 1045.

Lieutenant Commander Blair Walliser, USCGR, on board *Samuel Chase* later described the horror of the air attacks.

The dive-bombers were over the beaches now, skimming the ramp boats and the tank lighters and the various landing ships. And we saw "skip-bombing," where the plane lays a few sticks in the water at low altitude, and then watches them ricochet as the bombs leapfrog among the ships on the beach, ending up in a mountainous splash.

---

* The survivors swam in shark-infested waters for 17 hours before being rescued. *Maddox's* commanding officer, Lieutenant Commander E. S. Sarsfield, was posthumously awarded the Navy Cross for heroism displayed in supervising the abandoning of the ship.

Even though there were no friendly fighters in the area at the time for protection USS *Boise* (CL-47) and *Savannah* launched Curtiss SOC Seagull observation seaplanes at 0600 to locate targets and perform gunnery spotting. Messerschmitt Bf 109s had shot down both *Savannah* planes by 0730.

Walliser witnessed the slaughter:

> Two of them came by in a hurry, spied the scout plane from one of the cruisers busy spotting gunfire, and closed in on it. The battle was short and had an unhappy ending. What chance could a slow-flying scout biplane have against two Focke-Wulf fighters? The scout plane dove desperately, but the fighters swarmed all over it. There was something sickeningly unequal about it, like two wolves chasing a chicken. Wounded and smoking, she tumbled to the water. There was hardly time for her crew to get over the side before she sank, but a Coast Guardsman in a nearby landing boat picked up her men.

Ashore, troubles began piling up. The soft sand, shifting sandbars, and difficult exits had created congestion on the beaches that was further aggravated by enemy air and artillery barrages. *Dime* Yellow and Blue beaches were very bad due to enemy land mines. Casualties were being evacuated to transports by the ships' boats. Throughout the morning enemy artillery fire on *Dime* Red Beach 2 was so accurate that landing craft were temporarily diverted from landing. Stores piled on the beaches were being hit as well as craft.

The engineers efficiently cleared the land mines for the infantry. However, spotting and disarming vehicle mines was another matter. Buried four or more feet deep, a man could walk across them without difficulty. However, the first jeep that rolled over them was not so lucky and three bulldozers in a row also got blasted by the big Teller mines. By mid-morning artillery fire, rough surf, and poorly charted beach approaches resulted in between 150 and 200 landing craft being stranding on the shoreline. Walliser reported:

> It all added up to terrific congestion, and, in the midst of it, one bomber scored a lucky hit, and we had to evacuate two of the beaches. Then came an urgent call from the Army. Unload all possible antitank equipment at once. Other cargoes were hastily shoved aside; boats already loading were

unloaded and full priority was given the howitzer equipment. We didn't know why the urgency then. We found out later.

The reason for the priority unloading was because Italian and German tanks accompanied by infantry had been spotted closing in on the beaches – these were the spearhead of the enemy's counterattack.

The Italian General Guzzoni made strenuous efforts to throw the Americans back into the sea. Reinforcing his coastal troops, Guzzoni planned a counterattack against the beachhead, using General Chirieleison's Livorno Division, much of General Conrath's Herman Göring Division, and assorted Italian mobile units. At 0826 the cruiser USS *Boise* (CL-47) and destroyer *Jeffers* (DD-621) fired on the advancing columns.

An Italian tank-infantry team of reinforced company size came south down Highway 17 toward Gela. Gunfire from USS *Shubrick* (DD-639) disrupted their advance, knocking out some of the tanks. Around 0900 men of A and B companies, 4th Ranger Battalion, under Captain James Lyle reported nine enemy light tanks of the Renault type approaching from the north. Four tanks stopped at a grove of trees at a range of about 5,000 yards. The remaining five of these Italian tanks entered Gela, but without their accompanying infantry.

Rangers, waiting in ambush, attacked the tanks from basement windows and rooftops, using bazookas, sticky grenades, and satchel charges. Men, including Lieutenant Colonel Darby, climbed on the tanks, trying to open the hatches so that grenades could be dropped into the crew compartment. Captain Jack Street dropped 15lb explosive charges onto the tanks from the roof of a building. As the surviving tanks moved deeper into town, Darby and Captain Charles "Chuck" Shunstrom brought up a 37mm antitank gun by jeep, positioned it in the square, and with Darby as gunner and Shunstrom as loader, destroyed a tank. In 20 minutes the Italian tanks were badly beaten up and hurriedly withdrew under fire. At Lyle's direction the four tanks that had remained in the grove were attacked using 4.2in mortars. One tank was left smoking, and the others fled.[17]

General Conrath's Herman Göring Panzer Division posed a more serious threat to the landings that afternoon at 1400. First, a Tiger tank regiment struck the 2d Battalion, 16th Infantry, which had prepared defensive positions on ground overlooking the road junction at the coastal highway and had sent patrols almost to Casa del Priolo. Spotters called for naval gunfire support and soon 5in and 6in shells enveloped the Tigers, blunting the attack.

Conrath's infantry force had also jumped off at 1400 and run into the 1st Battalion, 180th Infantry, which, together with some paratroopers picked up along the way, was moving toward Biscari. Their attack stopped by the relatively small American force supported by one battery of the 171st Field Artillery Battalion, the Germans had come to a halt by 1530. However, the panzers weren't finished.

The next attack was better coordinated. Once again the Tigers led off, but this time the infantry followed close behind. Breaking through the thin American lines, the Germans overran the positions of the 1st Battalion, 180th Infantry, and took prisoner the battalion commander, Colonel Schaefer, and most of the surviving troops. The remnants of the battalion streamed south toward the coastal Highway 115. The way seemed open for German exploitation that would endanger the 1st Division beaches, when the 3d Battalion, 180th Infantry, suddenly appeared. Released from corps reserve to counter the German attack, this American force took defensive positions and held fast. Imminent disaster for the Americans was averted as the Germans unexpectedly panicked. German soldiers broke and ran in wild disorder, their officers finally stopping the rout just short of Biscari.[18]

The *Kool* Reserve force began landing on the Gela beaches at 1500. By nightfall all beaches were secured, although air attacks continued relentlessly throughout the day and well into the night. LST-313 was the victim of one such attack. Again, Donald Hunt tells what happened:

Late in the afternoon, we noted LST *313* off the beach and approaching with her a pontoon causeway, married to the bow. Around 15:00 hours, she beached alongside of LST *311* and prepared to start to unload her vehicles. But, as we started up the causeway ramp from the beach to rejoin the ship, we heard antiaircraft fire up the beach. Realizing that we were being subjected to another strafing attack, we had to make a quick decision. Should we run the 200 foot length of causeway and seek the safety of the ship's tank deck or to run back on the beach and get behind our pile of rations?

Incredibly, we chose the pile of rations. From there we witnessed the total destruction of ship and men. It appeared as slow motion, with the enemy approaching so low and close, that we all thought we could reach out and grab hold of the wings. Then we watched in horror as the bomb was released from under its wing, expertly arching downward, through the upper deck of

LST *313*. The bomb exploded on our tank deck, with a huge flash. It ignited the ammo and gas in the vehicles on the tank deck, and smaller jeeps, trucks and ambulances on the upper deck were blown up and off the ship like toys. Needless to say, had we not made the decision to run back to the beach, we too would have been in that tremendous explosion. Practically everyone in the tank deck and in the lower area of the open bow doors were killed. In all, it is believed that about 150 soldiers were killed or wounded. Men, who had been hailing us on to the ship only moments earlier, were gone. The pain of loss, at that instant, was monumental for us.

LST *311*, which was beached right next to *313*, used her stem anchor and engines to retract off the beach to escape the fire and explosions from *313*. The hours immediately following the explosion were spent pulling burned survivors and dead soldiers from the surf, with their monument of war burning behind us. The ship continued its furious burn, with sporadic explosions from stored ammo.

As we proceeded with our rescue efforts, the bodies and survivors were mostly flash-burned, making it very hard to handle them or provide any kind of comfort. They had the appearance of over barbequed meat, with leathery surfaces, and crackled edges. Uniforms were melted into the skin, and hair, eyes and nails were, in many cases, dissolved or melted, but somehow non-existent. There is no doubt that many of the survivors of the attack, died from their wounds. We worked as best we could, gathering the men, and finally huddling together on the beach for the night.[19]

The greatest threat to the American forces came at 0615 on July 11, when General Guzzoni renewed his attack against the shallow center of the American line – Piano Lupo, Gela, and the beaches beyond. He sent the three task forces of General Conrath's Hermann Göring Division forward. At the same time, one Italian task force, the one nearest Highway 117, jumped off, but on its own initiative, apparently after seeing the German tank battalion start south from Ponte Olivo airfield. To help support the converging attacks on Gela, German and Italian aircraft struck the beaches and the naval vessels lying offshore.

The Italian column passed the 26th Infantry, bumped into K Company, which was trying to get back to Gela, and headed directly for the city. Colonel Darby's force in Gela laid down heavy fire on the approaching enemy. The 33d Field Artillery Battalion began pounding away at both columns, and the two batteries from the 5th Field Artillery Battalion soon joined in. The 26th Infantry's Cannon Company and the 4.2in mortars in Gela also opened fire. The combined assault stopped the Italians.

First to feel the weight of the German attack was the 2d Battalion, 16th Infantry, at Abbio Priolo, where the infantrymen and paratroopers had little time to complete more than hasty foxholes and weapons emplacements. German tanks, a conglomeration of Mark IIIs and IVs, appeared, flanking the 2d Battalion from the west. The tanks rushed in, shooting their machine guns and cannon at almost point-blank range. The infantrymen and the paratroopers fought back with only a few bazookas plus their regular weapons. Aided by fires from eight howitzers of the 7th Field Artillery Battalion and part of the regiment's antitank company, the battalion held its ground.

General Conrath regrouped his forces and again sent them rushing at the American positions. This time, the tanks rolled directly down and tried to circle both flanks. The swinging German movement to the right brought the 1st Battalion at Casa del Priolo into the fight. As German tanks swept past the embattled Americans and joined with other German tanks at the eastern edge of the Gela plain, the Americans pulled slowly back to Piano Lupo under cover of supporting fires, both artillery and naval. By 1100, the Americans were back where they had started from around midnight. Despite heavy losses the Americans held on and the beaches remained secure.[20]

Due to the day's heavy fighting and casualties General Patton ordered that the 1st and 2d Battalions, the 504th PIR, the 376th Parachute Field Artillery Battalion, and a company from the 307th Airborne Engineer Battalion be dropped near Gela on the night of July 11 as reinforcements. Because of the heavy air attacks senior Army and Navy officers went to great lengths to inform everyone of the impending nighttime paratroop drop to prevent the planes being fired on by U.S. ships.

After more than a day and a half of heavy air attacks antiaircraft crews were on edge and that evening there was no let up. At 2000 Bf 109s attacked *Cent* shipping. At 2155 approximately 15 enemy aircraft attacked the *Dime* Attack Force transport area; near Gela, the *Boise* and all the destroyers except one were straddled by bombs falling on either side. Many ships were damaged by near misses. The transports weighed anchor and dispersed. The fighting raged for over an hour, and just as it ended the C-47s and gliders arrived overhead.

Captain Willard E. Harrison, Commander, A Company, 504th PIR, remembered later:

On the night of July 11–12, 1943, I flew in the leading plane of the first serial and reached the coast of Sicily near Punta Socca at approximately 2230 hours, thence flew in a northwesterly direction along the coast toward Gela. The left wing plane flew just over the water line, and the squadron of nine planes continued perfect formation up to the coast at an altitude of approximately 900 feet, We encountered no fire of any kind until the lead plane reached the lake [Lake Biviere], when one .50 caliber machine gun, situated in the sand dunes several hundred yards from the shore, opened fire. As soon as this firing began, guns along the coast as far as we could see toward Junta Socca, opened fire and the naval craft lying off shore, both towards Junta Socca and toward Gela, began firing anti-aircraft guns along the coast as far as we could see.

The antiaircraft fire, particularly from naval units, grew more intense, and to it was added fire from machine gunners and riflemen who attacked descending parachutists. The entire formation was badly scattered. The pilot of one of the planes that did return told of his difficulties:

A few minutes before reaching the drop point with the paratroopers, a shell smashed into the starboard side of the fuselage and knocked out a hole four by six feet while a fragment from the shell slit the aluminum and every rib from hole to rudder. Passing through the plane the fragment ripped off a door as a second ack-ack blast carried away a portion of the left stabilizer. The explosions also blew away a large piece of equipment, and the impact was so great that it felt like a motor crash in the pilot's cabin.

The airplane spun at a right angle and nearly pulled the controls from my grasp. For a second I didn't realize what had happened, then finding myself out of formation I began a violent evasive action. I saw three planes burning on the ground and red tracers everywhere as machine gunners sprayed us as if potting a flight of ducks.

Meanwhile I had cut into a less dangerous spot to give the parachutists a fighting chance to reach the ground. But I've got to hand it to those boys; one, who had been hit pretty badly by shrapnel insisted on leaping with the others although he'd been ordered to remain in the plane.

One of the more harrowing reports was that of First Lieutenant C. A. Drew, F Company, 504th Regimental Combat Team:

I was jumpmaster in Plane 531. This plane was leading a formation of 3 planes and was Number 7 in our Company, The pilot of my plane gave me the warning 20 minutes out from the DZ. After the red light came on he had to give me the green light in about 1 minute, due to the plane being on fire.

We jumped into a steady stream of AA fire, and not knowing that they were friendly troops. There was four men killed and four wounded from my Platoon. Three of these men were hit coming down and one was killed on the ground because he had the wrong password. After landing we found out this had been changed to "Think" – "Quickly".

The AA we jumped into was the 180th Infantry of the 45th Division. They also were not told we were coming. Later we found out that the 45th Division had been told we were coming but word never had got to the 180th Infantry of the 45th Division,

About 75 yards from where I landed, Plane No. 915 was hit and burned. To my knowledge, only the pilot and three men got out. The pilot was thrown through the window.

Another plane was shot down on the beach and another plane was down burning about 1,000 yards to my front. Altogether there were three planes I know of being shot down.

One aircraft passed low over the bow of *Susan B. Anthony* (AP-72) (off Scoglitti) and close by *Procyon* (AKA-2). Not identifying the C-47 as friendly, both ships opened fire. The plane crashed in flames just off the stern of the cruiser *Philadelphia*. Seconds later, fire from all the nearby ships blasted another C-47 out of the sky.

Flight Officer J. G. Paccassi (of the 61st Group) lost sight of his element leader after the turn to the northwest had been made and he went on alone to the drop zone, encountering heavy antiaircraft fire all the way. Paccassi's plane was hit just as the paratroopers went out the door and he quickly turned and headed out to sea, flying almost at surface level. Just off the coast, the plane was hit again; the rudder was shot away, and then both engines failed. As naval vessels still fired, Paccassi crash-landed into the sea. The destroyer USS *Beatty* (DD-640) fired on the downed aircraft for five seconds with 20mm guns before realizing that the plane was American, so then dispatched a small boat to pick up survivors.

The planes that returned carried four dead and six wounded parachutists, and eight full loads who had not been given an opportunity to jump. These included ten officers, two warrant officers and 95 men.

The following day, D-Day+2, more gliders were loaded and men of the Division Headquarters were ready to embark, when an order was received from Force 141 (15th Army Group) cancelling all projected movements by air.

Allied antiaircraft guns had shot down 23 and damaged 37 of the 144 American transport planes. The 504th Combat Team suffered a total of 229 casualties: 81 dead, 132 wounded, and 16 missing. In addition, the 52d Troop Carrier Wing casualties were reported as seven dead, 30 wounded, and 53 missing. Of the 23 destroyed planes, six were shot down before the parachutists had jumped. One of the C Battery planes was shot down at sea, carrying all its nine parachutists down with it, but from the other three there were five men saved by their reserve chutes – two struggled out of their plane after it had been hit twice and was on fire, and three were actually blown clear as their planes were demolished by antiaircraft fire.

General Matthew Ridgway later stated:

> Deplorable as is the loss of life which occurred, I believe that the lessons now learned could have been driven home in no other way, and that these lessons provide a sound basis for the belief that recurrences can be avoided. The losses are part of the inevitable price of war in human life.

George Henderson, Gunnery Officer on an LST, said, with deep emotion: "I don't know how many German planes we shot down that night but I can tell how many Americas we shot down."[21]

At 1600 on July 14, D-Day+4, a message from Vice Admiral H. K. Hewitt, Naval Commander Western Task Force, marked the end of the Assault Phase:

> Due to careful planning, excellent seamanship, gunnery, and engineering, and a high standard of proficiency and devotion to duty by all hands, the most difficult and complicated task of landing our troops on hostile shores has been successfully accomplished. Informed reports of especially meritorious acts and accomplishments have been many. I consider that all,

from the Task Force commanders to the lowest ratings, have performed splendidly and are deserving of the highest praise. Well done. It is now our duty to support, maintain, and build up the forces which have been landed. Carry on.[22]

The Assault Phase was over, but the battle for Sicily wasn't. Indeed, it went on until August 17 when the last Axis troops, an eight-man Italian patrol, was picked up by a German assault boat and ferried across the Straits of Messina to Italy. They were the tag end of a massive German and Italian evacuation of over 100,000 men and 10,000 vehicles between August 1 and 17.

Lessons Learned

Operation *Husky* was the first time Allied U.S., British, and Commonwealth forces operated in contiguous battle zones. Although Eisenhower, Cunningham, Tedder, and their respective staffs overall worked well together, dropping parachutists in unfavorable weather at night not only derided their capability to achieve their objects but also led to unnecessary casualties as well as alerting the enemy that an invasion was underway. This exacerbated an Allied intelligence failure, which underestimated the reaction times of Italian and German forces to the invasion. Unfortunately, the questionable advantage of night parachute operations was to be put to the test again when such operations were repeated on a larger scale at Normandy.

Another major failure was insufficient beach reconnaissance, which led to significant delays in securing and reinforcing the assault beaches. This, coupled with night landings on poorly marked beaches, led to confusion and loss of life and material. These mistakes were not repeated in subsequent assaults.

The introduction of LSTs, LCIs, and DUKWs significantly improved the ability to get men, equipment, and supplies quickly and efficiently onshore. DUKWs proved particularly useful because they could move inland without having to offload at the beach.

The U.S. Army's bazookas proved to be effective against light and medium tanks but were of little or no use against German heavy tanks. They were effective against hardened positions such as pillboxes, although for success, the operator had to expose himself to counter fire, which often killed him.

Although the lack of sufficient air cover and fighter protection was anticipated, its absence was felt in the lack of aerial reconnaissance, close air support, and fighter cover for the ships. This situation was avoided in future operations.

At the end of Operation *Husky* American losses totaled 2,237 killed and 6,544 wounded and captured. The British suffered 12,843 casualties, including 2,721 dead. German and Italian casualties were approximately 29,000 killed or wounded and over 140,000 captured.

Regardless of the cost, Sicily was a testing ground for new equipment and provided the necessary staging area needed to invade Italy, the first step into Hitler's *Festung Europa*.

Invasions of Italy

Based on the success in the early stages of Operation *Husky* and Italy's surrender on September 3 and the resulting Italian Army's collapse as a fighting force, General Marshall proposed an initiative to seize the port of Naples and the airfields at Foggia, some 50 miles northeast, followed by a drive on Rome. The operation, codenamed *Avalanche*, would be conducted by the U.S. Fifth Army commanded by Lieutenant General Mark Clark.

The Fifth Army plans called for coordinated assaults on the Salerno beach by two corps, one British and one American. After securing the beaches, the army was to advance inland to the mountains, then swing northwest to Naples. The Sele River, which bisects the Salerno plain, was to be the boundary between the British X Corps on the left and the United States VI Corps on the right. Under the command of Lieutenant General Sir Richard L. McCreery, X Corps included the British 46th and 56th Divisions, 7th Armoured Division, 2 and 41 Commando, and the U.S. 1st, 3d, and 4th Ranger Battalions. The support and service units of the Fifth Army were to be drawn largely from the Seventh Army in Sicily, and they included artillery battalions, field hospitals, and Quartermaster truck companies.

The plan was for four landing areas, designated by colored lights and panels, to extend southward from the Fiumarello River for a distance of two miles. Red Beach was to be 800 yards in length; Green, 500 yards; Yellow, 1,000 yards; and Blue, 1,500 yards. During the operation, the frontage was narrowed because of initial heavy opposition, particularly on Yellow and Blue beaches, so that each of the beaches was about 600 yards long.

Clark expected to meet some 39,000 enemy troops on D-Day and about 100,000 three days later after German reinforcements rushed to Salerno. Before that occurred, he hoped to land 125,000 Allied troops.

Vice Admiral H. Kent Hewitt, commanding the Western Naval Task Force, would be responsible for planning the employment, and directing the operations, of a fleet of warships, assault transports, landing ships and craft, and other vessels that would perform such diverse tasks as gunfire support, escort duty, mine sweeping, air support, motor boat patrol, and diversionary or cover operations. Subordinate commands of the Western Naval Task Force were the Northern Attack Force (under Commodore G. N. Oliver, RN) and the Southern Attack Force (under Rear Admiral John L. Hall, Jr., USN), which were the assault convoys; a Naval Air Support Force (under Rear Admiral Sir Philip Vian, RN), which was to provide air cover; and a separate Naval Covering Force (under Vice Admiral Sir Algernon Willis, RN), which was primarily to protect the assault convoys from the potentially dangerous Italian Fleet.

The combined strength of the Western Task Force was 201 warships, 41 troop and supply ships, and 333 major landing ships and craft. In addition to the grand total of 586 Allied naval units directly engaged in the landings, most of which were in their respective British or American sectors, there was a strong Royal Navy cover force and carrier support group.

D-Day was set for September 8.

Beach Terrain

Beaches near Naples were unsuitable for landings partly because of the sloped terrain, particularly around Mt. Vesuvius, which dominated the beaches, and the heavily fortified routes inland. Additionally, Naples was out of Allied fighter aircraft range from bases in Sicily.

Salerno, 50 miles south of Naples, which has a 20-mile stretch of beach, favorable landing gradients, and numerous exits to the main coastal highway linking Salerno to Naples and Rome, was chosen as the alternate landing site. However, the site also had some drawbacks. The mountains surrounding the Salerno plain would limit the depth of the initial beachhead and expose the invading troops to enemy observation, fire, and attack from higher ground. The steep vertical banks of the Sele River, which divides the plain into two sectors, would require assault forces to bring ashore bridging equipment to link the forces on either side of the river. On the positive side, Salerno was within range of Allied fighter aircraft based in Sicily, and Salerno's Montecorvino airfield, once captured, could sustain four fighter squadrons.

The Run Up to Operation *Avalanche*

While the Allies battled their way up the coasts of Sicily an event occurred in Italy that had a huge impact on the Allies and the future course of the war. On July 25, 1943, King Victor Emmanuel III of Italy informed Benito Mussolini that the Grand Fascist Council had just resolved by 19 votes to seven to remove him from office. As he left the meeting Mussolini was arrested. Following Mussolini's removal the new Prime Minister, Marshall Pietro Badoglio, initiated negotiations for an armistice with the Allies. Negotiations were completed and the Armistice of Cassibile was signed on September 3. However, the announcement was delayed until September 8. It was hoped the delay would prevent German forces under Field Marshal Albert Kesselring from having time to reinforce the area around Naples prior to the landings. It proved to be a false hope.

In fact German strength on the Italian peninsula had increased in mid-August when Field Marshall Rommel moved five infantry and two panzer divisions from Germany into northern Italy. A few days later, approximately 102,000 Axis forces fighting in Sicily withdrew to Italy, crossing the Straits of Messina when Allied forces failed to disrupt their retreat. The 45,000-man German Tenth Army, commanded by General Heinrich von Vietinghoff, was established on August 8 to facilitate Kesselring's control of operations. Its mission was to defend the heel of Italy (Puglia) and evacuate Calabria (the toe) when the Allies attacked. Kesselring, in conjunction with Vietinghoff, had three German divisions to hold the Naples–Salerno area and secure routes of withdrawal to Rome. The Hermann Göring Division was on the Naples plain, the 15th Panzer Grenadier Division was to its north, and the 16th Panzer Division had responsibility for defending the Salerno area to the south.

Hitler had also developed plans in case Italy deserted the Axis coalition. In such a situation, Rommel, responsible for the defense of northern Italy, was to occupy all important mountain passes, roads, and railroads and disarm the Italians. Kesselring was to disarm the Italians in the south and continue withdrawing north. [23]

Axis air reconnaissance over Allied-held North African ports revealed the massing of an invasion fleet, so the Germans knew the Allies were coming. The only question was where and when.

On September 3, six days prior to *Avalanche*, British and Canadian troops of the British Eighth Army, under General Sir Bernard L. Montgomery, launched Operation *Baytown* and landed at Reggio di Calabria at the southwestern tip of Italy, intending to tie down German troops in southern Italy and draw German troops away from the Salerno area further north.

Ray Ward, an officer with the Argyll and Sutherland Highlanders, wrote about the landing:

> We boarded our landing craft and cast off at 1900. At 0335 on 3 September 1943 – the fourth anniversary of the start of the war – the night exploded with an "Alamein barrage," a ferocious 600-gun bombardment. The sky sang with shells from Sicily as we chugged across the straits in the dark, watching in frozen fascination as the barrage straddled the enemy coast.
>
> All this turned out to be a complete waste of ammo. When we hit the beach at 0615, four kilometers north of Reggio di Calabria, our landing was unopposed. We were slightly dazed by the silence after the profligate bombardment. If someone had bothered to recce the beaches, I thought, or checked aerial reconnaissance photos, the shelling of an undefended coastline should surely have been avoided. But Monty had the firepower and there was an inevitability in its use.
>
> The Germans chose not to defend Calabria, preferring to concentrate further north towards Naples. We saw no Jerries but we bagged Italians – hundreds of the blighters, whose white flags had been waved the moment we landed – an instant labour force.[24]

Kesselring correctly deduced the main Allied target was further north up the coast, so instead of keeping troops south to counter the British–Canadian attack, Kesselring gradually pulled the German LXXVI Panzer Corps back.

Operation *Avalanche* D-Day

General Eisenhower announced the surrender of Italy at 1830 on September 8. Men in the invasion fleet heard the announcement and began cheering. The general feeling among the men was the landing would be unopposed, simply a matter of hitting the beach and marching into Naples. However, Italy's surrender posed a problem regarding the pre-assault bombardment. Since the Italians were no longer belligerents, should the shore defenses be shelled? If the Germans were manning the defenses then the beaches needed to be shelled. The Northern Attack Force carrying the British X Corps had been bombed and strafed by enemy aircraft, though with little effect, during the voyage, so the British concluded that the element of surprise had been lost. They decided in favor of a naval bombardment.

In the Southern Attack Force Major General Fred L. Walker, the U.S. 36th Infantry Division commander, and Rear Admiral John L. Hall discussed the option, but for multiple reasons decided against pre-assault bombardment, primarily because when he studied recent air photographs of the beaches and the surrounding high ground, Major General Walker could find no fixed or organized defenses in his zone. There would instead be short-range fire from destroyers along with rockets and mortars from LCIs standing close inshore.

By sundown of Wednesday, September 8, the Salerno invasion fleet passed Cap d'Orlando, Sicily, and headed straight for the Gulf of Salerno. H-Hour was 0330 on the morning of September 9.*

The Landing

At one minute past midnight on September 9, loudspeakers on the transports called the first boat teams to their stations. Soldiers clambered down the nets into landing craft. Motors sputtered and then roared as the first boats pulled away. Soon the calm sea was alive with snub-nosed craft, circling to reach their proper positions.

The night was oppressive. Not a breeze rippled the still water. The landing craft loaded with hot, sweating, wool-clad men, circled while waiting for the signal to go in. In the darkness some of the coxswains failed to locate their leaders. Lanes had been previously swept through the minefields, but occasionally mines broke free and drifted into the paths that the boats were trying to follow. Spray drenched the men and their equipment and many of the soldiers became seasick.

But at length the LCMs (Landing Craft, Mechanized) and LCVPs (Landing Craft, Vehicle, Personnel), carrying the first assault waves, turned east behind the guide boats toward the rendezvous deployment line, 6,000 yards from the Salerno beaches.[25]

---

* Concurrently with these two main landings, smaller landings were made along the coast west of Salerno for the purpose of seizing important military objectives. A Task Group, partly U.S., partly British, and including the Royal Netherlands Navy gunboats *Soemba* and *Flores*, was assigned the duty of occupying the islands off the Gulf of Naples – Ventotene, Ponza, Prociga, Ischia, and Capri.

Lieutenant Junior Grade Arthur Farter, USCGR, whose LCI was part of the large invasion force at Salerno, vividly remembered the landing:

It was D-day and H-hour was a few minutes away; we could see Mt. Vesuvius sputtering and flaring up on our port side, every minute or so. Though the night was dark, there were all kinds of lights to be seen – flares, gun flashes, and the colored signal lights: red lights, green lights, white lights, flashing and steady. We stared at our watches, awaiting H-hour. Suddenly we knew it had arrived. Countless gun flashes and explosions rent the air, both from ship to shore and vice versa. Tracer streams crisscrossed everywhere, and in several places we could see lines of fire running parallel to each other, but from opposite directions. The heavy batteries on the cruisers and destroyers opened up and displayed a beautiful yet awe-inspiring sight.

You could see, following the yellow gun flashes, the path of the large projectiles as they took flight, not rapidly in a breath-taking ruse, but slowly. The shells appeared as red-hot rivets, easily recognized that rose slowly in a curving path till they leveled off, moved on a few more seconds, then dipped, fell slowly to earth, and exploded in a glaring flash. There was so much to see that it was difficult to watch and grasp the intensity of the whole operation. It was tremendous. And it appeared more so when we realized that here, before our eyes, an alien force was present, and with its power and military might was seeking to destroy the defenders of a whole nation so that it might conquer that nation![26]

The 4th Ranger Battalion was selected to point the way in the assault, followed successively by the 1st and 3d Rangers, the 83d Chemical Mortar Battalion, and finally the engineers. After the 4th secured a beachhead, they would become a blocking unit so that the 1st and 3d Battalions could move up the road to capture Chiunzi Pass.

The small boats carrying the Rangers rendezvoused with a British destroyer that was their guide to the Sorrento Peninsula beaches north of Salerno. Colonel Darby wrote of the landings beginning with the rendezvous:

The captain shouted from the bridge, "I say, are you there?"

I answered, "I'm here."

The captain then said, "Off we go." The LCAs lined up in column behind the destroyer, very much like a mother duck and her brood.

In going towards Maiori the destroyer moved out, changed course a couple of times, and finally swung into the lane from which the small boats had only to continue straight ahead. The captain leaned over the rail with a farewell, "You are now on course."

The flotilla leader of the small boats blinked his rear light on, saying in effect, "No matter what happens, from now on you're on course. Don't change it even if your compass is pointing in reverse direction from what it ought to be."

In the darkness only the mountains of the Sorrento Peninsula could be seen in the distance, so we did not sight the small beach until the flotilla boat was about two hundred yards offshore. When the first assault craft hit the beach, it was exactly in the center of the thousand-foot landing strip. This landing was a complete surprise to the enemy. We broke radio silence when we hit the beach, telling the navy in code that we had landed.

Passing quickly through the beachhead held by the 4th Battalion, the 1st and 3d Rangers headed north up the highway into the mountains toward Chiunzi Pass. With scouts ahead, the men marched in single file on the edges of the road, advancing swiftly. It was pitch dark and the only sounds were the shuffle of combat shoes and the singing of crickets. An occasional toad jumped out on the road.

Suddenly the main party of Rangers came upon a parked car that the scouts had overlooked in the intense darkness. A not-unfriendly German voice hailed them. Guns whipped around, and after a few shots the enemy surrendered. A group of fourteen Germans had been laying mines on the road. Several of their number had gone off for a few hours, and when the Rangers approached, they thought their missing members were returning.[27]

British Commandos captured the town of Salerno against light opposition. X Corps landed under a heavy naval bombardment, meeting significant opposition as its soldiers fought their way inland.

Ahead of VI Corps, the beaches of Paestum were dark and silent. Then a strident voice over a loudspeaker, apparently from the landing area, called out in English, "Come on in and give up. We have you covered." Disregarding the taunting voice the first wave landed on all four beaches exactly at H-Hour.

To those first waves of first assault troops, the beaches seemed clear of the enemy. Some areas were not even marred by the black web of barbed wire. Mine-detecting squads felt their way ahead with their round, flat, lily-pad detectors, like humped, biped anteaters, clearing paths through the mines and marking them with white tape. Then in came the DUKWs, the amphibious trucks, and the light artillery, and more landing craft grated to a stop on the steep beaches. For five minutes after the first soldier stepped ashore the landing was unopposed.

Then the Germans in their well-hidden pillboxes and gun positions opened up. Unsurprised by the invasion, they had been waiting for the moment when the beaches were full, and it would be unnecessary to aim to find a target. Flares went up immediately, and the enemy guns opened fire as soldiers leaped into the shallow water, waded to the narrow strip of sand, and started inland toward the assembly areas.

Machine guns and rifles chattered, spat and snarled from positions 150 yards behind the waterline, and, beyond these, 88mm and larger shells belched from pillboxes. One shell struck a landing craft and it sank in a geyser of splinters, gray paint and water.

Combat engineers and attached special units, coming in behind the assault troops, encountered many difficulties. They found little wire to impede them, but mines caused both casualties and damage to vehicles. Six engineer officers were shot down by tank fire, and the first bulldozer ashore was destroyed by a shell from a tank at a range of 150 yards.

Landing craft struck by enemy fire burned near the shore or drifted helplessly. Equipment floated in the water and radios were lost in the surf. Men swam for shore as boats sank under them. As a 60mm mortar squad debarked, the gunner tripped on the ramp and dropped the piece into the water, machine-gun fire scattered the men in the darkness, and individuals joined whatever unit happened to be near them. An 81mm mortar platoon came ashore intact but without ammunition, as the boat carrying its shells had sunk. Staff Sergeant Quillian H. McMichen, hit in the chest and shoulder by machine-gun bullets before his assault boat grounded on the beach, found the ramp stuck. Despite his wounds, McMichen kicked and pounded the ramp till it fell. Then he led his men to a firing position on the beach where he received a third and fatal wound.

In the sand dunes, Sergeant Manuel S. Gonzales crept under machine-gun fire toward an enemy weapon. A tracer bullet creased the pack on his back and set it alight. Slipping out of his pack, he continued to crawl even after grenade fragments wounded him. At last he was close enough to toss hand grenades into a German machine-gun position and destroy the crew.

Private J. C. Jones gathered a few disorganized men around him, led them against several enemy machine guns, and took them inland to his unit's objective. Sergeant Glen O. Hiller, though painfully wounded, refused medical treatment in order to lead his squad across the sand.

Sergeant James M. Logan, lying on the bank of an irrigation canal, killed several Germans coming through a gap in a rock wall 200 yards away. He then dashed across open ground, seized a machine gun position after destroying the crew, swung the gun around, and opened fire on the enemy.

Almost from the moment the enemy had started firing, scattered enemy tanks had made it difficult for all combat teams to reach their objectives. However, they did not field a large-scale attack until around 0700. The troops on Yellow and Blue beaches suffered the first concentrated tank assault when, as the battalions of the 141st RCT were still attempting to reorganize after their landing, they were attacked by 15 or more Mark IVs, belonging to the 2d Tank Regiment, 16th Panzer Division. Some of these tanks had apparently just come from the south while others had been stationed close by when Allied troops landed. Five or more were on each flank and four were in the center. Maneuvering back and forth across the flat terrain along the regimental front, the Mark IVs had the advantage of protection from machine guns set up in the shelter of 4ft stone walls and inside many small farm buildings.[28]

The tanks worked in small groups, supported by infantry units usually no larger than platoon size. A lone tank, reaching the shoreline shortly after dawn, fired on approaching craft. Antiaircraft guns on LSTs, machine guns on landing craft, and men on the beaches took the tank under fire and soon drove it off. Other tanks spotted on the road behind the dunes were also fired upon.

It was the individual American infantryman who kept the German tanks at bay during the early morning hours. Corporal Royce C. Davis destroyed a tank after crawling under machine-gun bursts to a place where he could use his rocket launcher effectively. He pierced the armor, then crept beside the disabled and immobile vehicle to thrust a hand grenade through the hole and kill the crew. Sergeant John Y. McGill jumped on a tank and dropped a hand grenade into the open turret. Private First Class Harry C. Harpel kept at least one group of tanks from reaching the beach when, under enemy fire, he removed loose planking from a bridge across an irrigation canal and rendered it impassable.

Enemy snipers and machine gunners kept up their fire while the tanks were attacking. On the left flank, Captain Hersel R. Adams, Operations Officer of the 3d Battalion, led a group of K Company men in an infantry charge against the oncoming vehicles. Captain Adams was wounded but he urged his men to leave him beside a nearby canal and continue the fight. Their steady resistance broke up the tank formation for a time. Later, when the tanks reformed and came back, Captain Adams was exposed to their fire and killed. Private First Class Edward L. Rookey and Private Lavern Counselman, members of a machine-gun squad of M Company, saw four enemy tanks approaching their position. Obtaining a bazooka from a wounded man, they crawled to within 30 yards of the tanks and fired on them. Their fire and that of other men in their squad forced the Mark IVs to withdraw.[29]

Although a number of tanks were destroyed, at least one hit back hard as witnessed by Lieutenant O. J. "Jack" Elliott, First Naval Beach Battalion, who landed on Green Beach:

I was embarked in an LCI (Landing Craft Infantry), below decks until we grounded and the ship's control officer opened the doors to the deck. Simultaneously with grounding on the proverbial sandbar, a barrage of gunfire greeted us. With no real reason to hold back, I made my way down the landing ramp which ran down the bow of the landing craft, followed closely by Ensign Randy Herman, a very gutsy, very young kid who was to perform many duties preparatory to bringing in the following landing craft waves. We waded through waist deep water to the point where water meets sand and instinct told us to drop. We did.

We had not been told of the fact that there was a farmhouse and a canal tollhouse, directly behind this beach. It was now daylight. The firing from the gun emplacements behind the dunes, tanks having been added to the armament in the farmhouse and the canal toll house, stopped. Almost immediately we understood why. A heavily laden LST, loaded main deck and top deck with trucks also loaded, was slowly approaching the beach a short distance from where we had taken cover. They couldn't seem to understand our efforts to wave them off and get them to retreat from this area. It was a tragic mistake.

Since we had landed we had tried to get word up to Red Beach to stop all incoming landing to Green Beach. Nothing worked in time to save this one. The German forces in the tanks, farmhouse, and canal house, deliberately held their fire until the LST had grounded, anchored, and opened the bow doors and let the ramp down. It was really a horrible sight. Before the first truck had started down the ramp the barrage began. The ship was literally torn to pieces, truck after truck hit, and caught fire. Then the shells began to pierce the hull, igniting fires and explosions on the tank deck. We could only lie there and watch. The only possible good to come of this incident was its obvious message to the Task Force Commanders, "Don't send anything else in here until you wipe out those gun emplacements behind the beach."

Green Beach was closed down immediately. The battalion elements were ordered to Red Beach and joined the forces there shortly after dark.[30]

On the left at Red and Green beaches, the 142d Regimental Combat Team, commanded by Colonel John D. Forsythe, began the push that was designed to take it eventually to the high ground extending from Ponte Sele through Altavilla, Albanella, and Roccadaspide to Mount Vesole and Magliano. On the right at Yellow and Blue beaches, the 141st RCT, under Colonel Richard J. Werner, was already under fire as it moved to maintain contact with the 142d at Mount Vesole and Magliano and to occupy key points in the mountain arc as far as Agropoli at the southern end of the Gulf of Salerno.

After H-Hour the second and third assault waves hit the beaches at eight-minute intervals. On Red and Green beaches, the men of the 142d worked their way through barbed wire and around enemy machine guns and tanks. Behind them shells formed geysers in the water, and equipment from stricken craft floated offshore. On the left flank of the regiment, the 3d Battalion Combat Team, commanded by Lieutenant Colonel Thomas H. McDonald, was to reorganize at the railroad east of Paestum, advance north about three miles, then turn east to Tempone di San Paolo. On the right flank of the regiment, the 2d Battalion Combat Team, under Lieutenant Colonel Samuel S. Graham, was also to reorganize at the railroad before advancing inland along the Capodifiume River to occupy the nose of Mount Soprano, northwest of Hill 386. Under Lieutenant Colonel Gaines J. Barron, the 1st Battalion, in reserve at the beginning of the assault, was to land after the 2d and 3d Battalions, assemble, and take up a position at the southeast end of Hill 140.

While the first elements of the infantry combat teams were hurrying from the landing craft to the dunes, engineers began their work of organizing the beachhead area for communication and supply, cutting gaps in the barbed wire, and searching for mines. The initial invasion plans had directed that the

531st Shore Engineers (reinforced), a regiment of veterans from the African and Sicilian campaigns, under the command of Lieutenant Colonel Russell S. Lieurance, was to support the assault troops on the beaches. One company of engineers was to work with each battalion combat team, while one battalion would be held in reserve and be available for defense and assistance wherever needed. They arguably had one of the most dangerous tasks of the invasion – the construction of exit routes off the beaches – as the bulldozers were especially vulnerable targets for enemy fire, and a number of engineers were killed while bravely undertaking this task under heavy enemy fire.

The engineers also took an active part in the fighting. First Lieutenant George L. Shumaker, commanding Company D, 531st Shore Engineers, led a small group of his men in an attack against the Tower of Paestum in the village of Licinella where enemy snipers were firing on Green Beach. With the help of several infantrymen, including Corporal Howard J. Tucker who picked off the snipers, the party destroyed the machine guns and even drove off tanks hidden behind the buildings. Shumaker was wounded in both arms, but Tucker, Technician Fifth Grade Nathan S. Perlman, and Sergeant John J. Schneider carried on the fight until all the Germans at the target were killed or captured.

Offshore, a scout boat, commanded by Lieutenant Junior Grade Grady R. Calloway, USCG, supported the 142d by launching rockets at Green Beach, where enemy machine gunners and snipers were concealed in the grove and behind the dunes. Shortly before dawn army units ashore and support boats laid down a smoke screen which proved effective in protecting landing craft against shell and machine-gun fire.

At about 1020, 13 Mark IV tanks rumbled down from the direction of Battaglia between Highway 18 and the beaches, approaching the 142d Infantry command post which had been set up at Capaccio Station, and endangered both the division command post and the beachhead. Fortunately, about 30 minutes earlier a DUKW had come up the road, pulling a 105mm howitzer of the 151st Field Artillery Battalion. The gun crew immediately started firing, and despite having absolutely no cover, destroyed five tanks and forced the remaining eight tanks to withdraw.

Around 1145 13 more tanks launched an attack from the north near the 36th Division Command Post in the tobacco warehouse at Casa Vannulo. The Americans, watching from ditches along the railroad, waited for them to get within easy range. When the Germans opened fire at noon their barrage was met by 142d and 143d Infantry Regiment bazooka teams, a 143d Infantry Cannon Company 75mm self-propelled howitzer, and a 37mm antitank gun of the 36th Cavalry Reconnaissance Troop. Second Lieutenant John W. Whitaker's 75mm howitzer crew destroyed three tanks and the 37mm antitank gunners claimed two tanks knocked out at 170 yards. The surviving tanks withdrew.

An hour later the Germans attacked again, this time with ten tanks. When the attack hit, three howitzers of the 133d Field Artillery Battalion added their fire power to the melee. Three of the ten tanks were destroyed before the rest. After losing eight tanks in less than two hours there were no more tank threats against the beaches from the north.

In spite of enemy activity in the air and on all the beaches, the work of disembarkation continued. Ships, landing craft and personnel all became casualties. The order that the assault was "to be pressed home with relentless vigor, regardless of loss or difficulty" was obeyed to the letter. The beaches were seized and held, in spite of enemy gunfire and counterattacks. Despite contact having been made almost immediately with Germans, who put up a strong opposition, the Allied troops successfully established bridgeheads.

By 1530 the airfield at Monte Corvino, east of Salerno, was in Allied hands. Late in the evening tank destroyer and tank units began to arrive from the beach, and were mostly sent to the north flank, as air reconnaissance, statements of prisoners, and other information about the enemy indicated an attack from this direction was probable. The 29th Panzer Division was reported to be concentrated 30 or 40 miles to the northeast, while the 16th Panzer Division, now in contact with the 36th Division, was expected to withdraw and join the 29th.

These combined German units might attack down the corridor between the Sele and Calore Rivers. The Division's Commander, Major General Walker, meanwhile, directed that at dark all units were to hold in place, reorganize, and be prepared to move out next morning to their assigned objectives.

On the whole, VI Corps met with considerable success on D-Day. Allied troops controlled the plain south of the Sele River and occupied the high ground, an average distance of five miles from the beaches. Only on the right flank was the issue in doubt. There the infantry had absorbed vicious enemy attacks without being routed. Men, vehicles, artillery, and supplies continued to pour on to the beaches where the engineers labored efficiently under constant fire. Dumps were set up, exit roads were operating, antiaircraft batteries were in position, and communications were finally working. The U.S. had secured the beachhead.

September 10–17

While a temporary calm settled on the beaches during the night, for the landing ship crews the hours after dark were the worst time. Enemy bombers struck just after dusk, their raids lasting from a few minutes to an hour and a half. Men rushed to battle stations as General Quarters was sounded as many as four times during one sea watch – a total of four hours. Lieutenant Greene, USCGR, on board a Coast Guard-manned LCI(L), reported:

> These attacks presented the worst aspect of the whole operation, for we, on the small craft, could not see the planes or shoot at them, our guns being of too small a caliber, but we could hear the roar of engines as they dove, dropped flares, then came back to lay their eggs. Very discernible above the noise of anti-aircraft gunfire were the high-pitched whine and whistle of bombs which fell and struck nearby. Close ones always detonated with a terrific roar, and small craft like ours would vibrate from the concussion.
>
> The raids forced the officers and men to stay awake practically all night long, and when you remember that our work of unloading transports of their troops and supplies took all the daylight hours and then you may well realize how much sleep was gotten. No one, I am sure got more than one hour's unbroken rest at any one time. Men would be relieved from gun stations, but would fall to the deck where they were and try to catch a few minutes sleep. Chow was carried to the men at their gun stations by mess cooks. After three days and nights of this, human nerves became taut. Men would jump, startled at noises caused by the slamming of a hatch or the clatter of a falling helmet.[31]

On September 10, Fifth Army troops captured Salerno and began making steady progress inland.

Even though the Luftwaffe increased the number and intensity of attacks, the Northwest African Tactical Air Force headquarters proposed to reduce the fighter cover over the assault area. Admirals Hewitt and House protested the decision in vain.

By September 10 Kesselring and the other German commanders realized Salerno would be the decisive action. Having failed to coordinate counterattacks on September 9, Kesselring gathered the XIV Panzer Corps (including the 16th Panzer and 15th Panzer Grenadier Divisions, and the Luftwaffe 1st Parachute Panzer Division Hermann Göring) in the north, operating in an area that included the Sorrento peninsula and Salerno, with the 15th Panzer Grenadier and the Hermann Göring Divisions, in the south. He also increased the amount of air power directed at the beaches.

Luftflotte 2 began to employ all its available aircraft against the Fifth Army, and enemy air activity was at its height during that night of September 10 and throughout the next day. Of the 625 German planes based in southern France, Sardinia, Corsica, and the Italian mainland, no more than 120 single-engine fighters and 50 fighter-bombers were immediately available at bases in central and southern Italy. However, their short distance from the Allied beachhead made it possible for a plane to fly several sorties each day. During the night of September 10 and the following day, the Germans flew about 120 sorties, concentrating mainly on shipping and naval craft. One ship badly damaged was *Savannah*, which was forced to withdraw due to the destruction and number of casualties that resulted from a square hit from a German bomb or rocket.

Lieutenant Greene described what it was like to be strafed by a German Bf 109F:

All guns were manned as the plane approached but we were forced to hold our fire because a sister ship was abeam to port, about 150 yards distant, and the approaching aircraft made its approach from that bearing, thus presenting us with the situation of killing our own friends in the nearby vessel. We held our fire as he dove, watching for a chance to give him a few bursts, but as he came down, a Flak ship and destroyer fired at him, from long range.

The Flak ship scored a hit, but as the enemy plane came down at terrific speed, all his guns were blazing at us. The other LCI(L) commenced firing and later claimed several hits also, but the Messerschmitt's guns never ceased till he crashed between our two LCIs, showering us with shrapnel and debris. His aim was good, unfortunately, for we received numerous bullet holes in our vessel, and had five men hit. One of the wounded was our No. 2 gunner, who was shot above the heart. The other four men received shrapnel wounds;

one in his eyes, causing permanent blindness, and the others minor wounds in face, legs, and arms.

LCT-624 was hit squarely by a bomb and burst into flames. The survivors were picked up and the craft sank in a few minutes. The oil slick on the surface burned for hours. "Miraculously, we were not attacked again that afternoon or evening," Lieutenant Greene reported, "for by that evening our large convoys with bigger ships had arrived, and were a few miles astern of us. The enemy bombers went after them and let us go." That evening, just after dusk, the convoys astern were subjected to an air attack, but they defended themselves well and men in the flotilla observed three flaming airplanes streak out of the sky in as many minutes and crash into the sea, illuminating the horizon where they fell.

Even hospital ships displaying the internationally recognized Geneva Red Cross weren't immune from Luftwaffe attacks. Despite the bands of green lights and brilliantly illuminated red crosses clearly identifying it as a hospital ship, on the night of September 13 Luftwaffe planes bombed the British hospital ship HMS *Newfoundland* while it was en route to Salerno carrying nurses. Before the ship sank, British vessels rescued all 103 nurses aboard and evacuated them to Bizerte, Tunisia.

The Allies fought their way off the beaches, across the surrounding plain, and into the surrounding mountains. From the south, units from the 26th Panzer Division had joined XIV Panzer Corps by September 12. The combined forces entered the fight against the U.S. VI Corps around Salerno. To the north the Hermann Göring Division with detachments of the 15th Panzer Grenadier Division formed concentrated on the British X Corps. Added to the German forces was at least one 3rd Panzer Grenadier Division battalion in the line on September 14. Elements from the combined German divisions were also readying a counterattack against the Fifth Army.[32]

Landings on September 12 saw increasingly savage fighting as British, Canadian and U.S. units attempted to break through the encircling German units and head north to Naples. The Germans made full use of their advantages in position and in mobility. Tanks, followed by infantry carried in half-tracks, concentrated quickly at exposed parts of Allied lines and made rapid stabs.

Typically, whenever a position did not offer opportunity for further exploitation, the Germans withdrew, and in a few hours were ready to strike in another direction. If the position was important for future plans, they immediately fortified it with a small group of infantry, well equipped with machine guns and mortars, and held it against all odds, even when bypassed by counterthrusts. In the mountains, one 88mm gun, strategically placed on a bare nose along Highway 91 north of Contursi, delivered direct fire on almost the entire length of the valley floor. It seems that the piece was not camouflaged, but the light haze in the mountains and the flash suppressor so concealed the gun that only an observer directly in line with the barrel could spot it. Four hundred to five hundred yards behind the gun, a panzer armed with a 75mm gun supported the 88mm. This combination of weaponry caused the greatest possible delay to the advancing U.S. forces, and once the advancing troops had been slowed, the 88mm pulled out and moved farther back up the road.

It wasn't until the night of September 17 that the last German forces were cleared from in front of the 45th Division's positions on the hills surrounding Salerno. Two days later 36th Division units pushing east finally secured the last part of the Salerno plain. It took until October 6 for the Allies to reach Naples, the main objective of Operation *Avalanche*.

As the Allies clawed their way north against German resistance, weather became a major factor. The bitter cold in the mountains affected men and equipment. Units of the Fifth Army had fought since early September and by December were tired and discouraged. Every gain was paid for with more dead and wounded, but they fought on. However, the offensive was at a stalemate along the Gustav Line, which extended across the Italian peninsula from Minturno to Ortona. The line, buttressed by snow-capped peaks flanking the Liri Valley, and protected by the rain-swollen Garigliano and Rapido Rivers, was a formidable barrier. Unless a plan could be devised to defeat the defenses of the Gustav Line, the Fifth Army faced another long and arduous mountain campaign.

Winston Churchill believed that the solution would be to land at Anzio, approximately 60 miles behind the German lines and 30 miles south of Rome, with the aim of drawing German troops away their defensive positions.[33]

Anzio – Operation *Shingle*, January 24–29, 1944

Planning for the Anzio landings began in earnest on November 8, 1943, when an order came from General Alexander to the U.S. Fifth Army under General Mark Clark instructing it to plan an amphibious landing on the Italian west coast. Then, at the Tunis conference on December 25, 1943, Prime Minister Winston Churchill and the ranking Mediterranean commanders decided that an amphibious landing of not less than two assault divisions behind the enemy's right flank was essential for a decision in Italy.

The amphibious operation was timed to coincide with a general Fifth Army offensive calculated to tie up the German Tenth Army's 13 divisions. At the same time, Allied air power would hit the German lines of communication around Rome and between the beachhead and the German land front.

Initially D-Day was set for December 20, but for numerous reasons it was postponed several times until January 22, 1944. The lack of landing ships and craft and the failure of the Fifth Army and British Eighth Army to reach their objectives against German opposition were some of the reasons for the postponement.

The landing area chosen was a stretch of the narrow Roman coastal plain extending north from Terracina across the Tiber River. It included the port of Anzio and was approximately seven miles deep by 15 miles wide around the port. Forces designated for the assault included the U.S. 3d Division, the British 1st Infantry Division from the Eighth Army front, the British 46th Royal Tank Regiment, the U.S. 751st Tank Battalion, the U.S. 509th Parachute Infantry Battalion, the U.S. 504th PIR, British 9 and 43 Commandos, the U.S. 1st, 3d and 4th Ranger Battalions, and other supporting troops. This force was the largest that could be lifted by the limited number of landing craft available. It was estimated that the turnaround would require three days. As soon as the convoy returned to Naples, the U.S. 45th Division and the U.S. 1st Armored Division (less Combat Command B) would be brought in as reinforcements, bringing the total strength to approximately 40,000 troops. Major General John P. Lucas, U.S. Army, commander of the Fifth Army's VI Corps, was overall force commander and Major General Lucian K. Truscott, Jr. was commander of the U.S. 3d Division.

VI Corps' scheme of maneuver planned simultaneous landings on the Anzio and Nettuno beaches. The U.S. 3d Division would land three regiments over X-ray Beach, two miles south of Nettuno. In the center, the 6615th Ranger

Force (Provisional), as well as the 83d Chemical Battalion and the 509th Parachute Infantry Battalion, would land on Yellow Beach, adjacent to Anzio Harbor, with the mission of seizing the port and clearing out any coastal-defense batteries there.

The British force – the 2nd Brigade Group of the British 1st Division – would land on the Peter beaches, six miles northwest of Anzio. The 2nd Special Service Brigade of 9 and 43 Commandos would also land on the Peter beaches, but rather than taking part in the main assault would advance eastward to establish a roadblock on the main road leading from Anzio to Campoleone and Albano. The forces landing at Anzio and at Nettuno would link up to consolidate a beachhead, seven miles deep, centering on the port of Anzio.

The naval component, under the overall command of Rear Admiral F. J. Lowery, USN, consisted of the British and Allied Task Force Peter under Rear Admiral T. Troubridge with 215 ships and the U.S. Task Force X-Ray under Lowery with 154 ships.

The Mediterranean Allied Air Forces (MAAF) had about 2,600 aircraft, organized in roughly 60 squadrons (22 fighter, six fighter-bomber, four light bomber, 24 medium bomber, and two and a half reconnaissance). About 75 percent of the Allied aircraft were operational. B-25 Mitchell, B-26 Marauder, and Wellington medium bombers were used for attacking targets between 50 and 100 miles behind the enemy front. The MAAF's medium bombers, A-20 Havocs and the Martin 187 Baltimores, were used to destroy installations and facilities closer to the front. De Havilland's Mosquitoes and A-36 Apaches (also listed as "Invaders") provided direct support for the ground troops. Spitfires, Hurricanes, P-38 Lightnings, P-40 Hawks, P-47 Thunderbolts, and P-51 Mustangs escorted Allied bombers and intercepted and destroyed enemy fighters.

The planners assumed initial heavy German resistance and, therefore, provided a strong floating reserve – the bulk of the British 1st Division, with the 46th Royal Tank Regiment. In addition, the 24th Field Regiment, the 80th Medium Regiment, and the 504th PIR would land behind the 3d Division and assemble in a corps reserve.[34]

Time was of the essence since the majority of shipping allocated for the assault was needed for the Normandy landings in six months' time.

Assault landings were practiced, first from mock-ups on dry land and then in battalion and regimental landing exercises. The final exercises, codenamed Operation *Webfoot*, were held six miles south of Salerno between January 17 and 19 with craft provided by the U.S. Navy. The British portion went well but the U.S. units encountered bad weather during the night of January 17–18. In the darkness a navigational error caused the LSTs to open their doors far from shore. The DUKWs rolled down the ramps into heavy seas, too rough for the tiny vessels, and many were swamped. That night, the 3d Division lost 43 DUKWs; 19 105mm howitzers with fire-control equipment; and several antitank guns – an unrecorded number of men drowned. By mid-morning there was chaos on the beaches, and the whole rehearsal was completely disrupted. The loses were so severe that the battalion involved was replaced by a battalion of the 45th Division before the 3d Division sailed for Anzio.

General Lucas wrote about his reservations regarding the operation:

> I have the bare minimum of ships and craft. The ones that are sunk cannot be replaced. The force that can be gotten ashore in a hurry is weak and I haven't sufficient artillery to hold me over but, on the other hand, I will have more air support than any similar operation ever had before. A week of fine weather at the proper time and I will make it … the whole affair has a strong odor of Gallipoli and apparently the same amateur [Churchill] was still on the coach's bench.[35]

At 0005 on January 22 assault transports dropped anchor off Anzio. All was quiet except for the subdued rumble of landing craft headed for their assigned beaches. There was no preliminary long-range naval bombardment. Instead, just before the landing, at H-Hour-10 to H-Hour-5, two British LCT(R)s, each carrying 798 5in rockets, launched a short, terrific barrage, which burst with a deafening roar upon the beaches. Their mission was to make certain the enemy was not withholding his fire and to knock out defenses and minefields along the beach. Surprisingly, there was no return fire.

The first waves of craft nosed onto the beach at H-Hour, 0200. As ramps dropped, assault troops swarmed ashore. However, for the first time in any assault, the beaches were empty – the Allies had in fact achieved complete surprise. Except for a few small coast artillery and antiaircraft detachments, the only immediate resistance to the Anzio landing came from scattered elements of the 29th Panzer Grenadier Division.

The Ranger Force landed over the small beach just to the right of Anzio harbor and swiftly seized the port. The Rangers scrambled up the steep bluff, topped with pink and white villas overlooking the beach, and spread through the streets of the town, rounding up a few bewildered defenders. Except for a gap in the mole and some battered buildings along the waterfront, caused by Allied bombing, the port was captured intact.

After daylight four enemy 88mm batteries began sporadically shelling the port and Peter Beach. In spite of naval gunfire they could not be silenced that day. Floating mines were also encountered, although far less than the navy had expected. The minesweeper *Portent* struck a mine and sank, and another vessel was damaged. The Luftwaffe was not long in reaching the beaches. From 0850 an estimated 18 to 28 fighter-bombers made three raids on the landing areas. They caused only negligible damage except for one LCI sunk with 12 soldiers wounded. The number of craft lost for whatever reason on D-Day was very light for an amphibious operation.

The only medical installation ashore on D-Day was the 2d Platoon of the 33d Field Hospital, which landed its personnel and attached surgical teams at 1330, received its equipment three hours later, and was ready to accept patients at around 1800. The hospital was set up on the beach southeast of Nettuno. The 95th and 96th Evacuation Hospitals and battalion aid stations went ashore with the combat units to which they were attached, and litter squads from the 52d Medical Battalion accompanied the 3d Division as well as the Rangers and paratroops.

By midnight some 36,000 men, 3,200 vehicles, and large quantities of supplies were ashore – roughly 90 percent of the equipment and personnel of the assault convoy. Casualties were 13 killed, 97 wounded, and 44 captured or missing.

Although the Germans were driven from the immediate areas around the beaches, the beach and port areas, still within range of German artillery, were vulnerable targets for the shelling, which was increasing in intensity. Long-range 88mm and 170mm batteries dropped their shells sporadically on ships offshore and among troops working along the beach.

After the landing, the Allied forces advanced and expanded the beachhead. By the evening of D-Day advance elements of the 30th Infantry and 3d Reconnaissance Regiment had seized all the bridges across the Mussolini Canal. However, the Hermann Göring Panzer Division recaptured most of them that night. The next morning Lieutenant Colonel Lionel C. McGarr, commander of the 30th Infantry, brought up the remainder of his regiment, supported by tanks and tank destroyers. In sharp fighting it drove the enemy back across the bridges along the west branch of the canal.

The landings caught the German High Command and Field Marshall Albert by surprise, although they had anticipated a landing to the rear of their forces. Their reaction was swift and sure. By the end of D-Day, January 22, major German units including I Parachute Corps, the 65th Infantry Division (less one regiment), the 362nd Infantry Division (less one regiment), and two regiments of the 16th SS Panzer-Grenadier Division were en route to block Allied advances off the beaches.

Although the attack had caught the enemy momentarily off guard, General Lucas failed to act aggressively. Instead of pushing quickly to capture the Alban Hills, 20 miles away, he chose to consolidate the beachhead and wait for the German counterattack.

From D-Day unit the end of January 24, there were minor skirmishes on the beachhead, which was, as planned, roughly seven miles deep and 15 miles wide, centered on the port of Anzio. Its 26-mile perimeter was considered the maximum that could be held by VI Corps. However, the beachhead was too small – all of it could be reached by enemy artillery, and the forces within it had little space for maneuver. The chance for a quick advance off the encircled beachhead disappeared. By the evening of the 24th, the Germans were confident they could contain the beachhead forces and, as soon as they had substantially completed consolidating their forces, launched a counterattack that would wipe out the Allied beachhead.

By January 29 it was believed the German had not progressed beyond roadblocks, hasty field fortifications, and minefields along likely avenues of approach. General Lucas felt the beachhead was secured and decided to launch a drive toward Colli Laziali to coincide with a renewed offensive by the Fifth Army against the Gustav Line on January 30.

The plan was for one force to cut Highway 7 at Cisterna before moving east into the Alban Hills while a second advanced northeast up the Albano Road, before breaking through the Campoleone salient, exploiting the gap by moving to the west and southwest. A quick linkup with Fifth Army forces in the south was still believed possible.

To spearhead the assault General Truscott picked his Ranger Battalions. Jumping off one hour before the main attack, the 767 men of the 1st and 3d Rangers supported by a platoon of 43 men of the 3rd Reconnaissance Troop were to infiltrate under cover of darkness four miles across the fields to seize Cisterna by surprise and then, reinforced by the 4th Ranger Battalion and the 3rd Battalion, 15th Infantry Regiment, hold it until the 3d Division broke through and relieved them. Patrol reports and a careful reconnaissance of approach routes indicated that the Germans had not yet succeeded in consolidating their defenses, and Colonel Darby, force commander, believed his men could filter through. At the time VI Corps had 61,332 troops ashore. However, while Lucas was building up the beachhead Kesselring had amassed 71,500 troops backed by tanks and artillery.

At 0100 the 1st and 3d Ranger Battalions along with the 3d Recon troopers slipped across the Mussolini Canal on their mission to Cisterna. Concealed beneath a moonless, cloudy sky, the long column crept silently up the narrow Pantatto ditch, which runs northwest across the fields to the right of the Conca–Cisterna road. By dawn the head of the leading battalion had come out of the ditch where it crossed the road and was within 800 yards of Cisterna.[36]

The town of Cisterna was only a few hundred yards ahead, and the Rangers were in open fields, with light just breaking. The Rangers began running toward Cisterna in the hope of reaching it before the sun rose. When about 600 yards outside the town they passed through what seemed to be a German bivouac area and killed a large number of surprised enemy troops with bayonets and knives. When they had run 400 yards farther and reached the edge of Cisterna, all hell broke loose.

German forces consisting of the 715th Infantry Division and Herman Göring Panzer Division, including at least 17 German Mark IV Panzer and Mark V Panther tanks along with Nebelwerfer rocket mortars and flak wagons carrying quad 20mm antiaircraft guns, ambushed the Rangers.

Tracers burned through the air; mortars crump-crumped in sudden showers. Fire blossomed through the fields, from stone houses, from entrenchments dug before Cisterna, and from tanks hidden behind haystacks.

The Rangers who had infiltrated through to Cisterna were trapped.

Digging in along an irrigation ditch and fighting hard, they waited for the planned reinforcements. But this was not to be.

Moving out later than the 1st and 3d Battalions, the 4th Ranger Battalion ran into a roadblock made by two damaged jeeps and an Italian truck. They pulled these wrecks to the side of the road and six to eight medium tanks came up behind the Rangers to support their advance. All night the 4th Battalion had a running fight, and by dawn they were still short of the town of Isola Bella, the key point for the opening of radio communications.

Machine-gun tracers stabbed out of the night: men dropped. The leading company attacked, hurling grenades, slashing in with bayonets. Quickly, two machine-gun nests were overrun. But behind these, more guns opened up. The battalion had run into a strong point in the German line, organized in depth.

Lieutenant George Nunnelly, the leading company commander, ordered two violent assaults against the strong point. During the second attack he was killed. The German automatic weapons poured fire over the ground in front of them, covering every inch with bullets. The remnants of the company took cover in a shallow ditch.

Desperately, the 4th's CO, Colonel Murray, ordered A and B Companies to advance on the right flank. They ran into a vicious fusillade of fire and steel and two more company commanders died. The Rangers were forced to halt, while the firefight raged with mounting intensity.

Colonel Darby was with the 4th Rangers. In radio contact with the 1st and 3d Battalions in front of Cisterna, he knew these units had halted, and that the 4th must break through. The battalion moved forward, but with frightful losses. One platoon lost a lieutenant, four NCOs, and five men attacking one machine-gun nest.

German machine guns were seemingly everywhere, and German mortars spat a rain of death into the Ranger ranks. A German paratroop battalion had moved up to block the way. On Darby's staff, Major Bill Martin died, killed by mortar shards. Darby's personal runner, Corporal Stroud, was killed seconds later. Despite costly attempts to break through, the Ranger force had been fought to a standstill south of Isola Bella.

In front of Cisterna the Rangers halted 300 yards from the enemy when they spotted two enemy tanks hidden in the bushes on the opposite side of the road some 50 yards away. One tank began moving, and its cannon turned ominously in the direction of the Rangers. Two soldiers armed with bazookas slid forward and knocked out the tanks at practically point-blank range.

Major Alvah Miller ran forward, charging a heavy tank at the head of his men. The tank gun flamed with an ear-splitting crash. Alvah Miller never knew what killed him.

"One tank came out of a driveway behind a house ahead of us," said Sergeant Thomas B. Fergen.

One of my squad climbed aboard it while it was moving and dropped an incendiary grenade into the open turret. At the same time a bazooka gunner hit it head on, and I was up beside it with a sticky grenade. The grenade exploded while I was getting away. I ducked in time to see the tank blow up and start burning. One of the crew got out and tried to get under the tank, but I shot him.

Between sunrise and 0700, when radio silence was broken, we came to the realization that the battle was lost. Sunrise doomed us and marked the beginning of the hopeless, heroic fight that continued until the last Ranger was killed or captured, until the last few members of the two battalions made their escape.

"When it got light, we saw one big building ahead with trees around it," recalled Corporal Ben W. Mosier. "Behind us there was one tank and when we saw it, we cheered. We thought it was ours. We couldn't see very well, and then it opened up on us."[37]

The Rangers attacked the tank, set it aflame with a sticky grenade and a bazooka shot killed the crew when they tried to climb out of the turret. But with this tank gone, ten more appeared to take its place, and those ten were followed by German infantry armed with automatic weapons.

"The tanks caused most of the trouble," said Sergeant Fergen. "I was in a field with the rest of my men when the tanks moved in. They came from Highway No. 7, swinging into the field, racing after us. You could run about twenty yards and then hit the ground. If you waited longer, they got you. They got three next to me with a direct hit."

Major Jack Dodson, commanding officer 3d Ranger Battalion, knew he was cut off; there was no going back. The only hope for the Rangers was to move into Cisterna. The enemy had the Rangers pinned down with automatic fire in an area about 300 yards in diameter.

Reinforced by the 2d Parachute Lehr Battalion, the German attack continued with tanks, Nebelwerfer rocket mortars, flak wagons carrying quad 20mm antiaircraft guns, and artillery firing at point-blank range in to Ranger positions.

Soon after noon, German paratroopers backed by armored personnel carriers marched about a dozen captured Rangers toward the center of the 1st and 3d Ranger Battalions' position in an attempt to force the remaining Rangers to surrender. Ranger marksmen shot two German guards, but the Germans retaliated by bayoneting two of the prisoners and continued to march the rest forward. This scenario was repeated two more times. The third time several Americans were killed by mistake along with one or two Germans. Unnerved by what was happening a few men surrendered despite orders not to.

Heavily armed and armored German units split the remaining Rangers into smaller units and either capturing or killing them as they advanced.

The battalion doctor, taken prisoner while caring for his wounded, protested about being taken from the wounded men he was treating. The German soldier ignored him. The doctor seized the German's pistol and shot him. As he tried to return to his wounded, he was killed.

It had been seven hours from when the first shots were fired until the last American was killed or captured. When it was over 703 Rangers and 3rd Recon troops had been killed, wounded, or captured. Only six Rangers and one 3rd Recon trooper made it back to Allied lines.[38]

Although the Rangers failed to capture Cisterna at a suicidal cost, they contributed to the eventual successful breakout from the beachhead. The battle for Cisterna forced the Germans to delay their plans for two days until February 4. The attack which lasted until February 22 almost succeeded in breaking the Allied lines. The intensity caused so many casualties and came so close to Allied lines that some American artillery units were firing over open sights and others had to dragoon clerks and cooks from the rear echelons to serve as riflemen. The Allied breakout attempt proved costly. The 1st Armored Division lost 100 armored vehicles in the first day alone while VI Corps took over 4,000 casualties in the first five days of the offensive. Allied troops, however, took 4,838 enemy prisoners, including 1,000 in Cisterna, and destroyed or damaged 2,700 enemy vehicles.

From D-Day the Luftwaffe made a huge effort, its biggest since Sicily, to try to cut off Allied supplies. Small flights of fighter-bombers strafed and bombed the beach and port areas every few hours. At dusk, they would skim in low from the sea, through the smoke and hail of antiaircraft fire, and release bombs, torpedoes, and Henschel Hs 293 (nicknamed "Fritz X") radio-controlled anti-ship glider bombs onto the crowded shipping in the harbor. In a major raid on January 22 LCI-20 was sunk. The next night an aerial torpedo claimed the destroyer HMS *Janus* while a glider bomb damaged the destroyer HMS *Jervis*.

The night of January 24 three British hospital ships, HMS *St. David*, HMS *St. Andrew*, and HMS *Leinster*, were also attacked by Luftwaffe aircraft while evacuating casualties from the beachhead. As in the case of *Newfoundland*, the ships were well lighted and clearly marked with the Red Cross. *St. David*, with 226 medical staff and patients aboard, received a direct hit and sank. The two

Army nurses on board were among 130 survivors rescued by the damaged *Leinster*. One of these nurses, Second Lieutenant Ruth Hindman, had already survived the earlier bombing of *Newfoundland*.[39] USS *Plunkett (DD-431)* was also damaged.

The two heaviest raids came at dusk and midnight on January 29, when 110 Dornier Do 217s, Junkers Ju 88s, and Messerschmitt Me 210s sank the Liberty ship *Samuel Huntington* and the British antiaircraft cruiser *Spartan*.

Mines also took a heavy toll on shipping and men. The minesweeper *Portent* was lost on the 22nd. On January 24 an LST, carrying C and D Companies of the 83d Chemical Battalion, struck a mine. Most of the men were transferred to an LCI alongside, which also hit a mine and sank. The total number of casualties were five officers and 289 men. YSM-30 fell victim to a mine the same day.

Six days after the initial landing, many of the 200 Army nurses assigned to the 33d Field Hospital and the 95th and 93d Evacuation Hospitals waded ashore on the beachhead. Less than 30 minutes after their arrival, the men of the 33d Field Hospital, who had landed on the first day, warned the nurses to take cover during bombing or shelling wherever it was possible for them. No one, of course, left patients, no matter how heavy the attack, but if the nurse was off duty and there were no major hits, it was wise to head for a foxhole.

The rest of that day, the evening and the night passed with no further German attacks, underscoring the nurses' belief that Anzio "was just another beachhead." Many of the nurses, doctors, orderlies and other hospital staff had indeed been in North Africa and Salerno.

Their second night on Anzio would turn that belief around. With the evening and gradual darkness came the German planes beginning another in their series of unrelenting attacks. The night was filled with the sounds of exploding bombs and antiaircraft fire. Tracers from antiaircraft shells threaded the night skies with ribbons of fire. This was a standard night on Anzio.

"We learned fast," former Second Lieutenant Jessie Paddock said, as she thought of those first nights on the beachhead:

> After that second night, at the first sounds of an attack, all the nurses grabbed their helmets and headed for foxholes if they weren't on duty. That foxhole was like water in a desert to us. We'd crouch there with our faces toward the wall until the shelling or bombing finally stopped.

Of course, if you were on duty, it was another story. We just kept on working. You couldn't leave your patients no matter how bad it got. I remember one young corpsman who arrived on the beachhead about one week after us. We were veterans by then. Anyway, this kid thought that he should head for a foxhole whenever the shelling or bombing started. We had to tell him in no uncertain terms that when a person was on duty, they didn't head for a foxhole under any circumstances. It took him one more time and some kind of disciplinary action to convince him we were serious. After that, he just stayed on duty like the rest of us. At some very basic level, we were all scared, but we were too busy to worry about it.[40]

On February 7, a Luftwaffe plane attempting to bomb the port at Anzio was intercepted by a British Spitfire. While trying to gain altitude, the German pilot jettisoned his antipersonnel bombs on the 95th Evacuation Hospital. The direct hit on the surgical section killed 26 staff and patients, including three nurses; 64 others were wounded.

On February 10, in broad daylight, Second Lieutenant Jessie Paddock was walking from a hospital ward toward her tent where she was to meet her two tent mates and spend an hour or so of off-duty time. She could see her tent about 50 yards ahead of her, when the terrible sound of metal-on-metal brakes filled the air over the hospital, and her heartbeat quickened as she realized another shelling attack was about to hit the hospital area. She began to run toward her tent, calling for her friends Glenda and LaVerne to take cover. Her feet seemed to stick in the mud and take on a new weight as she strained to run faster.

There was a loud explosion behind her, and Lieutenant Paddock knew that one of the German antiaircraft shells had struck and exploded in the hospital area. A wave of energy seemed to be pushing her forward. She was calling out to Glenda and LaVerne again, then everything went black.

The German shell had exploded squarely in the middle of the cross arrangement of Unit C where 48 critically ill patients were hospitalized. The explosion partially destroyed the ward and sent huge chunks of shrapnel flying in all directions. The first thought of the 33d's personnel was for the helpless patients. Every available nurse, doctor and corpsman ran toward the disaster. They worked as fast as they could, transferring patients to litters for transportation to the 56th Evacuation Hospital, which was out of range of this particular attack.

When Second Lieutenant Paddock opened her eyes, she was looking up at the familiar faces of nurses and corpsmen. It took a few seconds to realize where she was, to remember what she had been doing. She glanced at the devastated tent that had been her home. Much of its canvas was in shreds, and there were several large holes in what remained.

"Where are Glenda and LaVerne? What happened to them?" Jessie Paddock asked. She was not at all sure she wanted to hear the answer.

"Don't you remember?" one of the nurses asked. "You went into the tent before you passed out."

Jessie Paddock could feel her heart beating against her chest, her mouth was dry and for a moment she felt she was going to lose consciousness again. She took a deep breath. "I don't remember being in the tent," she said, and forced the next words from her mouth. "Are they hurt bad? Are they going to be all right?"

One of the nurses put her arm around Jessie's shoulders. "Paddy, they're dead. They were both killed instantly."

"I don't remember who actually told me," Jessie Paddock said almost 50 years later, "but I'll never forget what they said. Glenda had been decapitated. LaVerne was eviscerated."[*][41]

Meanwhile, another shell smashed the generator of the operating tent, which caught fire. Medical personnel evacuated the 42 patients. The attack also killed one enlisted man and wounded four medical officers and another seven enlisted men.

It wouldn't be until May 25 that VI Corps fought its way clear of the Anzio beaches at a cost of over 29,200 combat casualties (4,400 killed, 18,000 wounded, 6,800 taken prisoner or missing) and 37,000 noncombat casualties.

---

[*] Two of the nurses of the 33d Field Hospital, First Lieutenant Elaine Rice and Second Lieutenant Rita V. Rourke were awarded Silver Stars for "gallantry in the face of enemy action." Three nurses were awarded the Purple Heart for combat wounds received on Anzio: Second Lieutenant Ruth D. Buckley, Elmswood, Wisconsin; Second Lieutenant Mary W. Harrison, Belyre, Ohio; and Second Lieutenant Fern Winegerd, Omaha, Nebraska.

First Lieutenant Glenda Spelhaug, Crosby, North Dakota, ANC and Second Lieutenant LaVerne Farquhar, Sidney, Texas, ANC of the 33d Field Hospital, and the nurses of the 95th Evacuation Hospital who were killed in the German bombing on February 7 – First Lieutenant Blanche F. Sigman of East Akron, Ohio, and First Lieutenant Marjorie Morrow, of Audulon, Iowa – were buried in the beachhead cemetery on Anzio, alongside infantrymen, tank drivers, physicians, and corpsmen also killed on Anzio.

Of the combat casualties, 16,200 were Americans (2,800 killed, 11,000 wounded, 2,400 taken prisoner or missing) as were 26,000 of the Allied noncombat casualties. German combat losses, suffered wholly by the Fourteenth Army, were estimated at 27,500 (5,500 killed, 17,500 wounded, and 4,500 taken prisoner or missing).

The fighting in Italy continued until the German surrender on May 8, 1945.

Lessons Learned

Operation *Shingle* was conceived as a military necessity when the Allies were stalemated in their drive to Rome and beyond. The planners did not define an objective, include alternate plans to account for enemy action, and, as at Salerno, underestimated the enemy's ability to react swiftly to the assault.

On the British landing beaches the lessons learned from the Dieppe raid were either forgotten or ignored and, once again, troops went ashore in an urban area. Any tactical lessons learned at Anzio were too late for the Normandy landings and, since there were not any more amphibious assaults in Italy, were not pertinent to future combat in the theater.

CHAPTER 8

BREACHING THE BARRIER

CENTRAL PACIFIC, MARCH–DECEMBER 1943

As a result of the Washington Trident Conference between Churchill and Roosevelt in May 1943, plans were made for the invasion of the Marshall Islands. The operation was to be carried out in three phases:

(1) the seizure of Kwajalein, Wotje, and Maloelap Atolls in the center;
(2) the occupation of Eniwetok and Kusaie as outposts to the north and west; and
(3) mopping-up to seize or neutralize the entire Wake–Gilberts–Marshalls system.

For the first actions to succeed, the Gilberts and Nauru would need to be captured as these islands would serve as bases for air reconnaissance of the Marshalls to the northwest.[1]

Since these attacks would be the first assaults against defended atolls, the planners wanted battle-tested troops with amphibious training. This limited their options to either the 1st Marine Division in the Southwest Pacific or the 2d Marine Division in the South Pacific. At that time, both divisions were recuperating after the bloody battles on Tulagi and Guadalcanal. Substituting the Army 7th Infantry Division upon completion of the Aleutian Campaign for one of the Marine divisions was also considered. General MacArthur refused to release the 1st Marine Division arguing "a diversionary attack [in the Marshalls] would of course assist the main effort in this theater [Southwest Pacific]."[2]

He believed that from a strategic stand point the best way of defeating Japan was from Australia through New Guinea and then to Mindanao in the Philippines with land-based support during the entire series of campaigns. He felt that moreover "no vital strategic objective is reached until the series of amphibious frontal attacks succeed in reaching Mindanao."[3]After further discussion between the Navy, Army, and Marine Corps, the 27th Infantry Division under Major General Julian C. Smith, then training in Hawaii, was designated as the Army component of the Gilberts operation. They would land on Makin.

Rear Admiral Richmond K. Turner commanded the Makin invasion fleet, Task Force 52 (TF-52), consisting of the attack transports USS *Neville* (APA-9), *Leonard Wood* (APA-12), *Calvert* (APA-32), and *Pierce* (APA-50); attack cargo ship *Alcyone* (AKA-7); landing ship dock *Belle Grove* (LSD-2); and Task Group 52.1 – LSTs 31, 78, and 179.

The Gilbert Islands – Operation *Galvanic*

The Gilberts straddle the equator some 2,000 miles southwest of Oahu. Most of them are low, coral atolls, rising a few feet from the sea, supporting coconut palms, breadfruit trees, mangroves, and sand brush. The Japanese seized Makin on December 10, 1941, and converted it into a seaplane base. In September 1942 they occupied Tarawa and Apamama. They stationed a considerable garrison on Tarawa, built an airstrip, and established the administrative headquarters for the naval forces in the Gilberts. On Apamama an observation outpost was established.

The attack on Makin would not be the first time that U.S. forces had landed there. The island had been the target of an operation by the 2d Marine Raider Battalion under Lieutenant Colonel Evans F. Carlson on August 17–18, 1942. Major James Roosevelt, President Franklin Roosevelt's eldest son, was second in command. The raid was intended primarily as a diversion aimed at upsetting Japanese plans to reinforce Guadalcanal, with the goal of forcing the Japanese to divert some of those reinforcements to the relief of the Makin garrison. The raiders also had the objective of gathering valuable intelligence and destroying enemy personnel and installations on Makin and Little Makin. Naval intelligence reported that 250 Japanese were on Makin, and that a shore battery covered the entrance to the lagoon where there was a good protected anchorage. Actually, only 43 Japanese of the 62d Guard Unit, Combined Special Naval Landing Force, under the command of Chief Warrant Officer Kamemitsu, were on the island.[4]

Raiders on Makin

The Raiders were transported to Makin onboard two submarines, *Nautilus* (SS-168) and *Argonaut* (APS-1). On August 17 at 0330, the men disembarked into 20 rafts. The unloading was complicated by a one and a half-knot westward current that pulled the submarines in toward the reef and required them to maintain a constant reverse to keep at a 500-yard distance from the reef. All rubber boats were cleared on schedule despite confusion resulting from heavy swells and a last-minute requirement that several boats launched from *Argonaut* pick up landing force personnel from *Nautilus*.

Voice communication was very difficult due to the roar of the surf and the noise of the sea washing through the limber holes in the submarines' decks. Without outboard motors to assist, it was impossible for the boats to rendezvous before heading for the beach, which created an unmanageable confusion on the water.

The situation was further complicated by a change in plans. After assessing the swift current, the strong wind conditions, and the heavy swells, as well as the lack of working outboard motors, Carlson decided that both companies should hit the beach together. Carlson felt that the landing must be accomplished before daylight and the confusion in the water made changing the landing plans imperative. This change in orders did not reach everyone. Lieutenant Oscar F. Peatross and his 11 men failed to get the change of plans and landed their boat at the original beach about half a mile to the southwest of the rest of the battalion and well behind Japanese lines. Within minutes of hitting the beach, a Marine accidentally discharged his weapon and the chance for a surprise attack was gone.

Dean Winters recalled that night:

> We landed about 100 to 150 yards from the main landing point. We hid the boat as best we could and crossed a road, contacting B Company in the village. The Japanese were in trenches outside the village and

were manning several machine-gun nests. There was a lot of small-arms fire. I had the Boys [antitank] gun along with Tiny Carroll. A truck was coming down the road, so I hit the deck, braced myself, and fired, hitting the truck in the radiator. Steam poured out and several Japs tumbled out.

I also used the gun on two seaplanes that landed in the bay. All of us were firing at them. The smaller one caught fire and burned. The bigger plane was a four-engine seaplane. I remember firing about 20 rounds. It took off, and flames came up on it, and then it went down.[5]

Shortly before 0600, Company A reported its point at Government Wharf and stated that Government House had been captured without opposition. Proceeding south, the 1st Platoon of Company A ran into a Japanese defensive position armed with four machine guns, a flamethrower, two grenade launchers, and automatic weapons and supported by well-concealed snipers firing from coconut trees who accounted for the majority of Raider losses.

The fighting was close and soon became fierce with snipers and Japanese machine-gun positions hampering the Raider force, which had little cover. A number of brave Raiders as well as desperate Japanese defenders lost their lives.

As the Raiders pushed forward, the islanders awoke. The locals were friendly and willing to help. However, they unfortunately over-estimated the number of Japanese on the island. Carlson took the information at face value and ordered a withdrawal to the beach.

By 1915 all the boats were lined up on the beach with those on either flank entering the water first. The first was Carlson's. The effort to return to the submarines was an unmitigated disaster. The rapid succession of the breakers, combined with their great force, proved too formidable for even the highly trained Raiders. After nearly an hour of struggling, during which almost all the weapons and equipment were lost, about two-thirds of the Raiders gave up, and were washed ashore. Waters recalled:

In the evening when we were supposed to evacuate, we got into our boat and tried to get it out, but the surf was too high. The waves were 15 feet or higher and they were breaking three at a time. The boat kept tipping over backwards, and we lost everything. To keep from drowning, I took all my clothes off. The last thing we tried to do was swim out to the reef with a long rope and tow the boat with the rope. As we got near there the guy I was with yelled, "Shark!" I never saw him again. I immediately turned around and rode the waves back in to the beach.[6]

After daylight, a group of men fought a terrible battle with the surf and made it to the submarines. A little later another group was organized and also succeeded in reaching the submarines. Approximately 70 Raiders remained on the beach. During the remainder of the day, however, they completed the rest of their mission with the exception of capturing prisoners. Carlson's men reported that everyone seen that day was loaded into the remaining rubber boats and an outrigger canoe. The trip back to the submarines took three very difficult hours.

Forty hours had elapsed since the Raiders first left the submarines. Raider casualties were 18 confirmed dead, with five others believed killed in a strafing attack on their rubber raft while attempting a rescue mission, and seven men believed to have died in the surf attempting to return to the submarines. Carlson later stated:

> There can be no question about the eighteen that were killed in action, for I checked their bodies. The twelve "missing" were presumed to have been lost in the surf during the first night attempt at evacuation and during the strafing of the boat the following morning.

By his calculations, all Raiders were accounted for. However, in the confusion on board the submarines following the raid, his count wasn't accurate. After the war it was discovered that nine men had been left behind. They eluded capture until August 24. The Japanese then shipped them to Kwajalein. Arriving on September 2, the nine were imprisoned in cells measuring 6ft long by 30in wide with a 6ft ceiling. They were starved, tortured, and finally beheaded on October 16, 1942.[*][7]

The raid did yield intelligence information including plans, charts, air defense details on all Japanese-held Pacific islands, battle orders, one top-secret map that provided the air defense capabilities of all Japanese-held Pacific islands, and details of the strength of all Japanese-held Pacific islands, the strength of the air forces on them, and the forces' radius of operations, methods of alert, types of aircraft, and operation plans for future emergencies.[8]

---

[*] Sergeants Allard and Cook, Corporal Gifford, Privates First Class Davis, Pallesen and Olbert, and Privates Mattison, Kems and Roberton.

Japanese Reaction and Reinforcement

While the raid on Makin was a great U.S. propaganda victory, afterward the Japanese reevaluated their Gilbert Islands defenses which, to this point, had consisted of only token forces. On Betio the natural defense formed by a shallow reef surrounding most of the island was augmented with a log barricade around much of the island's perimeter. Concrete gun emplacements, bunkers, pillboxes, trenches, fire pits and machine-gun nests with interlocking fields of fire, and four 8in naval guns at Temakin Point and near Takorongo Point were added. In addition, there were multiple lines of barbed wire, tetrahedrons along the waterline, and a number of antitank ditches across the island.

U.S. Naval Intelligence estimated that on this tiny, narrow island, only three miles long and less than 600 yards across at its widest point, the Japanese had eight or nine coastal defense guns, 12 heavy antiaircraft guns ranging from 75mm to 12cm, 12 medium antiaircraft guns from 40mm to less than 75mm, 81 antiboat positions for weapons of sizes ranging from heavy machine guns to 40mm guns, and 52 light weapons.

Also based on a U.S. Naval Intelligence estimate, the garrison size was not less than 2,500 and not more than 3,100 men. Actually, there was a total of 4,583 men from the 3d Special Base Force, the 6th Yokosuka Special Naval Landing Force (SNLF), the 7th Sasebo SNLF,* the 111th Construction Unit, the 4th Fleet Construction Department, and the 755th Naval Air Group. Among the construction departments were several hundred noncombatant Korean laborers on the islands.[9]

Operation Planning

For the U.S. to succeed in taking the occupied islands meticulous planning and training were essential, and the responsibilities for the planning and training for the forthcoming landings eventually fell to six separate headquarters. In all Pacific operations outside General MacArthur's Southwest Pacific Theater, Admiral Nimitz, as Commander in Chief, Pacific Fleet and Pacific Ocean Areas (CINCPAC-CINCPOA), exercised supreme command and so held ultimate responsibility for the success of the endeavor. Next in the

---

*   Special Naval Landing Forces were Japanese "Marines" of the *Rikusentai*.

chain of command was Vice Admiral Raymond A. Spruance, designated Commander, Central Pacific Forces, the highest operational fleet command in the Central Pacific Theater. Under him was the Fifth Amphibious Force, an organization established on August 24, 1943, and commanded by Rear Admiral Richmond Kelly Turner.

On September 4 the V Amphibious Corps, commanded by Major General Holland M. Smith, USMC, was created to better coordinate training and control of troop elements involved in Central Pacific amphibious landings. The aim of the first assaults would be to capture the Gilberts and they would be undertaken in stages.

After reviewing the proposed invasion plans, V Amphibious Corps questioned the feasibility of attacking Nauru. They believed that Nauru offered too many hazards for an amphibious attack at that particular time. It was about 390 miles west of the westernmost of the Gilberts, which would place an additional strain on available shipping. Also simultaneous landings in the two places would necessitate a wide dispersal of supporting fleet elements, leading to a dangerous division of forces that would be risky, especially in view of the presumed possibility of a Japanese naval counterattack.

Makin Atoll was considered just as good as Nauru as the location for an air base to be used in operations against the Marshalls. It was also thought to be considerably less well defended. Furthermore, the fact that it was only about 105 miles north of Tarawa made it possible to concentrate the supporting fleet in one area and, therefore, avoid the danger of excessive dispersion. The capture of the small island of Apamama was also added to the plans. It was thought by capturing the island the Americans could better consolidate their hold on the Gilberts. Again, the primary consideration was to gain an air base from which to strike the Marshalls. Taking Apamama promised to be the least difficult of the three objectives.[10]

Based on the recommendation that Makin should be invaded instead of Nauru, it was decided that the 27th Infantry Division would land on Makin while the 2d Marine Division would seize Tarawa and Apamama. D-Day for *Galvanic* was set for November 20 and involved simultaneous landings on both Makin (Operation *Kourbash*) and the largest Tarawa Atoll island, Betio (Operation *Longsuit*). Apamama would be occupied after Tarawa was secure (Operation *Boxcloth*).

Preliminary operations, designed primarily to strengthen the American control of the air approaches to the Gilberts, were launched. The first preparatory operation for capture of the Gilbert Islands was the unopposed occupation of islands in the Ellice group southeast of the Gilberts in August. Then, early in September, occupation forces and engineers were put ashore at Baker Island, 350 miles northwest of the U.S. base on Canton Island and almost due east of Tarawa, to develop air facilities. The construction of airfields commenced immediately and by October aircraft of both the U.S. Army and Navy, operating from these fields, were harassing Japanese forces on Nauru and the Gilbert Islands and were obtaining valuable photographic intelligence of the latter group.

Carrier Task Force raids on Tarawa and Makin during September and on Wake in October reduced the force of Japanese air attacks on U.S. positions in the Ellice Islands and destroyed a substantial portion of Japanese reconnaissance aircraft strength in the area.[11]

So that the carrier raid against Tarawa would be as successful as possible it was decided that the runway on Betio would need to be put out of commission. To that end, on the night of September 18, 24 Seventh Air Force, 11th Bombardment Group, B-24s flew out of Canton Island;* 18 reached the target and achieved excellent results with frag clusters and general-purpose bombs. The next morning, planes from the carriers *Belleau Woods* (CVL-24), *Princeton* (CVL-23), and *Lexington* (CV-16) raided Tarawa with very little interference from the Japanese. They then set out for Tarawa again, followed by 20 of the B-24s, for a reconnaissance and final bombardment mission. In addition to obtaining complete photographic coverage of the island, the planes dropped 30 tons of general-purpose bombs. The enemy fought back with antiaircraft fire and the attackers were intercepted by 15 to 20 "Zekes," which shot down one B-24 and damaged ten others.[12]

Tarawa – Operation *Longsuit*

The assault plan called for landings on Betio's northern shore by three reinforced battalions landing abreast on the one-mile stretch of lagoon shoreline between the northwest end of the island and a point roughly halfway

---

*   Before the war Canton Island was claimed by both the U.S. and Britain until April 6, 1939, when the U.S. and Britain agreed to hold Canton under joint control. Pan American Airways built flying boat and hotel facilities on the island in May 1939 for its service to New Zealand. The *Pacific Clipper* (a Boeing 314) departed on December 4, 1941, and was the last civilian flight off the island until November 1946.

up the lagoon coast. Midway on the landing beach a long pier extended out from the shore for a distance of about 50 yards. This pier, along with a beached Japanese freighter nearby, was a key terrain feature of the beach area.

The assault regiment was the 2d Marines, under the command of Colonel David Shoup. Attached was a battalion from the 8th Marines. Each assault battalion was assigned to a beachhead of about 500 yards. From west to east, they were broken down as follows:

Red Beach 1, 3d Battalion, 2d Marines, commanded by Major James F. Schoettel.
Red Beach 2, 2d Battalion, 2d Marines, commanded by Lieutenant Herbert R. Amey, Jr.
Red Beach 3, 2d Battalion, 8th Marines, commanded by Major Henry P. "Jim" Crowe.
Regimental reserve, 1st Battalion, 2d Marines, commanded by Major Wood B. Kyle.

Other beaches were designated as contingencies, Green Beach along the western shore (the "bird's head") to the right of and adjacent to Red Beach 1, and Black beaches 1 and 2 on the southern shore.

Amphtracs (LVTs) would carry the first three waves, and the succeeding waves were to follow in LCVPs and LCMs. These waves would transship into the returning LVTs. Saturday, November 20 was D-Day and 0830 H-Hour.

As the Marines began debarking at 0320 Rear Admiral Harry W. Hill, the commander of the Southern Task Force (TF 53 was assigned to take Tarawa), noticed the troopships were in the wrong area, masking several ships providing pre-invasion bombardment. Marines had already begun crawling down the nets as the massive ships moved to the correct area with LCVPs desperately trying to catch up. There were further delays because the LVT(2) drivers had missed the rehearsal and were not familiar with signals, speeds, and load limitations, a factor which slowed both the transfer of men from the LCVPs and the forming of assault waves. The assault waves had to align themselves on the slowest tractors, and fully loaded LVT(1)s could not keep up with the LVT(2)s. H-Hour was delayed until 0900. Landing teams of 488 men from each of the three Assault Battalions were boarded in the 125 amphibian tractors.

The assault waves were preceded by the Regimental Scout/Sniper Platoon, led by First Lieutenant William Hawkins, and a detachment of combat engineers under First Lieutenant Alan G. Leslie, Jr. The Scout/Sniper Platoon consisted of troops chosen after Guadalcanal. In a divisional history Richard W. Johnston wrote about them:

> Their mission was to land on the end of the pier that reached 500 yards into the lagoon and clean out all Japs – Japs who might enfilade the assault waves. They made the pier, at 0855 – the first Americans to land in the Gilberts, the first men ashore in the Central Pacific offensive (if the pier could be called shore). On the way in, they learned a terrible truth: instead of the usually low neap tide which had been taken into account, we had an even lower "dodging tide," and the reef was almost bare. It would not float the shallow-draft Higgins boats. Only the amphibious tractors could be assured of reaching land. They learned something else, too. There were plenty of Japs left on Betio, and they were shooting with rifles, machine guns, antiboat guns, mortars, and mountain guns.[13]

Whip-sawed by machine-gun fire and pelted with shrapnel, the first three waves made the beach. LVTs from the first wave headed for Red beaches 1 and 2 got hit the hardest. Red Beach 1 presented the only irregular shoreline on Betio Island. It was in a deep cove indenting the island just east of its western tip. The boundary between the zone of action of the 3d Battalion on Red Beach 1 and that of the 2d Battalion, 2d Marines, just east of it on Red Beach 2, lay almost at the point where the shoreline straightened out to sweep in a fairly regular line toward the island tail. All along the reaches of Red Beach 1 lay a coconut log barricade, erected as an obstacle over which invading troops must crawl. The barricade was separated from the water on the western half of the beach by approximately 20 yards of coral sand. On the east the beach was much narrower, and in most places the water lapped at the base of the logs. High tide would cover all of the beach strip within the cove. The principal source of enemy fire seemed to be one large emplacement at the left extremity of Red Beach 1, between it and Red Beach 2.[14]

The first assault battalion to reach its assigned beach was Major Schoettel's 3d Battalion, 2d Marines, who landed on Red Beach 1. Their landing began at 0910 with Private First Class Moore ramming his LVT 4-9 "My Deloris" onto the seawall. On the right half of that beach, the Marines of Company I leaped from their LVTs, clambered over the palm log beach barricade, and began advancing inland. On the left of the beach, astride the boundary between Red Beach 1 and Red Beach 2, the Japanese raked K Company with flanking fire from their emplacement before that unit could gain the shelter of the barricade.

Private First Class Gilbert Ferguson recalled what happened on board his LVT: "The sergeant stood up and yelled 'everybody out.' At that very instant, machine gun bullets appeared to rip his head off."

Private First Class Newman M. Baird, a machine gunner aboard one of the first LVTs ashore recounted his ordeal: "We were 100 yards in now and the enemy fire was awful damn intense and getting worse. They were knocking [LVTs] out left and right. A tractor'd get hit, stop, and burst into flames, with men jumping out like torches." Baird's own vehicle was then hit by a shell, killing the crew and many of the troops. "I grabbed my carbine and an ammunition box and stepped over a couple of fellas lying there and put my hand on the side so's to roll over into the water. I didn't want to put my head up. The bullets were pouring at us like a sheet of rain."[15]

Among casualties was Privates First Class Donald M. Libby. He and Private Frank Joe Smith were the only Marines in their LVT who were not killed. Most of the men died when mortar fire blasted the tractor near the shore. Libby, who'd already been wounded by machine-gun fire, was thrown into the water when the mortars hit, losing his rifle. When he came to the surface he found the LVT wreckage shielded him from the enemy fire, so he grasped hold of a wheel, with only his nose and eyes showing above the water. He was without a weapon and had nine gunshot and shrapnel wounds including machine-gun bullets lodged in both of his thighs. Libby figured that the cold salt water of the lagoon might stop the bleeding, so he decided to stay there until darkness. The battle raged over the lagoon but no more Marines attempted a landing on that part of the beach. Libby remembers:

> The minutes passed like days, and I tried to think of faraway things. But all I could think of was what a hell of a note this was: me a boy from Bangor out in the middle of the Pacific with only my bill sticking above the waves and with a bunch of little monkey men waiting on shore ready to kill me if I made the slightest move.

A life preserver came floating by. Libby grabbed it, put it on, and decided he'd try swimming out to sea as soon as night came. Shortly after sunset, Libby was getting ready to shove off from his shelter when a man appeared around the wreckage and stared at him. The man wore an American helmet, had a long rifle strapped to his back and carried a bayonet in one hand.

He said to Libby, in good English: "What state are you from?"

"Maine. Where you from?"

The man made no reply but raised the bayonet, and Donald saw that there was a hook on the weapon. He saw, too, that this was no American Marine. The man jabbed at Donald's throat. Libby put up his left hand and the blade pierced his palm. The jab put the Japanese soldier off balance. Libby seized the bayonet by the blade with his right hand and twisted the weapon from the Japanese soldier's grasp. As he fumbled for his rifle, Libby hit him on the ear with the handle of the bayonet. The Japanese soldier groaned and slid into the water. Libby hit him on the forehead as he went under, then held him there for many minutes.

After that he started paddling out to sea with blood pouring from his bayonetted hand. He was almost unconscious and his body was wrinkled like a prune when he was picked up a few hours later by an American landing boat about 1,000 yards off shore.[16]

K Company suffered heavy casualties from fire from the Japanese strongpoint on the left, I Company made progress over the seawall along the "bird's beak," on Red Beach 1 but paid a high price, including the loss of the company commander, Captain William E. Tatom, who was killed before he could even debark from his LVT. Both units lost half their men in the first two hours. Major Michael P. "Mike" Ryan's L Company, who were forced to wade ashore toward Green Beach when their boats grounded on the reef, sustained 35 percent casualties. Ryan recalled the murderous enfilading fire and the confusion. Suddenly, "one lone trooper was spotted through the fire and smoke scrambling over a parapet on the beach to the right," marking a new landing point. As Ryan finally reached the beach, he looked back over his shoulder. "All [I] could see was heads with rifles held over them," as his wading men tried to make as small a target as possible. Ryan began assembling the stragglers of various waves in a relatively sheltered area along Green Beach to their right.[17]

Red Beach 2 was the most violently opposed landing. Lieutenant Colonel Amey's 2d Battalion, 2d Marines, F Company and most of E Company gained Red Beach 2 at 0922, but one platoon of Company E was driven off course by machine-gun and antiboat artillery fire and forced to land on Red Beach 1. Even though G Company arrived only three minutes behind the other companies, to lend its weight to the attack, the battalion could do no more than carve out a beachhead about 50 yards in depth. About half the men of F Company became casualties.[18]

Of the 552 men in the first three waves that struck Red Beach 3, fewer than 25 became casualties during the landing. The men who made it ashore made their way to a retaining wall of coconut logs immediately inshore from the beach, and this was the first shelter they found against Japanese fire.

Many of the 87 amphibian tractors in the first waves onto shore were lost, some to direct hits from enemy artillery and mortars, while others were holed by machine-gun fire and were leaking, and a number suffered mechanical trouble. The fourth wave in LCVPs and those who followed could not cross the reef, leaving the Marines to wade 500 yards to shore. The defenders zeroed in on the boats, blowing some of them out of the water. Sergeant Gene Ward was in one of the boats.

> We were well off the 1800-foot pier and just as I was thinking we had a helluva way to go yet, something smacked the water beside us. At the same time the boat rolled and grated to a stop atop the coral. The coxswain gunned her, but that was as far as we went on that line.
>
> The ramp went down. The men spilled and scrambled forward to stumble out into chin-deep water. Almost at once some of them were hit. Others, apparently from a boat which had sloughed into this coral patch just before us, were calling for corpsmen and struggling to get into our boat. They were the wounded.
>
> I was pinned behind the coxswain and had to climb onto the motor shield, over it and down the length of the tilted boat. When I hit the tepid water I first became aware of the wasp like sound of the bullets and the sharp slap they made biting the water around me. Ahead toward the shore I could see wrecked amtracs; behind me an upended Higgins boat. I struggled forward and the water became shallower. At the same time the fire became heavier. Like others around me I kept only my eyes and right hand, which clutched my carbine, above water.[19]

A Beach Party consisting of Lieutenant Junior Grade Robert Hoyle, USCG, along with two other officers and 43 enlisted men from the Coast Guard-manned transport USS *Arthur Middleton* (APA-25) were part of the first waves. Among the Beach Party was Carl Jonas, USCG, who later wrote about the landing:

We were barely inside the bay, six to eight hundred yards from the nearest shore – just within range and, it seemed, alone in this exploding no man's land. The circle of the beach was dotted with motionless shapes which were the dead and wounded and their equipment. In the water were more specks, a few of them moving toward the shore, but the bulk moving out, unaccountably heading for us. They were in bunches, so that they attracted fire and, for the most part, standing up, so that they were half out of the water. Suddenly, we realized with a shock that they were the wounded, part of the vast number of unlucky men who had stopped or would stop bullets today.

The first one to reach the boat was wounded in the leg, and we noticed the pale, hopeless look on his face. The next two men were together, helping each other as they staggered along. One was wounded in the arm, the other in the chest. When we got them into the boats, the first tried to help with the other casualties, but the second lay on the floor boards with pink foam forming over his lips, his face a dull green. The next man had fine channels of blood making a mesh over his cheek and neck. After this, there were too many to notice any one in particular, but all of them below the gunwale were reaching up, like the men in the Italian primitive paintings of the damned in hell, the manhood gone from their faces, which wore the same dull amazement and shock we had seen in the first one. A few died in the boat. The rest lay there. It was time to get going; so the Marines climbed out and we followed. The pity was that it seemed to be entirely futile.[20]

Second Lieutenant Toivo Ivary's three LVTs left the transport several thousand yards from the shore and when they were halfway to the shore, they rendezvoused with the rest of the second wave. Then the platoon's craft, in a column of files, started in over the coral shelf toward Betio's flaming beach.

They were 500 yards out when they ran into the first machine-gun fire, but the bullets didn't start penetrating the LVTs until they got close in. Ivary's platoon was supposed to land at 30-yard intervals near a blockhouse on the seawall. However, the three LVTs found themselves part of a considerable traffic jam in the blazing lagoon as many of the landing craft were unable to get over the reef. Mortar shells were exploding in the coral.

The platoon was on the extreme right flank of the battalion. Ahead of them, Sergeant Jim Bayer, on the platoon's right flank, saw a tractor of the first wave, an old-style Alligator, explode near the seawall. A square package of explosives, probably dynamite, had come sailing out of the blockhouses and landed behind the Alligator's cab. Marines were blown 30ft into the air, and the beach where the sergeant's group landed was littered with dead bodies.

Two of the sergeant's men were wounded in the LVT as they neared the beach. Fifteen yards from the seawall, the vehicles were stopped and the riflemen and machine gunners went over the sides and dashed toward the seawall through a crossfire of machine-gun bullets.

The lieutenant's group landed on a dry stretch of coral, to the left of the jutting-out blockhouse. Bayer's men were the hardest hit as they raced for the seawall. It had been planned that machine guns would be set up on the beach, but with so many members of the crews being killed or wounded, and parts of guns lost in the water, this was impossible. The surviving machine gunners grabbed weapons off dead Marines and became riflemen.

"It was like fighting in the center of a pool table without any pockets – there was no place to dig in," Bayer explained. "I have never seen any place so well fortified – Guadalcanal and Tulagi were never like Tarawa."[21]

Private First Class Gerald Robert Weisenbrun was in the first wave to land at Betio. He carried a flamethrower that he never got to use as Japanese machine-gun bullets knocked the muzzle off the weapon as he came ashore. Weisenbrun also packed an M-1 rifle, but unfortunately for him, he didn't bring along a bayonet. He was with a group of about 300 Marines who reached the beach, and here they ran into such heavy fire that after just a few minutes only 50 were left standing.

Japanese with bayonets fixed charged to finish off the 50 survivors but were in for a shock as more Marines were coming ashore. Weisenbrun rid himself of the useless flamethrower and had gone about 15 yards inland when he ran head-on into a bayonet-wielding Japanese soldier. The two men fenced for a few moments. However, without a bayonet on his rifle Weisenbrun was getting the worst of it. He was backing away when he fell over a coconut log. The Japanese jabbed, missed with the blade, but knocked out three of Weisenbrun's front upper teeth with a butt stroke. Weisenbrun kicked the man in the crotch. Then, still sprawled across the log, he managed to get his M-1 operational. He only fired once, but that was all that was needed as the round hit his enemy in the chest, killing him instantly.[22]

Weisenbrun's experience was not the only close action that day, and not all of the individual battles were won by Marines. One 19-year-old corporal, who was protecting a shell hole full of wounded comrades, had his head lopped off by a saber-wielding Japanese lieutenant when the enemy made a *banzai* charge, and a private first class was stabbed in the throat as he attempted to hurl a grenade into the tunnel entrance of a pillbox.

———————

M4A2 Sherman medium tanks were deployed by the Marine Corps in combat for the first time on Tarawa. Fourteen Shermans of C Company, 1st Corps Tank Battalion (medium), fought their way across the reef to provide much-needed fire support for the infantry. Under its skipper, First Lieutenant Edward Bale, C Company drove in two columns across the reef.

Joining the Shermans was the 2d Tank Battalion, which landed 36 of its M3A1 Stuart light tanks. Attempts to get light tanks into the battle did not go well. Japanese gunners sank all four LCMs laden with light tanks before the boats even reached the reef, leaving surviving tanks to slog across the reef like the infantry.

Six Shermans tried to land on Red Beach 1, each preceded by a dismounted guide to warn of underwater shell craters. The guides were shot down every few minutes by Japanese marksmen, and each time another volunteer would step forward to continue the movement. Among the men guiding the Shermans was Private James W. Tobey, 2d Tank Battalion. His Navy Cross citation told of his cool bravery on D-Day:

> When the lane of channel markers laid by his party over a shell-and-bomb-pocked coral reef was swept away, Pvt. Tobey unhesitatingly served as a human marker under intense, persistent enemy fire and, after the tanks had safely reached the island, immediately made his way forward one hundred and fifty yards inside the hostile lines to a disabled tank, guided it back through his own lines to the beach and was highly instrumental in restoring it to operating condition.

Sergeant James R. Atkins was a member of the 2d Tank Battalion reconnaissance party which laid a lane of channel markers over a shell-and-bomb-pocked coral reef for a distance of 1,200 yards. When the channel markers were swept away, Atkins made himself a human channel marker, during which time he was under heavy enemy fire. After the tanks were safely guided to the beach, he volunteered to lead tanks inland through the U.S. infantry lines. He bravely led the tanks to well within the enemy lines, daringly and courageously working his way forward under extremely heavy enemy fire while also pointing out targets to the tanks.

Combat engineers had blown a hole in the seawall for the tanks to pass inland, but the way soon became blocked with dead and wounded Marines. One tank commander, rather than run over his fellow Marines, reversed his column of six tanks and proceeded around the "bird's beak" towards a second opening blasted in the seawall. Operating in the turbid waters without guides, during the detour four tanks foundered in shell holes, and their engines were drowned, putting them out of action. Japanese shells hit the two surviving tanks, setting one on fire and leaving the other with only its bow machine gun working.

Three Shermans had landed on Red 3 and halted in a previously selected assembly area. This trio of tanks then supported the 2d Battalion, 2d Marines in its advance toward the runway by rolling up to pillboxes by firing at point-blank range through the openings in these structures.

One Sherman engaged a Japanese light tank. The Marine tank demolished its smaller opponent, but not before the doomed Japanese crew released one final 37mm round, a phenomenal shot, right down the barrel of the Sherman, destroying the tank.

By day's end, only two of the original 14 Shermans were still operational, "Colorado" on Red Beach 3 and "China Gal" on Red Beach 1/Green Beach. Maintenance crews worked through the night to retrieve a third tank, "Cecilia," on Green Beach for Major Ryan. Nineteen Stuarts were also lost to enemy fire, sunk, or suffered mechanical failures during that first day.[23]

Early in the evening of D-Day, pack howitzers of 1st Battalion, 10th Marines landed on Red Beach 2. Lugging their broken-down guns by hand, the artillerymen brought five sections to the beach and set them up in a confined space that would never be found in the training manual. By sunrise on D-Day+1, the gunners were ready for fire missions.

In the evening dusk, Sergeant Jim Bayer mopped the blood out of his eye as he fired his M-1. Private First Class Donald E. Brooks, lacerated by 11 shrapnel slugs, moved along the seawall firing at the enemy who showed themselves to lob hand grenades. Navy Pharmacist Mate Third Class "Doc" Rogalski of Chicago was busy ripping up skivvy drawers to make bandages for the wounded, pausing only to pick up his carbine and take pot shots at a Japanese blockhouse. Second Lieutenant Toivo Ivary was propped up against the seawall, his right leg shattered. Earlier he'd kicked a grenade into a small pothole in the coral so that it wouldn't go off in the face of one of his wounded men. The grenade blew faster than he'd expected, shattering his right leg just above the ankle. He also had a bullet wound in one arm. He was weak from shock and loss of blood but still very much in command. These four were the only men left of 40 who had ridden with Ivary over the coral shelf of the atoll that morning in LVTs.[24]

At the end of the first day's fighting the Marines held only three strips of beach, the longest not more than 100 yards and the widest just 70 yards. On the right, Major Ryan's composite unit, isolated from the remainder of Colonel Shoup's command, had withdrawn to a compact perimeter on the island beak. Another perimeter fanned out from the base of the long pier. With entrenching tools, picks, helmets, or whatever was available, all hands dug in to await the expected *banzai* attack. Men on the transports moved about restlessly, not sure if a Japanese counterattack would drive the beleaguered Marines back into the sea.

Captain Frank O. Hough wrote:

> All in all, it was quite a night. But when daylight found that thin perimeter still intact, a new feeling began to imbue the weary, hungry, thirsty men who held it: a conviction, tacit but implicit, that the crisis had passed. Although ninety percent of Betio smoked and smoldered in front of them, although enemy fire rose in frenzy and volume from every side, and there was no sign of weakening resistance anywhere, all hands knew now that the issue was no longer in doubt – if it ever had been really.[25]

In actual fact, on D-Day+1 the tactical situation was precarious. Marines paid a high price moving forward as landing supplies cost even more men. Dead Marines, shot-up vehicles, and shattered landing craft lay strewn about the beaches and reef. Lieutenant Lillibridge surveyed what he could see of the beach at first light and was appalled: "a dreadful sight, bodies drifting slowly in the water just off the beach, junked amtracks. The stench of dead bodies covered the embattled island like a cloud." [26]

Marines of Landing Team 1/8 commanded by Major Lawrence C. Hayes, Jr. spent 18 hours in LCVPs waiting to get ashore. They got their chance on the morning of D-Day+1. Again the falling tide forced them to disembark 500 yards offshore.

"It was the worst possible place they could have picked," said Colonel Merritt A. "Red Mike" Edson, General Smith's Divisional Chief of Staff. Japanese gunners opened up with unrelenting fire. Enfilade fire came from snipers who had infiltrated to the disabled LVTs offshore during the night. At least one machine gun opened up on the wading troops from the beached inter-island schooner *Niminoa* at the reef's edge.

First Lieutenant Frank Plant, the battalion air liaison officer, accompanied Hayes in the command LCVP. As the craft slammed into the reef, Plant recalled Hayes shouting, "Men, debark!" as he jumped into the water. The troops that followed were greeted by a murderous fire.

Plant helped pull the wounded back into the boat, noting that "the water all around was colored purple with blood."

More than 300 men were killed, wounded or drowned; others were scattered all along the beach and the pier. More seriously, all the unit's flamethrowers, demolitions, and heavy weapons were lost.[27]

By mid-afternoon on D-Day+2 the Marines were moving forward again although in the face of heavy opposition, but at least they were moving forward. However, the Japanese still controlled the approaches to Red beaches 1 and 2. On one landing run of Marine reinforcements, well-aimed machine-gun fire disabled the boat and killed the coxswain; the other occupants had to leap over the far gunwale into the water. At 1550, Edson requested a working party "to clear bodies around pier … hindering shore party operations."

As men worked to clear the area a blackened LVT drifted ashore, filled with dead Marines. At the bottom of the pile was one who was still breathing, somehow, after two and a half days of unrelenting hell. "Water," he gasped, "Pour some water on my face, will you?"

It was a small miracle in the midst of so much death and destruction.

During the night of D-Day+2–D-Day+3 the Japanese mounted a series of *banzai* attacks; the first at 1930 when 50 men infiltrated a 150-yard gap between the border of two companies south of the airstrip. Major William K. Jones, whose 1st Regiment, 6th Battalion (1/6) Landing Team was the first major unit to land intact on Betio, sensing his forces would be the likely target for any *banzai* attack, had already taken precautions. His reserve force, comprised of his mortar platoon, headquarters cooks, bakers, and admin people contained the penetration and killed the enemy in two hours of close-in fighting under the leadership of First Lieutenant Lyle "Spook" Specht.

The Japanese struck Jones' lines again at 2300, and the Marines repulsed this attack too. However, they were forced to use their machine guns, thereby revealing their positions. A third attack came at 0300 in the morning when the Japanese moved several 7.7mm machine guns into nearby wrecked trucks and opened fire on the Marines' automatic weapons positions. Marine NCOs volunteered to crawl forward against this oncoming fire and lob grenades into the improvised machine gun nest. They succeeded in silencing the guns. Jones called for star shell illumination over the area around his unit.

In the final attack at 0400, a force of some 300 Japanese hit the Jones's men south of the airstrip. Again, the Marines met them with every available weapon. Artillery fire from 10th Marines' howitzers on Red Beach 2 and Bairiki Island rained a murderous cross fire, and two destroyers in the lagoon, *Schroeder* (DD-301) and *Sigsbee* (DD-502), opened up on the flanks, while pockets of men locked together in bloody hand-to-hand fighting. Private Jack Stambaugh of B Company killed three screaming Japanese with his bayonet, before an enemy officer impaled him with his samurai sword. Another Marine subsequently killed the officer with a rifle butt blow to the head.

By dawn of D-Day+3, 40 of Jones's Marines were dead and 100 were wounded. An estimated 600 Japanese died in the four attacks. This was the last organized Japanese attack.

Seventy-six hours after "My Deloris" hit the seawall, the fighting was over. All that remained to do was the deadly job of clearing out the small pockets of Japanese spread over the 45 miles of small islands east of Betio. The story of Corporal Arlton K. Wallace's experiences in the mopping-up operation is typical of the operations:

> These crossings between islands were not without difficulties. Sometimes, the Marines went across the reefs in surf up to their armpits, holding their weapons and other gear over their heads. On these crossings, Wallace was holding over his head the same BAR which he had toted throughout the later stages of the Guadalcanal campaign. But he is six feet, two inches in altitude, a convenient height for crossing water-washed reefs.
>
> It was a trip not without interest. When the Japanese fortified Betio they moved out all of the Gilbert Islanders to other islets; they were well-populated these smaller islands. The Marines passed in review through native villages. In one of these they met the chief of Tarawa and his comely granddaughter.
>
> Wallace described the chief's granddaughter (she was known as the Queen of Tarawa) as follows: "Dorothy Lamour hasn't got a single thing on that gal."

The islets were only about 250 yards wide, on the average. So, it was easy to patrol them thoroughly. According to reports, around 500 Nippers were on a pinpoint of an islet at the northern end of the atoll known as Lone Pine Islet. Adjoining Lone Pine was a larger islet, 300 yards wide by four miles long.

On the third day of the march two companies of the battalion bivouacked on the southern tip of this island and set up a line for the night. During the night the 500 or so Nips crossed the lagoon and set up a line of their own on the island. They made a light attack on one of the American companies in the darkness and then withdrew when they got a hot reply from Marine rifles.

The next morning the two companies of Marines started moving forward in a skirmish line. They met heavy resistance from the start. There was little cover, save for coconut trees, which often did not turn bullets, and taro root beds. These taro root beds formed pretty good foxholes for they were several feet deep.

"But them 'elephant ear beds' of the natives was just like hog-wallows," said Wallace. "Anyway I looked like a hog after I'd fallen into a few of them as we moved up."

After about two hours of this sort of fighting Wallace ran out of ammunition for his BAR. He picked up the Thompson sub-machine gun and ammunition of a dead comrade. Wallace was lying in a taro root bed when he received a command from his company commander. Captain Tom Wheeler. For the patrol, Captain Wheeler had worn only an overseas cap complete with bars attached. But he was lying in a nearby root bed with a fine nonchalance despite all of the mud on his face.

"I am moving up to that cocoanut tree on the left," announced Captain Wheeler.

"And I'll take the tree on the right, sir," said Wallace.

The two men dashed for their trees through a heavy Jap fire, and both made it, except that Corporal Wallace was shot through the flesh of his left arm.

"This is right on!" shouted the ebullient Captain Wheeler, before he noticed that Wallace had been hit.

"Right on!" echoed Wallace.

Private First Class G. E. Rollins, a platoon runner and a very lion-hearted lad, attempted to move up beside Wallace, but was shot by a sniper as he ran and fell beside the corporal. He was dead, but Wallace didn't know it then. He tried to pull Rollins behind the tree. A pattern of machine gun bullets, fired by a sniper in a tree only 15 feet away, sprayed around Wallace's tree, hitting him in both hands. His right index finger was blasted off and there was a big wound in the palm of his left hand.

"With both my hands so buggered up," said Wallace, "I couldn't operate my Tommy gun."

Rollins had a pistol. Wallace reached out a bloody hand and got the pistol. Then he played dead. The lower part of his body was exposed to the sniper in the nearby tree. The sniper must have figured that both of the American Marines were dead. The Japanese's yellow face appeared through the fronds of the trees. Through nearly closed eyes, Wallace watched the Japanese. Then he raised the pistol and fired eight rounds into the yellow face. The sniper screamed, perhaps first in surprise, then in pain, and tumbled from his roost, bringing his submachine gun with him.

It was then that Wallace, on orders from Captain Wheeler, got to his feet and made a dash to the rear. He sprinted back to his "hog wallow" in the taro root bed. On the way he lost his belt. Anyway, with his dungaree trousers falling, he made it to the taro root bed.

The firing let up a bit (when the fight was over all of the 500 Japanese soldiers were slain), and Wallace walked three miles back to Sick Bay on an adjoining islet. He left a trail of blood all the way.

So did First Sergeant Vanderbeck, who'd also been wounded in the morning fire fight. On the way back, they got another glimpse of the Queen of Tarawa.

"She's really a beautiful dame. Dorothy Lamour doesn't have a thing" said Corporal Wallace.

She's only fair looking," interrupted the First Sergeant.[28]

Despite the light-hearted tone to Wallace's story 32 Marines were killed and 59 wounded clearing the islands.*

The final casualty figures for the 2d Marine Division at Tarawa were 997 Marines and 30 sailors (medical personnel) dead; 88 Marines missing and

---

*   Under the command of Lieutenant Colonel Raymond Murray, the 2d Regiment, 6th Battalion (2/6) landed on D-Day+1 on the small island of Bairiki, southeast of Betio. Starting at dawn on November 25, they began hiking northward across the small islands on the eastern flank of Tarawa Atoll. Struggling through dense jungles, wading across tidal flats, 2/6 cleared each island.

presumed dead; and 2,233 Marines and 59 sailors wounded. Total casualties: 3,407. The 2d Amphibian Tractor Battalion lost over half the command and all but 35 of the 125 LVTs employed at Betio.[29] Of the 1st Corps Tank Battalion's 14 Sherman tanks, only one escaped unscathed. However 12 of the 13 damaged tanks were recovered, repaired, and would fight again.

At the end of the Tarawa operation, 4,690 Japanese and Koreans defenders were killed; only 17 Japanese and 129 Koreans survived the battle.

Makin Atoll Landings on Butaritari – Operation *Kourbash*

Butaritari is shaped like a long, bending ribbon; its western end resembles a fishtail, or the armrest of a crutch, with two main points projecting westward from the central shore, forming a shallow curve. The islands are so flat that they afford no natural points of observation, and so low that after rains extensive areas, especially in the west, are covered by shallow ponds surrounded by marshland.

The Japanese on Makin, garrisoned on the main island of Butaritari, consisted of 660 men: 284 troops of the 3rd Special Base Force, 100 aviation land personnel, and 276 men of the 4th Fleet Construction Unit. Most troops had no combat training or weapons. The defensive perimeter around the seaplane base on Butaritari Island consisted mainly of dual-purpose 8mm guns, four heavy and four medium antiaircraft guns, and between 20 and 40 machine guns. There were also two tank-barrier systems stretching across the narrow island, one on each side of the seaplane base around King's Wharf.

The invasion plan set two separate landings, with the second coming about two hours after the first. The western beaches were designated as Red Beach 1 and Red Beach 2, and on them, at 0830, the Army's 27th Division, 1st and 3d Battalions, were to commence penetrating the island side by side, each being led by a special landing group in 16 Alligators. If all went according to plan on the Red beaches, at 1030 a second landing was to be made on the north (lagoon) shore, among the piers, designated Yellow Beach.

On November 20 carrier planes from a temporary attack group built around three escort carriers, *Liscome Bay* (CVE-56), *Coral Sea* (CVE-43), and

Corregidor (CVE-58), bombed, dive-bombed, and strafed the western beaches and inland Japanese positions between 0618 and 0630. As the planes drew away naval guns of the accompanying battleships, cruisers and destroyers opened fire and kept up a steady rain of shells until 0825, just five minutes before the first troops hit the shore. During the bombardment a turret explosion on the battleship USS *Mississippi* (BB-41) killed 43 men and wounded 19.

Yeoman First Class Everett L. Garner, Coast Guard combat correspondent on board *Leonard Wood* (commanded by Captain Merlin O'Neill, a veteran of the African and Sicilian invasions), wrote about D-Day morning:

Long before dawn a hand reaches out of the darkness and shakes us, indicating it is time to eat the last square meal for several days. Too keyed up to eat, we gulp down mugs of pineapple juice and hot coffee. A sobering note is struck as we pass through the wardroom now converted into an operating room, piled high with stacks of bandages and equipped with gleaming surgical instruments.

Hundreds of soldiers from New York's own "Fighting 69th" [Regiment] are rushing through the morning twilight to their places beside the landing boats. Landing craft are lowered to deck level. Hard-bitten attack troops clamber into them in orderly lines.

These picked fighters are traveling arsenals. In addition to modern weapons they carry long curved machetes, two or three daggers or trench knives, many of which they have carefully fashioned themselves in anticipation of this day.

Far above is heard the hum of plane engines, indicating that scores of naval bombers and fighters are on their way to smooth out the "rough spots" on the beach.

Shortly after six the sun rises dimly through the beating rain of a tropical squall and long, crutch-shaped Makin rises before us out of the sea. Bombers are blasting and strafing the beach. One is seen, apparently hit, plunging into the surf. With a grinding whirl the winches lower the boats into the water. The soldiers clamber in. The lines cleared, with the command, "Pins in fore and aft," the boats roar off to the boat assembly circle.

The veteran coxswains bend to their wheels with the confidence born of seamanship and shipshape boats. These men, most of them veterans of the African and Sicilian invasions, shuttle their roaring boats back and forth from ship to shore, white wakes billowing out behind them, dodging and twisting like broken field runners to avoid the fire from cocoanut trees and taro holes.[30]

The first wave landed on the western Red beaches 1 and 2 at 0833. On the run into Red Beach 2 enemy rifle fire wounded one seaman and killed another. Major Edward T. Bradt, commanding the 3d Battalion, 105th Infantry, who was in charge of the special landing groups, later described his action: "I jumped down from my boat and stood straight up for two or three minutes, waiting for somebody to shoot me. Nobody shot! I saw many other soldiers doing the same thing."

Although intelligence had revealed the presence of rocks and coral pinnacles along the approaches to the shore at Red Beach 1, Admiral Turner's staff was satisfied that landing boats could get ashore there at any time. They were wrong. The reef was studded with coral boulders about 40 yards offshore. Coming in on a rising tide, some of the landing craft were able to slip past the boulders and were stranded less than a boat's length (36ft) from the water's edge, but many were broached, stranded, or forced to put out to sea again.

Most of the following eight waves were directed to Red Beach 2 causing confusion, delay and damage to the landing craft. However, despite this, the initial landings on Red Beach 2 went largely according to plan with the assault troops facing little enemy resistance and moving rapidly inland after an uneventful trip on the ocean side of the island. Their progress off the beach was slowed only by an occasional sniper and the need to negotiate their way around the debris and water-filled craters left by the air and naval bombardment. The troops on Yellow Beach, however, experienced a rather different reception.

Between 0850 and 1025 Red beaches 1 and 2 (the south beaches) were bombarded and the first landings were made on Yellow Beach at 1041 from the transports and LSTs, which had moved inside the lagoon. As the first wave of LVTs approached Yellow Beach from the lagoon, they were hit by rifle and machine-gun fire. One hundred yards behind the first wave of LSTs came the LCMs with their medium tanks. They hit a reef 150 to 200 yards offshore and could proceed no farther since there was less than 3ft of water over the reef. Ramps were lowered and the medium tanks lumbered forward through the shallow water. All but two of the 15 tanks reached the shore safely. These two foundered in shell holes in the reef.

The miscalculation of the depth of the lagoon caused the following LCVPs to go aground, forcing soldiers to cover the final 250 yards to the beach in waist-deep water. Equipment and weapons were lost or water-soaked and three men were shot and killed approaching the beach.

The invasion plan had been conceived with the aim of luring the Japanese into committing most of their forces to oppose the first landings on Red Beach, thus allowing the troops landing on Yellow Beach to attack from the rear. The Japanese, however, did not respond to the attack on Red Beach and withdrew from Yellow Beach with only harassing fire, leaving the troops of the 27th Division no choice but to knock out the fortified strongpoints in the defensive perimeter one by one.

During the night of November 22 the Japanese attempted a series of suicide counterattacks. "We are convinced that they were drunk-drunk or crazy," one wounded lieutenant told Marine Corps correspondents:

First they sent a delegation of villagers to us and we let them through. The villagers were terror stricken but they claimed nobody was behind them. We heard sounds and challenged. A group of Jap officers and men came toward me, holding their swords high above their heads in an attitude of surrender.

We advanced carefully toward them. They were singing and shouting like madmen. They kept coming. So did we. As the officer who led them drew near he lunged and brought his sword down at my head. I threw up my arm, which was cut, and the force of the blow carried the tip of his sword to the ground and into my foot. One of my men shot him squarely between the eyes. He was deader than a mackerel. So were all the rest, in a minute or two.[31]

It took two days of determined fighting to reduce enemy resistance to the point that defeat was inevitable. After clearing the entire atoll, the 27th Division commander, Major General Ralph C. Smith, reported on November 23, "Makin taken."[32]

The island was secure, but the Japanese could still hit back at the invaders. On the morning of November 24 *Liscome Bay* was operating about 20 miles southwest of Butaritari. She had spent the last three days providing close air support to the troops on Makin, and it was to be another routine day of flight operations in support of the Army. Flight Quarters sounded at 0450 followed by General Quarters at 0505. However, at 0513 *Liscome Bay* was hit amidships by one or more torpedoes fired from an undetected enemy submarine (later identified as IJN I-*175*). A torpedo hit near the bomb magazine, causing stored bombs and torpedo warheads to detonate. The ensuing massive explosion knocked the majority of personnel off their feet. Terrific waves of heat could be felt coming up from the flight and hangar decks and nothing could be seen of the flight deck aft of amidships. The few planes remaining on the flight deck forward were knocked askew and were burning brightly. Ammunition in the wings of the planes was beginning to explode. All along the flight deck, on the catwalks, and through holes blown in the side of the ship, men slipped down lines or simply jumped into the dark sea to escape the spreading conflagration.

Survivors attempted to extinguish the fires in the hangar but no water pressure was available, and it was immediately apparent that the situation was not only hopeless insofar as saving the ship was concerned, but that the abandonment would be extremely difficult.

Ensign Selden N. May, a Wildcat pilot, was asleep in an upper bunk when the torpedo hit. The blast knocked him onto the steel deck. May recalled in a survivor's statement:

> I was stunned, and woke up when [men] started running through my room. I slept in the raw, but I grabbed my life preserver and started running to find a way off the ship. There were continuous explosions. I finally climbed through a hole in the port antiaircraft [guns' ammunition] clip room onto the port catwalk. The ship was listing about thirty degrees to the starboard. I saw two men with a rubber raft just below me [and] I went down the rope and joined them.

At 0533, just 23 minutes after the torpedo hit, *Liscome Bay* listed to starboard and then sank, carrying 53 officers and 591 enlisted men down with her. Of

---

* Just over three months later, on February 4, 1943, the sonar men on USS *Charrette* (DD-581) acquired a target on sonar near Wotje in the Marshall Islands. At 0003, *Charrette* dropped a salvo of eight depth charges, but then lost contact. *Fair* (DE-35) was ordered to assist. At 0040, *Fair* attacked with Mark 10 "hedgehog" projector charges. Four explosions were heard and the submarine was sunk. Source: Bob Hackett and Sander Kingsepp, IJN Submarine I-175: Tabular Record of Movement, 2001-2010 REV 4, http://www.combinedfleet.com/I-175.htm

the 916 crewmen, 702 died and only 272 were rescued by *Morris Hughes* (DD-417) and *Hull* (DD-350), and many of the survivors suffered from burns.[33]

Taking the Makin Islands was significantly less costly in dead and wounded than was Betio. Army casualties were 58 killed in action, eight died of wounds, 150 wounded in action, and 35 non-combat injuries. In the boat crews and the beach parties, seven were wounded or injured, while three died of wounds. Combat and operational losses on eight carriers, not including *Liscome Bay*, totaled seven killed and 18 injured. The submarine *Plunger* (SS-179), on rescue patrol to pick up a flier from the *Lexington,* was strafed by Japanese planes, wounding six of the crew. Besides the loss of 19 planes on *Liscome Bay*, nine other planes were lost in combat and 35 in operational mishaps – a total of 63 aircraft. Consolidated naval casualties were 752 killed or died of wounds, 291 wounded or injured. The total U.S. casualties were 816 killed and 475 wounded or injured.

The Japanese lost 700 killed; three Japanese and 101 Korean laborers were captured.

Apamama – Operation *Boxcloth* [34]

The Marine invasion of Apamama ("Atoll of the Moon"), located 95 miles southwest of Tarawa, began in the dark morning of November 21, one day after the landings on Tarawa and Makin. Seventy-eight Marines of V Amphibious Corps Reconnaissance Company, under the command of Captain James Logan Jones, were ordered to proceed to Apamama, land in the darkness, and scout out the island, determine the strength of the hostile forces, select suitable beaches for the use of occupying American troops who were to follow in a few days, and to guide these troops through the channels. The submarine USS *Nautilus* (SS-168), Commander Donald G. Irvine commanding officer, transported the Marine assault force and was "to render direct support within the limits of her capabilities."

Accompanying the Marines were three officers from other branches of service and ten Army combat engineers. Among the 13 men were Australian Lieutenant George Hard, who was well acquainted with the people of Apamama and was to act as a guide and Gilbertese interpreter; Lieutenant E. F. "Bing" Crosby, a Navy construction battalion officer, who was to make a preliminary survey of the Apamamese airfield; and Major Wilson Hunt, a Marine defense battalion officer, who had been sent to select gun positions on the atoll and to work out the right beaches and channels for bringing in a base defense battalion.

Each man took three "K" rations, one "D" ration and two fragmentary grenades. There were 45 rounds for each carbine, 48 rounds for the rifles, 260 rounds for the BAR, and 2,000 rounds for each .30-caliber machine gun.

Although the assault was well planned, *Nautilus* almost didn't make it to the island. At 2159 on November 19, mistaking her as an enemy, the destroyer USS *Ringgold* (DD-89) fired at her, sending a 5in shell through the conning tower, damaging the main induction valve. Diving as soon as the water depth permitted, the boat was rigged for depth charge and the damage control party went to work. Within two hours repairs were sufficient to allow *Nautilus* to continue with her mission.

Fortunately, there were no more attacks and *Nautilus* arrived safely at Apamama. Once there, the small force went ashore in rubber landing craft, most of them equipped with outboard motors. The sea was heavy, pouring water over the motors and only three of the motors started. The others had to be paddled or towed. However, soon after the start the little fleet was hit by violent rain squalls, and two of the craft became separated from the others. One motor drowned out in the downpour, and two boats were forced to start towing the others. All hands paddled with a will, but they made little headway against the wind, the current, and the waves.

At 0330 breakers on the reef were sighted and the Marines drew a deep breath of relief. Guide boats, under the commands of Lieutenants L. B. Shinn and H. C. Minnier, were paddled toward the beach. The rowing was easy now, for the tidal current weakened at 400 yards out. However, the surf boiling over the cruel coral was another obstacle. At 0415, the men in the guide boats signaled that all was clear and the other boats came in, with the coral mauling some of them badly.

Once ashore a beachhead and command post was established with First Lieutenant Merwin H. Silverthorn, Jr., in charge. Machine guns were set up and the Army engineers were assigned to guard the command post. One unit, under Lieutenant Shinn (accompanied by Lieutenant Hard), was sent to scout out the northwest portions while a second, under Lieutenant Minnier, and a third, under Lieutenant Russell Corey, went to the southwest. Shinn's unit discovered a sea-going Japanese barge with a diesel engine, which was fueled and ready for operation. The boat was lying in the reef passage on the lagoon side between two islets.

After discovering the barge, the Marines saw two islanders crossing the reef passage near the boat. The Marines hit the deck in the bushes. When the islanders were very close, Lieutenant Hard stood up and called out in Gilbertese. They stared at him, grinned, and one of them replied in English:

"Why, Mr. Hard. My word! I'm glad to see you. But were you wise to come and visit us now? The Sapanese are here." (The Gilbertese pronounce their Js like Ss when they speak English.)

The islanders informed the lieutenant that the Japanese were entrenched stoutly around a radio station on an islet across the reef passage to the northeast.

The Apamama men said that the Japanese had pillboxes facing the reef passage, and similar fortifications on the seaward and lagoon sides and to their rear. They were equipped with heavy and light machine guns, mortars, rifles, grenades, and enough ammunition for many days' fighting. According to the islanders, the Japanese were fewer than the invaders. However, they were in a very strong defensive position that would be hard for infantry to take alone.

The unit returned to the command post and made a report to Captain Jones. The entire outfit moved across the reef passage on the surf side to Apamama and a second beachhead and a command post was established. The unit under Corey then set out on the double for the Japanese barge. When it was about 150 yards from the boat, a Japanese patrol was seen near the boat. Private First Class Homer Powers, a powerfully built BAR man, killed one of the patrol. The others fled into a nearby coconut grove.

Lieutenant Corey had his boys partially field strip the enemy barge. Unless they had a lot of spare parts and were superlative mechanics, the Japanese escape route was now cut off.

Back at the command post, two islanders had returned with another report. The Japanese had gathered up their machine guns and other weapons and had moved across the reef passage, seemingly intending to leave the atoll in their barge on the next high tide. They had passed the Catholic mission at a lope and reached Kabangake village, when, apparently, they got word from a patrol that Marines were on the atoll and had found the boat. The Japanese did an about face, and, still at the lope, headed back to their fortifications around the radio station.

There was a thin sand spit protruding to the northeast out into the lagoon and this spit commanded a view of the Japanese fortifications. Jones crossed to the spit with all the company. Three Japanese rose from hiding places on the spit and one was killed at about 200 yards by a Marine rifleman. The company then came under light machine-gun fire and the other two enemy escaped.

It was only an hour until a dramatic Gilbertese sunset, and the tide was coming in. Jones decided his men were in an unfavorable position, so he broke off the firefight and returned to the command post.

The men were in pretty bad physical condition by now. The ordeal en route and the nightmarish voyage in the rubber boats had given them a poor start for the operation. None of them had slept in more than two days. They rested by turns until 2030, when radio contact was established with *Nautilus*. A motor launch from the ship and some of the rubber boats came in through the boiling black water with supplies for 15 days.

The men tried to rest some more, but between 0100 and 0300 blinker lights were seen out at sea. Apparently, a Japanese submarine was trying to contact the Apamamese garrison.

There were no attacks during the night and the men got some rest. With the morning, Jones located an islander boat pilot named George who was capable of steering the ships through the channels when the occupying troops arrived. Captain Jones pondered his situation. By disabling and guarding the boat he had the Japanese cut off from escape. However, he did not have the heavy weapons necessary to dislodge them from their strong position along the reef passage. Mortars would be needed to get troops across the exposed reef and onto the flanks of the Japanese fortifications. To try to get behind the Japanese by landing in the rubber boats behind them on their islet would be inviting disaster, for the enemy would be expecting something like that and they had a truck which could transport men quickly to meet any point of attack. Besides, the rubber boats were in bad shape from their passage over the reefs and couldn't be used to assault the Japanese positions.

At breakfast the men had their first hot meal since leaving their ship. Then Major Hunt, the ebullient Lieutenant Crosby, and the islander pilot, George, with Corey's unit as a guard, set out to survey the channels and beaches at the southern end of the atoll. They returned with a lot of helpful information and some supplies obtained from locals.

Gunnery Sergeant Charles E. Patrick led a small patrol to ascertain if it might be possible to cross along the reef on the seaward side of the Japanese and thus outflank the enemy's position. One man was wounded during a contact with a Japanese patrol, and the Japanese fled into the brush. Patrick returned with the report that the crossing might be made but it would entail some casualties.

Plans were made for an attack in force and arrangements were made for *Nautilus* to shell the Japanese at 0800 the following morning.

At 0330, on the morning of the third day ashore, the units moved up to positions just across the reef passage, about 150 yards from the Japanese. Lieutenant Silverthorn, the ten Army men, Lieutenant Crosby and Lieutenant Hard were left to guard the beachhead. Corey set up the machine guns directly opposite the center of the Japanese lines. This was to provide a base of fire from which the others could hit the flanks.

The *Nautilus'* 6in deck gun fired salvos from 4,000 yards into the enemy positions. The Marines also started shooting and the Japanese replied with remarkably intense machine-gun fire. The vessel fired 70 rounds with fair accuracy, but evidently the shelling wasn't inflicting many casualties for the Japanese continued to fire unabated. Captain Jones radioed a request that the firing stop.

Meanwhile, the firefight across the reef passage rose in fury. From 0800 until 1530, the heavy firing never ceased. Like most Japanese gunners shooting from entrenchments, the Japanese machine-gun fire was higher than it should have been. As long as the Marines kept prone they were comparatively safe. Private First Class William D. Miller, a husky BAR man, was wounded by machine-gun fire while in an exposed position. Private Bert E. Zumberge attempted to reach his wounded friend but was shot twice in the upper left arm while administering first aid. Navy Pharmacist Mates Second Class Morris C. Fell and James E. Fields exposed themselves to fire several times trying to haul Miller to safety, but Miller was hit again and died before his body could be recovered.

The superstructures of numerous American ships appeared on the horizon, so Captain Jones decided to break off the firefight for a while until some mortars arrived. The convoy approached the entrance to the lagoon and it was seen to include numerous men-of-war, transports and two hospital ships.

Jones decided that he would go out in the little motor launch for a conference with the commanding officer of the occupying troops. He set out across the lagoon with Major Hunt, Lieutenant Crosby, George, and Sergeant Daniel J. Bento aboard. Major Hunt, being the only Annapolis man in the crowd, was appointed coxswain.

When they reached the entrance to the lagoon and were about a mile from the ships, a strange thing happened. The entire convoy suddenly got underway and went over the horizon. Apparently, they'd picked up several submarine contacts and were taking no chances on being attacked while off the atoll.

The men in the launch were left alone, and about 700 yards off to their right the "feather" of a submarine periscope appeared.

"Submarine!" yelled Major Hunt.

The submarine didn't molest the men in the tiny boat, so they turned around and headed back, arriving back at the beachhead at about 1800.

During the afternoon USS *Vandervoort* (DD-608) had appeared on the other side of the atoll and had sent an officer ashore. The destroyer had agreed to shell the Japanese positions on the following morning. However, early on the morning of the fourth day, the Marines began to get some strange reports from the islanders.

"The Saps are all dead," reported one tall, English-speaking Apamamese boy. Then, puffing the cigarette that Lieutenant Hard had given him, the boy went on to tell how the Japanese commanding officer had made a long speech to his men, waving his samurai sword and brandishing a pistol.

"We shall kill all of the American devils!" he had howled.

Then the officer's pistol exploded, apparently accidentally, and he received a fatal wound in the belly. By late afternoon of the third day of the Marine landing, all of the remaining 22 Japanese who hadn't been killed by shellfire, machine-gun fire or rifle fire, committed suicide in a mass ceremony.

The Japanese had dug themselves graves, laid down in them and killed themselves with pistols. Most of them had neat, round bullet holes in the throat, just below the jaw.

The Marines started burying their enemies. This mass suicide was puzzling to the American troops. The Japanese had plenty of ammunition left. Each man still had between ten and 40 grenades. They could have sold their lives for a high price in American lives. However, they elected to slay themselves without offering further resistance. Why they chose suicide instead of attacking the Marines is unknown. Marine Recon losses on Apamama were two killed, two wounded, and one injured. The Apamama assault remains unique in that it was the only successful amphibious invasion launched from a submarine.

Operation *Galvanic* – Lessons Learned

Operation *Galvanic* was the first large-scale amphibious assault in the Pacific against a well-fortified enemy island. One of the lessons learned was the need for better preliminary and pre-invasion bombardment with heavier shells and better close air support. The island had been heavily bombed in the weeks preceding the landings. However, there was no preliminary bombardment prior to the landings, thus many enemy guns were still operable when the Marines went in.

On Tarawa the ships' gunfire had been interrupted on two critical occasions when it was most desperately needed. The first costly cessation of fire was early in the morning and it was ordered to permit a scheduled air strike to be executed. The air strike failed to materialize but the defenders manned their guns during the lull in supporting activity and opened fire on the ships. The transports were forced to retreat to seaward and finally the ships reopened fire without waiting any longer for the air strike. The second cessation was at H-Hour, 0900, when the ships' gunfire support stopped as previously planned. Unfortunately, many of the boats had grounded hundreds of yards to seaward of the beaches, and at 0900 many of the marines that had been embarked in the grounded boats were wading in to shore. The lull in ships' gunfire permitted the Japanese to again man their guns and this time they opened up with everything they had upon the Marines wading up to the beaches as well as upon the few who had reached shore. [35]

At Tarawa, the amphibious tractor (LVT) came into its own as an assault troop carrier. In the words of Admiral Nimitz:

> The ideal defensive barrier has always been the one that could not be demolished, which held up assaulting forces under the unobstructed fire of the defenders and past which it was impossible to run, crawl, dig, climb, or sail. The barrier reef fulfills these conditions to the letter, except when sufficient amphibious tanks and similar vehicles are available to the attackers.

The main lesson learned at Tarawa about LVTs in the field was there needed to be enough of the tractors available in future operations to carry ashore not only the first three assault waves, but the following reserve waves. In addition to these, there needed to be spares to take the place of those tractors destroyed by enemy fire or mines, or which had become inoperative due to mechanical failures. Also recognized was the need for amphibious tanks and LCI gunboats.[36]

Radios were not adequately waterproofed, disrupting communications between Marines on shore and supporting ships as well as between units on the beaches. Tanks were not equipped with external phones needed for the infantry to communicate with the crews. Infantry units needed heavier weapons, including flamethrowers, to counter well-entrenched strongpoints. LVTs required better armor and heavier defensive weapons.

The need for better beach reconnaissance was another lesson learned. For *Galvanic*, all reconnaissance had been by aerial photography or through a camera mounted on a submarine's periscope.

Although roughly 20 percent of the Tarawa assault forces were killed or wounded, General Holland Smith, commander of the V Amphibious Corps, declared that Tarawa, with its "terrible loss of life," had "no particular strategic importance."[37]

Admirals King, Nimitz, and Spruance, and General Julian Smith agreed. Capturing the Gilberts was neither strategically important nor a turning point in the Central Pacific, rather it was the beginning of the Central Pacific drive against Japan.

Before leaving Tarawa there was a combined Catholic, Protestant and Jewish service in the Betio cemetery. An epitaph was dedicated to the dead:

So let them rest on their sun-scorched atoll,
The wind for their watcher, the waves for their shroud,
Where palm and pandanus shall forever whisper
A requiem fitting for Heroes so proud. [*]

---

[*]   In the immediate aftermath of the fighting on Tarawa, U.S. service members who died in the battle were buried in a number of battlefield cemeteries on the island. In 1946 and 1947, the 604th Quartermaster Graves Registration Company conducted a remains recovery operations on Betio Island. As of the summer of 2015, 520 of the Marines and Corpsmen who died on Tarawa are still listed as MIA.

In 2012 Joint POW/MIA Accounting Command (JPAC) teams conducted excavation operations in the Republic of Kiribati and discovered human remains and equipment that appeared to be those of American servicemen from World War II. In June 2015, a nongovernmental organization, History Flight, Inc., notified the Defense POW/MIA Accounting Agency (DPAA) that they had discovered a burial site on Betio Island and had recovered the remains of what they believed were U.S. Marines who fought during the battle in November 1943. The remains of 132 were turned over to DPAA in July 2015.

There are 73,515 service personnel not recovered following WWII. Sources: i) Defense POW/MIA Accounting Agency (DPAA), www.dpaa.mil; ii) Doyle, Dan, *They Finally Found the Remains of 132 American Marines on a Small Pacific Island!* TheVeteransSite.com

CHAPTER 9

TO THE FAR SHORE

LANDINGS IN FRANCE, JUNE 6–AUGUST 15, 1944

After years of planning, the long-awaited Allied invasions of Europe were launched in the summer of 1944. The first, Operation *Overlord* was launched along the Normandy coast on June 6, 1944. Operation *Dragoon* took place on August 15 on the southeastern Mediterranean coast of France.

Operation *Overlord*

The decision to cross the channel and invade northern France in May 1944 had been made by Churchill and Roosevelt at the Trident Conference in May 1943, and so began a year's planning for what would be the most important amphibious action of the war. The code name *Overlord* covered not only the landing itself, but also the build-up of Allied troops in the beachhead and the initial stages of the fighting in Normandy. Within *Overlord* was Operation *Neptune* which covered the naval operation to convey the assault troops across the Channel and land them on the beaches. Airborne operations were codenamed *Neptune-Bigot*.

Assault landings would be confined to five beaches along the northern Normandy coast. They were designated Utah, Omaha, Gold, Juno, and Sword. Utah, the westernmost of the D-Day beaches, was added to the invasion plans at the eleventh hour so that the Allies would be within striking distance of the port city of Cherbourg.

British, Canadian, Free French, and Free Polish forces (the latter two operating with the British) were assigned Gold, Juno, and Sword beaches while the Americans were tasked with Utah and Omaha beaches.

Omaha Beach was divided into nine landing areas: Charlie, Dog Green, Dog Red, Dog White, Easy Green, Easy Red, Fox Red, Fox Green, and Pointe du Hoc. Utah Beach had two landing areas: Tare Green and Uncle Red.

On Omaha Beach the Landing Forces O and B, which landed later on the same beaches as Force O, were composed of elements of V Corps, U.S. Army and included the U.S. 1st Infantry Division, 29th Infantry Division, and the 2d and 5th Ranger Battalions. This force was supported by a shore party consisting of the 5th Engineer Special Brigade with the 6th and 7th Naval Beach Battalions.*

Twenty Assault Naval Combat Demolition Units (NCDUs) and Army Demolition Units (collectively known as Gap Assault Teams or GATs) were to blast 21 gaps through the obstacles on Omaha Beach. Each GAT consisted of 28 Army engineers and an NCDU made up of a Navy officer and 12 enlisted men – seven Navy and five Army. Also called "Boat Teams," the NCDUs went into action with engineer combat battalions, assigned to Regimental Combat Teams (RCTs). On Omaha Beach the method of clearance on the assault phase was accomplished by the use of the 2lb Hagensen pack. Each man was carrying about 20 of these 2lb charges, safety fuses and detonator assemblies, and continued working until the rising tide covered the obstacles and prevented further clearance. Post assault clearance (i.e. after the tide receded) was accomplished with tank dozers, caterpillar tractors, and salvage explosives.

As part of Assault Force O, the 299th Engineer Combat Battalion was attached to the 16th RCT and the 146th Engineer Combat Battalion to the 116th RCT.

For Utah Beach, the landing force – Assault Force U – was assigned to VII Corps, commanded by General Omar Bradley. It was organized along the same lines as Assault Force O. The major units of VII Corps were the 4th, 90th, and 9th Infantry Divisions. Added to the 4th Division were the 70th Tank Battalion, 746th Tank Battalion, 87th Chemical Mortar Battalion, the 1106th Engineer Combat Group, the 899th Tank Destroyer Battalion, one

---

* Naval Beach Battalions were tasked with moving men and equipment across the beach, providing battlefield medicine, establishing communications between ship and shore, marking sea lanes, boat repairs, removing underwater obstructions, and directing the evacuation of casualties.

battery of the 980th Field Artillery Battalion (150mm), the 2d Beach Battalion with attached GATs, the 1st Engineer Special Brigade plus antiaircraft artillery units, and a detachment of the 13th Field Artillery Observation Battalion. The GATs planned to set their demolition charges while down in the water, so as to gain some protection from enemy fire.[1]

The five assault divisions were to be put ashore on the two beaches by naval task forces that were not only tasked with the transport of the troops but also with protecting them during the crossing and giving naval gunfire support before and after the landings. The Western Naval Task Force, commanded by Admiral Alan G. Kirk, USN, would handle the landings on Utah and Omaha beaches. The three British assault divisions, similarly organized, came under the Eastern Naval Task Force commanded by Rear Admiral Sir Philip Vian, RN. The British had a greater initial strength so that they could establish a powerful left flank very quickly to counter the strong German attack expected to come from the north and east. Because of their larger manpower and productive capacity, the U.S. forces would overtake and later outnumber the British during the buildup.

The assault itself was to be supported by a naval gunfire bombardment from supporting ships and craft. Tanks embarked in LCT(A)s would then fire on targets of opportunity during the last 3,000 yards of their approach to the beach and 105mm artillery embarked in LCTs likewise would fire during their passage through the boat lanes. Nine LCT(R)s (Landing Craft Tank-Rockets) each carrying 1,050 5in British rockets were to obliterate specific objectives on Omaha Beach and beyond at H-Hour minus 15 minutes.[2]

The infantry assault troops were to be stripped to the barest combat essentials, landing with only basic infantry weapons, but no motors or artillery. To make up for the lack of heavy weapons, a tank battalion attached to each of the assault regiments would lead the attack.

Some tanks were to be carried in on LCTs timed to land at the same time or at nearly the same time as the first infantry wave. Others were modified for amphibious operation and were to be launched about 5,000 or 6,000 yards offshore and swim in ahead of the assault waves. These were M4 Sherman medium tanks equipped with detachable canvas "bloomers" – accordion-pleated screens that when deployed were capable of floating the 32-ton tanks by displacement. They had a duplex drive – twin propellers for swimming and the normal track drive for overland. From the duplex drive came their common name "DD."

It was anticipated that landing craft would be damaged or sunk by enemy fire and the men aboard would be lost without help, so a rescue flotilla was assembled. The flotilla consisted of 60 wooden, gasoline-powered 83ft Coast Guard patrol boats, 30 for the American beaches and 30 for the British and Canadian beaches. The boats, stripped of armor and weapons, would patrol 1,000 to 2,000 yards off the beaches.

The amphibious armada numbered 6,939 vessels: 1,213 naval combat vessels, 4,126 landing craft and ships, 736 ancillary ships and craft, and 864 merchant ships. Of the 6,939, 80 percent were British or Canadian, 16 percent American, and the remaining 4 percent from other Allied nations.

Airborne assaults were planned for the U.S. 82d and 101st Divisions, and the British 6th Division. Their primary mission was to secure the eastern and western flanks of the beachhead to allow the main invasion force to come ashore without the immediate threat of German flank attacks. They were tasked with laying mines as well as destroying bridges where the enemy was likely to stage a counterattack, and securing bridges where Allied forces were expected to go immediately on the offensive.*

The date of D-Day was not set in stone. The general timing of the invasion of France was determined by weather forecasts, the availability of resources, and co-ordination with the Russian attacks on the Eastern Front. The designation of June 1 as the target date meant that the actual assault would take place as soon as possible after that date. The selection of D-Day would be determined by the conditions required for H-Hour. H-Hour, in turn, would be chosen to secure an advantageous coincidence of light and tidal conditions.

Terrain

The coast of Normandy offers only a few areas favorable for large-scale landing operations. Cliffs, reefs, and the wide tidal ranges combine to present natural difficulties.

Utah Beach
The overall shoreline designated as Utah Beach extended from a point northeast of Ravenoville to Point de la Madeleine, a distance of approximately

---

*   Although the airborne operations were important to the invasion, they will not be covered
     in this work, as it focuses on the amphibious portion of Operation *Overlord.*

9,600 yards. The beach varied in width between 800 and 1,200 yards. It was backed for its entire length by a masonry seawall ranging in height from 4ft to 12ft. Behind this seawall was an embankment from 10ft to 20ft high and beyond this, a long line of sand dunes extended 150 yards inland along much of the beach. These dunes had been created by the fine sand of the beach being blown inland by the wind. Beyond the sand dunes the land sloped gently westward for a distance of half a mile to a mile to the main channel of a sluggish stream. From here it rose gently to the relatively high ground two or three miles inland from the beach. The Germans flooded the land beyond the dunes to form a strong barrier to landing forces.

Omaha Beach

The area that was considered suitable for landings and designated as Omaha Beach was five miles long, stretching east from the seaside village of Grandcamp. The shore curved landward and 100ft to 170ft bluffs, which merged into the cliffs at either end of the sector, rose sharply from the flat and dominated the whole beach area. The beach sloped very gently below high water mark.

It was expected that there would be a tidal range of 18ft at the period of the assault. This meant that low tide would expose a stretch of firm sand averaging about 300 yards in distance from the low to the high watermark. The Germans had made full use of this tidal flat and laid numerous obstacles to delay the enemy. As well as the German defenses, at high tide men and vehicles wading up the beach would face up to 4ft deep irregular runnels, parallel to the shore, which had been scoured out by the tidal current.

At the high watermark, the tidal flat terminated in a bank of coarse shingle rock, sloping up rather steeply to a height of some 8ft. In places, it was as much as 15 yards wide, and the stones averaged 3in in diameter. On the eastern two-thirds of the beach, the shingle lay against a low sand embankment or dune line and constituted a barrier that was impassable for vehicles. On the western part of the beach the shingle was piled against a seawall, first of stone masonry sloping seaward, then of wood. The wall varied in height from 4ft to 12ft and was broken by a gap several hundred yards wide where the tidal flat ended in shingle and embankment. Immediately behind the seawall ran a paved promenade beach road that then became a rough track.

Between the dune line (or seawall) and the bluffs lay a narrow area of beach that was flat. Very narrow at either end of the main landing zone, this level shelf of sand widened to more than 200 yards near the center of the stretch.

Except at the Vierville-sur-Mer at the west end, the flat had large patches of marsh and high grass, usually near the edge of the bluffs.

At four points along the beach small wooded valleys sloped back inland and provided natural exit corridors. These corridors were, inevitably, key areas both in the plan of attack and in the arrangement of defenses. The advance inland of assaulting units would depend on opening exit roads for traffic and supply from the beach, and armor used in the attack could only get up to the high ground through the draws (the narrow ravines leading up to the plateau above the beach).

Once up the steep slopes bordering the beach, attacking troops would get the impression of coming out onto a gently rolling plain.[3]

German Defenses

In 1944, at all main beaches practicable for massive landings the Germans began constructing an elaborate system of obstacles along the tidal flats between the high and low watermarks. These obstacles, designed to wreck or block off landing craft, had begun to appear in the Omaha sector early in April.

The first band of obstructions consisted of a series of gate-like structures – reinforced iron frames with iron supports – on rollers, about 250 yards out from the high waterline. The main support girders were 10ft high, and waterproofed Teller mines were lashed to the uprights. The second band, 20 to 25 yards further in, was composed of heavy logs driven into the sand at such an angle that the mine-tipped ends pointed seaward, or of log ramps, which were reinforced and mined. One hundred and thirty yards from shore the final row of obstructions included metal hedgehogs.* These 5 1/2ft high obstructions were made of three or more steel rails or angles that were crossed at the centers and so strongly set that the ends would stave in the bottoms of

---

* A Czech hedgehog is an antitank obstacle made of three pieces of iron, with notches for barbed wire. Even when tipped over, it still presents an obstacle for tanks, though infantry may find minimal cover behind it. These obstacles were between 4 1/2ft and 5 1/2ft high and weighed between 440lb and 550lb, depending on what they were made of and where they were made. Typically, they were manufactured, but makeshift hedgehogs were made out of anything that could withstand a head-on collision with a tank. However, their main purpose wasn't to block tanks – it was to get stuck underneath them, preventing the tank from moving anywhere at all.

landing craft. None of these bands were continuous, the elements being staggered at irregular intervals and interlaced with barbed wire.

Other obstacles consisted of concrete and masonry walls ranging in height from 3ft to 10ft, built primarily as seawalls, rows of fabricated steel obstacles at and above the high watermark and 12ft to 16ft below the high water mark, and bands of barbed wire on the beach and inland. In addition, the assault troops faced land mines on the beach above the high watermark and in the sand dunes behind the beach, portable concrete and steel obstacles on roads and beach exits, portable wire obstacles on roads, driven piling, steel rails at the low water mark, and extensive craters created by friendly aerial or naval bombardment, as well as prepared enemy charges.[4]

The natural barriers along Omaha Beach were augmented by the addition of many strongly protected and cleverly concealed gun emplacements, machine gun nests, and pillboxes. Slit trenches were dug for defending riflemen, and tank traps and antitank ditches were sited between beaches and road exits. The artillery and machine guns were generally sited so that they could deliver enfilading fire along the beaches. In some cases they were completely concealed from a direct view from seaward by concrete walls covered with earth that extended well beyond the muzzle of the gun. These acted as blast screens and prevented the guns from being located by the dust raised near their muzzles, so that when used with flashless, smokeless powder and without tracer bullets they were exceedingly difficult to detect. As a result of this arrangement of gun positions, nearly all of the defensive fire was delivered on the beaches themselves or on craft within 2,000 yards of the beach.[5]

In the Utah Beach area, fixed infantry defenses were more sparsely located than at Omaha Beach. Here the Germans relied on the natural obstacles provided by flooding the area directly behind the beach. Defenses immediately behind the beach, along the sea wall, consisted of pillboxes, "Tobruk Pits" built entirely underground to support machine guns, mortars, or tank turrets mounted on top, firing trenches, and underground shelters. These emplacements were usually connected by a network of trenches and protected by wire, mines, and antitank ditches.

At and near the roads leading to the beach the defense was a linear series of infantry strong points including turreted machine guns and artillery in open concrete emplacements with antitank hedgehogs and slanted rows of mined stakes along the beach.[6]

The Landings

With the loading of VII Corps (Force U), 1st Infantry Division (Force O), and the 29th Infantry Division (Force B, which consisted of the 175th Infantry Regiment attached to the 1st Division and the 26th Regimental Combat Team) the operation began on May 30. All troops were aboard by June 3 for the landings, which were scheduled for June 5, the provisional D-Day. Force U would land on the Utah beaches and Force O on the Omaha beaches at H-Hour. Force B would land on the Omaha beaches at noon on D-Day.

However, the weather was deteriorating and was predicted to be overcast and stormy with high seas and a cloud base between zero and 5,000ft. Therefore, General Dwight D. Eisenhower, SHEAF Supreme Commander, postponed D-Day for at least 24 hours. By that time, part of the assault force had already put out into the English Channel, but the seas were so heavy that the craft were compelled to turn about and seek shelter. By the morning of June 5, conditions in the Channel showed little improvement but the forecast for the following day was a bit better. Taking tides into consideration, the latest possible date for the invasion was 7 June, but a further 24-hour postponement was impracticable. Therefore, at 0400 on June 5, General Eisenhower made the final decision, scheduling the landings for 0600 on June 6, 24 hours and 30 minutes later than the original plan.[7]

Before the main assault, at 0430 (H minus 2 hours), 65 troopers of A Troop, 4th Cavalry Reconnaissance Squadron, Mechanized (Lieutenant Colonel E. C. Dunn overall commander) and 67 troopers of B Troop, 24th Cavalry Reconnaissance Squadron Mechanized (commanded by Captain Wales Vaughan), 4th Cavalry Group, landed on the Îles Saint-Marcouf, 6,000 yards off Utah Beach's northern flank. They were to capture what was suspected to be a hostile observation post or a casemate for minefield control. A Troop was assigned to the smaller Île de Terre and B Troop the larger Île du Large to the west.

Corporal Harvey S. Olsen and Private Thomas C. Killeran of A Troop, with Sergeant John S. Zanders and Corporal Melvin F. Kinzie of B Troop, each armed only with a knife, swam ashore to mark the beaches for the landing crafts. They became the first seaborne American soldiers to land on French soil on D-Day. As the troops dashed from their landing craft they were met with silence – the Germans had evacuated the islands after mining them heavily.

By 0530 all elements of the 132-man detachment were ashore and the island was occupied. From mines and a concentration of enemy artillery that hit the islands in the afternoon, the cavalry units lost two men killed and 17 wounded.* [8]

The morning of June 6 was overcast with heavy seas running in the English Channel and the Bay of the Seine. The heavy overcast skies forced the Eighth Air Force bombers assigned to hit the coastal defenses to bomb by instrument. Over Omaha Beach the planes were ordered to delay dropping their bombs by several seconds to ensure they didn't hit the assault craft. This resulted in the bombs being scattered miles inland. About a third of the lower flying 9th Air Force medium bombers assigned to Utah Beach dropped their loads to seaward of the high-water mark and many of the selected targets were not located by pilots.

The naval bombardment that began at 0550 that morning detonated large minefields along the shoreline and destroyed a number of the German defensive positions. However, they missed many of the camouflaged artillery and heavy machine-gun revetments lining the dunes behind Omaha Beach.

Minesweepers cleared ten lanes through old enemy minefields in the Channel and the huge convoys, under a constant air umbrella of fighter squadrons flying overhead, closed in on the beaches. On transports anchored 22,000 to 23,000 yards offshore, heavily laden troops began the perilous climb down cargo nets into landing craft bobbing below them while other troops in LCTs, LCMs, and LCIs made for shore.† [9]

Omaha Beach

The first assault missions were to be carried out by 96 tanks, Gap Assault Teams, the 6th and 7th Naval Beach Battalions, and eight companies of the 1st Infantry Division.

---

* The cavalry units were relieved on the June 8 and moved ashore to provide local security for VII Corps Headquarters.

† Troops as well as vehicles were overloaded in the assault, often with tragic consequences. While there is no precise record of the load men carried, it is clear that the equipage of the individual rifleman weighed at least 68lb. The additional personal items not specified in orders, which many men are known to have carried, brought the load of even the most lightly equipped rifleman to 70lb or more. BAR men and heavy weapons crewmen carried even greater burdens. The figure of 68lb is derived from orders and historical accounts and includes the entrenching tool which was not specified in orders but which other evidence indicates was carried. Source: Royce L. Thompson, *D-Day Personal Loads, a compilation and study of data on the equipment and supplies carried by individuals in the assault waves on D-Day*, MS, OCMH.

Harry Kennedy, an LCVP crewman on the Coast Guard-manned Attack Transport USS *Samuel Chase* (APA-26), recalled that morning:

> "Up all hands" was piped at 0500 hours June 6. After chow, we began loading our landing party aboard our Higgins boats. We were lowered by cable into the water, and as I unhooked the cable from the hook in the bottom of our boat the water was so rough the rim was torn loose from the wheel, leaving us to steer with the spokes for 10 hours.[10]

Once underway, the LCVPs and LCAs* were tossed about in the heavy seas, drenching the tightly packed troops with cold spray and making many seasick. Most of the landing craft began taking on water, and despite the bilge pumps working to full capacity, troops had to bail out the water using their helmets. Early morning mists and smoke from the naval bombardment hid crucial landmarks, and to make the situation even worse a strong undetected current, aided by strong winds, pushed the landing craft east of their intended targets by anything from a few hundred yards to as much as 1,000 yards.

"Ahead of us lay the deadly maze of underwater obstacles, through which we had to maneuver before unloading the troops," recalled Kennedy:

> The Germans had waiting for us whole fields of miserable devices designed to impale our boats. Great iron pronged spikes jutted from the water everywhere around us. They also had huge logs buried in the sand pointing upwards, their tops just below water. Attached to these logs were mines dangling from barbed wire. Preliminary bombing and advanced demolition parties had made little headway toward eliminating this mess, so there was nothing to do but weave our way shoreward and pray. We saw a large number of our boats hung up on these obstacles, but we were lucky and reached the shore.
>
> As we lowered our ramp and the soldiers started to charge, they were met with streams of machine gun bullets which brutally mowed down some soldiers. Enemy snipers had hidden nests on the forward slopes with cross fire taking in every inch of the beach, and gun emplacements from where they directed 88 millimeter shells onto incoming landing boats.

---

* The British Landing Craft Assault (LCA) was a slow-speed, shallow-draft landing craft that was less seaworthy than the American LCVP.

We can assure you that D-Day was no time for sightseeing in France. We will never forget the sheer guts, heroism, and fighting ability of the American Infantry man when the going was tough.

Emil H. Bachschmidt, a Coast Guard Landing Boat Engineer attached to *Chase*, was in the first Omaha Beach assault wave. He related:

The moment we dropped our ramp, rapid machine-gun fire opened up, spraying bullets all around us, but all of my soldiers got onto the beach safely. Close to the water, I saw many infantrymen who weren't so fortunate. We wasted no time backing off the beach. We were mighty lucky for a German .88 landed in the water a few yards away.

We returned to the line of departure and there got orders from a control vessel to stand by in case it became too hot on the beach for incoming LCIs to land. We felt pretty safe lying there beyond machine-gun range, until we saw two British landing craft get direct hits by .88s. One of them blew up in a great gust of flame. The other one was luckier, and we picked up a few survivors.

By now, the beach was blazing with gunfire, and the soldiers were stopped cold for the moment. We were told that we would have to make another trip in with men from a Coast Guard-manned LCI. I really dreaded the thought of facing those machine-guns again.[11]

Edward Wozenski, Captain, E Company, 16th Infantry, 1st Division, was among those on Omaha Beach that morning:

After we debarked into the small LVCPs, I recall any number of characters floating around in the waves with their life vests on. I thought the 9th Tactical Air Force or possibly the 8th Air Force had taken a hell of a beating and these people had gone in. Until it dawned on me what had happened. The amphibious tank battalion that was supposed to hit the beach four minutes prior to H-Hour, apparently all swamped.

The beach was bloody awful. We landed, per the navy's request, at low water and that meant approximately 400 yards of struggle over the sand. So there was 400 yards and we were horribly overloaded.

So picture: You hit the beach and you're up and down, you're in water and then you're ducking, small arms and everything's flying all around so you duck down. You're terrified as anyone would be. And every time I got up I thought that it was pure terror that was making my knees buckle until I finally hit the shale and I realized I had about 100 pounds of sand in those pockets that had accumulated on top of the maybe 50 or 60 pounds that we were all carrying in. So it wasn't just pure terror that was making our knees buckle.

Personally, I could not move out of my place. I just was pinned down. Everybody around me was being shot and I was willing to believe it [that we couldn't move]. You'd stick your head up and they would just hose you right down. My executive officer, I'm talking to him, and he had one drilled right through his forehead. Lt. Duckworth married an English girl just a week or so before the landing.

Looking back, I could look at these Landing Craft Infantry, there must have been at least two of them that I saw there, with their ramps down, and these people just running like mad, almost lock step down the ramps on both sides of the Landing Craft Infantry, down toward the beach and they were being shot down just as fast as they came. The Germans had machine guns trained right on those ramps and they were just bowling them off just as fast as they ran down.[12]

Frank W. Freeman, Coast Guard Second Class Motor Machinist's Mate, recalled the assault:

You have no idea how miserable the Germans made the beach. From half a mile off shore we could see rows upon rows of jagged obstructions lining the beach. Added to this was the debris of blown up landing crafts which had been destroyed before us.

Because there was no cleared channel to the beach which we hit shortly after H-hour, there was nothing we could do but plough straight over many submerged logs. Luckily the ones we crashed through were not mined.

When our ramp went down and the soldiers started to charge ashore, the Germans let loose with streams of hot lead which pinged all around us. Why they didn't kill everyone in our boat, I will never know. You can bet we wasted no time cranking up the ramp and backing off. But before leaving we took on six badly wounded soldiers who were lying in the water before us.

The poor suffering army men were on their last legs when we reached the ship.[13]

Dead men littered the beach. Many wounded were drowned in the surf. Others, too weak to move, were run over by incoming landing craft.

E and F Companies of the 16th Combat Team, 4th Brigade Combat Team, 1st Infantry Division, were headed for Easy Red (E to the right half of the beach and F to the left half). At 500 to 600 yards offshore, the LCVPs were subjected to a thick barrage of mortar, artillery, and automatic-weapon fire. A report detailed their landing:

> There were no DD tanks to cover the advance of the assault companies. There were no bomb craters on the beach for the men to find cover in from enemy fire ... Several men struck underwater mines and were blown out of the sea; others continued to cross the obstacle-covered beach to slowly work up the shale at the high water mark to obtain momentary cover.
>
> A hasty firing line was built up along the pile of shale. Company E discovered most of their weapons were jammed with sand. Personnel stripped, cleaned weapons and enemy guns were brought under small arms fire. Despite the fact that enemy MGs [machine guns] and snipers cut down anyone attempting to return to the water to drag wounded up to the lee of the shale, many men pulled casualties out of the water and were wounded. A few succeeded in face of point-blank enemy fire...
>
> A 7 yard deep beachhead was established... Shoulder to shoulder the men lay prone on the pebbles, stone and shale... Landing craft discharged more troops onto the 7 yard beachhead. The third wave, fourth wave, [and] fifth wave found the first wave assault infantry trapped on a beach... Casualties mounted with each succeeding wave.[14]

When E Company's 1st Platoon, led by Lieutenant Spalding, worked their way to the top of the high ground overlooking the beach, under the covering fire of a platoon from G Company, 16th Infantry, they moved west to reduce the strongpoints, which consisted of an antiaircraft gun, four concrete shelters, two pillboxes, and five machine guns. A close exchange of hand grenades and small arms fire ensued until the 1st Platoon cornered approximately 20 Germans and an officer who, overpowered, surrendered. When the battle ended and the rest of the E Company arrived, of the 183 men that landed, 100 were dead, wounded or missing.[15]

To provide fire support on the beaches B and C Companies of the 741st Tank Battalion in DD Sherman tanks were launched as scheduled at 0540 and immediately ran into trouble from the weather. The 6,000 yards of open water that the DD tanks had to traverse were whipped up by a ten- to 18-knot wind with waves averaging between three and four feet in height, with some reaching as high as six feet.

Of the 32 DD tanks of these two companies, 27 swamped on the way in, two swam in, and three were landed from an LCT that could not launch its tanks because of a damaged ramp. All five of these tanks reached shore in the Easy Red sector, and immediately went into action against enemy emplacements. Fortunately, the majority of the crews escaped from their tanks and gained the surface of the water where they were picked up by small craft and taken to larger landing craft and evacuated back to Britain. However, not all were so lucky – unable to escape their tanks, 33 tank crewmen drowned.

At the same time, on the right, in the zone of the 116th Infantry, it was decided that the seas were running too high for the DD tanks to run ashore under their own power. As a result of this decision, B and C Companies of the 743rd Tank Battalion were carried to shore in the LCTs. Direct hits on the LCTs meant that eight B Company tanks were sunk before reaching shore. One of the LCTs sunk was carrying the company commander. He and four other officers were killed or wounded, leaving just one lieutenant in B Company. The remaining eight tanks reached shore safely at Dog Green, while three minutes later C Company's 16 tanks reached Dog White and Easy Green sectors with no losses. However, one was put out of action immediately upon landing.

Two tanks successfully swam their way to shore, where they were joined by three more from LCT-600 which had been landed directly on Easy Red Beach. A Company, which was following with 16 M4A1 tanks equipped with wading equipment, lost three tanks on the way in, so only 18 of the 48 tanks allocated to the eastern beaches arrived intact. The two regiments' artillery suffered equally as badly. Many of the guns were lost when the DUKWs being used to transport them to shore foundered in the heavy seas.[16]

Most of the tanks that reached the shore were knocked out by enemy artillery fire and mines or were caught in the obstacles and flooded by the rising tide.

Coast Guard Captain Miles Imlay commanded LCI(L) Flotilla 10 which consisted of 21 Navy-manned and 13 Coast Guard-manned LCI(L)s and one

Navy-manned LCI(G) gun boat assigned to land troops on Omaha Beach.* Many of the LCI(L)s and their crews were veterans of the landings in North Africa, Sicily, and Italy, which they had come through pretty much unscathed. Their luck changed on Omaha Beach.

The first LCI(L)s to land troops on Omaha Beach were Navy LCI(L)-493 and Coast Guard LCI(L)-88 at 0735. Within the hour, Coast Guard LCI(L)s 90, 91, 94, 92, 83, 85 and 89 would also land troops under withering artillery and small-arms fire while other LCI(L)s would strike mines as they plowed through the beach obstacles.

At 0830 LCI(L)-83 was heading into the beach, but after three tries to find an opening in the obstacles, gave it up and began to call for small boats to come alongside.

"We got one [LC]VP alongside," Lieutenant G, F, Hutchinson, USCGR, the commanding officer, said:

> Right after this boat took 36 men off a shell smashed through the bulwarks, killing three men and wounding thirteen. We were not able to get another boat until an hour later, shortly after ten o'clock. This one took in another 36 men.
>
> But it became apparent that we would never get unloaded this way. The VPs were just not there. Too many of them had been shot up on the beach. I decided to try a beaching.

Engineering officer, Lieutenant Junior Grade A. R. Anderson, USCGR, told how they moved the troops up out of the compartments before going in to the beach. "We figured we might hit a mine and if we did it was better to have the men on topside."

As the ship went in to an apparently clear spot she hit an obstacle and set off the mine they had been fearing. Anderson recalls:

> This mine blew up through number two troop compartment. Shrapnel went through four tanks down below. One tank was completely gone – it blew out right on the weld as if someone had cut it with a torch.

---

* The Navy boats were: 409, 410, 408(G), 411, 412, 413, 487, 488, 489, 490, 491, 492, 493, 494, 495, 496, 497, 498, 540, 541, 553, 554, 555, and 557.
The Coast Guard boats were: 83, 84, 85, 86, 87, 88, 89, 90, 91, 92, 93, 94, and 520.

A lot of the force of the mine was taken by the big Chrysler pumper we had on the deck. This pumper toppled over on several men, injuring them. One soldier standing on deck was blown over the side. I saw him struggle to his feet in the shallow water. A burst of machine-gun fire cut him down and he floated away. A number of soldiers standing on the ladder of number two hatch were injured. We were trying to put a plywood patch on this when the word came to abandon ship.

All of the troops were ashore by this time except the wounded. The crew carried all the casualties to the beach and turned them over to the medics working at the water's edge. Anderson remembers:

A little cliff was right ahead of us. Most of us dug in there. Hutchinson and I made a trip around the ship before leaving to see that everybody was off. The worse thing I saw was the wounded men lying on the beach having chills. We couldn't watch those guys shaking and shivering. We returned to the ship with some Army men to get blankets and food. We threw all the 10 in 1 rations we had over on the sand and all the blankets we could find. The Army picked the stuff up and carried it up the beach. Navy demolition crews cleared the area around and behind the beached LCI while the officers and men decided how best to save their craft.

By six that afternoon the machine-gun fire had stopped and only shell fire was hitting our sector, so we began planning how we were going to save the ship.

The crew was able to refloat the LCI(L) and after a harrowing night trying to keep her afloat, eventually made it back to England.[17]

LCI(L)-88 under Lieutenant Henry K. Rigg, USCGR, carrying Army combat engineers and Beachmaster Ensign Vaghi's C-8 platoon of the 6th Naval Beach Battalion, was the first LCI on Easy Red Beach at 0735. As they neared the beach one large-caliber, armor-piercing shell went through the wheelhouse from fore to aft, missing the helmsman and O.D. [Officer of the Deck] but didn't detonate. While putting ashore Vaghi's platoon, exploding 88mm shells killed three of the men. Withdrawing from the beach at 0739, a shell hit the starboard side forward, damaging the starboard ramp beyond repair. A young seaman who volunteered to take the man rope ashore was hit at the bottom of the ramp, and splattered over the ship, literally drenching

New Yorker war correspondent A. J. Liebling in USCG blood so badly he couldn't see through his glasses. Coxswain Amin Isbir and Vaghi were helping a medic get a wounded soldier to get onto a stretcher when the shell hit. Vaghi was on his knees while Amin was standing at the other end of the stretcher. The blast knocked Vaghi unconscious and killed Amin.[18]

After successfully retracting from the beach, the crippled LCI carried her casualties and surviving crew out to the transport area.

LCI(L)-91 was commanded by Lieutenant Junior Grade, Arend Vyn, Jr., USCGR. With 201 troops aboard, she landed at the left center of Dog White Beach. The troops immediately came under heavy machine-gun and rifle fire. A man rope had been led by a member of the ship's crew, from the ship through a maze of stakes, each topped by a teller mine, to the beach.

About 20 minutes after grounding the rapidly rising tide and slow departure of troops made it necessary to move the ship forward to keep grounded. While doing so a teller mine on a stake at the port bow exploded injuring a few soldiers and blowing a hole about 2ft in diameter in the bow just above the waterline. However, it apparently caused no more serious damage to the ship. A portion of the remaining troops had disembarked after the second beaching when a violent explosion occurred forward, immediately followed by a blast of flames. Within seconds the entire well deck was a mass of flames and there wasn't adequate water pressure to fight them. Small-caliber enemy fire continued near the beach and intermittent German 88mm fire near the ship. The remaining troops disembarked over the side and proceeded in to the beach.[19]

The crew of Lieutenant Robert M. Salmon's LCI(L)-92, following an hour later with 192 troops on board, saw Vyn's LCI(L) in flames, and it was decided that she should beach to the left and in the lee of the burning vessel.

Seth Shepherd, a Coast Guard Combat Cameraman, later wrote about what happen that day:

> My heartbeat jumped when I looked over the starboard bow, near the beach, and saw the Coast Guard manned LCI-91 enveloped in flames and smoke. She was the first LCI to hit that sector of the beach. We were scheduled as the second.
>
> I was on the port side by the signal light with my camera, bracing myself to take a picture. Then it came. A terrifying blast lifted the whole ship upward with a sudden lurch from the bow. A sheet of flame and steel shot

out from the forward hold. The ship shook as if it were pulling apart. In the first blast, which set fire to the main fuel tanks and blew out a hole in the starboard side, big enough to drive a Higgins boat through, forty-one soldiers in the forward troop compartment were trapped. Most of them were killed instantly in the fiery cauldron. The first explosion blew two of the soldiers out of the hatch.

But the worst concentration of explosive fire centered forward, where many of our crew were working to lower the ramps, others on the antiaircraft gun. Flames and dense smoke were pouring from the hatch, the ramps were damaged, making it impossible to lower.

Some soldiers jumped overboard. Others slid or let themselves down a chain, forward of the damaged ramp, into the surf, which was covered with burning oil. German gunners raked them with machine-gun fire. Shepherd later wrote: "The cries of some of the helpless soldiers in the deep water were pitiful." All the while the terrific explosions, fire and heavy smoke filled the air, and the littered decks heaved under the impact of yet more shells as they ripped through the steel plates.

Shepherd continued:

Going aft I saw "Doc" Maleska and "Pop" Hursey, pharmacist's mates, aiding the wounded amidst the chaos. Without the cool stand of Ray Maleska and Rudie Hursey as they swabbed the burned faces, necks, and hands of soldiers and our own crew there would have been many more bad cases of burns.

By now the order to abandon ship had been passed, but because of the thunderous noise and condition of the ship not all the crew heard the order immediately. It seemed as if every few seconds an 88mm came "whooshing" over my head. As I ducked down, the violent explosion would vibrate against my head, echoing in my helmet.

Once up on the beach we sank exhaustedly on the pebbles, reaching the lowest point of human existence. The Army medics and Navy corpsmen ran back and forth aiding the wounded. Some of the soldiers stretched out along the beach were a horrible sight with parts of their bodies shot away. I was impressed time and again at the lack of moaning or cries. They lay still, waiting with haunted eyes, but not asking for help because they knew that every able soldier with a gun was needed forward in the lines.

Now as the tide went out it left our burning ship high and dry on the beach. It was nearing midnight when three LCMs managed to get into the beach about a quarter of a mile down from us. The full moon rising back of us gave a hideous light to the dead bodies lying stacked up along the beach road, but we made the boats without drawing fire.

When the LCMs hit the beach, we helped the wounded into the boats and then followed them on. We were taken to an LST waiting a few miles out to unload her cargo and troops. Just as we were climbing aboard we had our first German air raid of the night. A German raider swooped by the LST in a long arc, narrowly missing the barrage balloon, to fly along the beach and strafe. We had gotten off that beach just in time.[20]

Despite the death and destruction, these LCI(L)s were not the worst hit. That was Lieutenant Junior Grade Coit T. Hendley, Jr.'s LCI(L)-85 at 0830. As a result of the strong tide running along the beach, the control vessel had drifted until it was almost past Easy Red Beach. It actually landed on the left flank of Easy Red, or on the right flank of Fox Green, rather than the right flank of Easy Red as scheduled. Hendley later described what happened:

We were carrying units of a beach battalion, a mixture of about 220 Army and Navy men who were to go ashore right after the first assault waves. They were rather grim about the whole thing.

My ship was to beach at H plus 120 – two hours after the initial assault. As we approached, there was no immediate sign of trouble. There were flashes from the various warships shelling the shore, plus a few black puffs of shell fire at the water's edge. Closer to the beach we saw signs that the landing was not going to be easy. A great number of small craft were drifting, out of control and shot to pieces. The entire beach area was covered with heavy smoke.

The sector where we were to land was blocked by sunken LCIs and by a confused mess of small craft which were abandoned, broached or hung up on obstacles covered with mines. The only thing to do was to pick a likely spot and ram through. The ship headed in at around twelve knots. The thud of underwater obstacles could be heard on the bottom and sides of the ship.

Four tanks were on the sand directly in front of us. Three of them were burning and the fourth seemed to have been hit. Every now and then the fourth fired, but at long intervals. A thin line of troops was stretched out face down at the water line firing at the Germans.

Now there is a nice little thing about an LCI(L) that occurs at this point. It has to do with the man rope. The idea was that as the ramps go down, a member of the crew dashes off the ship, carrying a small anchor attached to a rope (or line as the Coast Guard called it). He makes it to the beach and plants the anchor and the soldiers have the line to help them wade through the water. They were carrying up to 50 pounds of gear and men had been lost in other invasions when they stepped into holes and couldn't get back to their feet with all that weight on their backs.

Well, Seaman Gene Oxley had volunteered for that duty. Oxley went down the ramp and stepped into water over his head. The ship was stuck on some sort of obstacle. It was impossible to disembark troops at this point on the beach. Oxley was hauled aboard and the ramps taken in. As the ship was backing away from the beach, a shell hit amidships and went into number three troop compartment.

We could hear the screams of the men through the voice tube. That was the only hit we suffered on this beaching, but we didn't have time to make a count of casualties. The beach battalion doctors went to work.

"We were on deck together as we approached the beach," wrote Lieutenant Junior Grade John F. Kincaid Jr., a 6th Naval Beach Battalion medical officer waiting to go ashore with Lieutenant Junior Grade Jack Hagerty II, a beachmaster with the 6th Naval Beach Battalion.

It was then the first casualties occurred, and Jack assisted me in treating them. He turned to lead his men ashore and I moved forward to treat another casualty. At this moment a heavy shell landed aboard, killing Jack instantly. He had left me with a big smile and an encouraging word of "See you on the beach." [*]

Hendley continues the story:

The engineering officer managed to get the stern anchor in but the winch sputtered out and he never got it going again. We went down the beach about 100 yards and there seemed to be one spot clear of debris.

[*]   Dr. Kincaid survived the invasion of Normandy only to be killed on a destroyer off Okinawa in April 1945.

We beached again, this time without a stern anchor. As the bow hit the sand, a mine went off just under the bow, splitting a forward compartment. We got the port ramp over and Seaman Oxley again took the man rope to the beach. This time the water was about chest deep. He crawled through the obstacles and hauled on the line until there was a strain on it. Several soldiers on the water's edge stopped firing to help him steady the line. One soldier with a bazooka was right under the bow of the ship firing rockets at a pillbox up further on the beach. The troops began to disembark.

Shells had been bouncing near the ship the whole time we were coming into the beach. There was heavy machine gun fire. They smashed through the massed men trying to get down the ramp. I remember waving to two friends – an Army officer and a Navy lieutenant – who were standing on the deck just below the pilot house. A shell hit, killing them both and wounding a number of other men. About two thirds of the troops managed to make it to the beach before a shell finished off the ramp. It went over the side taking all the men with it.

Men were hit and men were mutilated. There was no such thing as a minor wound. When the shells hit they blew off arms, legs, and heads. The guns seemed to concentrate on the forward part of the ship, and so well did they do their work that unloading was stopped because it was impossible to get past the pile of dead and wounded. Finally a hit finished off the ramp.

The ship was hit about twenty-eight times. Our radio man was in the worst shape. His name was Gordon R. Arneberg. A shell exploded in the radio shack, wrecking everything and cutting Arnsberg's leg off. The crew dragged him out. I found his leg lying on the deck and kept walking around it. Finally, one of the crew with more guts than I had kicked it over the side.

Unloading had to be stopped because the living could not climb over the dead. There is no need to describe all the pitiful cases. They were there and no one will ever forget. Only four of the ship's crew were wounded. The other casualties were all from the beach battalion. A check showed approximately 15 men dead and 40 wounded.

The damage control party began fighting the fires which had started in her three forward compartments, while the Army doctors on board and Coast Guard pharmacists' mates began doing what they could for the wounded. Small boats from the large transports came alongside and finished unloading the men who had not been able to get ashore. Luckily the fires were caught in time. The ship had a list from the water coming in through the shell holes.

We made it out to the transport area, 10 miles from the beach, taking water slowly. Our emergency pumps could not keep ahead of the water. The wounded and dead were transferred to the transport by cargo boom. The Army medics and doctors who had stayed to help with the casualties climbed into a small boat furnished by the transport and headed for the beach they had just left. They took their equipment and said nothing. They knew they were needed on the beach. How many of them are living now I do not know.

We backed away from the transport and a salvage tug came alongside to determine whether she could be saved. But even their pumps could not keep up with the water. Slowly she settled by the bow and finally began to turn on her side. The crew scrambled up on the tug, and she went over. She floated for a while, her stern just showing. The tug sent over a small boat with a demolition charge to finish her off. The charge went off, and that was the end of one LCI.[21]

At approximately 0945, Lieutenant Junior Grade Budd B. Bornhoft, USCGR, pushed LCI(L)-93 through the obstacles of Easy Red Beach and dropped her ramps. Soldiers of the veteran 1st Infantry Division including 166 from I Company, and 37 from M Company of the 18th Regiment began to scramble down into the 3ft deep water. Manning the starboard ramp winch, Seaman First Class Robert McCrory observed that there was no artillery fire directed at LCI(L)-93, but several soldiers were struck down by small-arms fire as they ran down the ramp. Bornhoft asked for volunteers to retrieve wounded soldiers at the base of the ramps. Under fire, Seaman First Class McCrory, Boatswain's Mate Second Class Glenn Nichols and other shipmates carried several soldiers to safety. Bornhoft then retracted LCI(L)-93 off the beach and headed for the transport, Coast Guard manned *Samuel B. Chase* (APA-26), to pick up another load of soldiers.

Upon arriving at *Chase*, LCI(L)-93 picked up a double load of soldiers – standing room only – including members of the 453rd Amphibious Truck Company, 5th Special Brigade, and started her second run to the beach.

While LCI(L)-93 was on the way back to the beach, Lieutenant Stewart F. Lovell's LCI(L)-487 made her run to Easy Red Beach with 36 soldiers of M Company and 167 soldiers of K Company, 18th Regiment, 1st Infantry Division. Among the men were First Lieutenant William Messer and a combat veteran Sergeant Roland Ehlers.

When the ramps were dropped, Coxswain Edward Siecienski ran forward from his station at #2 gun and descended the ramp with the man rope that would assist the heavily laden soldiers. He was concentrating on stretching the line to the beach and drawing the line tight, by lying on the small anchor at the end of it, so that the soldiers would have something to hold on to as they struggled through the surf.

Behind him, huddled around #1 gun on the bow of LCI(L)-487, were Boatswain's Mate Second Class Kennedy Coulter and Gunner's Mate Third Class Patrick O'Donnell. Coulter was wearing headsets and was to report observations to the bridge. He was looking down at the first soldiers scrambling down the port ramp when an artillery or mortar round struck in the midst of them. Horrified, he reported the casualties. Messer was killed on the ramp, and others suffered mortal wounds including Ehlers, who had already won a Purple Heart and had endured three major campaigns in three years with his brother Walter.

More artillery rounds slammed into both sides of the bow of LCI(L)-487. Coulter identified a bunker and gun emplacement on the hillside and asked for permission to engage it with his 20mm. The request was denied. The first artillery strike on the bow had knocked O'Donnell to the deck, breaking his thumb. As he got back to his feet, he watched as the troops descended the only remaining usable ramp on the starboard side. Meanwhile, Siecienski was still lying on top of the man rope anchor on the beach. As the artillery and mortar rounds crashed around him the casualties mounted. He was surrounded by 11 wounded and three dead soldiers. When the last soldiers had passed by him, Siecienski pulled himself up and dashed back to his LCI.

Faced with no means to winch off the beach, a rapidly falling tide, a sandbar to block them and artillery rounds punching holes in his ship, Lieutenant Lovell informed Siecienski that he should abandon ship with three quarters of the crew and seek shelter on the beach or escape on another landing craft. Lovell planned to remain on board with some of the crew and try to refloat LCI(L)-487 at the next high tide.

With orders not to stop and lend assistance to anyone, LCI(L)-93 passed an LCVP with dead and wounded hanging over the gunnels. She then managed to slip over a sandbar in the rapidly falling tide and advance another 20 yards before the ramps were lowered. The LCI(L) then struck a mine aft and the starboard engine was thrown against the port engine.

Meanwhile, on LCI(L)-487, the crew began to abandon ship. Some heard the order to abandon ship, and others merely followed those who had heard the order. All saw LCI(L)-93, which was landing troops a mere 100 yards to port, as their potential savior. At least 16 sailors from LCI(L)-487 made the wild dash for LCI(L)-93. The flight had immediate consequences for both LCIs. The German artillerymen who observed the flight of the LCIs ceased fire on the abandoned LCI(L)-487 and trained their guns on LCI(L)-93 instead.

Gunner's Mate Third Class Byron Spalding ran down the ramp of LCI(L)-93, anchor in hand, determined to get the man rope stretched to the beach as fast as he could. Having completed his task with mortar rounds exploding nearby, he scurried back on board in record time. He later declared "I could walk on water!" The soldiers then began descending the ramps into a storm of small-arms and mortar fire. Some who panicked began jumping over the side. Seaman First Class Robert McCrory and Quartermaster Third Class Aven Templeton, who were manning the starboard ramp winch, did their best to help the soldiers inflate their life belts before jumping overboard. Those who did not inflate their belts were dragged under the waves by their heavy loads. McCrory did not see them resurface. Finally, McCrory and Templeton were pushed aside by the frantic soldiers moving towards the ramps. McCrory then received a temporary reprieve from the horror when a projectile slammed into his helmet knocking him unconscious.

Steward's Mate Second Class John N. Roberts had just received instructions from Bornhoft to relay information to the engine room. Communications had been knocked out and the skipper wanted Roberts to order engines full astern in an attempt to back over the sandbar created by the rapid falling tide.

"I was taking a message from the Commanding Officer to the engine room, because the intercom was no longer working," said Roberts. He then continued:

> He told me to go down to the engine room and tell them to rev the engines full to try to get us off, as I was coming down from where he was to the main deck, about halfway down, that when a shell came through and exploded underneath me. It took my leg off from my knee down, my foot was gone completely and it was skin and bone from my knee down. I remember hopping off the ladder down to the deck and called for help. In the meantime, Pharmacist Mate Charles Midgett was there, he came and put a tourniquet on me, on my leg and that saved my life I'm sure. I had nothing but my two hands to hold my leg to control the bleeding until he got there.[22]

Boatswain's Mate Second Class Abbot who had been recently assigned to the LCI as an additional Pharmacist's Mate immediately came to help Midgett apply the tourniquet and administer first aid. Siecienski jumped off the ladder from the bridge to help Abbot. Not only had the Steward's Mate lost much of his right leg, he had also received painful shrapnel wounds to his left.

In the barrage two artillery rounds passed through the pilothouse. All told, LCI(L)-93 took at least ten hits from large-caliber artillery rounds. About 25 troops were still on board when the enemy found the range and concentrated several heavy batteries on the vessel. Four of the troops were seriously injured and were later evacuated with the crew; one soldier later died of his wounds. The crew suffered five shrapnel casualties and two others were seriously injured.

When McCrory regained consciousness he was alone on the bow. McCrory staggered back towards the fantail where his shipmates were seeking shelter from the artillery rounds that were concentrated on the forward part of the ship. Along the way he saw a thick trail of blood that led to the pathetic crumpled body of his friend Boatswain's Mate Second Class Glenn Nichols. Upon arriving at the fantail, he sought shelter behind an ammunition box with Gunner's Mate Third Class Byron Spalding. Spalding pointed to a large dent in McCrory's helmet and declared that he should be dead.

After the firing subsided, McCrory walked forward along the deck and recovered an Army blanket to cover the body of his friend Glenn Nichols. While placing the blanket over Nichols, McCrory was shocked when the "body" groaned "I'm not dead yet you son of a bitch!" Nichols had five pieces of shrapnel in his throat. Surgeons would later leave two of the pieces inside him for fear that they would cause more damage in the process of removing them.

After hours stranded on the beach, Bornhoft realized that LCI(L)-93 was finished. His Executive Officer, John J. O'Conner, was one of the severely wounded. There was much flooding below and the craft was shot to pieces. Even if they could move, a sandbar blocked their escape. He signalled two destroyers, USS *Doyle* (DD-494) and USS *Emmons* (DD-457), and asked for help. *Emmons* asked for volunteers and it too sent a gig and a whaleboat. Bornhoft ordered the crew to abandon ship. McCrory was the first over the side and they lowered his wounded friend Glenn Nichols to him. McCrory towed Nichols out to the waiting whaleboat.

Emmons' deck log states that at 1633, the gig returned with six wounded and 18 more were recovered in another small boat. Seventeen were "Coasties" from LCI(L)-93, three were sailors from LCI(L)-487 and the remaining four were probably four wounded soldiers reported "removed with crew" by Lieutenant Bornhoft. USS *Doyle* reported rescuing a total of 37 crewmembers of LCI(L)-93 and LCI(L)-487.

That was the end of LCI(L)-93 but not the end of LCI(L)-487. For approximately 12 hours the remaining crew of LCI(L)-487 patched her up and awaited another high tide for a chance to refloat her. They got her off and returned to England.[23]

The intended beach sector for LCI(L)-94, commanded by Lieutenant Gene R. Gislason, USCGR, was Dog Red, close to Easy Green. The Executive Officer was Lieutenant Junior Grade Albert Green. In addition to the crew, there were 36 men of the 29th Military Police, 101 soldiers of the 112th Combat Engineers, and 42 members of B Company, 104th Medical Battalion.

Motor Machinist's Mate First Class Clifford W. Lewis later wrote:

At 0715 we were called to General Quarters. While at gun I noticed hundreds of ships & crafts all about us. Spitfires & P-38s were constantly flying back and forth over the area. Smoke hovered over the beach and a number of ships could be seen to be burning furiously. Tracer shells began skipping out over the water towards us. They exploded very close & shrapnel clattered against the ship. At 0745 we were called to man our beaching stations. I made a dash for the engine room hatch and could feel and hear shrapnel & machine gun bullets careening by.

Gislason steered around numerous mined obstacles. He had initially headed west toward Vierville. However, as he approached the landing area it became clear that the same fate awaited LCI(L)-94 as had happened to LCI(L)-91 and LCI(L)-92 if they kept that same heading, so he turned east to between Saint Laurent and Colleville-sur-Mer on the border of Dog Red and Easy Green beaches, where today the Colleville Cemetery is located. At 0747 the landing craft crunched onto the beach and the soldiers on LCI(L)-94 went ashore in shoulder-high water that had even deeper swells.

"We disembarked our troops and started out when the Skipper noticed we had fouled an LCVP with a line and started back in to assist them," Lewis recalled.

> At that moment three shells burst into the pilot house and exploded killing three of my shipmates and wounding two including an officer. Couldn't do any more for the LCVP so we cut the line and started off the beach again after the pilot house was cleared and hand steering put into operation. We had been on the beach 50 minutes and were now high-tailing it out minus the port ramp which had to be cut away.
>
> The pharmacist mates were working over a couple of shapeless hulks lying in wire baskets and covered with blankets. It was a horrible sight with blood and flesh splattered over everything. DeNunzio had both legs blown off and part of his stomach, but was still living. I helped the doc give him plasma, but it was hopeless. He died fifteen minutes later. Buncik was decapitated and occupied only half a stretcher. Burton was still intact but was killed by the concussion. Anthony had shrapnel in the feet and legs and was in great pain. He was given morphine and him and Mr. Mead, who was shocked and had shrapnel in his back.
>
> The bodies were later put aboard an LST and were later buried on the beach. Most of our lighting and power from the pilot house had been shot away and we went about for some time with great difficulty.

After the attack, communications had to be provided by a line of the crew relaying information from the sides of LCI(L)-94 to Gislason at the helm. He was thus able to hand steer off the beach. Repairs were made and LCI(L)-94 stayed in the fight.[24]

The Gap Assault Teams riding LCMs in the first landing wave touched down between 0633 and 0635. Almost without exception every LCM was subjected to mortar, machine-gun and 88mm barrages while approaching the beach. Lieutenant Junior Grade H. L. Blackwell, Jr., USNR, summarized what happened to the NCDUs on Omaha Beach in his report to the Commander of Task Force 122:

> The Assault NCDUs and Army Demolition Units (collectively called Gap Assault Teams) touched down on OMAHA beaches at 0633 – 0635, with

a single exception all were to the left of their assigned beaches, starting with Team No. 1 on DOG WHITE, 700 yards east of their intended landing on DOG GREEN. Others were as much as 1500 yards east of their assigned landings, though still within the Omaha beaches. Almost all units proceeded at once to lay charges; and they were ready to fire in a maximum of 20 minutes. Six complete gaps, through all bands of obstacles, were blown during the assault low-tide, most of them by H plus 30 minutes. Three partial gaps, through either the seaward or the landward bands, were also blown at this time.

Death prevented three other Navy units from firing. Of these, one was caught aboard the LCM by machine gun fire, while they strove to off-load their rubber boat; another was eliminated, after setting its charges, by well-placed mortar fire. The third was blown up after bringing in its rubber boat, when a direct hit set off the auxiliary explosives in it and somehow also the charges at the obstacles where men still were.

A freak accident caused the failure of another naval group; the officer was about to pull the twin friction-igniters, when a bit of shrapnel cut the two fuses and his finger as well. The enemy saved one naval team the trouble of pulling its igniters, when a bullet or fragment managed somehow to set off the primacord and all the charges!

Despite the casualties, surviving units continued working, with general disregard for personal safety. A notable example of courage was given by men who voluntarily placed charges on Tellermines atop obstacles, 10 or 12 feet above the beach; in the face of accurate rifle and machine-gun fire, they climbed on each other's shoulders or shinnied up the pilings and [landing craft] ramps.[25]

Navy Ensign Lawrence S. Karnowski was the officer in charge of NCDU-45, part of GAT-10, assigned to the 6th Beach Battalion. For the three nights and two days prior to the invasion the men endured rough sea conditions aboard an LCT. Cold and wet, often forced to sleep exposed on decks awash with water from the cold English Channel, with poor rations, contaminated drinking water, and a bucket for a head, the men waited. In the early hours of June 6 they boarded an LCM and headed for shore.

Landing at 0625 on Easy Red Beach, Karnowski led his team as they disembarked and began placing small satchel charges on the obstacles in the water. Encountering little German resistance they successfully blew a

100-yard line of obstacles at 0650. Almost immediately after Karnowski's men fired their first shot, German machine guns and artillery zeroed in on the group from the bluffs above. Refusing to remain pinned down, Chief Constructionman Millis grabbed a roll of primacord and sprinted from obstacle to obstacle, placing and wiring charges before being cut down. Motor Machinist Mate Second Class Meyers raced out to Millis's body and continued his deadly work. As American infantry waded past the NCDU men, Gunner's Mate First Class Gale B. Fant took a machine-gun round through his leg and then a piece of shrapnel wounded Meyers. Gunner's Mate Third Class Robert L. Svendsen carried Fant on his back to the dune line as Karnowski waded out and carried another wounded team member to higher ground.

At 0700, thanks to Millis' sacrifice and Meyers' quick actions, Karnowski's men detonated their second shot and cleared obstacles up to a 26-man team under First Lieutenant Joseph Gregory of the Army Engineers working further along the beach. Army engineers proceeded to detonate their first shot at 0710 and a second one soon afterward, clearing almost the entire assigned 50-yard gap of steel hedgehogs from the surf to the dunes. Karnowski and his remaining men then began placing charges for a third shot, but advancing infantry precluded detonation.

By this point, Karnowski and Gregory were standing in the rising tide with water up to their knees. The two men swam out and cleared the remaining obstacles one charge at a time. With the gap open, LCIs moved in to unload fresh troops. Karnowski and Gregory rounded up the remaining Navy and Army personnel, and led them to the dunes for protection from increasing shelling. But a short time later a shell burst fatally wounded Gregory.*

Returning to his men, Karnowski learned four of his Army personnel had sustained shrapnel injuries. Though exhausted, he dug foxholes for the wounded. Between 0730 and 0830 the 16th and 116th RCTs, 1st Infantry Division, attacked the bluffs overlooking Easy Red, finally clearing by 0930.

Karnowski, NCDU-45, and GAT-10 managed to clear the largest gap along Omaha Beach. This enabled Army engineers to transform Exit E-1 at Easy Red into the principal egress off Omaha Beach, ensuring an American foothold on the bloodiest Normandy beach.† [26]

---

*   Gregory posthumously received the Distinguished Service Cross for his efforts on June 6.

†   For his actions on June 6, Karnowski was awarded the Navy Cross, the first CEC officer to receive the medal for actions in Europe, and the French Croix de Guerre with Palm. For his heroism that morning, Meyers received the Silver Star. The entire NCDU

The following account of what befell the NCDU units that day was written anonymously by Ensign S.F.I. at a hospital somewhere in England shortly after the landings.* He prefaced the account with the words "For Those Who Died":

> Glory isn't at all important, but recognition of a task well done is – both for the sake of those who gave their lives for that task, and for those at home who know only that a loved one died in France. Yet in all the accounts I have seen of the invasion there has been nothing about the part played by the boys of the Naval Combat Demolition Units.[27]

Here's his account of that bloody morning.

> Our mission was to land on D-Day, H-Hour, and remove obstacles placed in the water by the enemy to keep our invasion craft away from the beach or blow them up as they came in. My crew of eight men and myself, together with five Army men, were in the bow of an LCM. In the stern were 18 Army engineers. We also had aboard an ample supply of explosives and equipment.
>
> As we came within sight of the beach, the water around the obstacles appeared to be about waist dep. When we were about 200 yards out, an 88mm shell hit the stern of our craft, taking off the ramp and part of the port side together with most of the Army engineers, blown to bits. For a split second our two machine gunners opened fire – then, in the time it took me to look up, disappeared. The coxswain also was blasted from his station. As the force of the explosion turned the LCM broadside to the beach another 88 went through both sides about midship and exploded in the water.
>
> The Germans kept spraying us with machine-gun fire, so I ordered what men were still alive overboard. They swam out to sea in spite of the machine-gun bullets spattering all around them. I hope to God they were picked up.
>
> Our LCM was right among the obstacles now – irregular rows of wooden poles about 16 inches thick and 12 to 18 feet high, all mined on top – but, with our motor idling and the tide working strong to the port side, was

†   (*continued from previous page*)
        component of Force O received one of three Presidential Unit Citations awarded to the
        Navy for D-Day.

*   The author was unable to find who the initials S.F.I. belong to. There is not record of an
        officer with these initials listed in NCDU or other associated unit records.

soon swept clear. Each time we faced the beach, however, the Germans turned the machine guns on us. By then only two men on board were still living, besides myself. After opening and dumping the cans of gasoline in the bow, we lay still in hope that the enemy would think us dead and cease firing.

After a while the LCM scraped bottom, and I made a dive for the cliff on shore with my two men following me, one shot in the legs. We dug into the bottom of the cliff for protection against the hand grenades the Germans were dropping over on us. Soon, realizing that we were still alive, they drew back and directed heavy fire against the top of the cliff, caving it in on us. One of my men suffocated to death, and the other two of us were dug out some two hours later.

After regaining strength, we crawled along the beach – which by this time was littered with dead – until, by noon, I had located several demolition men from other crews. At receding tide we went to work, still under machine-gun fire, to clear a 100-yard gap through the obstacles. The job took several days – and nights. I was evacuated from the beach on D plus 7.

Gap Assault Team casualties on the Omaha Beach were 31 killed and 60 wounded, 30 percent of the right flank group and 50 percent of the left flank group, a casualty rate of 52 percent. NCDU-45 alone suffered a casualty rate of more than 50 percent, with one killed, one seriously wounded and five slightly wounded. All casualties were the result of enemy action and no casualties resulted from improper handling of explosives.

Coast Guard 83ft rescue boats stayed close by as landing craft fought their way through dangerously heavy seas and onto deadly beaches. Stripped of armaments and excess gear to better enable soaked and weary survivors to climb on board, the crews rigged scramble nets fore and aft on both sides and installed block and tackle on the iron davits to lift the wounded.

Just prior to sailing a small shipment of California brandy arrived for use in reviving the spirits of the survivors. "It was packed in small, two-ounce bottles," recalled the flotilla commander, "and when divided among the sixty boats of the Flotilla, the size of the spirited ration for each craft was conceivably less than the proverbial 'cask' carried by the Saint Bernards of the Swiss passes. These few drops of concentrated 'sunshine' were expended during the first few hours of D-Day."

Typical of the pre-invasion briefing was the one given the night before D-Day by Lieutenant Junior Grade Raymond M. Rosenbloom, Jr., USCGR, skipper of Rescue Cutter 16. "We're going to have to be callous," he warned his men. The rescue vessels were to take on board no more persons than they could safely carry. "When we get a load," he continued, "we're going to have to back away, no matter how many men are in the water [but as] soon as we've unloaded one batch of boys on a larger ship we'll go back for another."[28]

Minutes after H-Hour, Ensign Bernard B. Wood, commanding CGC-1, probably made the first rescue less than 2,000 yards from the German guns. With a fairly high bitterly cold sea, and the majority of the survivors weakened from shock and immersion, the Coast Guardsmen had to go over the side and lift the soldiers on board. Though surrounded by bursting shells, the cutter continued to cruise about picking up every swimmer the lookouts could see. Since the assault craft had the right of way, the matchbox cutters had to dodge skillfully out of the way of the rushing landing vessels.

CGC-5, captained by Ensign S. G. Pattyson, picked up 15 men from sinking amphibious trucks just off Omaha Beach. By noon on D-Day, CGC-5 had made 34 rescues, mostly of seriously wounded men. The little cutter's wooden decks "were red with blood this hectic morning," reported the flotilla commander. "Even when she reached our base across the channel, her crew was still trying unsuccessfully to scrub away the vivid reminders of badly hurt men – men with missing arms or legs – whose day of battle had come and now was gone forever."

Carter Barber, a Coast Guard combat correspondent aboard the Coast Guard Rescue Cutter 16, sent this description of his ship's duties on June 6:

> The cutter had just made a round trip to the DICKMAN standing out in the harbor mouth, to discharge some ninety casualties picked up earlier this morning when she saw a stricken LCT which was slowly capsizing as it sank, and dashed to the aid of the stranded personnel. On the decks of the LCT over thirty men were trapped, including a wounded man with nearly severed legs, dangling only by pieces of flesh, who was unable to leave his ship. When the rescue cutter was skillfully maneuvered under the slowly lowering side of the LCT, despite the choppy seas surrounding the craft, all the other men were safely brought aboard the smaller craft, except for the wounded sailor.

When the sailor's plight became apparent, Arthur Burkhard, Jr., a member of the cutter's crew, jumped over the side of the rescue cutter, rushed to the wounded man's side, and helped to secure a line around him, completely disregarding the smoke that was beginning to pour from the LCT's hatches. "At that time I didn't know that the LCT was doubling as a small-arms ammunition ship," said Burkhard. "It was a good thing that I was able to get the line around the lad before that gigantic, sinking bomb blew up. However, the man helped me get the line around him."

"He was the bravest man that we picked up," Burkhard continued. "He was unable to talk because of weakness, but he managed to keep a grin on his face. Even when we were cutting his clothes off him to administer morphine when we saw that his two legs were severed above the knees, he kept himself under control, and even winked at us."

Once the wounded sailor had the line about him, Burkhard unsuccessfully tried to lower him from the settling LCT to the smaller rescue cutter. The LCT's starboard side was dropping lower and lower as the whole ship began to capsize, and it was impossible for the skipper, Lieutenant Junior Grade R. V. McPhail, to keep his craft under the LCT's side lest his own be pinned beneath it. Barber continued:

The only alternative was for Burkhard to throw the wounded man off the LCT's deck into the water, where he could be pulled aboard the rescue craft. "I never saw anyone so game as that man," adds Burkhard. "I hated to throw such a badly wounded man into the water, but that was the only way I could get him to safety. But he helped himself, and pulled himself hand-over-hand up the side of our boat when our fellows had towed him to the boat's side." Once his charge was aboard, Burkhard himself had to plunge into the water and make his way back to his ship.

Although he couldn't swim himself, he was dragged aboard by his mates. "I've got a brother in the Navy, myself, and figured that he might be the man aboard the sinking LCT. So the fact that I couldn't swim didn't stop me," said Burkhard. No more than two minutes after Burkhard and the casualties were taken aboard the rescue cutter and the boat had left the LCT, the burning ship completely turned turtle and disappeared from sight.[29]

The distinction of rescuing the most survivors on D-Day went to CGC-16, skippered by Lieutenant Junior Grade R. V. McPhail, USCG. In all, this cutter delivered 126 casualties and one fatality back to the hospital ship in less than six hours.

While transferring the wounded, a doctor stated that one particular man need not be placed on the hospital ship, since he was "beyond all possibility of recovery" with one whole side of his abdomen ripped away by a shell. The Coast Guardsmen put him aside with the dead and, at the first opportunity, held a sea burial. During this ceremony, the man who had been given up for dead raised his head, looked around at the astonished crewmen, and exclaimed: "If you guys think you are going to do that to me you've got another guess coming. How about some hot coffee, but hot – and for …'s sake, gimme a cigarette."

As a rueful Coast Guardsman later recalled: "A half-hour later, chalk white but still alive and full of grit, this man was put aboard an LST especially equipped for handling hospital cases. Whether he survived or not is not known."

Cutter No. 35's commanding officer Lieutenant Clark's trip report for that period simply stated: "Survivors rescued, five. Corpses, none. Comments, none."[30]

In all, the Coast Guard rescued 1,438 men off the Normandy beaches on June 6.

As the day lengthened, conditions combined to produce a near-inferno on Omaha Beach. Enemy mortar and artillery batteries, unscathed by Allied fire, poured destruction upon the attackers while the invading force time and again appeared to fumble. Allied rocket ships responded from extreme range and when their missiles fell short, they hit the troops on the beach. Wreckage at the water's edge accumulated as timetables slipped and landing craft became hopelessly entangled in the barbed wire and projecting beams of uncleared beach obstructions. This was partly because the engineering task force was at 40 percent strength as most were killed in the first half-hour of the attack.

At approximately 0633 (H+3) two platoons of the 6th Naval Beach Battalion worked their way up to Easy Red's shingle bank with three surviving DD tanks, which were seen to knock out several enemy pillboxes, while another 6th Naval Beach Battalion detachment attempting to get ashore had to abandon its LCVP 100 yards out from Easy Red when it struck an obstacle and was badly damaged by machine-gun fire. Other battalion elements set up control stations on the beach to direct the landing of craft and salvaged equipment to mark safe lanes of approach.

A detail from Company C helped rescue two platoons of infantrymen from the water. These men had debarked in deep water and their load of equipment was pulling many men down. Dr. Lee Parker, a member of the 6th Naval Beach Battalion medical team, recalled:

> We lost many men to bullets but also we had many drown. The drowning of our soldiers was not publicized that much but we lost many to the icy water. Many of the wounded soldiers were in shock and it wasn't always easy to tell the living from the dead among the hundreds of bodies that lay on the beach or washed in the surf. You'd go up to them and look at them and they looked pretty good on one side, you get over there, the heads blown off on the other side. So you just ran into that type of thing all day long.[31]

Under punishing fire, battalion aid men worked up and down the beach and in the minefields, bandaging, splinting, and giving morphine and plasma. Army and Navy doctors, often themselves injured, worked as best they could to give emergency treatment. Wearing a Red Cross armband and a painted Red Cross on his helmet did not protect the corpsmen from mortars, mines, and artillery fire. German snipers picked off exposed medics and hospital corpsmen while they treated the wounded on the beach. The medical teams, forced to drag casualties from the surf toward the enemy's murderous guns, often became casualties themselves.[32]

Pharmacist's Mate Vincent Kordack recalled:

> We were maybe 50 or 100 yards from the beach when we stopped and unloaded. I was the last off the craft and I was up to my waist. They were already loading casualties on. The first casualty I saw was a man with one arm shot off and he was holding it in the air. And then all of a sudden I heard '88s and they were overshooting the LCT. I got on the beach and took off my medical pack and everything I had. The first person I saw was a young man I knew from the marshaling area. He was a Pharmacist's Mate Second Class Rickenback. I noticed that he had a bullet hole through his helmet. I met Rickenback back in the marshaling area. He was not B Company. For some reason, we got very close. We were sitting in a tent

talking and so forth and he said, "Vince, I'm not gonna come home. This is it. I'm not gonna make it." I always think of that because he was the first casualty I saw that day.[33]

A little more than one-third of the first wave of attackers reached dry land. Lacking most of their heavy weapons, those survivors had little choice but to huddle behind sand dunes and in the lee of a small seawall that ran along the base of the beach. What happened to A and B Companies, 116th Infantry Division Battalion, is tragically typical.

As Company A drew to within 700 to 800 yards of the beach, artillery and mortar fire began to fall among the boats. There had already been a loss – one boat foundered 1,000 yards out from taking on too much water; one man had drowned and the others had been picked up by naval craft. At first the enemy shell fire was ineffective, but as the first boats drew to within 50 yards of the sand, one was struck by a shell and two men were mortally hit, while the others took to the water.

The first ramps were dropped at 0656 in water that was anything from waist deep to over a man's head. It was as if this was the signal for which the enemy had waited, and the ramps were instantly enveloped in the accurate and heavy crossfire of automatic weapons. The onslaught came at the boats from both ends of the beach. A Company had planned to move in three files from each boat with the center file going first, and then the flank files peeling off to the right and left. The first men tried it. However, they crumpled forward into the water as they sprang from the ship. All order was then lost. It seemed to the men that the only way to get ashore with a chance of survival was to dive headfirst into the water.

Private Howard I. Grosser remembers:

A few had jumped off, trying to follow the SOP, and had gone down in water over their heads. They were around the boat now, struggling with their equipment and trying to keep afloat. In one of the boats, a third of the men had become engaged in this struggle to save themselves from a quick drowning.

Private First Class Gilbert G. Murdoek remembered that many were lost before they had a chance to face the enemy. Some of them were wounded while they were in the water and some of these then drowned. Others, wounded, dragged themselves ashore and upon finding the sands, lay quiet and gave themselves shots, only to be caught and drowned within a few minutes by the rushing tide. Some men managed to move safely through German assaults and make it to the sands. However, they then found that they could not hold there and returned to the water, using it as cover, with only their heads sticking out above it. Others sought the cover behind the obstacles, though many were shot while so doing. Those who did survive kept moving shoreward with the tide and in this way finally made their landing. They were still in this tide-borne movement when E Company came in behind them. Others who had made it onto the sands and had burrowed in, remaining in their holes until the tide caught them, then joined the men in the water.

Within seven to ten minutes of the ramps dropping, A Company suffered so many casualties the survivors were leaderless and almost incapable of action. All the officers were dead or badly wounded. Lieutenant Edward N. Qaring was shot in the back where the first boat haul foundered. Lieutenant Elijah Nance had been hit in the heel as he left the boat and then in the body as he reached the sands. Lieutenant Edward Tidrick was hit in the throat as he jumped from the ramp into the water.

Tidrick went on to the sands and flopped down 15ft from Private First Class Leo J. Hash. He raised up to give Nash an order. Nash saw him bleeding from the throat and heard his words: "Advance with the wire cutters." It was futile. Hash had no wire cutters and in giving the order Tidrick had made himself a target for just an instant, and Nash saw machine-gun bullets cleave him from head to pelvis. German machine gunners along the cliff directly ahead were now firing straight down into the party. Captain Taylor N. Eellers and Lieutenant Benjamin H. Kearfott had come in with 30 men from "A" aboard LCA 1015, but what happened to that boat team in detail will never be known. Every man was killed; most of the bodies were found along the beach.

In those first five to ten confused minutes when the men were fighting the water, dropping their arms and even their helmets to save themselves from drowning, and learning by what they saw, the landing had deteriorated into a struggle for personal survival, every sergeant was either killed or wounded. It seemed to the others that enemy snipers had spotted their leaders and had directed their fire so as to exterminate them.

A medical boat came in to the right of Tidrick's boat. The Germans machine-gunned every man in the section. Their bodies floated with the tide. By this time the leaderless infantrymen had foregone any attempt to get forward against the enemy, and where men moved at all, their efforts were directed toward trying to save any of their comrades they could reach. The men in the water pushed wounded men ahead. Those who had reached the sands crawled back into the water, pulling men to the land to save them from drowning, in many cases, only to have them shot out of their hands or to be hit themselves while trying to save others.

By the time B Company hit the beach a half hour later it is estimated that only one-third of A Company remained alive or unwounded.

The first boats from B Company hit the beach at H-Hour+26. When the ramps dropped automatic weapons fire swept in from both flanks. On the right flank a sailor in one of the boats froze on the rope and wouldn't let the ramp down; the men had to struggle with him and take the rope away before they could make the break for the beach. They then jumped into neck-high water and started ashore.

The beach was strewn with heavy boulders and was extremely difficult to traverse. However, the outward jutting of the cliff wall gave the men partial protection from the enemy fire, and little of it seemed to be bearing directly at them.

Private First Class Robert L. Sales was in the boat of the B Company commander, Captain Ettore V. Zappacosta. Three hundred yards out it was hit several times but the men were uninjured. About 75 yards from the beach, the ramp was dropped and the front of the boat came under automatic-weapon fire. Zappacosta jumped from the boat and managed to get about ten yards through the water before being hit in the leg and shoulder. Sales saw him go down and did not see him come up again. Then Technician Fifth Grade Thomas Kenser, the aid man, jumped toward Zappacosta and was shot dead as he jumped. Lieutenant Tom Dallas of C Company, who had come in to make a reconnaissance, also jumped out. He managed to get to the edge of the sand before being killed. Sales was fourth in line. He started out with his SCR 300 radio strapped to his back, tripped at the edge of the ramp and fell sprawling into the water, an accident that probably saved his life.

Man by man, all of those leaving the ramp behind him were either killed or wounded. Sales was the only one to get as far as the beach unwounded and it took him almost two hours.[34]

Caught between the overwhelming German firepower and rising tide, unit cohesion disintegrated. Slowly leaders emerged from the wreckage of men and equipment. Sergeants took over for their dead officers, and corporals and privates took over for dead sergeants. Colonel George A. Taylor, commander of the 1st Division's 16th Infantry Regiment, summed up the need to get moving: "Two kinds of people are staying on this beach, the dead and those who are going to die. Now let's get the hell out of here."[35]

D, E and F Companies of the 2d Ranger Battalion, under Lieutenant Colonel James E. Rudder, were due to land four miles west of Omaha Beach at Pointe du Hoc at 0630. They were then to climb the cliffs with mortar-launched rope ladders and to try and silence a German battery of six 155mm canons located at the top. Rudder would give a signal within 45 minutes of the landing if the attack was successful. If it was successful A Company and B Company, 2d Ranger Battalion, and the 5th Ranger Battalion under Lieutenant Colonel Max F. Schneider would reinforce the Rangers on the cliff. If Rudder didn't give the signal the second wave would land on Omaha Beach and advance through the lines of the 116th Infantry Regiment to attack the battery from the rear.

John C. Raaen, Jr., 5th Ranger Battalion, who was in one of the British LCAs waiting for Rudder's signal, recalls: "At H-Hour, 0630 hours, we circled offshore waiting for a signal from the 2nd Ranger Battalion. Had they been successful in their assault of the cliffs at Point du Hoc? No word. Circle. No word."

At 0710, ten minutes beyond his deadline, Schneider received by radio the code word "Tilt," a prearranged signal telling him to follow the alternate plan. He then ordered the three waves of 18 Ranger boats under his command to divert to Omaha Beach, landing at Vierville-sur-Mer.

Unbeknownst to Schneider, the Pointe du Hoc assault was delayed by 40 minutes because of the eastward drifting of the craft carrying the Rangers.

As the ramps of Colonel Schneider's first wave dropped, A and B Companies of the 2d Rangers landed at Vierville, where they were cut to pieces by a barrage of German machine-gun, mortar, and artillery fire. Colonel Schneider diverted his remaining forces, the entire 5th Rangers, to the east. Approximately one mile and ten minutes later the 5th Infantry Battalion landed intact astride the boundary between Omaha Dog White and Red beaches.[36]

"We ultimately got to a point where the British coxswain on our boat said, 'I'm aground, I'm aground.'" Staff Sergeant Victor, in the heavy weapons section (E Company), 5th Ranger Battalion, wrote later:

He dropped the ramp and Lieutenant Anderson who was in the front yelled "All out" and then he jumped out. He immediately disappeared beneath the waves, and some in front of the boat were just in time to reach down and dragged him back in the boat. Sergeant Charles VanderVoort then simply put his tommy gun in the ribs of the coxswain and said, "I think you had better get us ashore." I might say that our boat, under those circumstances, probably got closer to the actual sand beach than any other.

We were able to get out without getting in water more than to our knees. You couldn't really blame the ship's crew, because as soon as they got us out they were able to leave this dangerous spot, so it was no wonder they were eager to get us out.

Robert Edlin of the 2d Ranger Battalion recalled:

Our assault boat hit a sandbar. I looked over the ramp and we were at least seventy-five yards from the shore, and we had hoped for a dry landing. I told the coxswain, "Try to get in further." He screamed he couldn't. That British seaman had all the guts in the world but couldn't get off the sandbar. I told him to drop the ramp or we were going to die right there.

We had been trained for years not to go off the front of the ramp, because the boat might get rocked by a wave and run over you. So we went off the sides. I looked to my right and saw a B Company boat next to us with Lt. Bob Fitzsimmons, a good friend, take a direct hit on the ramp from a mortar or mine. I thought, there goes half of B Company.

It was cold, miserably cold, even though it was June. The water temperature was probably forty-five or fifty degrees. It was up to my shoulders when I went in, and I saw men sinking all about me. I tried to grab a couple, but my job was to get on in and get to the guns. There were bodies from the 116th floating everywhere. They were face down in the water with packs still on their backs. They had inflated their life jackets. Fortunately, most of the Rangers did not inflate theirs or they also might have turned over and drowned.

When I was about twenty yards from the seaway I was hit by what I assume was a sniper bullet. It shattered and broke my right leg. I thought, well, I've got a Purple Heart. I fell, and as I did, it was like a searing hot poker rammed into my leg. My rifle fell ten feet or so in front of me. I crawled forward to get to it, picked it up, and as I rose on my left leg, another burst of I think machine gun fire tore the muscles out of that leg, knocking me down again.

Staff Sergeant Victor Miller, E Company heavy weapons section, 5th Ranger Battalion, remembered the landing also:

The tide was now coming in a bit and this started to be a serious problem for a number of wounded that were scattered along the beach at the places they had been hit. They were crying out to us, but if they couldn't move themselves there was little we could do for them, at least from our point of view. Most of them eventually drowned.

We saw very few tanks on the beach. We later heard that the tanks that were supposed to swim to the beach simply sank when they drove off the transport ships. We did see one tank, it was running up and down the beach and didn't seem to be accomplishing anything, other than almost running over some of the wounded who couldn't get out of the way.

Schneider immediately ordered the battalion to proceed to rallying points by platoon infiltration. Four holes were blown in the wire that trapped the American forces on the beach. Rangers poured through those gaps in the wire and stormed the crest of the smoke-covered bluffs, taking the German defenders by surprise.[37]

Edlin picks up the story.

There were some Rangers gathered at the seaway – Sgt. William Courtney, Pvt. William Dreher, Garfield Ray, Gabby Hart, Sgt. Charles Berg. I yelled at them, "You have to get off of here! You have to get up and get the guns!" They were gone immediately. I looked up at the top of the cliffs and thought, I can't make it on this leg. Where was everyone? Had they all quit? Then I heard Dreher yelling, "Come on up. These trenches are empty." Then Kraut burp guns cut loose. I thought, oh God, I can't get there! I heard an American tommy gun, and Courtney shouted, "Damn it, Dreher! They're empty now."

There was more German small-arms fire and German grenades popping. I could hear Whitey yelling, "Cover me!" I heard Garfield Ray's BAR talking American. Then there was silence.

Miller led his squad through one of the gaps:

While going up the hill I suddenly realized that one of my squads was missing. Both squads had been by my side the whole time, but now one was gone. I decided to go back down the hill and there I found my men. When I asked for an explanation why they weren't yet on their way to the top, they told me that someone had told them that there was a minefield on the road to the top. I drove them up the hill and once there they too realized that they were safer there than on the beach. We could hear the shells go overhead on their way to the beach.

When we were at the top of the hill we came to the road that runs parallel to the beach through Vierville sur Mer. From there we looked back on the beach before we went inland. We saw an LSI with men disembarking down the stairways on both sides. Suddenly these men were engulfed in flames. Apparently one of the men carrying a flame-thrower had been hit by a shell or bullet and his tank had exploded. The front of the ship simply disappeared in flames. With that terrible image in our minds we turned our backs to the beach and moved on inland.

Crippled by his leg wound, Edlin lay on the beach as the Rangers stormed up the hill:

My years of training told me there would be a counterattack. I gathered the wounded by the seaway and told them to arm themselves as well as possible. I said if the Germans come we are either going to be captured or die on the beach, but we might as well take the Germans with us. I know it sounds ridiculous, but ten or fifteen Rangers lay there, facing up to the cliffs, praying that Sgt. White, Courtney, Dreher, and the 5th Ranger Battalion would get to the guns. Our fight was over unless the Germans counterattacked.

I looked back to the sea. There was nothing. There were no reinforcements. I thought the invasion had been abandoned. We would be dead or prisoners soon. Everyone had withdrawn and left us. Well, we had tried. Some guy crawled over and told me he was a colonel from the 29th Infantry Division. He said for us to relax, we were going to be okay. D, E, and F Companies were on the Pointe. The guns had been destroyed. A and B Companies and the 5th Rangers were inland. The 29th and 1st Divisions were getting off the beaches.

This colonel looked at me and said, "You've done your job." I answered, "How? By using up two rounds of German ammo on my legs?" Despite the awful pain, I hoped to catch up with the platoon the next day.

By late afternoon the beach exits were cleared, the Germans driven from the bluffs, and, as the tide dropped, the GATs returned to the tidal flat to carry out the mission that they had found impossible at H-Hour. Of the two loaded forces, O Force, with 29,714 men, and B Force, the follow-up force of 26,492 men, more than 34,000 are estimated to have crossed the beach on the first day, but at a cost of 2,000 killed and 1,000 wounded.

Pointe du Hoc

The objective of 225 men of D, E, and F Companies, 2d Ranger Battalion, along with Shore Fire Control Party (SFPC) #1 was to eliminate a battery of six 155mm guns of the German 726th Infantry Regiment.

They disembarked from the two converted British Channel steamers, *Ben Machree* and *Amsterdam*, into ten LCAs along with another two LCAs loaded with supplies and four DUKWs carrying the 100ft ladders.

Almost immediately the LCAs ran into heavy seas. Eight miles from shore LCA 860, carrying Captain Harold K. Slater and 20 men of D Company, was swamped by choppy waves and the men were picked up by Coast Guard rescue craft. Ten minutes later the seas claimed one supply craft, which sank leaving only one survivor. The other supply craft was soon in trouble and had to jettison the Rangers' packs in order to stay afloat. The other craft survived, with varying degrees of trouble – several took on so much water that the men had to bail out with their helmets to help the pumps.

The leading group of nine surviving LCAs kept good formation, in a double column ready to fan out as they neared shore. Unfortunately, the guide craft lost its bearings as the coastline came into sight, and headed straight for Pointe de la Percée, three miles east of the target.

When Lieutenant Colonel Rudder, in the lead LCA, realized the error he intervened and turned the column westward. This put them in range of German strongpoints on the cliffs. A DUKW was hit by 20mm fire. Five of the nine men aboard were killed or wounded.

First Sergeant Leonard Lomell remembered that morning:

It suddenly occurred to all of us, particularly D Company: "Hey, we're not going to be able to do what we were trained to do. D Company was assigned the mission of going around the Pointe and landing on the west side of it. Our assignment was to take out three gun positions – 4, 5 and 6. Because of the mistake in navigation by the British coxswains, we had lost about a half hour.[38]

The escort destroyer HMS *Talybont* (L-18), which had taken part in the early bombardment of Pointe du Hoc, saw the flotilla heading in on a wrong course. Her captain closed range and raked enemy firing positions with 4in and 2-pounder shells. Meanwhile, lookouts on USS *Satterlee* (DD-626), standing out 2,500 yards from Pointe du Hoc, saw enemy troops assembling on the cliff, and opened fire with her 5in and 40mm guns.

At 0710 the first landing craft grounded on a heavily cratered strip 30 yards from the 100ft high cliffs. Heavy machine-gun fire raked the men as they headed for the cliffs. The Germans also rolled grenades down the cliffs, causing more casualties.

"My whole psyche that day was like I was in a football game," Lomell said later:

I remembered my instructions, and we charged hard and low and fast. That was our secret, and we stayed together. The 2nd Platoon stayed together as a team on D-Day. We got in, and our ramp went down and all hell broke loose. The boat leader goes off the front straightaway. I stepped off the ramp, and I was the first one shot.

The bullet went through what little fat I had on my right side. It didn't hit any organs, but it spun me around and burned like the dickens. There was a shell crater there underwater. I went down in water over my head with the spare rope, the hand launcher and my submachine gun.[39]

The first two attempts to reach the cliff top failed when the line was cut by gunfire. Line-carrying rockets fired from other LCAs reached the top. Scrambling up, the Rangers finally struggled to the top after incurring 15 casualties. As the men reached the top, they went off in small groups to accomplish their missions.

Although wounded, Lomell made it up the cliff:

When I went over the top, I tumbled into a shell crater. There was Captain Gilbert Baugh. He was E Company's commander. He had a .45 in his hand, and a bullet had gone through the back of his hand into the magazine in the grip of the .45. He was in shock and bleeding badly and there was nothing we could do other than to give him some morphine and say, "Listen. We gotta move it. We're on our way, Captain. We'll send back a medic. You just stay here. You're gonna be all right.

It was then that we left the crater where we had gathered together as we came over the cliff. We jumped into a bigger crater, and it held maybe a dozen of our guys. We couldn't get all 22 together in one crater for the move toward 4, 5 and 6 gun emplacements. We hadn't counted on craters being a protection to us. We would have lost more men, but the craters protected us."[40]

Other climbing parties had gone ahead with speed, determination, and resourcefulness, ready to improvise when necessary. This was the main reason for their success, along with the fact that within 30 minutes from touchdown all the attacking force was on top except for casualties,* headquarters personnel, and some mortar men.

As they came up from the ropes they found themselves in a bewildering wasteland of ground that had been literally torn to pieces by bombs and heavy naval shells, only to find the guns had been moved and replaced with telephone poles. They later found the guns camouflaged in an apple orchard.

By 0725, First Lieutenant James W. Eikner of the SFCP had his equipment set up and flashed word by SCR 300 that Colonel Rudder's force had landed. Five minutes later he sent out the code word indicating "men up the cliff"; in reply to this message he got "Roger", again on SCR 300. When he sent the message "PRAISE THE LORD" ("all men up cliff") at 0745 for some reason there was no answer.

At 0728, *Satterlee* made its first contact with the Naval Shore Fire Control Party, and was immediately given target requests followed by spotting reports from the shore observers. However, radio transmission was uncertain, and a new difficulty arose when the signals party moved to the Command Post on top of the cliff. Attempts to communicate by radio drew enemy artillery fire immediately, suggesting that the Germans were picking up the transmissions and using them to register on the Command Post. Lieutenant Eikner then turned to other means, and made successful contact using signal lamps.[41]

*   Between 30 and 40 Rangers were killed or wounded out of about 190.

By nightfall the Rangers companies had lost a third of their men and were low on ammunition. They established a 200-yard defensive perimeter and settled in for the night. At the end of the next day their number was reduced to fewer than 100 men and there was almost no food.

It was June 8 when the 5th Ranger Battalion finally broke through from the west to join up with them. Only 90 of the original 225 Rangers who had led the assault on Pointe du Hoc were still able to man their positions.

Utah Beach

In the early morning twilight of June 6, approximately 865 vessels and craft waited 22,500 yards off the Utah beaches. After a breakfast of steak and eggs the troops climbed down debarkation nets into landing craft heaving in three-foot seas. Once loaded with 36 soldiers the boats headed to their designated assembly area.

Coast Guard Coxswain Marvin Perrett, an LCVP driver assigned to the Coast Guard-manned USS *Bayfield* (APA-33) well remembered that morning:

> It took time to fill that circle of 12 boats. So consequently these troops are in my boat now at 2:30 in the morning and H-hour for everybody; first wave is going to be 6:30 am. As it developed I probably didn't bring my troops ashore until maybe seven o'clock in the morning. So these guys are – all of us; Navy and Coast Guard personnel alike, in these slow moving circles. Every time you got to the top of the circle you're eating your own diesel fumes and as a result many of these fellows were a little worse for the wear before they ever hit the beach.
>
> Every one of these fellows had backpacks on with like 80 or 90 pounds of gear. Everything they owned was on their person because they didn't know whether it would be the next day or a month from now, and consequently when these guys are standing in this same area; restricted area, they're in there now packed like sardines. They can't move around. They are actually frozen in space and in time. They can't move. They can't even sit down in their own spot, so it was a tight assemblage of personnel.[42]

At 0550 Task Force 125's bombardment group's ships opened fire, splitting the dawn with deafening noise as tons of metal screamed toward the German batteries. Seventeen of these craft mounted rocket launchers and discharged their rockets when the first waves of assault craft were still 600 to 700 yards from shore. A few minutes later 276 Ninth Air Force B-26 Marauder bombers made their first strike on the beaches.

The plan was that the first wave would consist of 600 infantry in 20 LCVPs. Then would come an intermediate Wave 1A of eight LCTs, each carrying four 70th Tank Battalion DD tanks, which would be followed by Wave 2 comprising another 32 LCVPs with additional troops of the two assault battalions, some combat engineers, and eight NCDU teams. Sixteen M4 Sherman tanks and eight tank dozers came ashore in Wave 3. Wave 4, at H-Hour+15, would consist of eight LCTs carrying tank dozers, and immediately behind these tanks would be eight engineer combat demolition teams to clear obstacles above water. A reserve of three naval teams and four engineer teams was included in the fourth and fifth waves.

When the LCVPs were between 300 and 400 yards from the beach, the assault company commanders were to fire special smoke projectors to signal the lifting of naval gunfire support.[43]

Smoke from naval bombardment and aerial bombing hid landmarks on shore and swift, undetected currents carried the 4th Division's landing craft 1,500 to 2,000 yards south of their target onto a portion of the beach that was only lightly defended. It turned out there were fewer obstructions and the shore defenses there weren't as strong as the ones in the area originally targeted for invasion. However, the Germans, alerted by the shelling and aerial bombardment, quickly manned their defenses and laid down lethal barrages. Improving visibility enabled enemy shore batteries to inflict heavier damage on the landing craft approaching the beach.[44]

Within a few minutes of the planned H-Hour the first assault wave of LCVPs hit the beaches, dropped their ramps and 600 men ran down into waist-deep water 100 yards from shore. Somehow they had managed to get through an unsuspected minefield located in the Cardonet Shoals, which lay right across the boat lanes. Thirty DD tanks of the 70th Tank Brigade's B Company that were unloaded from their LCTs 1,000 yards off the beach also made it without either a tank or an LCT being lost. The following waves weren't so lucky.

August Leo Thomas, a coxswain on LCT-633, remembers the landing:

[D-Day]Our passengers were combat engineers and infantrymen. Our cargo – the vehicles, trailers, explosives and other gear that belonged to these soldiers. There was a lot of talk and speculation aboard. Some of the soldiers came out of the North African campaign and one of them told us he had a feeling he would not make it this time. I often wondered about him.

We headed to the beach in columns. The LCT 777 [loaded with 479th Amphibious Truck Company] was ahead of us as we headed for the beach. There was a terrific explosion, and the LCT 777 seemed to break in half. We learned later she had hit a mine. The skipper altered course slightly to avoid running over survivors who were in the water. It was heartbreaking not to be able to stop and render assistance to the men who were so desperately in need of help. And to make matters worse, some of these men were our friends.

As we got closer to the beach, we could see the sand being kicked up by exploding shells. The skipper altered course slightly to starboard and was immediately ordered to return to our original course. There was smoke rising along the beach from burning vehicles. By this time, Ensign Edwards, who was on Flotilla staff and standing next to the Skipper and I on the conning tower, said to me, "Thomas, it looks like they are playing for keeps." I said, "Yes, sir, they are."

A few minutes after this Ensign Edwards was killed, and the Skipper and I were wounded by an exploding shell. The Skipper and I were able to remain at our stations. As Ensign Edwards was falling, I grabbed hold of him and laid him on the deck and called for a medic. As help was coming up, I helped lower Ensign Edwards to a catwalk near the wheelhouse. I returned to my station next to the Skipper. He had suffered a head wound but was able to continue commanding the LCT 663. We continued to the beach for our initial landing. We beached and dropped our ramp, and the combat engineers and infantrymen and their equipment were discharged on French soil.[45]

At 0547 LCT(DD)-593 also hit a mine which blew the ramp, two DD tanks and the entire front section of the craft clear of the water before sinking with her load of four tanks and leaving only one survivor.

After disgorging the tanks the LCTs retracted and headed for the transport area, dodging the incoming LCVPs and LCTs. LCT-597 struck a mine on the way back to the transportation area and was lost with no survivors. Hit ten times by artillery, the Royal Navy LCT(A)-2310 lost its starboard engine, and the engine room was flooded, creating a heavy list; both the coxswain and throttleman were injured. Although the guide vessel was out of sight, LCT(A)-2310 successfully discharged its three Sherman tanks.

Eight minutes after LCT(DD)-593 was damaged, LCT(A)-2282, another Royal Navy LCT, beached amid considerable shelling and blasting by the NCDUs. While lowering its ramp, it took a shell through the ramp, which killed six men. Despite this, the crew managed to unload its three tanks successfully.

The next LCTs were scheduled for the 13th wave, landing at 1000. LCT-362 (one of five LCTs in this wave) was lost en route to Uncle Red Beach. On Tare Green Beach the 14th wave lost LCT-458. In Uncle Red Sector, three of the LCTs – 443, 486, and 489 – carrying men and guns of the 29th Field Artillery Battalion were sunk. Of the 11 14th wave LCTs, four were lost.*

British-manned Landing Craft Flak (LCF) 31 was providing antiaircraft fire support off Utah Beach in the early morning hours when it struck a mine. Carter Barber, an American war correspondent on USS *Bayfield*, wrote about it:

> When we saw the LCF get hit, and rushed to her aid, I noticed plenty of men floating face down in the water. They might have just been stunned, sure. But I had to agree with the skipper that we couldn't stop for them just then but we must keep on to get the other men foundering about. I went forward to throw heaving lines to other men in the water. Twos and threes of them were screaming "Oh save me... I'm hurt bad ... please please please."
>
> And I yelled back "Hang on Mac, we're coming" and looked astern at the guys on our boat hauling other wounded men aboard, and wondered at the inadequacy of everything. We needed ten pairs of hands. One big fellow who afterwards admitted he weighed 230 pounds, stripped, had two legs broken, and was in intense pain. We had a hell of a time getting him aboard because his clothing was waterlogged and he was weighed down with helmet, rifle, pack, ammunition, et al. The man screamed as we helped him aboard, but we had to be a little callous so that we could get the man on deck and move to another group of survivors.[46]

---

* Pursuant to their commitment, the Royal Navy provided two squadrons of LCTs ("O" and "G"), which the British manned and operated during the invasion. Lieutenant Commander C. P. McArmstrong commanded British Squadron "G." Lieutenant Commander C. J. Skiles commanded British Squadron "O," consisting of three flotillas of 22 Mark(5)s. Waves 15 and 16 contained British-manned LCTs – 14 Mark(4)s and nine lend–lease Mark(5)s. Wave 18 was manned by five LCTs from Flotilla 17 and another five LCTs from Flotilla 4. The British LCT commitment on D-Day was largely unknown to U.S. skippers and crew.

Lieutenant Junior Grade Rosenbloom's Coast Guard Rescue Cutter 16 was patrolling off Utah Beach that morning. In stark words the logbook records the loss of LCF-31 and PC-1261:

> 0730, LCF-31 hit by shell 800 yards off shore, sinking immediately. While engaged in picking up survivors, shell struck PC-1261, which disintegrated, scattering men and debris over a wide area. While so engaged, shells and bullets were falling nearby, and just after last man picked up, small landing craft only few hundred yards off shore blew up. Proceeded to spot and picked up all living survivors. Then proceeded to APA *Dickman* and unloaded survivors. Two men pronounced dead, but one was revived later and put aboard an LST. Departed again for invasion coast.

NCDU 127 veteran John Dittmer remembers getting into the water; one of the first things he noticed was a disembodied leg floating next to him. He held his nerve and pressed on. At the beach it was a matter of getting the supplies ashore and taking cover for the moment. Myron Walsh of NCDU 127 stated that he found the best method to advance on the beach was to go from shell crater to shell crater; "lightning never strikes twice in the same place."[*47]

Sergeant Frederick Peters, 237th Engineer Combat Battalion, has vivid memories of the landing:

> My place on the LCVP was at the ramp, because as a squad leader, I would lead the men off and issue orders. Each one of us was loaded down with 76 pounds of TNT. In addition, we had our rifles, grenades, gas masks, and full field packs. Others of our battalion were carrying Bangalore torpedoes which looked like stove pipes filled with powder and fragments used to blow barbed wire entanglements. Other engineers were carrying mine sweepers, and others had flame throwers.
>
> Our barge could not get close to the beach because of all the 88 shells dropping, so the ramp was dropped and we stepped off into water over our heads. We were weighted down so much that we had to hold our breath and jump forward to reach the beach without drowning. As soon as we got to dry land, we knew that we must run for a crater made by the 88's or mortars.

---

[*] The overall casualty rates on Utah Beach were lower than those of Omaha Beach. Utah had its share of losses – six men from the NCDUs died during the fighting and 11 were seriously wounded.

My orders were to have those carrying TNT to deposit their packs at a spot of my choosing along the sea wall, then to blow the 4x5 foot wall. Breaching this wall was extremely important because all of our jeeps, trucks, howitzers, tanks, destroyers, etc. would go through the gap we had made. PFC Harrison was to help me gather the TNT and place the detonator on the sea wall, and to set the charge.

After I set the charge, I was to signal with a colored smoke bomb. It was in a size 202 can and also had the new detonator that was set off by pulling the ring on the lid. I did this and got only about 30 feet away from the blast. I was bounced a foot off the ground, and as a result, I spit blood for a week.

As the smoke settled, I realized that there was a machine gun nest close by and it was mowing down our soldiers as they advanced. I knew it was in a concrete pillbox about 20 feet to my right. These pillboxes had slits in all four sides, but luckily for me, only the front one was being used. Now I had to make a decision – would one of my three grenades pass through the slit? I decided to go ahead and try it, so I pulled the pin and reached up, pushing the grenade through.

I hadn't silenced this machine gun nest soon enough, for I heard a soldier screaming at the water's edge. It is hard to imagine that through all the noise I could hear one scream, but it was a sound I shall never forget. This soldier had been cut in half at his belt, the lower half of his body was nowhere near, and each time the salt water tide would come up and fill his chest cavity, he would scream in agony. For someone in this condition to still be conscious was one of the horrors a soldier had to witness every day.[48]

Harassed by sniper fire and aided by tank dozers, A Company, 237th Engineer Combat Battalion, blew two gaps in the wall on Uncle Red Beach and C Company blew two on Green Beach while the NCDUs blasted lanes for more landing craft. The job cost six men killed and another 39 wounded. As soon as the gaps were opened the 1st Battalion, 8th Infantry Division, moved inland to the north through Exit 3 while the 2d Battalion with B and C Companies, 70th Tank Brigade, headed down the coast through Exit 1. As they passed the minefield, Company C's commander, First Lieutenant John Ahearn, saw a wounded paratrooper lying in the minefield behind the sea wall. Ahearn stopped his tank, told his crew to stay in it, and dismounted to rescue the wounded man. As he was picking his way through the minefield, he tripped one or more mines which blew his feet off. His crew dismounted and, with the aid of ropes, succeeded in getting both men out of the minefield without accident. They evacuated them to the beach for return to England.[49]

The 3d Battalion, 8th Infantry, unloaded on Uncle Red Beach and supported by the 70th Tank Battalion and engineers of the 237th Engineer Combat Battalion, began moving down the causeway to Exit 2. Halfway down the causeway they found the culvert over a small stream had been blown and that the road was covered by an antitank gun off to the right. The first tank was stopped by a mine, and another was knocked off the road by the antitank gun. It was not until a third tank silenced the enemy gun that the column proceeded to ford the stream. The blown culvert never really obstructed traffic as Major Tabb of the Beach Obstacle Task Force immediately brought up a platoon of engineers and built a small tread way bridge.

Approximately 75 minutes after the first wave reached the beaches the 3d Battalion, 22nd Infantry Division, waded ashore on Green Beach and moved north along the coast to reduce beach strong points.

At the same time the 3d Battalion, 8th Infantry, moving west beyond Exit 2, met little opposition until just north of Sainte-Marie-du-Mont. At Germain the battalion encountered enemy dugouts, underground shelters, three or four 88mm guns, and smaller weapons. In a short firefight 50 Germans were shot as they broke and ran and 100 were taken prisoner. At night the battalion bivouacked north of Les Forges. K Company took up a position far to the left and sent one platoon to Chef-du-Pont to establish contact with the 82d Airborne Division.

Late in the afternoon the advance elements of the seaborne "Howell Force," which was attached to the 82d Airborne Division and commanded by Colonel E. D. Raff, followed the 3d Battalion across Exit 2. They were to join the 82d Airborne Division at Sainte-Mére-Èglise.

Compared to Omaha Beach the assault on Utah Beach was accomplished with surprisingly few problems. The 4th Division's losses for D-Day were low. The 8th and 22d Infantry Regiments, which landed before noon, suffered a total of 118 casualties with only 12 of them fatalities. The division as a whole suffered only 197 casualties during the day, and these included 60 men missing through the loss (at sea) of part of B Battery, 29th Field Artillery Battalion. A total of over 20,000 troops and 1,700 vehicles reached Utah Beach by the end of June 6. The casualty count doesn't include an unknown number of tank and American and British landing craft crews killed or wounded.

Lessons Learned

There were new amphibious warfare lessons from Operation *Overlord*. The landings had been extensively rehearsed, but what happened in the airborne landing zones and on the beaches could not have been predicted or planned for. The lessons learned in combined arms coordination were invaluable. Tankers and infantrymen found that together they formed an effective combination. They learned respect for each other's capabilities, and they guarded each other's weaknesses as had the Marines and soldiers in the Pacific.

August Leo Thomas perhaps best sums up the survivors' feelings as June 6 faded into June 7:

> To me, on June 6th, 1944, time meant nothing, simply because things were moving too fast to even think of time or of food or of anything else. At 2400 hours, June 6th, 1944, passed into history, but on the beaches of Normandy, nobody was sleeping and wouldn't be for some time.
>
> The only people who can truly appreciate the significance of D-Day at Normandy are those people who participated in this great invasion. It was a terrible price to pay, but one we had to pay to ensure that our freedom would be secure.[50]

Southern France – Operation *Anvil/Dragoon*[*]

The plan called for the U.S. VI Corps (Kodak Force), consisting of the U.S. Army's 3d, 36th, and 45th Infantry Divisions, and the French Armored Combat Command Sudre, to land in southern France along a 30-mile wide front from Layet Point northeast to Deux Frères Point at 0800 on August 15. After securing

---

[*]   The code name *Dragoon* was changed to *Anvil* because it was believed *Dragoon* had been compromised. Two Center of Military History publications *Riviera to the Rhine* (CMH Pub7-10) and *Southern France* (CMH Pub 72-31) list the operation as *Anvil* as does *CSI Battlebook 3-D, Operation Anvil/Dragoon* by the Combat Studies Institute. Therefore, for clarity the operation will be termed *Anvil* throughout this section.

the beachhead the troops were to capture LeMuy, secure the airfield sites in the Argens valley against ground-observed artillery fire, and then continue the attack to the north and northwest.[*][†][51]

In conjunction with the amphibious landing were Operations *Rugby* and *Sitka*. Operation *Rugby*, conducted by a combined U.S.–British 1st Airborne Task Force[‡][§] was to land in LeMuy around first light on D-Day to prevent enemy movement into the assault area from LeMuy and LeCuc.

In Operation *Sitka* the American–Canadian 1st Special Service Force (the "Devil's Brigade") under Colonel Edwin A. Walker, U.S. Army, was to assault the islands of Île de Port-Cros and Île du Levant on the left flank during darkness at H-Hour minus1. They were instructed to capture the five forts on the islands and destroy the enemy coastal battery on the east end of Île du Levant. By taking them, the 1st Special Service Force would protect the rest of the invasion force from enfilading fire from the left flank.

As part of Operation *Anvil* the Allies staged a number of deception efforts before the main assault. These included dropping 300 dummy paratroopers between Marseilles and Toulon, and operations off the coast by Beach Jumper Units One, Three, and Five. The idea was to convince the Germans that the landing would come somewhere other than on the beaches of the French Riviera surrounding St. Tropez. One Beach Jumper unit would simulate a large landing force approaching Marseilles while the other Jumper unit, commanded by Lieutenant Commander Douglas Fairbanks, Jr., would do the same in the Nice–Cannes area. A portion of Fairbanks's unit, consisting of two British gunboats, a fighter–director ship and four PT boats, would

---

*　The chain of command was as follows: General Alexander Patch's Seventh Army; U.S. VI Corps commanded by Major General Lucian Truscott; 3d Infantry Division, Major General John W. "Iron Mike" O'Daniel commanding; 36th Infantry Division, Major General John E. Dahlquist commanding; and 45th Infantry Division, Major General William W. Eagles commanding.

†　Combat Command (CC) Sudre, one of French General Jean de Lattre's two armored divisions, was not crucial to the assault. The U.S. infantry divisions included highly mobile attached tank and tank-destroyer battalions and organic vehicles and each was roughly the equivalent of a full-strength German panzergrenadier division.

‡　The 1st Airborne Task Force consisted of the U.S. 509th Parachute Infantry Battalion, U.S. 517th Parachute Regimental Combat Team, U.S. 550th Glider Infantry Battalion, U.S. 551st Parachute Infantry Battalion, and the British 2nd Independent Parachute Brigade commanded by Maj. Gen. Robert T. Frederick.

§　Operation *Rugby* was subdivided into four missions: *Albatross*, the main assault, and reinforcement missions *Bluebird*, *Canary*, and *Dove*.

break off and land a group of Free French commandos at Theoule to cut German communication.* [52]

The French Commando Group (Romeo Force) was to land in darkness, destroy coastal defenses in the vicinity of Cape Nègre, block the coastal highway, and then seize the high ground in the vicinity of Biscarre. Demolition parties from the French Naval Assault Group (Rosie Force) were to land near Pointe Des Travas on the night of D-Day-1–D-Day and execute demolitions on the Cannes–St. Raphael and Cannes–Frejus roads. The II French Corps (Garbo Force) was to debark after D-Day within the established beachhead area then pass through Kodak Force, and capture Toulon.

Under the command of Vice Admiral Henry K. Hewitt, USN, commander of the U.S. Eighth Fleet, nearly 900 ships from the U.S., British, Australian, French, and Greek Navies were prepared for action in Operation *Dragoon*. The mix included five battleships, 30 cruisers, nine escort carriers with 216 aircraft, 88 destroyers, 15 destroyer escorts, 36 transports, and nearly 600 smaller landing craft of various types. The ships were divided into four Task Forces.† [53]

Anvil assault forces totaled approximately 151,000 troops along with 21,400

---

*   The Beach Jumpers were assigned ten 63ft Air-Sea Rescue Boats (ASRs). These ASRs were double hulled, plywood constructed, powered by twin engines, and operated with an officer and a six-man crew. The ASRs were equipped with twin .50-caliber machine guns and carried the unit's deception gear and equipment. The boats also had ten 3.5in window rockets, smoke generators and buoyant time delay explosive packs.

    The unit's specialized deception equipment included a wire recorder (precursor to the tape recorder); a five-phase amplifier; a 12-horn speaker; three generators for power; and naval balloons, to which strips of radar reflective window had been attached and could be towed behind the boats. Later, different models of jammer transmitters were in operation. The sound equipment was used to project the noise created by a large amphibious force – anchors dropping, landing craft engines revving up, even orders being shouted. To enemy radar operators, the balloons looked like much larger naval ships. Later on in the war, the ASRs would also carry radar-jamming equipment.

†   Task Force 84 was led by Rear Admiral F. J. Lowry who selected the U.S. Coast Guard cutter *Duane* as his flagship. Designated Alpha Force, Lowry's job was to land the U.S. Army's 3d Division on the beaches at Pampelonne and Cavalaire Bays.

    Rear Admiral Bertram J. Rodgers, who flew his flag in the seaplane tender USS *Biscayne* and commanded Task Force 85, was charged with putting the U.S. Army's 45th Division ashore at Bougnon Bay, just east of St. Tropez Gulf.

    Task Force 86, commanded by Rear Admiral L. A. Davidson in USS *Augusta* (CL-31), was responsible for delivering a strike force of American and French commandos to Îles d'Hyères and Rade de Bormes, 18 miles east of Toulon.

    Under the command of Rear Admiral S. S. Lewis, who flew his flag in the attack transport USS *Bayfield*, Task Force 87 put the U.S. Army's 36th Division ashore at Frejus and Saint Raphaël in the easternmost sector of *Dragoon*.

trucks, tanks, tank destroyers, prime movers, bulldozers, tractors, and other assorted vehicles.[54]

The need for a major port was driven by two considerations. Strategically, a major port in southern France would clearly be needed to support the cross-Channel forces in their advance into Germany. The amount of men, material, and ships assigned to Operation *Anvil* required the seizure and development of a major port in southern France. Only three of the many ports along France's Mediterranean coast were large enough to support *Anvil*: Sete, Marseilles, and Toulon. Sete was eliminated because of its limited capacity, easily blocked approaches, and difficult exits. Toulon, although capable of supporting the force in its initial stages, suffered from bad clearance facilities. Marseilles proved to be ideal with its extensive docking facilities, and road and railroad networks.

Terrain and Defenses

The sites selected for the 3d Division landings were the beaches facing Cavalaire and Pampelonne Bays, which are on either side of the headland upon which sits St. Tropez. The beaches themselves were flat and sandy, and the offshore gradient was so steep that, in some cases, landing craft were able to run up and drop their ramps onto the beach. The exits from the beaches were limited, and in some cases the approaches to the main road network were limited.

In both the bays there was an offshore sandbar covering roughly the southern half. The tidal range on this portion of the Mediterranean coast was almost negligible, with the result that the sand on the beaches was extremely soft, even floury, both above and below the waterline.

The defenses consisted of batteries and strongpoints, which were mostly constructed of timber and earth, although there were some concrete gun emplacements. The land area close to the beachhead was very heavily mined, while in areas not blocked by the sandbar the Germans had placed a combination of wooden and concrete barriers of upright posts sunk into the seabed, and concrete tetrahedrons. Sea mines were placed between the posts about 15ft apart, while Tellermines were installed inside the tetrahedrons, with an exposed pressure plug facing the seaward side.[55]

Landing Beaches

There were three main landing areas, Alpha, Delta, and Camel, running from Cape Nègre near Cavalaire-sur-Mer to Theoule-sur-Mer and Deux Frères Point. Alpha, Delta, and Camel were divided into Alpha Red and Yellow; Delta Red, Green, Yellow, and Blue; and Camel Green and Blue.

Alpha Red, along Cavalaire Bay, consisted of low sand dunes backed by a narrow band of pines 20 to 30 yards deep, and cultivated fields just beyond the eastern half of the beach with rocky, pine-clad foothills which rose just inland on the west. About six miles northeast of Alpha Red was Alpha Yellow. This beach consisted of over two good miles of excellent landing beach, however, exits were poor. The narrow, one-lane road leading north to St. Tropez might not hold up under heavy fire and there was no direct route west across the peninsula.

The southernmost of the Delta beaches, Delta Red, was located about a mile and a half north of Ste. Maxime, and the others, Green, Yellow, and Blue, were a few miles farther up the coast, separated by 500- to 1,000-yard stretches of fairly inhospitable shoreline.

Camel Green lay a little over three miles east of St. Raphael and was backed by a steep embankment on top of which ran Route N-98 and the main-line, standard-gauge railroad. Situated at the head of Antheor Cove, the tiny Camel Blue was three miles southwest of Camel Green, which gave way ten yards inland to the Route N-98 embankment, beyond which the main railroad crossed a narrow gorge via a bridge.

Assault

Operation *Anvil* began with the 1st Special Service Force executing Operation *Sitka*, landing on the Île du Levant and the Île de Port-Cros just after 0030, and the main assault waves arrived one hour later. The 1st Regiment, 1st Special Service Force, went ashore near the northeast corner of the Île de Port-Cros, while the 2d and 3d Regiments made their assault along the eastern shore of the Île du Levant. By 2030 the Île du Levant was secured. About 10 men had been killed and 65 wounded, for approximately 25 German soldiers killed and 110 captured.

On the Île de Port-Cros the 1st Regiment met stiffer opposition. The Germans withdrew to thick-walled old forts and châteaux at the island's

OPERATION *ANVIL* LANDING BEACHES, AUGUST 15–16, 1944

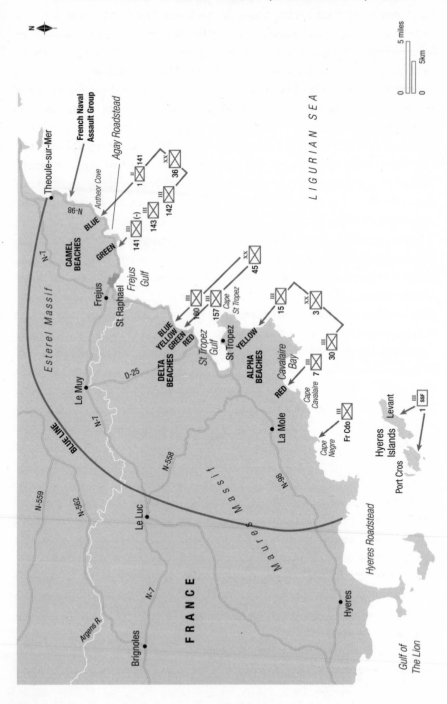

northwest corner. Infantry assaults failed to dislodge the defenders. Eight-inch shells fired by the heavy cruiser USS *Augusta* bounced off the walls, and aerial attacks using rockets and light bombs directed against the forts early on the 17th proved equally ineffective. It took 12 rounds from the 15in guns of the British battleship HMS *Ramillies* to beat down the German resistance. The capture of Île de Port-Cros cost the 1st Special Service Force five men killed and ten wounded, while the Germans lost ten killed and 105 captured.[56]

The 1st Special Service Force lost men due to unnecessary acts of bravado. "The men were too courageous," one 1st Special Service Force man said later. "They had a mistaken concept that courage and physical fitness were all that was necessary." [57]

While the 1st Special Service Force fought for the islands, Operation *Rugby* began when nine planes carrying 121 pathfinder troops left Marcigliana in Italy and headed west. All went well until they ran into heavy fog off the Riviera coast, which forced them to use poorly detailed maps and dead reckoning aided by SCR-717-C radar to find the drop zones. Trailing the pathfinders were 396 aircraft carrying 5,628 paratroopers and 150 artillery pieces.

At 0421 the first 600 paratroopers landed within a half mile of their DZ. However, those headed for other DZs weren't as lucky, landing between 10 and 15 miles away from their targets. Only the British 2nd Independent Parachute Brigade hit its DZ. Fortunately for the Americans no Germans were in the area, so there was not a repeat of what happened in Normandy. The 1st Airborne Task Force did not collect the last scattered elements of the parachute drop until D-Day+5. [58]

The amphibious assault began with naval gunfire and rocket attacks across the 30-mile front. Landing craft wallowed toward the beach behind minesweepers and Apex radio-controlled LCVPs loaded with high explosives, which blew channels through offshore obstacles and detonated mines on the beach. On the left, 3d Division troops hit Alpha Red and Yellow beaches. On Alpha Red one tank hit a mine and sank, as did two LCVPs carrying men of the 2d Battalion, 7th Infantry, resulting in 60 casualties. Mines rather than German fire caused the few casualties in the 15th Infantry's assault at Alpha Yellow.

In the center the 45th Division's Delta beaches Red, Green, Yellow, and Blue lay along the shores of Bougnon Bay, about eight miles north of Alpha

Yellow. There weren't any offshore obstacles and the troops ran into little trouble from the defenders, although four DD tanks were disabled by mines.

The 36th Division's Camel Blue, Green, and Red beaches were on the right flank. The 141st Infantry was tasked to secure the right flank of VI Corps. Once it landed, the regiment was to concentrate its efforts on clearing the shores of Agay Roadstead, between Camel Green and Camel Blue, so that the division could use an excellent strand at the top of the roadstead for general unloading.

At Camel Red the assault teams met heavy resistance. The Germans had a network of defenses including a minefield across the Frejus Gulf, single and double rows of mined concrete tetrahedrons at the shoreline, and, on the beach, two rows of double-apron barbed wire, a concrete antitank wall, which was 7ft high and over 3ft thick, a 12ft-deep antitank ditch on the seaward side of the wall, and extensive fields of land mines on the beach, on the nearby airfield, and on the roads and paths leading inland. These were backed up with machine gun positions in the antitank wall, and pillboxes and other strongpoints just behind it. Larger emplacements, a few holding 88mm guns, enfiladed the beach from the harbor front at St. Raphael.

Two hundred tons of bombs from 90 B-24s and a final 45-minute bombardment by four destroyers, two cruisers, and a battleship followed by a rocket barrage failed to neutralize the German defenders. Knowing surprise was lost and the assault waves would take heavy casualties, Captain Leo B. Schulten, USN, commanding the Camel Red assault group, cancelled the landing and shifted the troops to Camel Green.[59]

Every German attempt to mount a counterattack against the landing area failed. At the end of August 15 all VI Corps units, except the 7th Infantry in the west and the 1st Airborne Task Force, reached their objectives with only about 95 killed and 385 soldiers wounded.

Lessons Learned

The lessons learned from Operation *Anvil* focused more on land-based operations than amphibious ones. One of the primary lessons was regimental combat teams consisting of one infantry regiment and one artillery battalion proved the most effective means to face determined or scattered enemy resistance to fast-moving action on a wide front.

Another lesson that seems self-evident was "When approaching towns, we have found that shooting up the highest buildings pays dividends. This has reduced artillery and mortar fire. Two rounds of HE [high explosive] delay and one round of smoke discourage observers."[60]

One lesson learned the hard way in North Africa, Sicily, and Italy and apparently forgotten was that the Germans booby-trapped anything they could, especially stock piles of engineering materials. This was relearned when 48th Engineer personnel attempted to fill holes in the road from gravel left behind. It exploded when a shovel was thrust into it.

One lesson that wasn't learned was that airborne operations are costly in men and rarely succeed in reaching their objectives when planned. This occurred in Sicily, Italy, Normandy, and southern France. This failure to learn would lead to between 2,370 and 2,700 dead, wounded or captured out of 16,870 paratroopers during Operation *Varsity*, part of Operation *Plunder Field*, Field Marshal Bernard Montgomery's assault across the northern Rhine River on March 23, 1945. A month before, on March 16, 1,000 paratroopers from the 509th Parachute Regimental Combat Team jumped out over the rocky top of Corregidor in the Philippine Islands. The 509th lost 168 men killed, injured, or wounded, some of whom died hitting the rocks or were wind-blown over the edge and drowned.

Summary

In the ten weeks from June 6 to August 15 Germany's vaulted *Festung Europa* was irrevocably breached in two places. However, the losses at Normandy and in southern of France were just down payments on victory.

CHAPTER 10

REAPING THE WHIRLWIND

PACIFIC OPERATIONS, JANUARY 1944–JUNE 1945

During the *Sextant* Conference held in Cairo from November 22 through December 7, 1943, the Combined Chiefs of Staff (CCS) debated the question of strategy for the Pacific campaign for 1944. It was decided that the next operations should aim at securing bases for attacking the Luzon–Formosa–China area in early 1945.

MacArthur's Southwest Pacific Area (SWPA) forces were still engaged along the New Guinea coast and Nimitz's Central Pacific (CENPAC) forces had secured Makin and Tarawa. The CCS authorized the continued two-pronged drive with SWPA forces advancing through New Guinea and the Netherlands East Indies, with Mindanao in the Philippines targeted for mid-November. Nimitz's CENPAC forces would advance through the Marshall, Caroline, Mariana, and Palau Islands. The assault on the southern Marianas was to begin on June 15 and the Palau Islands would be invaded by September.

On January 31, 1945, the 4th Marine and 7th Army Divisions attacked Kwajalein Atoll (Operation *Flintlock*) in the Marshall Islands and secured it after a four-day battle. Eniwetok (Operation *Catchpole*) was the next of the Marshalls to fall. The 22d Marine Regiment, 6th Marine Division, and the 106th Regimental Combat Team, 27th Infantry Division, hit the beaches on

February 17 and completed the operation on February 23.*

A major Japanese naval and air base was located at Truk in the Caroline Islands. Plans to invade Truk were abandoned after a massive two-day U.S. carrier air and surface attack (Operation *Hailstone*) on February 16–17 effectively destroyed the base.†

With the Marshalls secured and the Carolines neutralized the next step was the Marianas.

The Marinas – Operation *Forager*, June 15

The Marianas were part of Japan's inner ring of defenses built to defend the home islands, its central Pacific islands, and its more recent victories in the western Pacific. They lay across Japan's lines of communication to the Netherland East Indies and Malaysia.

Saipan, Tinian, and Guam were directly across, or on the near flank of, the advance of the U.S. Central Pacific forces from their westernmost base at Eniwetok to almost any part of Japanese-held territory that was, or might become, an objective of future amphibious operations, including the Philippines, Formosa, the Volcano Islands, the Ryukyus, and Japan proper.

In meetings with the U.S. Joint Chiefs of Staff General Henry H. Arnold, Commanding General, Army Air Forces, emphasized that the Marianas would provide bases for the new B-29 bombers, and that bombs delivered in sufficient quantities would undoubtedly go far to shorten the war by destroying Japan's steel, airplane, and other factories, oil reserves, and refineries near extremely inflammable cities in which most houses were made of paper and wood. Success in the Marianas, of itself, would largely isolate the Central Carolines and cut the main Japanese aircraft pipeline to the Carolines. Also, bases on the Marianas would be within reach of targets in the Philippines, Palaus Islands, Formosa, and China.[1]

---

*　U.S. casualties on Kwajalein and Roi-Namur were 348 killed, 1,462 wounded, and 181 missing. Japanese losses were approximately 8,000 killed, wounded or captured. On Eniwetok U.S. casualties were 313 killed, 879 wounded, and 77 missing. Japanese losses were 3,380 killed and 105 captured.

†　U.S. losses were one aircraft carrier and one battleship damaged, 25 aircraft lost, and 41 men killed. The Japanese lost 15 warships, 32 merchant ships, and 270 aircraft.

Task Force Organization

The Fifth Fleet (Task Force 50) was commanded by Admiral R. A. Spruance. The various task forces were the Joint Expeditionary Force (Task Force 51), the Northern Attack Force (Task Force 52), the Southern Attack Force (Task Force 53), the Expeditionary Troops and Landing Force (Task Force 56), the Forward Area, Central Pacific (Task Force 57), the Fast, Carrier Task Force (Task Force 58), and the Land Based Air of Forward Area (Task Force 59). A total of 486 vessels, ranging from older-type battleships to small craft such as the PC, LCI(G), and YMS types, was assigned to Task Force 51, and this task force embraced many elements of other task forces such as 52, 53, and 56.[2]

Operation *Forager* was divided into three parts, one each for Saipan, Tinian, and Guam. There were 105,859 assault troops assigned to capture the three islands; 66,779 were allocated to Saipan and Tinian and the remaining 39,080 to Guam. The bulk of the force was composed of the 2d and 4th Marine Divisions and the Army 27th and 77th Infantry Divisions.

Geography

The Marianas are a chain of 15 volcanic islands fringed with coral reefs, behind which there are cliffs, 50ft to 500ft high, frequently rising sharply to tablelands above. The islands extend 450 miles from north to south. There are four major islands: Guam, Rota, Tinian, and Saipan. Guam is the southernmost and largest island and lies 101 miles southwest of Saipan. Rota is 37 miles northeast of Guam. Tinian lies just south of, and adjacent to, Saipan.

Saipan is 12¾ miles long and 5¾ miles wide with a barrier reef one to two miles offshore. Although mountainous in character, a considerable portion of the island is arable and was under sugar cane cultivation. In 1941 the civilian population was estimated to be between 30,000 and 35,000, the greatest part being Japanese, with the remainder mostly Chamorros and Korean natives.

Tinian is 10½ miles long and markedly narrower than Saipan, and Guam is 32 miles long and between four and eight miles wide. Both Tinian and Saipan's east coast have steep-sloped cliffs, and very narrow shallow beaches.

Guam's northern shore has high cliffs overlooking the beaches and strong surf and rugged offshore reefs, while the entire east coast is marked by a 400ft plateau and a narrow coastal flat.

The weather is warm with frequent showers during the summer monsoon season and the sky is overcast two-thirds of the time. Typhoons rarely hit the Marianas but do occur. Monsoon winds blow in from the southwest in August and September; the trade winds blow from the northeast for the rest of the year.

Saipan

Landing Beaches

All of the 6,500 yards of Saipan's landing beaches were at the southern end of the western shore. The 6th and 8th Infantry Regiments, and 2d Marine Division were assigned Red beaches 1, 2, and 3, and Green beaches 1, 2, and 3. Blue beaches 1 and 2, and Yellow beaches 1, 2, and 3 were tasked to the 23d and 25th Marine Regiments, and the 4th Marine Division. Although part of the initial planning, no landings were scheduled on Red 1, Green 3, or Yellow 3 when the operation was finalized.

The 68 amphibious tanks of the Marine 2d Armored Amphibian Tractor Battalion were divided over the four Blue and Yellow beaches, with 17 tanks on each beach. The Army 773d Amphibian Tractor Battalion followed the tanks onto the two Yellow beaches. Marine tractors landed the troops on the Blue beaches behind the Army 708th Amphibian Tank Battalion. In the Second Marine Division's sector to the north, Marine tanks were employed on the Red and Green beaches and a Marine tractor unit formed behind the tanks on the Red beaches. The Army 715th Amphibian Tractor Battalion carried assault forces to the two Green beaches where landings were made.

The Army 534th Amphibian Tractor Battalion was divided among the four Blue and Yellow beaches and used to land reserve troops and artillery reconnaissance parties for the 4th Marine Division and the 27th Infantry Division.[3]

A total of 393 Amphibious Tractors (LVTs) and 140 Amphibious Tanks (LVT(A)s) formed the assault waves. Of these, the Army units furnished 268 tanks.

Japanese Defenses on Saipan

In early August U.S. intelligence estimated there were 15,000 to 17,600 Japanese troops on Saipan, of which 9,100 to 11,000 were combat troops, 900 to 1,200 aviation personnel, 1,600 to 1,900 Japanese laborers (plus 400 to 500 Koreans), and 3,000 "home guards," recent recruits who were believed to be the scrapings from the bottom of the manpower barrel. The actual number of Japanese was approximately 30,000 soldiers and sailors plus hundreds of Japanese civilians willing to fight the invaders.

Aerial reconnaissance photographs identified 32 dual-purpose guns, 71 light antiaircraft cannon or machine guns, 16 pillboxes, a dozen heavy antiaircraft guns, and other miscellaneous weapons. Some 54 pieces of heavy artillery were located on the first high ground and on the reverse slopes about 3,000 yards inland and back of the proposed landing beaches. However, most of the highlands were continually obscured by cloud-making mortar positions, mountain guns, and other mobile weapons difficult to identify.

On June 11, U.S. carrier-based fighters destroyed a total of 150 enemy planes, about 75 percent of which were in the air at the time, effectively neutralizing Japanese air power on the island.[*] [4]

Assault

On the morning of June 14 three naval underwater demolition teams swam toward Red, Green, Yellow, and Blue beaches, as well as toward the Scarlet beaches, an alternate landing area north of Tanapag Harbor. Each team consisted of about 16 officers and 80 men, all naval personnel except for one Army and one Marine liaison officer per team. They undertook the difficult mission of daylight reconnaissance. Lieutenant Commander Draper L. Kauffman, leader of one of the demolition teams, had told Admiral Turner that "You don't swim in to somebody's beaches in broad daylight," but swim they did, close in to the shoreline in full daylight under the protection of ships' fire.

Despite a screen of naval gunfire, which had difficulty in silencing the weapons sited to cover the waters of the Blue and Yellow beaches, the teams lost two men killed and seven wounded, approximately 13 percent of their total strength. The swimmers reported the absence of artificial obstacles, the condition of the reef, and the depth of water off the beaches. No obstacles were reported and hence no demolition work was necessary.[5]

At dawn on the morning of June 15, fire support vessels took their stations, and soon thereafter began firing at Saipan and Tinian. In the meantime the transport and tractor groups, carrying the troops, artillery, tanks,

---

[*]   U.S. combat losses were 11 fighter planes and eight pilots; one plane was an operational loss.

ammunition, supplies and other equipment, arrived off the western coast of
Saipan. A heavy air strike along the landing beaches was made between
0700 and 0730, and intense pre-assault close-range naval bombardment of
the landing beaches commenced at 0800. H-Hour was originally set at 0830
but was later changed to 0840 to enable all the vehicles to form at the line
of departure.

Marshall E. Harris of the 2d Armored Amphibian Battalion remembers that
morning:

> Our LST booms out *Reveille* then *Chow down* at 0430. From my roost on
> the bow of our tank in the hold of our LST, I groan. Rolling over, I realize
> this isn't just another day at sea: it's D-Day. I square away the deck, check
> gear, make ready for the run into the beach, give up that wonderful
> mattress on loan from the Navy, then head for Mess Hall. Lo and behold,
> a great morning meal: sizzling steaks cooked to my liking, fried potatoes,
> eggs, bacon, ham and fresh milk, toast, butter, juice of all kinds.[6]

"Soon after sunrise we got our amtanks ready to go down the metal ramp
between our open LST's bow doors and head for the landing beaches," recalled
James A. ("Al") Scarpo, Company D, 2d Armored Amphibian Battalion.
"That's when Lewis Zimmer handed me a letter, saying 'Mail this for me'. I
looked at him and said: 'Why should I mail it, I'm going in too'. But I took
the letter anyway. Within a few hours Lewis was killed."

Coast Guard Yeoman First Class Herbert Baumgartner, a correspondent on
board one of the Coast Guard-manned attack transports, wrote about what he
saw that morning:

> At the debark stations along the first and second decks dungareed telephone
> talkers adjusted their headphones in anticipation of the heavy business to
> come. They didn't have long to wait. The crack Marine sniper party, in
> their camouflaged green and brown jungle suits, started filing out of one
> of the hatches.
>
> These were veterans and the nonchalance of their stride to the embarkation
> station was something to behold. They carried their rifles in waterproofed
> transparent cases. Their tightly fitted packs and foxhole shovels rode high on
> their backs. Some carried lunches in paper bags which already showed
> evidence of the peanut butter sandwiches inside.

The booms swung the barges to the rail and the troops clambered in and we watched with thoughtful eyes. Coast Guard and Navy barges were taking the troops in. From the distance we were riding off the beach it looked like an easy kind of war from five miles out.

And then a barge pulled up on the starboard side and a throng gathered at the rail. There were men lying on stretchers inside. They were wearing every form of temporary bandage, and some of the men were grimacing with pain. These were the first casualties.

"Rugged going, Mike?" inquired a Marine buddy of one of the lesser injured.

The wounded man, his face still caked with camouflaging, replied "Pretty rugged."

Another said "Toughest since Tarawa."[7]

Twelve LCI(G) gunboats led the first wave toward the offshore reef, the outer edge of which began anywhere from 1,400 to 1,100 yards offshore. Once there the gunboats had to flare right and left before crossing the reef, then fire into the flanks of the landing beaches as the first wave of amphibian tanks and amtracs climbed over the reef before plunging into the lagoon. Once in the lagoon they lumbered onto the beaches to battle several hundred yards inland to seize the first day's objectives at the first objective line (O-1).

The Japanese opened fire as the LVTs crossed the reef and crawled toward the beaches.

James D. Mackey recalled:

My periscope bubble was blown off. Opening the hatch, I saw a high tower in front of us and tracers racing out towards me from a dozen points on the beach. Those tracers whizzed past as we dropped into the lagoon. Tank #2 blew up.

"Crossing the lagoon I talked with Radio Man Robert B. Lewis in Tank #31 nearby. We went to radio school together, joined the 2d Armored together, trained in the same platoon, and now were going into Saipan side by side, best buddies, 18 years old", said Marshall E. Harris:

We were talking about whether we'd gone too far left when his voice vanished in the sound of an explosion. I felt the concussion then shoved up my periscope.

412

Peering out I scanned it. Smoke stopped me. Black smoke splotched with fire roiled off the water, flames boiled out of blackened bent metal hatches – Bob's Tank. Lt. Michael motioned for us to keep going, to hit to the beach. Then Tank # 31 was gone. That was the last time I saw it. Or Bob. Later I saw Bob listed as MIA, presumed dead, his body not found or identified if found. Our Platoon leader was in the same amtank.

Of the 68 tanks in the first wave that struck Blue and Yellow beaches, all but three arrived safely. One of these, an A Company tank, burned; one from B Company was swamped on the reef; and one from C Company received a direct hit from an antitank weapon that was firing from the shore at about a 25-yard range.

Astern of the tanks came the amphibious tractors of the Marine 10th Amphibian Tractor Battalion and the Army 773d Amphibian Tractor Battalion in four waves, spaced from two to six minutes apart. Of the 196 troop-carrying tractors, only two failed to land their cargo; one was hit by a shell on the reef and the other developed mechanical difficulties. Between 0843 and 0907 all of the leading waves with about 8,000 marines embarked were ashore.[8]

The 3d Battalion, 6th Marines, commanded by Colonel James P. Riseley and Amtank B Company landed on the 1200-yard front along Red 2 and Red 3. There was a 150-yard gap on Riseley's right flank between him and Colonel Clarence R. Wallace's 8th Marines assaulting beaches Green 1 and 2. The 3d Battalion, 8th Marines and Amtank C Company landed as planned on Green 1. Adding to the confusion the 2d Battalion, 8th Marines and Amtank D Company also landed on Green 1 instead of on Green 2 further south as planned. Thus two Battalions and Amtank Companies became densely packed on a single beach exposed to heavy fire from Afetna Point on their right flank to the south. No troops landed on Afetna Point for fear of a heavy concentration of Japanese artillery emplaced to guard the only channel through the reef to the pier at Charan Kanoa.

Gene Lewis recalled:

In from the beach our tank got hung up. Perched on a stump, angled up in the air, unable to fire our 75mm gun or get traction, we're stuck. A Jap 37mm shell passed between our ammo passer's legs, singing his pants and him too then exited our amtank's other side. We bailed out. I never saw several of my tank crew again. But wounded Marines lay all over the beach, corpsmen yelling for help. So I helped, going from one wounded Marine to another, putting sulfa drugs in their wounds then bandaging them, all we could do amid exploding shells, landing craft coming ashore, dropping off Marines. Mass confusion, I don't remember most of it, so focused was I on doing my job. But I do recall bullets hitting close by, smashing into a tree inches away.

The 715 Amphibian Battalion's 24 LVTs carried the first wave of the 8th Marines into Green Beach 1 when a bank topped with trees stopped 22 of the LVTs at beach. The Marines left the LVTs at the water's edge and took cover behind the bank. The second wave of assault troops arrived soon thereafter and within the next five minutes all five waves had landed, jamming troops between the tractors behind them and the Japanese in front. One LVT that did get over the bank drove a road through small trees to the airstrip road, and then managed to make it 150 yards north before the driver stalled its engine when confronted by three Japanese tanks. All aboard bailed out and returned to beach.

By 1000, Sherman tanks loaded on LCMs arrived at the reef but heavy Japanese interdicting fire made it difficult to get in through the Charan–Kanoa Channel. Mounting seas during the afternoon increased the hazards of the trip. Of the 60 tanks of the 4th Tank Battalion, 21 failed to reach the 4th Marine Division's beaches. One sank with the LCM on which it was boarded, another settled into a pothole off the reef, and others were unable to locate landing craft to take them ashore or had their wiring systems fouled en route. Finally, six tanks were misdirected to Green Beach 2, a 2d Division beach. Of these, five were immobilized in deep water inside the lagoon.[9]

By noon Red 3 was clear enough to allow Army shore parties to land. The first team came ashore at 1300, and supplies began moving over the two central beaches. Additional shore parties landed later in the day.

As darkness fell the Marines had established a beachhead approximately 10,000 yards in length and over 1,000 yards in depth in most places, only about two thirds of the area to the first objective line. However, the landings were considered successful. It was six days before the beachhead could be considered completely secured and on July 9, Lieutenant General Holland M. Smith declared the Island of Saipan secured although much mopping up of Japanese remnants remained to be done.

U.S. casualties were heavy with 3,225 killed, 13,061 wounded, and 326 missing. The Japanese suffered 23,811 confirmed dead, 5,000 suicides, and 736 taken prisoner. There were also 22,000 civilian dead. Many Japanese committed suicide by jumping off the cliffs near Marpi Point; they included women holding their children when they jumped.* One group of children standing in a circle pulled the pin from a grenade then tossed it around until it exploded. Some civilians were killed by Japanese soldiers as witnessed by Marine Second Lieutenant Charles T. Cross and his men. Marine correspondent David Dempsey wrote about the incident:

> In a secluded spot in a canyon well behind our own lines two Marines passing by heard Japanese voices. They listened, decided the voices were corning from a cave, and crept as close as they could to the top of the cliff where the cave was located.
>
> As the men approached the cave, they could hear the crying of babies and the moaning of women. It was evident that civilians as well as soldiers were hidden inside.
>
> By removing a large slab of stone on top of the cliff the Marines could see down into the cave. Women, children, old men, and soldiers were huddled together in mixed postures of fear and defiance. An old man looked up at them pitifully. "Mizu," he groaned. "Mizu ... mizu..." ("Water ... water...")
>
> Through an interpreter Cross told him to send a child out and that water would be supplied for all of them. The Marines waited, but no one came. The sound of the old man groaning "Mizu ... mizu" was all they heard.
>
> Cross crawled closer and spoke to them again. Suddenly he heard the sound of hand grenades clicking as the pins were knocked out against the rocky walls of the cave. Lieutenant Cross jumped back just in time as the grenades began to explode in the cave. Jap soldiers were committing suicide, killing and wounding their own people as they did so.
>
> The Marines waited in awe-struck terror. From inside the cave came a pitiful chorus of wailing babies and the screams of women and old men. For an hour Lieutenant Cross lay near the mouth of the cave, pleading with the Japanese to come out. Occasionally, there would be a movement inside the dim tunnel, as though someone were struggling to crawl out. Invariably, it was followed by a rifle shot, and silence.
>
> They waited four hours – "four of the longest hours of my life," Cross said. "During that time there were more grenade explosions, more rifle shots. The groaning and wailing inside increased. The old man kept crying for water."

---

* The author has seen a number of uncensored films taken by U.S. Coast Guard cameramen showing this happening.

Finally, there was silence. The explosions and the screams had stopped. Marines, still wary of going directly into the cave, crawled back to the top of the cliff and lifted the stone slab.

Four of them were lowered 15 feet to the floor of the cave. What they saw will go down in their memories as the most gruesome of all sights in war. The bodies of men and women and children were blown apart and lay splattered against the walls of the tunnel.

The soldiers had disemboweled themselves with grenades. The bodies of 30 Japanese – ten of them soldiers – literally had been blown together. There were four survivors: two girls, eight and 12 years old, whose throats had been slit; a baby whose face had been cut by grenade fragments, a young boy who had been overcome by the concussion.[10]

Guam

W-Day was July 21 and H-Hour set for 0830. The objectives were along an eight-mile stretch of the coast in the vicinity of Apra Harbor, and included the series of four villages of Asan, Piti, Sumay, and Agat.

In the assault, 56,715 troops were employed – 19,423 Army and 37,292 Marines. The ships off Guam included the 12 transports of the 3d Marine Division and the eight of the 1st Provisional Marine Brigade, as well as the destroyers that screened the transports. The 77th Infantry Division had 12 transports, five cargo ships, and three LSTs. Five assault cargo ships carried supplies for the assault forces.

The 3d Marine Division, the Northern Transport Group, was to go ashore on Red, Green, and Blue beaches at Asan, north of Apra Harbor. Yellow and White beaches, at Agat, were assigned to the 1st Provisional Marine Brigade and the 77th Infantry Division, which made up the Southern Transport Group.

Japanese Defenses

The Japanese on Guam numbered 18,500 Army and Naval personnel. The beach defenses were well organized. There were 19 Japanese 8in, eight 5.9in and 22 4.9in coast defense guns and approximately 40 heavy and 96 medium antiaircraft guns. Concrete pillboxes were built into the coral cliffs and an elaborate trench system extended from the water's edge. Machine gun emplacements and tank traps buffered the strong points. Small arms and mortar fire backed up the other weapons and several 70mm guns in concrete blockhouses enfiladed the beaches. The beaches themselves were strung with barbed wire and in some places aerial bombs were embedded in the sand just inland of the wire. Antitank obstacles were also installed on the beaches by lashing coconut logs across trees or setting them vertically in the ground.

The Japanese placed coral-filled palm cribs and wire cages to interrupt and impede the approach of landing craft to, and over, the offshore reef. A series of antiboat mines of between 40lb and 50lb was placed along the reef or between the obstacles.[11]

Assault

On July 17 Underwater Demolition Teams (UDTs) started to clear the obstacles and clear paths for the LVTs, LCTs, and LCMs. The following excerpts from the UDT Three Action Report shows how much they accomplished:

17 July 1944

1945: Started approach for night operations to remove antiboat obstacles on landing beaches at Asan. Orders were to remove obstacles close to shore first. Operation delayed due to grounding of LCI-348 on reef. After attempts to remove LCI, which was taken under heavy mortar fire by enemy, it was decided to abandon it and crew was removed by UDT #3's, Boat No. 4.

18 July 1944

0100: Delayed operations to remove obstacles started. Platoons 1 and 3 failed to locate obstacles assigned them. Platoons 2 and 4 removed 60 obstacles each from Blue, Red 2 and Green beaches. Mortar fire from DDs. Result 120 obstacles removed; used 2400 pounds Tetrytol.

1400: 3 LCPRs sent to reef edge under heavy fire cover and smoke screen, and launched 5 rubber boats. 150 obstacles removed, using 3000 pounds Tetrytol. The edge of the reef, contrary to what was indicated by aerial reconnaissance, did not break off sharply, but had a gradual slope from 18 inches of water at edge of reef to about 6 feet of water, 100 feet from edge of reef... The enemy had placed obstacles in an almost continuous front along the reef. These obstacles were piles of coral rock inside a wire frame made of heavy wire net... They were 3 to 5 feet in diameter, 3 to 4 feet high and 5 to 8 feet apart...

21 July 1944. [W Day]

0730: Dispatched all UDT Boats to respective beaches to guide LCMs and LCTs with tanks ashore and over reef.

0925: All tanks landed safely... The intensity and accuracy of fire cover during the two days prior to W-Day were amazing, considering the fact that while demolition personnel were working within 50 yards of the beach, the beach itself was covered with fire from LCIs, destroyers, cruisers, and also from bombing and strafing planes.[12]

W-Day dawned bright and clear with a light wind and calm sea. Ahead of the first waves of landing vehicles went a line of nine LCI(G)s firing 4.5in rockets and 40mm and 20mm guns as they came within range of the shoreline. Following the gunboats was the 1st Armored Amphibian Battalion, its turreted LVT(A) amtanks firing their 37mm guns at targets on the beach. Following close behind were 360 LVTs carrying six waves of assault troops.

At the northern Asan areas smoke and dust from the bombardment obscured the areas where the men were to land. The first two waves made it to the beach safely but as the third and fourth waves landed the reef and beach areas came under Japanese mortar fire. Once ashore both assaults were met by the usual stubborn to fanatical Japanese defense.

On the southern beaches there was no enemy activity until the Marines were within the last few yards of the beaches. The cumbersome amphibian tractors had negotiated the reef successfully when fire from Japanese small arms and antiboat guns destroyed nine LVTs and LVT(A)s.

The Marines moved forward. Some of them were wounded; some were without weapons. An amphtrac took three hits from an antiboat gun. Six of its occupants were killed. The seventh was injured, but he went ahead, unarmed.

Crossfire from Gaan Point and Yona Island raked White Beach 2, a 300-yard strip of sand, and casualties mounted. A shell from a 75mm field gun on Yona burst on the aid station party debarking at the beach. The group's only uninjured member tended the wounded for more than four hours until medical reinforcements arrived.

Assault troops of the 22d Marines under Colonel Merlin F. Schneider faced moderate opposition, and managed to move rapidly inland. Successive waves mopped up remaining pockets of enemy resistance. Two hours after landing the Marines had advanced 1,000 yards inland between the southern outskirts of Agat and Bangi Point.

To the southwest, elements of the 4th Marines under Colonel Alan Shapley pushed toward Mount Alifan. They eliminated snipers in a grove of decapitated coconut trees, and their spearhead of tanks neutralized pillboxes and blockhouses. In wide rice paddies, which were broken up by tiny streams, they were hit hard by machine-gun bullets and mortar shells. Sherman tank fire sealed caves on the steep hillside. Up one hill and into a valley, stumbling over the shale, clutching roots, hugging ridges, the Marines went onward and upward. By evening they held a thin, twisted 1,600-yard line rolling from the beach to the mountain.[13]

As evening approached, men along the perimeter dug in with the expectation of a Japanese night counterattack. The predicted attack started at 2230 with reconnaissance parties milling about the front of Marine positions on the right and in the center of the perimeter.

A half-hour later, a knee mortar barrage hit the seaboard flank, and the Japanese came over, throwing demolition charges and small land mine-like hand grenades. Six Marines were bayoneted in their foxholes before the enemy was repulsed with rifle fire and grenades.

At 0100 in the morning of July 22, the Marines smashed ahead again. Their attack centered on Hill 40, a slight rise 300 yards from the beach. A platoon of Marines defending the mound was cut down, taking heavy casualties. At the base of the hill the unit reformed and forged ahead. The Japanese were killed, but the Marines could not withstand a surge of enemy reinforcements. Again Hill 40 fell to the enemy.

The platoon was battered. The few remaining Marines could not retake the hill. Help came with two squads under First Lieutenant Marvin C. Plock who, in the black night, led his men across a rice paddy raked by enemy automatic fire. They covered the 400 yards without a casualty to join the Marines at the base of Hill 40. The Marines attacked, and took their objective. They counted 63 dead Japanese on the heights and 350 between the beach and Hill 40.

On the right flank, Japanese tanks, supported by guns mounted on trucks and followed by foot troops, rolled toward Marine positions near a reservoir northwest of Mount Alifan. The mobile attack began at 0230 with the elemental noise of motors and guns and tank treads grinding the limestone shale. *Banzai* screams pierced the flare-lit night. Marines fought off the charge with small arms fire. One Marine sliced off the lead tank's turret with his bazooka. From static positions along a road leading to the reservoir Sherman tanks knocked out the remaining enemy tanks as they approached in column. The Japanese infantry attack grew listless with the immobilization of their armored vehicles. They retired behind Mount Alifan.

A second prong of the counterattack hit the lower slopes of Mount Alifan using knee mortars and light and heavy machine guns. The Japanese surged through a draw, throwing grenades, swinging samurai swords, and shouting in their frenzy. They were led by an officer waving a battle flag on the end of a bamboo pole to which a long knife was affixed. They aimed for Marine artillery positions in the rear; they died clutching magnetic mines, makeshift explosives, and picric acid blocks. Another cluster of attackers was cut down by machine-gun fire as they broke from a bush forest near Mount Alifan.

The enemy gathered its strength and prepared for its final, greatest bid for victory. The Japanese were strangely silent as they formed on a hill 400 yards to the south of Mount Alifan. Marines saw the dark shadows on the skyline under the eerie light of naval flares. They checked their weapons; they lined their remaining grenades on the edge of their foxholes; they dug deep into their helmets as they watched and waited for the next attack.

The Japanese struck hard again at 0300, hammering a wedge westward into a sector commanded by First Lieutenant Martin J. "Stormy" Sexton. Wave after wave pushed past the Marine periphery. The Japanese threw antitank mines into the defenders' foxholes like quoits. Even though BAR men wiped out the first line, the second rushed on. Marine casualties were heavy. The wounded were bayoneted to death by the advancing horde. Ammunition ran low as Japanese and Marines fought and died in the same foxholes.

Remnants of the tattered first echelon infiltrated into the Marine's pack howitzer positions 400 yards from the beach. The Japanese were too close for the field pieces to fire, so artillery men grabbed carbines and wiped out the attackers.

On the east flank, the 22d Marines withstood several abortive night attacks. A few Japanese infiltrated along the sparsely defended front and a number of them were cut down behind the lines. A company of three officers and 66 Japanese soldiers hid on the rim of the 22d's command post, where they were surprised at dawn by sentries on the crest of a knoll 50 yards from the command post. Regimental personnel, including office clerks and runners, tangled with the enemy.

First Lieutenant Dennis Chavez, Jr., led 25 men of a reconnaissance unit into the sharp skirmish. Their firepower totaled a few automatic weapons and two light machine guns. The three officers and the 66 Imperial soldiers were annihilated. Six Marines were wounded.

The counterattack along the entire front disintegrated at 0445. The Marines pushed forward with local reserves and restored their lines. More than 600 enemy dead were counted.[14] At dawn troops began mopping up any survivors from the night's attacks. Tanks provided fire for the attacks that were made to restore and strengthen the perimeter.

On August 10, after 20 days of fighting, Guam was declared secure. The Japanese garrison lost 18,337 combatants, and 1,250 were taken prisoner. The number of U.S. casualties amounted to 7,800, of which 2,124 were killed in action or who died. Of this total, the Army accounted for 839, the Navy for 245, while the remaining 6,716 were Marines. Another 7,122 soldiers, sailors, and Marines were wounded. Added to this total should be the 1,880 U.S. servicemen who died in 1941 when the Japanese invaded Guam, and the 1,170 people of Guam who died and the 14,721 who suffered atrocities of war from 1941 to 1944.

A the end of the campaign Marine Brigadier Lemuel General Shepherd said:

> On this hallowed ground, you men and officers of the First Marine Brigade have avenged the loss of our comrades who were overcome by a numerically superior enemy five days after Pearl Harbor. Under our flag, this island again stands ready to fulfill its destiny as an American fortress in the Pacific.[15]

Tinian

Since Tinian is only three and a half miles off Saipan's southern coast, invasion plans called for a shore-to-shore amphibious attack. This meant that most of the necessary troops, equipment, and supplies could be lifted from Saipan directly to Tinian in LCIs and landing boats, or in amtracs and DUKWs carried aboard LSTs and LCTs.

The 2d and 4th Marine Divisions were tasked to land on White beaches 1 and 2 along the northwestern coast. Both beaches were narrow. White 1 was only between 65 and 75 yards long and 15 to 20 yards deep. White 2 was between 15 and 17 yards in width, 200 yards long, and sandy and smooth except for a few scattered rocks. Both beaches were on the lee side of the island and within range of artillery support from Saipan.

For the defense of Tinian the Japanese had approximately 8,039 men from the Army's 50th Infantry Regiment and the Navy's 56th Guard Force augmented by Home Guards. The basic force was the 50th Infantry Regiment, a veteran unit recently transferred from the Manchurian area. The three battalions of this regiment, with artillery and the attached engineer and tank companies, numbered about 3,600. Attached, and under the command of the 50th's commander, Colonel Ogata, was the First Battalion of the 135th Infantry. With hospital, motor transport, and such units, the army component of the defense numbered close to 5,000.

The 56th Naval Guard Force manned the British-manufactured three 6in coast defense guns, ten 5½in coast defense guns, ten 4.6in dual-purpose guns, and four 3in dual-purpose guns that collectively protected the island from sea or air assault. Naval gun crews, armed with rifles, and instructed to fight as infantry when their guns were knocked out, formed another source of manpower. The troops on Tinian were better individual soldiers than those met on Saipan. The condition of their equipment, their exceptionally good rifle and machine-gun marksmanship, and the physical condition of the men showed a high standard of military perfection.[16]

J-Day was July 24. As the day broke, a small fleet of ships and landing craft sailed from Saipan's Tanapag Harbor for the brief voyage to Tinian's northwest coast. The collection of vessels included eight transports, 37 LSTs, two LSDs, 31 LCIs, 20 LCTs, 92 LCMs, 100 LCVPs, 533 LVTs, and 140 DUKWs.

Despite heavy bombing and shelling by 156 Army and Marine artillery and howitzers, one Japanese 20mm gun near White Beach had survived. It came to life on July 24 as the following report indicates:

At 0735 all ships were ready to launch. At about 0745 the right flank of the formation was fired upon ... (by) a 20mm gun ... The fire was too close for comfort ... At 0758 a hit causing 4 casualties was observed on the signal bridge of LST 272. The same burst struck the LST forward. Another burst ... resulted in a hit on LST 340 causing an additional 4 casualties and on subsequent bursts, at least one hit was observed on a line of LVTs on starboard bow of LST-225 ... Considering the character of the main deck cargo (gasoline drums and ammunition) it was an unpleasant 15 minutes.[17]

Besides the 20mm gun shooting at the LSTs, the larger ships were not immune from Japanese guns firing heavier shells. *Colorado* (BB-45) was hit 22 times resulting in 39 killed and 109 wounded. *Norman Scott* (DD-690) was badly hit. She suffered 19 killed, including the captain, and 47 wounded.[18]

At 0721, 24 LVTs took the first wave of Marines across the line of departure. Preceding them were LCI gunboats firing rockets and automatic cannon. In eight of the craft were E Company, 2d Battalion, 24th Marines, ready to land on White Beach 1. The beach defenders employed hand grenades, rifles, and machine guns against the Marines as the troops approached the shore. E Company destroyed the Japanese in their caves and crevices in a brief and bitter fight before pushing inland.

The other 16 LVTs lifted G Company, 2d Battalion, 25th Marines, and I Company of the 3d Battalion, and landed them on White Beach 2, abreast of E Company. The Japanese defenses on White Beach 2, which was undamaged by the bombardment, were built around two pillboxes that were situated so that anyone on the beach would be caught in crossfire. The beach had been seeded with mines, including powerful antiboat and deadly antipersonnel ones, and there were booby traps inland.

Because of the unknown number of mines lacing the beach and waters offshore it was decided not to send LVTs over the beach until engineers could get at the mines. Initial waves were to avoid the beach, and instead the first troops would have to climb rocky ledges, which rose 3ft to 10ft above the surf.

Despite all precautions, two LVTs which ventured inland were blown up 30 yards from the shore, killing 15 men. A third detonated a mine while attempting to turn around on the beach.

By dark amphibians had landed the entire 4th Division and one battalion of the 2d Division including 48 tanks, several 77mm pack howitzers, many bulldozers, cherry picker cranes, and a lot of other cargo.

As the light faded the Marines dug in, waiting for the Japanese counterattack that always came after every landing. The attack, when it came, consisted of three separate and seemingly uncoordinated thrusts against the American front – one along the western shore against the Marines' left, one in the center at the boundary between the 25th and 24th Marines, and a third against the 23d Marines on the American right flank.

At 0200, men of the 1st Battalion, 24th Marines made out a compact group of the enemy some 100 yards away. Emerging from the darkness into the bright light of the Marines' flares some 600 Japanese naval troops hastily deployed to attack. The white gloves of some of the naval officers gave a curious dress formality to the scene of carnage that, after more than three hours of bitter fighting, left 476 Japanese dead.

The first indication of the enemy's movement on the right flank, where the lines crossed the main north–south road from Tinian Town, was six light Japanese tanks coming down the road. Some had men riding on them. All were camouflaged with leaves and branches. The Marine antitank weapons and artillery took them under direct fire at 400 yards, and the tank threat was over. One got away.

Thereafter, until dawn the next morning, the enemy continued attacking, never infiltrating more than a few men into the lines. On the right, in front of the 23d Marines, the 1st Battalion of the 50th Infantry destroyed itself against bands of machine-gun fire and charges of canister shot. Two companies of the 2d Battalion of the 50th Infantry were thrown into the fight. They, too, were destroyed on the wire. Crack troops, well-armed and healthy, they were expended in futile *banzai* charges. A company of engineers, armed and fighting as infantry, also died during the night on the wire in front of the perimeter.

On the night of July 31–August 1 Colonel Ogata, the Japanese commander, personally led a final counterattack. Ogata was killed in the attack along with over 100 Japanese in an area no larger than 70 square yards.

The battle for Tinian was over. The Marines lost 328 dead and 1,571 wounded in action and the Navy, 68 killed and 56 wounded. For the Japanese, losses were 5,592 dead, 252 captured, and 2,265 missing.

Summary

The major U.S. construction effort on all three islands was primarily devoted to constructing airfields and other facilities for very long-range bombers. The first B-29 airdrome to be completed was Isely Field on Saipan. Work started on June 24, 1944, and by mid-December Saipan boasted two B-29 runways plus storage space for 60 spare bombers at nearby Kobler Field.

On Tinian U.S. forces succeeded in capturing one of the best airfield sites in the Central Pacific. Two fields were developed. The first one was designated

North Field, the second, West Field, located just above Tinian Town. Both bases became operational in the next month.

Guam became the Pacific Fleet forward headquarters and Apra Harbor was dredged and given the additional protection of a lengthy breakwater. An extensive tank farm was erected, several major supply depots were established, and hospitals and administration buildings were constructed.[19]

Operation *Forager* confirmed the belief that the current amphibious doctrine – that the combination of land, sea, and air power could be used to defeat any Japanese-held territory – was sound.

Where Next?

Throughout July and August and into September the Joint Chiefs of Staff, General MacArthur, and Admiral Nimitz discussed bypassing the then selected next major objective (Leyte in the Philippines on November 15) and landing amphibious assault forces directly on either Formosa with a further operation into China or on to Japan proper. MacArthur was adamant about returning to the Philippines. He believed landing on Formosa would be "unsound" and invading Japan "utterly unsound."[20]

In a conference with President Roosevelt and Admiral Nimitz, MacArthur predicted his loses on Luzon would be "inconsequential" and personally guaranteed that "a Luzon Campaign could be completed in thirty days to six weeks."[21]

MacArthur's plan to keep his "I shall return" promise made after he left the Philippines in March 1942 was approved. However, it would start with Leyte not Luzon in October. It was to follow attacks on the Palaus islands of Peleliu, Ngesebus, and Agaur as a maneuver to protect MacArthur's right flank.[*] MacArthur's homecoming (Operation *King II*) began on October 17.[†‡]

---

[*]   On Peleliu the Marines lost 2,336 killed and 8,450 wounded. Angaur cost the Army 260 killed and 1,354 wounded. Halsey recommended the attacks be cancelled but was overruled by Nimitz. For the Marines Peleliu was the bitterest battle of the war, more so than either Tarawa before it or Iwo Jima afterward.

[†]   Taking Luzon was a ten-month battle and the 47,190 U.S. casualties beggars the description of "inconsequential."

         On another note, the famous photograph of MacArthur wading ashore in the Philippines took three tries. The Coast Guard coxswain who drove the LCVP MacArthur stepped out of said it was the only time anyone got their feet wet leaving his boat.

[‡]   Author's Note: The multiple amphibious landings and parachute assaults undertaken in the Philippines is beyond the scope of this work.

Finally, at the end of September, Admiral Nimitz convinced Admiral King to bypass Formosa and move against Iwo Jima in the Volcano Islands then onto Okinawa in the Ryukyus Islands. Located only 670 miles south of Tokyo the Japanese considered Iwo Jima to be very important. In June 1944, a young Japanese officer wrote in his diary: "Iwo Jima is the doorkeeper to the Imperial capital."[22]

Iwo Jima – Operation *Detachment*

Iwo Jima is a volcanic, pear-shaped island, four and a half miles long and between 800 yards and nearly two and a half miles wide with a southwest to northeast axis. It has no barrier reef on the eastern side, and the one on the western side is not formidable.

Mount Suribachi is an extinct volcano 546ft high, rising from the narrow neck of the pear at the southwesterly end of the island. Mount Motoyama, which was still jetting steam sulphur fumes in 1945, rises up about 350ft in the bulge of the pear on the northwesterly part.

Between Mount Suribachi and the northern plateau there were two miles of volcanic sand beaches on either side of the head of the pear. Between 5ft and 35ft from the water's edge the cinder-laden, volcanic black sand beaches are a nearly perpendicular 12ft high ledge. The water is very deep right up to the very narrow beaches with the surf breaking right at the edges. In the late winter the easterly beaches are in the lee of the island and the temperature is comfortable with some rain and drizzle.

In preparing Iwo Jima's defenses the Japanese applied lessons learned from defensive failures on other islands. Their beach defenses were organized in depth with open areas covered by extensive antitank defenses and machine guns laid on final protective lines. The light artillery of infantry units was emplaced to bring flanking fire against the beaches. The island was riddled with interconnected, camouflaged trenched pillboxes and strong points strengthened by antitank defenses and mines. Intelligence, based on submarine reconnaissance, failed to discover any guns or emplacements on the slopes of Mount Suribachi itself, nor could individual pillboxes be identified, though a number of caves were visible.

Intelligence estimates placed the number of Japanese defenders at 13,000 to 14,000 when the garrison actually numbered over 23,000 men. The backbone of this force was the 2nd Mixed Brigade of the 109th Division, commanded by Major General Koto Osuka, and Colonel Masuo Ikeda's 145th Infantry Regiment. There was a detachment of the 26th Tank Regiment with approximately 23 medium and ten light tanks. In addition to the tanks there were artillery units and five antitank battalions with a combined strength of 326 guns augmented by rockets. [23]

Assault Plan and Forces

As commander of the Fifth Fleet's Task Force 50 (TF 50), comprised of over 900 vessels, Admiral Raymond A. Spruance was the operation's overall commander. Vice Admiral Turner commanded the Joint Expeditionary Force (TF 51). The Amphibious Support Force (TF 52), commanded by Rear Admiral W. H. P. Blandy, included an Air Support Group with eight escort carriers, an Air Support Control Unit, an Underwater Demolition Group and a Gunboat Mortar Support Group with rocket LCIs and gun LCI units. Task Force 53 Attack Force was commanded by Rear Admiral Harry W. Hill and comprised of an air support control unit, embarked assault troops, two transport squadrons, amphibious tractor groups, LSM groups, a control group, a beach party group, and a pontoon barge, causeway, and LCT group. Rear Admiral Bertram J. Rodgers commanded Task Force 54 Gunfire and Covering Force, which was composed of three battleship divisions, one cruiser division, three destroyer divisions, and was reinforced on D-Day by an additional two destroyer divisions from Task Force 58.[24]

Lieutenant General Holland M. Smith commanded the Expeditionary Troops (TF 56), and Major General Harry Schmidt commanded the Landing Force Task Group 56.1. Marine units assigned to the Landing Force were the 3d Division (commanded by Major General Graves B. Erskine) supported by the 9th Regiment, 21st Regiment, and 12th (Artillery) Regiment; the 4th Division (under Major General Clifton B. Cates) with the 23d Regiment, 24th Regiment, 25th Regiment, and 14th (Artillery) Regiment; and the 5th Division (under Major General Keller E. Rockey) augmented by the 26th Regiment, 27th Regiment, 28th Regiment, and 13th (Artillery) Regiment.

The designated landing beaches, on the southeast shore of Iwo Jima, covered 3,500 yards. For the purposes of organization and control of the invasion force, these beaches were divided into 500-yard segments, which, from left to right, were designated as Green, Red 1 and 2, Yellow 1 and 2, and Blue 1 and 2.

The 4th and 5th Divisions were to be landed abreast on 3,000 yards of these beaches. The 4th Division was assigned to Yellow 1, Yellow 2, and Blue 1 while the 5th Division assaulted Green 1, Red 1, and Red 2. No assault troops were assigned to Blue 2. The 3d Division was designated Expeditionary Troop Reserve and when released not before D-Day+1 would land over the same beaches.

The 4th Marine Division had the specific mission of moving into the center of the isthmus, from Yellow beaches 1 and 2, and Blue beaches 1 and 2 while its right flank swerved to the north to seize Motoyama Plateau, the high ground above the East Boat Basin.

Green, Red 1, and Red 2 beaches were tasked to the 5th Marine Division. Once ashore it was to advance straight across the island, which at that point formed a narrow isthmus, until it reached the west coast. At the same time, it was to hold along the right, while part of the division wheeled to the south to capture Mount Suribachi. The 3d Marine Division was held as a floating reserve.

Sixty-eight LVT(A)s were in the lead wave, and 83 LVTs in Wave 2, with a varying lesser number of craft in Waves 3 through Wave 5. Wave 6 on Green and Red beaches contained LCMs and LCVPs. Wave 6A consisted of LCTs and LSMs carrying tanks. Altogether, 482 amtracs were to participate in the assault.[25]

Assault

On February 17, D-Day-2, Navy battleships and cruisers sallied close inshore to provoke Japanese fire. It worked, but the *Tennessee* (BB-43) was lightly hit and the cruiser *Pensacola* (CA-24) was hit hard – there were 115 casualties including 17 men killed, one of whom was her Executive Officer, and the Combat Information Center was wrecked.

At 1045 swimmers from Underwater Demolition Teams 12, 13, 14, and 15 headed toward the beach. Their mission included checking beach and surf conditions, searching for obstacles and destroying said obstacles on the beach and in the water approaches. Their small boats reached the beach under withering fire. Shells were dropping so closely that spray soaked everyone and twice the boats were lifted out of the water by concussion. Zigzagging all the while, the boats made their runs and dropped swimmers at 100-yard intervals. They then retired astern of the line of LCI Gunboats (LCI(G)s).*

---

* LCI(G)s mounted a mix of weapons including two to three twin mount Bofors 40mm guns, three to four Oerlikon 20mm guns, six .50-caliber machine guns, and ten Mark 7 and two Mark 22 rocket launchers.

Swimmers fluttered off toward the beach, cautiously but speedily. Their last swim had been at Ulithi, in the Carolines, in 85-degree water, but at Iwo Jima the water was reported to have a temperature of 59 degrees. Their combat uniform was bathing trunks, face mask, swim shoes, swim fins, webbed belt, knife, mine detonators, and a plastic plate to record information. The only protection from the cold was a layer of grease over their near naked bodies, applied before they left their ships.[26]

Periodically one of a pair would take a sounding (with a three-fathom lead line) and give his results to his partner who would write it on a plexiglass slate. Some dispensed with the writing as they were too busy. By swimming under the surface out of sight, casualties were averted.

The schedule called for all swimmers to be back in their LCPRs in 90 minutes after they were dropped off. They worked fast. Although they were dropped at about 700 yards, the men had to come back to about 900 yards to be picked up, as endangering the boat was endangering many more lives. Orders were for the boat officers to keep away from the beaches and only in an extreme emergency could they go as close as 300 yards, and only then to pick up a stranded swimmer. The swimmers were very important as they had the information.

Although there were some close calls, the swimmers all made it back safely. Radio contact was made with Admiral King and he ordered the return to the ship. The operation was almost over when the unfortunate happened. In spite of the zigzagging and swerving, Frank W. Sumpter, the stern gunner for Platoon Four's boat, was hit in the head by the Japanese equivalent to the U.S. .50 cal. He was rushed to the nearest destroyer and put aboard – he was later transferred to a battleship for further surgery, but he died there.[27]

At 1100, 12 LCI(G)s had moved in to less than 1,000 yards offshore to provide close gunfire support for the personnel of the Underwater Demolition Teams. Enemy heavy mortars and three previously unlocated guns in a four-gun Japanese battery overlooking the beach from Mount Suribachi, as well as a considerable number of mortars on the high ground on the north flank of the beaches, came to life just after the gunboats let go their rockets. In the following 45 minutes 11 of the 12 LCIs were hit and one was sunk. The LCIs gallantly carried out their mission despite suffering 170 casualties including UDT men acting as spotters stationed on board as their teammates went ashore. One of these was Lieutenant Junior Grade Frank Jirka, a member of UDT 12:

Just as we were about 400 yards off our beaches, all hell broke loose. Mortars, coast guns, machine guns and small arms fire was being fired all around us and at us from what looked like a rather dead island ten minutes before. We tried to call for some fire support, but it was of no avail, since we couldn't tell exactly where the firing was coming from due to the Japs' crisscrossed pattern of defenses, with interlocking trenches, gun positions and rat hole-like caves.

While the morning operation was still underway and after some of us finished our reconnaissance, a marine captain, two of his men, and I went out to where our supporting LCI was to be located. We found that it was hit and out of action. Just then a large shell hit near our craft and raised the aft end up with quite a force. After looking around we noticed an LCI that wasn't the one assigned to us, but which was off our beach. We decided to go aboard and try to spot our gunfire from it. We came alongside and the four of us climbed aboard. I went up to the bridge, told them what I was there for and what team I represented.

I said to the captain that it looks like we're getting in pretty close, when the next thing I knew I was flat on the deck, wounded. I tried to stand but was unable to do so. Since I was not suffering from any pain I looked down to see just why I was unable to stand. It was then that I noticed a pair of blown up feet at right angles to my body, without shoes or stockings. I thought surely those couldn't be mine for I was wearing shoes when I came aboard.

Then I suddenly felt a painful drawing sensation and upon noticing carefully found that those mangled pieces of skin and bone were all that was left of my good nine and a half C's. I then crawled to the after end of the bridge, for the spot that I was standing on was no longer there. I asked for some morphine and gave myself a shot. I then had a fellow mark the time of the injection on my "T" shirt and had him help me apply tourniquets.

I perched myself up on my elbows in order to see just how bad the ship was hit. I glanced down on the main deck and there I saw men covered with blood, sprawled all over the place. The ship was hit three times. In an hour or so they finally took 27 casualties out of 48 men off and onto the USS *Tennessee* where at last we saw a doctor. Around ten hours later they took me to the operating room and there they removed what remained of my feet.[28]

The Commander Task Force 52 After Action Report stated:

The personnel of these little gunboats displayed magnificent courage as they returned fire with everything they had and refused to move out until they were forced to do so by materiel and personnel casualties. Even then, after undergoing terrific punishment, some returned to their stations amid a hail of fire, until again heavily hit. Relief LCI(G)s replaced damaged ships without hesitation.[29]

Ship and air attacks continued on D-Day-1 with negligible results. For USS *Blessman* (ADP-48) and UDT-15 it was to prove deadly. At 2121 that evening *Blessman* was steaming at flank speed from the vicinity of Iwo Jima to the outer screening area. While she was speeding at 22 knots a twin engine "Betty" flew very low over the port quarter, strafing, and dropped a 500lb bomb that exploded in the starboard mess deck, blowing it open. The midsection of the ship was engulfed in flames and the smell of burning flesh was everywhere.

Some of the men went through the troop compartments pulling injured men from their bunks and helping others to struggle to the stern. It was a hectic race to see if the injured men could be cleared from the troop compartment before they were burned to death. In a short time all the injured men had been rescued from the troop compartment but there were still dead men in there that the survivors were not able to get out until the next day. In all, 40 men were killed including 18 from UDT-15 – another 23 team members were badly wounded.[30]

D-Day, February 19

The flag signal to "Land the Landing Force" was executed at 0645 on February 19, H-Hour was 0900. The weather was clear with a ten-knot trade wind.

At 0805 naval guns lifted their fire as 72 fighter and bomber planes from Admiral Mitscher's Fast Carrier Force roared in to attack the eastern and northern slopes of Mount Suribachi, the landing areas, and the menacing high ground on the north flank of the eastern beaches with rockets, bombs, and machine guns. Following on their heels, 48 additional fighters, including 24 Marine Corsairs (F4Us) from Marine Fighter Squadrons 124 and 213, led by Lieutenant Colonel William A. Millington, came in to ravage the same areas with napalm, more rockets, and machine-gun bursts. Colonel Vernon E. Megee, Air Officer on the Expeditionary Troops staff, urged Millington to put on a special show for the troops in the assault waves, telling him to "Drag your bellies on the beach."[31]

Men in the three surviving Underwater Demolition Teams led the first wave of 68 LVT(A)4 armored amtracs, mounting snub-nosed 75mm cannon, followed by 380 troop-laden LVT4s and LVT2s, into the beaches that they had reconnoitered.

Colonel Robert H. Williams, executive officer of the 28th Marines, recalled that "the landing was a magnificent sight to see – two divisions landing abreast; you could see the whole show from the deck of a ship."[32]

The first waves struck the beaches at 0900 on a front of about 3,000 yards, receiving only a small amount of gunfire, which still destroyed five LVTs. Within minutes 6,000 men were ashore and rapidly moved 350 yards forward with the assistance of a rolling barrage of naval gunfire. The second wave was the initial troop wave. As the Marine Commander reported: "No anti-boat gunfire was reported by the initial waves."[33]

Beach conditions were bad. As LVTs landed some became bellied up on the ledge and as the surf broke over the sterns of the LVTs their cargo compartments were filled with water and sand. The LVT(A)(4)s preceding the troop-carrying LVTs could not fire because the ledge immediately behind the beaches was too high. The surf picked up and threw landing craft broadside on the beach, swamping them, and then, wrecked by succeeding waves, the craft sank deeper into the sand. Wreckage piled higher and higher, extending seaward to damage the propellers of landing ships. Many of those coxswains whose boats were hit, or had become stranded, immediately joined Marines ashore and assisted with any task necessary.

Beside and under this wreckage was a scattering of dead and wounded. A few uninjured men were trying to salvage a bit of radio or other equipment. Wounded men lay helplessly in shell holes a few yards in, along the entire beach area. The fire was so heavy that they could not be carried down to the boats even when boats were available. Many of the hospital corpsmen themselves were wounded. Boats going back to the transport carried casualties – as many as could be brought down to the water's edge and taken aboard before enemy fire made it necessary to shove off.

On Yellow beaches 1 and 2 no one ever could be graphic enough to cover what the 12 Navy Medical Corpsmen did under heartbreaking and impossible circumstances.* Soon after landing, 11 of the corpsmen had been wounded or killed leaving only Pharmacist Mate 3d Class Richard Dreyfuss.

---

* The Navy provided corpsmen to the Marines and wore the same uniforms as the Marines in combat.

THE IWO JIMA LANDINGS, FEBRUARY 19, 1945

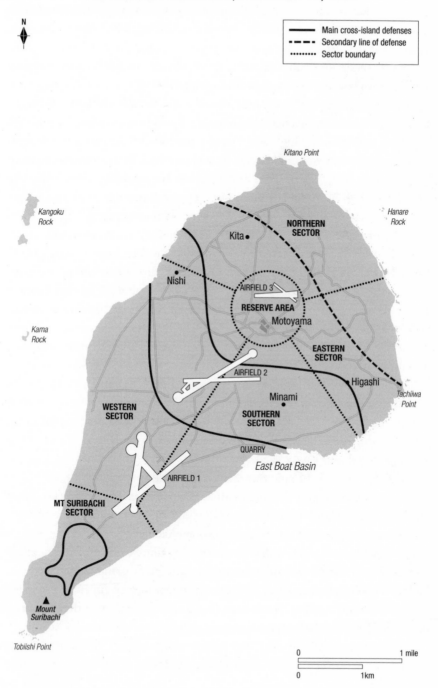

——	Main cross-island defenses
- - -	Secondary line of defense
········	Sector boundary

N

Kitano Point

Kangoku Rock

Hanare Rock

NORTHERN SECTOR

Kita •

Nishi •

AIRFIELD 3

RESERVE AREA

Motoyama

Kama Rock

EASTERN SECTOR

AIRFIELD 2

Higashi

Tachiiwa Point

WESTERN SECTOR

Minami •

SOUTHERN SECTOR

QUARRY

East Boat Basin

AIRFIELD 1

MT SURIBACHI SECTOR

Mount Suribachi

Tobiishi Point

0   1 mile

0   1km

He faced almost impossible odds, and without regard for his own life, crawled, dodged, and staggered up and down the beach through enemy fire, from one shell hole to another, from one line of wounded to another, everywhere he thought he was needed. He moved inland later with his regiment. Deserving equal credit is H. J. Kelsch who followed Dreyfuss, keeping him covered as best he could with a BAR.[34]

The fire on the beach was murderous. It came from both flanks; from the heights of Mount Suribachi on the left, which was being assaulted by the 5th Division; and from the high area forming the bulk of the island to the right – the deadly territory of pillboxes, gun emplacements, machine guns, mortars, mines, and snipers, which were all manned by Imperial Japanese troops who had orders to fight to the last man. Fire from both these areas came together on the invasion beachhead, making it one maelstrom of explosion.

To Lieutenant Paul F. Cook, commander of A Company, 133 Naval Construction "Seabees" Battalion attached to the 23d Regiment, the shore looked okay. It didn't look bad as his LCVP dipped in on a rough sea toward the blackish colored line. It was H-Hour plus 30 minutes, and it didn't seem logical that the beach would be tough. It had been strafed, rocketed, bombed from the air, and shelled from battlewagons and cruisers, taking more bombardment with more explosives for its area than any other island to date.

Just in front of the high square prow of the LCVP, and to either side, high fountains of water sprayed upward. The boat's coxswain, Seaman First Class Caisey Kidd, from Wheelwright, Kentucky, smiled reassuringly. "It's all right," he yelled. "It's our own shells moving in ahead of us to keep the Japs dazed and glassy-eyed."

Right after that they found out that Caisey Kidd was wrong.

They realized suddenly that the outlines along the beach were wrecked Navy and Coast Guard landing craft. One Seabee said he saw a bunch of the advance assault waves of the 23d up the slope running like hell.

Two beach parties, each with 45 men and one officer, one under Lieutenant Commander Loomis and the other under Lieutenant Commander Baldwin, had tried to move in early to set up their regular beach party direction system for landing men and supplies. The wrecked boats were evidence that they had been unsuccessful; both beach parties were put out of action with heavy casualties.[35]

On other assault beaches in previous operations there had been beachmasters, salvage parties, and beach parties to keep the landing area clear. There was none of that on D-Day at Iwo Jima because no one could remain on the beach.

Those of the assault forces who were still alive had to keep moving forward. To run, even to crawl, in the soft gravelly volcanic sand was like trying to move through foot-deep mud. It was impossible to move at much more than a fast shuffle. However, to remain near the water's edge for any length of time was to invite certain death. Snipers hid in wrecked landing craft and picked off men. One sniper in particular played hell from a demolished Japanese lugger on the right flank of Yellow Beach 1. Finally, on D-Day+1, some Marines went in and got him. Machine gun emplacements above the beach on the terraces, and in sandstone pillboxes at the base of the airfield, kept a chattering death raining down on the area.

Through this hell the Pioneers, Seabees, and Marines of the 23d were trying to get vital equipment and supplies ashore. Tanks were groping to find a road inland, but in the shifting sands, there weren't any roads. Other tanks struggled over the first and second terraces, and even made it up to the third, only to be blasted by mortars. A few did make it up and over the crumbling sand hills. Ensign R. H. Ross saw one tank blown up 50 yards away as he was struggling with a 37mm, trying to drag it through the sand.

"It was trying to edge over the first terrace toward the airstrip," he said that night. "It was hit by a mortar that blew off its right tread. Marines began trying to get out of the turret. Another mortar lit right in the turret. The tank spread apart a little. All the Marines were killed."

It seemed impossible to get ashore all the supplies and equipment necessary to keep the advancing assault troops going. The Seabees hugged the sand. Many of them hadn't been able to get more than ten yards inland. Men were falling with a certain horrible steadiness. Mortar craters appeared everywhere, all the time.[36]

None of the assault units found it easy going to move inland, but the 25th Marines almost immediately ran into a buzz saw trying to move across Blue Beach. General Cates would say of it later: "That right flank was a bitch if there ever was one." Lieutenant Colonel Hollis W. Mustain's 1st Battalion, 25th Marines, managed to scratch forward 300 yards under heavy fire in the first half hour, but Lieutenant Colonel Chambers' 3d Battalion, 25th Marines, took the heaviest beating of the day on the extreme right trying to scale the cliffs leading to the Rock Quarry.[37]

Progress straight across the southern belt of the island was rapid and by 1030 Marines had reached the cliffs overlooking the western beaches of Iwo Jima, and by 1130 these cliffs were in the possession of the 5th Marine Division. Progress on the right flank was slower, much slower, as the Marines met gradually intensifying fire from the quarry and plateau area, and from undestroyed pillboxes. They also encountered land mines.

Sherman tanks were called for, but it was hell getting them into action. It was tough disembarking them on Iwo Jima's steep beaches. The LSMs' stern anchors could not hold in the loose sand, and bow cables run forward to "deadmen" LVTs parted under the strain. On one occasion the lead tank stalled at the top of the ramp, blocking the other vehicles and leaving the LSM at the mercy of the rising surf. A few tanks stalled in the surf and were swamped. Other tanks bogged down or threw tracks in the loose sand. Many of those that made it over the terraces were destroyed by huge horned mines or disabled by deadly accurate 47mm antitank fire from Mount Suribachi. However, the tanks kept coming; their relative mobility, armored protection, and 75mm gunfire were most welcome to the infantry scattered around Iwo Jima's lunar-looking, shell-pocked landscape.[38]

By the end of D-Day a total of 30,000 men from both Marine divisions had been landed. Heavy opposition had developed from the high ground on both flanks, but the 5th Marines on the left had advanced rapidly across the narrow part of the island, capturing the southwest end of Airfield No. 1, then pivoting southwest against Mount Suribachi. The 4th Marines on the right advanced across the steep and open slopes leading up to Airfield No. 1.

Veteran Marine combat correspondent, Lieutenant Cyril P. Zurlinden, who was soon to become a casualty himself, described that first night ashore:

> At Tarawa, Saipan, and Tinian, I saw Marines killed and wounded in a shocking manner, but I saw nothing like the ghastliness that hung over the Iwo beachhead. Nothing any of us had ever known could compare with the utter anguish, frustration, and constant inner battle to maintain some semblance of sanity.[39]

Personnel accounting was a nightmare under those conditions, but the assault divisions eventually reported the combined loss of 2,420 men: 501 killed, 1,755 wounded, 47 dead of wounds, 18 missing, and 99 suffering from combat fatigue.

The first night on Iwo Jima was ghostly. Sulfuric mists spiraled out of the earth. The Marines, used to the tropics, shivered in the cold, waiting for Kuribayashi's warriors to come screaming down from the hills.[*] They would learn that this Japanese commander was different. There would be no wasteful, vainglorious *banzai* attacks on Iwo Jima.

The Last Attack

About 0515 on March 25, 200 to 300 Japanese moved down from the north along the west side of the island in the vicinity of Airfield No. 2 and attacked Army pilots, Seabees, and Marines of the 5th Pioneer Battalion, and the 28th Marines' bivouacs nearby. The Marines, who were due to board transports the next day, had been required to turn in their ammunition the day before, so they were pretty much unarmed when the attack struck.

The attack was not a *banzai* charge. Instead it appeared to have been a well-laid plan aimed at creating maximum confusion and destruction. The Japanese were well armed with both Japanese and American weapons. Forty of the officers were dressed with careful attention and one was wearing a white shirt. Each officer carried his samurai sword with its ornate hilt and keen, shiny blade. These swords were not only used for decoration, and later examination disclosed that most of them had fresh blood stains from Marines who had tried to parry a vicious blow. Most of the Japanese were wearing the "belt of a thousand stitches," a Japanese prayer belt.

Grenades, apparently taken from dead Marines, were hurled at Marines from behind scrubby bushes and tufts of grass on the sandy dunes of the area. Small arms fire cracked at them. One Japanese knee mortar shook the ground with a cluster of closely bunched hits.

Over the crack of rifle fire and the bang of exploding grenades could be heard shouts of "There he goes, don't let 'im get away."

The cry of "Stretchers, stretchers" would break through the noise of the battle and Marine Pioneers dodged Japanese fire to take the litters to the wounded.

After daylight, when the Marines could see one another and fire was more easily directed, the hunt for the attackers bubbled with activity. One group of Japanese, who tried to hide in a shell crater at the northern end of the Pioneers' bivouac area, was pelted with grenades. Whenever a Japanese soldier came into sight he was riddled with fire.

---

[*] Lieutenant General Tadamichi Kuribayashi, overall commander of the Volcano–Bonin Defense Sector.

The battle lasted for about 90 minutes with the Americans suffering 53 killed and 120 wounded in exchange for 196 enemy dead. Two Marines from the 36th Depot Company, an all-African-American unit, received the Bronze Star and First Lieutenant Harry Martin of the 5th Pioneer Battalion was the last Marine to be awarded the Medal of Honor during the battle for Iwo Jima.[40]

There was one other assignment for the UDTs at Iwo Jima, and it was an assignment for volunteers only. The Marine Corps and Navy had both lost many men in the close-in waters. These were those who did not survive the wrecking of the landing craft. After about 4 days, the bodies would surface and float in the ocean in front of the beach approaches. UDTs were asked to man their rubber boats, and were supplied with short pieces of railroad iron and non-corrosive wire. The men were told to take the identification tags, "dog tags," off the deceased men, tie the iron to the bodies, and sink the bodies.[*][41]

When the Marines left Iwo Jima on March 26, they had lost 5,453 killed, 19,217 wounded, and 1,986 who were suffering from fatigue. The total does not reflect the dead, wounded or missing Navy sailors, aircrews, and Coast Guardsmen.

The operation was planned and executed because of the grim necessities of the air war against Japan. By the end of the war a total of 2,251 B-29s carrying 24,761 crewmen made emergency landings on the island, aircraft and crews that might have otherwise been forced to ditch in the ocean.

Iwo Jima's biggest cost to the V Amphibious Corps was the loss of so many combat veterans in taking the island.

"They died so fast," Captain Jim Headley, 3d Division, 25th Regiment, said, "that the whole business of heroes and death is a little mixed up in my mind. You'd see a man do something almost unbelievable and a minute later you'd see him die. It's pretty hard to pick out any outstanding man or men."[42]

Okinawa – Operation *Iceberg*

The Japanese Empire's strategic need to hold Okinawa was absolute. The Japanese considered the Ryukyus Islands (Nansei Shoto) an effective barrier against incursions against Japan from the east and southeast toward Japan and

---

*   There were 21 Underwater Demolition men killed, 26 wounded, and one missing at Iwo Jima. The missing man was from Team 12 and he was later declared killed in action. His body was never found.

Korea. For the U.S. and her allies Okinawa, only 325 miles from the southern Japanese homeland island of Kyushu, was the main link in the island chain. Its capture would secure command of the East China Sea and open approaches to the Yellow Sea and the Straits of Tsushima, which connect the Sea of Japan and the East China Sea.

The Ryukyu Island chain stretches almost 800 miles between the Japanese homeland and Taiwan (which was then known as Formosa). Okinawa, the only really large island in the Ryukyu Island chain, is 60 miles long, generally oriented northeast to southwest, and varies in width from two to 18 miles. The northern portion, constituting two-thirds of the island, is mountainous, heavily wooded, and rimmed with dissected terraces – areas which were once essentially flat, but which have been so cut up by erosion that the high portions between ravines are the only remnants of the former flatland. The island is covered with a dense growth of live oak and conifers, climbing vines, and underbrush. The highlands of the north rise to jagged peaks of 1,000ft to 1,500ft which extend the entire length of the region.

Rainfall is heavy, and the high humidity makes the summer heat oppressive. The prevailing winds are monsoonal in character, and between May and November each year the islands are hit by typhoons.

Japanese Forces

The total strength of the Japanese forces on Okinawa was about 100,000; 67,000 of these were in the Army, 9,000 were in the Navy, and 24,000 were impressed Okinawans used mostly in service support roles under the 32nd Army, which was commanded by Lieutenant General Mitsuru Ushijima.

U.S. intelligence estimated that the Japanese had 198 pieces of artillery of 70mm or larger caliber, including 24 150mm howitzers. The Japanese were also presumed to have about 100 antitank guns of 37mm and 47mm calibers in addition to the guns carried on tanks. The tank regiment on Okinawa had, according to Japanese Tables of Organization, 37 light and 47 medium tanks, but one estimate in March placed the total number of tanks at 90. Intelligence also indicated that rockets and mortars up to 250mm could be expected.[43] In addition, the Japanese prepared squadrons of special *kamikaze* attack boats. These small, 18ft plywood speedboats, powered by a Chevrolet automobile engine, which carried two 250lb depth charges on a rack behind the one-man crew, the steersman, were designed to damage amphibious ships and craft in their vulnerable underbellies.

What the intelligence did not know was that the Japanese had abandoned its policy of seeking out the enemy aggressively in decisive battle in favor of a war of attrition. The Japanese would not oppose the landing, but rather dig deep, contest the ground foot by foot, and selectively use bold defensive counterattacks, primarily at Okinawa's southern end.[44]

To keep the soldiers' morale at a high peak, Army headquarters had devised the following battle slogan:

> One Plane for One Warship
> One Boat for One Ship
> One Man for Ten of the Enemy
> or One Tank.[45]

Plan of Attack and U.S. Forces

Love Day (selected to avoid planning confusion with "D-Day" being planned for Iwo Jima) would occur on April 1, 1945, April Fool's Day and, coincidentally, Easter Sunday.

The landings would be a massive four-division assault over the Hagushi beaches by the Tenth Army (under Lieutenant General Simon Bolivar Buckner, Jr.). The Marines III Amphibious Corps, composed of the 1st Marine Division (under Major General Pedro A. del Valle) and the 6th Marine Division (under Major General Lemuel C. Shepherd, Jr.), would land on the north beaches. The Army XXIV Corps (under Major General John R. Hodge), consisting of the 7th Infantry Division (under Major General Archibald V. Arnold) and the 96th Infantry Division (under Major General James L. Bradley), was assigned the southern beaches.

The naval component consisted of the Fifth Fleet Central Pacific Task Forces (commanded by Admiral Raymond Spruance) with overall command of Covering Forces and Special Groups (Task Force 50) directly under Spruance, Fast Carrier Force (Task Force 58) under Vice Admiral Marc A. Mitscher, British Carrier Force (Task Force 57) under Vice Admiral Sir Bernard Rawlings, and Joint Expeditionary Force (Task Force 51) under Vice Admiral Richmond K. Turner.

The U.S. plan of attack called for the advance seizure of the Kerama Retto Islands off the southwest coast on March 26 by the 77th Infantry Division (Reinforced). The invasion of Kerama Retto involved a complicated amphibious assault that required initial assault landings on eight small

THE OKINAWA PLAN OF ATTACK, APRIL 1, 1945

beaches on four different islands and subsequent assault landings on three additional islands.

The Fleet Marine Force Amphibious Reconnaissance Battalion was to reconnoiter the reef islets of the island group. First they were to investigate Keise Shima for the presence of enemy troops, and in the following days and nights prior to L-Day they were to land on Aware Shima, Mae Shima, and Kuro Shima. Field artillery and antiaircraft guns would land on Keise Shima on March 31 (L-Day-1).

Assault

Coast Guard-manned LST-829 had the special distinction of landing the first troops in World War II to invade and secure Japanese colonial soil (Iwo Jima was a Japanese mandate). In the early morning of March 26, the LST landed A Company, 1st Battalion, 306th Infantry, 77th Division, on Geruma Shima in the Kerama Retto. After swiftly overrunning the island and smothering Japanese resistance, these troops raised the American flag over Geruma Heights.

That afternoon the troops were reloaded and on the 27th were sent against Tokashiki Shima. They also uncovered and destroyed scores of Japanese *kamikaze* attack boats, hidden in caves and underbrush all over the island, and captured charts and intelligence papers that showed the proposed use of these craft to combat the invasion of Okinawa.

Before Kerama Retto was secured 15 separate assault landings had been made, including five shore-to-shore landings. In these preliminary operations the 77th Division suffered 31 dead and 81 wounded, while Japanese dead and captured numbered over 650.[*][46]

Okinawa Landings

At 0830 on April 1 the Marine 3d Amphibious Corps under Major General Roy S. Geiger and the 24th Army Corps commanded by Major General John R. Hodge landed on Okinawa on an eight-mile stretch of beach opposite Yontan and Katena airfields, about 20 miles north of Naha, the capital. Before noon the two airfields had been seized. Resistance on the beaches was unexpectedly light, and within 48 hours U.S. forces had driven across to the east coast.

Marine correspondent James Finan described the landing:

---

[*] On April 16, 1945, the 77th landed on Ie Shima, captured the airfield, and engaged in a bitter fight for "Government House Hill" and "Bloody Ridge." It was during this operation that journalist Ernie Pyle was killed.

A huge moon came up last night and Marines hanging on the starboard rail of our personnel assault ship watching the horizon, could see the arching flare shells our battleships were throwing at the beaches and strongpoints of Okinawa.

We were filled with foreboding. This was to be worse than our last bloody landing, we thought. Instead, so far, it has been for us a literal "walkaway."

We saw four big mortar splashes among the wave of landing craft over to our left – on Beach Blue One. We figured it was just about time for the Japs to open up with mortar barrages on our beach. But the driver of the amtrac said. "It's easy. We didn't get anything and the first wave's in."[47]

One observer caught the drama of the landing in these words:

The approaching landing waves possessed something of the color and pageantry of medieval warfare, advancing relentlessly with their banners flying. In the calm sunlight of the morning, it was indeed an impressive spectacle.[48]

The morning's tranquility had already been shattered at about 0514 when three planes were seen approaching the Coast Guard-manned LST-884 off Okinawa. All port guns opened fire and one plane immediately burst into flames, nosed into a shallow dive, and crashed into the port side of the LST, plunging through the ship fitter's shop, and into the tank deck, where it exploded with intense flame. The plane had crashed through the 81mm and 60mm mortar ammunition, causing it to explode. By 1100, however, the fire was deemed under control, but the tank deck and both engine rooms were flooded. Amazingly, Motor Machinist Mate First Class F. D. Flockencier was the only man killed.[49]

Less than an hour later *kamikazes* struck again. USS *Hinsdale* (APA-120) was steaming toward the transport area with the 3d Battalion, 2d Marines and its reinforcing units preparing to disembark. *Hinsdale*'s lookouts spotted an enemy plane skimming low over the water at 0600. The *kamikaze* plane crashed into her port side and ripped into the engine room. Three bombs exploded deep inside her and tore the engine room apart – only one member of the watch was not killed by the scalding steam from the exploding boilers.

Hinsdale came to a dead stop in the water. Below decks *Hinsdale*'s crew were groping through the smoke-filled darkness trying to fight fires and jury-rig patches. Despite the damage *Hinsdale* carried out her job to put the Marines ashore. Eight Marines were reported killed, 37 were wounded, and eight were listed as missing in action. The crew of *Hinsdale* suffered one dead, 34 wounded, and ten missing. First Class Metalsmith James O. Perry saw the *kamikaze* plane approaching and cleared the topside of Marines and sailors, saving many lives.[50]

By the end of the day the front lines were 4,000 to 5,000 yards from the assault beachhead along an eight-mile front and 50,000 troops were ashore. It was a day of major accomplishments by the amphibians. Admiral Spruance reported in his Action Report:

> Naturally, all attack commands were highly elated with this unexpected situation. The fierce fighting and heavy casualties considered unavoidable in taking this area had not materialized due to the sudden withdrawal of the unpredictable Jap.[51]

After staying all day onshore Finan hitched a ride on a landing craft back to his transport. There, all hell broke lose:

> Suddenly, a twin 40mm gun began throwing tracers into the sky from a nearby ship. Then all the guns in the world seemed to be firing. Orange and red tracers made a woven pattern over our heads. Flak began to fall around us and the coxswain steered toward a nearby ship to avoid being run down by one of our dodging, zigzagging vessels. It was pitch black and you could see nothing. Suddenly a vessel nearby became suffused with orange-red, like a neon sign, and seemed to burst in a great sheet of flame. Then all was quiet.
>
> Easter is over now. The general quarters bell is ringing. Through the steel skin of the bulkhead I can hear the steady pounding of hundreds of antiaircraft guns again.
>
> The Japs will exact their price for Okinawa. But on the first day, we got a lot of this crucial island virtually free. Tomorrow may be a different story.[52]

It took until June 22 to secure the island. Total American battle casualties were 49,151, of which 12,520 were killed or missing and 36,631 wounded. Army losses were 4,582 killed, 93 missing, and 18,099 wounded; Marine losses, including those of the Tactical Air Force, were 2,938 killed or missing and

13,708 wounded. Navy casualties totaled 4,907 killed or missing and 4,824 wounded, and 560 members of the Navy Medical Corps assigned to the Marine units were killed or wounded. Non-battle casualties during the campaign amounted to 15,613 for the Army and 10,598 for the Marines. Thirty-six ships were sunk, including 15 amphibious ships and 12 destroyers, and 368 other ships were damaged, most of them as a result of air action. In the air 763 planes were lost between April 1 and July 1.[53]

It was a bloody struggle.

EPILOGUE

The war in Europe ended on May 8, 1945. Europe and much of Britain lay in ruins with tens of thousands of men, women, and children without shelter or food, and with little hope for the future. Even before the fighting ended men and material were being loaded onto transports bound for the Pacific.

By July Okinawa and the Philippines were secure, and, plans for Operation *Downfall*, covering the invasion of Japan, were complete.

Operation *Downfall* was in two parts. The first, Operation *Olympic*, targeting the Japanese southern home island of Kyushu, was to take place on November 1. The invasion fleet included 42 aircraft carriers, 24 battleships, and over 400 destroyers and destroyer escorts. The fleet would escort the 14th Army and Marine Corps divisions that formed the initial assault force.

The second part, Operation *Coronet*, the invasion of Honshū at the Kantō Plain south of Tokyo, was to take place on March 1, 1946. Planning was based on the assumption that Operation *Olympic* had secured airfields so that additional land-based air support would be available. It was to be the largest amphibious operation in history, with 25 divisions participating in the initial invasion, including those in floating reserve; the great invasion force was to include those combatants transferred from Europe.

In a study done by the Joint Chiefs of Staff in April it was estimated that a 90-day *Olympic* campaign would cost 456,000 casualties, including 109,000 dead or missing. If *Coronet* took another 90 days, the combined cost would be 1,200,000 casualties, with 267,000 fatalities. Japanese casualties, including civilians participating in the defense, ranged between five and ten million dead or wounded.[1]

As invasion forces gathered, the 509th Composite Bomb Group issued Operations Order No. 35 to the 393d Bombardment Squadron on Tinian. On August 6 the B-29 *Enola Gay*, piloted by Brigadier General Paul W. Tibbets, carrying an atomic bomb named "Little Boy," took off from Tinian's

North Field for an estimated six-hour flight to Hiroshima. Accompanying the *Enola Gay* was Major Charles Sweeny's *The Great Artiste*, carrying instruments and a then unnamed B-29 piloted by Captain George Marquardt assigned as the photography aircraft.*

At 0809 Tibbets started his bomb run and handed control over to his bombardier, Major Thomas Ferebee. The release at 0815 (Hiroshima time) went as planned, and "Little Boy" exploded above the city. An estimated 70,000 to 80,000 people were killed, including 20,000 Japanese soldiers and 20,000 Korean slave laborers, and another 70,000 were injured by the blast and resultant firestorm.

After the bombing President Harry S. Truman warned Japan that "If they do not now accept our terms, they may expect a rain of ruin from the air, the like of which has never been seen on this earth. Behind this air attack will follow sea and land forces in such numbers and power as they have not yet seen and with the fighting skill of which they are already well aware."[2]

The Japanese government did not respond to Truman and there was no indication that Japan would surrender. A second bomb named "Fat Boy" was readied. The 509th's Operations Order No. 39 of August 8 assigned Major Charles W. Sweeney, commanding officer of the 393rd Squadron and pilot of *Bockscar*, to lead the mission. For this mission Kokura was the primary target with Nagasaki as an alternative. However, heavy smoke obscured Kokura, and after three runs over the city, with fuel running low because of a failed fuel pump, the B-29s headed for Nagasaki.

At 1101, a last-minute break in the clouds over Nagasaki allowed *Bockscar*'s bombardier, Captain Kermit Beahan, to visually sight the target as ordered and drop "Fat Boy." In Nagasaki casualty estimates for immediate deaths vary widely, and the numbers range from 22,000 to 75,000.†

Compounding Japan's already desperate situation, Soviet infantry, armor, and air forces had launched the Manchurian Strategic Offensive Operation at two minutes past midnight on August 9, Tokyo time. Four hours later, word reached Tokyo of the Soviet Union's official declaration of war.

On August 15 Emperor Hirohito announced Japan's surrender to the Japanese people and ordered Japanese forces to lay down their arms. Despite

---

*   This B-29 was later dubbed *Necessary Evil*.

†   There are numerous sources for the dropping of "Fat Boy" over Nagasaki. However, for the most part, they give different casualty figures, making it impossible to give a more accurate estimate of fatalities.

their earlier suicidal resistance, they immediately did so. The formal surrender occurred on September 2 on board the USS *Missouri* anchored in Tokyo Bay.

Aftermath

Over the next months thousands of ships, aircraft, tanks, and weapons were laid up or scrapped. The American factories that had made victory possible retooled to once again make consumer products. Tens of thousands of men and women returned to civilian life, each trying to put the war behind them. Uniforms and medals were packed away along with the memories they carried. No one forgot what he or she had been through, but there were families and futures to build, so there wasn't time to dwell on the past. When asked what they did in the war only the funny stories were told. The hard and painful ones weren't for public consumption.

Decades later new generations with a renewed interest in the war began asking the same questions. Now with families grown and more time to reflect veterans were more willing to tell the hard, painful stories in recorded oral histories. However, without knowing the context of what the veterans went through, the right questions never got asked, the opportunity was wasted and, with few exceptions, the real stories died with the men. Perhaps this is for the best.

Now most are with their old friends swapping stories, smoking cigarettes, sitting on a ship's mess deck or perched on empty ammo boxes or around a bar in club where the coffee's hot, chow always good, and the beer free. There are no reveilles, work details, inspections, or someone shooting at them.

I hope they're enjoying themselves. They earned it the hard way.

ABBREVIATIONS

AA	Anti-Aircraft
AK	Auxiliary Cargo Supply Ship
AKA	Auxiliary Cargo Assault
AP	Auxiliary, Personnel, Armor Piercing
APA	Auxiliary, Personnel, Assault
APC	Armoured Personnel Carrier
APD	Auxiliary Personnel Destroyer
AT	Anti Tank
ATAF	Allied Tactical Air Force
BAR	Browning Automatic Rifle
BB	Two-letter designator for a battleship
Brig. Gen.	Brigadier General (rank) – U.S.
CA	Heavy Cruiser (ship)
Capt.	Captain (Navy rank O–6 equivalent to an Army Colonel)
	Captain (Army rank O–3)
CIC	Combat Information Center
CJTF	Combined Joint Task Force
CL	Light Cruiser (ship)
CO	Commanding Officer
CPO	Chief Petty Officer (Coast Guard and Navy)
CV	Fleet Air Craft Carrier
CVE	Escort (or Jeep) Aircraft Carrier
DD	Destroyer (ship), Duplex Drive (amphibious tank)
DE	Destroyer Escort (ship)
DUKW	amphibious truck
ETO	European Theater of Operations
1stSgt	First Sergeant (1st Grade, today's E-8)
GAT	Gap Assault Team

LCA	Landing Craft, Assault (British)
LCI	Landing Craft, Infantry
LCI(G)	Landing Craft, Infantry (Gunboat)
LCI(L)	Landing Craft, Infantry (Large)
LCI(R)	Landing Craft, Infantry (Rocket)
LCM	Landing Craft, Mechanized
LCP	Landing Craft, Personnel
LCP(R)	Landing Craft, Personnel (Ramped)
LCR	Landing Craft Rubber
LCT	Landing Craft, Tank
LCT(R)	Landing Craft, Tank (Rocket)
LCV	Landing Craft, Vehicle
LCVP	Landing Craft, Vehicle and Personnel
LSD	Landing Ship, Dock
LSM	Landing Ship, Medium
LSM(R)	Landing Ship, Medium (Rocket)
LST	Landing Ship, Tank (aka "Large Slow Target")
Lt.	Lieutenant
Lt. Cdr.	Lieutenant Commander (Naval Rank)
Lt. Col.	Lieutenant Colonel – U.S.
Lt. Gen.	Lieutenant General
LVT	Landing Vehicle Tracked
LVT(A)	Landing Vehicle, Tracked (Armoured)
MAAF	Mediterranean Allied Air Forces
MAC	Mediterranean Air Command
MACAF	Mediterranean Allied Coastal Air Force
Maj.	Major
Maj. Gen.	Major General
MG	Machine Gun
MSgt	Master Sergeant (1st Grade, today's E-8)
NCDU	Naval Combat Demolition Unit
PO	Petty Officer (Coast Guard and Navy)
PTO	Pacific Theater of Operations
Pvt.	Private (Army and Marine Corps)
RAAF	Royal Australian Air Force
R. Adm.	Rear-Admiral (naval rank, O-8)
RAF	Royal Air Force (UK)

RBG	Reserve Brigade Group
RCA	Royal Canadian Artillery
RCAF	Royal Canadian Air Force
RCT	Regimental Combat Team
Sgt.	Sergeant (4th Grade, today's E-5)
SHAEF	Supreme Headquarters Allied Expeditionary Force
SOP	Standard Operating Procedure
S/Sgt.	Staff Sergeant
SWPA	Southwest Pacific Area
UDT	Underwater Demolition Team
USAAC	United States Army Air Corps
V. Adm.	Vice Admiral, three-star naval flag officer (O9)
XO	Executive Officer (Navy); 2nd in command, reports to the CO

BIBLIOGRAPHY

Books

Anderson, Bern, *By Sea and by River: The Naval History of the Civil War*, Da Capo Press, Boston, Massachusetts 1962

Bale, Richard H., *Currier's Travels – the history of USS Currier DE-700*, Carlsbad, CA, 2002

Barbey, Daniel E., *MacArthur's Amphibious Navy: Seventh Amphibious Force Operations, 1943–1945*, United States Naval Institute, Annapolis, Maryland, 1969

Bradley, Omar N., *A Soldier's Story*, Henry Holt and Company, New York, 1951

Carrigan, Paul E., *The Flying, Fighting Weathermen of Patrol Wing Four, 1941-1945 U.S. Navy*, Volume I, Regal-Lith Printers, Forked River, NJ 2002

Chan, Gabrielle, *War On Our Doorstep. Diaries of Australians At the Frontline in 1942*, South Yarra, Victoria: Hardie Grant Books, Melbourne, Australia, 2003

Churchill, Winston S., *The End of the Beginning*, Cassell, London, 1943

Cooper, Marvin, *The Men From Fort Pierce* [Note: The author was unable to locate any more information about this book. All quotes are taken from Underwater Demolition Team Histories (see Websites)]

Crumley, B. L., *The Marine Corp: Three Centuries of Glory*, Amber Books, London, UK, Revised January 2013

Cuttle Fish Five, *The Aleutian Invasion: World War Two in the Aleutian Islands*, Unalaska, AK, 1981

Darby, William O., Baumer, William H., *Darby's Rangers, We Led The Way*, The Random House Publishing Group, 1980

Dictionary of American Naval Fighting Ships Naval Historical Center, Washington, D. C.

Donovan, Robert, *John F Kennedy In World* War II, International Marine/Ragged Mountain Press; anniversary edition, Camden ME, 2001;

Dwyer, John B., *Seaborne Deception - The History of U.S. Navy Beach Jumpers*, Praeger Publisher, 1992

History of the Second Engineer Special Brigade: United States Army, World War II, Telegraph Press, 1946

Hough, Frank O, Capt., USMC, *The Island War*, J.B. Lippincott, 1947

Hunt, Donald J., *USS LST 313 and Battery A – 33rd Field Artillery, 26th Regimental Combat Team of the 1st Division, The Unpublished Facts And Personal Accountings Of The Invasion Of Diamond Beach,* privately printed, December 1994

Jomini, Le Baron de, *Précis de l'Art de la Guerre: Des Principales Combinaisons de la Stratégie, de la Grande Tactique et de la Politique Militaire.* Brussels: Meline, Cans et Copagnie, 1838. English translation: Jomini, Baron de, trans. Major O.F. Winship and Lieut. E.E. McLean [USA], *The Art of War*, G.P. Putnam, New York 1854

Kelly, Robert H, *Volume II: 1943 – Year of Expansion and Consolidation, Allied Air Transport Operations in the South West Pacific Area in WWII*, Buderim, Queensland, 2006

Kahn, Jr. E. J. WO, *G. I. Jungle,* Simon and Schuster, New York, 1943

Maguire, Eric, *Dieppe, August 19*, Jonathan Cape, London, 1963

Manchester, William, *The Glory and the Dream*, Little Brown & Company, Boston, 1974

McMillan, George, *The Old Breed, A History of the First Marine Division in World War II*, Infantry Journal Press, Washington, D.C., 1949

Merillat, Henry L., Captain, *U.S.M.C.R, THE ISLAND: A History of the Marines on Guadalcanal August 7 – December 9*, 1942, Houghton Mifflin Company, Boston, 1944

Moen, Marcia and Heinen, Margo, *Heroes Cry Too, A WWII Ranger Tells His Story of Love and War*, Meadowlark Publishing, Inc., Elk River, MN, 2002

Moskin, J. Robert, *The U.S. Marine Corps Story (3rd Revised ed.)*, Little, Brown and Company, 1992

O'Dell, James Douglas, *The Water Is Never Cold: The Origins of the U.S. Navy's Combat Demolition Units, UDTs, and SEALs*, Brassey's UK Ltd, 2000

O'Donnell, Patrick K., *Into the Rising Sun: In Their Own Words, World War II's Pacific Veterans Reveal the Heart of Combat*, Free Press, March 5, 2002

Reed, Ken, *the Hand-me-down Ships*, Fleet Hargate, Spalding, Lincolnshire, England, 1993

Richter, Don, *WHERE THE SUN STOOD STILL! The Untold Story of Sir Jacob Vouza and the Guadalcanal Campaign*, Toucan Publishing, Calabasas, CA, 1992

Rzheshevsky, Oleg, *War and Diplomacy: The Making of the Grand Alliance*, Taylor & Breach, Abingdon, 1996

Sears, David, *AIR Fearless Flyboys, Peerless AIRCRAFT, and FAST FLATTOPS Conquered the Skies in the War With Japan*, Da Capo Press, Perseus Book Group, Philadelphia, PA, 2011

Vey, W.D. and Elliot, O.J., *The Beach Boys, A Narrative History of the First Beach Battalion Amphibious Force, U.S. Atlantic Fleet, World War II*, privately distributed

Zimmerman, John L., Major, USMCR, *The Guadalcanal Campaign*, Historical Division, Headquarters, U.S. Marine Corps, 1949

Official Sources

Airborne Missions In The Mediterranean 1942-1945, USAF Historical Studies: No. 74, USAF Historical Division, Research Studies Institute, Air University, September 1955

Alexander, Joseph H., Col. USMC (Retired), *Across the Reef: The Marine Assault of Tarawa*, Marine Corps Historical Center, Washington, D.C., 1993

Alexander, Joseph H., Col., USMC (Retired), *Closing In: Marines in the Seizure of Iwo Jima*, Marines in World War II Commemorative Series, Marine Corps Historical Center, Building 58, Washington Navy Yard Washington, D.C., 1994

AMPHIBIOUS OPERATIONS, INVASION OF NORTHERN FRANCE, WESTERN TASK FORCE JUNE 1944, COMINCH P-006, UNITED STATES FLEET, HEADQUARTERS OF THE COMMANDER IN CHIEF NAVY DEPARTMENT, WASHINGTON, D.C., 1944

ANNEX KING TO OPERATION PLAN No. A3-24, NAVAL HEADQUARTERS AND NAVAL LOCAL DEFENCE FORCE TASK FORCE SIXTY-TWO, U.S.S. McCAWLEY, Flagship, July 30, 1942

Appleman, Roy E.; Burns, James M.; Gugeler, Russell A.; and Stevens, John, *United States Army In World War II, The War in the Pacific, Okinawa: The Last Battle*, Center of Military History, United States Army, Washington, D.C., 1993

Armed Forces in Action Series, Makin, Historical Division, War Department, 1946

Army Air Forces Historical Studies: No. 17, *Air Action in the Papuan Campaign 21 July 1942 to 23*

BIBLIOGRAPHY

January 1943, Assistant Chief of Air Staff, Intelligence, Historical Division, August 1944

Australian Military Forces, *Reconquest, New Guinea, 1943 – 1944, The Australian Army at War,* Melbourne, Victoria: Director General of Publication Relations, 1944, Archived from the original (PDF) on 16 February 2015

Bartley, Whitman S., Lt. Col., USMC, *Iwo Jima: Amphibious Epic,* Historical Branch, G-3 Division, Headquarters, U.S. Marine Corps, 1954

Biennial Report of the Chief of Staff of the United States Army, 1 July 1939-30 June 1945, Center of Military History, United States Army, Washington, D.C., 1996

Blumenson, Martin, *United States Army In World War II, The Mediterranean Theater of Operations SALERNO TO CASSINO,* Center of Military History, United States Army, Washington, D.C., 1993,CMH Pub 6-3-1

Bradsher, Greg, *Operation Blissful: How the Marines Lured the Japanese Away From a Key Target — and How "the Brute" Got Some Help from JFK,* Nation Archives and Records Administration Prologue Magazine Fall 2010, Vol. 42, No. 3

Casey, H. J., ed. (1959), *Volume IV: Amphibian Engineer Operations. Engineers of the Southwest Pacific 1941–1945,* Washington, DC: Government Printing Office

Cater, Kit C. and Mueller, Robert, U.S. Army Air Forces in World War II Combat Chronology 1941-1945, Center for Air force History, Washington, D.C., 1991

Chapin, John C., Captain, U.S. Marine Corps Reserve (Retired), *Top of the Ladder: Marine Operations in the Northern Solomons,* Marine in World War II Commemorative Series, Marine Corps Historical Center, Washington, D.C., 1997

Combat Narratives, The Aleutians Campaign, Office of Naval Intelligence, United Sates Navy, Washington, D.C., 1945

Commander-In-Chief South Pacific Force Item No. 877 dated 2 Dec43, SE Detachment Command Report to Seventeenth Army Chief of Staff, late JUL43.

Craven, Wesley Frank and Cate, James Lee, eds., *The Army Air Forces in World War II, Volume II, Europe: TORCH to POINTBLANK, August 1942 to December 1943,* Office of Air Force, History; USAF Historical Division, University of Chicago Press, Chicago, 1948–1958

Cressman, Robert J., *A Magnificent Fight: Marines in the Battle for Wake Island,* World War II Commemorative Series, Marine Corps Historical Center, Washington, D. C., 1992

Crowl, Philip A. and Love, Edmund G., *United Sates Army In World War II, The War in the Pacific, Seizure Of The Gilberts And Marshalls,* Office of the Chief of Military History, Department of the Army, Washington, D. C. 1955, CMH Publication 5-6

Daniels, Gordon, ed., *A Guide To The Reports of the United States Strategic Bombing Survey, The Campaigns of the Pacific War,* United States Strategic Bombing Survey (Pacific),Naval Analysis Division, United States Printing Office, Washington, 1946

Department of Defense Dictionary of Military and Associated Terms, Joint Publication 1-02, 8 November 2010 (as amended through 15 March 2015)

Fifth Air Force in the Conquest of the Bismarck Archipelago, November 1943 to March 1943, Army Air Forces Historical Studies No. 43, AAF Historical Office, Army Air Forces, 1946

Frank, Benis M. and Shaw Jr., Henry I., *Victory and Occupation, HISTORY OF U. S .MARINE CORPS OPERATIONS IN WORLD WAR II, VOLUME V,* Historical Branch, G-3 Division, Headquarters, U. S. Marine Corps, 1968

Frierson, Major William C. *THE ADMIRALTIES: Operations of the 1st Cavalry Division 29 February - 18 May 1944* , Center of Military History, United States Army, Washington, D.C., CMH Pub 6-2-1, 1999

Garland, Albert N., Howard McGraw Smyth, and Martin Blumenson, *The Mediterranean Theater of Operations: Sicily and the Surrender of Italy.* Washington, DC: Government Printing Office, 1965

Garland, Albert N., Lieutenant Colonel and Smyth, Howard McGaw, *UNITED STATES ARMY IN WORLD WAR II, The Mediterranean Theater of Operations, SICILY AND THE SURRENDER OF ITALY,* Center of Military History, United States Army, Washington, D.C., 1993

Harrison, Gordon A., *The European Theater of Operations, Cross-Channel Attack*, United States Army in World War II, Center of Military History, United States Army, Washington, D.C., CMH Pub 7-4-1, 1951

Hough, Frank O., Lt Col, USMCR, Ludwig, Verle E., Maj, USMC, Shaw, Jr., Henry I., *Pearl Harbor to Guadalcanal, HISTORY OF U. S. MARINE CORPS OPERATIONS IN WORLD WAR II, VOLUME I*, Historical Branch, G-3 Division, Headquarters, U. S. Marine Corps

Howe, George F., *The Mediterranean Theater of Operations, NORTHWEST AFRICA: SEIZING THE INITIATIVE IN THE WEST*, UNITED STATES ARMY IN WORLD WAR II, Center of Military History, United States Army, Washington, D.C., CMH Pub 6-1-1

Howe, George F., *UNITED STATES ARMY IN WORLD WAR II - The Mediterranean Theater of Operations, NORTHWEST AFRICA: SEIZING THE INITIATIVE IN THE WEST*, Center for Military History, United States Army, Washington, D.C. 1993, , CMH Pub 6-1-1

Japanese Monograph No. 88, Aleutian Naval Operation, March 1942-February 1943, translated by the U.S. Army, United States Army, Headquarters, Army Forces Far East, Office of Military History, n.d.

John N., Major, USMCR, *Marines in the Central Solomons*, Historical Branch, Headquarters, U.S. Marine Corps, 1952

LCI(L) file, Coast Guard Historian's Office

Leighton, Richard M. and Coakley, Robert W., *United States Army In World War II, The War Department, Global Logistics and Strategy 1940-1943*, CMH Pub 1-5, Center of Military History, United States Army, Washington, D.C., 1995

Maryland National Guard Military Historical Society, Inc., 116 Regiment, 1st Battalion, SLA Marshall Post Invasion Interviews

Melson, Charles D., Major, U.S. Marine Corps (Retired), *Condition Red: Marine Defense Battalions in World War II*, Marines in World War II Commemorative Series, Marine Corps Historical Center, Washington, D.C., 1996

Miller, John, Jr., *UNITED STATES ARMY IN WORLD WAR II, the war in the Pacific, CARTWHEEL: THE REDUCTION OF RABAUL*, CMH Pub 5-5, Office of the Chief of Military History, Department of the Army, Washington, D.C., 1959

Mitchell, Robert J, 1st LT and Tyng, Sewell Tappan. *The Capture of Attu, A World War II Battle as Told by the Men Who Fought There*, prepared by the War Department, Washington, D.C., 1944

Morton, Louis, *United States Army In World War II, The War in the Pacific, Strategy And Command: The First Two Years*, U.S. Army Center of Military History, United States Army, Washington, D. C., CMH Pub 5-1, 2000

Naval Combat Demolition units; report of, From Lt. (jg) H.L. BLACKWELL, Jr. D-V(G) USNR, To: Commander Task Force ONE TWO TWO, 15 July 1944

Nicholson, G. W. L. LT. COL., Deputy Director, Historical Section, General Staff, Official History of the Canadian Army in the Second World War Volume II, *The Canadians In Italy 1943-1945*, Edmond Cloutier, C.M.G., O.A., D.S.P., OTTAWA, 1956, Queen's Printer And Controller Of Stationery, Published by Authority of the Minister of National Defence

Office of Naval Intelligence Combat Narrative, *Battle of Midway June 3-6, 1942*, United States Navy, 1943

Office of Naval Intelligence, *Combat Narratives Solomon Islands Campaign: I The Landings in the Solomons 7-8 August 1942*, Publications Branch, Office of Naval Intelligence, United States Navy, 1943

Office of Naval Intelligence ONI-226 Allied Landing Craft And Ships, Office of the Chief of Naval Operations, NAVY DEPARTMENT, Washington, 7 April 1944

Omaha Beachhead (6 June-13 June1944), American Forces in Action Series, Historical Division, War Department, Center of Military History, United States Army, Washington. D.C., CMH Pub 100-1

Operations Plan 712-H "Advanced Base Operations in Micronesia", 23 July 1921

Papua, The U.S. Army Campaigns of World War II, Center of Military History, Washington, D.C., CMH Pub 72-7

Papuan Campaign, The Buna-Sanananda Operation 16 November 1942 – 23January 1943, Center of Military History, United States Army, Washington, D. C., CMH Pub 100-1, 1990

Put 'em Across: a History of the 2d Engineer Special Brigade, 1942-1945 : United States Army, World War II, Office of History, U.S. Army Corps of Engineers, Fort Belvoir, VA, 1988

Rentz, John N., Major, USMCR, *Marines in the Central Solomons*, Historical Branch, Headquarters, U.S. Marine Corps, 1952

Report of the Commanding General Buna Forces on the Buna Campaign, Dec. 1, 1942 – Jan. 25, 1943

Reports of General MacArthur, *The Campaigns of MacArthur in the Pacific Volume I*, Prepared by His General Staff, Washington, D. C., CMH Pub 13-1, 1996, 1994 edition

Robert J., *At Close Quarters: PT Boats in the United States Navy, Part IV, Southwest Pacific -- Conquest of New Guinea*, Naval History Division, Washington, 1962

Ruppenthal, Roland G., *UNITED STATES ARMY IN WORLD WAR II, The European Theater of Operations Logistical Support of the Armies In Two Volumes Volume I: May 1941–September 1944*, Center Of Military History, United States Army, Washington, D.C., CMH Pub 7-2-1, 1995

Salerno, American Operations From the Beaches to the Volturo, 9 September – 6 October 1943 Center of Military History, United States Army, Washington, D.C., CMH Pub 100-7, 1990

Shaw, Henry I, Jr. and Kane, Douglas T., Major, USMC, *Isolation of Rabaul, HISTORY OF U.S. MARINE CORPS OPERATIONS IN WORLD WAR II, VOLUME II*, Historical Branch, G–3 Division, Headquarters, U.S. Marine Corps, 1963

Shaw, Jr. Henry I., *First Offensive: The Marine Campaign For Guadalcanal*, Marines in World War II Commemorative Series, Marine Corps Historical Center, Washington, DC, 1992

Shaw, Henry I., et al, *History of the U.S. Marine Corps Operations in World War II, Central Pacific Drive, Volume III*, Historical Branch, G-3 Division, Headquarters, U.S. Marine Corps, 1966

SKILL IN THE SURF, A Landing Boat Manual, Chapter II Landing Craft Form Troy To Tokio [sic], Training and Operations Staff, Landing Craft School Amphibious Training Base Coronado, California, February 1943

Stockman, James R., Captain, USMC, *The Battle For Tarawa*, Historical Section, Division of Public Information, Headquarters, U.S. Marine Corps, 1947

The Amphibians Came to Conquer, The Story of Admiral Richmond Kelly Turner, Volume II, U.S. Marine Corps, Fleet Marine Force Reference Publication (FMFRP) 12-109-II, September 1991

The Coast Guard At War, Public Information Division, U.S. Coast Guard Headquarters, Washington, D.C., 1946

The Official History of New Zealand in the Second World War 1939–1945, *The Pacific, Part II The Treasuries*

The U.S. Army Campaigns of World War II, Aleutian Islands, CMH Pub 72-6

The U. S. Army Campaigns of World War II, *New Guinea 24 January 1943 – 31 December 1944*, Center of Military History, Washington, D. C., CMH Pub 72-9

The U. S. Army Campaigns of World War II, *Normandy 1944*, Center of Military History, Washington, DC, CMH Pub 72-18

The U.S. Army Campaigns of World War II, *Northern Solomons*, Center of Military History, CMH Pub 72-10

The U.S. Army Campaigns of World War II, *Sicily*, Center for Military History, Washington, D.C., CMH Pub 72–16

The U.S. Army Campaigns of World War II, *Southern France*, Center of Military History, Washington, D.C., CMH Pub 72-31

Updegraph, Charles L, Jr., *U. S. MARINE CORPS SPECIAL UNITS OF WORLD WAR II*, HISTORY AND MUSEUMS DIVISION, HEADQUARTERS, U. S. MARINE CORPS WASHINGTON, D. C., printed 1972, reprinted 1977

U. S. S. LISCOME BAY (CVE56) LOSS IN ACTION GILBERT ISLANDS. CENTRAL PACIFIC 24 NOVEMBER, 1943, WAR DAMAGE REPORT No. 45, Preliminary Design Branch Bureau of Ships Navy Department10 March, 1944, Printed By U. S. Hydrographic Office

UTAH BEACH TO CHERBOURG 6 - 27 JUNE 1944, Center Of Military History, United States Army, Washington, D.C., 1990

Watson, Mark Skinner, *United States Army In World War II, The War Department, Chief Of Staff: Prewar Plans And Preparation*, Center of Military History, United States Army, Washington, D.C., 1991, CMH Pub 1-1

Wings of War Series, No. 6, *The AAF in Northwest Africa, An Account of the Twelfth Air Force In The Northwest African Landings And The Battle For Tunisia, An Interim Report*, Office of Assistant Chief of Air Staff, Intelligence, Headquarters, Army Air Forces, Center for Air Force History, Washington, D. C., New Imprint, 1992

Papers

Armor In Operation Neptune (Establishment Of The Normandy Beachhead), Prepared by Committee 10, Officers Advanced Course, The Armored School, 1948 – 1949, Fort Know, KY, May 1949

Huber, Thomas M., PhD, *Japan's Battle of Okinawa, April-June 1945*, Leavenworth Papers Number 18, Combat Studies institute, U.S. Army Command and General Staff College, Fort Leavenworth, KS

Lemay, John C., Major, US Army, OPERATION HUSKY: OPERATIONAL ART IN LARGE FORMATION COMBINED ARMS MANEUVER Monograph, School of Advanced Military Studies, United States Army Command and General Staff College, Fort Leavenworth, Kansas, 2013-02

Low, James L. Major, US Army, *Operations of Task Group 87 (Elements of 87TH, 153RD, and 184TH Infantry Support Units) Kiska 15 July – 25August 1943 (Aleutian Campaign)(Personal experience of an Assistant S-3), Type of Operation Described: Amphibious Operation*, THE INFANTRY SCHOOL, GENERAL SECT ION, MILITARY HISTORY COMMITTEE, FORT BENNING, GEORGIA, ADVANCED OFFICERS COURSE 1946 - 1947

Majors Stewart, Anton, Costello, LTC Domi, Majors Pingel, Gaylord, Myers, McFetridge, Pankey, Peknev, Edie, Smerz, Townsend, *OPERATION ANVIL/DRAGOON, The Invasion of Southern France by The 3D Infantry Division and Other Seventh Army Units, August 15 – 1 September 1944*, Combat Studies Institute U.S. Army Command and General Staff College, Fort Leavenworth, Kansas, May 1984

Powell, Scott, *Learning Under Fire: A combat Unit In The Southwest Pacific*, Doctoral Dissertation, Office of Graduate Studies, Texas A&M University, 2006

Thornton, Gary J. E., Commander, USCG, *THE U.S. COAST GUARD AND ARMY AMPHIBIOUS DEVELOPMENT*, US Army War College, Carlisle Barracks, PA, 23 March 1987

Tooke, Lamar, Colonel, US Army, *Infantry Operations in the Aleutians: The Battle for Attu* ,Student Paper, U.S. Army War College, Carlisle Barracks, PA, 16 March 1990

Ward, Kenneth, Lt.Col., US Army, *THE OPERATIONS OF AMPHIBIOUS TASK FORCE NINE IN THE REOCCUPATION OF KISKA, 15 AUGUST 1943. (ALEUTIAN CAMPAIGN) (Personal experience of Reconnaissance Troop Commander and Hq. Commandant Southern Sector), Type of operation described: Amphibious Operation*, THE INFANTRY SCHOOL, GENERAL SECT ION, MILITARY HISTORY COMMITTEE, FORT BENNING,

BIBLIOGRAPHY

GEORGIA, ADVANCED OFFICERS COURSE 1946 – 1947
Wiles III, M. Emerson, *The Forgotten Raiders*, A Professional Paper Submitted in Partial Fulfillment
of the Requirements for the Degree of Master of Arts in Diplomacy and Military Studies,
Hawaii Pacific University, Fall 2001

Interviews

Author interview with George Henderson
Author interview with Ray Evans
*D-Day: Interview with Two U.S. 2nd Ranger Battalion Members Who Describe the Attack at
Pointe-du-Hoc*, HISTORYNET, 6/12/2006, http://www.historynet.com/d-day-interview-
with-two-us-2nd-ranger-battalion-members-who-describe-the-attack-at-pointe-du-hoc.htm
Edward Wozenski Military Record, interviewer: Thames Television (1972). Edited as a narrative by
War Chronicle. http://warchronicle.com/16th_infantry/soldierstories_wwii/wozenski.htm
Interview with Marvin Perrett, (USCGR), World War II U.S. Coast Guard Veteran, U.S. Coast
Guard Oral History Program, U. S. Coast Guard Headquarters, Washington, D.C., 18 June
2003
MEMOIRS OF SGT. FREDERICK PETERS, A WWII COMBAT ENGINEER, The Genealogy
Center, Allen County Public Library, Fort Wayne, IN
Navy Lieutenant Junior Grade Frank Jirka for presentation before Ceska Beseda, an association of
Croatian Czechs in the United States
Oral History with Dr. Lee Parker, U.S. Navy Medical Department Oral History Program,
conducted by Jan K. Herman, Historian, BUMED, telephone interview, 10 September 1999
Oral History with Pharmacist's Mate (Retired) Vincent Kordack, USN, U.S. Navy Medical
Department Oral History Program, conducted by Jan K. Herman, Historian, BUMED,
telephone interview, 20 June 2000
SLA Marshall Post Invasion Interviews, The Maryland National Guard Military Historical Society,
Inc., Baltimore, MD

Websites

3 / 4 Cavalry chapter website http://www.3-4cav.org/index.php
82D Airborne Division In Sicily And Italy, JULY 9 1943, SEPT 13 1943, JAN 22 1944, http://
www.ww2-airborne.us/division/82_overview.html
Antill, Peter, *Operation Galvanic (1): The Battle for Tarawa November 1943*, 22 January 2002,
http://www.historyofwar.org/articles/battles_tarawa.html
Australia's War 1939-1945, 'Rats in New Guinea', http://www.ww2australia.gov.au/pushingback/
huonpeninsula.html
Australian War Memorial https://www.awm.gov.au/blog/2013/09/09/remembering-war-new-
guinea/
Blazich, Frank Jr., PhD, Historian, Navy Seabee Museum, *Opening Omaha Beach: Ensign
Karnowski and NCDU-45*, SEABEE Online, June 6, 2014
Budge, Ken G, The Pacific War Online Encyclopedia, 2012-2013, http://pwencycl.kgbudge.
com/D/e/Decisive_Battle_Doctrine.htm
Chen, C. Peter, British Attacks on the French Fleet, 3 Jul 1940 – 25 Sep 1940, http://ww2db.com/
battle_spec.php?battle_id=96
Chen, C. Peter, *Preparations for Invasion of Japan, 14 Jul 1945 – 9 Aug 1945*, http://ww2db.com/
battle_spec.php?battle_id=54
Commanding Officer, Beachmaster Unit Two History, http://www.bmu2.navy.mil/

Defense POW/MIA Accounting Agency, www.dpaa.mi

Doyle, Dan, *They Finally Found The Remains Of 132 American Marines On A Small Pacific Island!*, TheVeteransSite.com

Edlin, Robert, "Invasion of Normandy, June 6, 1944: On the Beach EyeWitness to History", 2010, www.eyewitnesstohistory.com

Flowers, Mark, *World War II Gyrene, Dedicated to The U.S. Marine 1941-1945*, http://www.ww2gyrene.org/2ndmardiv_history_part_4A.htm

Global Security Amphibious Operations History http://www.globalsecurity.org/military/systems/ship/amphib-hist.htm

Global Security, *1942 – SLEDGEHAMMER*, http://www.globalsecurity.org/military/world/war/ww2/ww2-op-sledgehammer.htm

Hackett, Bob, et al, *RISING STORM* - THE IMPERIAL JAPANESE NAVY AND CHINA 1931-1941, The "China Incident" (USS PANAY) – 1937, 2012, http://www.combinedfleet.com/Panay_t.htm

Hickman, Mark, The Pegasus Archives, The British Airborne Forces 1940 – 1945, http://www.pegasusarchive.org

Hughes, Warwick, *Hughes14th Brigade, INVASION OF GREEN ISLANDS FEBRUARY 1944, 3rd NZ Division in the Pacific, Second NZEF World War II 1939-1945*, http://web.archive.org/web/20061015162402/http://au.geocities.com/third_div/green.html

Jersey, Stanley C. *the Battle for Betio Island, Tarawa Atoll, A Japanese Perspective: Operations in the Gilbert Islands by the 4th Fleet and the6th Base Force*, Tarawa on the Web, http://www.tarawaontheweb.org/stanjersy1.htm

Midway Memorial Foundation, *Losses in the Battle of Midway June 3-7, 1942*, http://www.immf-midway.com/midwaylosses.html

Naval Combat Demolition Unit #127 at Utah Beach: One Man's Experience – JUNE 6, 1944, http://ncdu127.com/

Psychological Operations, U.S. Navy Beach Jumpers, http://www.psywarrior.com/beach.html

Raaen, John C., Descendants of WWII Rangers http://www.wwiirangers.com/history/history/battalion%20pages/fifth.htm

Rickard, J., *Battle of Arundel Island, 27 August-20 September 1943* , 22 April 2013, http://www.historyofwar.org/articles/battles_arundel_Island.html

Rickard, J, *Land Battle of Vella Lavella, 15 August-7 October 1943* , 16 May 2013 http://www.historyofwar.org/articles/battles_vella_lavella_invasion.html

Rickard, J., *Operation Cleanslate, The Occupation of the Russell Islands, 21 February 1943*, 3 April 2013 http://www.historyofwar.org/articles/operation_cleanslate.html

Ross, Wesley, *Journey with the COMABT ENGINEERS in WWII "ESSAYONS"*, American D-Day http://www.americandday.org/Veterans/Ross_Wesley.html

Ross, Wesley, *JOURNEY with the COMBAT ENGINEERS in WWII "ESSAYONS"*, VI Combat Engineers of WWII ,www.6thcorpscombatengineers.com

Spark, Nick T., *Suddenly and Deliberately Attacked! The Story of the Panay Incident*, The USS PANAY Memorial Website, http://usspanay.org/attacked.shtml

The Aleutians Home Page, World War II in the Aleutians A Brief History, http://www.hlswilliwaw.com/aleutians/Aleutians/html/aleutians-wwii.htm

The Eisenhower Center for American Studies, University of New Orleans transcript, created July 30, 1994, and provided to Military.com, *http://www.military.com/Content/MoreContent1/?file=dday_0009p2*

The First Special Force web site: http://www.firstspecialserviceforce.net/history.html

The History of War, The Fate of the Tanks, http://www.historyofwar.org/articles/battles_omaha_beach.html

The Kokoda Track Casualties, List of casualties for Kokoda, Milne Bay and Buna-Gona, www.kokoda.commemoration.gov.au

Underwater Demolition Team Histories, WWII UDT Team Fifteen, complied by Robert Allan King for the UDT-SEAL Museum from public records at the Operational Archives of the Naval Historical Center, http://www.navyfrogment.com/wwii%20UDT.html

U.S. Coast Guard-manned LCI(L)-88, U.S. 6th Naval Beach Battalion, http://www.6thbeachbattalion.org/uscg-lci.html

U.S. Militaria Forum, posting 08 June 2009, http://www.usmilitariaforum.com/forums/index.php?/topic/44654-d-day-posthumous-navy-purple-heart-grouping/

US Naval Institute Blog: Operation Vengeance, https://blog.usni.org/2009/10/12/the-solomons-campaign-operation-vengeance-the-shootdown-of-yamamoto

Victor Miller - *Victor Miller 5th Ranger Bat., Omaha Beach, Dog Green, 0730*, Normandy 1944 http://normandy.secondworldwar.nl/vicmiller.html

Other Sources

Frankin Delano Roosevelt, "Fireside Chat 18: On The Greer Incident" (September 11, 1941)

Kassner, Ken, Major, USMC, Amphibious Warfare PowerPoint presentation, University of Texas Naval ROTC, PowerPoint Presentation, Fall 2001

National Archives (College Park, Maryland), Rg. 407, 301-INF (16) 0.3.0, "Invasion of France-Combat Team 16"

Rosenman, Samuel, ed., Public Papers and Addresses of Franklin D. Roosevelt, vol.10 (1938–1950)

Statement by the President Announcing the Use of the A-Bomb at Hiroshima., Harry S. Truman Presidential Library and Museum. August 6, 1945.

Wintermute, Ira F, Major, USAAF, *War in the Fog*, Wintermute Family News Letter, January 2013

World War II Database: Operation Vengeance

Zebel, Sydney H., *HAROLD MACMILLAN'S APPOINTMENT AS MINISTER AT ALGIERS, 1942: The Military, Political, and Diplomatic Background*, Rutgers University, Newark, N.J

NOTES

Briefing

1   Department of Defense Dictionary of Military and Associated Terms, Joint Publication 1-02, November 8, 2010 (As amended through March 15, 2015)
2   Sources: i) *SKILL IN THE SURF, A Landing Boat Manual, Chapter II Landing Craft From Troy To Tokio [sic]*, Training and Operations Staff, Landing Craft School Amphibious Training Base Coronado, CA, February 1943; ii) Powell, John, *Great Events from History: The 18th Century 1701–1800*. Pasadena, CA: Salem Press, 2006
3   Global Security Amphibious Operations History, http://www.globalsecurity.org/military/systems/ ship/amphib-hist.htm
4   Jomini, Le Baron de, *Précis de l'Art de la Guerre: Des Principales Combinaisons de la Stratégie, de la Grande Tactique et de la Politique Militaire*. Brussels, Meline, Cans et Copagnie (1838). English translation: Jomini, Baron de, trans. Major O. F. Winship and Lieutenant E. E. McLean [USA], *The Art of War*, New York, G. P. Putnam (1854)
5   Dempsey, David, S/SGT, USMC, *The Three Rs of Invasion, Marine Corps Gazette*, Volume 29, Issue 5, April 4, 1945
6   Vey, W. D. and Elliot, O. J., *The Beach Boys, A Narrative History of the First Beach Battalion Amphibious Force, U.S. Atlantic Fleet, World War II*, privately distributed
7   *Amphibious Operations – The Shore Part* (PHIB-16), Marine Corps Schools, Quantico, VA, 1945; and Commanding Officer, Beachmaster Unit Two History, http://www.bmu2.navy.mil/
8   Heinl, Jr., R. D., *Naval Gunfire Support in Landings, Marine Corps Gazette*, Volume 29, Issue 9
9   Browning, Miles R., Captain, USN, *Carrier Air Support of Assault Landings, Military Review*, Command and General Staff School, Fort Leavenworth, KS (November 1944), Volume XXIV, Number 8
10 Kassner, Ken, Major, USMC, Amphibious Warfare PowerPoint presentation, University of Texas Naval ROTC, Fall 2001

Chapter 1

1   Sources: i) Hough, Frank O., Lieutenant Colonel, USMCR, Ludwig, Verle E., Major, USMC, Shaw, Jr., Henry I., *Pearl Harbor to Guadalcanal, HISTORY OF U. S. MARINE CORPS OPERATIONS IN WORLD WAR II, VOLUME I*, Historical Branch, G-3 Division, Headquarters, U. S. Marine Corps; and ii) Operations Plan 712-H "Advanced Base Operations in Micronesia", July 23, 1921, pages 37 and 41

2   Thornton, Gary J. E., Commander, USCG, *THE U.S. COAST GUARD AND ARMY AMPHIBIOUS DEVELOPMENT*, US Army War College, Carlisle Barracks, PA, March 23, 1987

3   Sources: i) Spark, Nick T., *Suddenly and Deliberately Attacked! The Story of the Panay Incident*, The USS PANAY Memorial Website, http://usspanay.org/attacked.shtml; ii) Hackett, Bob, et al, *RISING STORM* – THE IMPERIAL JAPANESE NAVY AND CHINA 1931–1941, The "China Incident" (USS PANAY) – 1937, 2012, http://www.combinedfleet.com/Panay_t.htm

4   Morton, Louis, *United States Army in World War II, The War in the Pacific, Strategy and Command: The First Two Years*, U.S. Army Center of Military History, United States Army, Washington, D.C.(2000), CMH Pub 5-1, page 69

5   Ibid., pages 69–70

6   Op. cit. *United States Army In World War II*, CMH Pub 5-1, page 81

7   Op. cit. *United States Army in World War II*, CMH Pub 5-1, page 82

8   Watson, Mark Skinner, *United States Army in World War II, The War Department, Chief of Staff: Prewar Plans and Preparation*, Center of Military History, United States Army, Washington, D.C., 1991, CMH Pub 1-1, pages 376–377, summarized from ABC-1, paragraph 12, given in full on pages 1490–1491 of *Pearl Harbor Attack Hearings*, Pt. 15

9   Ibid., page 377

10   Author's research and interviews.

11   Op. cit. Thornton, *THE U.S. COAST GUARD AND ARMY AMPHIBIOUS DEVELOPMENT*

12   Leighton, Richard M. and Coakley, Robert W., *United States Army in World War II, The War Department, Global Logistics and Strategy 1940–1943;* CMH Pub 1-5, Center of Military History, United States Army, Washington, DC 1995. Chapter II, War Plans and Emergency Preparations, pages 63–67

13   Ibid., pages 65–67

14   Rosenman, Samuel, ed., Public Papers and Addresses of Franklin D. Roosevelt, vol. 10 (1938–1950), page 314

15   Manchester, William, *The Glory and the Dream*, Little Brown & Company, Boston, 1974. A formal document was later drawn up and signed by fourteen nations, including the Soviet Union, in September.

16   Franklin D. Roosevelt, "Fireside Chat 18: On the Greer Incident" (September 11, 1941)

17   Walling, Michael G., *Bloodstained Sea: The U.S. Coast Guard in the Battle of the Atlantic, 1941–1944*, McGraw-Hill, 2004. Reprinted Cutter Publishing, 2009

18   Op. cit. *Pearl Harbor Report*

19   i) McLellan, "Officer mistook radar warning of Pearl Harbor Raid," *Los Angeles Times*, February 25, 2010; and ii) Author interview Joseph Ritz who knew George Elliott in Long Branch in 1962–64.

20   Conn, Stetson; Engleman, Rose C.; and Fairchild, Bryon, *UNITED STATES ARMY IN WORLD WAR II, The Western Hemisphere, GUARDING THE UNITED STATES, AND ITS OUTPOSTS*, Center of Military History United States Army, Washington DC, 2000, CMH Pub 4-2

21   Cressman, Robert J., *A Magnificent Fight: Marines in the Battle for Wake Island*, World War II Commemorative Series, Marine Corps Historical Center, Washington, DC (1992), page 32

22   Barde, Robert E., "Midway: Tarnished Victory." *Military Affairs* 47 (4), December 1983

23   Sources: i) Office of Naval Intelligence Combat Narrative, *Battle of Midway June 3–6, 1942*, United States Navy, 1943; and ii) Midway Memorial Foundation, *Losses in the Battle of Midway June 3–7, 1942*, http://www.immf-midway.com/midwaylosses.html

24   Op. cit., *Strategy And Command: The First Two Years*

25   Global Security, *1942 – SLEDGEHAMMER*, http://www.globalsecurity.org/military/world/war/ww2/ww2-op-sledgehammer.htm

26   Churchill, Winston S., *The End of the Beginning*, Cassell, London (1943), p 205

27   Sources: i) Thompson, Julia, *The Dieppe Raid*, updated March 30, 2011, http://www.bbc.co.uk/history/worldwars/wwtwo/dieppe_raid_01.shtml; and ii) Stacey, C. P., Colonel, *Official History of the Canadian Army, Six Years of War, Volume I, Chapter XI, The Raid on Dieppe, 19 August 1942*, Department of National Defense, Queen's Printer, Ottawa, 1955

28 Sources: i) Lowe, Bill, "Dieppe and Tarawa," *Marine Corps Gazette*, February 1946; and ii) Maguire, Eric, *Dieppe, August 19*. Jonathan Cape, London (1963)

29 Op. cit, *Global Logistics And Strategy*, page 389

Chapter 2

1   Author interview with Ray Evans

2   Cooke, F. O., "Solomons Spearhead!", *Leatherneck Magazine*, Volume 25, Issue 10, October 1942

3   Ibid.

4   Ibid.

5   Story source: Merillat, Henry L., Captain, U.S.M.C.R, THE ISLAND: A History of the Marines on Guadalcanal August 7–December 9, 1942, Houghton Mifflin Company, Boston (1944)

6   Ibid.

7   Source: Office of Naval Intelligence, *Combat Narratives Solomon Islands Campaign: The Landings in the Solomons 7–8 August 1942*, Publications Branch, Office of Naval Intelligence, United States Navy, 1943

8   Op.cit *Leatherneck Magazine*, October 1942

9   Op. cit. Office of Naval Intelligence, *Combat Narratives Solomon Islands Campaign*

10 Ray Evans's letter to the author "Guadalcanal Revisited," July 2004

11 The Army P-400s made some air kills, but were generally useless as intercept fighters because of their rate of climb, low operating ceiling, and lack of proper oxygen equipment. Their most valued contributions were many low-altitude and strafing missions in support of the ground troops.

12 "Valor's Reward," *Harpoon Magazine*, U.S. Coast Guard Training Station, Manhattan Beach, Volume II, Number 19, December 1, 1943

13 Miller, John, Jr., *Guadalcanal: The First Offensive*, United States Army In World War II, The War in the Pacific, Center of Military History, United States Army, Washington, D.C., 1995, CMH Pub 5-3

14 Op. cit. Ray Evans

Chapter 3

1   *Biennial Report of the Chief of Staff of the United States Army, 1 July 1939–30 June 1945*, Center of Military History, United States Army, Washington, DC (1996)

2   Sources: i) Zebel, Sydney H., *HAROLD MACMILLAN's APPOINTMENT AS MINISTER AT ALGIERS, 1942: The Military, Political and Diplomatic Background*, Rutgers University, Newark, NJ, and ii) Howe, George F., *The Mediterranean Theater of Operations, NORTHWEST AFRICA: SEIZING THE INITIATIVE IN THE WEST*, UNITED STATES ARMY IN WORLD WAR II, Center of Military History, United States Army, Washington, DC, CMH Pub 6-1-1

3   Op. cit. *NORTHWEST AFRICA: SEIZING THE INITIATIVE IN THE WEST*

4   Wings of War Series, No. 6, *The AAF in Northwest Africa, An Account of the Twelfth Air Force In The Northwest African Landings And The Battle For Tunisia, An Interim Report*, Office of Assistant Chief of Air Staff, Intelligence, Headquarters, Army Air Forces, Center for Air Force History, Washington, D.C. New Imprint (1992)

5   *The Coast Guard At War, North African Landings, Volume IX*

6   Vey, W. D. and Elliott, O. J., *The Beach Boys, A Narrative History of the First Naval Beach Battalion Amphibious Forces. U.S. Atlantic Fleet*, privately printed (February–March 2001)

7   Anderson, Charles R., *The U.S. Army Campaigns of World War II: Algeria–French Morocco*, Center for Military History, CMH Pub 72-11

8   *The Coast Guard At War, North African Landings, Volume IX*, The Historical Section, Public Information Division, U. S. Coast Guard Headquarters, Washington, DC, June 1, 1946

9   Op. cit, *The Beach Boys*

10   Op. cit, *The Coast Guard At War*

11   Ibid.

12   Ibid.

13   Ibid.

14   Ibid.

15   Leopold, James E., Captain, 47th Regiment, 9th Infantry Division

16   Op cit. Anderson, Charles R., *The U.S. Army Campaigns of World War II*

17   *Dix, Titania*, and *Lyon* Action Reports. Coxswain Henry B. Kulizak was particularly commended.

18   Op. cit. Anderson, Charles R., *The U.S. Army Campaigns of World War II*

19   Darby's report of action at Arzew, 1 January 1943, WWII Ops Reports, INBN 1-0, RG 407, WNRC; Darby and Baumer, Darby's Rangers, pp. 8–10, 17–23; Altieri, *The Spearheaders*, p. 137. From: http://www.army.mil/cmh-pg/books/wwii/70-42/70-422.htm

20   Moen, Marcia and Heinen, Margo, *Heroes Cry Too, A WWII Ranger Tells His Story of Love and War*, Meadowlark Publishing, Inc., Elk River, MN (2002)

21   Cooke, F. O., "They Took Thirty Marines", *Leatherneck Magazine*, Volume 26, Issue 7, July 1943

22   Op. cit., Wings of War Series, No. 6

23   Sources: i) Reed, Ken, *The Hand-me-down Ships*, Fleet Hargate, Spalding, Lincolnshire, 1993; ii) Op. cit., "They Took Thirty Marines", *Leatherneck Magazine*

24   A large part of this section was drawn from *The U.S. Army Campaigns of World War II: Algeria–French Morocco*, Center for Military History, CMH Pub 72-11 and *The Coast Guard At War, North African Landings, Volume IX*.

25   Op. cit. *The Coast Guard At War*

26   Ibid.

27   Ibid.

28   Ibid.

29   Howe, George F., *UNITED STATES ARMY IN WORLD WAR II - The Mediterranean Theater of Operations, NORTHWEST AFRICA: SEIZING THE INITIATIVE IN THE WEST*, Center for Military History, United States Army, Washington, DC 1993, , CMH Pub 6-1-1, pp 241–244

30   Ibid.

31   Op. cit. *The U.S. Army Campaigns of World War II*

32   Op. cit. *The Beach Boys*.

Chapter 4

1   Army Air Forces Historical Studies: Number 17, *Air Action in the Papuan Campaign 21 July 1942–23 January 1943*, Assistant Chief of Air Staff, Intelligence, Historical Division, August 1944

2   Chan, Gabrielle, *War on Our Doorstep. Diaries of Australians at the Frontline in 1942*, South Yarra, Victoria: Hardie Grant Books, Melbourne, Australia (2003)

3   *Papua, The U.S. Army Campaigns of World War II*, Center of Military History, Washington, DC, CMH Pub 72-7

4   Report of the Commanding General Buna Forces on the Buna Campaign, December 1, 1942–January 25, 1943

5   Op. cit. *Papua, The U.S. Army Campaigns of World War II*

6   Kahn, Jr. E.J., WO, *G. I. Jungle*, New York; Simon and Schuster, 1943, pp. 121–122.

7   Sources: i) *Papuan Campaign, The Buna-Sanananda Operation 16 November 1942–23 January 1943*, Center of Military History, United States Army, Washington, DC. 1990, CMH Pub 100-1 ii) Op. cit. *Papua, The U.S. Army Campaigns of World War II*

8   U.S. Army Campaigns of World War II, *New Guinea 24 January 1943–31 December 1944*, Center of Military History, CMH Pub 72-9

9   Op. cit. Army Air Forces Historical Studies, Number 17

10   Sources: i) Craven, Wesley Frank, *THE ARMY AIR FORCES In World War II, Volume Four, THE PACIFIC: GUADALCANAL TO SAIPAN, AUGUST 1942 TO JULY 1944*, New Imprint by the Office of Air Force History, Washington, DC , 1983; ii) Shaw, Henry I, Jr. and Kane, Douglas T., Major, USMC, *Isolation of Rabaul, HISTORY OF U.S. MARINE CORPS OPERATIONS IN WORLD WAR II, VOLUME II*, Historical Branch, G–3 Division, Headquarters, U.S. Marine Corps, 1963; iii) Miller, John, Jr., *UNITED STATES ARMY IN WORLD WAR II, the war in the Pacific, CARTWHEEL: THE REDUCTION OF RABAUL*, CMH Pub 5-5, Office of the Chief of Military History, Department of the Army, Washington, DC, 1959

11   Ibid *CARTWHEEL: THE REDUCTION OF RABAUL*

12   Rickard, J. (3 April 2013), *Operation Cleanslate, The Occupation of the Russell Islands, 21 February 1943*, http://www.historyofwar.org/articles/operation_cleanslate.html

13   Sources: i) World War II Database: Operation *Vengeance*; and ii) US Naval Institute: Operation *Vengeance*

14   Shaw, Jr., Henry I. and Kane, Douglas T., Major, USMC, *Isolation of Rabaul*, History of U.S. Marine Corps Operations in World War II, Volume II, Historical Branch, G–3 Division, Headquarters, U.S. Marine Corps, 1963

15   *The Coast Guard at War*, Consolidation of the Southern Solomons, Volume VI

16   Sources: i) Op. cit. *The Coast Guard at War*; ii) The U.S. Army Campaigns of World War II, *Northern Solomons*, Center of Military History, CMH Pub 72-10

17   Op. cit. *Northern Solomons*

18   Anonymous, *The Capture of Enogai, Marine Corps Gazette*, Volume 27, Issue 5, September 1943

19   Op. cit. *Up the Slot*

20   Sources: i) Op. cit. *Up the Slot*; ii) Rentz, John N., Major, USMCR, *Marines in the Central Solomons*, Historical Branch, Headquarters, U.S. Marine Corps, 1952; iii) McDevitt, Frank J., Technical Sergeant, USMC, *The Capture of Enogai, Marine Raiders and Naval Medicine Men Write a Saga in the new Georgia Jungle*, Bureau of Naval Personnel Bulletin, Bureau of Naval Personnel, Washington, DC, Number 319, October 1943; and iv) Anonymous, *The Capture of Enogai, Marine Corps Gazette*, Volume 27, Issue 5, September 1943

21   Commander-in-Chief South Pacific Force, Item Number 877, December 2, 1943, SE Detachment Command Report to Seventeenth Army Chief of Staff, late JUL43.

22   Melson, Charles D., Major, U.S. Marine Corps (Retired), *Condition Red: Marine Defense Battalions in World War II*, Marines in World War II Commemorative Series, Marine Corps Historical Center, Washington, DC, 1996

23   Op. cit. *Northern Solomons*

24   Rickard, J., *Land Battle of Vella Lavella, 15 August–7 October 1943* , May 16, 2013 http://www.historyofwar.org/articles/battles_vella_lavella_invasion.html

25   Op. cit. *The Coast Guard at War*

26   *The Dictionary of American Naval Fighting Ships*

27   Op. cit. *The Isolation of Rabaul*

28   Op. cit. *Land Battle of Vella Lavella*

29   Sources: i) Op. cit. *Isolation of Rabaul*; ii) Op. cit. *Cartwheel*; and iii) Op. cit. *Condition Red*

30   Chapin, John C., Captain, U.S. Marine Corps Reserve (Retired), *Top of the Ladder: Marine Operations in the Northern Solomons*, Marine in World War II Commemorative Series, Marine Corps Historical Center, Washington DC, 1997

31   *The Official History of New Zealand in the Second World War 1939–1945, The Pacific, Part II The Treasuries.*

32   Op. cit. *Top of the Ladder*

33   Sources: i) Op. cit. *The Isolation of Rabaul*; ii) Bradsher, Greg, *Operation Blissful: How the Marines Lured the Japanese Away From a Key Target – and How "the Brute" Got Some Help from JFK*, National

Archives and Records Administration Prologue Magazine, Fall 2010, Volume 42, Number 3, http://www.archives.gov/publications/prologue/2010/fall/blissful.html; iii) Donovan, Robert, *John F. Kennedy in World War II*, International Marine/Ragged Mountain Press; anniversary edition, Camden, ME, 2001; and iv) Hubler, Richard C., *Mission: to Raise Hell, The Raid on Choiseul Island*, *Marine Corps Gazette*, Volume 28, Issue 27, October–4 November 1943

34 9th Marine Regiment Operation Order 57-43, October 24, 1943

35 Sources: i) Op. cit. *Bougainville and the Northern Solomons*; ii) Op. cit. *Top of the Ladder*; iii) Op. cit. *Cartwheel: the Reduction of Rabaul*; and iv) Op. cit. *Isolation of Rabaul*

36 Devine, Frank, *How We Captured Cape Torokina*, *Leatherneck Magazine*, Volume 27, Issue 5, April 1944

37 Tolbert, Frank X., *Puruata Was No Pushover*, *Leatherneck Magazine*, Volume 27, Issue 7, June 1944

38 Sources: i) Warder, Murray, *"D" Day for Dogs*, *Leatherneck Magazine*, Volume 27, Issue 6, May 1944; and ii) Helfer, Harold, *Dog Tales*, *Leatherneck Magazine*, Volume 28, Issue 7, July 1945

39 Hughes, Warwick, *Hughes' 14th Brigade, INVASION OF GREEN ISLANDS FEBRUARY 1944, 3rd NZ Division in the Pacific, Second NZEF World War II 1939–1945*, http://web.archive.org/web/20061015162402/http://au.geocities.com/third_div/green.html

40 Op. cit. *The Coast Guard at War*, Volume VI

Chapter 5

1 The majority of this information was excerpted from James Scott Powell's doctoral Dissertation, *Learning Under Fire: A Combat Unit in the Southwest Pacific*, Office of Graduate Studies, Texas A&M University, 2006

2 Barbey, Daniel E., *MacArthur's Amphibious Navy: Seventh Amphibious Force Operations, 1943–1945*. United States Naval Institute, Annapolis, Maryland United States Naval Institute. 1969

3 Sources: i) Op. cit. *CARTWHEEL: THE REDUCTION OF RABAUL* and ii) Op. cit. *Learning Under Fire*

4 Op. cit. *CARTWHEEL: THE REDUCTION OF RABAUL*

5 Shaw, Henry I., Jr. and Kane, Douglas T., Major, USMC, *Isolation of Rabaul*, History of the U.S. Marine Corps Operations in World War II, Volume II, Historical Branch, Headquarters, U.S. Marine Corps, 1963

6 MacKechnie, A. R., Colonel, U.S. Army (Retired), *The Salamaua Campaign, A Brief Account of the First Campaign of the 162nd Infantry in New Guinea*, The Sunset Division Bulletin, The 41st Infantry Division Association, Volume 2, No. 1, Portland, Oregon, 1948

7 Ibid.

8 Ibid.

9 Sources: i) Op. cit. *CARTWHEEL: THE REDUCTION OF RABAUL*; ii) Bulkley, Robert J., *At Close Quarters: PT Boats in the United States Navy, Part IV, Southwest Pacific – Conquest of New Guinea*, Washington: Naval History Division, 1962; and iii) Op. cit. *The Salamaua Campaign*

10 Op. cit. *Campaigns in the Pacific*

11 *Australia's War 1939–1945*, "Rats in New Guinea", http://www.ww2australia.gov.au/pushingback/huonpeninsula.html

12 Dawes, Allan, *Soldier Superb, The Australian Fights in New Guinea*, F. H. Johnston Publishing Company, 1943

13 Op. cit. *CARTWHEEL: THE REDUCTION OF RABAUL*

14 Australian War Memorial https://www.awm.gov.au/blog/2013/09/09/remembering-war-new-guinea/

15 History of the Second Engineer Special Brigade: United States Army, World War II, Telegraph Press, 1946

16 Op. cit. Australian War Memorial

17 Op. cit. *CARTWHEEL: THE REDUCTION OF RABAUL*

18 The U.S. Army Campaigns of World War II, *New Guinea 24 January 1943–31 December 1944*, Center of Military History, Washington, DC, CMH Pub 72-9

19 The original 2-503 PIR was detached to Europe and made the first U.S. combat jump during Operation *Torch* (see Chapter 3: Lighting the Torch). Unbeknownst to the 2-503 PIR it was re-designated the 509th Parachute Infantry during the North African Campaign. It was not informed of such until after the war. When the remaining 503d battalions were transiting the Panama Canal Zone en route to Australia the 501st Parachute Battalion was picked up. This battalion was re-designated as the Second Battalion of the 503d PIR (2-503), replacing the original Second Battalion.

20 Sources: i) Kelly, Robert H., *Volume II: 1943 – Year of Expansion and Consolidation, Allied Air Transport Operations in the South West Pacific Area in WWII*, Buderim, Queensland, 2006 and ii) Op. cit. *CARTWHEEL: THE REDUCTION OF RABAUL*

21 Reports of General MacArthur, *The Campaigns of MacArthur in the Pacific, Volume I*, Prepared by His General Staff, Washington, DC, 1966, 1994 Edition, CMH Pub 13-1

22 *Casey, H. J., ed. (1959). Volume IV: Amphibian Engineer Operations. Engineers of the Southwest Pacific 1941–1945, Washington, DC: Government Printing Office*

23 Australian Military Forces, *Reconquest, New Guinea, 1943–1944, The Australian Army at War* Melbourne, Victoria: Director General of Publication Relations, 1944, Archived from the original (PDF) on February 16, 2015

24 Ibid.

25 Private Van Noy, a towheaded youth aged 19 years, was from Preston, Idaho. He was nicknamed "Junior" or "Whitey." A skilled machine gunner, he had shot down a low-level Japanese bomber at Lae during a strafing attack. On D-Day at Scarlet Beach, Van Noy received five shell fragment wounds in his wrist, back, and side, but he refused to be evacuated.
Sources: i) *Put 'em Across: a History of the 2d Engineer Special Brigade, 1942-1945 : United States Army, World War II*, Office of History, U.S. Army Corps of Engineers, Fort Belvoir, VA, 1988; and ii) Op. cit. *Amphibian Engineer Operations. Engineers of the Southwest Pacific*

26 Op. cit. *New Guinea* CMH Pub 72-9

27 Op. cit. *CARTWHEEL: THE REDUCTION OF RABAUL*

28 Fifth Air Force in the Conquest of the Bismarck Archipelago, November 1943 to March 1943, Army Air Forces Historical Studies Number 43, AAF Historical Office, Army Air Forces, 1946

29 Op. cit. *Learning Under Fire*

30 Op. cit. *CARTWHEEL: THE REDUCTION OF RABAUL*

31 Op. cit. *Learning Under Fire*

32 Sources: i) Op. cit. *CARTWHEEL: THE REDUCTION OF RABAUL*; ii) Op. cit. *Campaigns in the Pacific*; iii) Op. cit. *Isolation of Rabaul*; and iv) Op. cit. *Learning Under Fire*

33 Op. cit. *CARTWHEEL: THE REDUCTION OF RABAUL*

34 Op. cit. *The Coast Guard at War*

35 Op. cit. *Isolation of Rabaul*

36 Op. cit. *Put 'em Across*

37 McMillan, George, *The Old Breed, A History of the First Marine Division in World War II*, Infantry Journal Press, Washington, DC 1949

38 Op. cit. *Isolation of Rabaul*

39 Captain Joseph A. Terzi was posthumously awarded the Navy Cross for heroism while leading the attack. When General Rupertus learned the Hansen brothers were the sons of a widow who had already lost an older son in the war, he sent the survivor, Paul, stateside immediately with orders that he should never be sent into combat again, no matter how long the war lasted. Leslie Hansen and the other gunner, Sergeant Robert J. Oswald, Jr., were awarded the Navy Cross posthumously, while Paul Hansen received the Silver Star.
Sources: i) Hough, Frank O., Major, USMCR, *The Island War, The United States Marine Corps In The Pacific*, J.B. Lippincott Company, New York, 1947; and ii) Naulty, Bernard C., *Cape Gloucester: The Green Inferno*, Marines in World War II Commemorative Series, Marine Corps Historical Center, Washington, DC 1994

40 Op. cit. *The Island War*

41 Joseph Gerczak was posthumously awarded the Silver Star. The citation read in part: "By his expert marksmanship, unwavering perseverance and cool courage in the face of tremendous odds, he contributed materially to the success of this as well as previous assault and reinforcement landings in the New Guinea Campaign, and his constant devotion to duty throughout was in keeping with the highest traditions of the Naval Service."
Sources: i) *United States Coast Guard Book of Valor*, U.S. Coast Guard Public Relations Division, 1945; and ii) Op. cit. *The Coast Guard at War*

42 *Dictionary of American Naval Fighting Ships*, Naval Historical Center, Washington, DC

43 Op. cit. *The Army Air Forces in World War II*

44 Op. cit. *Put 'em Across*

45 Op. cit. *Isolation of Rabaul*

46 Op. cit. *The Island War*

47 Op. cit. *The Old Breed*

48 Op. cit. *Put 'em Across*

49 Op. cit. *CARTWHEEL: THE REDUCTION OF RABAUL*

50 Sources: i) Op. cit. *Isolation of Rabaul*; ii) Op. cit. *CARTWHEEL: THE REDUCTION OF RABAUL*; iii) Op. cit. *New Guinea*; and iv) Op. cit. *The Army Air Forces in World War II*

51 Frierson, Major William C. *THE ADMIRALTIES: Operations of the 1st Cavalry Division 29 February–18 May 1944* , Center of Military History, United States Army, Washington, DC 1999, CMH Pub 100-3

52 Task Force Brewer Assault Echelon Units
Brigadier General William C. Chase
2d Squadron, 5th Cavalry Regiment
Battery B, 99th Field Artillery Battalion
673rd Anti-Aircraft Machine Gun Battery (Airborne)
Reconnaissance Platoon, HQ Troop. 1st Cavalry Brigade
Communications Platoon, HQ Troop. 1st Cavalry Brigade
1st Platoon, TroOp.B (Clearing), 1st Medical Squadron
30th Portable Surgical Hospital
ANGAU Detachment
Air Force Detachment
Naval Gunfire Support Party
Air Liaison Party
Task Force Brewer Supporting Echelon Units
Colonel Hugh Hoffman
5th Cavalry Regiment (less 2d Squadron)
99th Field Artillery Battalion (less Battery B)
1st Platoon, Troop.A, 8th Engineer Squadron
1st Collecting Troop. 1st Medical Squadron
Signal Detachment, 1st Signal Troop
40th Naval Construction Battalion
Battery C, 168th Anti-Aircraft Artillery Battalion (Gun)
Battery A, 211th Coast Artillery Battalion (Anti-Aircraft) (Automatic Weapons)
Company E, Shore Battalion, 592d Engineer Boat and Shore Regiment
Source: Krueger, Walter, Report on Brewer Operation, 2 August 1944

53 Ibid.

54 Ibid.

55 Op. cit. *Put 'em Across*

56 Subsequently, McGill was awarded the Medal of Honor for his courage and selflessness. Source: Op. cit. *Bismarck Archipelago*

57 Op. cit. *Put 'em Across*

58 Sources: i) Op. cit. *CARTWHEEL: THE REDUCTION OF RABAUL* and ii) Op. cit. *Put 'em Across*

59 Casey, Hugh J., Major General, US Army, *Amphibious Engineer Operations, Engineers of the Southwest Pacific 1941–1945, Volume IV*, Washington, DC, 1959

60 Six of the perpetrators were sentenced for war crimes in 1947. Sentenced to death by hanging, Tamura was executed at Stanley Prison on March 16, 1948. Source: Dunbar, Raden, *Kavieng Massacre: A War Crime Revealed*, Binda, New South Wales: Sally Milner Publishing, 2007

61 Op. cit. *The Isolation of Rabaul*

62 Op. cit. *The Admiralties*

Chapter 6

1 Japanese Monograph No. 88, Aleutian Naval Operation, March 1942–February 1943, translated by the U.S. Army (United States Army, Headquarters, Army Forces Far East, Office of Military History, n.d.), 1.

2 Ibid.

3 Carrigan, Paul E., *The Flying, Fighting Weathermen of Patrol Wing Four, 1941–1945 U.S. Navy*, Volume I, Regal-Lith Printers, Forked River, NJ, 2002. Reprinted with permission from Mrs. Jean Carrigan.

4 Sources: i) The U.S. Army Campaigns of World War II, Aleutian Islands, CMH Pub 72-6, page 6; ii) Craven, Frank Wesley and Cate, James Lee, Eds., THE ARMY AIR FORCES In World War II, Volume I, Plans and Early Operations January 1939 to August 1942, United States Air Force. Air Historical Group, New Imprint by the Office of Air Force History Washington, DC (1983), pages 464–465; iii) Cater, Kit C. and Mueller, Robert, U.S. Army Air Forces in World War II Combat Chronology 1941–1945, Center for Air Force History, Washington, DC (1991); and iv) *The Coast Guard At War, Alaska*, Volume III, Public Information Division, U.S. Coast Guard Headquarters, Washington, DC (1946)

5 Op cit. *The Flying, Fighting Weathermen of Patrol Wing Four, 1941–1945 U.S. Navy*, Volume I

6 Combat Narratives, The Aleutians Campaign, Office of Naval Intelligence, United States Navy, Washington, DC (1945), page 10

7 Sources: i) Cuttle Fish Five, *The Aleutian Invasion: World War Two in the Aleutian Islands*, Unalaska, AK, 1981, http://www.hlswilliwaw.com/aleutians/Attu/html/attu_charles_foster_and_etta_jones.htm; and ii) The Aleutians Home Page, World War II in the Aleutians: A Brief History, http://www.hlswilliwaw.com/aleutians/Aleutians/html/aleutians-wwii.htm

8 Wintermute, Ira F., Major, USAAF, *War in the Fog*, Windemuth Family News Letter, January 2013, www.windemuth.org/adobe/january-2013.pdf. Reprinted with permission from Commander H. Rand Wintermute, USCG (Retired).

9 Sources: i) Tooke, Lamar, Colonel, U.S. Army, *Infantry Operations in the Aleutians: The Battle for Attu*, Student Paper, U.S. Army War College, Carlisle Barracks, PA, March 16, 1990; and ii) Op. cit. *Combat Narratives, The Aleutians Campaign*, pages 1–4, with additions and clarifications by the author.

10 Op. cit. *The Coast Guard At War*

11 Op. cit. *The Flying, Fighting Weathermen of Patrol Wing Four, 1941–1945 U.S. Navy*, Volume II

12 Sources: i) Op. cit. Aleutian Islands June 3, 1942–August 24, 1943, CMH_Pub_72-6, page 12; and ii) Op. cit. Craven, THE ARMY AIR FORCES In World War II, Volume One, page 369

13 Op. cit. *The Flying, Fighting Weathermen of Patrol Wing Four, 1941–1945 U.S. Navy*, Volume II

14 Sources: i) Dwyer, John B., "Remembering the Alaska Scouts," *American Thinker*, November 12, 2005, reprinted with permission; ii) Adak Historical Guide, Kuluk Bay Landing Site, Castner's Cutthroats Memorial

15 Sources: i) op. cit. US Navy Combat Narrative: The Aleutians Campaign June 1942–August 1943; ii) op. cit. Aleutian Islands June 3, 1942–August 24, 1943, CMH_Pub_72-6; iii) op. cit. *The Coast Guard At War*; iv) *Dictionary of American Naval Fighting Ships*, Office of the Chief of Naval

Operations, Naval History Division, Washington, DC (1959)

16 Dull, Paul S., *A Battle History of the Imperial Japanese Navy (1941–1945)*, Annapolis (1978), page 261

17 Sears, David, *AIR Fearless Flyboys, Peerless AIRCRAFT, and FAST FLATTOPS Conquered the Skies in the War with Japan*, Da Capo Press, Perseus Book Group, Philadelphia, PA (2011), page 486

18 Op. cit. Tooke, Lamar, Colonel, US Army, *Infantry Operations in the Aleutians*

19 Mitchell, Robert J., 1st Lieutenant and Tyng, Sewell Tappan. *The Capture of Attu, A World War II Battle as Told by the Men Who Fought There*, Prepared by the War Department, Washington, DC (1944)

20 Dwyer, John B., "Remembering the Alaska Scouts," *American Thinker*, November 12, 2005

21 Op. cit. Mitchell

22 Op. cit. Carrigan

23 Thompson, Erwin N., *Attu Battlefield and U.S. Army and Navy Airfields on Attu*, National Register of Historic Places Registration Form, Washington, DC: U.S. Department of the Interior, National Park Service (1984)

24 Op. cit. Carrigan

25 From an transcription of an a interview with Joseph Sasser conducted by Janis Kozlowski, National Park Service, July 21, 2011. Transcription: http://www.nps.gov/aleu/learn/photosmultimedia/interview-sasser.htm. Original file: aleu-Joseph-Sasser-July-21-2011.mp3

26 Op. cit. Mitchell

27 Ibid.

28 Ibid.

29 Ibid.

30 Op. cit. Tooke

31 Op. cit. Mitchell

32 Ward, Kenneth, Lieutenant Colonel, US Army, *THE OPERATIONS OF AMPHIBIOUS TASK FORCE NINE IN THE REOCCUPATION OF KISKA, 15 AUGUST 1943. (ALEUTIAN CAMPAIGN) (Personal experience of Reconnaissance Troop Commander and HQ. Commandant Southern Sector), Type of operation described: Amphibious Operation*, THE INFANTRY SCHOOL, GENERAL SECTION, MILITARY HISTORY COMMITTEE, FORT BENNING, GEORGIA, ADVANCED OFFICERS' COURSE 1946–1947

33 Low, James L. Major, U.S. Army, *Operations of Task Group 87 (Elements of 87th, 153d, and 184th Infantry Support Units) Kiska, July 15–August 25, 1943 (Aleutian Campaign)(Personal experience of an Assistant S-3), Type of Operation Described: Amphibious Operation*, THE INFANTRY SCHOOL, GENERAL SECTION, MILITARY HISTORY COMMITTEE, FORT BENNING, GEORGIA, ADVANCED OFFICERS' COURSE 1946–1947

34 Bureau of Naval Personnel Information Bulletin, September 1943, Number 318, Washington, DC

35 Op cit. Ward, Kenneth A., Lieutenant Colonel, U.S. Army

36 Op cit. Dictionary of American Naval Fighting Ships

37 Sources: i) Op. cit. The U.S. Army Campaigns of World War II, Aleutian Islands, p. 26; and ii) Op. cit. Ward, Kenneth A., Lieutenant Colonel, U.S. Army

Chapter 7

1 Note by Minister of Defence, November 25, 1942, WP (42) 543, annex to 3d Br COS Casablanca Mtg. SHAEF SGS file 337/5, British Minutes of SYMBOL Conference

2 Alexander *Despatch*, 1009. SYMBOL Conference, Combined Chiefs of Staff 151/1, January 19, 1943

3 Nicholson, G. W. L. Lieutenant Colonel, Deputy Director, Historical Section, General Staff, Official History of the Canadian Army in the Second World War Volume II, *The Canadians In Italy 1943–1945*, Edmond Cloutier, CMG, OA, DSP, Ottawa (1956), Queen's Printer and Controller of Stationery, published by Authority of the Minister of National Defence

4   Craven, Wesley Frank and Cate, James Lee, eds., *The Army Air Forces in World War II, Volume II, Europe: TORCH to POINTBLANK, August 1942 to December 1943*, Office of Air Force, History; USAF Historical Division, University of Chicago Press, Chicago (1948–58), pages 419–430

5   Ibid.

6   Lemay, John C., Major, US Army, OPERATION HUSKY: OPERATIONAL ART IN LARGE FORMATION COMBINED ARMS MANEUVER Monograph, School of Advanced Military Studies, United States Army Command and General Staff College, Fort Leavenworth, Kansas, 2013-02. Major Lemay's sources include: i) Eisenhower, Dwight. *Commander in Chief's Dispatch, Sicilian Campaign, 1943*, Allied Force Headquarters (1943), page 16; ii) Bradley, Omar N. *A Soldier's Story*, New York: Henry Holt and Company (1951), page 120; and iii) Garland, Albert N., Howard McGraw Smyth, and Martin Blumenson, *The Mediterranean Theater of Operations: Sicily and the Surrender of Italy.* Washington, DC: Government Printing Office (1965), CMH Pub 6-2-1

7   The U.S. Army Campaigns of World War II, *Sicily*, Center for Military History, Washington, DC, CMH Pub 72-16

8   Ibid., United States Naval Administration in World War II, Volume III, Action Report

9   Brown, John Mason, Lieutenant, USNR, *To All Hands, An Amphibious Adventure*, McGraw-Hill (1943)

10 Mark Hickman, The Pegasus Archives, The British Airborne Forces 1940–1945, http://www.pegasusarchive.org

11 Garland, Albert N., Lieutenant Colonel and Smyth, Haward McGaw, *UNITED STATES ARMY IN WORLD WAR II, The Mediterranean Theater of Operations, SICILY AND THE SURRENDER OF ITALY*, Center of Military History, United States Army, Washington, DC (1993)

12 Parle Genealogy http://www.parle.co.uk/genealogy/ww2johnjosephparle.htm

13 The Coast Guard At War, Volume X, *Sicily, Italy Landings*, Historical Section, Public Information Division, U.S. Coast Guard Headquarters, Washington, DC, 1946

14 Hunt, Donald J., *USS LST 313 and Battery A – 33rd Field Artillery, 26th Regimental Combat Team of the 1st Division, The Unpublished Facts and Personal Accountings of the Invasion of Diamond Beach*, privately printed, December 1994. Author's Note: There was not a Diamond Beach in Operation *Husky*; the unit landed on DIME Beach.

15 Op. cit. *SICILY AND THE SURRENDER OF ITALY*

16 Ibid.

17 Darby, William O., Baumer, William H., *Darby's Rangers, We Led the Way*, Random House, 1980

18 Op. cit. Sicily and the Surrender of Italy

19 Op. cit. Hunt. LST-311's Captain, Lieutenant Robert Coleman, USNR, placed the bow of his own ship against the stern of the stricken 313, saving about 80 survivors trapped by the flames.

20 Op. cit. *Sicily and the Surrender of Italy* and *Sicily, U.S. Army Campaigns of World War II*

21 Sources: i) *82D Airborne Division in Sicily and Italy, JULY 9, 1943, SEPT 13, 1943, JAN 22, 1944*; ii) Op. cit. *Sicily and the Surrender of Italy*; iii) Op. cit. *Sicily*; and iv) Author interview with George Henderson

22 Op. cit. Action Report – Western Naval Task Force

23 The U.S. Army Campaigns of World War II, *Naples–Foggia, 9 September 1943–21 January 1944*, Center for Military History, CMH Pub 72-17

24 World War II Today, *Operation Baytown: The Invasion of Italy*, http://ww2today.com/3rd-september-1943-operation-baytown-the-invasion-of-italy

25 *Salerno, American Operations from the Beaches to the Volturo, 9 September–6 October 1943*, Center of Military History, United States Army, Washington, D.C., 1990, CMH Pub 100-7,

26 Op. cit. *Coast Guard At War*

27 Op. cit. Darby

28 Op. cit. *Salerno*, CMH Pub 100-7, page 27

29 Ibid.

30 Vey, W. D. and Elliott, O. J., *The Beach Boys, A Narrative History of the First Naval Beach Battalion, Amphibious Force, U.S. Atlantic Fleet, World War II*, privately printed

31   Op. cit. *The Coast Guard At War*

32   Op. cit SALERNO, American Operations from the Beaches to the Volturno, page 53

33   Sources: i) *Infantry Combat Part Three: Beachhead at Salerno*; ii) Op. cit. *Naples–Foggia*; iii) Op. cit. *Salerno*; iv) Op. cit. *Salerno to Cassino*; and v) Op. cit. *The Coast Guard At War*

34   Vego, Milan, *the Allied Landing at Anzio–Nettuno, 22 January–4 March 1944, Operation Shingle.* Naval War College Review, Autumn 2014, Volume 67, Number 4, 2014

35   Fifth Army History, 16 January 1944–31 March 1944, Part IV Cassino and Anzio

36   Ibid.

37   Fehrenbach, T. R., *The Battle of Anzio*, Monarch Books, Derby, Conneticut, 1962

38   Sources: i) Op. cit. Darby, *Darby's Rangers, We Led the Way*; ii) Op. cit. *The Battle of Anzio*, 1962; and iii) King, Michael J., Dr., *Rangers: Selected Combat Operations in World War II*, Leavenworth Papers, Combat Studies Institute, U.S. Army Command and General Staff College, Fort Leavenworth, Kansas, June 1985

39   Bellafaire, Judith L., *The Army Nurse Corps: A Commemoration of World War II Service*, The Campaigns of World War II, U.S. Army Center of Military History, Washington, DC, CMH Pub 72-14 Paper

40   Monahan, Evelyn M and Niedel-Greenlee, Rosemary, *Women who were there recall bravery on the beachhead, Purple Heart Magazine*, May–June 1992. Reprinted with permission.

41   Ibid.

Chapter 8

1   Crowl, Philip A. and Love, Edmund G., *United States Army In World War II, The War in the Pacific, Seizure of the Gilberts and Marshalls*, Office of the Chief of Military History, Department of the Army, Washington, DC (1955), CMH Publication 5-6, pages 19–22

2   Ibid., page 21

3   Ibid.

4   Updegraph, Charles L, Jr., *U.S. MARINE CORPS SPECIAL UNITS OF WORLD WAR II*, History and Museums Division, Headquarters, U.S. Marine Corps, Washington, DC (1972, reprinted 1977)

5   O'Donnell, Patrick K., *Into the Rising Sun: in their Own Words, World War II's Pacific Veterans Reveal the Heart of Combat*, Free Press, March 5, 2002

6   Ibid.

7   Sources: i) Op. cit. *U.S. MARINE CORPS SPECIAL UNITS OF WORLD WAR II*; ii) Haughey, David W, Colonel, USMC (Retired), "Carlson's Raid On Makin Island," *Marine Corps Gazette*, August 2001, https://www.mca-marines.org/gazette/carlsons-raid-makin-island; and iii) Wiles III, M. Emerson, *The Forgotten Raiders*, A Professional Paper Submitted in Partial Fulfillment of the Requirements for the Degree of Master of Arts in Diplomacy and Military Studies, Hawaii Pacific University, Fall 2001, www.hpu.edu/CHSS/.../2001TrippWiles.pdf.
    Mr. Wiles conducted a telephone interview with Louis Zamperini on April 16, 2001. Here is an excerpt from that interview:
    "According to Zamperini, the first thing his eyes focused on were the crudely engraved words on the wall: Nine Marines marooned on Makin Island – August 18, 1942." The nine Marines' names were inscribed on the wall under the heading and Zamperini would spend the next 43 days memorizing these names and contemplating their fate and his."

8   Bradsher, Greg, Dr., *Seventy Years Ago:the Makin Island Raid, August 1942*, The National Archives, The Text Message Blog, November 14, 2012, http://text-message.blogs.archives.gov/2012/11/14/seventy-years-ago-the-makin-island-raid-august-1942-2/

9   Sources: i) Jersey, Stanley C. *The Battle for Betio Island, Tarawa Atoll, A Japanese Perspective: Operations in the Gilbert Islands by the 4th Fleet and the 6th Base Force*, Tarawa on the Web, http://www.tarawaontheweb.org/stanjersy1.htm; ii) Antill, Peter, *Operation Galvanic (1): The Battle for Tarawa November 1943*, January 22, 2002, http://www.historyofwar.org/articles/battles_tarawa.html; and iii) Op. cit. *U.S. Army in World War II, War in the Pacific, Seizure of the Gilberts and Marshalls*.

10 Lieutenant Commander Fifth Amph Force to COMCENPAC, September 23, 1943, sub: GALVANIC Opn, Discussion of Substitution of Makin as Assault Objective Instead of Nauru, Ser 0037, File 1975 Operation and Training (GALVANIC), Folder I, VAC files, Naval Records Management Center, Mechanicsburg, Pennsylvania.

11 Sources: i) Craven, Wesley Frank, and Cate, James Lea, ed., *The Army Air Forces in World War II, Volume Four, The Pacific: Guadalcanal To Saipan August 1942 to July 1944*, Office of Air Force History, Washington, DC 1983, pages 292–293; and ii) Daniels, Gordon, ed., *A Guide to the Reports of the United States Strategic Bombing Survey, The Campaigns of the Pacific War*, United States Strategic Bombing Survey (Pacific), Naval Analysis Division, United States Printing Office, Washington (1946)

12 Op. cit. *The Army Air Forces in World War II, Volume Four*

13 Johnston, Richard W., *Follow Me: The Story of the Second Marine Division in World War II*, Battery Press, Nashville, TN, 1987

14 Op. cit. *U.S. Army in World War II, War in the Pacific, Seizure of the Gilberts and Marshalls*

15 Alexander, Joseph H., Col., USMC (Retired), *Across the Reef: The Marine Assault of Tarawa*, Marine Corps Historical Center, Washington, DC, 1993

16 Tolbert, Fran X., USMC, "Death at Close Quarters," *Leatherneck Magazine*, Volume 27, Issue 8, July 1944

17 Op. cit. *Across the Reef*

18 Shaw, Henry I., et al, *History of the U.S. Marine Corps Operations in World War II, Central Pacific Drive, Volume III*, Historical Branch, G-3 Division, Headquarters, U.S. Marine Corps, 1966

19 Ward, Gene, Sergeant, col., USMC, "The Dead Were Too Close Around Us," War Orphans Scholarships, Inc., (1945)

20 Jonas, Carl, USCG, *My First Day on Tarawa*, Curtis Publishing Company

21 Anonymous, "Amphibious Operation: the Story of Tarawa," *Leatherneck Magazine*, February 1944

22 Op. cit. *Death at Close Quarters*

23 Sources: i) op. cit. *Across the Reef*; ii) Metcalf, Clyde H., USMC, "This Was Tarawa," *Marine Corps Gazette*, Volume 28, Issue 5, May 1944; and iii) Flowers, Mark, *World War II Gyrene, Dedicated to The U.S. Marine 1941–1945*, http://www.ww2gyrene.org/2ndmardiv_history_part_4A.htm.

24 Op. cit. *Amphibious Operation: the Story of Tarawa*

25 Hough, Frank O., Captain, USMC, *The Island War*, J. B. Lippincott (1947)

26 Op. cit. *Across the Reef*

27 Ibid.

28 Tolbert, Frank X., "Mop-Up Beyond Betio," *Leatherneck Magazine*, Volume 27, Issue 7

29 Op. cit. *Across the Reef*

30 Garner, Everett, USCG, "Coast Guard Assault Transport at Makin Island," *Harpoon Magazine*, February 15, 1944

31 Taken from: *Will to Die Wins the Gilberts, 76-Hour Battle for Pacific Atolls is Bloodiest in Marine Corps History*, Bureau of Naval Personnel Information Bulletin, Number 322, January 1944

32 Sources: i) Op. cit. *U.S. Army in World War II, War in the Pacific, Seizure of the Gilberts and Marshalls*; ii) Armed Forces in Action Series, *Makin*, Historical Division, War Department (1946)

33 Sources: i) *U.S.S. LISCOME BAY (CVE56) LOSS IN ACTION GILBERT ISLANDS. CENTRAL PACIFIC NOVEMBER 24, 1943, WAR DAMAGE REPORT No. 45*, Preliminary Design Branch Bureau of Ships Navy Department, March 10, 1944, printed by U.S. Hydrographic Office; ii) Noles, James L., Jr., "All Guts, No Glory: What they lacked in strength, World War II escort carriers made up in numbers … and the perseverance of their crews", *Air & Space Magazine*, July 2004, http://www.airspacemag.com/military-aviation/all-guts-no-glory-6028074/#MM1MCcKUTq1gtFO7.99

34 The following was taken from Sergeant Frank X. Tolbert's excellent *Leatherneck Magazine* article "Apamama: a Model Operation in Miniature" (Volume 28, Issue 2, February 1945). It is the basis for most descriptions of the invasion, the only successful one conducted from a submarine.

35 Miller, I. E., USMC, "Naval Gunfire at Roi-Namur", *Marine Corps Gazette*, Volume 32, Issue 7, July 1948

36 Stockman, James R., Captain, USMC, *The Battle For Tarawa*, Historical Section, Division of Public Information, Headquarters, U.S. Marine Corps (1947)
37 Op. cit. *Central Pacific*, CMH Pub 72-4

Chapter 9

1   O'Dell, James Douglas, *The Water is Never Cold: The Origins of the U.S. Navy's Combat Demolition Units, UDTs, and SEALs*, Brassey's UK Ltd (2000)
2   Sources: i) AMPHIBIOUS OPERATIONS, INVASION OF NORTHERN FRANCE, WESTERN TASK FORCE JUNE 1944, COMINCH P-006, UNITED STATES FLEET, HEADQUARTERS OF THE COMMANDER IN CHIEF NAVY DEPARTMENT WASHINGTON, DC (1944); and ii) Ross, Wes, *JOURNEY with the COMBAT ENGINEERS in WWII "ESSAYONS,"* VI Combat Engineers of WWII, www.6thcorpscombatengineers.com
3   Sources: i) Harrison, Gordon A., *The European Theater of Operations, Cross-Channel Attack*, United States Army in World War II, Center of Military History, United States Army, Washington, DC (1951), CMH Pub 7-4-1; ii) *Omaha Beachhead (6 June–13 June 1944)*, American Forces in Action Series, Historical Division, War Department, Center of Military History, United States Army, Washington. DC, CMH Pub 100-1; and iii) *Armor in Operation Neptune (Establishment of the Normandy Beachhead)*, prepared by Committee 10, Officers Advanced Course, The Armored School, 1948–1949, Fort Knox, KY, May 1949
4   Op. cit., *Armor in Operation Neptune*
5   Op. cit. *AMPHIBIOUS OPERATIONS, INVASION OF NORTHERN FRANCE, WESTERN TASK FORCE JUNE 1944*, COMINCH P-006
6   *Utah Beach to Cherbourg, 6–27 June 1944*, American Forces in Action Series, Historical Division, War Department Center of Military History, United States Army, Washington. DC, CMH Pub 100-12
7   Op. cit. *Armor in Operation Neptune*
8   Sources: i) Op. cit. *Armor in Operation Neptune*; ii) 3/4 Cavalry chapter website http://www.3-4cav.org/index.php; and iii) 4th Cavalry Group After Action Report
9   Ruppenthal, Roland G., *UNITED STATES ARMY IN WORLD WAR II, The European Theater of Operations Logistical Support of the Armies in Two Volumes, Volume I: May 1941–September 1944*, Center of Military History, United States Army, Washington, DC (1995), CMH Pub 7-2-1
10 U.S. Coast Guard interview with Harry Kennedy, December 9, 1987
11 *Coast Guard at War, The Landings in France*, Volume XI, Historical Section, Public Affairs Division, U.S. Coast Guard Headquarters, Washington, DC, March 1946
12 Edward Wozenski Military Record, interviewer: Thames Television, UK (1972). Edited as a narrative by *War Chronicle*. http://warchronicle.com/16th_infantry/soldierstories_wwii/wozenski.htm
13 Op. cit. *The Coast Guard at War*
14 National Archives (College Park, MD), Rg. 407, 301-INF (16) 0.3.0, "Invasion of France-Combat Team 16"
15 Ibid.
16 Sources: i) Op. cit. *Armor in Operation Neptune* and ii) *The History of War, The Fate of the Tanks*, http://www.historyofwar.org/articles/battles_omaha_beach.html
17 Op. cit. *The Coast Guard at War*
18 Sources: i) LCI(L) file, Coast Guard Historian's Office; and ii) U.S. Coast Guard-manned LCI(L)-88, U.S. 6th Naval Beach Battalion, http://www.6thbeachbattalion.org/uscg-lci.html
19 Op. cit. LCI (L) file, Coast Guard Historian's Office
20 Sources: i) Op. cit. LCI (L) file, Coast Guard Historian's Office and ii) Shepherd, Seth, USCGR, *Hell on the Beach*, Challenge Publications, Sea Classics, 1995

21 Sources: i) Hendley, Coit, "D-Day: A Special Report," *The Washington Times*, Wednesday, June 6, 1984; ii) Op. cit. *The Coast Guard at War*; and iii) Lieutenant Jack Hagerty II, Duties of the 6th, U.S. 6th Naval Beach Battalion, ,http://www.6thbeachbattalion.org/lt-jack-hagerty.html

22 U.S. Coast Guard Oral History Program, Interview with Steward Second Class John Noble Roberts, USCGR, African-American U.S. Coast Guard D-Day Veteran, Conducted by C. Douglas Kroll, Ph.D., U.S. Coast Guard Auxiliary, Santa Maria, CA, July 3, 2012

23 Sources: i) France, John, *The Story of the LCI 93 and LCI 487 at Normandy*, Elsie Item, Issue #63, April 1, 2008, USS LCI National Association, http://www.usslci.org/Archive/Archive.htm; and ii) Op. cit. LCI(L) file, Coast Guard Historian's Office

24 Sources: i) Johnson, Mark, Colonel, USA (Retired), *104th Medical Battalion, 29th Division Aboard LCI(L)-94 on D-Day*, U.S. Coast Guard, https://www.uscg.mil/History/webcutters/ JohnsonDDayhistoryLCI94.asp; and ii) Young, Stephanie, Lieutenant, *D-Day through the eyes of a Coast Guardsman*, LCI(L)-94 Motor Machinist's Mate 1st Class Clifford W. Lewis, Coast Guard Compass, Official Blog of the U.S. Coast Guard, Lieutenant Stephanie Young, Wednesday, June 6, 2012. http://coastguard.dodlive.mil/2012/06/d-day-through-the-eyes-of-a-coast-guardsman/

25 Naval Combat Demolition units; report of, from Lieutenant Junior Grade H. L. BLACKWELL, Jr. D-V(G) USNR, to: Commander Task Force ONE TWO TWO, July 15, 1944

26 Blazich, Frank Jr., PhD, Historian, Navy Seabee Museum, *Opening Omaha Beach: Ensign Karnowski and NCDU-45*, SEABEE Online, June 6, 2014

27 *Clearing Normandy Obstacles*, Bureau of Naval Personnel Information Bulletin, September 1944. Number 330, page 23

28 Strobridge, Truman R., *St. Bernard's of Normandy*, Sea Classics Challenge Sea Special, Volume 1, 1995

29 Op. cit. Coast Guard at War, *The Landings In France*

30 Op. cit. *St. Bernard's of Normandy*

31 Sources: i) Oral History with Dr. Lee Parker, U.S. Navy Medical Department Oral History Program, Conducted by Jan K. Herman, Historian, BUMED, telephone interview, September 10, 1999; and ii) Op. cit. U.S. 6th Naval Beach Battalion

32 Op. cit. U.S. 6th Naval Beach Battalion

33 Oral History with Pharmacist's Mate (Retired) Vincent Kordack, USN, U.S. Navy Medical Department Oral History Program, conducted by Jan K. Herman, Historian, BUMED, telephone interview, June 20, 2000

34 SLA Marshall Post Invasion Interviews, The Maryland National Guard Military Historical Society, Inc., Baltimore, MD, http://www.marylandmilitaryhistory.org/

35 The U. S. Army Campaigns of World War II, *Normandy 1944*, Center of Military History, Washington, DC, CMH Pub 72-18

36 Sources for the quotes in the following: i) Robert Edlin, "Invasion of Normandy, June 6, 1944: On the Beach EyeWitness to History", www.eyewitnesstohistory.com (2010); ii) Victor Miller, *Victor Miller 5th Ranger Battalion, Omaha Beach, Dog Green, 0730*, Normandy, 1944, http://normandy. secondworldwar.nl/vicmiller.html; and iii) John C. Raaen, Descendants of WWII Rangers, http://www.wwiirangers.com/history/history/battalion%20pages/fifth.htm

37 Op. cit. John C. Raaen

38 *D-Day: Interview with Two U.S. 2nd Ranger Battalion Members who Describe the Attack at Pointe-du-Hoc*, HISTORYNET, December 6, 2006, http://www.historynet.com/d-day-interview-with-two-us-2nd-ranger-battalion-members-who-describe-the-attack-at-pointe-du-hoc.htm

39 Ibid.

40 Op. cit. *D-Day: Interview*

41 *American Forces in Action Series SMALL UNIT ACTIONS*: *France: 2d Ranger Battalion at Pointe du Hoe* [sic] *Saipan: 27th Division on Tanapag Plain Italy: 351st Infantry at Santa Maria Infante France: 4th Armored Division at Singling*, Historical Division, WAR DEPARTMENT, WASHINGTON, DC, Center of Military History, Facsimile Reprint, 1982, 1986, 1991, CMH Pub 100-14

42 Interview with Marvin Perrett, (USCGR), World War II U.S. Coast Guard Veteran, U.S. Coast Guard Oral History Program, U.S. Coast Guard Headquarters, Washington, DC, June 18, 2003

43 Op. cit. *Armor in Operation Neptune*

44 *UTAH BEACH TO CHERBOURG, JUNE 6-27, 1944*, Center of Military History, United States Army, Washington, DC, 1990

45 The Eisenhower Center for American Studies, University of New Orleans transcript , created July 30, 1994, and is provided to Military.com, *http://www.military.com/Content/MoreContent1/?file=dday_0009p2*

46 U.S. Militaria Forum, posting June 8, 2009, http://www.usmilitariaforum.com/forums/index.php?/topic/44654-d-day-posthumous-navy-purple-heart-grouping/

47 Naval Combat Demolition Unit #127 at Utah Beach: One Man's Experience – JUNE 6, 1944, http://ncdu127.com/

48 MEMOIRS OF SGT. FREDERICK PETERS, A WWII COMBAT ENGINEER, The Genealogy Center, Allen County Public Library, Fort Wayne, IN

49 Op. cit. *Armor in Operation*

50 Op. cit. August Leo Thomas interview transcription

51 Majors Stewart, Anton, Costello, LTC Domi, Majors Pingel, Gaylord, Myers, McFetridge, Pankey, Peknev, Edie, Smerz, Townsend, OPERATION *ANVIL/DRAGOON*, *The Invasion of Southern France by the 3d Infantry Division and Other Seventh Army Units, August 15– September 1, 1944*, Combat Studies Institute U.S. Army Command and General Staff College, Fort Leavenworth, KA, May 1984

52 Sources: i) Psychological Operations, U.S. Navy Beach Jumpers, http://www.psywarrior.com/beach.html; ii) Dwyer, John B., *Seaborne Deception – the History of U.S. Navy Beach Jumpers*, Praeger, 1992

53 Bale, Richard H., *Currier's Travels – the history of USS Currier DE-700*, Carlsbad, CA, 2002

54 The U.S. Army Campaigns of World War II, *Southern France*, Center of Military History, Washington, DC, CMH Pub 72-31

55 Op. cit. Operation *ANVIL/DRAGOON*

56 Op. cit. *Riviera to the Rhine*

57 Whitlock, Flint, "U.S. –Canadian 1st Special Service Force in World War II," *World War II Magazine*, January 2000

58 *Airborne Missions in the Mediterranean 1942–1945*, USAF Historical Studies: Number 74, USAF Historical Division, Research Studies Institute, Air University, September 1955

59 Op. cit. *Riviera to the Rhine*

60 Op. cit. *CSI Battlebook*

Chapter 10

1 Sources: i) Shaw, Henry I., Jr., Natly, Bernard C., Turnbladh, Edwin T., *HISTORY OF U. S. MARINE CORPS OPERATIONS IN WORLD WAR II, Central Pacific Drive, Volume III*, Historical Branch, G-3 Division, Headquarters, U.S. Marine Corps (1966); and ii) Crowl, Philip A., *United States Army in World War II, The War in the Pacific, Campaign in the Marianas*, Center of History, United States Army, Washington, DC, 1960, CMH Pub 5-7-1

2 *U.S. Coast Guard at War, Volume VI, The Marianas*

3 Gugeler, Russell A., Lt., U.S. Army, *Army Amphibian Tractor and Tank Battalions in the Battle of Saipan 15 June–9 July 1944*, 1st Information and Historical Service, January 20, 1945, Historical Manuscripts Collection (HMC) under file number 8-5.3 BA, http://www.army.mil/cmh-pg/documents/wwii/amsai/amsai.htm

4 Sources: i) Op. cit. *U.S. Coast Guard at War*; and ii) Op. cit. *Central Pacific Drive, Volume III*

5 Sources: i) Op. cit. *The War in the Pacific, Campaign in the Marianas*; and ii) Op. cit. *Central Pacific Drive, Volume III*

6 This and all following quotes in this section from men in the 2nd Armored Amphibian Battalion are taken from *2nd Armored Amphibian Battalion, USMC, WWII: Saipan, Tinian, Iwo Jima*, 2nd

Armored Amphibian Battalion Association, 1991, http://2ndarmoredamphibianbattalion.com/saipan/

7   Baumgartner, Herbert, Y1C, U.S. Coast Guard, "Saipan," *The Bug Magazine*, U.S. Coast Guard, August 1944

8   Op. cit. *The War in the Pacific, Campaign in the Marianas*

9   Ibid.

10 Dempsey, David, "Cave of Horror," *Leatherneck Magazine*, Volume 27, Issue 10, September 1944

11 Sources: i) Op cit. *Coast Guard at War*; ii) Op. cit. *The War in the Pacific, Campaign in the Marianas*; and iii) Op. cit. *Central Pacific Drive, Volume III*

12 Commander UDT Three Action Report, August 18, 1944

13 Kaufman, Millard, Marine Corps Public Relations Officer, "Attack on Guam," *Marine Corps Gazette*, Volume 29, Issue 4, April 1945

14 Excerpted and edited from "Attack on Guam"

15 Op. cit. "Attack on Guam"

16 Sources: i) Thomson, III, John W., "The Fourth Division at Tinian," *Marine Corps Gazette*, Volume 29, Issue 1, January 1945; and ii) Op. cit. *Campaign in the Marianas*

17 Op. cit. *The Amphibians Came to Conquer*

18 *The Amphibians Came to Conquer, The Story of Admiral Richmond Kelly Turner, Volume II*, U.S. Marine Corps, Fleet Marine Force Reference Publication (FMFRP) 1-2-109-II, September 1991

19 Op. cit. *Central Pacific Drive, Volume III*

20 Op. cit. *The Amphibians Came to Conquer*

21 Ibid.

22 Ibid.

23 Sources: i) Bartley, Whitman S., Lieutenant Colonel, USMC, *Iwo Jima: Amphibious Epic*, Historical Branch, G-3 Division, Headquarters, U.S. Marine Corps, 1954; and ii) Crumley, B. L., *The Marine Corp: Three Centuries of Glory*, Amber Books, London, UK, revised January 2013

24 Sources: i) Bartley, Whitman S., Lieutenant Colonel, USMC, *Iwo Jima: Amphibious Epic*, Historical Branch, G-3 Division, Headquarters, U.S. Marine Corps, 1954; and ii) Op. cit. *The Coast Guard at War*

25 Sources: i) Op. cit. *Iwo Jima: Amphibious Epic*; and ii) Op. cit. *The Amphibians Came to Conquer*

26 Cooper, Marvin, *The Men from Fort Pierce*. Note: The author was unable to locate any more information about the book. All quotes are taken from Underwater Demolition Team Histories, WWII UDT Team Fifteen, compiled by Robert Allan King for the UDT-SEAL Museum from public records at the Operational Archives of the Naval Historical Center, http://www.navyfrogmen.com/WWII%20UDT.html

27 Ibid.

28 The text is a transcription of a speech written by Navy Lieutenant Junior Grade Frank Jirka for presentation before Ceska Beseda, an association of Croatian Czechs in the United States. Lieutenant Jirka passed away in 2000. http://www.viewoftherockies.com/Frank%20speech1.pdf

29 Commander Task Force Fifty-Two, Amphibious Support Force, After Action Report Iwo Jima, February 1945

30 Op. cit. *The Men from Fort Pierce*

31 Sources: i) Op. cit. *Iwo Jima: Amphibious Epic*; and ii) Alexander, Joseph H., Colonel, USMC (Retired), *Closing In: Marines in the Seizure of Iwo Jima*, Marines in World War II Commemorative Series, Marine Corps Historical Center, Building 58, Washington Navy Yard Washington, DC (1994)

32 Op. cit. *Closing In: Marines in the Seizure of Iwo Jima*

33 Op. cit. *The Amphibians Came to Conquer*

34 Walton, Bryce, "D-Day on Iwo Jima," *Marine Corps Gazette*, Volume 28, Issue 5, May 1945

35 Ibid.

36 Ibid.

37 Op. cit. *Closing In: Marines in the Seizure of Iwo Jima*

38 Op. cit. *The Amphibians Came to Conquer*
39 Op. cit. *Closing In: Marines in the Seizure of Iwo Jima*
40 Sources: i) Moskin, J. Robert, *The U.S. Marine Corps Story (3rd Rev. edn)*, Little, Brown and Company, 1992; ii) Cunningham, Charles B., "Last Banzai on Iwo," *Marine Corps Gazette,* Volume 28, Issue 6, June 1944; and iii) Op. cit. *Iwo Jima: Amphibious Epic*
41 Op. cit. *The Men from Fort Pierce*
42 Op. cit. *Battle for Iwo*
43 Appleman, Roy E.; Burns, James M.; Gugeler, Russell A.; and Stevens, John, *United States Army in World War II, The War in the Pacific, Okinawa: The Last Battle*, Center of Military History, United States Army, Washington, DC, 1993
44 Huber, Thomas M., PhD, *Japan's Battle of Okinawa, April–June 1945*, Leavenworth Papers, Number 18, Combat Studies Institute, U.S. Army Command and General Staff College, Fort Leavenworth, KS
45 Frank, Benis M. and Shaw Jr., Henry I., *Victory and Occupation, HISTORY OF U.S. MARINE CORPS OPERATIONS IN WORLD WAR II, VOLUME V,* Historical Branch, G-3 Division, Headquarters, U.S. Marine Corps, 1968
46 Sources: i) Op. cit. *The Coast Guard at War;* and ii) Op. cit. *The Amphibians Came to Conquer*
47 Finan, James, "Damndest Battlefield," *Leatherneck Magazine*, Volume 28, Issue 6, June 1945
48 Op. cit. *Amphibians Came to Conquer*
49 Op. cit. *Coast Guard at War*
50 *Dictionary of American Naval Fighting Ships Online*, http://www.hazegray.org/danfs/
51 Op. cit. *Amphibians Came to Conquer*
52 Op. cit. Finan
53 Op cit. *Okinawa: The Last Battle.*

Epilogue

1 Chen, C. Peter, *Preparations for Invasion of Japan*, July 14, 1945–August 9, 1945, http://ww2db.com/battle_spec.php?battle_id=54
2 *Statement by the President Announcing the Use of the A-Bomb at Hiroshima*, Harry S. Truman Presidential Library and Museum, August 6, 1945

INDEX

INDEX